D1395897

Revise
AS

Psychology

Cara Flanagan

Contents

Chapter 5 Individual differences

Chapter 6 Social psychology

Chapter 7 Research

Specification lists

AQA A Psychology

MODULE	SPECIFICATION TOPIC	CHAPTER REFERENCE	STUDIED IN CLASS	REVISED	PRACTICE QUESTIONS
Unit 1	**Cognitive psychology: Human memory**	2.1			
	Short-term and long-term memory	2.2			
	Forgetting	2.3			
	Critical issue: eyewitness testimony	2.4			
	Developmental psychology: Attachments in development	3.1			
	The development and variety of attachments	3.3			
	Deprivation and privation	3.4			
	Critical issue: day care	3.5			
Unit 2	**Physiological psychology: Stress**	4.1, 4.2			
	Stress as a bodily response	4.4			
	Sources of stress	4.5			
	Critical issue: stress management	4.6			
	Individual differences: Abnormality	5.1			
	Defining psychological abnormality	5.3			
	Biological and psychological models of abnormality	1.1, 5.4			
	Critical issue: eating disorders – anorexia nervosa and bulimia nervosa	5.5			
Unit 3	**Social psychology: Social influence**	6.1			
	Conformity and minority influence	6.3			
	Obedience to authority	6.4			
	Critical issue: Ethical issues in psychological research	6.5			
	Research methods				
	Quantitative and qualitative research methods	7.1			
	Research design and implementation	7.2			
	Data analysis	7.3			

(Chapter references include complete coverage of the specification)

Examination analysis

The specification comprises six compulsory modules (3 examination units).

Unit 1	Two structured questions on cognitive psychology, candidates must choose one. Two structured questions on developmental psychology, candidates must choose one.	1 hr test 33.33%
Unit 2	Two structured questions on physiological psychology, candidates must choose one. Two structured questions on individual differences psychology, candidates must choose one.	1 hr test 33.33%
Unit 3	Two structured questions on social psychology, candidates must choose one. One compulsory structured question on research methods.	1 hr test 33.33%

AQA B Psychology

MODULE	SPECIFICATION TOPIC	CHAPTER REFERENCE	STUDIED IN CLASS	REVISED	PRACTICE QUESTIONS
Unit 1 PSO1	**Introducing psychology**	10.1			
	Key approaches and the study of psychology	1.1, 2.1, 5.4			
	The biological approach	4.1, 4.2			
	Methods of research	7.1, 7.2			
	Representing data and descriptive statistics	7.3			
	Ethics	6.5			
	Studying gender	5.2			
	Explaining gender	–			
Unit 2 PSO2	**Social and cognitive psychology**	2.1, 6.1			
	Attitudes	6.2			
	Social influence	6.3, 6.4			
	Social cognition	–			
	Social psychology of sport	–			
	Perception and attention	–			
	Remembering and forgetting	2.2, 2.3			
	Language and thinking	–			
	Cognition and law	2.4			
Unit 3	**Practical work**	–			

('–' means not covered in this book as they are optional modules)

(Chapter references cover some but not necessarily all of the specification)

Examination analysis

The specification comprises three units. There is considerable choice in units 1 and 2 of the examination.

Unit 1 Candidates must answer three structured questions:
- one on either key approaches or the biological approach
- one on either explaining gender or studying gender
- one compulsory question on research methods.

1 hr 30 min test   35%

Unit 2 Candidates must answer three structured questions:
Eight questions set, one from each of the eight sections in social and cognitive psychology (see list above).
- a minimum of one on social psychology
- a minimum of one on cognitive psychology
- plus one from either cognitive or social psychology.

1 hr 30 min test   35%

Unit 3 Practical investigation: one 1500 word report, externally assessed.   30%

Edexcel Psychology

MODULE	SPECIFICATION TOPIC	CHAPTER REFERENCE	STUDIED IN CLASS	REVISED	PRACTICE QUESTIONS
	Cognitive, social and development processes				
	The cognitive approach (key assumptions, methods)	2.1			
	Memory and forgetting	2.2, 2.3			
	Key application (eyewitness testimony)	2.4			
Unit 1	*The social approach (key assumptions, methods)*	6.1			
	Obedience	6.4			
	Key application (prejudice)	6.2			
	The cognitive-developmental approach (key assumptions, methods)	3.1			
	Cognitive development	3.2			
	Key application (education)	3.2			
	Individual differences, physiology and behaviour				
	The learning approach (key assumptions, methods)	1.1			
	Classical and operant conditioning	1.1			
	Key application (behaviour modification)	5.4			
Unit 2	*The psychodynamic approach (key assumptions, methods)*	1.1			
	Freud's theory	1.1			
	Key application (mental health)	5.4			
	The physiological approach (key assumptions, methods)	4.1, 4.2			
	States of awareness	4.3			
	Key application (shift work and jet lag)	In A2 book			
	Data gathering exercise				
Unit 3	Ethics	6.5			
	Methods used in psychological research	7.1, 7.2, 7.3			

(Chapter references cover some but not necessarily all of the specification)

Examination analysis

The specification consists of three compulsory units.

Unit 1	A set of compulsory structured questions.	1 hr 30 min test	33.33%
Unit 2	A set of compulsory structured questions.	1 hr 30 min test	33.33%
Unit 3	Practical investigation: one 1500 word report, no inferential statistics, externally assessed.		33.33%

OCR Psychology

MODULE	SPECIFICATION TOPIC	CHAPTER REFERENCE	STUDIED IN CLASS	REVISED	PRACTICE QUESTIONS
Units 1&2	**Cognitive core studies**				
	Loftus and Palmer (eyewitness)	2.4			
	Deregowski (perception)	–			
	Baron-Cohen et al. (autism)	–			
	Gardner and Gardner (Washoe)	–			
	Social core studies				
	Milgram (obedience)	6.4			
	Haney, Banks and Zimbardo (prison simulation)	6.3			
	Piliavin et al. (subway samaritan)	6.1			
	Tajfel (ethnocentricism)	6.2			
	Developmental core studies				
	Samuel and Bryant (conservation)	3.2			
	Bandura et al. (imitating aggression)	1.1			
	Hodges and Tizard (attachment)	3.4			
	Freud (Little Hans)	1.1			
	Physiological core studies				
	Schachter and Singer (emotion)	–			
	Dement and Kleitman (dreaming)	4.3			
	Sperry (split brains)	4.1			
	Raine et al. (murderers)	–			
	Individual differences				
	Gould (IQ testing)	4.2			
	Hraba and Grant (doll choice)	–			
	Rosenhan (sane in insane places)	5.3			
	Thigpen and Cleckley (multiple personality)	–			

(Chapter references cover some but not necessarily all of the specification)

Examination analysis

The specification comprises twenty key studies, examined in units 1 and 2, plus a unit on practical work.

Unit 1	Core Studies 1 (questions on the core studies) 16–20 compulsory short answer questions	1 hr	33.3%
Unit 2	Core Studies 2 (essay questions related to core studies) Part A: choice of 1 from 2 structured essays (50%) Part B: choice of 1 from 2 structured essays (50%)	1 hr	33.3%
Unit 3	Practical work examination. Candidates should complete a practical folder containing notes about four specified practical activities. The examination will ask about 10–12 compulsory questions about these four practical activities, as well as questions on general issues of methodology.	1 hr	33.3%

AS/A2 Level Psychology courses

AS and A2

All Psychology A Level courses being studied from September 2000 are in two parts, with three separate units or modules in each part. Most students will start by studying the AS (Advanced Subsidiary) course. Some will then go on to study the second part of the A Level course, called the A2. It is also possible to study the full A Level course, both AS and A2, in any order.

How will you be tested?

Assessment units

For AS Psychology, you will be tested by three assessment units. For the full A Level in Psychology, you will take a further three units. AS Psychology forms 50% of the assessment weighting for the full A Level.

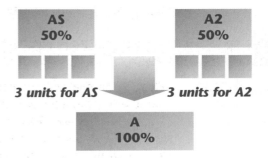

Each unit can normally be taken in either January or June. Alternatively, you can study the whole course before taking any of the unit tests. There is a lot of flexibility about when exams can be taken and the diagram below shows just some of the ways that the assessment units may be taken for AS and A Level Psychology.

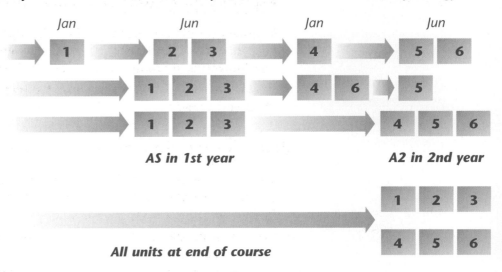

If you are disappointed with a module result, you can resit each module once. You will need to be very careful about when you take up a resit opportunity because you will have only one chance to improve your mark. The higher mark counts.

A2 and Synoptic assessment

For those students who, having studied AS, decide to go on to study A2, there are three further units to be studied. Similar assessment arrangements apply except some units, those that draw together various elements of the course in a 'synoptic' assessment, have to be assessed at the end. The question style is intended to be a progression from AS.

Coursework

Coursework will form part of your A Level Psychology course. In some specifications this does not come until the A2 part of the course.

Key skills

It is important that you develop your key skills throughout the AS and A2 courses that you take, as these are skills that you need whatever you do beyond AS and A Levels. To gain the key skills qualification, which is equivalent to an AS Level, you will need to demonstrate that you have attained Level 3 in Communication, Application of number and Information technology. Part of the assessment can be done as normal class activity and part is by formal test. It is a worthwhile qualification, as it demonstrates your ability to put your ideas across to other people, collect data and use up-to-date technology in your work.

What skills will I need?

Following an examination course means that much of your learning is guided by how it will ultimately be assessed. Examination boards set out their assessment objectives: these are skills and abilities you should have acquired by studying the course. In the new A Level examinations there are three skill clusters, which in brief are: describe (AO1), evaluate (AO2), and conduct (AO3). There is also an assessment of the Quality of Written Communication (QoWC).

These objectives are shown below.

Knowledge and understanding (AO1)

- Knowledge and understanding of Psychological theories, terminology, concepts, studies and methods in the core areas of cognitive, social, developmental, individual differences and Physiological Psychology.
- Communicate knowledge and understanding of Psychology in a clear and effective manner.

Analyse and evaluate (AO2)

- Analyse and evaluate psychological theories, concepts, studies and methods in the core areas of cognitive, social, developmental, individual differences and Physiological Psychology.
- Communicate knowledge and understanding of Psychology in a clear and effective manner.

In general, the AS assessment contains more AO1 assessment than AO2.

Design, conduct and report (AO3)

- Design, conduct and report psychological investigation(s), choosing from a range of methods, and taking into account the issues of reliability, validity and ethics.
- Collect and draw conclusions from data.

Quality of Written Communication (QoWC)

The Quality of Written Communication is assessed in all AS and A2 assessment units where candidates are required to produce extended written material. Candidates will be assessed according to their ability to:

- select and use a form and style of writing appropriate to a complex subject matter
- organise relevant information clearly and coherently, using specialist vocabulary when appropriate
- ensure text is legible, and spelling, grammar and punctuation are accurate, so that meaning is clear.

AQA A Key Studies:

The AQA A specification requires that you know certain studies in depth. Only the topics are specified for these studies, for example 'one study of eyewitness testimony' or 'one study of privation'. Throughout this book suitable examples have been provided for all of the topic areas.

OCR core studies:

The OCR specification requires that you know certain studies in depth. The studies are specified (see page 7). Some of these studies have been covered in this book.

IMPORTANT INFORMATION
(This book is based on the latest versions of specifications, however these do change and candidates should always consult the website of the appropriate examining board to check the latest versions.)

Key Term   Throughout the book AQA Key Terms are highlighted with this symbol.

Different types of questions in AS examinations

Short-answer questions

A short-answer question may test recall or it may test understanding by requiring you to recall information from your studies. This style of question is used in OCR units 1 and 2. For example:

> Milgram's study of obedience is often criticised for being unethical, though Milgram himself made a robust defence of it. Give **two** examples of how the ethics of this study can be defended. *(Specimen paper for Unit 1)*

Structured questions

Structured questions are in several parts. The parts are usually about a common context and they often become progressively more difficult and more demanding as you work your way through the question. They may start with simple recall, then require more elaborate description of a study or a theory. The most difficult part of a structured question is usually at the end, where the candidate is asked to analyse the evidence related to a specific issue.

When answering structured questions, do not feel that you have to complete one question before starting the next. The further you are into a question, the more difficult the marks are to obtain. If you run out of ideas, go on to the next question. Five minutes spent on the beginning of that question are likely to be much more fruitful than the same time spent wracking your brains trying to think of an explanation for an unfamiliar phenomenon.

Here is an example of a structured question that becomes progressively more demanding.

(a) Explain what is meant by the terms obedience and conformity (majority influence). [3+3 marks]

(b) Describe the procedures and finding of **one** study that has explored minority influence. [6 marks]

(c) Milgram's and Zimbardo's studies provoked public outcry because of the ethical issues raised.

Outline some ethical issues raised in social influence research and consider to what extent such ethical issues can be justified. [18 marks]

The AQA specification A examination uses the following mark scheme to assess parts (a) and (b) of this question, and the AOI component of part (c):

Skill cluster A01

Band 3: 5-6 marks
The description is **accurate** and **detailed**.

Band 2: 3-4 marks
The description is **limited**. It is **generally accurate** but **less detailed**.

Band 1: 1-2 marks
The description is **basic, lacking detail** and may be **muddled**.

0 marks
The description of a research study of conformity is **inappropriate** or the description is **incorrect**. Where an answer is marked out of 3, then the marks are changed accordingly.

Extended answers

In AS Level Psychology, questions requiring more extended answers will usually form part of structured questions *(AQA A)* or be the last question on the question paper *(Edexcel and OCR)*. They will be characterised by having more than 6 marks. These questions are also used to assess your abilities to communicate ideas and put together a logical argument. For example:

> To what extent can forgetting be explained in terms of repression? *(AQA A)*

> Discuss **two** contributions of either Freud or Rogers to the development of Psychology. *(AQA B)*

> Discuss the effects of shift work on circadian rhythms. *(Edexcel)*

> What impact have the findings about human behaviour and experience had on everyday life, good or bad? *(OCR)*

The 'correct' answers to extended questions are less well-defined than those requiring short answers. Examiners may have a list of points for which credit is awarded up to the maximum for the question, or they may first of all judge the 'quality' of your response as poor, satisfactory or good before allocating it a mark within a range that corresponds to that 'quality'.

The AQA specification A uses the following mark scheme for extended answer questions:

Skill cluster A02

12–11 marks
There is an **informed commentary** and **reasonably thorough analysis** of the relevant psychological studies/methods. Material has been used in an **effective** manner.

10–9 marks
There is a **reasonable commentary** and **slightly limited analysis** of relevant psychological studies/methods. Material has been used in an **effective** manner.

8–7 marks
There is a **reasonable commentary** of relevant psychological studies/method and a **slightly limited analysis** of the relevant psychological studies/methods. Material has been used in a **reasonably effective** manner.

6–5 marks
There is a **basic commentary** but a **limited analysis** of the relevant psychological studies/methods. Material has been used in a **reasonably effective** manner.

4–3 marks
There is **superficial commentary** and **rudimentary analysis** of the relevant psychological studies/methods. There is **minimal interpretation** of the material used.

2–1 marks
Commentary is **just discernible** (for example, through appropriate selection of material). Analysis is **weak** and **muddled**. The answer may be **mainly irrelevant** to the problem it addresses.

0 marks
Commentary is **wholly irrelevant** to the problem it addresses.

Exam technique

Links from GCSE

AS Level Psychology is a step up from GCSE. You can take a GCSE in Psychology but this would mean covering very much the same information. The advantage of this is that the work will be quite easy because it is familiar, and you can focus on tackling slightly more difficult assignments and focus on those areas that are new.

Most students doing AS Level Psychology will be new to the subject but there are still links to your earlier GCSEs. Physiological Psychology is concerned with the same subject matter as Biology, and some of the things you have studied in Mathematics will come in useful here (such as drawing graphs and calculating statistics).

The most important thing to realise is that the level of this AS exam is designed to be just the right sort of step up for you, after studying GCSE. You will be required to learn about more complex ideas and, in the examination, to answer more extended questions than during your GCSE studies.

What are examiners looking for?

Psychology examiners are looking for evidence of your knowledge, but often there are no 'right' answers. There are a range of correct answers and any of these will receive credit. The examiners mark your answers *positively*. They do not subtract marks when material is missing. Instead they award marks for any material that is relevant. You must aim to demonstrate your knowledge and understanding.

Whatever type of question you are answering, it is important to respond in the correct way to the **command words** at the beginning of the question:

Recall

To identify and reinforce knowledge gained at Key Stage 4 through the study of the National Curriculum science programme, also through the study of other units in this specification.

Understand

To explain the underlying principles and apply the knowledge to novel situations (AO2).

Appreciate

To show awareness of the significance, without detailed knowledge of the underlying principles.

Discuss

To give a balanced, reasoned objective account of a particular topic.

Distinguish

To recognise comparable differences in a given context, e.g. different types of neurones within the nervous system.

Outline

To briefly describe without explanation, identifying main points.

Describe

To give details without explanation.

Evaluate

To comment on, giving advantages and disadvantages, or give a judgement.

Apply

To explain how a concept is significant when considering everyday issues or novel situations.

Some dos and don'ts

Dos

Do read all the questions first.

If you have to choose between questions make sure you choose the right question for you. Don't end up discovering that you could do parts (a) and (b) but haven't a clue about part (c).

Do answer the question.

This sounds obvious but, under examination conditions, students feel very anxious and write about anything they can think of. Sometimes they don't even read the whole question. They just look at the first few words and start writing.

Do use the mark allocation to guide you in how much you should write.

Two marks is likely to mean two valid points. If you write lots and lots for a question with very few marks you won't get extra credit and you will leave less time for the other questions.

Do write legibly and try to use technical terms and correct spelling.

There are marks in the examination for your quality of written communication, and this includes the use of technical terms. It also helps to use names and dates if you know them.

Don'ts

Don't regurgitate your prepared answer because you got a good mark for it in class. If it doesn't answer the question set, it will receive no credit.

Don't ignore features of a question.

If the question says 'describe one study of work stress', explain how the study you select demonstrates work stress. Explain any ambiguities to the examiner.

Don't leave out obvious material.

It is very easy to think 'the examiner knows this' and presume that you don't have to write down the obvious things. However, the examiner cannot be sure that you know it unless you demonstrate it.

Don't waste time.

An examination has a finite length, so don't spend time 'waffling' because you think the examiner might find something relevant in what you say. Spend time thinking and select what you say very carefully.

What grade do you want?

For a Grade A

- You must be able to cope with the evaluation as well as the description (skills AO1 and AO2).

- To do this type of work you need to practise by writing lots of answers to extended-type questions. In the AQA A questions the evaluation part of the question is always the last part.

- Increase your understanding by trying to discuss your studies with other people. For example, you might try to explain psychological research into conformity to your mother. What does it all mean?

For a Grade C

- You must have thoroughly learned the material. You will need to get virtually full marks on all the AO1 questions (description).

- Memory is improved by organising the material. Write your own notes using your own method of organisation.

- Practise examination questions and try to find out where you lost marks, and why.

For a Grade E

- Aim to get high marks on the most straightforward questions.

- Memorise the definitions of all key terms.

- Don't overlook any question. Try to write something.

- If your examination has a coursework component, make sure you get as high a mark as possible on this.

- Select one area that you especially enjoy and do the most work on this.

What marks do you need?

Each examination board publishes their own grade boundaries. Visit their website to find out:

www.aqa.org.uk

www.ocr.org.uk

www.edexcel.org.uk

Four steps to successful revision

Step 1: Understand

- Study the topic to be learned slowly. Make sure you understand the logic or important concepts.
- Mark up the text if necessary – underline, highlight and make notes.
- Re-read each paragraph slowly.

GO TO STEP 2

Step 2: Summarise

- Now make your own revision note summary:
  What is the main idea, theme or concept to be learned?
  What are the main points? How does the logic develop?
  Ask questions: Why? How? What next?
- Use bullet points, mind maps, patterned notes.
- Link ideas with mnemonics, mind maps, crazy stories.
- Note the title and date of the revision notes
  (e.g. Psychology: Attitudes and prejudice, 3rd March).
- Organise your notes carefully and keep them in a file.

This is now in short-term memory. You will forget 80% of it if you do not go to Step 3. GO TO STEP 3, but first take a 10 minute break.

Step 3: Memorise

- Take 25 minute learning 'bites' with 5 minute breaks.
- After each 5 minute break test yourself:
  Cover the original revision note summary
  Write down the main points
  Speak out loud (record on tape)
  Tell someone else
  Repeat many times.

The material is well on its way to long-term memory. You will forget 40% if you do not do step 4. GO TO STEP 4

Step 4: Track / Review

- Create a Revision Diary (one A4 page per day).
- Make a revision plan for the topic, e.g. 1 day later, 1 week later, 1 month later.
- Record your revision in your Revision Diary, e.g.
  Psychology: Attitudes and prejudice, 3rd March 25 minutes
  Psychology: Attitudes and prejudice, 5th March 15 minutes
  Psychology: Attitudes and prejudice, 3rd April 15 minutes
  ... and then at monthly intervals.

Chapter 1

The study of psychology

The following topics are covered in this chapter:

- *Key approaches and the development of psychology*

1.1 Key approaches and the development of psychology

What is psychology?

AQA A	general
AQA B	U1
EDEXCEL	general
OCR	U1, U2

Psychology is the scientific study of behaviour and experience. It differs from common sense in so far as it seeks to collect objective and verifiable facts about behaviour and construct empirically based theories.

The scientific process involves:

- making observations, and producing 'facts' (data about the world)
- constructing a theory to account for a set of related facts
- generating expectations (hypotheses) from the theory
- collecting data to test expectations
- adjusting the theory in response to the data collected.

Data can be collected in two ways:

- **empirically**, through direct experience or observation
- **rationally**, by constructing reasoned arguments.

> Sometimes 'approaches' are called 'perspectives'. Both describe a characteristic way of looking at the world. Every psychological theory grows out of a perspective or 'world-view'.

The psychodynamic approach

AQA A	U2
AQA B	U1
EDEXCEL	U2
OCR	U1, U2

'Psychodynamic' refers to any approach which emphasises the processes of change and development (i.e. dynamics). Freud's psychoanalytic theory is the best-known psychodynamic theory. The term psychoanalysis describes both a theory of personality and the therapy derived from it. Key assumptions of the psychodynamic approach are as follows:

- Human development is a **dynamic process** (i.e. it is driven or motivated by certain forces).
- Importance of **early experience**. Infants are born with innate biological drives, e.g. for oral satisfaction.
- **Ego defence.** If innate drives are thwarted or not satisfied, anxiety is produced. The ego defends itself against anxiety using ego-defence mechanisms (e.g. repression, denial, projection). Ego defenses can explain abnormal and/or unconscious behaviour.
- **The unconscious.** Many aspects of personality dynamics are unconscious, and their expression is indirect, for example through dreams and in 'Freudian slips'.

> Freud (1920) gave the following example of the Freudian slip: a British MP was speaking of his colleague from Hull but said 'the honourable member from Hell', thus revealing his private thoughts about the other MP.

Key concepts in psychoanalytic theory

The structure of the personality

- The **id** (or 'it'). This is the primitive, instinctive part that demands immediate satisfaction. Motivated by the **pleasure principle** ('it' gets what 'it' wants).
- The **ego** (or 'I') develops in the first two years of life as a result of the child's experience. Motivated by the **reality principle**, the child learns to accommodate to the demands of the environment and modifies the demands of the id.
- The **superego** (or 'above-I') develops at about the age of five. It is equivalent to the conscience.

Psychosexual stages of development

The three strands of Freud's theory of development are: driving forces (e.g. the pleasure principle), personality structure (e.g. the id), and the organ-focus (e.g. oral).

The child seeks gratification through different body organs during development. If conflicts arising from these developmental stages are not resolved satisfactorily they can lead to 'fixations' later in adult life.

- **Oral stage** (0–18 months). Oral fixation from too much or too little gratification of the id, may result in, for example, thumb-sucking.
- **Anal stage** (18–36 months). Anal fixation could be due to either strict toilet training, or pleasure taken in playing with faeces.
- **Phallic stage** (3–6 years). A fixation on genitals leads to the Oedipus Complex (desire for mother, jealousy and guilt towards father, resolved by identification with father; this is described further in Freud's case study of Little Hans – see p.20). Girls, on the other hand, realise they have no penis and blame their mother. 'Penis envy' is resolved by a desire to have babies. This conflict resolution is weaker for girls and therefore, according to Freud, girls don't develop as strong a sense of moral justice as boys. Jung proposed an 'Electra complex' – a young girl feels desire for her father and rejects her mother.
- **Latency stage** (7 until puberty): the in-between years. Little psychosocial development takes place but children develop socially by interacting with other children, e.g. at school (although boys and girls do not interact much).
- **Genital stage** (puberty). The development of independence is now possible if earlier conflicts have been resolved.

Therapy (see Chapter 5, p.116–117).

Evaluation of the psychodynamic approach

Freud did not mean the term 'sexual' in the way many people interpret it. 'Sexual' roughly means 'physical' or 'sensual'.

Positive points include the following:

- Freud's important contribution was to **recognise childhood** as a critical period of development, and to identify sexual (physical) and unconscious influences.
- The theory has been enormously **influential** within psychology, and beyond.
- It is an **idiographic** approach, meaning that it focuses more on the individual than on general laws of behaviour (the nomothetic approach). Psychoanalytic theory provides a rich picture of individual personality dynamics.

Criticisms of the theory are that:

- It lacks rigorous **empirical support**, especially regarding normal development. The 'evidence' comes largely from case studies of middle-class, European women, many of whom were neurotic. The data was retrospectively collected and given subjective interpretation (thus introducing potential **investigator bias** – see p.171).
- It reduces human activity to a basic set of structures, which are **reifications** (abstract concepts which are presented as if they are real things).
- It is **deterministic** (it implies that people have little if any choice or free will), suggesting that infant behaviour is determined by innate forces and adult behaviour is determined by childhood experiences.
- The original theory lays too much emphasis on **innate biological forces**.

Methods used in the psychodynamic approach

Case studies

Psychoanalytic studies focused on one person (see Freud's case study of Little Hans on p.20), though a case study could also be of one family, one school or a particular event. Case studies offer insight into unusual behaviour and provide rich details grounded in real life. They are an idiographic approach to data collection.

In a case study an individual may be interviewed to discover details of their present and past, or psychometric tests may be used to assess personality, intelligence and other abilities.

The drawbacks of case studies are that:
- they are **time-consuming** and unreliable (retrospective data, interviewer bias)
- they **can't be replicated** and it may not be reasonable to generalise the findings to all human behaviour
- there may be **ethical objections** in terms of invasion of privacy.

As already indicated, there are advantages to case studies, such as rich data.

Clinical interviews

The interview method is described on p.162–163. Clinical interviews, as used by doctors and therapists, start with a predetermined set of questions. As the clinical interview (like an unstructured interview) progresses, the questions are adapted in line with some of the responses given. This means that unexpected answers and individual differences can be accommodated. The method maximises the amount of information gained and may lead to new discoveries.

The drawback of interviews is that:

- the interviewer needs to be highly experienced because their questions may affect the kinds of answers given (**interviewer bias**).

The advantages of interviews are described on p.162–163.

Analysis of symbols in dreams

Freud proposed that the **latent content** of dreams may be represented in symbols (the **manifest content** being the dream as reported by the dreamer). Some symbols are personal, related to an individual's experiences, whereas others are universal. For instance, Freud suggested that guns or swords were representations of the penis, whereas vessels such as ships and jars represented the female genital organs. In order to interpret personal symbols, the therapist has to become familiar with an individual's life history.

A criticism of dream interpretation is that it lacks **falsifiability** (i.e. cannot be proven wrong). If the patient rejects the therapist's interpretation, this may be seen as resistance. If the patient accepts the interpretation, this confirms its accuracy.

Neo-Freudians

Other theorists, such as Erikson and Jung, produced psychodynamic theories which placed less emphasis on biological forces and more on the influences of social and cultural factors. Erikson's work with adolescents and Sioux Indians led him to believe that many aspects of behaviour were culturally rather than biologically based.

Progress check

1 Name one assumption of the psychodynamic approach.
2 Name one method used by the psychodynamic approach.

1 E.g. the importance of early experience; the influence of the unconscious.
2 E.g. case studies; analysis of symbols.

OCR core study: Little Hans

Freud (1909) Analysis of a phobia

Aims To document the case history of a boy who had developed an extreme phobia of white horses.

Procedures & Findings This was a case history of a 5-year-old boy whose father was a supporter of Freud. The case history was recorded by the father and discussed with Freud, who only met the boy twice. The chief findings of the case history (chronologically) were:

- *His 'widdler'.* Hans was fascinated by his 'widdler' (his penis). He observed that animals had big ones and probably so did both his parents because they were grown up.

- *His mother.* Hans spent a lot of time alone with his mother over the summer holiday and realised he liked having her to himself. He wished his father would stay away. He also felt hostile towards his new baby sister who further separated Hans from his mother. He expressed this indirectly in his fear of baths because he thought his mother would drop him (in fact, he *wished* his mother would drop his little sister – a desire which he projected elsewhere because of the anxiety it aroused).

- *Horses and anxiety.* There were two strands to Hans' anxiety: (1) Hans once heard a man saying to a child 'Don't put your finger to the white horse or it'll bite you'. (2) Hans asked his mother if she would like to put her finger on his widdler. His mother told him this would not be proper. Therefore Hans learned that touching a white horse or a widdler was undesirable. Hans' desire (libido) for his mother created a sense of anxiety and fear that she might leave him if he persisted in asking her to touch his widdler. Unconsciously this anxiety was projected elsewhere: he became afraid of being bitten by a white horse.

- *More anxiety* was created by the fact that Hans' mother told Hans that, if he played with his widdler, it would be cut off. Hans' father told Hans that women have no widdler. Hans reasoned that his mother's must have been cut off – and she might do the same to him.

- *Dream about giraffes.* Hans dreamt that there were two giraffes – one crumpled and one big. He took away the crumpled one and this made the big one cry out. This might represent Hans' wish to take away his mother (crumpled one) causing his father to cry out (big giraffe – possible symbol of penis). Hans sat on the crumpled one (trying to claim his mother for himself).

- *Symbolism.* Freud suggested to Hans that the black around horses' mouths and the blinkers in front of their eyes were like his father's moustaches and glasses. Hans might envy these symbols of adulthood because they might give him the right to have a woman's love.

- *Further horse anxieties.* Hans told his father that he was afraid of horses falling down, and if they were laden (e.g. with furniture) this might lead them to fall down. Hans also remembered seeing a horse fall down and thinking it was dead. Since he secretly wished his father would fall down dead this made Hans feel more anxious.

- *The 'lumf' obsession.* Hans now became preoccupied with bowel movements ('lumf'). Freud suggested that laden vehicles represented pregnancy and when they overturn it symbolises giving birth. Thus the falling horse was both his dying father and his mother giving birth.

- *The plumber.* Hans was in the bath and the plumber stuck a big borer into his stomach. Freud called this a 'fantasy of procreation'. The bath is the mother's womb (and Hans is in it). The borer is his father's penis, which created him.

- *The resolution.* Hans became less afraid of horses because he had worked through his fantasies and understood their real meaning – they were no longer unconscious and he could deal with them. He developed two final fantasies which showed that his feelings about his father were resolved: (1) 'The plumber came and first he took away my behind with a pair of pincers, and then he gave me another, and then the same with my widdler', (2) Hans told his father that he was now the daddy and not the mummy of his imaginary children, thus showing that he had moved from wishing his father dead to identifying with him.

Conclusions This provides support for Freud's theory of psychosexual development, and evidence for Freud's explanation of the origins of disordered behaviour.

OCR Revision question
a) In the study by Freud, Little Hans is referred to as 'a little Oedipus'. Briefly describe the Oedipus complex. [2]

b) Outline **one** piece of evidence from the study that is used to support the claim that Hans is a 'little Oedipus'. [2] (January 2001, Core Studies 1, question 4)

The behaviourist approach

AQA A	U2
AQA B	U1
EDEXCEL	U2
OCR	U1, U2

Introspectionism was a highly formalised investigative technique. Individuals were trained to produce evidence about their thoughts and mental states.

This approach has its roots in nineteenth-century empirical philosophy (e.g. that of Locke) which believed that we should only study what can be directly observed (**positivism**). Watson (1913) coined the term 'behaviourism', suggesting that Pavlov's **classical conditioning** theory could be used to explain all behaviour, and that this approach was preferable to Wundt's **introspectionism**.

Thorndike (1913) expanded learning theory to include 'instrumental learning', later adapted by Skinner (1938) into **operant conditioning**. Skinner's views represent 'radical behaviourism' – the position that there are private, less accessible activities (mental events or the contents of the 'black box') but these are not needed in the explanation of behaviour.

Key assumptions of the behaviourist approach are as follows:

- Humans and non-human animals are only **quantitatively different**, i.e. they differ in terms of having more or less of something rather than differing qualitatively.
- There is no need to look at what goes on inside the 'black box' – it is sufficient to be concerned with external and **observable behaviour** only.
- All behaviour can be explained in terms of **conditioning theory**: stimulus and response (S–R) links which build up to produce more complex behaviours.
- All behaviour is determined by **environmental influences**, i.e. learning. We are born as a blank slate.

Key concepts of behaviourist (learning) theory

Classical conditioning

Learning to associate a stimulus with a response.

Before	NS (neutral stimulus, bell)	→ no response
	UCS (unconditioned stimulus, food)	→ UCR (unconditioned response, salivation)
During conditioning		NS and UCS are paired by occurring together
After	CS (conditioned stimulus, bell)	→ CR (conditioned response, salivation)

Operant conditioning

Learning due to the consequences of a behaviour (response).

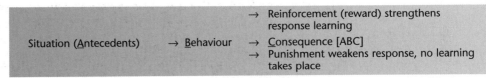

Situation (Antecedents)	→ Behaviour	→ Reinforcement (reward) strengthens response learning
		→ Consequence [ABC]
		→ Punishment weakens response, no learning takes place

The probability of a behaviour being repeated depends on strengthening or weakening S–R links:

- **Positive reinforcement** increases the probability of a response recurring because the response is pleasurable – for example, receiving a smile when you give someone a kiss.
- **Negative reinforcement** – escape from an unpleasant stimulus. This is also pleasurable and increases the probability of the same response in the future. For example, finding that a smile stops your mother shouting at you.
- **Positive punishment** (punishment by application), receiving something unpleasant, decreases probability of a future behaviour. For example, being told off for smiling at an inappropriate moment.
- **Negative punishment** (punishment by removal), removing something desirable, also decreases probability of future behaviour. For example, not being allowed your dessert because you didn't finish the main course.

All reinforcement (positive or negative) increases the likelihood of a response.

Features of conditioning

- **Generalisation.** Animal responds in the same way to stimuli which are similar.
- **Extinction.** The new response disappears because it is no longer paired with the original stimulus or is not reinforced.
- **Shaping.** Animal gradually learns a target behaviour by being reinforced for behaviours which are closer and closer to the target.
- **Reinforcement schedules.** Partial reinforcement schedules are more effective and more resistant to extinction. This may be because, under continuous reinforcement, the organism 'expects' it on every trial and therefore 'notices' its absence more quickly. Partial reinforcement includes fixed or variable ratios, and fixed or variable intervals. An example of a fixed ratio would be a reward once in every ten trials; an example of a fixed interval would be a reward every 10 minutes.

Skinner's approach concentrated on the effects of emitted behaviour rather than Pavlov's focus on the elicited behaviours themselves. ('To emit' means to spontaneously produce, whereas 'to elicit' means to draw forth.)

Evaluation of the behaviourist approach

Positive points include the following:

- Classic learning theory has had a major influence on all areas of Psychology – **methodological behaviourism** is the view that all approaches use some behaviourist concepts to explain behaviour.
- Behaviourism has given rise to many **practical applications**.
- It is an empirical perspective which lends itself to **scientific research**. Broadbent (1961) argued that it is the best method for rational advance in psychology.

Criticisms of the theory are that it:

- **is a mechanistic (machine-like) perspective** which ignores consciousness, subjective experience, and emotions
- **excludes the role of cognitive factors** and cannot explain, for example, insight learning and cognitive maps
- denies the role of **innate factors**
- **is deterministic**: behaviour is determined by the environment
- **is reductionist**: reduces complex behaviour to stimulus–response links
- is largely based on work with **non-human animals**. Behaviourists argue that the theory of evolution shows that human and non-human animals are quantitatively not qualitatively different and therefore such research is meaningless

Reductionism refers to the process of reducing complex matters to a set of simple rules or components. Behaviourism is a very reductionist approach.

- can lead to the use of behaviourist principles to control others (as in some prisons and psychiatric institutions) and this could be considered **unethical**.

Methods used in the behaviourist approach

Laboratory experiments

These are described later in Chapter 7, on p. 160–161.

Non-human-animal learning experiments

Skinner (1938) placed a pigeon in a 'Skinner box' and if it pecked a lever, a door would open and food (the reinforcer) was delivered. The pigeon first pecks randomly around the box as part of its natural exploratory behaviour. Accidentally it pecks the lever a few times and receives food. Each experience strengthens the S–R link. Reinforcement is positive (when the lever is pecked) and also any unrewarded behaviour is 'stamped out' (when pecking elsewhere no food appears). Behaviour has thus been brought under stimulus control. If the pigeon learns to peck at a button whenever it is lit to get food, it is **learning** to discriminate between different states of illumination of the button (a discriminative stimulus).

The drawback of this approach is that it may not be appropriate to make generalisations from the study of non-human animals to human behaviour because much of human behaviour is influenced by higher-level thinking.

Social learning theory

Neo-behaviourist approaches are those which are based on behaviourist principles but use un-observable processes (mental events) in their explanations – for example, social learning theory which was developed by Dollard and Miller (1950). The key concepts for social learning theory are:

- As well as direct reinforcement and punishment, behaviour is learned through **indirect (vicarious)** reinforcement and punishment, i.e. by seeing others reinforced or punished. Much more can be learned indirectly.
- Individuals imitate the behaviour of others either because they see it **rewarded** and/or because they **identify** with significant others (e.g. people of the same gender, or TV idols, or parents). In order to imitate behaviour, one must store an internal representation of that behaviour.

Bandura *et al.* (1961) demonstrated how aggressiveness can be learned through modelling (see the OCR core study on p.24).

The advantage of this approach is that is goes beyond traditional learning theory in the inclusion of **un-observable** and **cognitive** and **social** factors. Its weakness is that it doesn't include the effects of **emotional factors**.

Progress check

1 Name one assumption of the behaviourist approach.
2 What is the difference between positive and negative reinforcement?
3 What is 'shaping'?

3 Receiving rewards for behaviours that are closer and closer to the target behaviour.

2 Positive reinforcement involves a reward whereas in negative reinforcement pleasure is derived by escaping from an aversive stimulus.

1 E.g. that everything is learned.

OCR core study: Imitating aggression

Bandura *et al.* (1961) Transmission of aggression through imitation of aggressive models

Aims Is aggression learned through imitation? Do observers imitate specific acts or do they just become more aggressive? Would children be more likely to imitate a same-sex model?

Procedures This was a laboratory experiment. The participants were children from a university nursery school, 36 boys and 36 girls aged approximately 3 to 5 years. Two adult 'models', a male and a female.

Phase 1: Exposure to aggression. Each child was taken on their own to a room where there were lots of toys including, in one corner, a 5-foot inflatable 'Bobo' doll and a mallet. The experimenter invited the 'model' to join them and then left the room for about 10 minutes. Participants had been allocated to one of three conditions on the basis of a pre-test for aggressiveness so that each group contained equally aggressive children:

- *Non-aggressive condition*: The model played with the toys in a quiet manner.
- *Aggressive condition*: The model spent some of the time being aggressive to Bobo, including some specific acts, e.g. repeatedly punching it on the nose.
- *Control*: The report does not say what treatment these children received.

Phase 2: Tests for imitation. In order to find out whether the children imitated the aggressive model it was necessary to 'mildly' provoke the children to behave aggressively – the children were taken to a room of attractive toys and then told they couldn't play with these. They were then taken to another room which contained some aggressive toys (e.g. a mallet, and a dart gun), some non-aggressive toys (e.g. dolls and farm animals) and a Bobo doll. The children were observed through a one-way mirror while they played. A record was made of any physical or verbal aggression and whether it was imitative of the model's behaviour.

Findings *Imitation*: Children in the aggressive condition imitated specific behaviours. Children in the non-aggressive condition displayed very few of these behaviours (70% had zero scores).

Non-imitative aggression: The aggressive group displayed much more non-imitative aggression than the non-aggressive group, ie. they were generally more aggressive.

Non-aggressive behaviour: Children in the non-aggressive condition spent more time playing non-aggressively with dolls.

Gender: Boys imitated more physical aggression than girls but not verbal aggression. There was some evidence of a 'same-sex effect' between model and children.

Conclusions This provides evidence that learning can take place in the absence of either classical or operant conditioning. The children imitated the model's behaviour in the *absence* of any rewards. Bandura *et al.* suggest that Freud's concept of identification may be useful in explaining how learning took place but more investigation is needed to understand the modelling process.

OCR Revision question
a) From the study by Bandura, Ross and Ross, outline **one** difference that was found between the aggressive behaviour of boys and that of girls. [2]
b) Outline **one** possible reason for the gender differences that were found. [2]
(January 2002, Core Studies 1, question 2)

> The pre-test (before the experiment) was done to ensure that there were a similar number of aggressive children in each condition, otherwise aggressiveness could have been a confounding variable.

> This study has been used as support in general for social learning theory yet the data is based on the imitative behaviour of children. Adults might not behave in the same way since they are less impressionable.

The humanistic approach

 AQA B   U1

Maslow called humanistic psychology the 'third force in psychology', in its rejection of determinism and reductionism. Humanistic approaches are a reflection of modern-day society in the same way that both psychoanalysis and behaviourism are a reflection of their times.

Key assumptions of the humanistic approach are as follows:

- Each individual is *unique*. What matters is each person's subjective view rather than some objective reality. Reality is defined by the individual's perspective.
- Human nature is positive and inherently good. Each person strives for growth and **actualisation**.
- Individuals are capable of **self-determination** (free will).

Evaluation of the humanistic approach

Positive points include the following:

- This **subjective approach** has encouraged psychologists to accept the view that there is more to behaviour than objectively discoverable facts.
- It has had **widespread application** in counselling and client- or person-centred therapy (Rogers, 1951).

Criticisms of the theory are that:

- it is largely a vague, unscientific and **untestable** approach.

> Rogers was the founder of client-centred therapy, or counselling. He believed that maladjustment stemmed from receiving conditional love as a child. This results in a conflict between the self and the ideal self, and means the individual is likely to try to be someone else in order to receive the love they want.

Methods used in the humanistic approach

Humanistic psychologists believe that psychological theories should be humanly rather than statistically significant, claiming that objective data can tell us little about subjective experience. New research methods are needed to properly investigate human behaviour, such as **new paradigm research** (Reason and Rowan, 1981) and **ethogenics** (Harré and Secord, 1972). Ethogenics involves a careful analysis of sequences of events, without quantifying them, to understand how successive episodes interlock.

Progress check

1   Name one assumption of the humanistic approach in psychology.
2   What is one advantage of the humanistic approach in psychology?

2 E.g. emphasises the importance of individual experience.
1 E.g. each person strives for self-actualisation.

Sample question and student answer

AQA B style question

from AQA B specimen paper Unit 1 Introducing psychology, question 1

(a) Identify and describe **one** characteristic of the scientific method. [3]

(b) Discuss **one** limitation of the scientific study of human behaviour. [4]

(c) Identify and describe **one** assumption of the behaviourist approach in psychology. [3]

(d) Discuss **two** contributions of either Freud or Rogers to the development of psychology. [10]

> The candidate has correctly identified a characteristic of the scientific method (1 mark) and made an attempt to describe this characteristic. Some understanding is apparent but the description is not entirely clear (1 mark). (Total of 2 marks for this part.)

(a) One characteristic of the scientific method is that it is objective. This means that observations are made from an objective point of view rather than one individual's view.

> The question requires a discussion rather than simply a description, as in part (a). 'Discuss' entails both description and evaluation. The candidate has offered both: a description of one limitation and then a consideration of why this is a limitation and a means of overcoming it. Additional credit might have been gained by elaborating on this final point. (3 marks)

(b) One problem with the scientific approach is that human behaviour does not lend itself to objective study. If you stand outside an individual and make objective observations of their behaviour you don't take their subjective experience into account. This latter approach is taken by humanistic psychologists.

> The candidate has identified two assumptions and not given a description of either. Only one can be credited. (1 mark)

(c) One assumption of the behaviourist approach is that all that matters is observable behaviour. Another assumption is that all behaviour can be explained in terms of learning.

(d) I will write about two contributions from Freud. His first contribution to psychology was to write a theory of development. He described how biological forces interact with experience to produce adult personality. In the first stage of development the primitive force, the id, makes demands and wants immediate gratification. If these biological demands are not met then the individual has repressed desires and these will surface in later life, being expressed in different ways. For example, a repressed desire during the oral stage of development might later be expressed as a parsimonious personality.

The other elements of the personality are the ego and super-ego. The ego is governed by the reality principle. The super-ego develops out of identification with the same-sex parent. The other stages of development after the oral stage are the anal, phallic, latency and genital stages.

Freud's theory has been very influential in psychology and many other areas such as literature. His approach of studying individuals in detail produced a lot of rich data concerning those individuals. On the other hand, these individuals were a very biased sample (female, middle-class, neurotic) and therefore his theory of personality may not actually account for all people all over the world. Another criticism of Freud's theory is that it is deterministic, suggesting that adult personality is the result of innate biological forces rather than being the result of an individual's decision to behave in a particular way.

> The candidate has identified two contributions from Freud and offered a good description for both, though the second one is slightly limited. Unfortunately evaluation is only offered for the first contribution which means that the overall mark would be 7. The candidate would have done better to spend less time on the descriptive material and include some evaluation of the second contribution. (7 marks)

Freud's second contribution was a therapy to treat mentally ill patients. The main features of this therapy are free association, where the therapist says something and then the patient talks freely about whatever comes into their head, and dream analysis, where the patient recounts their dreams and the therapist turns the manifest content into the latent content and tells the patient what they were really thinking. These methods give the therapist a chance to have insights into the patient's unconscious thoughts which can then be dealt with. Only that way can the patient resolve those things which are causing their neurotic behaviour.

TOTAL: 13 out of 20 marks

Practice examination questions

1

(a) Ivan Pavlov studied how dogs learned to salivate to the sound of a bell using the procedure shown in the table. Complete the table by writing the appropriate terms in the boxes. [3]

When answering the question, ensure that you write *enough*. The detail required is indicated by the number of marks allocated to each question. The kind of answer required is also indicated by the injunctions that are used (e.g. 'describe', 'discuss', 'evaluate').

Before learning	Food	→	Salivation
	Unconditioned stimulus		*Unconditioned response*
During learning	Food + bell	→	Salivation
After learning	Bell	→	Salivation
			Conditioned response

(b) Describe **one** advantage and **one** disadvantage of classical conditioning as an explanation of learned behaviour in humans. [4]

(c) Describe **one** other way in which humans can learn behaviour. [3]

Edexcel specimen paper Unit Test 2 question 1

2

Some psychologists argue that behaviour is learned through imitation. From the study by Bandura, Ross and Ross on the imitation of aggression:

(a) Give **two** examples of behaviours that were imitated by the children.. [2]

(b) Suggest **one** possible implication for society if children do learn by imitation. [2]

OCR Core studies 2 June 2001

3

(a) From Freud's study on 'Little Hans', outline **one** piece of evidence that suggests Hans's phobia resulted form the Oedipus complex. [2]

(b) Outline an alternative explanation for Hans's phobia. [2]

OCR Core studies 1 May 2002

4

'Why do I behave as I do?' Do I have the freedom to choose what I do or is my behaviour determined by forces which are beyond my control such as the environment in which I live, my family or my culture? Using the Core Studies listed below, answer the questions which follow.

> Freud (Little Hans)
> Sperry (split brain)
> Hodges and Tizard (social relationships)
> Bandura, Ross and Ross (aggression)

(a) Describe what each study tells us about the factors that influence our behaviour. [10]

(b) Comment on the problems psychologists may have when they investigate factors that influence our behaviour. [10]

(c) Is all our behaviour determined? Give a reason for your answer. [10]

OCR Core studies 2 May 2002

Chapter 2
Cognitive psychology

The following topics are covered in this chapter:

- The cognitive approach
- Short-term and long-term memory
- Forgetting
- Critical issue: Eyewitness testimony

2.1 The cognitive approach

After studying this topic you should be able to:

- define the term 'cognitive'
- describe key assumptions of the cognitive approach and evaluate its advantages and limitations
- discuss some of the methods used by the cognitive approach

LEARNING SUMMARY

Key assumptions of the cognitive approach

AQA A — U1
AQA B — U1, U2
EDEXCEL — U1
OCR — U1, U2

The word 'cognitive' comes from the Latin word *cognitio* meaning 'to apprehend, understand or know'. Cognition is the activity of internal mental processing. Early psychologists such as Wundt investigated mental activity using introspection. Behaviourists such as Watson and Skinner rejected this approach, regarding mental concepts as 'explanatory fictions', i.e. mental concepts don't actually exist and only *appear* to explain behaviour. For the first half of the 20th century, cognitive psychology lay dormant and it was only revived due to the advent of the computer age.

Cognitive psychologists are primarily interested in thinking and related mental processes such as memory, perception, attention, forgetting, learning, thinking, and language. You will come across the word again when you look at *cognitive* development (Chapter 3) and social *cognition* (Chapter 6).

The key assumptions of the cognitive approach are:

An *assumption* is something which is taken as being true without any proof. It is the basis of an approach or belief.

- Behaviour can largely be explained in terms of how the **mind** operates.
- The mind works in a manner which is **similar to a computer**: inputting, storing and retrieving data.
- Cognitive psychologists see psychology as a **pure science**.

Evaluation of the cognitive approach

Weaknesses of this approach

The cognitive approach has been criticised as overly mechanistic and lacking in social, motivational and emotional factors. It is mechanistic because cognitive explanations are based on the behaviour of machines. Inevitably, this de-emphasises the importance of emotion.

Strengths of this approach

The approach has numerous useful applications, including: advice about the validity of eyewitness testimony (see p.43–47).

Methods used in the cognitive approach

Laboratory experiments

Most cognitive research takes place in laboratories. The main advantages of this method are that cause and effect can be determined and that there is good control of variables. The main weakness is that such research doesn't always apply to the real world (low ecological validity). For example, memory research focuses on one kind of memory – **explicit memory**.

Explicit memory is based on conscious recollection, as distinct from implicit memory which occurs without any conscious direction to remember something. The key study on p.31 illustrates this.

Field experiments

Field experiments involve the use of more natural situations. For example, Abernethy (1940) showed that students performed better if they were tested in the same room where they were taught and tested by the same person. The context (same room, same lecturer) must have acted as a cue to recall. Field experiments have greater ecological validity but less control than laboratory experiments.

Natural experiments

Natural experiments are also used in cognitive research. For example, Myers and Brewin (1994) found that individuals who were classed as 'repressors' were less able to recall negative childhood memories as compared with other personality types, thus taking advantage of naturally occurring difference between people. We can not truly claim that cause and effect have been demonstrated because the experimenter has not manipulated the independent variable nor were participants randomly allocated to conditions.

Case studies of brain-damaged patients

If a person incurs damage to part of his or her brain, we may be able to associate this with changes in behaviour. This allows us to determine what parts of the brain might be related to particular behaviours, as in the case study of HM (Milner, 1959). The man referred to as HM suffered from epilepsy of such severity that it couldn't be controlled by drugs. As a final measure, surgeons removed the hippocampus from both sides of his brain. HM's personality and intellect remained intact but his memory was affected. He had no memory for events subsequent to the operation. His memory for events prior to the operation was reasonable, though not as good as before. He could still talk and recall all the skills he previously knew (semantic and procedural memory) but his memory did not incorporate new experiences. In short, his LTM was intact but he appeared to have no ability to update it, i.e. use his STM. This case study suggests that the hippocampus may be a specific location for STM. Without STM, HM couldn't transfer data to LTM, but he could still use his long-term memory. However, there are criticisms. HM's epilepsy may have caused general brain damage and this could explain his abnormal behaviour. We also don't know whether his subsequent behaviour was caused by the trauma of the operation, rather than the loss of part of the brain. Finally, it is not reasonable to generalise from a sample of one person. However, other studies have supported the importance of the hippocampus. For example, Baddeley (1990) described similar symptoms in a man, Clive Wearing, whose hippocampus was damaged by infection.

The hippocampus is a small structure found in both hemispheres of the forebrain.

Imaging techniques

A more recent method of studying brain activity is the use of brain scans. There are a variety of these: CAT, MRI and PET scans which produce images of the brain in action. For example, Squire *et al.* (1992) used PET scans to show that blood flow in the right hippocampus was much higher when the participants were performing one kind of memory task (cued recall) than another memory task (word-stem completion).

2.2 Short-term and long-term memory

After studying this topic you should be able to:

- *define the term 'memory' and outline the main methods used to investigate it*
- *identify the stages in, and structure of, memory*
- *distinguish between short-term memory and long-term memory*
- *explain the main models of memory and assess their strengths and limitations*

LEARNING SUMMARY

Research into the nature and structure of memory

AQA A   U1
AQA B   U2
EDEXCEL   U1

There are close links between learning and memory. So, in what ways are they different from each other? Something which is learned is lodged in memory. The two terms are almost synonymous, though learning theorists (behaviourists) do not acknowledge internal mental states (therefore the concept of memory has no place in learning theory).

Definitions

Key Term Memory is the process by which we encode, store and retrieve information. It includes sensory memory, short-term memory and long-term memory. These concepts are defined on page 31.

A **memory trace** is the physical representation of the information in the brain.

Memory research usually involves asking a participant to learn a set of material and then to recall it, in order to assess how much they have memorised or learned. The typical methods and means used to test memory and recall are:

- **Nonsense syllables** – a participant is given information devoid of meaning, such as trigrams (e.g. BDT) or CVCs (consonant-vowel-consonant, e.g. HIG).
- **Paired associate learning** – participants are given a pair of stimuli, such as a syllable and a digit. Recall is tested by presenting the participant with a member of the pair and recording if its partner can be remembered.
- **Interference task** – participants are given a task to perform between exposure to stimulus and recall of information. (It is used to prevent rehearsal.)
- **Free recall** – information is directly retrieved from memory at will. Participants are allowed to recall items in any order they please.
- **Recognition** – identifying familiar information. Participants are shown a list of items to remember, and then later shown another longer list that contains the original items. Their task is to recognise the original items. It is a better test of memory than recall because participants recall all the items that are not available, not just those that are currently accessible.

Progress check

1 Why are interference tasks necessary?
2 Is a person likely to recall more when given a free recall task or a recognition task?

2 Recognition task.
1 To prevent rehearsal.

The nature and stages of memory

The stages involved in the operation of memory are:

1 **Input (registering/encoding information).** Sensory data is translated into a memory trace.
2 **Storage.** This may be temporary or permanent.
3 **Output.** Memories are useless unless they can be retrieved through recall, recognition, reconstruction, reproduction (rote learning), and/or confabulation.

The structure of memory

Memory can be divided into the following parts:

Sensory memory (SM)

The sensory form of a stimulus remains unaltered in the mind for a brief time. This could be an auditory or visual trace. It is rapidly lost through spontaneous decay (i.e. the trace disappears).

Short-term memory (STM)

Key Term Short-term memory refers to a temporary storage place for information where it receives minimal processing. It is relatively limited in capacity (about seven items) and decays rapidly unless maintained through rehearsal. It may be held in a visual or auditory form (code), though it is mainly the latter.

Long-term memory (LTM)

Key Term Long-term memory refers to relatively permanent storage, which has unlimited capacity and uses a semantic code. Different kinds of long-term memory have been identified:

- Procedural memory: knowing how. Our knowledge of how to do things, skills such as riding a bicycle.
- Declarative memory: knowing that. Memory for specific information or facts. This is either semantic or episodic.

  - Semantic memory: storage for language, other cognitive concepts and general knowledge. This is well organised, usually isn't forgotten, and doesn't disappear in cases of amnesia. Theories of loss of availability can't account for the behaviour of semantic memory.

  - Episodic memory: memory for personal events and people, the episodes of your life. It is this kind of memory that is tested in experimental work. It is unstructured and more rapidly lost, particularly as new information arrives and interferes.

Distinguishing between short-term and long-term memory

The evidence for separate stores comes from empirical studies of:

An empirical study is a study (such as an experiment or interview) where data has been collected through direct observation or experience.

Duration

Key Term Duration refers to how long a memory is stored. Short-term memories last a short time, between 15 and 30 seconds if not rehearsed. Long-term memories may last forever. See key studies on duration in STM (page 32) and LTM (page 33).

Capacity

Key Term Capacity refers to how much can be held in a memory store. STM has a very small capacity, estimated by Miller (see page 33) to 7±2 chunks of information. LTM is potentially unlimited. Merkle (1988) estimated (using the number of synapses) that LTM may have a capacity of between one thousand and one million gigabytes.

Encoding

Key Term Encoding describes the form or code used to store data in memory. This may be based on the sound of the information (an acoustic code), the way the information appears visually (a visual code) or may be in terms of meaning (a semantic code). STM tends to be stored acoustically whereas LTM is more semantic. (See the key study on encoding on page 34.)

Serial position effect: primacy and recency effects

Glanzer and Cunitz (1966) asked participants to recall word lists; if this was done immediately there was a primacy and a recency effect (early and later words were better recalled) due to STM and LTM effects. If there was delay of 10 seconds or more there was only a primacy effect – STM alone was affected. Primacy is due to the fact that the first items are more likely to have entered LTM. Recency occurs because the last items in the list are still in STM.

Brain damage

Amnesia affects LTM. In anterograde amnesia, permanent memories remain intact but sufferers cannot remember any new information for more than the normal STM span. This is probably because transfer from STM to LTM is lost. Examples include the case study of HM (described on page 29) and Korsakoff's syndrome, which is due to severe alcohol poisoning.

Brain injury can affect STM. The patient KF (Shallice and Warrington, 1970) performed poorly on many short-term memory tasks (e.g. digit span) after a motorbike accident. However his long-term memory was normal.

> What are some of the weaknesses with evidence from brain-damaged individuals?

Forgetting

Explanations for forgetting are different for STM and LTM. See pages 38–42.

AQA (A) Key study: Duration of STM

Peterson and Peterson (1959) Recall of trigrams without rehearsal

Aims
To test the hypothesis that information held in STM disappears within about 20 seconds if rehearsal is prevented. If participants are allowed to rehearse (repeat) information, this maintains information indefinitely. An accurate 'reading' of STM requires no rehearsal.

Procedures
This was a laboratory experiment. Participants were given trigrams to remember – three letters that did not form a meaningful unit, such as TVG. After each trigram they were given a three-digit number and were asked to count backwards in 3s and 4s until told to stop. This task was done to prevent rehearsal. On each trial they were stopped after different times: 3, 6, 9, 12, 15 or 18 seconds. This is called the 'Brown-Peterson technique'.

Findings
If participants had to wait 3 seconds before recalling the trigram they could recall the trigram correctly 80% of the time; if they had to wait 6 seconds, 50% were recalled; and after 18 seconds, recall was reduced to 2%.

Conclusions
This suggests that STM is limited to a maximum of 18 seconds when rehearsal is prevented. This supports the idea that STM and LTM are distinctly different kinds of memory as STM has a very limited duration.

Criticisms
A particular kind of memory was tested in this experiment, as in many memory experiments (called 'episodic memory', see page 31). Other kinds of memory may behave somewhat differently. This means that this study lacks ecological validity (cannot be easily applied to other settings).

The fact that participants were counting numbers during the retention interval means that the numbers may have *displaced* the information in STM. This means that poor recall may not be due to decay but could be explained in terms of displacement (see explanations of forgetting in STM on page 38) – which means that the experiment does not reflect the duration of STM after all.

AQA (A) Key study: Duration of LTM

Bahrick *et al.* (1975) Recalling names and faces

Aims To investigate recall over a long period of time (very long-term memories, VLTM). In particular, to look at the sort of memories where an individual is highly motivated to remember details rather than the typically artificial circumstances of many memory experiments. In this case, participants' recall of classmates' details was tested decades after leaving school.

Procedures Nearly 400 participants were tested in this natural experiment, some of them had recently left school whereas others had left over 40 years ago. They were given many tasks including being asked to list all the names of the pupils in their graduating class and being asked to select familiar photographs from a set of high-school photographs (not all familiar) and to name them.

Findings Participants who were tested within 15 years of graduation were about 90% accurate in identifying faces and names. After 48 years, this declined to about 80% for names and 70% for faces.

Conclusions Despite the fact that recall was not perfect, these findings still show that participants are able to remember information over long periods of time, certainly more than is claimed for short-term memory! The study supports the existence of VLTM in a real-life setting.

Criticisms A positive feature of this study was that it investigated memory in a real-life context (high ecological validity). This gives us information about how memory functions in the real-world rather than in limited laboratory experiments in which participants have little motivation to recall information.

At the same time, such real-world investigations often lack suitable control of extraneous variables. For example, it is possible that participants actually saw their ex-classmates frequently and this might explain their high recall. In addition, as it is a natural experiment, we cannot truly claim a cause-and-effect relationship.

AQA (A) Key study: Capacity of STM

Miller (1956) The magic number seven

Aims Miller noted that there are many things that come in sevens (seven days of the week, seven notes on the musical scale) and wondered whether this 'Magic number 7' might be related to an individual's span of immediate memory – that is, the amount that can be held in STM at any time. This study aimed to review other research to see what support there was for this hypothesis.

Procedures The method used was a review of previous research, all laboratory experiments. Such studies presented participants with ranges of stimuli, such as dots or words. The experimenter would show participants displays with varying numbers of dots to find out how many could be identified. Or, the experimenter would give participants words to remember; the words varied in the number of letters (or bits of information) in the word or the number of syllables (chunks) in the word.

Findings Participants could reliably report up to 5 or 6 dots in a display but then accuracy deteriorated. Another finding was that participants could remember as many 5-letter words as they could 10-letter words. Participants were able to remember about 7 words no matter how many bits of information were in the word. It was the number of chunks in the word that appeared to affect recall.

Conclusions These findings led Miller to conclude that the span of absolute judgement (counting dots) is about 5 or 6 items, and that the span of immediate memory is about 7±2 chunks. This supports the view that STM is very limited and that its limit is between 5 and 9 items. However, an 'item' may consist of small chunks. The ability to chunk data is a way to increase the capacity of STM.

Criticisms Subsequent research has found that the size of the chunk does actually matter. For example, Simon (1974) found that he could remember fewer 8-word phrases than he could one-syllable words.

The concept of chunking has many useful applications. It is used in designing phone numbers and postcodes. This is a positive criticism of such research.

AQA (A) Key study: Encoding in STM and LTM

Baddeley (1966) The influence of acoustic and semantic similarity

Aims Previous research (Conrad, 1964) found that participants made mistakes when trying to recall words that sounded the same (acoustic similarity) when recall was immediate (i.e. testing STM). Baddeley sought to investigate this further: to see whether acoustic similarity affected long-term recall and to see what effect semantic encoding (i.e. when words are placed in memory on the basis of meaning) had on STM and LTM.

Procedures This was a laboratory experiment, using an independent groups design. One experiment tested STM (recall was tested immediately), and in another experiment LTM was assessed (recall was after 20 minutes). In each experiment there were 4 groups of participants: group 1 were given acoustically similar word lists (e.g. man, cab, can, cad, mad), group 2's words were acoustically dissimilar (e.g. pit, few, cow), group 3's words were semantically similar (e.g. great, large, broad, tall) and group 4's words were semantically dissimilar (e.g. good, huge, hot, safe).

Findings In the experiment testing STM it was found that group 1 (acoustic similarity) did worst. Participants recalled about 55% of the words. In the experiment testing LTM it was found that group 3 (semantic similarity) again recalled about 55% of the words. In both experiments, recall of the other three groups was about 75%.

Conclusions These findings suggest that in STM information tends to be acoustically coded (and that is why acoustically similar words were muddled up) and in LTM information tends to be semantically coded (and that is why words with similar meaning tended to be muddled up).

Criticisms This study again tests a particular kind of memory (episodic memory). Other kinds of memory may behave somewhat differently. This means that this study lacks ecological validity (cannot be easily applied to other settings).

Other research has found that STM doesn't always use an acoustic code. This depends on whether verbal rehearsal is prevented and/or whether recall is tested in an acoustic manner. For example, Brandimote *et al.* (1992) found that participants used visual encoding in STM if they were given pictures to remember (a visual task) and verbal rehearsal was prevented (they had to say 'la la la') and they were asked to recall the items by drawing them (visual recall task).

Models of memory

AQA A ▶ U1
AQA B ▶ U2
EDEXCEL ▶ U1

A model or theory of memory aims to describe the structure of memory and explain how information is transferred from STM to LTM.

The multi-store model

Key Term The **multi-store model** is a representation of memory based on having more than one different kind of store for remembered information. Atkinson and Shriffrin (1968) proposed this model based on evidence related to the separate stores of memory (see pages 31–34). Information enters SM, and is initially stored in STM. If it is not rehearsed, it is lost. Continued rehearsal leads to LTM storage.

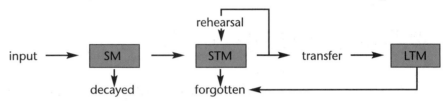

The multi-store model of memory

Evaluation

The strengths of this model are as follows:

- There is general agreement that there is an STM/LTM distinction, and this is well supported by the empirical evidence.
- The multi-store model is the basis of many later models, even if they were subsequently divided into further STM and LTM stores.

The limitations of this model are as follows.

- Rehearsal doesn't adequately explain LTM. It may *appear* that rehearsal creates a long-term memory but this may be an artefact of memory experiments where participants are asked to remember things. In most situations we do not actively try to store something in our memory.
- Alternative explanations can account for the empirical findings, e.g. the levels of processing model (see p.36) can explain differences in material recalled.
- The model is over-simplified; in practice there are no clear distinctions between stores of memory.
- It presents a passive view of memory and cannot account for active processes such as reconstruction.

The working memory model

Key Term The **working memory model** was proposed by Baddeley and Hitch (1974) as a way to represent short-term memory in terms of further sub-divisions. The use of the term 'working memory' reflects the idea that this is the area of memory that is active when you are working on information. Working memory consists of the following components:

1 The **central executive**. This component of working memory is modality-free (i.e. not visual or auditory). It is roughly the same as 'attention' (the concentration of mental effort on sensory or mental events). The central executive allocates resources to other components. Empirical support comes from studies (e.g. McLeod 1977) which show that task similarity impairs performance, e.g. playing the piano and singing a song (both are auditory). This must be due to competition within the one component.

2 **Phonological loop** deals with verbal material and consists of:
- An articulatory process. Baddeley and Lewis (1981) found that articulatory suppression did not affect decisions involving acoustic (phonological)

Articulatory suppression refers to a task which stops you articulating, i.e. speaking. The **articulatory process** is the process of speaking.

35

The phonological store allows an individual to rehearse information acoustically.

differences and therefore there must be a separate store for this.

- A phonological store. Baddeley (1975) gave participants a sequence of words to recall. Normally they could perform the task better with short rather than long words (called the word-length effect), but when an articulatory suppression task (counting backwards) was included there was no difference, demonstrating that the word-length effect depends on having access to an articulatory process.

3 A **visuo-spatial sketchpad** (or scratchpad) is used to hold visual memories, such as faces. Baddeley *et al.* (1975) gave participants the task of visualising a matrix of digits which was presented auditorially. If this was combined with tracking a moving light, the ability to visualise was impaired.

Evaluation

The strengths of this model are as follows:

- The model is supported by empirical evidence, especially Hitch and Baddeley (1976) who showed that dual task performance is reduced when both tasks involve the same component (e.g. the central executive is involved in a verbal reasoning task, and saying random digits, but is not involved when saying 'the, the, the'). This is hard to explain within the multi-store approach.
- It can explain how we can do two tasks at one time if they involve different stores and why we have trouble with some tasks that involve the same store.
- It concerns active processing and therefore is relevant to a wider set of activities such as verbal reasoning and comprehension.
- It describes rehearsal (the articulatory process) as only one component, which seems preferable to the central importance given in the multi-store model.
- Its division of STM into further components more accurately reflects evidence from brain-damaged patients. For example, Shallice and Warrington (1970) studied KF, who was injured in a motorcycle accident. His LTM was not affected, but his STM was much reduced in capacity. In addition, his short-term forgetting of auditory stimuli was much greater than his forgetting of visual stimuli. He could remember meaningful sounds but not words.

The weakness of this model is that the description of the central executive is somewhat vague and it may not be one thing but in fact a number of different stores/processes.

The levels of processing model

The key point here is that memory is a by-product of the processing that takes place. Therefore this can explain both implicit and explicit memory.

Whenever you read the description of a study, ask yourself 'What does this show?' It is vital to understand what was demonstrated in order to communicate this in an exam.

Key Term   The **levels of processing model** (approach) is the view put forward by Craik and Lockhart (1972) that memories become enduring not through rehearsal but because information is processed in a meaningful way. Rehearsal is a kind of processing but it is not very deep. Craik and Lockhart believed that it is the *depth* of processing that determines whether information is stored over a long period.

The main problem with this theory is defining what constitutes 'depth'. Craik and Lockhart defined it in terms of a continuum: an example of shallow processing would be to say whether a word was written in capital letters, whereas an example of deep processing would be to say if the word would fit in a given sentence (this involves semantic processing or a consideration of meaning). A study by Craik and Tulving (1975) illustrates this point. They showed participants a list of words, each followed by a question with a yes/no answer. The questions belonged to one of three levels of analysis:

1. **Shallow** or structural, for example 'Is the word in capital letters?'

2. **Phonemic**, for example, 'Does the word rhyme with able?'

3. **Semantic** or sentence, for example, 'Would the word fit in the sentence "They met a ---- in the street?"'

Those words which had been given semantic-type questions were remembered most. The phonemic coding was next best. This shows that semantic processing creates an automatic memory, supporting the levels-of-processing theory.

There are a number of ways that complex processing can take place.

- **Elaboration**. Craik and Tulving (1975) also tested the effects of elaboration. Participants were shown a word and a sentence containing a blank, and asked whether the word fitted into the incomplete sentence. Elaboration was manipulated by varying the complexity of the sentence between the simple (e.g. 'She cooked the ….') and the complex (e.g. 'The great bird swooped down and carried off the struggling ….'). Participants recalled twice as many words for the complex sentences. The improved performance was not due to increased time spent on the task because some phonemic questions in the original study required as much time. Depth of processing involves elaboration.
- **Organisation**. Mandler (1967) asked participants to repeatedly sort a pack of cards into categories of their choosing, using anything from 2 to 7 categories and according to any system they wished. They were asked to repeat the sorting until they had achieved two identical sorts. At the end they were given an unexpected free-recall test. Mandler found that recall was poorest for those who had decided to use only 2 categories, and best for those who used 7 categories. Those participants who used several categories in sorting were imposing more organisation on the list and thus remembered more.
- **Distinctiveness**. Eysenck and Eysenck (1980) manipulated distinctiveness by using words containing silent letters or irregular pronunciation, such as 'comb'. Some participants were asked to say these words as they were spelled (e.g. pronouncing the 'b' in 'comb'). This was the shallow (non-semantic), distinctive condition. There was also a non-semantic, non-distinctive condition where the nouns were pronounced normally; as well as a semantic, non-distinctive condition and a semantic, distinctive condition, where the nouns were processed in terms of their meaning. On an unexpected test of recognition memory, words in the non-semantic, distinctive condition were much better remembered than those in the non-semantic, non-distinctive condition and almost as well as the two semantic conditions. This demonstrates that distinctiveness was as importance as depth.

> You can use this evidence to enhance your revision – the more you organise your notes, the better you will remember it! Other ideas are to elaborate it and make it **distinctive**!

Evaluation

The strength of this approach is that there is considerable empirical evidence to support the role of depth of processing, as outlined above.

The weaknesses are as follows:

- It is possible that the better recall of meaningful material is due to the way the participants' memories were tested. Morris *et al.* (1977) found that if participants were given a rhyming recognition test they remembered the words which had received shallow processing better than the more deeply processed ones.
- This model *describes* rather than explains. The concept of 'depth' is hard to define and it is circular (something which requires deeper processing is better remembered, and something that is better remembered was more deeply processed).
- The model ignores the evidence that supports the distinction between STM and LTM.

Progress check

1 How does the multi-store model suggest that data is transferred from STM to LTM?
2 How does the levels of processing (LOP) theory suggest that data enters permanent memory?

2 Complexity or depth of processing.

1 Verbal rehearsal.

2.3 Forgetting

After studying this topic you should be able to:

- describe and evaluate explanations of (and research into) forgetting in short-term memory
- describe and evaluate explanations of (and research into) forgetting in long-term memory
- explain and assess research on the effects of emotion on memory

LEARNING SUMMARY

Explanations of forgetting in short-term memory

AQA A — U1
AQA B — U2
EDEXCEL — U1

What do you think would happen if you didn't forget most of the information that enters your mind?

Key Term **Forgetting** is the inability to recall or recognise information that was once stored in memory and has now disappeared (not available), or can't be 'brought to mind' (not accessible). Since STM has limited capacity and duration, the explanations for forgetting in STM are likely to be due to lack of availability (it has disappeared) rather than accessibility (being unable to 'find' it).

Trace decay

The physical trace simply disappears because it is not rehearsed or processed sufficiently. As we saw in the previous section, Peterson and Peterson provided evidence that data in STM disappears (see p.32).

Evaluation

The disappearance of a memory trace may be due to interference rather than spontaneous decay, i.e. if nothing else entered STM it wouldn't disappear.

Displacement

Information stored in STM is displaced by new information entering STM because STM has a limited capacity. This might explain Peterson and Peterson's findings (page 32) where the second set of information (participants had to count backwards in threes) displaced the initial material and caused information to disappear, i.e. be forgotten.

The serial probe technique has been used to investigate displacement. Waugh and Norman (1965) asked participants to listen to a sequence of numbers, after which the participants were given a probe (one of the numbers in the list) and asked to recall the number that came next. If the probe was near the end of the list, recall was good; if the probe was early in the list, recall was poor. This demonstrates that early numbers were displaced by later ones.

Evaluation

Waugh and Norman (1965) repeated the experiment, this time reading digits out at different speeds: at a rate of 1 per second (faster) or 4 per second (slower). If the numbers were presented faster, recall improved – which must be because the numbers had less time to decay rather than because they had been displaced; displacement would have led to the same recall no matter what the timing. This suggests that short-term forgetting is due to decay *and* displacement. Shallice (1967) found that displacement is more important. In the serial-probe task, forgetting was less if the numbers were presented faster, but there was a stronger effect when the position of the probe was moved.

Progress check

1. Why is STM explained by lack of availability rather than lack of accessibility?
2. Name two explanations for forgetting in STM.

2 Trace decay, displacement.
1 Because it is a limited capacity store and any information would be accessible.

Explanations of forgetting in long-term memory

AQA A   U1
AQA B   U2
EDEXCEL U1

Forgetting in LTM can be explained as lack of availability or accessibility.

Failures of availability in LTM

Encoding failure

This means that the memory is not available because you never remembered it! You may think you've forgotten something, whereas in fact you had never stored it.

Evaluation

Ebbinghaus (1885) demonstrated **re-learning savings** – that you may think you have forgotten something, but the next time you try to learn it you will be better at it. This suggests that some memory trace is there but it is possibly fragmentary.

Trace decay

This means that the physical form of memory disappears with time.

Evaluation

This is unlikely to apply to LTM. Some kinds of memory clearly do not decay, e.g. you never forget how to ride a bicycle even if you haven't done it for a long time (procedural memory). Other kinds of memory may not decay but they become inaccessible.

Interference

One set of information competes with another, causing it to be 'overwritten' or physically lost. There are two forms of interference:

* **retroactive (RI)** – a second set of information 'pushes out' earlier material
* **proactive (PI)** – previous learning interferes with current learning/recall.

This can be demonstrated by a **paired-associate** task. Participants are asked to learn two similar lists (see margin). In each list the same nonsense syllable is paired with different words (word B or C). An example of an A–B pair would be 'BEM and lawn,' and an A–C pair would be 'BEM and aisle'. If participants learn List 1 (A–B), *then* List 2 (A–C), and are asked to recall List 1 their performance will be affected by RI. If they learn List 2 followed by List 1, and are tested on List 1 again, their performance will be affected this time by PI.

Findings include:

* **Similarity causes greater interference.** McGeoch and McDonald (1931) found that if the interference task was a list of synonyms to the original list, recall was poor (12%), nonsense syllables interfered less (26% recall), and numbers even less (37% recall). Only interference can explain such findings.
* **RI is stronger than PI.**

Evaluation

Interference has limited application. It is relevant to occasions when two sets of data are very similar. This is rare in everyday life but it does occur.

Tulving and Psotka (1971) showed that the effects of interference disappear when cued-recall rather than free recall is used. Participants had to learn lists of 24 words, each organised into 6 categories. There were two tests of recall: 1. **Noncued recall:** after seeing each of their lists three times, they were asked to recall the words. They then were given another list to learn and recall. In total participants were given either 1, 2, 3, 4, or 5 lists to learn; 2. **Cued recall:** after learning all the lists they were given an interference task for 10 minutes, and then told the category names for each list they had learned, and asked to recall the words again. In the noncued recall, the more lists the participants were given the fewer words they recalled. In

Margin notes:

The concept of *re-learning savings* means that even though you don't think you have learned anything when you read a textbook, it hasn't all been to waste. Why is that?

There are many different kinds of memory – such as remembering how to ride a bicycle and remembering what you learned in psychology class today. If there are different kinds of memory, then there are likely to be different kinds of forgetting.

List 1

A	B
BEM	lawn
TAQ	barge
MUZ	host
PEZ	tube
LUF	weed
ROH	mate

List 2

A	C
BEM	aisle
TAQ	cave
MUZ	bass
PEZ	vine
LUF	dame
ROH	file

One common everyday example of interference is if you are given a new locker at school – for a while you still go to the old locker (PI). If you are later given your old locker back you may go to the 2nd one for a while (RI).

the cued recall performance remained the same (about 70% recalled for each list) no matter how many words the participant learned. This demonstrates the effects of both retroactive and proactive interference, and that, given suitable cues, the participants' memories recovered from the effects of interference. This suggests that forgetting is due to a lack of good-enough cues at the time of recall.

Progress check

1 Why is trace decay an unlikely explanation for forgetting in LTM?

2 How did Tulving and Psotka demonstrate that interference doesn't affect what is actually stored in memory?

2 When they used a cued–recall task, participants were able to recall much more.

1 E.g. some memories do last forever.

Failures of accessibility in LTM

Cue-dependent forgetting

People always perform better on a recognition task than on free recall. This can be explained by cue-dependent forgetting, which is the same as cue-dependent remembering because forgetting and remembering are two sides of the same coin – if you can't remember something then you have forgotten it. A recognition task provides cues for better recall.

Tulving (1962) presented participants with a list of words followed by three recall trials. The words recalled each time differed, though the response rate remained a fairly steady 50%. This suggests that information is there but not always retrieved. Presumably, on each recall trial the participants were using different retrieval cues. Tulving and Pearlstone (1966) found that performance was three times better when participants were given appropriate retrieval cues.

- **Encoding specificity principle:** The closer the retrieval cue is to the information stored in memory, the greater the likelihood that the cue will be successful in retrieving the memory. Thomson and Tulving (1970) demonstrated this by showing that cues which are strongly associated (e.g. white paired with black) lead to better recall than weak associations (e.g. train paired with black).
- **Context-dependent recall:** Cues do not have to be a significant word, they may also be the context or state in which something was learned. In Abernethy's study (1940) on p.29, the participants may have looked around the room and certain things acted as cues which jogged their memory.
- **State dependent recall:** Goodwin *et al.* (1969) reported that drinkers who hid money when drunk, couldn't remember where it was when they were sober. However, they could recall where it was when drunk again.

Police reconstructions of crimes are based on context-dependent recall. When a person revisits the scene of the crime their memory is jogged. A more common example is the smell of something, e.g. the smell of the sea may jog your memory for a particular incident at the seaside.

Repressed memories

Key Term **Repression** is a form of forgetting. Freud (see Chapter 1) argued that painful or disturbing memories are put beyond conscious recall as a means of protecting one's ego from anxiety. The kinds of memory that are 'forgotten' or repressed range from the serious, such as childhood incidents of sexual abuse or extreme unhappiness, to more commonplace situations like 'forgetting' to clean your room.

Freud initially used hypnosis with his patients, in order to access repressed memories, but ultimately concluded that it was too unreliable.

Empirical support

Levinger and Clark (1993) gave participants word lists, including some emotionally charged words (such as 'fear'). Subsequent recall was poorer for the emotional words. However, when Parkin *et al.* (1982) repeated this experiment with delayed recall, they found improvement, which suggests that arousal had led to initial repression. Finally, there are case histories of event-specific amnesia such as Bower's (1981) report that Sirhan Sirhan, the man who assassinated Robert Kennedy, claimed he could recall nothing of the crime. (See also key study opposite.)

Evaluation

Repression is hard to prove or disprove. Someone may simply say they can't recall something (though it is there), or their eventual recall may be inaccurate.

AQA (A) Key study: Repressed memories

Myers and Brewin (1994) Repression

Aims Some individuals are classed as 'repressors'. They are characterised by having low anxiety and high defensiveness, i.e. they tend to use repression as a coping strategy and that is why they are low on anxiety. Truly non-anxious people score high on tests of defensiveness. Do repressors have restricted access to negative childhood memories?

Procedures This was a natural experiment using semistructured interviews. A psychological test was used to classify 27 female undergraduates as repressors, or other types such as defensive high-anxious. The participants were asked to recall unhappy childhood memories as quickly as possible, and were also questioned about the quality of parenting experienced (to check that the repressors did have something to repress).

What makes this a natural experiment? You can read about natural experiments on page 161.

Findings The repressors took about twice as long to recall unhappy memories but not positive ones. The repressors free-recalled fewer negative childhood memories than nonrepressors, and the age of first memory was older in both free recall and cued recall conditions. Repressors were more likely to report poor or negative relationships with their fathers.

Conclusions This suggests that individuals with anxiety-provoking memories are more likely to repress such memories. The reason why repressors took longer to recall unhappy childhood memories and fewer were recalled was repression rather than a lack of unhappy memories.

Criticisms Repression in this study was probably 'inhibited recall' rather than total forgetting. On the other hand, participants may have been reluctant to report certain memories in the experimental situation.

Speed of recall does not necessarily mean that a memory was repressed, only that it may be more difficult to *report* a painful memory. McGinnies (1949) showed lists of words to participants, including emotionally toned words such as 'raped'. Participants were significantly slower at recognising these words, showing the effects of emotion on perception.

Emotional factors in forgetting

Repressed memory

As seen above, this *inhibits* recall. It is an example of lack of accessibility, or restricted access due to emotion.

Flashbulb memories

Key Term A flashbulb memory is a long-lasting and vivid memory of the context in which a person heard about an important and/or dramatic event. The memory is for the context and not the event itself. It is as if a flash photograph was taken at the moment of the event and every detail indelibly printed in memory. Brown and Kulik (1977) first coined the term, after noting that many people were able to vividly recall what they were doing at the time of President Kennedy's assassination.

What flashbulb memories can you recall? Many people have a clear picture of exactly what they were doing when they heard the news of Princess Diana's death. But flashbulb memories need not involve major public events – they might be related to some special personal moment which was either intensely happy or sad.

Empirical support

Are flashbulb memories accurate? McCloskey *et al.* (1988) interviewed people shortly after the explosion of the space shuttle *Challenger* and then re-interviewed the same people nine months later, finding that recall was not particularly accurate. However, Conway *et al.* (1994) felt that the *Challenger* explosion lacked distinctiveness for many people and therefore would not evoke flashbulb memories. Using the incident of Mrs Thatcher's resignation as the flashbulb event, Conway *et al.* tested people a few days after the event and again later, finding that 86% of their UK participants still had flashbulb memories after 11 months compared with 29% in other countries.

An experimental attempt to produce flashbulb memories had mixed success. Johnson and Scott (1978) arranged two experimental conditions:

- high stress – a 'witness' watches as a confederate runs through the room carrying a letter-opener covered in blood
- low stress – the confederate holding a pen covered in grease.

When later asked to identify the culprit, some participants in the high-stress condition did have better recall but it was not true for all participants.

Evaluation

It is difficult to test the accuracy of flashbulb memories without affecting later recall. Immediate testing may enhance subsequent recall.

AQA (A) Key study: Flashbulb memories

Schmolck *et al.* (2000) O.J. Simpson verdict

Aims	To investigate the recall of the context in which an individual heard about an emotionally arousing event. Previous research has found that the length of time after the event has little effect on the accuracy of such memories, supporting the concept of a flashbulb memory. This study set out to investigate how such memories change over time.
Procedures	This was a natural experiment, using a naturally occuring event (the announcement of the verdict in the O.J. Simpson murder trial). Psychology students were interviewed 3 days after the verdict to record their flashbulb memories associated with this event.
	The participants were divided into two groups, matched on the emotional significance of the event to them, and whether they agreed or not with the verdict. Group 1 was re-interviewed 15 months later, and group 2 were re-interviewed 32 months later.
Findings	After 15 months, 50% of the recollections were highly accurate, and 11% contained major errors or distortions. After 32 months, 29% of the recollections were highly accurate, more than 40% containing major distortions.
Conclusions	The findings show that retention interval is important in the recall of flashbulb memories. They do decay and are not accurate over a long period of time.
Criticisms	The big issue is whether the event (trial verdict) was significant enough to produce a flashbulb memory. It may not have been significant for all participants, which challenges the validity of these findings. The sample used was restricted (students) and it is not reasonable to generalise to the whole population, i.e. the study lacked population validity.

Progress check

1 What effect can emotion have on memory?
2 Name one study of flashbulb memory.

2 E.g. McCloskey *et al.*, Conway *et al.*, Johnson and Scott.
1 It can inhibit or enhance recall.

2.4 Critical issue: Eyewitness testimony

After studying this topic you should be able to:

- *assess the accuracy and value of eyewitness testimony*
- *use the concept of 'reconstructive memory' in relation to eyewitness testimony*
- *discuss the effects of language on recall*
- *discuss the effects of emotion on recall*
- *discuss research into memory for faces*

How accurate is eyewitness testimony?

AQA A   U1
AQA B   U2
EDEXCEL   U1
OCR   U1, U2

Defining terms

Key Term Eyewitness testimony (EWT) refers to the descriptions given in a criminal trial by individuals who were present during the crime. This includes identification of perpetrators, details of the crime scene (such as how fast a car was travelling in an accident), and/or peripheral information (such as the weather that day).

Key Term Reconstructive memory describes how memory is more than passive recall. It is the active process of building up a memory using fragments of an event plus expectations (schema). These schema are socially constructed so that the way we alter memory is socially (culturally) determined.

The concept of a 'schema' is fundamental to cognitive psychology. The concept may not, at first, seem to be easy to understand, but it is important that you grasp it.

Schema (or schemata) are organised packets or clusters of information which facilitate understanding and generate expectations. For example, we each have a schema for what a 'mother' is like, or what a football game will be like.

Why is eyewitness testimony so unreliable?

AQA A   U1
AQA B   U2
EDEXCEL   U1
OCR   U1, U2

There are many answers to this question, some of which are examined below.

Reconstructive memory

'Schema theory' is a general approach to understanding cognitive processes and doesn't just apply to memory. Here, it is used to explain the reconstructive nature of memory.

Bartlett (1932) suggested that recall is not simply a matter of accessing a piece of information and 'reading it'. Instead, memory involves active reconstruction. Prior knowledge, or schema, leads to distortions of memory during both storage and recall. Bartlett demonstrated this (see key study on page 44).

Initial learning

Past experience or schema affect what you 'see'. For example, Cohen (1981) described a woman in a videotape as either a waitress or a librarian, and showed her doing a variety of things. When participants were later asked a series of questions, such as 'What was she drinking?' they tended to remember those features which were consistent with their stereotypes.

Subsequent recall

Schema affect recall. Bransford and Johnson (1972) found that ability to understand a passage and subsequent recall were greater if participants were told the title ('Washing clothes') before rather than after reading a passage. The title generates schema which are helpful in interpreting the meaning of otherwise meaningless text and this comprehension facilitates recall.

Evaluation

- In terms of EWT, this evidence suggests that, when people try to recall what they witnessed, their recall is likely to be affected by previous experience.

- However, the reconstructive theory of memory does not explain why memory is sometimes very accurate, as when an actor has to learn his or her lines.

AQA (A) Key study: Reconstructive memory

Bartlett (1932) War of the ghosts and other stories

Aims
To investigate how a person's memory for stories is affected by his or her attitudes, beliefs, motivation and general cognitive style. Bartlett's hypothesis was that memory is largely a reconstructive process. When we store and retrieve data we reconstruct it according to our expectations or schema.

Procedures
Bartlett used a technique he called 'repeated reproductions'. This involved showing a story, or simple drawing, to a participant and asking them to repeat it shortly thereafter (e.g. 15 minutes later) and then repeatedly over weeks, months and years. One of the best-known stories was a legend about North American Indians, 'The War of the Ghosts'. The tale belongs to a culture very different from ours, with unexpected concepts. This makes it ideal for persistent transformation.

Bartlett used a number of participants for each story and, for each one, kept a record of successive recall (a protocol).

Findings
Participants distorted the story rather than remembering it exactly. The distortions (or transformations) were consistent with the participants' Western expectations. The distortions included omissions, using a dominant theme to organise the story, and transformation of information into more familiar terms. The stories become more dramatic, and more stereotyped (according to the stereotypes of the tellers). Each retelling was different.

Conclusions
The process of remembering is not a passive recording but rather active processing, altering material to a form that can be readily dealt with. This is done by making connections with existing schemas.

Criticisms
The study may lack ecological validity because the findings don't apply to more naturalistic conditions. Wynn and Logie (1998) tested students' recall of real-life events over a 6-month period. Recall was relatively accurate and little transformation took place, suggesting that there was very little use of reconstruction.

There was a lack of rigorous methodology. For example, participants were not given very specific instructions and therefore some of the distortions may be a result of conscious guessing. Gauld and Stephenson (1967) found that when accurate recall was stressed at the outset, then errors fell by almost half.

Effects of language on the accuracy of memory

The language that is used by police, when interviewing witnesses, and by court officials, during a trial, may influence the answers given by witnesses. Language may affect initial perception and subsequent recall. Both of these effects are shown in the study on page 45 by Loftus and Palmer (1974).

Initial perception

Carmichael *et al.* (1932) gave two groups of participants different descriptions for the same set of drawings, e.g. a picture which looked as follows: C was described as a 'crescent moon' or 'the letter C'. Subsequent recall was related to the labels provided. It is likely that the labels affected initial encoding, though they may also affect subsequent recall.

Subsequent recall

A leading question is one that prompts the desired answer. Loftus and Zanni (1975) showed how the use of 'a' or 'the' in a question changes the way people answered a question. 'Did you see the broken headlight?' assumes that there was a broken headlight whereas 'Did you see a broken headlight?' is more open-ended. Participants were shown a short film of a car accident. There was no broken headlight in the film, but 17% of those asked about *the* broken headlight said there was one, whereas only 7% of those asked about *a* broken headlight said there was.

Loftus *et al.* (1978) conducted an experiment that showed that leading questions did affect recall. The participants were divided into two groups. One group were given consistent information (they saw a car stopping at a 'YIELD' sign in an original set of slides and were later asked about a YIELD sign). The other group had inconsistent information (they were shown the 'YIELD' sign in the initial set of slides but were later asked about a 'STOP' sign). Finally all participants were shown pairs of slides and had to identify which slides were in the original sequence. 75% of participants who had consistent questions picked the correct slide, whereas only 41% who had a leading or misleading question picked the correct slide.

However, when Bekerian and Bowers (1983) repeated this study and showed the final slides in the same order as originally shown (not a random order as Loftus *et al.* had done) they found that recall was now the same for the consistent and misleading groups. This shows that the participants' memories were intact in spite of misleading post-event information. Therefore misleading questions (post-event information) would appear to affect the retrieval of memories rather than their storage.

Effects of emotion on the accuracy of memory

We have seen that emotion may enhance recall (flashbulb memories) or suppress it (repressed memories). Loftus (1979) was called as an expert witness on the psychology of memory in a trial where a shop assistant, Melville, had identified a robber, José Garcia. One of the points she made, in relation to memory research, was about the effects of emotion. Melville was in a state of extreme distress after seeing a colleague shot, and psychologists have found that arousal and stress have a negative effect on recall – especially short-term memory (the memory trace may not be consolidated).

Real life studies of eyewitness testimony

Most studies are laboratory-based. In real life other factors may operate to enhance or reduce recall. In one study (Yuille and Cutshall, 1986) interviewed 13 real life eyewitnesses to an armed robbery in Canada. The witnesses were interviewed at the time of the crime and again, four months later. Their recall was very good, despite the fact that some misleading questions were included in the recall test, which suggests that in real life eyewitness testimony can be very reliable.

Progress check

1 What is a schema?
2 How do schema affect memory?

2 They lead to predictable distortions in initial learning and in subsequent recall.

1 A packet or cluster of related concepts.

OCR core study and AQA (A) Key Study: Eyewitness Testimony

Loftus and Palmer (1974) Reconstruction of automobile destruction

Aims
Eyewitnesses are often asked to provide details of a complex event. This study aimed to investigate the effects of leading questions on recall, using a situation where participants are asked to estimate speed – a task that most people find difficult and therefore, one where where accurate recall is more likely to be affected.

Part I

Procedures

The 'critical question' contained the independent variable – a word was expected to affect memory. All other questions were there to distract the participant from guessing the experiment's purpose.

This was a laboratory experiment using an independent groups design. Participants (students) were shown film clips of automobile accidents, and asked a set of questions, one of which was a *critical* question: 'About how fast were the cars going when they [hit] each other?'. Participants were in one of 5 conditions determined by the word used in the critical question, 'hit' was replaced by: smashed, collided, bumped, hit or contacted.

Findings
Participants in the 'smashed' group reported the highest speeds, followed by collided, bumped, hit and contacted groups.

Conclusions
Some words imply speed more than others and act as leading questions, i.e. the questions influenced the answers given by participants, demonstrating how recall can be biased by language/schema.

Part II

Procedures
A one-minute film was shown which contained a 4-second multiple car accident. The participants were divided into 3 experimental groups:

- Group 1 were asked: 'How fast were the cars going when they *hit* each other?'
- Group 2 had the words 'smashed into'
- Group 3 were asked no question about the speed of the vehicles.

A week later the participants were asked some further questions including the critical question 'Did you see any broken glass?'

Findings
The group with the word 'smashed' were twice as likely to answer 'yes' to seeing broken glass (though there was none) than either of the other two groups.

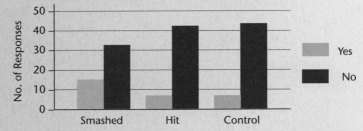

Responses to 'Did you see any broken glass?'

Conclusions
Post-event information (information supplied after an event) was shown to affect later recall of the video.

Criticisms
The experiment lacked ecological validity because participants only witnessed a video clip. This would lack the emotional effects of witnessing a real-life accident. Foster *et al.* (1994) found that if participants thought they were watching a real-life robbery and also thought that their responses would influence the trial, their identification of a robber was more accurate than if they didn't think it was real-life.

The findings may be due to demand characteristics – participants in an experiment are uncertain about how to behave (especially on questions about speed) and therefore look for cues about what answer to give. This leads to systematically similar responses from all participants.

OCR Revision question The study on eyewitness testimony by Loftus and Palmer includes two experiments. In the second experiment, the use of the verbs 'smashed' and 'hit' led to different responses from the participants.

a) Outline one of these differences. [2]

b) Give one explanation of why these differences were found. [2]

(January 2002 Core Studies 1, question 1)

Sample question and student answer

(a) Outline **two** factors that may influence the likelihood of information being retrieved from long-term memory. [3 + 3]

(b) Describe **one** model or theory of memory. [6]

(c) 'Research into eyewitness testimony suggests that information from eyewitnesses is not reliable.' Describe and evaluate research (theories **and/or** studies) into eyewitness testimony. [18]

> The candidate has provided one detailed and accurate response but the second one is in name only, and it isn't entirely clear in what way familiarity might increase or decrease retrieval from LTM. (3+1 marks)

(a) One factor that might influence retrieval from LTM is the availability of a suitable cue. Many memories are available, i.e. they are there, but they aren't accessible. A second factor is familiarity.

> The candidate has identified and described the essential details of the model. The answer is generally accurate but limited. The candidate might have been a bit more careful in explaining the transfer between stores, and the rehearsal loop. (4 marks)

(b) One model of memory is the multi-store model. This suggests that memory consists of more than one kind of store – specifically a sensory memory, short-term memory and long-term memory. The way information is passed from one store to another is as a result of verbal rehearsal. If material is not rehearsed then it disappears and is not remembered.

(c) There have been lots of studies on eyewitness testimony and most of it suggests that it is very unreliable. The best known study is by Loftus and Palmer. They showed participants slides of a car accident and then asked some questions. One question was the important one where they were asked how fast the car was going when the accident happened. For some participants the word 'hit' was used in this question, others were asked the question using the word 'smashed' or other words. The answer given was related to the word that had been used. If the word 'smashed' was used then participants gave the fastest speed. This shows that the testimony provided was affected by leading questions. A policeman may deliberately or not deliberately ask questions in such a way that leads eyewitnesses to give certain answers.

The main thing is that such answers at the scene of a crime may then influence how people remember the details later. Loftus and Palmer re-interviewed the participants a week later and found that those who were given the word 'smashed' were twice as likely to say there had been broken glass when there was none. So this shows that the leading questions altered recall of information.

This is a well-constructed response to the question that certainly includes sufficient AO1 material (description of research) but rather too little AO2 (commentary/evaluation). The information about relevant studies is detailed and accurate and appropriate for 6 marks therefore AO1 = 6 marks. There is about the same amount of AO2 material whereas there should be twice as much for the 12 AO2 marks available. AO2 credit is given for the comments that indicate what the research shows us and also for the well-expressed comments about laboratory studies. Further analysis might have included a consideration of demand characteristics and the effects of emotion. AO2 is 'basic', though close to 'limited' = 6 marks (see marking allocation on page 12).

Loftus did other research on leading questions and showed that whether you use 'a' or 'the' in a question affects recall. The problem with all of these studies is that they are laboratory experiments and are artificial. People do not behave in the same way in real life when other factors influence their recall. Real life studies of eyewitness testimony have found better recall. For example, one study in Canada found that the recall of eyewitnesses even 4 months later was still the same as their initial reports despite the use of some misleading questions. This suggests that in real life eyewitness testimony can be very reliable. [310 words]

TOTAL: 20 out of 30 marks

Practice examination questions

1

(a) Describe **three** differences between short-term and long-term memory.
[2 + 2 + 2]

(b) Describe the procedures and findings of **one** study on the capacity of short-term memory. [6]

(c) Outline and evaluate **one or more** theories of forgetting in long-term memory. [18]

AQA A style question

2

(a) The table below outlines three features of long-term memory. In your **answer book** write down what should be included in boxes (i) and (ii) to complete the table. [2]

(i)	Memory for events
Procedural memory	Memory for motor skills
Semantic memory	(ii)

(b) Atkinson and Shiffrin's multi-store model describes the way information is transferred to the Long Term Memory store. Outline how this happens.　[2]

(c) A researcher reads out a list of 20 words, which are all similar in length and familiarity. Immediately afterwards the researcher asks participants to write down all the words they can remember from the list. Participants remember more words from the beginning and from the end of the list than from the middle.

(i) Explain why the first few words are more likely to be remembered than words from the middle of the list.　[3]

(ii) Explain why the last few words are more likely to be remembered than words from the middle of the list.　[3]

(d) Describe and discuss **at least two** psychological explanations why a person who does not suffer from amnesia may forget things in the course of everyday life. Illustrate your answer with reference to examples.　[10]

AQA B January 2003

> 'Describe and discuss' is a phrase used in the AQA specification B exam. You are required to present description and evaluation.

3

(a) Identify **two** general assumptions of the cognitive approach to psychology.　[2]

> The term 'identify' requires you to simply name these assumptions and offer no further elaboration.

(b) Psychologists have conducted many investigations into the accuracy of eyewitness testimony. Describe **three** factors that have been shown to influence the accuracy of eyewitness testimony.　[6]

(c) Give **one** criticism of psychological research into eyewitness testimony and assess this criticism.　[4]

Edexcel specimen paper Unit Test 1 question 2

4

In the study by :Loftus and Palmer (eyewitness testimony), the participants were shown film clips of car accidents. Suggest **two** ways in which the ecological validity of this study could be improved.

OCR Core studies 2 January 2002

5

(a) Using an example, explain what is meant by the term *procedural memory*.　[3]

(b) The Working Memory model includes the following components:

- the articulatory loop;
- the visuo-spatial scratchpad;
- the primary acoustic store.

Which **one** of these components is most likely to be used by a person who is

(i)　running over uneven rocky ground;

(ii)　counting silently?

(c) Describe **one** study in which the levels of processing model of memory was investigated. Indicate why the study was conducted, the method used, results obtained and conclusion drawn.　[5]

(d) Sam and Ella are looking theough an album of their holiday photographs from many years ago. The photographs remind them of events which happened at that time, although their memories differ. For example they disagree about the details of several holidays they spent together in the South of France.

Describe and discuss at least two psychological explanations of forgetting which might explain Sam's and Ella's memories of their holidays.　[10]

AQA B May 2003

Chapter 3

Developmental psychology

The following topics are covered in this chapter:

- *The developmental approach*
- *Cognitive development*
- *Attachments in development:*
  The development and variety of attachments

- *Attachments in development:*
  Deprivation and privation
- *Critical issue: Day care*

3.1 The developmental approach

After studying this topic you should be able to:

- *define the concepts of nature and nurture*
- *describe the key assumptions of the developmental approach in psychology*
- *evaluate the developmental approach in terms of its advantages and limitations*
- *outline some of the methods used in the developmental approach*

Key assumptions of the developmental approach

AQA A	U1
EDEXCEL	U1
OCR	U1, U2

You can think of nature and nurture in terms of a plant. One seed (nature) may thrive when planted in a sunny corner of garden with fertile soil (nurture). Another seed may not do as well despite enjoying the same conditions (nurture) due to genetic differences (nature).

The term 'development' refers to the changes that take place over a person's lifetime. These changes may be the result of:

- inherited factors (**nature**), which include events that occur as a result of maturation, such as puberty
- lifetime experiences (**nurture**), which include interactions with other people.

Psychologists used to talk about 'nature *versus* nurture', meaning that development could be explained in terms of either nature or nurture. They now recognise that all behaviour is a result of an *interaction between* both nature and nurture. But they still argue about which has the greater influence.

There are many aspects to a person's development:

- *Cognitive* (mental abilities). Your thinking changes as you get older (we look at cognitive development later in this chapter, p.53–59); your knowledge increases, and your language develops.
- *Social*: for example, gender development, making friends, and learning pro- and anti-social behaviour
- *Personal*: for example, development of your emotional self (this is considered later in the chapter under 'Attachments in development' see p.60–74) and your self-concept generally (self-esteem, self-efficacy, and so on).

The cognitive-developmental approach focuses on the development of cognitive activity, and explanations of how behaviour changes in terms of cognition. So, for example, moral behaviour could be explained in terms of how a child's *thinking* about right and wrong changes over time.

Evaluation of the developmental approach

Weaknesses of this approach

Until recently, developmental psychology focused on childhood as the only time when changes took place, describing life thereafter as a plateau with little change. Psychologists are now increasingly aware of the cognitive, social and personal development that takes place *after* the age of 18.

Strengths of this approach

- Developmental psychology is a dynamic view of behaviour, emphasising the changes that occur over time and the factors that influence those changes.
- Developmental psychology has many applications, ranging from providing advice about education (see p.59), to providing information on the effects of day care on cognitive and socio-emotional development (see p.75–77) and better ways to raise children.

Methods used in the developmental approach

The experimental approach

The experimental method is unsuitable for developmental psychology for two reasons:

- Children are not ideal participants in experiments because they tend to behave very unnaturally in an artificial situation and they are highly sensitive to an experimenter's unconscious cues (**demand characteristics**). It is better to observe children in a naturalistic environment.
- In any developmental study the independent variable (IV) is likely to be age. For example, in a typical study, you want to know in what way a 5-year-old's behaviour differs from that of a 10-year-old. Age is the IV and the differences in behaviour are the DV (dependent variable). We cannot manipulate age directly (i.e. you cannot make one participant a 5-year-old and another a 10-year-old) and therefore the study is called a quasi-experiment, which is longitudinal or cross-sectional.

The methods which *are* suitable for the developmental approach are as follows:

Naturalistic observation

In this method, behaviour is observed in a natural environment. All variables are free to vary (unlike in an experiment) and interference is kept to a minimum. The participants may not be aware that they are being observed (undisclosed observation can be used, e.g. one-way mirrors, though this raises ethical concerns). On the other hand, if participants know they are being observed, this can affect their behaviour.

Evaluation

This method gives a more realistic picture of spontaneous behaviour but one cannot infer cause and effect. There are also problems with observer bias.

Controlled observation

Some observational studies, such as the Strange Situation (see p.62), involve observations made within a set of strict guidelines.

Evaluation

This means that the environment may still be fairly natural but some degree of control is exerted – which increases comparability from one participant to another, and from one observer to another (observer reliability).

Longitudinal studies

One group of individuals is studied over a period of time, taking periodic samples of behaviour. This makes it possible to determine what factors may influence development – see, for example, the study by Hodges and Tizard (p.74).

Demand characteristics are those features of an experiment which cause participants to try to work out what is expected of them, and lead them to behave in certain predictable ways.

Some of these methods are discussed in Chapter 7, along with a look at their strengths and weaknesses.

Evaluation

The main strength of these are that they use a repeated measures design (see p.167) and therefore personal variables are well controlled. The main weakness is that such studies take a long time, requiring a large investment of time and money. A further problem is that some participants 'drop out' and this may bias the results because one is left with a particular kind of sample (e.g. one which has lost all the 'difficult' participants because they couldn't be bothered to reappear continuously).

Cross-sectional studies

An alternative approach is to compare different age groups at the same point in time, as in the study by Samuel and Bryant (see p.57).

Evaluation

This is a cheaper method but one that offers less control of personal variables. One particular problem is that different age groups may not be comparable because of the **cohort effect** (social changes at certain points in time result in cohorts of children who are unique – such as those who grew up in the 1960s hippie culture).

Twin and family studies

The word 'zygote' means fertilised egg, so 'monozygotic' means the twins come from one egg and therefore share the same genetic material.

An obvious way to make comparisons between nature and nurture is to look at identical and non-identical twins – called monozygotic (MZ) and dizygotic (DZ) twins respectively. MZ twins share 100% of the same genes and therefore in terms of nature they are the same – so any differences in their behaviour must be due to environment. There are cases of twins brought up in different homes and in this instance any *similarities* are presumed to be due to nature. The term **concordance rate** is used to express the extent to which a certain trait in both twins is in 'concord' or agreement.

Evaluation

Twins who are reared together also share the same environment, so it isn't always possible to claim that any behaviour is due to similar nature or shared nurture.

Progress check

1 Give another word for the terms 'nature' and 'nurture'.
2 What is the difference between a longitudinal and a cross-sectional study?
3 What is a MZ twin?

3 This refers to monozygotic twins who come from one egg and who are therefore genetically identical.
2 In a longitudinal study the same participants are compared at different ages, in a cross-sectional study different participants are compared of varying ages.
1 E.g. innate (nature) and experience (nurture).

3.2 Cognitive development

After studying this topic you should be able to:

- *outline and evaluate Piaget's theory of cognitive development*
- *outline and evaluate Vygotsky's theory of cognitive development*
- *discuss the empirical evidence related to both theories*
- *describe and evaluate practical applications of these theories*

Piaget's theory of cognitive development

EDEXCEL U1
OCR U1, U2

Cognitive development is the study of how mental activities develop.

The essence of Piaget's theory

The essence of this theory of cognitive development is as follows:

- There are **qualitative** differences between child and adult thinking. Before Piaget the view was that children simply knew less than adults and cognitive development involved quantitative changes.
- It is a **biological** approach: cognitive development is mainly a consequence of physical maturation. Progress occurs only when the child is *ready* and then appropriate experiences will enable cognitive development to occur.
- **Language** is the outcome of a generalised cognitive ability. Language does not create cognitive development, it is the *result of* general cognitive maturity.

The structure of the intellect

Variant cognitive structures develop with age:

- **Schemas (or schemata)** are cognitive representations of things or activities. A child is born with innate schema. These are reflex responses, such as grasping schema or sucking schema. These schema integrate with each other, and new ones form in response to the environment.
- **Operations** are things that involve physical or symbolic manipulations (as in **pre-operational thought** – see p.54).

Invariant cognitive structures: The process of adaptation (learning) remains the same through life:

- **Assimilation.** A new object or idea is understood in terms of existing schema. For example, you see a furry thing and realise that it is a dog. You have understood the new experience in terms of existing schema.
- **Accommodation.** Schema are modified to fit new situations or information. For example, you realise the furry thing is not a dog nor does it belong to any other group of animal with which you were familiar. It is in fact a llama and you must modify your existing schemas to cope with this new information.
- **Equilibrium.** If existing schema are inadequate, a state of disequilibrium occurs, and this drives the person to accommodate the schema – thus ensuring cognitive development.

Piaget's theory is sometimes called an 'ages and stages theory' because of the concept of stages. However, the structure of the intellect and the way development takes place (through disequilibrium and accommodation) is just as important.

Stages in cognitive development

A child moves from one stage to the next as a consequence of maturity. **Horizontal décalage** describes the fact that not all aspects of the same stage appear at the same time – for example, the ability to conserve number and volume.

- **Sensorimotor stage** (0 to approximately 2 years). Early reflex activities (e.g. sucking) are built up into more complex routines through **circular (repetitive) reactions**. The infant co-ordinates sensory and motor activity. By the end of this stage symbolic activity has started (e.g. language).

- **Pre-operational stage** (2–7 years). Using symbols but not adult logic (i.e. logic that is internally consistent). Pre-operational children use **transductive reasoning** (logic which is centred on one particular aspect of a thing and therefore cannot be transferred to other situations), e.g. 'if a thing has four legs and a dog has four legs, the thing must be a dog'. The stage is subdivided into:

  - **Pre-conceptual** (2–4 years). Concepts not fully formed, e.g. Daddy owns a blue car – therefore all blue cars are called 'Daddy's car'.
  - **Intuitive** (4–7 years) e.g. child displays animism, egocentric behaviour (as in the three mountains experiment described on p.55), and cannot conserve (see also below).

- **Concrete operational stage** (7–11 years). Children now use logical mental rules, but only for concrete rather than abstract tasks, e.g. they cannot cope with the transitive interference task problem 'Mary is taller than Susan, Susan is taller than Anne, who is tallest?' unless the problem is presented using dolls (i.e. in concrete form). The child can cope with conservation, class inclusion, and using numbers to perform calculations. However, problem solving still tends to be random rather than systematic (scientific).

- **Formal operational stage** (11+ years). Abstract and systematic thought possible, organised deduction/induction, more scientific approach.

> Note the use of the word 'operational' which refers to the kind of mental logic which the child is using. Addition is an example of an 'operation'.

Empirical evidence

Piaget's methods involved naturalistic observation and semi-structured interviews, using small samples of (often) his own children. However, he did spend over 50 years amassing a detailed record of individual behaviour (idiographic approach). Piaget also conducted research with Inhelder of a more experimental nature, which did involve large samples of children. Piaget's research led him to several conclusions, as outlined below.

Object permanence (sensorimotor stage)

This refers to a child's realisation that objects continue to exist even when they cannot be seen. Piaget claimed that this developed after the age of 8 months.

- However, Baillargeon and DeVos (1991) showed that infants aged 3–4 months demonstrated object permanence when tested on various tasks. In the rolling car task (see below) there was a large or small carrot sliding along a track and hidden at one point by a screen with a large window. The track is arranged so that the large carrot should be visible as it passes behind the window whereas the small carrot (not as broad) should remain hidden. The infants looked longer at the large carrot presumably expecting the top half to be visible behind the window.

- It would seem that children develop object permanence before the age suggested by Piaget but that it is still a developmental stage.

The rolling car task

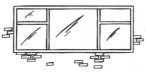

Small carrot is invisible behind window – child expects this.

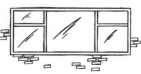

Large carrot remains invisible because window contains opaque glass – child shows surprise.

Piaget's three mountains scene

Egocentrism (intuitive pre-operational stage)

Pre-operational children find it hard to take the perspective of another.

- In the three mountains experiment Piaget and Inhelder (1956) asked children aged 4–12 to say how a doll, placed in various positions, would view a model of a mountain range (see diagram). The youngest children could only work from their own perspective, but by the age of nine they were sure of the doll's perspective.
- However, Hughes (1975) achieved better performance by hiding a doll from a toy policeman and Borke (1975) used the character Grover from Sesame Street driving along in his fire engine, again finding that younger children were not as egocentric as Piaget suggested.

Conservation (intuitive, pre-operational stage)

This refers to the ability to understand that quantity is not changed even when a display is transformed.

- In the number conservation experiment, Piaget showed a child two identical rows of counters and asked whether they were both the same. He then made one row longer by moving the counters in it further apart and again asked whether they were the same. A child over 7 (concrete operational stage) recognises that quantity can not change and says 'yes'. Similar experiments were done with volume (water in a jar) and mass (balls of clay).
- Rose and Blank (1974) and Samuel and Bryant (1984 see p.57) found that using two questions confuses younger children. If one question was asked younger children performed better, but there were still age differences.
- McGarrigle and Donaldson (1974) found that a less artificial task led to success at a younger age. They used 'naughty teddy' to rearrange a row of counters. However, subsequent research (Moore and Frye, 1986) has suggested that the naughty teddy may have unduly distracted the children and they didn't realise that any transformation had taken place and that's why they were not 'fooled' by the transformation.

Formal operational thinking

- Bryant and Trabasso (1971) showed that difficulty on transitive inference tasks (see p.54) may be due to memory failure rather than lack of ability. They trained children until they could perform a transitive task successfully, and found that they could then perform a more lengthy series of comparisons.
- Piaget and Inhelder (1956) tested deductive reasoning using the beaker problem. Children are given four beakers of colourless, odourless liquid and asked to find which combination turns yellow. They found that concrete thinkers try to solve the problem randomly whereas formal thinkers are systematic.

The influence of language on thought

Sinclair-de-Zwart (1969) produced evidence that the inability to conserve was related to linguistic development (i.e. children who could conserve had more extensive vocabularies using words such as 'larger' instead of absolute terms such as 'big'). However, training in verbal skills did not increase the ability to conserve (i.e. teaching the children to use other words for 'small' such as 'short', 'thin' or 'few'). 90% of the non-conservers remained unable to conserve, which supports the view that children only move from one stage to the next when they are ready – not when given extra practice.

1 Outline one study that has investigated the sensorimotor stage of development.
2 What is the key characteristic of the pre-operational stage of development?

2 Intuitive rather than adult logic, egocentric thought.

1 E.g. Bower (1981) moved objects behind a screen to test object permanence.

Criticisms of Piaget's theory and the empirical evidence

- **Age.** Many studies have found that children develop certain cognitive structures earlier (or later) than Piaget claimed but the *stage sequence* remains unchallenged by this evidence.
- **Appropriateness of the task.** Piaget's tasks may have confused children, e.g. the three mountains task.
- **Form of questioning.** Children aim to please and so they respond to demand characteristics and/or experimenter bias, e.g. the conservation experiment.
- **Practice.** If the development of cognitive structures is related to maturity then practice should not improve performance. Danner and Day (1977) coached students aged 10, 13 and 17 in three formal operational tasks. The effects were limited with the younger participants but very marked at 17 years, showing that training does make a difference although it is still related to cognitive maturation.
- **Effects of language.** Frank (1966) claimed that language can help overcome concrete thinking. He tested 4–6-year-olds on the volume conservation task with a screen in front of the beakers so the level was not visible. Almost all the older children coped, and half the 4-year-olds. However, Sinclair-de-Zwart (see p.56) did not find that language training led to improved performance.

Evaluation

The strengths of Piaget's theory are as follows:

- Piaget's theory was the first **comprehensive account** of cognitive development.
- It **changed the traditional view** of the child as passive and stimulated an enormous amount of research.
- It had a **large impact on education**, particularly in primary schools.

Weaknesses of Piaget's theory have been identified as follows:

- Piaget's evidence often **lacked scientific rigour**. The samples were small and open to experimenter bias. Bryant (1995) claimed that Piaget's experiments lacked control (which means that he did not rule out other possible explanations for the behaviours he observed).
- Piaget suggested that disequilibrium would be the driving force in cognitive development. However, although conflict would create a sense that something is wrong it does not tell a child **how to solve the problem**.

OCR core study: Conservation

Samuel and Bryant (1984) Asking only one question

Aims Do younger children fail to cope with Piaget's conservation task because they are not sufficiently mature, or is it because they find being asked two questions is confusing? The child may well think that the reason the experimenter asks the same question again is because he wants a different answer. This would be especially *true* because children are susceptible to demand characteristics.

Procedures This was a laboratory experiment, with a cross-sectional design. The children (252 boys and girls aged between 5 and $8\frac{1}{2}$ years) were divided into four age groups, whose mean ages were: 5 years 3 months, 6 years 3 months, 7 years 3 months, 8 years 3 months. Each group was further subdivided into 3 subgroups.

- *Standard*: Traditional conservation task, asked two questions.
- *One judgement*: Only one question asked, after the display was changed.
- *Fixed array control*: Only saw one display, the post-transformation one.

A control group was necessary in order to be able to explain the performance of the other two groups in terms of the information they had from the pre-transformation display. If the control group couldn't cope with the task then failure might be due to problems understanding just the one question.

The children were tested on:

- *Mass*. Two equal plasticine cylinders. One cylinder is squashed so it looks like a sausage or a pancake.
- *Number*. Two rows of 6 counters each, arranged identically. One row was either spread out or bunched up so the two rows were not of equal length.
- *Volume*. Two identical glasses, with the *same* amounts of liquid. The liquid from one glass is poured into a narrower or wider one.

Findings The table below shows the mean number of errors for each child (rounded to the nearest whole number). An error is a failure to give a conserving response.

Age	Standard	One question	Control
5	8	7	9
6	6	4	6
7	3	3	5
8	2	1	3

Table of results from Samuel and Bryant's study

Conclusions Younger children did cope better with the one question task but there were still age differences.

Criticisms The younger children may still have felt intimidated by the experimental situation and been less able to cope.

OCR Revision question
a) In the study by Samuel and Bryant on conservation, in the 'one question condition' children are asked a question about number, mass or volume, only after they have seen the substance changed in front of them. Identify the **two** other conditions of this experiment. [2]

b) In addition to these conditions, **two** other factors affected the children's ability to conserve. Identify **both** these factors. [2] (June 2001, Core Studies 1, question 3)

Vygotsky's theory of cognitive development

EDEXCEL U1

The essence of his theory is as follows.

- Cognitive development is the result of the **child's active construction** of their knowledge rather than passive conditioning (Pavlov's view).
- The **social construction of knowledge**: Social and cultural influences, especially *language* and other cultural symbols (e.g. mathematics), are the driving force behind cognitive development. Vygotsky's theory grew out of the political world he lived in (Marxist Russia) which believed that the only way to bring about psychological change was by altering social conditions.
- The **guidance of experts** (people with greater knowledge) is the main reason why children move forward in their thinking (as opposed to Piaget's notion of biological readiness).
- The role of **scaffolding** (see p.59) in constructing a framework to promote effective learning.

The structure of the intellect

- **Elementary mental functions**: these are innate capacities (such as attention and sensation) that will develop to a limited extent through experience. This kind of thinking is not dissimilar to that of other primates.
- **Higher mental functions**. In the main it is cultural influences that are responsible for transforming elementary functions into higher mental functions, such as problem solving and thinking. Culture is transmitted via language, shared symbol systems such as mathematics, and the help of 'experts'.
- The **zone of proximal development (ZPD)** is the distance between a child's current and potential abilities. The aim of instruction is to stimulate those functions which lie waiting in the ZPD.

Stages in cognitive development

Vygotsky's theory was not a stage theory in the same way that Piaget's was, nevertheless he did identify certain phases of development:

- **Pre-intellectual, social speech** (age 0–3 years). Language serves a social function. At the same time, thought is pre-linguistic.
- **Egocentric speech** (3–7 years). Language is used to control one's own behaviour but often spoken aloud.
- **Inner speech** (7+ years). Self-talk becomes silent and differs in form from social speech. Throughout life, language serves these dual purposes – for thought and social communication.

Empirical evidence

- Gredler (1992) argued that if higher mental functions depend on cultural influences, we would expect to find different higher mental functions in different cultures. One example of this can be seen in the children of Papua New Guinea who are taught a counting system which begins on the thumb of one hand and proceeds up the arm and down to the other fingers, ending at 29 (which means that it is very difficult for them to add and subtract).
- Shif (Vygotsky, 1987) asked pupils to complete sentences which ended in 'because' or 'although' and found that they were better able to finish the sentences which dealt with scientific rather than everyday concepts. Vygotsky argued that this demonstrates a greater understanding of scientific concepts – because these are learned through instruction with expert guidance, whereas everyday concepts are assimilated through self-directed activity.

- Freund (1990) arranged for one group of children to play on their own with a doll's house, and another to play with their mothers. At the end, the children who worked with experts (mothers) showed a dramatic improvement in their ability to perform a furniture sorting task.

An evaluation of Vygotsky's theory

- Vygotsky's approach has produced comparatively little empirical support (so far), but lots of interest from psychologists and educationalists.
- The central role of language and culture in cognitive development has important implications for education.

> Piaget and Vygotsky need not be seen as opposites. Glassman (1999) argues that in fact the two theories are remarkably similar, especially at their central core. An attempt to integrate the two approaches would be productive.

Practical applications to education

EDEXCEL U1

> 'Each time one prematurely teaches a child something he could have discovered for himself, that child is kept from inventing it and consequently from understanding it completely' (Piaget, 1970).

Piaget's theory

- **Readiness.** Children advance their knowledge because of biologically regulated cognitive changes. Children should be offered stimuli which are moderately novel only when they are ready.
- **Self-discovery and self-motivation.** If you tell a child how to do something you prevent their complete understanding.
- **Individualised.** Since each child matures at a different rate and has different schema, their learning programme should be unique.
- **Discovery learning.** The teacher should set tasks which are appropriate for pupils and intrinsically motivating. The teacher's role is not to impart knowledge but to ask questions or create situations which 'ask questions', thus creating disequilibrium and forcing children to make accommodations.
- **Logic** is not an innate mental process, it is the *outcome* of cognitive development. Logic, maths and science should be taught in primary schools.
- Use of **concrete materials** in teaching children, in the stage of concrete operations.

Vygotsky's theory

> 'What a child can do with assistance today he/she can do by him/herself tomorrow' (Vygotksy)

- **Expert intervention** (by peers or adults) should be most effective when the expert is aware of the limits of the ZPD. Thus, the more sensitive an adult is to a child's competence the more the child should improve.
- **Scaffolding.** An adult advances children's thinking by providing a framework (scaffolding) on which children can climb. Wood *et al.* (1976) observed mothers and children (aged 4–5 years) working together. When the learner ran into difficulty, the mothers gave specific instructions. When the learner is coping well only general encouragement is needed. The learner is given a scaffold by those more expert and the scaffold enables them to 'climb higher' i.e. achieve more. In time, we all learn to scaffold ourselves (self-instruction).
- **Peer tutoring.** Peers can also be experts and co-operative group work successful in schools. Bennett and Dunne (1991) found that children who were engaged in co-operative group work were less competitive, less concerned with status and more likely to show evidence of logical thinking than those who worked alone.

Progress exercise

1 What is the difference between elementary and higher mental functions?
2 Whose theory of cognitive development emphasises the role of experts?

2 Vygotsky's.

1 Elementary functions are innate, higher mental functions develop as a result of cultural influences

3.3 Attachments in development: The development and variety of attachments

After studying this topic you should be able to:

- describe the nature, consequences and development of attachment
- discuss individual and cultural variation in attachment
- explain and evaluate the main theories of attachment

The nature and consequences of attachment

AQA A ▶ U1

Key Term Attachment is a mutual and intense emotional relationship between two individuals. It is especially used to describe the relationship between an infant and his/her caregiver(s). There are four characteristic behaviours associated with attachment:

- seeking proximity, especially at times of stress
- distress on separation (**separation anxiety**)
- pleasure at reunion
- general orientation of behaviour towards primary caregiver.

The purposes of attachment are as follows:

- **Safety.** It may be no accident that attachment bonds develop at the time when the infant becomes mobile.
- **Secure base.** Provides an emotionally safe place from which to explore.
- **Anxiety reduction.** The presence of the attachment figure reduces anxiety.
- **Promoting emotional and self-development** – an attachment figure may act as a model for later emotional relationships.

> Notice that some benefits of attachment are *short-term* ones while others are *long-term*.

The development of attachments

Schaffer and Emerson (1964) and Bowlby (1969) have identified the following key phases in the development of attachment.

Phase 1 Pre-attachment: Indiscriminate social responsiveness (Birth–2 months)
In this phase infants behave in characteristic and friendly ways towards other people but their ability to discriminate between them is very limited, e.g. they may just recognise familiar voices. They are equally friendly to inanimate objects, though towards the end of this period infants are beginning to show a greater preference for social stimuli (such as a smiling face).

> The words 'mother' and 'maternal' are used to refer to a 'mother-figure' – this need not necessarily be a woman.

Phase 2 Attachment-in-the-making: Recognition of familiar people (2–6/7 months)
Infants continue to be generally social but there is beginning to be a marked difference of behaviour towards one primary caregiver. They continue to be relatively easily comforted by anyone, and do not yet show anxiety with strangers.

> Separation protest and stranger anxiety are both forms of distress displayed by an infant who can now distinguish between known and unknown people. Both behaviours are related to the formation of attachments.

Phase 3 Specific attachments: Separation protest and stranger anxiety (7 months–2 years)
The infant shows attachment to one special person by protesting when that person puts them down (**separation protest**), and showing especial joy at reunion with that person. Around the same time, the infant begins to display **stranger anxiety** and also starts to be mobile. The infant will follow his or her caregiver and use this person as a safe base for exploration.

Phase 4 Multiple attachments (8 months approximately)
Very soon after the main attachment is formed, the infant also develops a wider circle of attachments depending on how many consistent relationships he or she has. The quality of these attachments is a matter of some debate. Some

Monotropy means 'turning towards one person'. Monotropy doesn't exclude multiple attachments but is the view that there is one special relationship that is at the top of the hierarchy of the infant's other relationships.

psychologists believe that there remains one special attachment figure (**monotropy** is the term used to represent this view). Bowlby felt that this was important for emotional development. Other psychologists have suggested that all attachments are equivalent though qualitatively different (for example, mum is used for comfort, older brother for play, dad for encouragement).

Phase 5 Formation of a goal-corrected partnership (From age 2 onwards)
The child develops insight into the mother-figure's behaviour and this opens up a whole new relationship where the infant can consciously influence what the caregiver does. This is the beginning of a real partnership.

An evaluation of the sequence of development
More recent research suggests that very young infants are far more social and discriminating than was once thought. For example, Bushnell *et al.* (1989) found that infants who were less than 24 hours old looked longer at their mother than at another woman. They could discriminate between people and showed a preference for one special person.

Progress check

1 Name one consequence of being attached.
2 What behaviours indicate that an infant is attached?

2 E.g. separation protest or stranger anxiety.

1 E.g. safety, emotional security or development.

Variation in attachment: Individual differences

AQA A U1

Secure and insecure attachment

One of the ways in which children differ is in terms of how securely they are attached to their primary caregiver.

Key Term Secure attachment is the optimal form of attachment, which is associated with healthy emotional, social and cognitive development. A securely attached child shows mild protest (separation anxiety) on their caregiver's departure. On the caregiver's return the child seeks out the caregiver and is relatively easily comforted. Securely attached children are more likely to display stranger anxiety than insecurely attached children.

Key Term Insecure attachment is associated with less optimal emotional, social and cognitive development. There are two main forms of insecure attachment: avoidant (child avoids contact with caregiver at reunion) and resistant (child resists contact with caregiver at reunion). These are described in more detail on page 62.

Measuring security of attachment

Ainsworth and Bell (1970) developed the Strange Situation as a method of measuring an infant's attachment. This method has been revised so that it can be used with older children as well. The study and its findings are reported below.

Explaining security of attachment

- **Bowlby's theory** (see page 67). Secure attachment is the result of sensitive and responsive caregiving.
- **Temperamental hypothesis.** Kagan (1982) suggested that some children are innately more vulnerable to stress due to inherited temperamental differences. Such differences mean that some children are less easy to care for and maternal rejection leads to insecure attachment.

AQA (A) Key study: Secure and insecure attachment

Ainsworth and Bell (1970) The Strange Situation

Aims To establish a method of assessing strength of attachment. The theory of attachment suggests that one of the functions of attachment is to provide a secure base. If you place young children in situations of mild stress, how do they respond? Are there individual differences? This study aimed to test how different children respond to stranger anxiety and separation anxiety.

Procedures The method used was a controlled observation, called the **Strange Situation**. The procedure consists of seven 3-minute episodes designed to be used with children aged 12–18 months old:

1. Parent (or caregiver) and infant enter a room, infant plays.
2. Stranger enters and talks with caregiver, gradually approaches infant.
3. Caregiver leaves. Stranger leaves child playing unless appears distressed and then offers comfort.
4. Caregiver returns, stranger leaves.
5. Caregiver leaves, after the infant has again begun to play.
6. Stranger returns and behaves as described in 3.
7. Caregiver returns and the stranger leaves.

The Strange Situation provides a measure of the security of a child's attachment on the basis of four behaviours:

- **Separation anxiety.** This is the unease the child shows when left by its caregiver.
- **Infant's willingness to explore.** A more securely attached child will explore more widely.
- **Stranger anxiety.** Security of attachment is related to greater stranger anxiety.
- **Reunion behaviour.** Insecurely attached children often greet their caregiver's return by ignoring them or behaving ambivalently.

Findings When separation anxiety, willingness to explore, stranger anxiety and reunion behaviour were examined, certain patterns of behaviour emerged. The infants could be classified within one of these three groups:

- **Secure attachment** (Type B). 71% of infants showed mild protest on their caregiver's departure. On the caregiver's return the infants sought the caregiver and were relatively easily comforted.
- **Insecure/avoidant attachment** (Type A). 12% showed indifference when their caregiver left, and did not display stranger anxiety. At reunion they actively avoided contact with their caregiver, and the caregiver generally ignored the infant during play.
- **Insecure/resistant attachment** (Type C). 17% were seriously distressed when their caregiver left and not easily consoled when the caregiver returned. The infant sought comfort and rejected it at the same time. The caregiver was also inconsistent: either rejecting and angry toward the infant, or overly responsive and sensitive.

Conclusions The distinct patterns of behaviour observed suggest that this is a valid method of assessing individual differences. Secure attachment was regarded as the optimal type of attachment and is associated with healthy socio-emotional development.

Criticisms On the positive side, there is support for the validity of this measurement. A number of studies have found that children who were classified as secure in infancy do show more positive social and emotional development. For example, Sroufe (1983) found that infants rated as secure in their second year were later

The concept of validity refers to the extent to which a measurement is actually assessing something that is real. Reliability concerns the extent to which a measure is consistent – the test should give the same result every time it is used.

found to be more popular, have more initiative, and were higher in self-esteem, less aggressive and more likely to be social leaders.

On the other hand there is evidence that this method of assessment lacks validity. The Strange Situation may test the child's relationships rather than some characteristic that has developed in the child (as a result of caregiver interaction). Children can have different attachment classifications with different caregivers, e.g. Lamb (1977) found that some children were securely attached to their mothers but avoidantly attached to their fathers. This makes the Strange Situation classification meaningless (lacking validity).

Cross-cultural variation

Key Term **Cross-cultural variation** refers to the differences that exist between people from different cultures. A culture is all the rules, customs, morals and ways of interacting that bind together members of a society or some other collection of people. These rules affect the way we behave and, in relation to attachment, lead to different methods of child-rearing – and these may lead to differences in kinds of attachment.

To what extent does security of attachment vary across cultures? Van Ijzendoorn and Kroonenberg (1988) compared results from studies using the Strange Situation with the results shown below:

Country	Number of studies	Percentage of each attachment type (to the nearest whole number)		
		Secure	*Avoidant*	*Resistant*
West Germany	3	57	35	8
Great Britain	1	75	22	3
Netherlands	4	67	26	7
Sweden	1	74	22	4
Israel	2	64	7	29
Japan	2	68	5	27
China	1	50	25	25
United States	18	65	21	14
Overall average		65	21	14

A comparison of results from Strange Situation studies

The noteworthy features are:

- **Considerable consistency across cultures:** Bee (1995) concluded that it is likely that the same caregiver–infant interactions contribute to secure and insecure attachments in all cultures.
- **Some differences.** In Japan, infants very rarely leave their mother (Miyake *et al.*, 1985). Therefore, the Strange Situation is a particularly stressful event for them, which might explain the large number of insecure-resistant children. Using a 'tool' developed in one culture and applied to another culture may produce meaningless results – see also study by Grossman and Grossman in the key study on p.64.
- Van IJzendoorn and Kroonenberg found that the variation of attachment within cultures was $1\frac{1}{2}$ times greater than the variation between cultures. This means that the Strange Situation may also be an **imposed etic** (i.e. meaningless form of assessment) for many sub-cultures in the Western World.
- Some of the studies involved **small samples** and in some countries there were only a few studies that were analysed. This would bias the results.

AQA (A) Key study: Cross-cultural variations

Grossmann and Grossmann (1991) Study of attachment in Germany

Aims The aim of this study was to investigate whether the Strange Situation can be used in a different cultural context and whether similar attachment types exist in another culture. The study also explored the relationship, proposed by Ainsworth, between maternal sensitivity and attachment type.

Procedures This was a longitudinal study following 49 'normal' German families over a period of time using controlled observation (the Strange Situation) and naturalistic observation (observing the children with their parents).

Findings More of the infants were insecurely attached (anxious and avoidant) than securely attached.

Maternal sensitivity was positively related to secure attachment.

There was high stability in attachment over a 10-year period (80% of the children were classified the same).

Early attachment experiences with mothers showed a stronger influence on the child's socio-emotional development than attachments to fathers.

Children who were securely attached to their mothers as infants enjoyed close friendships later in childhood, whereas those who were avoidant or anxious reported either having no friends or few friends.

Conclusions The findings suggest that there are important cross-cultural similarities (maternal responsiveness) but also there are important differences in attachment. The different distribution of attachment types, compared to Ainsworth and Bell's findings, suggests that secure attachment is not always optimal. In other cultures other attachment types are associated with preferred outcomes.

Criticisms As suggested on page 64, it may not be appropriate to use the Strange Situation in a culture other than the one it was designed in (the US). German culture requires keeping some interpersonal distance between parents and children, therefore the norm would be for infants who appear to be insecurely attached within the Strange Situation classification scheme. The scheme does not have the same meaning in Germany.

This study provides a useful cross-cultural perspective for interpreting studies of attachment in the US and Britain. It shows that there are many similarities, which suggests that some aspects of attachment and parent–child relationships may be universal, whereas others are related to child-rearing methods specific to the culture.

Progress check

1 Name two types of insecure attachment.
2 Why is it inappropriate to use the Strange Situation in a culture other than the one it was designed for?

2 E.g. infants in different cultures experience different child-rearing styles so the Strange Situation has different meaning for them.

1 Avoidant and resistant.

Explanations of attachment

AQA A ▶ U1

What factors determine the formation of attachments? Why do infants become attached to one person rather than another?

Learning theory

Learning theory is described in Chapter 1, but as a reminder: learning theorists (behaviourists) believe that all behaviour is acquired through conditioning.

Classical conditioning

Food (the unconditioned stimulus) produces a sense of pleasure (unconditioned response). The food becomes associated with the person doing the feeding, who then becomes a conditioned stimulus also producing a sense of pleasure.

According to behaviourists, infants become attached to the person who feeds them, or gives them pleasure.

Operant conditioning

Dollard and Miller (1950) adapted the principles of operant conditioning to incorporate the concept of mental states. The hungry infant feels uncomfortable and this creates a drive to lessen the discomfort. Being fed reduces the discomfort and the drive. Drive reduction is rewarding and the infant learns that food is a reward or primary reinforcer. The person who supplies the food is associated with the food and becomes a secondary (or conditioned) reinforcer, and a source of reward in their own right.

Social learning theory

This proposes that learning can take place indirectly through vicarious reinforcement and modelling. Hay and Vespo (1988) suggested that attachment occurs because children learn to imitate the affectionate behaviour shown by their parents. Parents/caregivers also teach children in an explicit way to show affection.

Evaluation

Learning theory accounts suggest that infants should become most attached to the person who feeds them. However, Schaffer and Emerson (1964) found that fewer than half of the infants in their study had a primary attachment to the person who usually fed them. Harlow's (1959) classic study of rhesus monkeys also showed that feeding was less important than contact comfort. In this study each monkey was given two 'mothers', a wire one and a cloth one. Milk was provided through a nipple in one of the mothers. Half of the monkeys received milk from the wire mother, the other half from the cloth mother. Harlow found that all of the monkeys spent more time with the cloth mother, whether or not this 'mother' provided milk. When the monkeys were frightened they went to the cloth mother (a secure base). This appears to indicate that physical contact is more important than feeding with regard to attachment. In addition, it would seem that 'contact comfort' alone is not sufficient for healthy development because later in life the monkeys had difficulty mating and became rejecting mothers.

There may have been a confounding variable in the study, insofar as the shapes of the "mothers'" heads were different: a possible confounding variable.

Progress check

1 How does the caregiver become a conditioned reinforcer?
2 In what way does Schaffer and Emerson's research provide evidence against the learning theory explanation of attachment?

2 They found that the person who fed the child was more often *not* the primary attachment figure.

1 By being associated with drive reduction and providing a reward.

Psychodynamic theory

Freud's psychodynamic theory of development (see Chapter 1) suggests that an infant is born with innate drives to seek pleasure. Love has its origins in the attachment formed with the person who first satisfies those needs. If the infant is deprived of such satisfaction, he or she will become fixated on the earliest stage of development – the oral stage.

Evaluation

This account also suggests that it is the person who provides food that will become the primary attachment object, but the evidence does not support this.

Ethological theory

Ethology is the study of animal behaviour in its natural environment, focusing on the importance of innate capacities and the functions of behaviours.

Imprinting

Imprinting is the process of learning an indelible impression of another individual. The imprint thus formed has both short-term consequences (for following and safety) and long-term consequences (for reproduction).

- **Following response (short-term)**: Lorenz (1937) divided a clutch of gosling eggs into two groups: one group was left with their natural mother, and the others were hatched in an incubator and saw Lorenz when they hatched, following him around thereafter.
- **Reproduction (long-term)**: Imprinting acts as a template for future reproductive partners. For example, Immelmann (1972) arranged for zebra finches to be raised by Bengalese finches, and vice versa. In later years, when the finches were given a free choice, they preferred to mate with the species which they had imprinted on.

Critical period

Biological (innate) characteristics tend to have a 'window' for development. If the characteristic does not develop at a particular time, then it won't happen. Hess (1958) found that ducks showed the strongest following response (imprinting) about 16 hours after hatching and that, after this period, the imprint was irreversible. Furthermore, 32 hours after hatching, the ducklings showed almost no ability to acquire a following response if they hadn't acquired one already.

Sensitive period

Sluckin (1961) found that some birds will imprint beyond the normal critical period, and suggested that it might be more appropriate to use the concept 'sensitive' instead of 'critical'. Imprinting is possible at all times but happens more easily and effectively during a certain window of time.

Imprinting in humans

Imprinting research generally involves non-human animals though some psychologists have applied the same principles to humans. For example, Klaus and Kennell (1976) argued that there is a sensitive period immediately after birth in which bonding (an initial part of the attachment process) can occur through skin-to-skin contact (thus it has been called the **skin-to-skin hypothesis**). To test this, they arranged for a group of mothers to have extra contact time with their newborn babies, including skin-to-skin contact. A year later these infants and mothers had stronger attachments. However, Goldberg (1983) reviewed a number of studies and concluded that the effects of early contact are neither large nor long lasting.

Evaluation

- There is some question as to whether imprinting is any different from learning in general. This suggests that it is a superfluous concept.
- Using the concept of a sensitive rather than critical period means that learning can actually occur at any time, though perhaps less easily.

Bowlby's theory of attachment

Bowlby developed the most influential theory of attachment which drew on both psychoanalytic theory (he was a trained psychoanalyst) and ethological theory.

The main strands of Bowlby's theory

- **Attachment is adaptive:** Attachment behaviour promotes survival because it ensures safety and food for offspring. This makes it an adaptive behaviour because it enables the individuals with this characteristic to be better adapted to the environment and more likely to survive to reproduce themselves.

- **Social releasers:** Infants are born with innate social releasers, such as crying and smiling, which elicit caregiving.

- **Critical period:** Bowlby claimed that if attachment does not take place before the age of $2\frac{1}{2}$, then it is not possible thereafter.

- **Quality rather than quantity of care:** Ainsworth *et al.* (1974) proposed the **caregiving sensitivity hypothesis**. Secure attachments are the result of mothers being responsive to children's needs. Isabella *et al.* (1989) found that mothers and infants who were more responsive to each other at one month were more likely at twelve months to have a secure relationship. Those that had a more one-sided pattern of interaction tended to have insecure relationships. Schaffer and Emerson (1964) also found that responsiveness was important, as did Grossmann and Grossman (1991).

- **The internal working model:** Infants have many mental models (schema) of their environment, one of these 'internal working models' represents the infant's knowledge about his or her relationship with the primary caregiver. The model generates expectations about other relationships so that, whatever this child's primary relationship was like, will lead the child to have similar expectations about other relationships and serve as a template for all future relationships. Hazan and Shaver's (1987) research provided support for this hypothesis. They devised a 'Love Quiz' and analysed over 600 responses, classifying individuals (1) as secure, ambivalent, or avoidant 'types' based on their description of their childhood experiences, and (2) in terms of their adult style of romantic love. They found that secure types had happy, trusting and lasting love relationships; anxious-ambivalent types worried that their partners didn't really love them and experienced love as extremes of high and low; and avoidant lovers typically feared intimacy, and believed that they did not need love to be happy. This suggests that there is a consistent relationship between early attachment type and later, adult styles of romantic love, supporting the concept of the internal working model. However the data is correlational and relies to some extent on recall of childhood experiences.

- **Monotropy:** Bowlby claimed that infants need one special attachment relationship, which is qualitatively different from all others, because this intense emotional relationship forms the basis of the internal working model and underlies the ability to experience deep feelings.

Evaluation

- **Influential:** This theory has had an enormous effect, which will be examined in the next topic on deprivation and privation.

- **Evolutionary argument:** The notion that attachment is adaptive is unfalsifiable (can't be proven wrong) though it is highly plausible insofar as being close to a caregiver is protective and helps the infant find food.

- **Critical period:** The concept of a critical period may be too strong. Ethologists now prefer the idea of a **sensitive period**, which would lead us to believe that children might well be able to form attachments at any time if the opportunity presents itself (this will be discussed in the next topic).

- **Internal working model:** This would lead us to expect children to form similar sorts of relationships with all people because they are always working from the same template. However, the correlations among a child's various relationships are actually quite low (Howes *et al.*, 1994). Even if there are positive correlations there could be an alternative explanation to that of the internal working model – namely that some infants may simply be better than others at

According to Bowlby, attachments are to those individuals who are most responsive to the infant's social releasers.

All psychologists agree that an infant has multiple attachments. The issue is about whether there is one primary attachment which serves a special purpose in emotional development and that it is qualitatively different from all others.

forming relationships, and they do this as infants and again later in life.

- **Monotropy:** Some psychologists believe that the infant's many attachments are **qualitatively equivalent**. Thomas (1998) suggested that a network of close attachments provides an infant with a variety of social and emotional interactions that meet their various needs.

  Bowlby agreed that the infant had multiple attachments but he believed that one attachment was at the top of the hierarchy. Support comes from various studies – for example, Fox (1977) studied infants raised on Israeli kibbutzim, and found that they remained most attached to their mothers despite the fact that they spent more time with their metapelet (nurse or childminder). The fact that there is quite a high turnover rate of metapelets might explain the low attachment there.

- **Secure base for exploration:** Attachment is important for cognitive as well as emotional development because secure attachment promotes independence. Hazen and Durrett (1982) found that securely attached young children were more independent explorers of their environment and more innovative.

Progress check

1 How is a 'sensitive period' different from a 'critical period'?
2 Identify two key features of Bowlby's theory.

2 E.g. adaptiveness, internal working model, monotropy, social releasers, responsiveness.

1 A sensitive period means that behaviour can be acquired at any time in development but may happen most easily during a 'window', whereas the concept of a critical period is that behaviour must be acquired at that time or it will never happen.

3.4 Attachments in development: Deprivation, separation and privation

After studying this topic you should be able to:

- explain Bowlby's maternal deprivation (separation) hypothesis
- distinguish between the concepts of deprivation (separation) and privation
- describe and evaluate research into the effects of both deprivation (separation) and privation
- assess the impact of both deprivation (separation) and privation on development

LEARNING SUMMARY

Defining deprivation and privation

Again, note that the use of the term 'maternal' was to describe mothering – this does not necessarily have to be done by a woman.

Key Term **Deprivation** occurs when something is taken away. In the context of attachment, deprivation occurs when a child who has experienced attachment, is separated for a period of time from their primary attachment figure. Short-term effects of deprivation have been described by the protest–despair–detachment model (see page 69). The maternal deprivation hypothesis describes the long-term effects of deprivation.

Key Term **Separation** occurs when a child is physically separated from his/her primary caregiver, for example when attending a nursery. The child may receive suitable replacement emotional care during this separation, in which case emotional bonds are not disrupted and no harm may occur. When there is no suitable substitute emotional care there may be short- and/or long-term developmental effects.

Key Term **Privation** occurs when a child has never been able to form any attachments. Rutter (1981) suggested that one important distinction is between deprivation (loss of an attachment figure) and privation (lack of any attachment figure). It is privation that may have permanent consequences.

The effects of deprivation

Short-term effects of deprivation: separation protest

The protest–despair–detachment (PDD) model

Robertson and Bowlby (1952) observed young children who were separated from their mothers, often as a result of hospitalisation (mother or child). They noted three stages in the child's response to separation:

1 Protest: crying but able to be comforted, inwardly angry and fearful.
2 Despair: calmer, apathetic, no longer looking for caregiver, may seek self-comfort through, for example, thumb-sucking.
3 Detachment: if the situation continues for weeks or months, the child may appear to be coping but is unresponsive, caregiver may be ignored on return.

AQA (A) Key study: Short-term effects of deprivation

Robertson and Robertson (1952) Young children in brief separation

Aims   Husband and wife, James and Joyce Robertson, sought to demonstrate how brief separations were extremely emotionally damaging for young children but that this damage can be reduced if substitute emotional care is offered.

Procedures   James Robertson filmed children during periods of short separation. It was important that he used a rigorous sampling method when filming because otherwise he could be accused of just filming when the children were distressed. He used a method of time sampling where he took films at regular intervals.

Findings   The details of two of the cases are:

John, 17 months, spent 9 days in a residential nursery. He gradually broke down under the cumulative stresses of the loss of his mother, the lack of mothering care from the nurses, the strange foods, institutional routines, and the attacks from the other toddlers. He refused food and drink, stopped playing, cried a great deal, and rejected his mother when reunited.

Jane, 17 months, in foster care for 10 days. Food and routines were kept similar to those at home, her father visited daily, and the foster mother (Joyce Robertson) was fully available to meet her needs. She showed signs of missing her mother but she slept and ate well and related warmly to the foster family. Jane's reunion with her natural mother was not difficult.

Conclusions   The observations suggest that good physical care is not sufficient to help a child cope with separation/deprivation; loss of emotional care during short-term separation (deprivation) has profound effects. However, the films show that substitute emotional care (avoiding **bond disruption**) can compensate for this.

Criticisms   These are case histories. Even though there were a number of children filmed they may have had unique characteristics. This means it may not be reasonable to generalise to all children from these findings.

Barrett (1997) re-examined the original films, and noted that there were significant individual differences – securely attached children coped relatively well, whereas the insecurely attached children did become despairing.

Long-term effects of deprivation

Bowlby's maternal deprivation hypothesis

Before Bowlby formulated his theory of attachment he proposed the **maternal deprivation hypothesis**. This stated that deprivation of attachment during a critical period of development would result in permanent emotional damage. Bowlby (1953) said 'prolonged deprivation of a young child of maternal care may have grave and far reaching effects on his character … similar in form … to deprivation of vitamin(s) in infancy'.

Supporting evidence came from Bowlby's own study (1946, see key study p.71).

Material deprivation reassessed

Rutter (1981) wrote a book *Maternal deprivation reassessed* in which he offered support for Bowlby's hypothesis but felt that refinements were needed. He identified three key criticisms:

- **Bowlby had confused 'cause and effect' with correlation:** Early separation and later maladjustment may be linked but that doesn't mean that one caused the other. Rutter suggested that early separation and maladjustment may both be caused by family discord. Rutter *et al.*'s 'Isle of Wight study' (1976) involved interviews with over 2,000 boys, aged between 9 and 12, and their families. They found that boys were four times more likely to become delinquent (i.e. emotionally damaged) if separation was related to family discord rather than through illness or death of their mother.

- **Deprivation is not a homogeneous concept:** It includes a variety of different experiences including short- and long-term deprivation and also privation.
- **Individual differences are important:** Some children are harmed by early deprivation/privation, whereas others are quite resilient.

Anaclitic depression

> The term 'anaclitic' means 'arising from emotional dependency on another'.

Spitz (1945) used this term to describe the severe depression found in institutionalised infants as a result of prolonged separation from their mothers. Spitz and Wolf (1946) studied 100 apparently normal children who were hospitalised. They became apathetic and sad but recovered quickly when restored to their mother if the separation lasted less than three months. However, longer separations were rarely associated with complete recovery. It is possible that other factors associated with being in hospital were also distressing.

Effects of hospitalisation

Douglas (1975) used data from a longitudinal study of all the children born in Great Britain during one week in 1946. The children were tested every two years over the next 26 years. He found strong evidence that a hospital admission of more than a week, or repeated admission in a child under 4, was associated with an increased risk of behaviour disturbance and poor reading in adolescence.

However, Clarke and Clarke (1976) reanalysed Douglas' data and found that many of the children were in hospital because of problems associated with disadvantaged homes, and felt this might explain the children's subsequent problems rather than early separations (deprivation).

AQA (A) Key Study: Long-term effects of deprivation

Bowlby (1944) Forty-four juvenile thieves

Aims
To test the maternal deprivation hypothesis by looking at the possible causes of habitual delinquency. Individuals who are delinquent (thieves) lack a social conscience, which may be due to early experiences of separation that would damage the child's emotional development.

Procedures
Children and parents attending a child guidance clinic were interviewed about the children's early experiences. The group consisted of: 44 'thieves' or delinquents, children referred to a child guidance clinic who had been involved in stealing. There was also a control group of 44 emotionally-disturbed teenagers, seen at the child guidance clinic. Their ages ranged from 5 to 16 years. It was presumed that the 'thieves' lacked a social conscience (i.e. lacked emotional sensitivity) whereas the control group were disturbed but remained emotionally functional.

Findings
There were two distinctive features of the children studied.

- Some displayed an 'affectionless' character, a lack of normal affection, shame or sense of responsibility.
- Many of these affectionless children (86%) had, before the age of 2, been in foster homes or hospitals, often not visited by their families.

Conclusions	Bowlby termed this disaffected state '**affectionless psychopathy**' and concluded that it was caused by attachment bonds being disturbed in early life. This supports the maternal deprivation hypothesis.
Criticisms	The key data were collected retrospectively, and may be unreliable because people do not recollect past events accurately.
	The evidence is correlational, we cannot be certain that the cause of affectionless psychopathy was maternal separation.

The effects of privation

AQA A   U1
OCR   U1, U2

In Chapter 4, we will see that stress causes certain hormones to be produced and these can affect physical health.

Case studies

Genie

Curtiss (1989) reported the case of Genie, who spent most of her childhood locked in a room at her home in Los Angeles. She came to the attention of the social services department when she was $13\frac{1}{2}$. She looked like a child half her age, could not stand erect, and could not speak. She never fully recovered, socially or linguistically. This may have been due to her extreme early emotional privation, as suggested by Bowlby. It may also have been for a variety of other reasons, such as that she might have originally been retarded.

Czechoslovakian twins: PM and JM

Koluchová (1976) studied twins who had spent the first seven years of their lives locked up. When they were discovered, they couldn't talk. They were then looked after by two loving sisters and by age 14 had near normal intellectual and social functioning. By the age of 20, they were of above average intelligence and had excellent relationships with the members of their foster family (Koluchová, 1991).

Other case studies

Isabelle (Mason, 1942), Anna (Davis, 1947), sisters Mary and Louise (Skuse, 1984), and a Japanese brother and sister (Fujinaga *et al.*, 1992). All these children, when discovered, were extremely underdeveloped physically (**deprivation dwarfism**, a lack of physical development resulting from emotional deprivation) and showed cognitive, social and emotional delays. If they were relatively young when discovered, they were able to recover reasonably well.

Conclusions

- **Age matters:** Those children who were discovered early enough appeared to have a better chance to recover. Genie may have been too old.
- **Experiences during privation:** Some of the children were able to form attachments with peers or siblings, protecting them from total privation.
- **Subsequent care:** Some children had good care after discovery which assisted their recovery. Without this they might not have recovered.

Evaluation

It is difficult to draw any real conclusions from these cases because:

- they are small samples
- the data about the children's early childhood were collected retrospectively
- any lack of development might be due to innate backwardness
- it is difficult to separate emotional from physical deprivation.

Reactive attachment disorder

This is a mental disorder with symptoms such as being unable to form relationships, showing little emotion, and engaging in very aggressive and controlling behaviour. Children with this disorder have often been adopted after the age of 6 months, subsequently experiencing multiple foster homes or institutional care. This means that they have little or no early experience of attachments.

Institutionalisation

Research by Skeels

Privation may affect cognitive development (remember that attachment is important for both emotional and cognitive development).

- Skeels and Dye (1939) observed how two apparently retarded children developed near normal IQs when transferred from their orphanage to a women's ward in an institution for the mentally retarded. The increased attention (attachments) presumably helped.
- Skodak and Skeels (1949) tested this by transferring 13 mentally retarded infants aged under 2 from their orphanage to an institution for the mentally retarded. After 19 months in the new institution the transferred infants' mean IQ had increased from 64 to 92, whereas another group who had stayed in the orphanage showed a decrease in IQ from 87 to 61 over the same period.
- Skeels (1966) assessed the children 20 years later and found that the differences between the groups remained.
- One criticism should be considered: the children may have been responding to the researcher's expectations and it was this, as much as the increased stimulation, which led to the intellectual improvements of the two.

Research by Hodges and Tizard

Classic longitudinal study is described on page 74.

Research by Rutter

Recovery from extreme privation can be achieved given adequate care. Rutter *et al.* (1998) studied 111 Romanian orphans adopted in the UK before the age of two. By the age of 4 they had recovered to normal levels of cognitive and physical development. There was a negative correlation between age at adoption and rate of recovery (the later the adoption, the slower was recovery). This suggests that the longer children experience emotional deprivation, the longer it will take for them to recover. Alternatively, the more damaged children may not be so readily adopted because they are less appealing.

Conclusions

Children who suffer early deprivation are also likely to continue to experience disruption, and later maladjustment may be due to this rather than early privation. When children have better experiences later, they may cope well. Triseliotis (1984) recorded the lives of 44 adults who had been adopted late and whose prognosis had been poor. However, these adults showed good adjustment.

Progress check

1 What is the 'maternal deprivation hypothesis'?
2 What is 'privation'?

2 The lack of any attachment figures.
1 The theory that early deprivation of attachment leads to permanent emotional damage.

OCR core study and AQA (A) Key Study: Long-term effects of privation

Hodges and Tizard (1989) Social relationships of ex-institutional adolescents

Aims To investigate the long-term effects of early institutionalisation, further exploring the maternal deprivation hypothesis. If this hypothesis is correct, children who experience early privation should experience permanent emotional damage.

Procedures This was a longitudinal study and a natural experiment, following 65 children placed in care before the age of four months. There was an institutional policy against the 'caretakers' forming attachments with the children. They were physically well cared for but, it was assumed, emotionally privated. Some of the children remained in the institution, some were adopted and some returned to their natural homes.

Findings Early follow ups at age 4 and 8 (Tizard and Rees, 1975, and Tizard and Hodges, 1978) found that the adopted children were doing best in virtually every way when compared with those who returned home ('restored' children), although they were having more social and cognitive difficulties than a control group of children who had never been in care. This shows that some recovery is possible after the age of 4 and that a child's natural home may not necessarily be best.

> Bowlby had claimed that bad homes were better than good institutions but this study suggests he was wrong.

> Five of the original children had remained in the institution but were not included in the final analysis because their behaviour could tell us little about recovery from the effects of institutionalisation.

At age 16 twenty-three adopted children and eleven 'restored' children were again assessed, and compared with a matched 'normal' control group:
- Those who were adopted formed close bonds with their adoptive parents, whereas the 'restored' group were much less likely to be closely attached.
- Both groups of children (adopted and restored) had problems with relationships in school, both with adults and peers. They were less likely to have a special friend, to be part of a crowd, or to be liked by other children.

Conclusions *At home* the adopted children maintained good relationships because their parents presumably put a lot of effort into the relationship, whereas in the 'bad' homes the children still had ongoing problems.

Outside the home, the adopted children and the restored children had the same difficulties. This may be for a number of reasons.
- The adopted children may have suffered from poor self-esteem stemming from being adopted, which affected their relationships outside the home.
- The ability to form and maintain peer relationships is especially affected by early emotional deprivation, more so than family relationships.
- It may be that all the ex-institutional children lagged behind their peers in emotional development and that is why they couldn't cope.

This suggests that recovery is possible up to a point, but it depends on having continuing supportive relationships.

Criticisms Only some of the children were included in the final sample because of 'drop out' (some participants couldn't be found or refused to take part). This results in a biased sample. Hodges and Tizard reported that those adopted children who were left in the study were the ones who, at age 4, had fewer adjustment problems. In contrast, the restored children who remained in the study had earlier shown somewhat more adjustment problems than the restored children who dropped out. This left a 'better' sample of adopted children.

As this is a natural experiment we can comment on an association between early privation and later maladjustment but cannot conclude that one causes the other because the IV was not directly manipulated, and participants were not randomly allocated to groups.

OCR Revision question
a) Hodges and Tizard's study on social relationships is an example of a natural experiment. What is a 'natural experiment'? [2]

b) What was the independent variable in this study? [2] (June 2001 Core Studies 1, question 4)

3.5 Critical issue: Day care

After studying this topic you should be able to:

- outline different forms of day care
- describe and assess research into the effects of day care on cognitive, emotional and social development
- explain individual differences in relation to the effects of day care
- recommend ways of improving day care in terms of attachment

Forms of day care

 U1

Key Term Day care refers to situations where children are regularly looked after by temporary caregivers during the day and thus separated from their main caregivers for regular periods. Children in day care do not stay overnight, as in a residential nursery or hospital care. The maternal deprivation hypothesis would predict that such separations could have permanent consequences for both cognitive and socio-emotional development.

Day nurseries

Large numbers of children are cared for in a specially designed environment. Kagan *et al.* (1980) studied 33 infants over a two-year period while they attended a day-care centre in Boston, and 67 control infants cared for by their mothers in their homes. The staff at the school each had special responsibility for a small group of children, thus ensuring close emotional contact. Kagan *et al.* found no consistently large differences between the two groups of children on social, emotional or cognitive variables.

Childminding

A person registered with the local authority cares for a small number of children in his or her own home. Mayall and Petrie (1983) observed and interviewed 66 pairs of mothers and minders in London. The children were under 2. They found that the quality of care was very variable. They concluded that the things which moderate the effects of child-care arrangements are: (1) the quality of the care, (2) the stability of the arrangement, (3) the original attachment bond.

The effects of day care

 U1

Three features of the day-care environment are especially important for development:

- stimulation – affects cognitive development
- attachment with substitute caregiver(s) – affects cognitive, emotional and social development
- interaction with peers – affects social development.

Effects of day care on cognitive development

Key Term Cognitive development describes the changes that occur as a child gets older in terms of their cognitive (mental) abilities. This includes the development of the child's intelligence and abilities at school such as in reading and maths.

Day care may harm cognitive development

Day care may affect the security of attachment between child and caregiver because of bond disruption, resulting in insecure attachment and impaired cognitive development. Bus and van Ijzendoorn (1988) found that children who were securely attached at age 2 showed more interest in written material three years later than did the insecurely attached children, regardless of their intelligence and the amount of preparatory reading instruction.

Why might nursery care be good for cognitive development whereas childminding has been associated with a 'failure to thrive'?

Tizard (1979) found that the conversations between mother and child were more complex, had more exchanges and elicited more from the children than conversations between the child and their nursery school teachers. This is in part due to a teacher's lack of time and divided attention but also because they inevitably know the children less well.

Day care may boost cognitive development

Operation Head Start was an enrichment programme begun in 1965 in the USA. The rationale was that some children begin school at a disadvantage and therefore are destined for failure. If they were given an early boost through intensive preschool care, involving both health and education, this might break the cycle of failure. When the Headstart children did start school, they showed IQ gains in comparison to those disadvantaged children who had not attended daycare programmes, but these differences soon disappeared. Follow up studies, e.g. Lazar and Darlington (1982) found that participants were less likely to, for example, need welfare assistance, and become delinquent; and/or to continue in further education.

Andersson (1992) studied Swedish children in day care and assessed their performance at age 8 and 13. School performance was rated highest in those children who entered day care before the age of one. School performance was lowest for those who did not have any day care. This suggests that day care is not harmful in terms of development and may even be beneficial. It should be remembered that day care in Sweden is high in quality.

Broberg *et al.* (1997) compared Swedish children in nursery care with those looked after by a childminder and those who remained at home. When these children were assessed at the age of 8, the children who had been in day care were consistently better than other groups on tests of verbal and mathematical ability.

Effects of day care on emotional development

Day care disrupts attachment

Belsky and Rovine (1988) found that there was an increased risk of an infant developing insecure attachments if they were in day care for at least four months and if this had begun before their first birthday.

Day care has no ill effects on attachment

All studies assess attachment using the Strange Situation. However, children who are used to separations because of day care may react differently in this controlled observation to children who spend most of their time with one caregiver.

Clarke-Stewart *et al.* (1994) compared security of attachment in 15-month-old children who spent a lot of time in day care (30 hours or more a week from age 3 months) with children who spent less time (less than 10 hours a week). There was no difference between the groups in terms of attachment security.

Effects of day care on social development

Key Term Social development describes the changes that occur as a child gets older in terms of their relationships with others ('social' refers to interactions between two or more members of the same species). This includes the number of friendships they form, their popularity with peers, their abilities to negotiate in social situations and their desire to be with others.

Day care increases sociability

Shea (1981) videotaped play times at nursery school and found that the children became more sociable from the start of the year. The children stood closer together and engaged in more rough-and-tumble play and peer interactions. They were less aggressive and had less need to cling to the teacher.

Clarke-Stewart *et al.* (1994) studied 150 children attending school for the first time and found that those who had attended day care could cope better in social situations and negotiate better with peers.

Individual differences in social development

Not all children benefit. Pennebaker *et al.* (1981) found that the nursery experience was threatening for those children who were shy and unsociable.

Individual differences in response to day care

The reason why some of the studies have contradictory findings may be because:

- some children are insecurely attached and they cope less well with day care
- some day-care provision is poor – the children lack stimulation and/or lack close emotional contact with substitute caregivers.

An NICHD (The National Institute of Child Health and Human Development) study (1997) looked at about 1,000 infants and their mothers at age 6 months and again at 15 months. In general, there were no differences between children looked after at home or in day care, but children whose mothers lacked responsiveness and who were in low-quality day care were less secure.

Egeland and Hiester (1995) studied about 70 children either at home or in day care. The children all came from poor backgrounds and were assessed at age one and again at $3\frac{1}{2}$ years, using the Strange Situation procedure. Day care appeared to have a negative effect for secure children but had a positive influence on the insecure children.

Improving day care

The evidence generally indicates that day care need not be harmful and can be positively beneficial, given the right circumstances, which are as follows.

- **Consistent care:** avoid high staff turnover, low adult : infant ratio, assign each child to one member of staff. The institutionalised children in Hodges and Tizard's study (see p.74) experienced high staff turnover and the staff were told not to form attachments with the children.
- **A stimulating environment.**
- **Increased emotional sensitivity to avoid bond disruption.** The NICHD study (1997) found that one fifth of the caregivers were 'emotionally detached' from the infants under their care.
- **Trained staff.** Howes *et al.* (1998) found that a short course aimed at improving caregiving practices of day-care providers led to increased attachment in the two-year-old children they cared for, as compared with caregivers who received no extra training.

Sample question and student answer

AQA A style question

(a) Describe the procedures of **one** study of cross-cultural variations in attachment and give **one** criticism of this study. [3 + 3]

(b) Outline **one** explanation of attachment. [6]

(c) Describe and evaluate **one or more** studies of the effects of privation. [18]

(a) One study by Ijzendoorn looked at the findings from lots of different studies around the world. The procedures used in all of the studies was called the Strange Situation where an infant, mother and stranger go through varies steps to show how the infant responds to separation, reunion and strangers. This is a controlled observation. The mother leaves the stranger with the infant, then the mother comes back and the stranger goes and then the mother goes too.

One criticism of this study is that the Strange Situation may not be relevant in different cultures.

(b) Bowlby proposed a theory of attachment which explained how attachment is an adaptive behaviour because it helps survival and also acts as a basis for emotional development. The child's first main attachment relationship provides a template for later relationships in the form of an internal working model. Bowlby also claimed that attachments have to form before the child is $2\frac{1}{2}$ years old, otherwise it will be too late and the child will be forever emotionally scarred. A further part of his theory was that attachment acts as a secure base for exploration. For this reason good attachment is important for cognitive development because otherwise the child won't be able to wander from its caregiver, and this affects cognitive development.

(c) Bowlby's study about 44 thieves was called a study of deprivation but it might also be regarded as privation as some of the children spent prolonged time away from their families and this might explain the long term effects. In this study the case histories of 44 juvenile delinquents were studied and it was found that those who had suffered early privation were more likely to later become affectionless psychopaths.

One of the problems with this study is that we don't know if the early separations were the cause of the affectionless psychopaths, we only know that there was a correlation. To support this Rutter showed in his Isle of Wight study that family discord may equally be a cause of later delinquency. Another criticism of the 44 thieves study was that the data collected about the children's early lives was retrospective and therefore we cannot rely on it being correct.

Another well known study of privation was by Hodges and Tizard who followed children who spent their early lives in an adoption home before returning to their own homes or to adopted homes. Initially it seemed that the children who were adopted had recovered well which suggests that privation is reversible but later findings showed that all of the children found it difficult to form friendships.

This study also had criticisms because of the problems of drop out. The final sample may have been biased because some of the children (possibly some of those who were most disturbed) refused to take part. Also it may well be that the adopted children were 'nicer' because families preferred to adopt the nicer children. Again this is a natural experiment

---

The reference to the study is not exact (it was a study by van Ijzendoorn and Kroonenberg) but this is enough to make it clear to the examiner the precise study being described, which is important. The study described must be identifiable to attract credit. The procedures used in the various studies summarised by this meta-analysis are accurate and detailed for 3 marks. The criticism is not explained at all; there is a mininal explanation but it is not clear *why* this would be weakness (or a strength) and why it applies to this study, thus 1 mark.

The candidate wisely chose Bowlby's theory because there is so much that can be written. The description of the theory is both accurate and well detailed, and covers various features of the theory. It clearly deserves full marks. (6 marks).

This is a detailed and thoughtful answer to the question in the time allowed. It has been clearly structured into paragraphs that are AO1 and paragraphs that are AO2. This helps when writing the answer and also helps an examiner to pick out the main points. Two appropriate studies have been described. The inclusion of Bowlby's 44 thieves study has been justified thus making it creditworthy (it did concern deprivation but might equally apply to privation). The commentary is informed and reasonably thorough. Evidence such as Rutter's study has been used effectively as commentary rather than simply being described. Thus the essay receives full marks for AO1 (6 marks) and AO2 (12 marks).

and therefore we cannot draw causal conclusions from the findings. We can only say that early privation and later maladjustment appear to be associated.

This research is very important because children do experience early privation and we need to know what to do to make this better. In fact the research tends to focus on the question of whether there are effects rather than looking at what things might reduce the effects which would be a more productive thing to research. [360 words]

TOTAL: 28 out of 30 marks

Practice examination questions

1

(a) Explain what is meant by secure and insecure attachment. [3 + 3]

(b) Outline findings from research into the effects of day care on cognitive development. [6]

(c) Describe and evaluate research (theories **and/or** studies) into cross-cultural variations in attachment. [18]

AQA A style question

2

(a) The following table describes Piaget's four developmental stages. Give the correct name for each stage of cognitive development. [4]

Name of stage	Brief description
	Recognises self as agent of action and begins to act intentionally – for example, pulls a string to set a mobile in action or shakes a rattle to make a noise.
	Learns to use language to represent objects by images and words. Thinking is still egocentric.
	Achieves conservation of number, mass and weight.
	Can think logically about abstract propositions and test hypotheses systematically.

(b) Outline **two** research methods used in the cognitive-developmental approach to psychology. [6]

(c) Evaluate **one** of the methods you have outlined in (b) above, in terms of one of its strengths and one of its weaknesses. [6]

Edexcel specimen paper

3

The study by Samuel and Bryant looks at cognitive development.

(a) Describe **one** way in which the results show cognitive development has taken place. [2]

(b) Suggest **one** problem that psychologists face when studying development. [2]

OCR Core studies 2 June 2001

4

From the study on social relationships of adolescents by Hodges and Tizard

(a) Outline **one** of their research questions. [2]

(b) Give **one** conclusion the researchers made from their data. [2]

OCR Core studies 1 Jan 2001

Chapter 4

Physiological psychology

The following topics are covered in this chapter:

- The physiological approach
- Genetic explanations of behaviour
- Bodily rhythms

- Stress: Stress as a bodily response
- Stress: Sources of stress
- Critical issue: Stress management

4.1 The physiological approach

After studying this topic you should be able to:

- outline the key assumptions of the physiological approach in psychology
- evaluate the physiological approach in terms of its strengths and weaknesses
- discuss some of the methods used by the physiological approach
- describe the usefulness of split-brain studies in understanding the human brain

LEARNING SUMMARY

Key assumptions of the physiological approach

AQA A	U2
AQA B	U1
EDEXCEL	U2
OCR	U1, U2

Biology refers to the study of living organisms, **physiology** is concerned with the functioning of body parts. Genetic explanations are biological but not physiological.

Behaviour and experience can be reduced to the functioning of physiological systems.

The nervous system

The nervous system consists of the central nervous system and the peripheral nervous **system** – which is further subdivided into the somatic nervous system and the autonomic nervous system (ANS).

Central nervous system (CNS)

This comprises the brain and spinal cord, containing about 12 billion nerve cells (neurons). The brain consists of the following parts:

- The **forebrain**: the **cerebral cortex**, the outer, much-folded grey matter responsible for higher cognitive functions. It is divided into two halves (hemispheres) joined by fibres, including the corpus callosum. Each half has 4 lobes: **frontal** (fine motor movement, thinking), **parietal** (bodily senses, e.g. pain), **occipital** (vision), **temporal** (hearing, memory, emotion, language) lobes. The forebrain also contains various subcortical structures such as the **hypothalamus** (which integrates the ANS, and is important in stress and emotion).
- The **midbrain** contains, e.g., the reticular activating system (**RAS**) (which deals with sleep, arousal, consciousness and attention).
- The **hindbrain** contains, e.g., the **cerebellum** (controlling voluntary movement) and the **medulla** (controlling heart beat, respiration).

Somatic nervous system

(soma = body) Messages are sent out to control voluntary movement and sent back regarding sensations.

The autonomic nervous system

Controls involuntary muscles, such as the stomach and the heart, and the endocrine system which produces and distributes hormones. The ANS is largely self-regulating (automatic or autonomous). There are two branches of the ANS that work in a correlated but antagonistic fashion to maintain internal equilibrium (homeostasis):

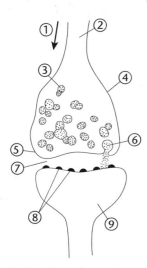

1 Direction of neural impulse
2 Axon
3 Vesicles containing neurotransmitter
4 Synaptic knob
5 Axon terminal
6 Neurotransmitter
7 Synaptic gap
8 Receptors
9 Receiving neuron

A synapse

- the **sympathetic branch**, which activates internal organs for vigorous activities and emergencies, 'fight or flight'
- the **parasympathetic branch**, which conserves and stores resources, monitors the relaxed state, promotes digestion and metabolism.

See p.93–95 for more details of the ANS.

Communication in the nervous system

Neurons

A nerve is a bundle of neurons.

- **Electrical transmission** occurs along the **axon** due to changes in potassium and sodium ions.
- **Chemical transmission** occurs at the **synapses** (see diagram opposite). Each neuron ends in numerous **dendrites** where it is connected to many other neurons across the synapse. The electrical signal stimulates **presynaptic vesicles** which release chemical messengers (**neurotransmitters**) – these may be excitory or inhibitory. Some common neurotransmitters are: dopamine, serotonin (sleep and arousal), adrenalin, GABA (decreases anxiety), endorphins (pain blockers).

Hormones

These are chemical substances produced by the **endocrine system** – a group of ductless glands controlled by the ANS. Hormones are secreted directly into the bloodstream and have a profound effect on behaviour and development. They are present in very small doses and the individual molecules have a very short life, so their effects quickly disappear if they are not secreted continuously.

The main endocrine glands and their functions are as follows:

- The **pituitary gland** in the forebrain controls much of the endocrine system by producing hormones, such as: growth hormone, prolactin (responsible for milk production), anti-diuretic hormone (ADH regulates the amount of water secreted by the kidneys), vasopressin (which acts on the kidneys and controls blood pressure) and adrenocorticotrophic hormones (ACTH).
- The **pineal gland** in the forebrain secretes melatonin, which regulates sleep and other bodily rhythms.
- The **adrenal gland** produces many hormones, especially adrenalin and noradrenalin (see p.93).
- Other glands include the thyroid (metabolism and growth), pancreas (insulin), gonads (sex hormones promote and maintain secondary sexual characteristics).

Progress check

1 What is the difference between the CNS and ANS?
2 What is a synapse?

2 The junction between neurons.

1 The CNS is the brain and spinal cord, the ANS controls involuntary muscles and the endocrine system.

Localisation of cortical function

Localisation refers to the fact that particular areas of the cerebral cortex are associated with specific physical or behavioural functions. Localisation of function allows more specialised development – for example, if an area of the brain is pre-set to interpret visual information, it reduces the amount of learning which is necessary.

- **Language** is directed by areas of the frontal and temporal cortex on the left side of the brain, as illustrated in Sperry's OCR core study on p.83. **Broca's**

area is in the anterior frontal lobe and is involved with language production. **Wernicke's area** is in the posterior temporal lobe and is mainly concerned with language comprehension. In some people the language centres are on the right or present in both hemispheres (which may lead to stuttering).

- **Vision** is controlled bilaterally by the visual cortex in the occipital lobe.

Evaluation of the physiological approach

Weaknesses of this approach

- Physiological explanations offer an **objective**, **reductionist** and **mechanistic** (machine-like) explanation of behaviour, which is oversimplified. There are, however, positive aspects of this oversimplification (see below).

> The term 'reductionist' means that one is reducing something to its most basic components.

- It overlooks the **experiential aspect** of behaviour.
- Physiological explanations are more appropriate for some kinds of behaviour (such as vision) than other kinds where higher order thinking is more involved (e.g. emotion) – although all human behaviour, even vision, involves some higher order mental activity. Therefore physiological explanations on their own are **usually inadequate**.
- Physiological explanations are also very **deterministic**, suggesting that all behaviour is entirely predictable. We may not yet be able to explain everything in physiological terms, but this approach suggests that such explanations are theoretically possible and then *everything* can be described in terms of biology.

Strengths of this approach

- The objective, reductionist nature of physiological explanations **facilitates** experimental research.
- Physiological explanations can be used to **treat behavioural problems**, as in drug therapies (see p.101).

Methods used in the physiological approach

Brain-scanning

X-ray tomography (CAT and PET scans). Brain tissue is dyed using radioactive substances which are injected into the bloodstream. Active areas of the brain take up more of these substances. One can determine what part of the brain is working and relate this to concurrent behaviour, such as learning activity. MRI and NMR (which are types of brain scanner) use magnetic fields and radio waves to construct a picture of the brain.

> Non-human animals are often used in physiological research because of the ethical problems involved with human participants. The methods listed here are the 'more' ethical approaches.

Evaluation

These methods cause no permanent damage, and allow one to observe the brain in action.

EEG (electro-encephalogram)

Micro-electrodes are attached to the patient's scalp to detect electrical activity in specific parts of the brain.

Evaluation

This is useful in understanding states of awareness but cannot tell us much about precise regions of the brain.

Lesioning

Cutting connections in the brain and therefore 'functionally' destroying a section of the brain. Temporary lesions can be created using sodium amytal, an anaesthetic, to deactivate a hemisphere for short periods in a fully conscious patient (the Wada test). For example, Jones (1966) used sodium amytal to establish where patients' speech centres were located so that he could operate on tumours (if they could still talk when the left side was paralysed, the centre must be on the right). He found that all patients with mixed dominance stuttered but after the left hemisphere centres were removed (with the tumour) their stuttering stopped.

Evaluation

You cannot be certain that a primary cause has been located. For example, if you sever a person's vocal chords they cannot speak but that doesn't mean the chords are central to speech.

Neurosurgery

Split brain operations (see Sperry's OCR core study below) have been used to demonstrate the functional asymmetry of the brain. Individuals may require surgery for removal of tumours which results in damage to specific areas, and indicates the function of that area. For example, HM (see p.29).

Evaluation

Patients may have suffered brain damage as a result of their condition and therefore their brains are atypical.

OCR core study: Split brains

Sperry (1968) Hemispheric deconnection and unity in consciousness

Aims What happens when the two hemispheres of the brain are disconnected, and there are therefore two minds in one body?

Procedures This was a natural experiment and controlled observation. The participants were a group of individuals who suffered from severe epileptic seizures, which were alleviated by a commisurotomy – an operation where all the connecting fibres between the two hemispheres are cut. This reduces the electrical storm which is the basis of an epileptic seizure.

Pictures were presented to the participants' left or right visual field. The participant covered one eye and looked at a fixed point in the centre of a projection screen. Slides were projected onto either the right or left of the screen at a very high speed. Below the screen there was a gap so that the participant could reach but not see objects.

Why do you think that Sperry had to project the slides at such a fast rate?

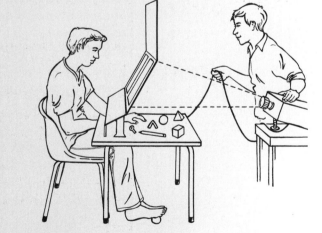

Split brain patient shown pictures to right and left visual fields and asked to identify objects manually, out of sight

Findings The participant did not recognise a picture shown to the right visual field that had previously been shown to the left visual field.

OCR core study *(continued)*

Material in the right visual field could be described in speech and writing.

Visual material in the left visual field could be identified by the right but not left hand.

If visual material was presented to the left visual field the patient consistently *reported* seeing nothing or just a flash of light to their left. However, the participant could point to a matching picture or object with their *right* hand.

Conclusions These findings show that:

- The right visual field of both eyes feeds information to the right hemisphere.
- The left hand is connected to the right hemisphere and vice versa.
- The right hemisphere cannot speak or write.
- However, the right hemisphere can *comprehend* language, i.e. read and understand words.
- The left hemisphere is the 'major' hemisphere (because of its role in language functions) but the right or 'minor' hemisphere is not simply an automaton because it has a capacity for logical thought as well as language comprehension.

Other variations Sperry flashed $ to the left and ? to the right. Participants would draw a dollar sign with their left hand. Participants would *say* that they saw the question mark. If the patient was asked what he had just drawn he would say the question mark (which was the wrong answer).

Composite words were flashed on the screen so that, for example, 'key' was in the left visual field and 'case' in the right. The left hand would identify a key from a collection of objects and the right hand would spell out the word case.

If asked what their left hand was holding they would say something like 'This hand is numb', strategies for explaining their strange behaviour.

If two objects were placed one in each hand and then the participant was given a pile of objects containing the original object to search through, each hand would locate its own object.

The right hemisphere is not totally word blind. Some split-brain patients, when shown words to their left visual field, could identify the item with their left hand (right hemisphere). However, they were still not able to say what it was.

The right hemisphere demonstrates more appropriate emotional responses. If a nude figure was shown in amongst a series of geometric shapes, the participant typically denied seeing anything (left hemisphere is talking) but at the same time the participant might blush or display a cheeky grin (controlled by right hemisphere).

Criticisms The participants were not normal: they may have suffered brain damage from the severe epileptic seizures, or the seizures were the result of brain damage. However, the findings of Sperry's study have been confirmed in studies using the Wada test.

OCR Revision question In the study by Sperry (split brain) patients had problems with material presented to their left visual field.

a) Give **one** example of these problems. [2]

b) Suggest **one** way in which patients could overcome these problems in everyday life. [2] (January 2002, Core Studies 2, question 3)

4.2 Genetic explanations of behaviour

After studying this topic you should be able to:

- *outline the key assumptions underlying genetic explanations of behaviour*
- *evaluate genetic explanations in terms of their advantages and limitations*
- *discuss some of the methods used in the genetic approach*
- *critically consider research into the inheritance of intelligence (the nature–nurture debate)*

Key assumptions underlying genetic explanations of behaviour

AQA A	U2
AQA B	U1
EDEXCEL	U2
OCR	U1, U2

This is an example of a contemporary debate on a biological topic.

The question is to what extent is intelligence due to genetic factors (nature) and to what extent environmental factors (nurture)?

- All behaviour can be explained in terms of genetic determination. **Genes** are the units of inheritance.
- Genetically determined traits evolve through **natural selection**. A behaviour that promotes survival and reproduction will be 'selected' and the genes for that trait survive. As the environment changes (or an individual moves to a new environment) new traits are needed to ensure survival. New genetic combinations produce **adaptation** and the individual who best 'fits' the environmental niche will survive (**survival of the fittest**).

The inheritance of intelligence

Genetic factors

Twin studies

Monozygotic (MZ) twins have more similar IQs than dizygotic (DZ) twins, which indicates a genetic component. Through an appeal on the BBC, Shields (1962) gained access to a sample of 44 sets of twins, some of whom were reared apart and some together. The concordance for MZ twins reared apart was 0.77, and for those reared together was 0.76. This suggests little environmental influence. Bouchard *et al.* (1990) used data from over 100 twins in the Minnesota Study of Twins Reared Apart. They found that about 70% of the variation in IQ scores is due to genetic factors.

Evaluation

Kamin (1974) criticised Shield's study and twin studies generally on the grounds that:

- the samples were relatively **small**
- in reality the twins had often spent a substantial amount of **time together**. In Shields' study 14 sets of MZ twins were only separated after the age of one year and many were raised by relatives, often visiting each other
- those twins who were genuinely adopted might still have had **similar environments** because adoption agencies try to match backgrounds
- if intelligence was entirely inherited, the MZ correlations **should be +1.00** – the fact that scores are lower shows a significant environmental component
- a correlation is not evidence that one factor **caused** another. A third (or more) factor may have been involved.

Family studies

Bouchard and McGue (1981) surveyed over 100 studies looking at familial correlations of IQ, and found that the closer the genetic link, the higher the correlation between IQ. For example, siblings reared together had a correlation of 0.45 and adopted siblings had a correlation of 0.31.

Evaluation

- This would seem to support the genetic position, but it could be taken equally as evidence for environment, as genetically related people usually also live in the same environment.
- Comparisons from one study to another involve grouping together many different tests.

Adoption studies

To compare a child and its natural parents, Skodak and Skeels (1949) followed 100 adopted children and their natural mothers. At the age of 4 the IQ correlation was 0.28 and at 13 it was 0.44. It appears that the effects of environment become less with age, and that the decline of environmental influence may be due to early enrichment and extra attention levelling out, and genetic factors showing through. Horn (1983) reported on the Texas Adoption Study which looked at about 300 families with adopted children. The biological mothers had all given the children up within one week of birth. The children at age 8 had a correlation of 0.25 with their biological mother (genetic link) and 0.15 with their adopted mother (environmental link). Plomin (1988) reported on the same children at age 10. They had a correlation of 0.02 with their adoptive siblings.

Evaluation

- There is usually a higher correlation between children and their biological rather than adoptive parents.
- Adoptions are often made to similar environments. Any differences tend to be in a positive direction.

Environmental factors

Adoption studies

The concept of a 'reaction range' proposes that genetically there are certain upper and lower limits for your development. You are born with certain genetic predispositions (genotype), such as your potential height. You might have the potential to grow six feet but even with the best diet in the world you would never have become taller. This is the upper end of your reaction range for height.

Schiff *et al.* (1978) found that children born to low socio-economic status (SES) parents who were subsequently adopted by high SES families, showed significant IQ gains when compared with siblings who had remained at home. Scarr and Weinberg (1977) found that, on average, adopted children have IQs that are 10 to 20 points higher than those of their natural parents.

Evaluation

- Adoptive families are generally smaller, wealthier and better-educated than natural families. This means that adopted children develop the higher end of their reaction range and become more similar to better-educated adopted parents. This would cause environmental factors to appear stronger.
- Early adopted children do better, favouring the idea that environment is important under suitable circumstances.

Social class

Bernstein (1961) introduced the notion of restricted language (code) as opposed to elaborated code. He argued that children from low SES groups learn a limited form of language which lacks, for example, abstract concepts. This affects their cognitive development and verbal intelligence. Labov (1970) rejected this idea and claimed that Bernstein was confusing social and linguistic deprivation, and had failed to recognise the subtleties of non-standard English. Sameroff *et al.* (1987, 1993) conducted the Rochester Longitudinal study, which has followed over 200 children from a range of socio-economic backgrounds since birth, keeping a record of IQ and life events. They found a clear negative (about 0.60) association between number of risk factors and IQ; (risk factors include: parental mental health, education, occupation, family support, stressful life events, and family size).

Evaluation

- It is factors associated with low social class that cause low IQ, not social class *per se.*

- It is possible that low socio-economic parents are biologically less intelligent: those with more intelligence become better educated and are able to have higher living standards.

Family influences

- **Stimulation:** Yarrow (1963) found a correlation of 0.65 between IQ at six months and the amount of time the mother spent in social interaction with her child.
- **Birth order:** Zajonc and Markus (1975) examined the IQ data of 40,000 Dutch males born in 1944 and found that IQ declines with family size and birth order. In larger families each child has a smaller share of parental attention, less money and more physical deprivation.
- **Diet:** Harrell *et al.* (1955) gave low income, expectant mothers supplementary diets. When their children were tested at three years they had higher IQs than those whose mothers had been given placebos. Benton and Cook (1991) demonstrated that IQ scores increased by 7.6 points when children were given vitamin supplements rather than a placebo.

Evaluation of the genetic approach

The genetic approach is deterministic and assumes a 1:1 correspondence between genes and behaviour. In reality, there is a difference between genotype and phenotype.

- **Genotype:** an individual's genetic constitution, as determined by the particular set of genes it possesses.
- **Phenotype:** the observable characteristics of an individual, which results from interaction between the genes he or she possesses (i.e. the individual's genotype) and the environment.

An example of this would be hair colour. Your genes determine the colour of your hair, but the fact that you live in a sunny country may mean that your hair is bleached in the sun and this produces your phenotype: your observable hair colour which results from your genetic make-up and an environmental influence.

> You can think of your height in terms of genotype and phenotype. What environmental factors influence your height?

Progress check

1 What is a 'gene'?
2 Name three kinds of study used to demonstrate the genetic inheritance of intelligence.

2 Twin, familial, adoption.
1 The units of inheritance.

Methods used in the genetic approach

Twin and family studies

(See p.85).

Adoption studies

As described on p.86, these enable comparisons between nature and nurture.

Selective breeding

Animals are identified for certain characteristics, such as a dog who is good at hunting. These individuals are bred together to produce offspring with the same behavioural traits, which is evidence of the inheritance of behavioural characteristics.

OCR core study: IQ testing

Gould (1982) A nation of morons

The text provided here summarizes a review by Gould which considers the history of intelligence testing, aiming to indicate the flaws in IQ tests.

A new age for Psychology

Mental testing offered a way to help psychology appear more scientific. Yerkes saw the potential usefulness of such tests and the advent of World War I gave him an ideal opportunity to develop them. Army recruits could be tested so that the most able could be given jobs with greater responsibility. Yerkes and other psychologists wrote a set of mental tests which aimed to test innate abilities. The kind of questions they used were:

- *Analogies*, such as 'Washington is to Adams as first is to ...' [second, because Washington was the first US president and Adams was the second]
- *Number sequences*, such as 'What number comes next: 1, 3, 6, 10, ...'
- *Multiple choice*: 'Crisco is a: patent medicine, disinfectant, toothpaste, food product?' [It is a food product]

> What would you say is wrong with these questions? What skills are being tested?

The alpha and beta tests

Yerkes and his team tested 1.75 million recruits using two forms of the test.
- The *Army alpha* test was a written exam.
- The *Army beta test* was a set of pictures. This was given to any recruit who failed the Alpha test or who could not read – though even this test involved *writing* the answers.

Problems
- The standards varied from camp to camp.
- The large numbers of illiterate recruits meant there were huge queues for the Beta test and therefore some of these men had to do the alpha tests!
- The pressure for results meant that the re-testing of men who failed the beta test was not possible. This was especially true for the Black 'failures' who were treated with less concern. When such individuals *were* recalled their scores improved dramatically.
- Exam anxiety was also a problem. It is very likely that a foreign or an illiterate Black recruit would feel especially anxious at the strange experience of taking an exam, especially if they didn't understand English very well.

After the war

Once the war was over and Yerkes' tests became widely known, inquiries flooded in from schools and businesses to use the tests to select students and employees. The army data was also used politically. Another psychologist (Boring) analysed the test results from 160,000 men and concluded that:

- *White Americans* had an average mental age of 13, just above being a 'moron'
- *European immigrants* were all 'morons' but those from northern Europe (fair-skinned) were better than were those from the south ('darker' people).
- *Negroes* were at the bottom of the scale, scoring an average of 10.41.

It was concluded that cultural/racial differences in IQ were due to innate differences. Politicians argued that immigration laws should be passed to limit people coming from abroad because they were intellectually inferior.

Criticisms

Yerkes admitted that those who could not speak English inevitably were penalised. He also noted that test scores rose in relation to the number of years an immigrant had lived in the US. This strongly suggested that learning, not innate intelligence, was involved – familiarity with American ways (learning) was related to higher IQ.

OCR Revision question

In the paper on IQ testing, Gould identified three 'facts' that were created from the data collected by Yerkes.

a) Identify **one** of these 'facts'. [2]

b) Outline a difficulty with accepting this 'fact'. [2] (1998 Paper 1, question 18)

4.3 Bodily rhythms

After studying this topic you should be able to:

- *describe and evaluate research into the sleep/wake cycle, and outline sleep stages*
- *describe and evaluate theories of sleep*
- *critically consider theories of dreaming*

The sleep/wake cycle

| Edexcel | U2 |
| OCR | U1, U2 |

Biological rhythms are periodically repeated behaviours. The sleep/wake cycle is an example of a **circadian rhythm**. A circadian rhythm repeats itself once a day.

Causes of the sleep/wake cycle

External stimuli: zeitgebers

This is a German word meaning 'time-giver'. Light is the dominant zeitgeber, but meal times can also affect sleepiness, as can learned factors such as bedtimes.

Internal (endogenous) stimuli: the body clock

> This shows an interaction between the internal mechanism or 'clock' and external stimuli such as light.

The suprachiasmatic nucleus (SCN) generates circadian rhythms from protein synthesis and is 'fine tuned' by light and other stimuli, receiving information about light directly from the retina. The SCN regulates production of melatonin in the pineal gland – increases in melatonin are associated with decreases in arousal.

Research into the sleep/wake cycle

Demonstrating an endogenous (internal) pacemaker

- **Cave experiments:** Siffre (1972) spent 6 months in an underground cave finding that his sleep/waking cycle settled down to a naturally (endogenously controlled) cycle of 25–30 hours.
- **Transplanting the SCN:** Morgan (1995) transplanted SCNs from mutant hamsters who had a different circadian rhythm into non-mutant animals. The recipients quickly changed their rhythm to that of the donor, mutant hamster.
- **Different light conditions:** Luce and Segal (1966) recorded that people living near the Arctic circle still sleep the normal 7 hours a day despite the fact that in winter the sun doesn't rise.

Demonstrating the effects of external cues

- **Cave experiments:** Folkard *et al.* (1985) used artificial light to reduce the clock cycle – participants coped at a 23-hour cycle, but when it was reduced to 22 hours their bodies reverted to an endogenously controlled natural cycle. It appears that light can have a profound influence.

Stages of sleep

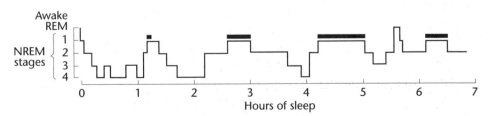

Sleep stages alternate through the night, starting with a rapid descent into deep sleep, followed by progressively increased episodes of lighter sleep and REM sleep (coloured area)

Theories of sleep

Edexcel U2

Restoration theory

Sleep allows various physiological and psychological states to be recovered. During slow-wave sleep the body makes repairs – for example, removing waste products. Certain metabolic processes also increase at night – for example, there is increased protein synthesis, particularly in REM sleep.

Evaluation

If restoration was the only function of sleep we would expect to observe deprivation effects, and increased sleep in relation to increased activity.

- **Case studies of sleep deprivation:** Dement (1972) reported the cases of a disc jockey, Peter Tripp, and a student, Randy Gardner, both of whom went for days without sleep. Towards the end, Tripp experienced hallucinations and profound delusions but Gardner wasn't affected except finding it difficult to perform some tasks. At the end Gardner only slept for 15 hours but this sleep consisted of mainly **core sleep** (stage 4 and REM). It's possible that Gardner benefited from episodes of **micro-sleep** (staring into space for a moment).
- **Controlled studies:** Webb (1985) found that sleep loss over 48 hours had little effect on precision and cognitive-processing tasks, whereas subjective and attention measures suffered. Depressed performance may be more due to motivational factors than cognitive components. Hüber-Weidman (1976) found that after 1 night there was an increased urge to sleep, after 4 nights increased episodes of micro-sleep, and after 6 nights a loss of identity and sense of reality (sleep-deprivation psychosis).
- **Increased activity:** Shapiro *et al.* (1981) found that marathon runners did require extra sleep, whereas Horne and Minard (1985) tried to exhaust their participants with numerous activities and found that they went to sleep faster but not for longer.

Conclusion

Empson (1989) reports that it is impossible to go without sleep and remain okay and Horne (1988) points out that sleep-deprived participants do show a rebound effect. It may be that only core sleep is essential and that some recovery can take place during relaxed wakefulness and micro-sleep.

Evolutionary theory

Sleep is an adaptive response to environmental and internal demands, akin to hibernation. There are two evolutionary theories:

- **Protection from predation** (Meddis, 1975). Animals have evolved an innate programme to protect them when they can't be gathering food and at times of danger (such as darkness). The more dangerous your world, the less time you should spend sleeping.
- **Hibernation theory** (Webb, 1982). Sleep is adaptive because it is a means of conserving energy in the same way that hibernation enhances survival by reducing physiological demands. An animal who is constantly active requires more food, and this is likely to decrease survival.

Evaluation

- If protection was the only function of sleep we would expect an inverse relationship between the time needed to search for food and the time needed for sleep. This is true for cows which graze all the time and sleep little, and cats who eat rapidly and sleep a lot.
- We would also expect that animals likely to be attacked will sleep little and

Infant sleep could be explained as an adaptive behaviour to help exhausted parents cope with finding food and other things.

lightly. Predators do sleep more than animals who are preyed upon, and animals who are preyed upon often sleep in burrows and feed at night, such as rabbits. But, taken to its logical conclusion, this would mean some animals shouldn't sleep at all in order to ensure their safety.

- Support for the evolutionary theory comes from looking at how species adapt their mode of sleep to suit their lifestyle. For example, dolphins sleep one hemisphere at a time which probably is related to the fact that they need to remain partly conscious to breathe.

> Beware of evolutionary arguments which sound as if the animal has made some deliberate choice about behaviour, the 'choice' is made through natural selection.

A combined approach

Neither theory accounts for why animals lose consciousness when sleeping. It is not necessary for restoration, and from a safety (adaptive) point of view it makes little sense. The fact that all animals sleep means that it must perform some restorative function. The fact that each species evolves a particular style suggests an adaptation.

Progress check

1 What is a circadian rhythm?
2 What is restored during slow-wave sleep?

2 E.g. neurotransmitters, bodily repairs.
1 A biological rhythm that is repeated once a day.

Theories of dreaming

Edexcel U2
OCR U1, U2

The classic study by Dement and Kleitman (see OCR core study on p.92) demonstrated the link between dreaming and REM sleep.

Reverse learning

> Many theories make the assumption that REM sleep = dreaming. This assumption in part comes from the study by Dement and Kleitman, reported on p.92. But the two are not necessarily equivalent.

Crick and Mitchison (1983) used a computer analogy to liken dreams to updating memory files and discarding redundant data, processes which are necessary to avoid wasted space. We dream to forget. The actual content of dreams is an accidental by-product and has no meaning.

Evaluation

- Animals that have a large cortex, such as a dolphin, don't appear to have REM sleep. This could be because they don't need to discard vast quantities of redundant data because they have plenty of room. However, the lack of folding of their cortical surface means there may not actually be as much storage space as is apparent.
- This theory doesn't explain dreams such as the common dream of falling, and why we have bizarre dreams that contain 'novel' experiences.
- The idea of wasted space doesn't fit with modern connectionist ideas. There are plenty of potential connectionist pathways in the brain.

Emotional catharsis

Freud (1900) suggested that dreams are 'the royal road' to the unconscious and enable repressed desires or memories to become known. Dreams are not accidental by-products but important ways of coping with anxieties. Dreams have manifest content (i.e. how one would describe the dream) which is arbitrary and meaningless but also have latent content (i.e. features of the dream symbolise deeper meanings such as a cave representing female sexual anatomy).

Evaluation

- This approach cannot explain why animals dream, if they do.
- The interpretation of a dream is entirely subjective.

> One of the main issues is the extent to which dreams have real meaning.

Activation-synthesis

Hobson and McCarley (1977) suggested that the brain is activated during REM sleep and this random activation is interpreted in a meaningful way.

Evaluation

- This account can explain common experiences like feeling one is falling, and explains both why we dream and why the dream contains a particular content.

Progress check

1 What theory of dreaming suggests we need to save wasted space?
2 What is the latent content of a dream?

2 The underlying meaning.
1 Reverse learning theory.

OCR core study: Dreaming

Dement and Kleitman (1957) The relation of eye movements during sleep to dream activity

Aims To what extent are dreams related to REM activity? Does the length of the dream and movements of the eye relate to the content of the dream?

Procedures This study involved a controlled observation. Each participant reported to the sleep laboratory on a number of occasions just before their usual bedtime. Electrodes were attached around the participant's eyes to measure eye movement, and to their scalp to record brain activity as a measure of depth of sleep.

Findings REM activity was accompanied by a relatively fast EEG pattern, compared with the slower activity during deeper sleep.

REM periods lasted between 3 and 50 minutes. During that time the eyes were not constantly in motion but there were bursts of activity.

REM activity occurred at regular intervals for each individual. For one participant they were every 70 minutes, for another every 104 minutes.

Most (but not all) dreaming occurred during REM sleep.

It proved difficult for participants to estimate the length of their dream. Therefore participants were woken after 5 or 15 minutes of REM and asked to state how long it felt like. All but one participant gave very accurate responses.

> Dreams are subjective experiences and it is difficult to study such things empirically.

Relationship of type of eye movement to imagery of dream. There did appear to be some support for a relationship – for example, when one participant displayed horizontal eye movements (which were quite rare) they dreamt they were watching two people throwing tomatoes at each other!

Conclusions It appears that REM activity is roughly equivalent to the experience of dreaming. Without this objective measure the study of dreaming would be difficult.

Criticisms It may be that people do dream in NREM sleep but it is deeper sleep and therefore the dreams are forgotten when a person is woken, or wakes up.

OCR Revision The study by Dement and Kleitman (sleep and dreaming) involved participants' self reports of dreams and the use of equipment to measure REM and NREM.

a) Outline **one** finding of the relationship between sleep and dreaming. [2]

b) Give **one** reason why the conclusions of the study might not be valid. [2]

(January 2002, Core Studies 2, question 5)

The effects of stress on cardiovascular disorders

Key Term **Cardiovascular disorders** are any disorder of the heart (e.g. coronary heart disease) and circulatory system (e.g. hypertension – high blood pressure).

- **Coronary heart disease (CHD):** The link with stress was demonstrated in a study by Friedman and Rosenman (1959, see Key Study below).
- **Hypertension:** This is diagnosed when a person has experienced raised blood pressure for at least several weeks. It is a major risk factor for coronary heart disease. Cobb and Rose (1973) found that hypertension rates were several times higher in air-traffic controllers, and especially in those controllers working in busy airports, than other people working at the airport.

AQA (A) Key study: Stress and cardiovascular disorders

Friedman and Rosenman (1959, 1974, 1996) Type A and heart disease

Aims Friedman and Rosenman proposed that some individuals (Type A) are typically impatient, competitive, time pressured, and hostile. Type B individuals lack these characteristics and are generally more relaxed. Type Bs are nice, industrious, conventional, sociable but tend to be repressed and react to stress or threat with a sense of helplessness. Friedman and Rosenman predicted that Type As would be less able to cope with stress and therefore more likely to experience coronary heart disease (CHD). They set up the Western Collaborative Group Study to test the long-term effects of stress on certain types of people.

Procedures This was a longitudinal study. Participants (3,154 healthy men aged between 39 and 59, living around San Francisco) were assessed using a set of 25 questions that looked at how a person typically responds to everyday pressures that would create feelings of impatience, competitiveness or hostility. For example, they were asked how they would cope with having to wait in a long queue or working with a slow partner. The interview was conducted in a provocative manner to try to elicit Type A behaviour. For example, the interviewer might speak slowly and hesitantly, so that a Type A person would want to interrupt.

Both the participants' answers and the way they answered were recorded. Participants were then classed as A1 (Type A), A2 (not fully Type A), X (equal amounts of Type A and B), and B.

Findings Eight and a half years later (Friedman and Rosenman, 1974) 257 of the total sample had developed CHD, 178 of these had been assessed as Type A (69%), whereas half as many were Type B.

Twenty-two years later (Friedman, 1996) 214 men had died from CHD, 119 were Type A and 95 Type B – a rather less impressive difference.

Conclusions This offers strong support for the idea that aspects of a person's temperament are associated with CHD, in particular a link between Type A personality and CHD.

The fact that the death rate was lower in the second study may be because some people take preventive measures once they know they are ill.

Criticisms Hostility rather than stress may explain the findings. Matthews *et al.* (1977) suggested that high levels of hostility produce increased activity within the sympathetic nervous system.

The findings have been applied to improving health. Friedman *et al.* (1986, the Recurrent Coronary Prevention Project) found that, after 5 years, those CHD patients taught how to modify their behaviour had fewer second heart attacks than those who received just counselling or no treatment.

Someone with AIDS is suffering from an immunosuppressive effect because the HIV virus attacks T-helper cells. AIDS doesn't kill in itself but it prevents the body from protecting itself against other viruses and tumours.

The effects of stress on the immune system

Key Term The **immune system** protects us from disease. The main components are antibodies, and white blood cells (leucocytes and lymphocytes), which include T-cells. The presence of cortisol and adrenaline seem to inhibit the production of these components.

- **The common cold:** Cohen *et al.* (1991) exposed participants to the cold virus. Those who had highest stress levels (as measured in life change units, see p. 97) were twice as likely to become ill as those with lower levels of stress.
- **Tumours:** Riley (1981) created stress in mice by placing them on a turntable rotating at 45 rpm. After 5 hours of continual rotation their lymphocyte count was reduced. In another study cancer cells were implanted in mice. Those mice who were given 10 minutes of rotation per hour for 3 days (high stress) developed large tumours whereas mice exposed to no stress had no tumours.
- T-cell activity. See Kiecolt-Glaser *et al.* (1984, key study below).

Evaluation of link between stress and illness

- The functioning of the immune system in people who say they are very stressed is actually within the **normal range**.
- The link between illness and stress **oversimplifies** a complex system.
- The correlation between stress and illness doesn't mean one causes the other. There may be other indirect factors, such as **lifestyle**. Cohen and Williamson (1991) found that people who are stressed tended to smoke more, to drink more alcohol and take less exercise, than people who are not stressed.

AQA (A) Key study: Stress and the immune system

Kiecolt-Glaser *et al.* (1984) Immunocompetence in medical students

Aims One reason why stress may be associated with illness is because the immune system in a stressed individual is not functioning as normal. This study set out to test this hypothesis and also aimed to see if other factors such as loneliness were associated with lowered immune function.

Procedures This was a natural experiment, using a questionnaire. The participants were 75 first-year medical students who volunteered to take part. The researchers took a blood sample one month before the students' final examinations, and again during their exams. The samples were tested for T-cell activity. On both occasions the students were also given questionnaires on psychiatric symptoms, loneliness and life events.

Findings T-cell activity was significantly lower on the second occasion, when the students were presumably most stressed. It was particularly low for students who reported feeling most lonely, and those experiencing other stressful life events and psychiatric symptoms such as depression or anxiety.

Conclusions The findings suggest that stress arising from exams is associated with a lowered immune response. This effect is stronger where social support is lacking. This suggests that social support reduces the effects of stress.

Criticisms The study lacked population validity as only students were tested and, in addition, it lacked ecological validity as stress was tested in one setting (exams) and the findings may not generalise to other settings.

The findings are supported by many other studies. For example, Kiecolt-Glaser *et al.* (1987) analysed blood samples from married, separated and divorced women. Happily married women had better immune functioning than those who were dissatisfied. Separated and divorced women who found their separation hard to bear also had weaker immune functions.

4.5 Stress: Sources of stress

After studying this topic you should be able to:

- *outline research into the sources of stress*
- *discuss the effects of life changes and workplace stresses*
- *discuss the role of individual differences in modifying the effects of stressors*

LEARNING SUMMARY

Research into sources of stress

AQA A U2

To use the SRRS, you should circle events which have happened to you in the last 12 months. Each event is awarded a value measured in 'life change units' (LCUs). Your LCU total is an estimate of the amount of life stress you have experienced.

Life changes

Key Term **Life changes** are events in a person's life that cause stress because they require the person to make adjustments. It is said that they use 'psychic energy'. Such events may be positive (such as marriage) or negative (such as divorce).

Two doctors, Holmes and Rahe (1967), observed in their patients that poor health was associated with life events which involved change from of a steady state, even when the change was for the better. They developed the Social Readjustment Rating Scale (SRRS) as a means of measuring life change units (LCUs). They did this by analysing 5,000 patient records and identifying 43 life events which seem to precede illness. Then they asked people to rate the events using marriage as a reference point. Some examples are shown below.

Rank	Life event	Mean value
1	Death of spouse	100
2	Divorce	73
3	Marital separation	65
4	Jail term	63
5	Death of close family member	63
6	Personal injury or illness	53
7	Marriage	50

Evaluation

- The scale muddles different kinds of life events. Those over which you have least control may be most stressful (see 'lack of control' on p.99 and p.103).
- The scale does not allow for the fact that different people interpret the same event differently, and therefore a single value cannot be assigned for stress.
- Studies using the scale have found only a small correlation between life events and illness (see key study by Rahe *et al.* 1970 below).
- The importance of this scale is not in its usefulness but in its status as a breakthrough. It triggered off a wealth of research.
- **Daily events.** DeLongis *et al.* (1982) noted that most people do not often experience major life events, therefore the strains of everyday life might be a better measure of stress and a better predictor of physical illness.

Key study: Life changes

Rahe *et al.* (1970) Illness in navel personnel

Aims Are life events associated with physical illness? Rahe *et al.* set out to test the hypothesis that life events may lead to stress and illness, using the SRRS that had been designed to measure life events.

Procedures This was a correlational study using the SRRS to assess life events. The participants were 2,500 naval personnel.

Just before a tour of duty, participants were asked to fill in a questionnaire relating to significant changes in their life over the past six months. This meant that a LCU (life change unit) value could be calculated for each participant.

A health record was kept by the ship's physician for each participant during the six months tour of duty.

Findings They found a small but significant positive correlation of 0.118 between LCUs and illness. This means that as life events increased so does illness. The fact that the findings were significant means that the relationship is not simply due to chance.

Conclusions This seems to suggest that life events do cause physical illness, though since the study was correlational this means we cannot draw conclusions about cause and effect. We can only state that life events and physical illness are positively associated. The findings support the view that changes associated with major life events absorb 'psychic energy', leaving less available for other matters such as physical defence against illness.

Criticisms The data collected about life events was retrospective. It is likely that individuals did not recall these events accurately. They might have forgotten which events had happened in the past 6 months, included ones from longer ago, and excluded ones they preferred to forget. This means the data might be unreliable.

The study lacked population validity because the sample consisted of American males (and in the Navy). This means we cannot justifiably generalise these findings to other cultures or to women.

Progress check

1 What is an LCU and what does it measure?
2 Give one criticism of the SRRS.

2 E.g. it assumes that life events mean the same thing to everybody.
1 Life change unit which measures amount of stress in terms of change experienced.

Workplace stressors

Key Term **Workplace stressor** is any feature of the workplace that creates stress. This can affect paid workers, volunteers, students or housewives, and may be due to the factors described below.

- **Effects of workplace stress:** absenteeism; high job turnover; alcohol and drug abuse; and poor performance in terms of quantity and quality.
- **Causes of workplace stress:** job uncertainty; organisational change; work overload; under-utilisation of skills; difficult tasks; decision-making and dangerous, unpleasant or uncomfortable work environments.

Further causes of workplace stress have focused on a number of areas:

Shift work

Having to adjust one's body clock to different sleep patterns results in considerable stress and has been associated with major industrial accidents. Czeisler *et al.* (1982) found that shift work amongst manual workers in an industrial setting in Utah, USA correlated with raised accident rates, absenteeism and chronic feelings of ill health.

Overcrowding

Calhoun (1962) placed a population of rats in a limited space. Once their population reached a certain level, their behaviour became pathological (males became hypersexual, and attacked females and young, females became poor mothers). The overcrowding created stress.

Remember that a stressor is any physical or psychological stimulus that threatens an individual's psychological and/or physiological well-being.

One comment that is made about many psychological experiments is that they involved American male undergraduates – a population sample that is by no means typical of the rest of us. Glass' research involved *female* students, different but still potentially biased.

There is evidence that density also causes stress in humans. Freedman (1973) found correlations between urban density and pathological behaviour such as admissions to mental hospitals. However, in other situations, such as a football match, density can be an uplift rather than a hassle.

Noise

Glass *et al.* (1969) arranged for participants to complete various cognitive tasks, such as number work and letter searches, while listening to noisy tapes. Later the participants had to complete four puzzles. Two of them were insoluble. Frustration was measured in terms of the time that participants persisted at these tasks and stress was measured throughout using galvanic skin response (GSR). Participants did adapt to the noise as shown by the fact that their GSR levels and number of errors were considerably reduced by the end of the first set of tasks. However, if the noise was intermittent, participants made more errors and showed less task persistence.

Lack of control

Glass *et al.* (1969) tried a further variation where some participants were given a button to ostensibly control the noise. These participants showed greater task persistence than those who thought they had no control. Perceived control avoids a sense of helplessness and anxiety, which would increase stress and frustration. In Cohen *et al*'s. study (1991 see p.96) those participants who felt their lives were unpredictable and uncontrollable were twice as likely to develop colds as those suffering low stress.

Responsibility

In contrast with 'lack of control' studies, other research has found that increased responsibility (greater control) is linked to higher stress. Brady's (1958) classic study which showed that control was associated with increased stress is described below.

AQA (A) Key study: Workplace stressers

Brady (1958) Ulcers in executive monkeys

Aims

If you use this study in an exam make sure you link it to workplace stress.

Brady conducted research where monkeys were strapped in a chair and given electric shocks unless the monkey pressed a lever every 20 seconds. Many of them died and postmortems showed they had stomach ulcers. The question was whether these ulcers were due to the physical restraint and electric shocks (physiological stress) or to psychological stress (the task they had to perform).

Procedures

The study with monkeys may be considered unethical, though we should weigh up the costs versus the benefits. Do you think that usefulness of the findings 'excuses' the harm done to the participants?

This study used non-human animals and was a laboratory experiment. Brady used a yoked control technique – the executive monkey received the shocks but had control over the lever, a yoked control was also restrained but had no control over the shocks and received the shocks whenever the first monkey failed to press the lever regularly.

A number of variations were tried: 6 hours on and 6 hours off; 18 hours on, 6 hours off; 30 minutes on, 30 minutes off.

Findings

After 23 days the executive monkey died due to a perforated ulcer. The control monkey had no ulcers nor any gastrointestinal abnormalities. This happened when using the 6 hours on, 6 hours off schedule. None of the other timings produced ulcers. An investigation of stomach secretions showed that stomach acidity increased during rest periods when in the 6 on, 6 off schedule, and such acidity was related to the development of ulcers.

Conclusions

First, these findings show that the ulcers were due to psychological stress not physiological stress. Second, they suggest that it is being in control that creates the psychological stress. Third, the study of stomach acidity suggests that the greatest danger period for an individual under stress is during rest.

Criticisms	It may not be reasonable to draw conclusions about human behaviour. However, research with humans has supported Brady's findings. For example, Margolis and Kroes (1974) found that foremen (more responsibility) were seven times more likely to develop gastric ulcers than shop-floor workers.
	Subsequent research on ulcers found that a bacterium (helicobacter pylori), not stress, is a major cause of ulcers (Marshall *et al.*, 1985).

Progress check

1 What is GSR?
2 In what ways is a managing director likely to suffer different levels of stress to a shop-floor worker?

2 A managing director probably has a greater sense of control (less stress) but increased responsibility (higher stress).

1 Galvanic skin response: a test of skin conductivity, sweating and ANS activity.

Individual differences in modifying the effects of stress

AQA A ▸ U2

Personality

- **Type A** individuals are more likely to be affected by stress, as indicated in a study by Friedman and Rosenman (see key study on p.95).
- **Hardiness:** Kobasa *et al.* (1982) found that managers for large companies who were psychologically 'hardy' suffered less illness. Hardiness characteristics are:
  - greater sense of commitment to work and personal relationships, seeing stressful situations as a challenge and an opportunity, a stronger sense of personal control.

Culture

Black-African Americans are more likely to have cardiovascular problems than White Americans. This may be due to:

- **Biological factors** arising from racial differences. However, Cooper *et al.* (1999) compared hypertension rates of Africans living in Western and African countries. They were highest in urban societies, suggesting that hypertension is due to social factors and not to race.
- **Social factors.** Different cultural groups learn to manage stress differently. Wade and Tavris (1993) note that the Japanese deal with stress by trying to accept problems; westerners try to control a stressful problem.
- **Cognitive factors.** Black Americans experience high levels of prejudice.

Gender

Men are more likely to have cardiovascular problems than women. This may be due to:

- **Biological factors:** Women appear to be less affected by stress than men. It may be that women's hormones (such as oxytocin and oestrogen) protect them. Hastrup *et al.* (1980) found that women had lowered stress responses at the time in their menstrual cycle when their oestrogen levels were highest.
- **Social factors:** It may be that women engage in fewer unhealthy behaviours than men. Carroll (1992) reported that women are now smoking and drinking more, and their CHD rates have risen, which suggests that lifestyle could be important.
- **Cognitive factors.** Females may think differently about stressful situations. Vögele *et al.* (1997) suggest that females learn to suppress anger and therefore show low reactivity in stress situations.

4.6 Critical issue: Stress management

Physiological approaches to stress management

 AQA A ▶ U2

> There is no clear distinction between physiological and psychological therapies since all physiological treatments have psychological effects.

Key Term Stress management refers to techniques for coping with the negative effects of stress. One group of techniques is physiological and the other is psychological.

Key Term Physiological approaches to stress management are techniques that aim to reduce stress by altering the body's natural stress responses. Examples include the use of drugs and biofeedback.

Drugs

What are they?

Anxiolytic drugs reduce anxiety. These include:

- **Benzodiazepines:** (e.g. Valium and Librium). These are most common today. They act on synapses and neurotransmitters, especially by promoting **GABA** (the body's natural form of anxiety relief). GABA reduces **serotonin** levels, a neurotransmitter related to arousal and aggression. The common side-effects of benzodiazepines are sleepiness and dependence.
- **Buspirone** enhances the effects of serotonin, thus reducing anxiety, but also has side effects (e.g. depression).

How do they work?

All drugs are related to the bodily processes involved in the stress response, i.e. they intervene in the activity of the ANS.

Evaluation

- Drugs can be effective in reducing stress in the **short term**.
- They do not tackle the **real problem**.
- Drugs often have unpleasant **side-effects** and problems of **dependence**.

Biofeedback

What is it?

This is a technique to learn voluntary control of involuntary muscles that control, for example, blood pressure and heart rate. Learning occurs through:

- **feedback** – a patient is connected to various monitoring devices and a light or tone signals when a correct alteration occurs
- **relaxation** – in order to reduce blood pressure the patient is told to relax, and this leads to changes in muscle tone and ANS activity.

> Remember that operant conditioning involves a behaviour being 'stamped in' as a result of rewards or reinforcement.

How does it work?

There are two possible explanations.

- **Operant conditioning** occurs. Certain behaviours are reinforced because they result in a desirable state of affairs. Miller and DiCara (1967) demonstrated this by paralysing rats with curare (they had respirators to keep them breathing).

This was to ensure that the rats could not use any form of voluntary control. Half of the rats were rewarded whenever their heart rates slowed down by electrically stimulating the pleasure-centre in the brain. The other half were rewarded when their heart rates speeded up. In both groups there were significant changes in heart beats after repeated reinforcement.

- Relaxation leads to restoration of **homeostasis** (the body's normal state of balance). Selye's GAS model suggested that stress disrupts the body's normal state, so relaxation helps the body to regulate the various physiological activities that are out of control, e.g. high blood-pressure.

Empirical support

- Dworkin and Dworkin (1988) used biofeedback to teach sufferers of scoliosis (curvature of the spine) to control their back muscles and alter their posture.
- There are reports of its usefulness with asthma, hypertension, migraine, circulatory problems, pain control, and bed wetting (Underhill, 1999).

Evaluation

- Biofeedback certainly works with **voluntary** responses. However, apparent changes in **involuntary** control may be due to relaxation and control of unused voluntary muscles.
- Such strategies are costly, time-consuming and require effort and commitment.
- On the other hand, biofeedback is non-invasive, has virtually no side-effects, and can be effective over the long term.

Psychological approaches to stress management

AQA A   U2

Key Term **Psychological approaches to stress management** are techniques that aim to reduce stress by helping to cope better with stressors now and/or in the future. Such techniques require considerable effort on the part of the 'patient' but offer long-term solutions.

Meichenbaum: Stress inoculation therapy

The term 'cognitive' refers to mental activity, so cognitive therapies are those techniques concerned with thinking.

What is it?

Meichenbaum (1985) proposed a form of therapy to protect an individual ('inoculate') *before* dealing with stress rather than coping with it afterwards. This is a form of cognitive therapy because it aims to change the way the individual *thinks* about their problem rather than changing the problem itself.

How does it work?

- **Assessment:** therapist and patient discuss potential problem areas.
- **Stress reduction techniques** are taught, e.g. relaxation and using self-coping statements (such as 'Stop worrying, because it's pointless').
- **Application and follow-through:** patient practises stress-reduction techniques in role play, and then uses them in real-life situations.

Empirical evidence

Fontana *et al.* (1999) found that students benefited from a 6-week peer-led stress inoculation programme. They had lower heart rate and state-anxiety levels than did controls even 6 months later.

Meichenbaum (1977) compared stress inoculation with desensitisation (a form of learning therapy where patients learn to relax with their feared object). Patients had both snake and rat phobias, one of which was treated with one of the methods. Meichenbaum found that both methods were effective but stress inoculation also greatly reduced the non-treated phobia, showing that the patient had learned general strategies for coping with anxiety.

Evaluation

- Stress inoculation therapy is good for coping with **moderate stress** but not as effective for severe stress.
- **Not all individuals** are able to use this method effectively.

Kobasa: Increasing hardiness

What is it?

Kobasa (1986) suggested that people who are psychologically more hardy find it easier to cope with stress.

How does it work?

- **Focusing**: People often are unaware that they are stressed, so they should become more aware of signs of stress, such as tight muscles.
- **Reconstructing stress situations**: Think of a stressful situation and write down how it could have turned out better and worse.
- **Compensating through self-improvement**: Find tasks that can be mastered. This reassures you that you can cope.

Empirical evidence

Wiebe (1991) found that individuals rated high in hardiness showed lower rates of heart rate when performing a stressful task.

Maddi (1999) found that hardy individuals had lower blood pressure and reported less stress than individuals who measured low in hardiness.

Evaluation

Some people find this sort of strategy doesn't work. It requires **considerable effort** and determination – the characteristics of a hardy personality.

The role of control in stress

Key Term **Control** refers to the extent to which an individual feels able to direct his/her life. Research indicates that control may either reduce (e.g. Glass *et al*, see page 99) or increase stress (e.g. Brady, see page 100). In addition it is the perception of control that is significant, not whether an individual *is* actually in control.

Seligman (1975) proposed that individuals acquire **learned helplessness** when placed in situations where they have no control. In one experiment animals were placed in a cage and given shocks which were impossible to escape from. Later, when placed in a cage where there were opportunities to escape the animals didn't try. They had learned to be helpless.

Rotter (1966) introduced the concept of **locus of control**. People who have an internal locus of control believe they are responsible for the things that happen to them. They control their world. People with an external locus of control blame someone or something else. Locus of control moderates the perception of stress. For example, Kim *et al.* (1997) found that children with an internal locus of control showed fewer signs of stress when parents divorced.

Progress check

1 Give one drawback to using drugs to manage stress.
2 What did Kobaso mean by 'hardiness'?

2 The ability to cope with stress.

1 Side effects, may mask the problem.

Sample question and student answer

AQA A style question

(a) Describe **two** sources of stress. [3 + 3]

(b) Explain how the body responds to stress. [6]

(c) Describe **two** methods of stress management and consider their strengths **and** weaknesses. [18]

Two sources of stress are identified and both described in detail for 3+3 marks.

(a) One source of stress is the workplace. Many factors in the workplace lead to stress such as job dissatisfaction, too much responsibility, lack of control, too much noise, overcrowding, heat and tiredness from shiftwork. The workplace is cited as one of the main causes of stress.

A second source of stress is life changes. This was investigated by Holmes and Rahe who said that major changes in a person's life, whether good or bad, cause you stress because they require psychic energy. Examples include marriage and divorce.

This is a detailed and accurate description of the physiological response of the body to stress. Further details might have been included (such as the name of the pituitary hormone ACTH) but what has been included is sufficient for a 6 mark question, thus a full 6 marks.

(b) When an animal is exposed to a stressor the brain sends signals to the pituitary which releases a hormone which activates the adrenal glands to produce adrenaline and noradrenaline. These activate the ANS ready for fight or flight. After a while, if the animal remains in a state of stress, the body recovers some balance so that normal metabolic functioning can take place. The levels of stress hormones are reduced but the body remains in a state of alertness. After a long period these hormones are depleted and a state of exhaustion occurs.

(c) Two psychological methods are stress inoculation and increasing hardiness. Meichenbaum's stress inoculation aims to teach people to be able to cope with stress when it comes, rather than trying to treat stress where it already exists. This should enable them to cope better. The individual is taught how to relax and to use self-coping statements. These are first tried out in role play and later applied in real life.

One study by Meichenbaum showed that stress inoculation was better than other forms of therapy for coping with phobias and their associated anxiety. Even though a patient was only treated for one phobia they were able to cope better with other phobias as well. It seems that stress inoculation therapy is good for coping with moderate stress but not as effective for severe stress. Also it requires a lot of effort on the part of the patient but again has no side effects.

The descriptions of both methods are accurate and detailed, and would receive the full 6 marks. The commentary is disappointing. Strengths and weaknesses have been identified for stress inoculation and evidence used effectively. The overall quality of the commentary is reduced because there is very little for the second method (though there is mention of a strength and a weakness). The last paragraph improves the situation as a general commentary on psychological techniques and a valuable contrast with biological methods. So overall, this is limited and reasonably effective AO2 = 8 marks.

Kobasa suggested that people could learn to be more 'hardy' and therefore cope better with stress, in the same way that some people are just naturally better at coping with stress. She said you should recognise that you are stressed (people often just get used to being slightly stressed and fall apart when stress levels get too high), then you should rethink the stress situation by writing a list of how it could have turned out better and worse. This allows one to focus on the positive and see that it could have been worse. This method appears to be effective and certainly Kobasa's own research has shown that people who are more hardy are better able to cope with stress.

It is clear that there are many ways to manage stress and each has its own advantages and disadvantages. The effectiveness of any technique is related to individual differences and the kind of stress. If the stress is extreme it may be necessary to use drugs to reduce the anxiety levels

Sample question and student answer *(continued)*

first. Some individuals could never cope with the level of commitment required by the psychological techniques. [340 words]

TOTAL: 26 out of 30 marks

Practice examination questions

1

(a) Describe the main features of Selye's General Adaptation Syndrome. [6]

(b) Describe the findings and conclusions of **one** study relating to workplace stressors. [6]

(c) Describe and evaluate the role played by gender **and/or** culture in modifying the effects of stress. [18]

AQA A style question

2

Some of the core studies take a physiological approach to human behaviour and experience. This approach considers how our hormones, nervous system, and functions of the brain interact to determine our behaviour. Using the studies below answer the following questions.

Schachter and Singer (emotion)

Sperry (split brain)

Dement and Kleitman (sleeping and dreaming)

Raine, Buchsbaum and LaCasse (brain scanning)

(a) Describe what each study tells us about physiological psychology. [10]

(b) What are the strengths and weaknesses of the physiological approach? [10]

(c) 'All behaviour is caused by physiological processes'. To what extent do you agree with this statement? [10]

OCR Core studies 2 June 2001

3

(a) What method is used to obtain the records of patterns of sleep shown in the diagram? [1]

(b) Describe **one** theory of sleep [4]

(c) Describe **one** method of studying genetic influences on individual differences. [3]

(d) Assess correlational techniques as a means of studying genetic influences on individual differences. [6]

Edexcel specimen material

Chapter 5
Individual differences

The following topics are covered in this chapter:

- *The individual differences approach*
- *Studying gender*
- *Abnormality: Defining psychological abnormality*
- *Abnormality: Biological and psychological models of abnormality*
- *Critical issue: Eating disorders*

5.1 The individual differences approach

After studying this topic you should be able to:

- *outline key assumptions of the individual differences approach*
- *distinguish between nomothetic and idiographic approaches in psychology*
- *evaluate the individual differences approach in terms of its strengths and weaknesses*
- *discuss some of the methods used in the study of individual differences*

LEARNING SUMMARY

Key assumptions of the individual differences approach

AQA A — U2
EDEXCEL — U2
OCR — U1, U2

This approach focuses on the way that people differ. Traditionally, this has involved the study of personality and intelligence. However, clearly, there are many other ways in which individuals differ: for example, in terms of hair colour, skin colour, gender, willingness to conform, and mental health.

The nomothethic approach to individual differences:

- aims to make **generalisations** about the differences between people;
- involves the study of **a large number of people** and then seeks to make generalisations about them. For example, research on gender differences highlights the way that men **on the whole** and women **on the whole** differ from one another.

The idiographic approach to individual differences focuses on the unique characteristics of individuals – for example, research based on case studies. Many psychological theories are written in a way that assumes all people are the same: all men are the same, all Americans are the same and so on, i.e. a nomothetic view. The idiographic approach is different and emphasises the fact that there is considerable individual variation:

- within any group of people;
- between cultures. Many psychological theories are **eurocentric** in that they are based on White, middle-class Europeans and assumed to apply to all classes of people. Even more research is based on American sources – possibly as many as 90% of the research studies in psychology are conducted with American participants.

Evaluation of the individual differences approach

Strength of this approach

The aim of psychology is to explain behaviour and clearly individual differences are an important part of this explanation: both in terms of making generalisations about groups of people (nomothetic) and focusing on individual cases (idiographic).

Weaknesses of this approach

- The danger with the nomothetic approach is that individual variation is overlooked.
- The danger with the idiographic approach is that we can not make generalisations about human behaviour from the study of individuals.

Methods used in the individual differences approach

Psychometric testing

A psychometric test is an objective and standardised measure of a small but carefully chosen sample of some aspect of human psychological ability. A 'good test' must have **reliability** (consistency) and **validity** (it must measure what it claims to measure). Tests also need to be standardised so we know whether any score is within the normal range or outside it. This is achieved either by **norm referencing** (establishing norms for a target population) or **criterion referencing** (establishing objective criteria of what is expected).

Evaluation

The strength of such tests is that one can collect large amounts of data about people. The disadvantage is that they are inevitably biased (e.g. culture bias) because they are based on the views of the test designer. They also give an illusion of reality, i.e. each individual can be given a score such as their IQ score which makes it appear that this is a absolute thing (like their shoe size). However, there is little evidence that this single number provides an accurate overall picture of the individual's capabilities.

Cross-cultural research

> Different historical periods are examples of different cultures. Britain today is as different from Britain in the 1800s as it is from life in a Third World country.

Research may be conducted in different cultures in order to make comparisons. This can demonstrate universal behaviours and/or the effects of specific cultural practices.

Evaluation

The problems are that often psychologists use measures designed for one cultural group that are inappropriate for another group. In addition, observers are culture-biased and are only able to *sample* behaviour in that culture, a sample that may be biased.

Progress check

1 What does 'idiographic' mean?
2 What is the aim of cross-cultural research?

2 To compare behaviour and practices in different cultures and determine what human behaviours are universal and what are due to social influences.

1 An approach related to the unique characteristics of the individual.

5.2 Studying gender

After studying this topic you should be able to:

- *distinguish between the terms sex and gender*
- *outline gender concepts*
- *describe factors affecting gender role identity and development*
- *discuss methods used to study gender differences*

Gender concepts

AQA B   U1

> Many people use the terms 'sex' and 'gender' as if they refer to the same thing, but this is not true.

Sex and gender

- **Sex** is a biological fact – i.e. whether someone is male or female.
- **Gender** refers to being male or female, i.e. masculinity and femininity.

Androgyny

> Androgyny is defined as 'having a partly male, partly female appearance'. This can be applied to physical and psychological characteristics.

Bem (1974) proposed that it was not necessary to regard 'male' and 'female' as mutually exclusive categories. A person can be both male and female, i.e. androgynous. For example, a person might be independent (normally considered as masculine) and at times show vulnerability (normally considered as feminine).

Bem further proposed that a person who is androgynous will be psychologically more healthy than an individual who is tied to being like a male or a female. Individuals who are less sex-stereotyped are freer to do things which are appropriate for a *situation* rather than being appropriate to their *gender*.

Sex-role stereotype

> Can you think of an example of a behaviour which would be reinforced in boys but not in girls?

This is a set of related concepts (**schema**) which tells us what behaviours are appropriate for our sex/gender, i.e. how males and females should behave. They are learned through direct and indirect reinforcement and exposure to role models.

Role and identity

A key feature of any individual's self-identity is their gender. Martin and Halverson's **gender schema theory** (1981) proposes that once a child has a basic gender identity they are motivated to learn more about gender and incorporate this information into their gender schema. Like all schemas, this serves to organise relevant information and attitudes, and will influence behaviour.

Nature and nurture

Some aspects of gender role are biologically determined (nature) whereas other aspects are learned (nurture).

- **Nature:** Hormones (e.g. testosterone in males and oestrogen in females) control many sex-related behaviours (such as puberty). Money and Ehrhardt (1972) found that girls who were exposed prenatally to male hormones were more tomboyish in later life.
- **Nurture:** Maccoby and Jacklin (1974) reviewed over 1,500 studies of gender differences and concluded that sex-role stereotypes are 'cultural myths' that have no basis in fact. They are perpetuated by expectations arising from gender stereotypes.

Cultural diversity

Williams and Best (1982) explored gender stereotypes in 30 different national cultures, finding that men were seen as more dominant, aggressive and autonomous, whereas women were more nurturant, deferent and interested in affiliation. Mead's classic studies (1949, described in the next section) found that, for example, in some cultures both men and women behaved in a way Westerners would regard as feminine. This must be due to social influences. At the same time, in all cultures men were always more aggressive, indicating the effects of nature.

Progress check

1 What does the term 'gender' mean?
2 What is meant by 'sex-role stereotype'?

2 The schemas you have about what is appropriate behaviour for males or females.

1 Your masculinity or femininity, not whether you are a male or female.

Methods used to study gender

 AQA B   U1

Case studies

Goldwyn (1979) described the case of Daphne Went. She was a married woman who sought help because she could not become pregnant. Internal examination revealed that she didn't have a womb and was in fact a male. Since she was content with her female role, she continued to live happily as a woman and adopted two children. This suggests that gender is a result of rearing not biological sex. However, any conclusion drawn from a single case history must be treated with caution as other unique factors may be involved.

Content analysis

Crabb and Bielawski (1994) compared children's books from 1938 and 1989 in terms of the way they represented how men and women use equipment such as washing machines and lawn mowers, and so on, and found relatively little change. Such stereotypes act as **social representations** of our culture. They reflect the way that society thinks, and they also shape the way people continue to think.

Observation

Lamb and Roopnarine (1979) observed the behaviour of 3–5-year-old children during free-play periods. They found that children generally reinforced peers for sex-appropriate play and were quick to criticise sex-inappropriate play, and that they responded more readily to reinforcement by the same sex rather than opposite sex peers. This suggests that children already know what is sex-appropriate, and that their peers are just reinforcing that knowledge. This supports gender schema theory.

Experiments

Laboratory experiment: Smith and Lloyd (1978) showed how reinforcement of gender stereotypes takes place very early on. Participants were asked to play with a baby who was referred to as a male or female. They were given toys to use while playing: e.g. a squeaky hammer (masculine); a doll (feminine); a rattle (neutral). If a participant thought she was playing with a boy, she verbally encouraged more motor activity and offered masculine toys.

Natural experiment: Williams (1985) studied the effects of television on sex stereotypes in a community that had recently got access to TV. The children's sex role attitudes became more traditional and sex-stereotyped. American television portrays men and women in traditional roles. This may considerably influence sex-attitudes in other cultures.

Cross-cultural research

Mead (1935) recorded observations of tribes from New Guinea.

- The Mundugumour tribe were all aggressive (masculine quality) regardless of sex. Neither gender gave much attention to childrearing.
- The Arapesh were all warm, emotional and non-aggressive (feminine qualities).
- The Tchambuli exhibited a reversal of our own gender roles. Women reared the children but also looked after commerce outside the tribe. The men spent their time in social activities, and were more emotional and artistic.

Mead (1935) initially concluded that gender was culturally determined. Later (1949) she changed her view to one of **cultural relativism**: in all tribes the men were more aggressive in comparison with the women. This suggests that some aspects of gender behaviour are innate. However, Freeman (1983) suggested that Mead was selective in reporting her results, and that the natives told her what she wanted to hear.

Ethical issues: socially sensitive research

Research that has direct social consequences creates particular problems because it often concerns issues where there is little agreement, much bias and serious implications. This applies to psychological research concerning 'alternative' sexuality. For example, Hamer *et al.* (1993) found evidence of a 'gay gene' by looking at the genes of homosexual brothers. If this is true, it could lead some people to testing unborn children.

5.3 Abnormality: Defining psychological abnormality

Attempts to define abnormality

AQA A ▶ U2
OCR ▶ U1, U2

Key Term **Abnormality** means to deviate from what is usual or from some sort of standard. The problem lies in establishing a standard. Possible approaches are described below.

Statistical infrequency

Key Term The **statistical infrequency** approach suggests that the standard can be defined statistically, i.e. in terms of what most people in the population are like. We can test a population for any behaviour, such as depression, and plot its frequency. If only 10% of the population exhibit this behaviour then it is abnormal.

Advantages of this approach

It is relatively easy to determine abnormality using psychometric tests.

Limitations to this approach

- Many unusual behaviours, such as genius, are statistically uncommon but not aberrant, in fact they may be **highly desirable**.
- Some undesirable behaviours or disorders, such as chicken pox, anxiety, or depression, are **statistically normal**.
- What is **common at a certain age** or in a certain context, is not universally applicable. For example, thumb sucking is normal at a certain age but not later.

Deviation from social norms

Key Term The **deviation from social norms** approach proposes that abnormality can be defined in terms of certain standards of social behaviour. Many people who are labelled as clinically abnormal do behave in a socially deviant way, for example schizophrenics behave anti-socially and erratically.

Advantages of this approach

Includes some consideration of the **effect** of deviant behaviour on others.

Limitations to this approach

- This approach allows serious **abuse of individual rights**. Examples of deviation through history have been witchcraft, homosexuality and political dissent.
- Social deviation is related to **social and cultural context**. What is deviant behaviour in Britain may not be deviant elsewhere.
- Social deviation can be a **good thing**, as in the case of people who resisted German occupation during World War II.

Failure to function adequately

Key Term The **failure to function adequately approach** suggests that certain behaviours are distressing or dysfunctional for the individual. For example, they disrupt the ability to work and/or to conduct satisfying relationships. Rosenhan and

Seligman (1989) suggested that certain elements jointly determine abnormality – singly they may cause no problem but when several co-occur they are symptomatic of abnormality:

- psychological suffering
- irrationality and incomprehensibility
- vividness and unconventionality
- violation of moral and ideal standards
- maladaptiveness (personally and socially)
- unpredictability and loss of control
- observer discomfort.

Advantages of this approach

Using the concepts of dysfunction and distress acknowledges the subjective experience of the individual.

Limitations to this approach

- In some situations apparently dysfunctional behaviour **may be functional** – for example, depression can be an adaptive response to stress.
- Personal distress may **not be a good indicator** of an undesirable state. Although many people do seek psychiatric help because they feel distressed, not all mental disorders are accompanied by a state of distress.
- Diagnoses of dysfunction and distress require **judgements to be made by others**, which are inevitably influenced by social and cultural mores.

Deviation from ideal mental health

Key Term The **deviation from ideal mental health** approach likens mental health to physical health. Doctors use the concept of physical health as a yardstick to measure ill-health (for example, a body temperature outside the normal range indicates illness) so why shouldn't we do the same with mental health? Jahoda (1958) suggested that the key features would be:

- self-acceptance
- autonomy
- environmental competence
- potential for growth and development
- accurate perception of reality
- positive interpersonal relations.

Advantages of this approach

- This is a **positive approach**.
- It is preferable to have some **absolutes** (signs of healthiness) rather than relying on a reference population to establish norms.

Limitations of this approach

- Such approaches are influenced by **cultural attitudes** – for example, autonomy is not a universal ideal.
- The list is **idealistic**, and few people achieve most of the behaviours identified.
- It is possible to measure physical illness objectively (e.g. temperature and blood pressure) but the concepts for mental health are **vague**.

Progress check

1 Outline one disadvantage of the 'deviation from statistical norm' explanation.
2 Which of the four explanations takes the most positive approach?

2 The deviation from mental health model.

1 E.g. some behaviours which are undesirable are statistically common.

Limitations associated with attempts to define abnormality

Reliability

The aim of diagnosing abnormality is to offer treatment to those who might be considered abnormal. This only makes sense if the diagnosis is reliable, i.e. two people would give the same diagnosis. The study by Rosenhan (1973 on page 115) demonstrates how the diagnosis of mental illness may lack reliability.

Cultural relativism

Key Term Cultural relativism is the view that behaviour must be viewed in the cultural context in which it occurs otherwise it doesn't make sense. This is because the meaning and causes of any behaviour are relative to the culture of the person.

Cultural relativism was a key problem for all of the definitions outlined above. Each standard is relative to cultural context. However, if one considers Rosenhan and Seligman's list, there are some universal indicators of undesirable behaviour, such as distress to oneself or others.

OCR core study: Diagnosing mental illness

Rosenhan (1973) On being sane in insane places

Study 1

Aims Can diagnoses of mental illnesses ever be reliable? If 'normal' people were diagnosed as mentally ill this would suggest that the diagnosis was unreliable.

Procedures A field experiment involving eight sane people who acted as pseudo-patients (i.e. not real). The pseudo-patients presented themselves in different US mental hospitals saying that they had been hearing voices (a symptom of schizophrenia). All other details were drawn from their real lives, i.e. were normal. If and when the pseudo-patient was admitted, they continued to behave entirely as normal. They spent their time making notes. To be released they had to convince staff that they had now recovered

> Note that the participants in this study were not the pseudo-patients but were the staff in the mental hospitals.

Findings All but one pseudo-patient was admitted. When they were released it was with the label 'schizophrenia in remission'. The length of stay ranged from 7 to 52 days (average 19 days). Visitors and staff found that the pseudo-patients 'exhibited no abnormal indications'. Real patients were suspicious.

Conclusions It was possible that doctors were biased towards making **type-two errors** (making a false judgement to avoid failing to diagnose a real illness).

Study 2

Aims To test whether the tendency to err on the side of caution could be reversed.

Procedures Field experiment. The staff in another mental hospital were told the results of the first study, and that during the next 3 months, one or more pseudo-patients would attempt to be admitted to the hospital.

Findings There were no pseudo-patients but of 193 patients admitted 41 were judged as such by at least one staff member.

Conclusions The staff were now making more **type-one errors** (calling a sick person healthy).

Study 3

Procedures Rosenhan conducted a mini-experiment in four of the original hospitals. The pseudo-patient asked a staff member 'Pardon me, Mr/Mrs/Dr X, could you tell me when I am likely to be discharged?'

Findings Only 4% of the psychiatrists and even fewer nurses answered the question posed by the pseudo-patient. Whereas, in a control test, all people stopped.

Overall conclusions It is the setting (situation) as much as the individual's behaviour (disposition) which leads to the diagnosis. The medical model does not work with mental illness, partly because mentally ill individuals do not have objective symptoms and partly because people can recover from physical illnesses whereas mental illness carries a lifelong stigma.

OCR Revision question The study by Rosenhan (sane in insane places) broke a number of ethical guidelines.
a) Outline **one** way in which the hospital staff were treated unethically. [2]
b) If the study had been ethical, suggest what effect this would have on results. [2]
    (June 2001, Core Studies 2, question 5)

5.4 Abnormality: Biological and psychological models of abnormality

After studying this topic you should be able to:

- describe assumptions of the biological (medical) model of abnormality in terms of views on the causes and treatment of abnormality
- describe assumptions of psychological models of abnormality—including psychodynamic, behavioural and cognitive models in terms of their views on the causes and treatment of abnormality

LEARNING SUMMARY

The biological (medical) model of abnormality

 AQA A   U2

Assumptions of the biological (medical) model

- Psychological symptoms are manifestations of an **underlying biochemical or physiological dysfunction**, which may or may not have a known cause.
- **Symptoms** need to be identified and **syndromes** diagnosed, followed by appropriate somatic treatment(s).

Explanations for the cause of mental illness

Infection

Mental illness is caused by a virus or bacteria. For example, general paresis (a mental disorder known since the 16th century) was found to be caused by the syphilis bacterium. Crow (1984) proposed that schizophrenia is caused by a retrovirus, which becomes incorporated into DNA.

Genetic transmission

> A 'concordance rate' is the extent to which two things are related, in this case how frequently both twins have the same disorder.

Mental illness is the result of an inherited gene. For example, Gottesman and Shields (1972) found that **concordance rates** for schizophrenia in non-identical twins is about 9% whereas it rises to 42% in identical twins, indicating some environmental influence but a larger genetic component. Other studies have used **gene-mapping** to demonstrate the location of the actual gene that caused the disorder. For example, Sherrington *et al.* (1988) found evidence of a link between schizophrenia and a gene located on chromosome 5.

Biochemical abnormalities

Teuting *et al.* (1981) who analysed the urine of depressed and normal people and found lower levels of products associated with noradrenaline in the former. Some forms of depression are related to disordered hormone levels, such as post-partum depression, premenstrual syndrome and seasonal affective disorder (SAD).

Neuroanatomy

Chua and McKenna (1995) reported that the brains of schizophrenic patients were smaller and had larger ventricles than the brains of normal individuals.

Methods of treatment

> Until fairly recently the medical model was the dominant model for explaining and treating mental illness. It tends to be favoured by psychiatrists, whereas clinical psychologists favour psychological models.

If one believes that mental illnesses have a physical basis, then they can be treated using physical (or somatic) methods. Some such methods are described on p.115.

ECT (electroconvulsive therapy)

Today, this involves little physical discomfort, as the patient is given an anaesthetic

The diagnosis of mental disorder is officially done using a classification scheme. The DSM-IV is used in America and the ICD-10 in Britain.

and muscle relaxant. An electric shock is applied to the non-dominant cerebral hemisphere to produce a seizure. The individual awakens soon after and remembers nothing of the treatment (which is desirable).

Evaluation

- The method is **potentially dangerous** and there are ethical concerns about it.
- ECT appears to be **successful** for cases of severe depression. Janicak *et al.* (1985) found that 80% of all severely depressed patients respond well to ECT, compared with 64% recovery when given drug therapy.
- Some criticise the fact that we don't know **how ECT works** and therefore it shouldn't be used. It has been suggested that the seizure may re-structure disordered thinking or it may alter the biochemical balance of the brain.

Psychosurgery

Moniz (1937) introduced the practice of lobotomy. The operation involved removing large portions of the frontal cerebral cortex to make a patient more controllable. Today the technique is much refined, electric probes destroy specific nerve fibres and cause minimal intellectual damage.

Evaluation

- It is **used only rarely**, in cases of severe depression, obsessive-compulsive disorder or pain where all other treatment has failed (Griest, 1992).
- The effects are **not consistent** and it is **irreversible**.

Drug therapy (chemotherapy)

The main classes of drugs are:

- **Anxiolytic drugs** (anti-anxiety) such as Valium and benzodiazepines (see p.101).
- **Neuroleptic drugs** (anti-psychotic) such as chlorpromazine, used to treat schizophrenia. They block dopamine receptor sites. Possible side-effects include blurred vision and a decrease in white blood cells (which can be fatal).
- **Anti-depressant drugs** (stimulants), e.g. Prozac. They promote activity of noradrenaline and serotonin, which leads to increased arousal. Side-effects include heart problems.
- **Anti-manic drugs**, e.g. Lithium, used to control mania in bipolar depression.

Evaluation

- The use of drug therapies has offered **significant relief** to many sufferers.
- There are problems of **addiction** and **dangerous side-effects**.
- Drugs are **not cures** – they are short-term remedies.
- **Effectiveness varies** considerably between individuals; questions usefulness.

Evaluation of the biological (medical) model

Strengths

- The medical treatment of insanity was a move in the direction of **humaneness**: the illness rather than the patient was blamed. On the other hand, control is taken away from the patient, who relies on expert guidance.
- At least some disorders have a **biological basis**; however, an exclusive emphasis on biological bases may mean that other factors are overlooked.

Weaknesses

- In many cases it is not clear whether the physical factor is actually an **effect rather than a cause**.
- The medical model may be appropriate for **physical illness** but not for mental illness where symptoms are less objective.
- The medical approach purports to be **value-free** and scientific, but is just as subject to prevailing attitudes as other models.

A combined approach: The diathesis-stress model

It may be more realistic to combine the biological and psychological models. Mental illness arises:

- Diathesis – a genetic vulnerability or predisposition.
- Stress – some environmental event which triggers the predisposition.

This would explain why, when one identical twin develops a disorder, their twin does not always go on to develop the disorder. It also explains why we don't all develop eating disorders even though we are all exposed to slim models.

Progress check

1 Identify one assumption of the medical model.
2 Name one therapy derived from the medical model.

2 E.g. drug therapy.

1 E.g. mental illnesses have a physical cause, symptoms can be identified and diagnosed.

Psychological models of abnormality: The psychodynamic model

AQA A	U2
AQA B	U1
EDEXCEL	U2
OCR	U1, U2

Assumptions of the psychodynamic model

This model is largely based on Freud's psychoanalytic theory (see Chapter 1).

- Mental illness is the result of **psychological** rather than physical causes.
- Mental illness arises from **unconscious** and **repressed conflicts**.

Explanations for the cause of mental illness

- Behaviour can be explained in terms of the factors (dynamics) that motivate it.
- Unresolved, unconscious conflicts form in early childhood and create anxiety.
- Ego defences, such as projection and repression, form to protect the ego from anxiety.
- These defences lead to neurotic behaviour.
- Recovery depends on insight and working through past problems.

Methods of treatment

Psychoanalytic theory implies that recovery can only take place if the unconscious is made conscious, and patients resolve their conflict. This is done through psychoanalysis which involves the following techniques.

Free association

The therapist asks a question and the patient is encouraged to talk freely about anything that comes into their mind, i.e. to verbalise their stream of consciousness so that the therapist can identify where the patient may be repressing material.

Rich interpretation

The therapist explains the patient's thoughts and feelings.

Analysis of dreams

Dreams are considered to express the innermost workings of the mind (see p.91).

Transference

The patient transfers their feelings about others onto the therapist which gives the therapist insight into the patient's other relationships, both past and present. This may have to be dealt with as an additional 'problem'.

Evaluation of psychoanalysis

- The emphasis on early conflicts means that **present conflicts** may be overlooked.
- Psychoanalysis has somewhat **limited applicability**, being suitable for motivated intelligent and verbally able patients.
- It is only suitable for those mental illnesses where some **insight is retained**.

Evaluation of the psychoanalytic model

Strengths

- It was the **first attempt** to explain mental illness in psychological terms.
  - It is supported by **extensive theory** and practice.

Weaknesses

- It is **not a scientifically rigorous** approach, the model is based on research with a limited sample (Freud's middle-class Viennese neurotic clients).
- It is a **reductionist** model, suggesting that the patient is controlled by instinctual forces and help must come from an expert.
- It is also a **determinist** model based on innate, biological mechanisms of psychosocial development with some room for cultural influences.
- Freud was overconcerned with **sexual factors**, and this may reflect the culture in which he lived. Subsequent psychoanalytic theories (e.g. Erikson) have replaced sexual with social influences.

Progress check

1 Identify one explanation for abnormality offered by the psychoanalytic model.
2 What is 'free association'?

2 The therapist says a word and the patient talks freely about whatever comes into their head.

1 E.g. unresolved conflicts create anxiety, ego defences against anxiety lead to neurotic behaviour.

Psychological models of abnormality: The behavioural model

AQA A	U2
AQA B	U1
EDEXCEL	U2
OCR	U1, U2

Assumptions and explanations of the behavioural model

- Behaviourists (see Chapter 1) suggest that **abnormal behaviours are learned**, like any other behaviours.
- Only behaviours which are currently **observable** are important, the patient's history doesn't matter.
- **Thoughts and feelings** are not relevant. There is no conscious activity involved in learning. It occurs through conditioning techniques:
- What can be learned can be **unlearned**.

Methods of treatment

If abnormal behaviours are learned then these can be unlearned and/or new behaviours can be learned in their stead. The behavioural model suggests that this can be done with either classical or operant conditioning techniques.

Classical conditioning techniques (Behaviour therapy)

- Aversion therapy: For example, alcoholics are injected with a drug which makes them vomit when drinking, and eventually the nausea becomes a conditioned response to the presentation of alcohol (conditioned stimulus). Meter and Chesser (1970) found that at least half their patients abstained for a year after therapy. The use of an unpleasant stimulus is ethically questionable. The drop-out rate tends to be high and patients may become anxious.

- **Systematic desensitisation (SD)** is used to treat phobias. The patient learns to pair the feared thing with relaxation rather than anxiety. Wolpe (1958) described the following steps: (1) Patient learns deep muscle relaxation; (2) Patient constructs a hierarchy of increasingly threatening situations; (3) Patient is asked to imagine each scene while deeply relaxed. At any time, if the patient feels anxious, the image is stopped and relaxation regained.
- **Implosion therapy and flooding:** Both techniques aim to present the patient with maximum exposure to the feared stimulus, with exposure continuing until their fear subsides, thus extinguishing the conditioned response. This can be done in one's imagination (implosion therapy) where the person imagines a very fearful situation (such as being in a room full of spiders). There is evidence that real-life exposure (flooding) is more effective but it does involve placing the patient in an intensely anxiety-provoking situation.

Operant conditioning techniques (Behaviour modification)

- **Modelling:** The patient first watches the therapist experiencing the phobic situation calmly, then the patient does the same.
- **Token economy (TE):** Patients living in an institution are given tokens as secondary reinforcers when they engage in correct/socially desirable behaviours. The tokens can then be exchanged for primary reinforcers – food or privileges. The drawback to this therapy is that it often fails to transfer to life outside the institution. The effectiveness of tokens may be due to other factors, such as the fact that the system is being positively reinforcing for the nursing staff (because the patients respond to the rewards and the staff feel they are making positive gains, and therefore are stimulated to persist). They also help to structure the situation and ensure consistent rewards. Paul and Lentz (1977) found the chronic mental patients with TE did as well as those in a therapeutic community in terms of full release or reduction of medication, and they did considerably better than those in a hospital setting.

Mental institutions are therapeutic communities, but other groups of people living together can also be described as a 'therapeutic community' if the whole social environment is designed to have a beneficial and therapeutic impact on the residents.

Evaluation of the behavioural model

Strengths

- The therapies are **successful for the target range of disorders**, e.g. phobias, obsessive-compulsive and developmental disorders. In fact, for some disorders it is the only viable option – e.g. the brain injured.
- The firm scientific basis and operationalised procedures make the theory and therapies **easy to research**.

Weaknesses

- There are **ethical** questions about manipulating behaviour.
- Treatment is of **symptoms not underlying causes**, which may remain – but behaviourists argue that the symptoms are all that matters.
- The success of behavioural therapies may be quite **unrelated to learning theory**, for example it may be a matter of receiving increased attention.

Psychological models of abnormality: The cognitive model

AQA A U2
AQA B U1

Assumptions and explanations of the cognitive model

The cognitive model emphasises the role of thoughts, expectations and attitudes (i.e. cognitions) in mental illness, either as causes or mediating factors.

- It is the way you think about a situation which is maladaptive, which is different to maladaptive behaviour (as suggested by the behavioural model).

The cognitive (or cognitive-behavioural) model grew out of the behavioural model because the latter was seen as inadequate in its focus on external behaviour only.

- 'Cure' can be achieved by **restructuring** a patient's thinking and enabling them to change their self-beliefs and motivations.
- The psychotherapy is **client-centred** – only the client knows their own cognitions.

Methods of treatment

This model assumes that disturbance lies in the way one thinks about things and therefore treatment should focus on training an individual's ways of thinking. Examples include the following.

Rational-emotional therapy (RET)

Ellis (1962) suggested that patients develop a set of irrational beliefs which lead them react to situations with undesirable emotions (ABC – **A**ctivating event – **B**eliefs about the activating event – **C**onsequences). For example, a person might believe that he must be competent in everything he does in order to be worth – while. When he fails at something, he is plunged into despair. The therapist is directive and aggressive and challenges beliefs, e.g. 'who says you must be perfect?', leading the patient to ask the same questions. Bradsma *et al.* (1978) reported that RET is effective with certain types of patient (those who are perfectionist and capable of rational thought).

Cognitive restructuring therapy

Beck (1976) developed a therapy for depression. The therapist identifies the patient's self-defeating assumptions and substitutes more adaptive ones. This should disprove the patient's negative self-image. The therapy may be effective with eating disorders and even schizophrenia. Hollon *et al.* (1988) gave 64 adults suffering from major depression either drug or cognitive therapy, or both for 12 weeks. Each treatment led to improvements. In the 'drug only' group there were no changes in 'explanatory style' but there were considerable changes in the other groups. There was some evidence of relapse in the 'drug only' group over the next two years but not in the other patients.

Stress inoculation therapy

Meichenbaum (1975), see p.102.

Evaluation of the cognitive model

Strengths

- In general these therapies are **quick**, and are becoming **increasingly popular**.
- They are successful for a **target range of disorders** (depression, anxiety and eating disorders, and sexual problems).
- It is an **objective approach** that lends itself to research.

Weaknesses

Like the behavioural model, this approach **does not investigate causes** but just treats behaviours – which appeals to some patients who prefer not to search for deep meanings.

Progress check

1 What is the behaviourist view on thoughts and feelings?
2 What is one limitation to the behavioural approach?
3 Which therapy involves patient insight?

3 Psychoanalysis.
2 E.g. doesn't treat underlying problems, unethical to manipulate behaviour.
1 They are not relevant to understanding behaviour.

5.5 Critical issue: Eating disorders

After studying this topic you should be able to:

- describe the clinical characteristics of both anorexia nervosa and bulimia nervosa
- outline and evaluate biological explanations for eating disorders
- discuss psychological, (psychodynamic, behavioural and cognitive explanations) for eating disorders

LEARNING SUMMARY

The clinical characteristics of eating disorders

AQA A ▶ U2

The DSM-IV lists four criteria for the diagnosis of anorexia: weight, anxiety, body-image distortion and amenorrhoea.

Key Term Eating disorders are one category of mental disorder. Individuals with eating disorders have some problem with food, for example they may overeat (e.g. obesity), undereat (e.g. anorexia), or vomit repeatedly (ruminative disorder). There is evidence that such disorders may have a genetic basis but are also triggered by environmental stressors.

Anorexia nervosa

Key Term Anorexia nervosa is literally a 'nervous lack of appetite'. The main characteristics are as follows.

- There is a deliberate and prolonged **restriction of calorie intake** and considerable weight loss (weight falling to less than 85% of normal weight).
- They have an intense **fear of gaining weight**, but anorexics are often very hungry and preoccupied with food.
- Anorexics have a **disturbed body image** – they usually continue to see themselves as overweight despite large weight loss.
- It is accompanied by **amenorrhoea** (no menstrual cycle).
- It is largely a problem of **middle-class**, **adolescent girls** (although the percentage of males is increasing).
- It is sometimes seen as a **modern problem**, however Tolstrup (1990) documents cases prior to 1600, when the condition was described in connection with religious life.
- Two types of anorexia have been identified: the **restricting type** (constant fasting) and the **binge eating/purge type** (those who periodically binge and purge). The 'restricting type' tend to be more introverted, younger, and deny their distress.

One difference between anorexia and bulimia is that anorexics are characteristically concerned with perfection, whereas bulimics suffer from a constant craving for food/attention.

Bulimia nervosa

The DSM-IV lists five key characteristics of bulimia: binge, purge, frequency, body-image and that it occurs independently of anorexia.

Key Term Bulimia nervosa is a more common problem than anorexia and probably more related to dieting. The main characteristics are as follows.

- It is characterised by periods of **compulsive bingeing** followed by forced vomiting or the use of laxatives or other means (**purge**).
- Binge-purge eating is reasonably common among dieters, i.e. some dieters eat a lot and then make themselves sick. However, when it occurs **more than 2 times a week** for over 3 months it is abnormal. The abnormal behaviour also involves eating enormous amounts of **high-calorie food** and then purging.
- Bulimics are **obsessed about their weight**, though it is usually nearer normal than anorexics. Most of them are within 10% of their correct body weight.

Explanations of anorexia nervosa

 AQA A   U2

Biological (medical) explanations

Genetic transmission

Twin studies illustrate this. Holland *et al.* (1984) found a 55% concordance rate for identical (MZ) twins compared with only 7% for non-identical (DZ). See also Holland *et al.* (1988) below.

Evaluation

The fact that not all MZ twins develop the disorder means that genetic transmission cannot be the sole explanation.

Biochemical abnormalities

Disordered hormones may be a cause. Amenorrhoea may occur before weight loss, which suggests a disorder of the endocrine system. Fava *et al.* (1989) found changes in the levels of serotonin and also noradrenaline in anorexics.

Neuroanatomy

Damage to the hypothalamus may result in a loss of appetite, as well as disturbances to menstruation.

Evaluation of biological explanations

Strengths

- Biological models can explain why anorexia is related to adolescence – because it is a time of hormonal change.
- The diathesis-stress model proposes that **genetic vulnerability** must be part of the explanation, though there also needs to be some trigger ('stress').

Weaknesses

- Biological explanations can't explain the **recent increase** in cases of anorexia.
- It isn't always possible to distinguish **cause and effect**.

AQA (A) Key study: Biological explanation of anorexia nervosa

Holland *et al.* (1988) Evidence for a genetic basis

Aims This study aimed to find out whether anorexia nervosa is related to genetic factors. One way to investigate this is to look at twins who develop the disorder. If anorexia is genetic then we would expect more MZ twin pairs to develop anorexia than DZ twin pairs because they have identical genes (whereas DZ twins share 50% of their genes). Both kinds of twins are assumed to share the same environment during development.

Procedures Twin studies are natural experiments. The participants in this study were 34 pairs of twins (males and females) and one set of triplets. Participants were selected because they were a twin and one member of the pair (or triplet) had been diagnosed with anorexia nervosa at a London hospital. Genetic relatedness (i.e. whether they were MZ or DZ) was established by blood group analysis or by use of a physical resemblance questionnaire. Both twins were interviewed to establish presence or absence of an eating disorder, and this data was used to confirm or diagnose anorexia.

Findings Far more MZ twins (56%) were concordant for anorexia nervosa than DZ pairs (7%). Concordant means that both members of the pair had the disorder.

In three cases the partner twin was found to have had other psychiatric illnesses, and two others had minor eating disorders.

Conclusions These findings suggest that anorexia has a strong genetic basis because it occurred more when individuals shared the same genes than when they were simply related. However, concordance was not 100% which suggests that genes simply predispose individuals to develop an eating disorder (or other disorder). Only in certain circumstances (environmental triggers) does anorexia develop.

Criticisms Since the twins were reared together they also shared environmental influences and this may be greater for MZ twins who look and behave more similarly than DZ twins, and therefore are treated more the same.

It could be that one twin imitates the twin who developed the disorder first. However, some of the twins developed the disorder when living in separate countries. This would also not explain the difference between MZ and DZ twins.

Progress check

1 Suggest one limitation with the biological explanation for anorexia.
2 Suggest one strength of the biological explanation.

2 E.g. supported by twin research.

1 E.g. can't account for recent increases.

Psychological models: Psychodynamic explanations

Family systems theory

> In early childhood the child first establishes his or her identity. This is the first period of 'individuation'. During adolescence this process starts again.

Minuchin *et al.* (1978) suggested that anorexic's families are **enmeshed**. The members don't have a clear identity and the family finds it hard to resolve conflicts. This leads to anxiety which may be projected onto the 'ill' child, i.e. the eating disorder arises as a means of dealing with family conflict. Humphrey *et al.* (1986) did find that such families have more negative and fewer positive interactions than families with a normal adolescent.

Autonomy

Anorexics tend to be somewhat obsessive personalities, with low self-esteem and a fear of their own autonomy. Bruch (1987) suggested that certain mothers wish their daughters to remain dependent and therefore encourage anorexia. Anorexia develops as a means of asserting autonomy by exerting control over their body. The fact that most anorexics come from middle-class families where there are high expectations supports this.

Evaluation of psychodynamic explanations

Strength

The role of autonomy could explain why anorexia **is common during adolescence**. Blos (1967), a psychodynamic theorist, proposed that adolescence is a time of reindividuation.

Weaknesses

- Psychodynamic theories can't explain the **recent increase** in anorexia.
- Parental conflict may be an **effect rather than a cause** of anorexia.
- The accounts are difficult to prove wrong (**falsify**).

> Adolescence may be a prime time for anorexia because it is then that girls especially are aware of making themselves attractive. They also often put on weight with puberty and this triggers off slimming.

Psychological models: Behavioural explanations

Classical conditioning

Leitenberg *et al.* (1968) suggested that anorexics have learned that eating is associated with anxiety, because eating too much makes people overweight.

Operant conditioning

Weight loss is reinforcing because people praise it (positive reinforcement) and the individual has escaped from an aversive stimulus (negative reinforcement).

Social learning theory

Feminine stereotypes in the media and the current emphasis on dieting promote a desire to be thin which is exaggerated in vulnerable individuals. This explanation is supported by cross-cultural studies, see the key study by Lee *et al.* (1992) on p.126.

Evaluation of behavioural explanations

Strengths

- Social learning theory can account for **increased incidence** of anorexia.
- Conditioning theory can explain how the disorder is **maintained**.
- **Behavioural therapies have been successful** in treating anorexia.

Weakness

- **Social factors alone** can't explain anorexia because otherwise more people would suffer from it.

Psychological models: Cognitive explanations

Distortion of body image

Garfinkel and Garner (1982) found that anorexic patients typically overestimate their body size compared with 'normal' controls. This distorted thinking may explain why they lose more weight than normal individuals.

Evaluation of cognitive explanations

The disordered thinking may be an *effect* rather than a cause of anorexia.

AQA (A) Key study: Psychological explanation of Anorexia nervosa

Hennighausen *et al.* (1998) Distorted perception of body shape

Aims Previous research has not consistently found that anorexic patients overestimate the size of their body or body parts in comparison with controls. Some studies have found no difference and others have found large inaccuracy. These inconsistent findings have led to a suggestion that the body-shape criteria be dropped from the DSM. This study aimed to investigate the importance of body shape.

Procedures The participants were all female, 36 anorexic patients and a matched control group of 18 patients who had diagnosed mental disorders but not any that might produce perceptual distortions (e.g. schizophrenia).

Participants were asked to record (1) their real body image (RBI) and (2) their ideal body image (IBI). This was done using a computer representation of each patient in a swimsuit which could be altered on screen to change the measurements.

Participants were also given an eating disorder questionnaire to complete.

Findings There was no significant difference between the anorexic patients and the control group for RBI but there was a significant difference for IBI.

Many anorexic patients correctly estimated their real body size, as did the control patients. However, some anorexic patients over- or under-estimated their real body size considerably.

Both anorexic and control preferred a slimmer ideal body shape than they actually were. Despite this, the controls expressed lower body dissatisfaction on the eating disorder questionnaire.

Conclusions The findings show that anorexic patients do not systematically overestimate their body size, which challenges this criteria in the DSM. However, the individual differences in anorexic patients may be significant. It may be that some anorexic patients have some form of perceptual disturbance.

The findings also indicate that all women have a desire for thinness but controls are not as dissatisfied about this. The key factor in anorexic patients may be the willingness to do something about this desire whereas the control patients accepted the discrepancy between actual and ideal body shape.

Criticisms The control group were also patients and therefore the findings cannot be generalised to normal individuals (low population validity). Mental patients may have disturbed body images because of low self-esteem.

This is a natural experiment as the independent variable (anorexic or not) varies naturally. This means that we cannot draw conclusions about cause-and-effect, i.e. that anorexia is the cause of disturbed perceptions.

Progress check

1 Name one psychodynamic explanation for anorexia.
2 How can operant conditioning explain anorexia?

2 Individuals are rewarded for weight loss and therefore continue to lose weight.

1 E.g. family systems theory.

Explanations of bulimia nervosa

There is a considerable degree of overlap in the explanations offered for anorexia nervosa and bulimia nervosa, so the following account will be less comprehensive.

Biological explanations

Genetic transmission

Kendler *et al.* (1991) found a 23% concordance rate for bulimia in identical twins compared with about 9% in non-identical twins (see detailed report below).

Biochemical abnormalities

Decreased serotonin activity may be responsible for bulimia. People with bulimia suffer specifically from carbohydrate craving (Turner *et al.*, 1991) and increased consumption of carbohydrates increases production of serotonin. This has led to the use of selective serotonin reuptake inhibitors (SSRIs) in the treatment of bulimia. Blouin *et al.* (1992) suggested that there is seasonal variation in bulimics similar to seasonal affective disorder, i.e. in the darker months they become depressed/more prone to binge/purge. This could be related to increased levels of serotonin.

Psychodynamic explanations

Family conflicts have also been identified in families with bulimics.

Behavioural explanations

- **Conditioning.** Rosen and Leitenberg (1985) suggest that bingeing causes anxiety; purging reduces that anxiety: a cycle which is reinforcing.
- **Social learning theory** explains **cultural differences.** For example, Nasser (1986) found that 12% of Egyptian women who were studying in London developed bulimia compared with no cases in Cairo.

Cognitive explanations

- **Disinhibition hypothesis:** Ruderman (1986) suggested that when a dieter has a rigid cognitive style they respond to situations of overeating by going over the top (becoming disinhibited). Once they have overeaten they purge to rectify their mistake.
- **Distorted body image:** Cooper and Taylor (1988) reported that bulimics usually show a substantial discrepancy between their estimation of their true body size and the size they would ideally like to be. This distorted thinking would encourage the desire to lose weight.
- **Coping style.** Vanderlinden *et al.* (1992) suggested that bulimics have a tendency to perceive events as more stressful than most people do, and use binge/purge as a means of coping with the stress or gaining a sense of control.

Progress check

1 What is the 'disinhibition hypothesis'?
2 Name one other explanation for bulimia.

2 E.g. genetic, socio-cultural factors (social learning).
1 Overeating results in a disinhibition of normal rigid self-control.

AQA (A) Key study: Biological explanation of bulimia nervosa

Kendler *et al.* (1991) Evidence for a genetic basis

Aims Kendler *et al.* sought to see whether bulimia (like anorexia) had a genetic basis. Evidence from the study of MZ and DZ twins was again used.

Procedures This was a natural experiment. Over 2,000 female twins were found using a register of American twins where one member of the twin pair had been diagnosed with bulimia. The other twin was interviewed and a diagnosis determined using standard criteria.

Findings In MZ twins there was 26% concordance between twin pairs and 16% for DZ twins. Of the sample interviewed, there were 123 cases of bulimia. Most of these participants also reported other mental disorders at some time in their lives including anorexia (10% of them), depression (51%), phobia (42%) and anxiety disorder (11%).

Conclusions This suggests that bulimia has a strong genetic component, though it is not as strong as found for anorexia. About half of the variation in bulimia is due to genetic factors and half to environmental factors.

The data also suggests that there is a link between all mental disorders. An individual may inherit a risk for mental disorder rather than just for bulimia, and life events act as triggers for specific disorders.

Criticisms Twins may not be representative. Klump *et al.* (1999) studied individuals with eating disorders who were MZ, DZ or non-twin and found differences between the groups in terms of the symptoms. This suggests that twins may not be representative of the general population for eating disordered behaviour.

A more recent study by Bulik *et al.* (2000) concluded that bulimia is 83% genetically influenced and anorexia nervosa is 58% genetic, which both supports and contradicts Kendler *et al.*'s findings. It is supportive because it is further evidence of a genetic cause. It is contradictory because it suggests a greater genetic component.

AQA (A) Key study: Psychological explanation of bulimia nervosa

Lee *et al.* (1992) Bulimia in Hong Kong chinese patients

Aims Lee *et al.* note that bulimia is rare among the Chinese living in Hong Kong. If it is a genetic disorder then we would expect the incidence to be the same in any country. This study aimed to consider the explanations for the low incidence.

Procedures This research study involves no direct investigation but is a review of other research and a consideration of possible explanations. Thus it is not empirical research but research through reasoning. It is a form of observation and qualitative research.

Findings
- Clinical psychologists in Hong Kong are unfamiliar with the disease and are not making the diagnosis.

- Obesity is rare among the Chinese and dieting is uncommon. Chinese girls do not have a fear of fatness (leading to anxiety) and fatness is even valued.

- The Chinese diet is generally low in fat whereas in the West fatty foods are desirable, but also associated with shame and guilt.

- There is less role-conflict among Chinese women because in their society success is more related to 'family' values than to a good personal appearance or career accomplishment.

- Less exposure to role models. Chinese women are not aware that self-induced vomiting is an effective method of weight control.

Conclusions The conclusion that can be drawn from these observations is that the rarity of bulimia nervosa in Hong Kong is related mainly to the absence of the relevant sociocultural factors. This, in turn, suggests that when bulimia is common it is due to sociocultural factors – factors in the society that enable the disorder to develop, such as fear of fatness, association between eating and guilt, role conflict for women and exposure to role models

Criticisms It is possible that cultural differences are due in part to genetic differences in predisposition to the disease. Biological (genetic) differences can be seen in the fact that the Chinese do tend to be slimmer than Westerners. Biological differences might make them less genetically predisposed to weight problems.

As this study is not an experiment we cannot claim that sociocultural factors cause bulimia. We can only consider the value of the arguments and look for supporting empirical evidence from other studies to confirm the findings.

Sample question and student answer

1

(a) Outline **two** attempts to define abnormality. [3 + 3]

(b) For **one** of the definitions in part (a) suggest **two** limitations to this definition. [3 + 3]

(c) 'Eating disorders, such as anorexia nervosa and bulimia nervosa, are becoming a major problem throughout the world'. Describe and evaluate **one or more** psychological explanations of eating disorders. [18]

> The question requires an outline of two definitions and the candidate has fulfilled this requirement. Both definitions are clearly outlined and accurate. (3 marks + 3 marks)

(a) One way to define abnormality is in terms of statistical norms. The standard for what is normal is set in terms of what most people in any population are like. Any behaviour that is statistically infrequent is then regarded as abnormal. A second way to define abnormality is in terms of mental health. This means that we say what kind of psychological behaviours are signs of good mental health, such as a lack of depression or a lack of distress. If these are lacking in an individual then they are psychologically abnormal.

> The candidate has identified two (possibly three) limitations. There would not be an extra credit for a third limitation but it adds to the detail provided for the first limitation described. The second limitation is adequate but an actual example of a behaviour (such as hearing voices) would have extended this answer. (3 marks + 2 marks).

(b) I will consider the statistical infrequency model. One limitation is that it overlooks the fact that many statistically infrequent behaviours are quite desirable, such as genius. At the same time some statistically frequent behaviours would be regarded as undesirable (such as overeating) and therefore should really be abnormal. A second limitation is that this definition is related to the culture that sets the norm. Behaviours that are statistically infrequent in one country (and therefore regarded as abnormal) might not be infrequent in another culture.

> Social learning theory is described in the first paragraph and used to explain eating disorders. This is all credited as description (AO1). The remainder of the answer evaluates (AO2) this explanation. This means there is about the right ratio of AO1:AO2 (1:3). The commentary is reasonably informed though no actual studies are cited, the candidate nevertheless displays a reasonable psychological knowledge and the structure indicates good skills of analysis (AO2=12 marks). The description is accurate but key details about social learning theory are omitted, such as reference to vicarious reinforcement (AO1=5).

(c) Cultural differences can be best explained with reference to social learning theory. People learn behaviour by imitating other people. If the other person is reinforced for doing something then the observer will be more likely to imitate the behaviour. If the other person is seen as highly desirable then it will also be more likely that they will be imitated. In our culture the ideal woman is portrayed by fashion models, rock stars and TV personalities who are very slim. Therefore, young girls want to imitate this in order to be desirable. In other cultures girls are not exposed to the same models and this would explain why there is less anorexia and bulimia — though the rates are increasing, which would be reasonable as other countries are more exposed to things like Barbie dolls and the Spice Girls.

However, this cannot be the whole explanation for eating disorders because then all girls would develop the disorder because we are all exposed to these role models. The diathesis–stress model suggests that mental disorders arise first of all because an individual has a genetic predisposition for the disorder (and studies show that MZ twins are more likely to develop anorexia than DZ twins). Second because of some environmental stressor(s). Therefore, in the Western world it is only those individuals who have both the vulnerability and the stress who will then be susceptible to the effects of role models. Perhaps in other cultures, other mental disorders develop.

The social learning account of eating disorders also can't really explain why it is adolescent girls who are especially effected, though it could be that they are at a time of their life when their self-image is most vulnerable and their increasing self-awareness means that they want to

Sample question and student answer (continued)

be slim. On the other hand, psychodynamic theories suggest that anorexia comes from a desire to be independent and do this by controlling one's body.

The social learning explanation can explain why girls more than boys are affected because there are fewer slim role models for boys — though this too may be increasing. [345 words]

TOTAL: 28 out of 30 marks

Practice examination questions

1

(a) Give **two** limitations of the 'statistical infrequency' definition of psychological abnormality. [3 + 3]

(b) Outline **two** assumptions of the psychodynamic model in relation to the causes of abnormality. [3 + 3]

(c) Outline and evaluate **one** psychological model of abnormality. [18 marks]

AQA A style question

2

People often use the term 'normal' without thinking what it means. Perhaps if we looked at what is said to be 'abnormal' behaviour we could learn something about what is said to be 'normal' behaviour. Using the Core Studies below answer the following questions:

      Rosenhan (sane in insane places)
      Freud (Little Hans)
      Sperry (split brain)

(a) Describe what each study tells us about 'abnormal' behaviour. [10]

(b) Comment on the problems that psychologists have when they investigate 'abnormal' behaviour. [10]

(c) How useful is it to distinguish 'normal' from 'abnormal' behaviour? Give reasons for your answer. [10]

OCR Core studies 2 January 2001

3

(a) Define the following terms:

    (i) superego [2]

    (ii) id [2]

(b) Study the table below, which summarises Freud's psychosexual stages of development. Then complete the table by filling the gaps with the most appropriate word or words. [4]

Stage	Age (years)	Distinguishing feature
Oral	0-1	
	1-3	Pleasure derived from controlling the expulsion of faeces
Phallic	3-6	
	6-puberty	Sexual desires repressed
Genital	Puberty-maturity	The onset of adult sexuality

(c) Assess **one** strength and **one** limitation of the psychodynamic approach. [4]

Edexcel specimen paper

Chapter 6

Social psychology

The following topics are covered in this chapter:

- *The social approach*
- *Attitudes and prejudice*
- *Social influence: Conformity and minority influence*

- *Social influence: Obedience to authority*
- *Critical issue: Ethical issues in psychological research*

6.1 The social approach

After studying this topic you should be able to:

LEARNING SUMMARY

- describe the key assumptions of the social approach in psychology
- evaluate the social approach in terms of its advantages and limitations
- discuss some of the methods used by the social approach

Key assumptions of the social approach

AQA A	U3
AQA B	U2
EDEXCEL	U1
OCR	U1, U2

The **social approach** is a contrast to the **physiological approach**, which focuses on internal bodily processes. The **cognitive approach** also focuses on internal processes but there is a '**social cognitive' approach** in psychology which seeks to explain the influence of others in terms of how social factors affect our thinking.

A sub-culture is a group of individuals living in one culture who share a distinct set of rules, morals, etc.

'Social' refers to any situation involving two or more members of the same species.

The assumptions of the social approach are that:

- An individual's behaviour can be explained in terms of the way that other **conspecifics** (members of your species) affect you.
- Other **individuals** may influence you. For example, you may imitate what others do (social learning theory) or obey someone else (see 'Obedience' on p.148).
- **Groups** of people may influence you. For example, people conform to group norms (see 'Conformity' on p.141).
- **Society** (culture) in general may influence your behaviour, e.g. methods of child rearing tend to be cultural or sub-cultural.

Social psychology is distinct from **sociology**, which is less concerned with the individual as a separate entity and more with the structure and functioning of reference groups such as the family and social classes.

Evaluation of the social approach

Weaknesses of this approach

- There is always a danger in relying on **one kind of explanation alone**. Social explanations, like all others in psychology, are unlikely to be the whole story. In a sense 'social' is equivalent to 'nurture', and we always need to consider the 'nature' (biological/physiological) explanations as well.
- In addition, the social approach **overemphasises the group** at the expense of individual psychology. For example, **social constructionists** aim to explain behaviour in the way that groups of people construct reality. The shared meanings held by groups influence behaviour. This approach overlooks the individual's role by focusing on group/cultural influences.

Strengths of this approach

- The social approach is a **major contribution** to psychology in that it involves the human element of the environment. There are social explanations within many other approaches, e.g. developmental social psychology.

Methods used in the social approach

Field experiments

Social psychology utilises field experiments to make conditions more naturalistic. The key feature of a field experiment is that participants do not know they are taking part in an experiment. There is still control of the IV, but extraneous variables are not as closely controlled. An example of a field experiment in social psychology (Piliavin *et al.*, 1969) is in the OCR core study on p.133.

Evaluation

The advantages and disadvantages of field experiments are discussed on p.161. It is important to recognise that such experiments overcome the problem of the psychology experiment as a social situation: issues such as **participant reactivity**, **demand characteristics** and **evaluation apprehension** are all social behaviours inherent in laboratory experiments.

Participant reactivity, demand characteristics and **evaluation apprehension** all concern the active involvement of the participant in research. They are discussed on p.171.

Surveys

Surveys (interviews and questionnaires) are also discussed later in this book (see p.161–163). Social psychologists often investigate people's attitudes and use attitude scales, a kind of survey (see p.132–133).

Evaluation

In brief, they enable large amounts of data to be collected but suffer from problems such as **social desirability bias** (the tendency to provide answers that make the interviewee appear nicer or better).

Discourse analysis

This methodology is related to social constructionism. The aim is to analyse discourses, i.e. the things people say or write (including music). Through such an analysis we can identify shared meanings and the things that influence behaviour. For example, one might analyse the lines of a popular song such as a lyric from a Beatles record of the 1960s to discover what the lyrics tell us about youth culture of that period.

Evaluation

This methodology is a contrast to the traditional experimental approach in psychology which aims to be objective. Discourse analysis recognises that objectivity is never actually obtainable and that intense scrutiny made of each discourse produces data that is as biased (or unbiased) as any other form of research.

Progress check

1 What is the main assumption of the social approach?
2 Suggest one drawback to the social approach.

2 E.g. the tendency to overlook biological or individual factors.

1 That behaviour can be explained in terms of the influence of two or more conspecifics (members of the same species).

6.2 Attitudes and prejudice

After studying this topic you should be able to:

L E A R N I N G
S U M M A R Y

- *outline the structure and function of attitudes, and the links between attitudes and behaviour*
- *describe and evaluate research into attitude change and persuasion*
- *explain the concept of stereotypes and the different kinds of prejudice that exist*
- *describe and evaluate research into the causes of prejudice and discrimination*

Attitudes

 U2

The word 'attitudes', refers to relatively permanent feelings and can be used to explain why people behave in certain ways.

Structure and function of attitudes

The structural approach

Attitudes have three components:

- **affective** – the extent to which you like or dislike a thing
- the readiness to **behave** in a certain way
- beliefs (**cognitions**) about the thing.

> If we put all three components together we have a definition for attitudes: 'A liking or disliking of an object based on cognitions about the object that leads to a readiness to behave in a certain way.'

The functional approach

Attitudes serve the following four functions.

- **Adaptive** – Attitudes help us to avoid unpleasant things and seek out favourable ones, e.g. feeling wary of dangerous sports might enhance your survival.
- **Knowledge** – Attitudes are part of our knowledge about the social world, and an integral part of stereotypes that help us simplify our social perceptions. (We look at stereotypes in a later section of this chapter.)
- **Self-expressive** – Attitudes are a means of expressing our emotions, we use them to show like or dislike.
- **Ego-defensive** (see 'The psychodynamic model on p.116) – Attitudes protect the ego by: (1) promoting a positive self-image through positive self-attitudes. For example, as a woman I make myself feel better by feeling good about women generally. (2) projecting feelings of threat or conflict onto others, (as in the case of prejudice).

Measuring attitudes

The Likert scale (Likert, 1932)

Probably the most widely used method, this involves, typically, about 30 statements being prepared on a topic, representing both pro- and anti- views. The respondent then rates each statement on a 5-point or 7-point scale.

A score is calculated by reversing the numerical value for anti-statements, and then adding the values up.

Semantic differential technique (Osgood *et al.*, 1957)

It is possible to measure the affective component of an attitude using bipolar adjectives. Respondents are asked to rate an attitude object, such as a person, thing or word.

This means that an attitude can be evaluated on **a number of different dimensions**, whereas the Likert scale only represents one dimension of an attitude (agreement or disagreement).

131

Projective techniques

Respondents are shown a picture and asked to give their interpretation. Their attitudes are projected on the picture and revealed in their descriptions.

- **The Rorschach test:** Respondents are asked to describe a set of standardised ink blots. Their responses are interpreted in terms of, for example, whether they have used the whole plot in their response, whether they have included unusual detail or whether they describe something animate or inanimate.
- **The Thematic Apperception test:** A series of pictures are presented and respondents are asked to make them into a story. The individual's story reflects their attitudes because the pictures are vague and open to all sorts of subjective interpretation.

Progress check

1 Name the three components of an attitude.
2 Which method of measuring attitude change represents one dimension only?

2 The Likert scale.

1 Affect, behaviour, cognition.

Attitudes and behaviour

Allport (1935) said 'Without guiding attitudes the individual is confused and baffled' – in other words, attitudes serve to organise behaviour. However, there is evidence that behaviour cannot be so simply predicted from attitudes.

Empirical studies

- LaPiere (1934) produced evidence that attitudes and behaviour are not consistent. He travelled around the USA for two years with a Chinese couple and noted that only once were they refused service by hoteliers. However, 92% of the same hoteliers claimed in response to a postal questionnaire that they did not serve Chinese. Critics have suggested that the fact that LaPiere was white and the Chinese couple were 'Americanised' may have affected the hoteliers' reactions.
- DeFleur and Westie (1958) asked white students to be photographed with black colleagues. Thirty per cent of the students behaved differently from their previously expressed views (either they were prejudiced and agreed to be photographed or were unprejudiced but refused to be photographed).
- On the other hand, Bagozzi (1981) questioned people about their attitudes, intentions and behaviour with respect to donating blood. He later checked to see which of his participants did actually give blood and found that, as expected, attitudes did affect intentions and ultimately behaviour.

So, what factors might lead to a discrepancy between attitudes and behaviour?

Availability

At any time your behaviour is a selection between possible courses of actions, and one attitude may take precedence over another. For example, a person may favour nuclear power but object to a nuclear power station being cited within view of their house.

Relevance

Our image of a prejudiced group may be different from the reality. In LaPiere's study, the Chinese couple spoke and dressed like Americans and were with an American, therefore they may not have been perceived as Chinese. Fishbein and Ajzen (1975) call this **correspondence**, the degree to which an attitude and action focus on identical objects in the same context at the same time.

OCR core study: Subway samaritan

Piliavin *et al.* (1969) Good Samaritanism: An underground phenomenon?

Aims In 1964, a young woman, Kitty Genovese, was murdered on her way home despite the fact that there were 38 witnesses. Why did no one help? It might be because there was a **diffusion of responsibility**. No one helps because everyone thinks someone else will do it. Latané and Darley (1968) conducted a laboratory experiment and found that as group size increased, helping behaviour decreased. This is called the **bystander effect**. Piliavin *et al.* wondered whether behaviour would be the same in a more naturalistic setting.

Procedures This was a field experiment: nearly 4,500 male and female passengers on a New York subway were observed on weekdays between 11 a.m. and 3 p.m. On average there were 43 people in a compartment on any one trial. Each trial lasted $7\frac{1}{2}$ minutes. On each trial, a team of 4 students boarded the train separately. Two females acted as observers, one male was a confederate and the other acted as a victim. There were four different teams, with a Black 'victim' in one of the teams.

> This study used an **opportunity sample** – a sample which is representative of a particular group of people. Can we make generalisations about all people from this data?

There were two experimental conditions used to test the hypothesis that 'People who are responsible for their own plight receive less help'.

- *'Drunk' condition:* The victim smells of alcohol and carries a bottle wrapped in a brown paper bag.
- *Cane condition:* The victim appears sober and carries a cane.

Seventy seconds after the train pulls out of the station, the male victim staggers and collapses. If no help is offered the confederate steps in to help after 70 seconds. The observers recorded how long it took for help to be forthcoming, as well as information about race and gender.

Findings The cane victim received spontaneous help 95% of the time whereas the drunk victim was spontaneously helped 50% of the time.

The cane victim was helped on average within 5 seconds whereas the drunk victim was helped after 109 seconds.

Black victims received less help less quickly, especially in the drunk condition.

The more passengers who were in the immediate vicinity of the victim, the more likely help was to be given. This is the reverse of the 'diffusion of responsibility' effect.

In terms of gender, 80% of the first helpers were males.

Conclusions Piliavin *et al.* proposed a **arousal-cost-reward model** to explain why people sometimes help, despite the presence of other bystanders.

- An emergency situation creates a sense of arousal in a bystander.
- The arousal can be reduced by helping (directly or indirectly).
- Help will not be forthcoming if the costs are too great, e.g. effort, embarrassment, disgusting experience, possible physical harm.

In the subway situation the **costs of not helping** (perceived censure from others) meant that people did help, whereas in the Kitty Genovese case the bystanders couldn't see each other and, in this case, the costs were too high and therefore help was not forthcoming.

OCR Revision question a) The subway Samaritan study was a field study. Describe **one** advantage and **one** disadvantage of conducting field studies and relate them to this study. [4] (January 2002, Core Studies 1, question 7)

Situation

If our personal attitudes run contrary to prevalent social norms we may well follow the crowd. Minard (1952) studied prejudiced whites in a West Virginian mining town. In a general survey only 20% admitted to having black friends. However, down the mines, where black and white worked together, 80% expressed friendship towards blacks. This can also be taken as an example of relevance.

Personality variables

A 'self-monitor' is someone who is very conscious of his or her behaviour.

Some people may be more or less consistent than others. Snyder (1979) found that low self-monitors behaved in consistent ways while high self-monitors are more influenced by the situation, and behaved in ways appropriate to the situation rather than their attitudes.

Theory of reasoned action (Ajzen and Fishbein, 1975)

This model was developed in relation to attitudes towards health behaviour and subsequent behaviour, but applies generally. An individual's behaviour (or rather their 'intention' to behave in a particular way) is determined by:

* perceived facts or beliefs about the behaviour, i.e. a person's attitude regarding the behaviour
* social or subjective norms that modify personal beliefs.

For example, smoking behaviour might be determined by 'smoking causes cancer' (a belief about the outcome) and 'my parents smoke' (a social norm) leading to 'I won't be so foolish' (an intention) which finally results in refusing a cigarette.

Evaluation

This model assumes that people behave rationally, whereas this is not always true.

Attitude change

Attitudes are resistant to change, but they do change. Methods of attitude change are of interest commercially (e.g. advertising) and in implementing new social policies (e.g. encouraging parents to have their baby vaccinated against whooping cough).

So, when and how do attitudes change?

Cognitive dissonance (Festinger, 1957)

Dissonance is 'a negative drive state which occurs whenever an individual holds two cognitions (ideas, beliefs, attitudes) which are psychologically inconsistent'. Dissonance leads to attitude change in order to restore a state of balance. Situations leading to dissonance include the following.

* **Forced-compliance or counter-attitudinal behaviour** – The classic cognitive dissonance experiment, conducted by Festinger and Carlsmith (1959), involved students performing a very boring task (turning pegs in a board). They were then asked to tell another participant who was waiting to do the task that the task was very interesting. Some of the participants were paid $20 others $1. When finally asked to rate the task, the more highly paid participants rated the task as boring whereas the low paid said it was enjoyable. The high paid have a reason for lying so they experience no dissonance, whereas the low paid have to overcome their dissonance by adjusting their assessment of the task.
* **Post-decisional dissonance** – These are the feelings of unease that arise after a person has made a decision. Such dissonance is reduced by enhancing the attractiveness of the elected choice. Brehm (1956) asked women to rate various household items in terms of their preferability, and then gave them one of their top two. When the women were asked to rate the items again, the rating for the one they now owned went up and the other went down.

Evaluation

- Dissonance produces novel and **counter-intuitive** predictions, and a great deal of interesting research.
- However, dissonance **can't be measured**, and it is difficult to identify the existence of a psychological state of tension as suggested by dissonance.
- The empirical findings can be explained in terms other than dissonance, e.g. Bem's (1972), **self-perception theory**. According to this theory, we acquire our attitudes by observing our behaviour in certain situations and thus we may also change our attitudes because we observe a change in behaviour. Attitude change occurs as a result of self-attributions not dissonance.

Persuasive communication

Persuasive communications aim to induce a person to adopt a particular set of values. Hovland *et al.* (1953) identified four basic variables called the 'Yale model'.

- **Source (who)** – e.g. power, expertise, credibility, motives, similarity, likeability and other personal attributes such as race and religion.
- **Message (what)** – Rhetorical questions, such as 'Isn't it clear that Daz is better than powder B?' are more persuasive. Where threats are made such as, 'smoking can kill', this may arouse a defensive response unless the viewer is given an effective means of avoiding the consequences. On the other hand, techniques using shock tactics, as in some of the drink-drive advertisements, have been successful.
- **Receiver (to whom)** – The more intelligent receiver is better able to remember the message, but also more likely to be more confident about already held attitudes and therefore more resistant to change. Sherif and Hovland's (1961) proposed a 'latitude of acceptance or rejection': where the view presented differs too much from the listener's initial stance, it is unlikely to be successful.
- **Context (where)** – whether the message is written, visual, spoken, audio-visual or face-to-face. It appears that more complex messages are best when written.

Evaluation

- Some of the original findings may be **oversimplifications**.
- Explains **when** and **how** people may change their attitudes but not *why*.
- People have a considerable ability to resist persuasion. One element in this is **reactance**: attempts to restrict or control personal decisions may lead to a move in the opposite direction.

Dual-process model of persuasion

Moscovici (1980) used the ideas of majority and minority conformity (described on p.146) to explain when attitude change is likely to occur. Moscovici claims that the two processes (majority and minority influence) are different in that:

- **Majority influence** is likely to result in a public change of behaviour but no private realignment as a result of normative and/or informational influences. This is because majority views are accepted passively.
- **Minority influence** produces conversion, i.e. a change of private opinion. This is because deviant ideas produce cognitive conflict and a structuring of thought. In a sense, obedience is a form of minority influence (see p.148)

Progress check

1 What is cognitive dissonance?
2 What two processes underlie the dual-process model?

2 Minority and majority influence.

1 The state of disequilibrium experienced when two conflicting attitudes are held.

Prejudice and discrimination

AQA B   U2
EDEXCEL   U1
OCR   U1, U2

The study of attitudes and prejudice comes within the area of **social cognition**, a branch of social psychology that joins cognitive psychology (how people think) with social psychology (the study of the interactions between people).

Clearly, this section on prejudice is related to the previous one on attitudes because prejudice is an attitude.

What is your stereotype of a bus driver? Do most people have similar stereotypes of a bus driver? How might you explain this?

A **prejudice** is a **biased attitude** towards others based mainly on group membership. Prejudice is literally the act of pre-judgement, an attitude held prior to direct experience about a group of people.

Discrimination is the behaviour arising from a prejudice, i.e. the manifestation of prejudice. Discrimination literally means to 'distinguish between', and prejudice leads you to distinguish between groups of people and favour one or the other group.

Stereotypes

Prejudices are often based on stereotypes. A stereotype is a social perception of an individual in terms of group membership or physical attributes rather than actual personal attributes. A stereotype is a fixed and often simplistic view of a group of people. Stereotypes are a kind of **schema**, organised packets of information.

Why do we have stereotypes?

They are an example of human cognitive processes: categorising, making generalisations and generating expectations.

How do stereotypes develop?

- **Social representations** – we learn them indirectly through exposure to cultural stereotypes in the media.
- **Conditioning** – we learn them directly through classical conditioning. Staats and Staats (1958) told participants to learn word pairs: a nationality name paired with another word. In one group, Dutch was always paired with a favourable word, and Swedish with an unfavourable word. This was reversed with the other group. When participants were asked to rate national groups this was correlated with the learned pairings.

Evaluation of stereotypes

- Their advantage is that they summarise large amounts of information and provide an **instant picture** from meagre data. We are 'cognitive misers' and stereotypes allow us to conserve cognitive energy.
- Their disadvantage is that they are, at least partly, **inaccurate** because they do not allow for exceptions and are based on superficial characteristics. They tend to be irrational, resistant to change and to lead to prejudice and discrimination.

Causes of prejudice

There are many explanations of how prejudice develops. We will consider three here.

Social identity theory (SIT)

A person's self-image has two components: personal identity and social identity. Social identity is determined by the various social groups to which you belong, such as your football club or your gender. There are three causal processes involved in the determination of social identity:

- **Categorisation:** we group people into social categories, which leads to the formation of in- and outgroups. This categorisation process simplifies interpersonal perception.
- **Social comparison:** comparisons are made between groups in order to increase self-esteem. **Ingroup favouritism** and **outgroup negative bias**

enhance social and personal esteem, and lead to biased perceptions of in- and outgroup members. Tajfel (1982) demonstrated this in his study of the minimal group (see OCR core study on p.139).

- **Social beliefs**: our beliefs/attitudes generate different social behaviours.

Empirical support

SIT generates various predictions that can be tested.

- **Illusion of outgroup homogeneity**: members of an outgroup are perceived as less diverse than members of the ingroup, thus confirming existing stereotypes. Linville *et al.* (1989) asked elderly people and college students to rate their own group and the other group in terms of traits such as friendliness. Both tended to perceive the ingroup as more differentiated (e.g. there were both friendly and unfriendly group members) and the outgroup as more homogeneous (all group members were much the same).
- **Reaction of group members to threat**: SIT would predict that individuals would enhance the perceived group differences as a means of coping with threat in order to maintain a positive social identity. Breakwell (1978) compared adolescent football fans who were classed as being fanatics or not. Those who were not fanatics might feel threatened when quizzed about being a fan because they might feel they weren't very good fans and therefore would be more likely to respond by emphasising their support – which was what the study found.

Evaluation of SIT

- It offers a **good explanation** of why members of an ingroup favour themselves over an outgroup, and that this might lead to prejudice.
- It generates a number of **testable propositions**.
- It can account for prejudice in situations of **minimal information**.
- It doesn't fully explain the **violence** associated with some prejudices.

Realistic conflict theory

Prejudice stems from direct competition between social groups over scarce and valued resources, such as unequal distribution of wealth, unemployment or disputes over territory. In- and outgroup attitudes are turned into hostility because the outgroup becomes the scapegoat for economic problems.

Empirical evidence

- **Robbers Cave Experiment** (Sherif *et al.*, 1961) is the classic study of how prejudice forms through the effects of in- and outgroup behaviour. Twenty-two White, well-adjusted, 11-year-old boys were selected to go on a summer camp for three weeks.
  - In Stage 1 the ingroup was developed. The boys were divided into two groups, they were given lots of co-operative activities and a sense of group identity (a name, hats and t-shirts).
  - In Stage 2 the groups became aware of each other and a tournament was organised (competition). There was aggression and fights after every match.
  - In Stage 3 the researchers resolved the conflict through co-operative activity involving superordinate goals, such as repairing a failed water supply.

  Three factors led to the prejudiced behaviour: ethnocentrism (in- and outgroups), competition and stereotypes.

- However, a similar study by Tyerman and Spencer (1983) observing an annual scout camp with conditions fairly similar to the Sherif study, concluded that the presence of competition did not lead to intergroup conflict and hostility.
- Hovland and Sears (1940) found a negative correlation between the number of lynchings (mainly Blacks) in the southern USA in the years 1882 to 1930 and the economic indices of the time. High aggression (measured by lynchings)

towards Blacks may be one consequence of prejudice. The economic index is an indication of frustration: when the price of cotton is low there will be fewer jobs and greater hardship.

Evaluation

- Prejudice is likely to exist prior to conflict, but **conflict is the trigger** to hostile behaviour.
- The theory **can be applied** to reducing prejudice by creating superordinate goals. Aronson *et al.* (1978) developed the jigsaw method to foster mutual interdependence. Schoolchildren worked in groups where each member had a piece of work to prepare and teach to other group members for an end-of-project test. This lead to moderate attitude change.

The authoritarian personality

Adorno *et al.* (1950) proposed that some individuals may be more prejudiced, conformist and obedient personalities. This hypothesis grew out of a desire to understand the anti-Semitism of the 1930s, believing that such prejudiced behaviour might be explained in terms of having an authoritarian upbringing and cognitive style. In order to test this, Adorno *et al.* developed a set of scales for testing authoritarianism, such as the potentiality for Fascism (F) scale. They tested about 2,000 White, middle-class Americans, finding that the authoritarian personality has the following characteristics:

- **Positive self-concept** of themselves, and of their parents.
- A **cognitive style** that tended to be rigid.
- **Values** that favoured law and order, and were more concerned with status, success, and traditional customs.
- A **personal style** that avoided psychological interpretations and tended to repress feelings.
- An **experience of child rearing** in which their parents tended to give conditional love, used strict discipline, expected unquestioning loyalty and were insensitive to the child's needs. Such experiences would create an insecure adult who respects authority and power, conforms more readily to group norms, and who may increase their self-esteem through ingroup favouritism (social identity). A person with repressed feelings will project these onto scapegoats (realistic conflict).

Evaluation

- This accounts for both the existence of **prejudices and the hostility element** which is often present in people who are highly prejudiced.
- There were a number of criticisms of the **data collected**, e.g. that the sample was biased, and some data was retrospective.
- There were also criticisms of the **questionnaires**, e.g. there may have been a response set on the F-scale (agreement leads to authoritarian-type answers), and authoritarianism of the left was overlooked.
- The study was **correlational** so we cannot say that parenting style *caused* the prejudiced personality.

> An authoritarian parenting style is one which relies on having a clear social hierarchy and expects obedience to those in authority.

Categories of prejudice

Racial prejudice

Moghaddam *et al.* (1994) note that some apparent racism may be in part explained by self-attitudes. They found that Haitians living in Canada overestimated the extent that they were outsiders and may expect to be rejected, and this led to a self-fulfilling prophecy.

Gender prejudice

Condry and Condry (1976) showed films of a baby, labelled alternatively as a boy or girl, and asked participants to rate emotional responses. They found that assumed gender led to different interpretations of the same behaviour. Fidell (1970) sent personnel profiles about a man or woman (e.g. Patrick or Patricia Clavel) to over 200 psychology professors – people who might have been expected to know better. The professors were asked to rate the applicants in terms of potential job prospects. They rated the man more highly. Mischel (1974) used the essay-assessment technique to show how gender affected rating of academic abilities, again favouring men (John was better than Joan) but only if the essay was on masculine topics such as law or city planning; women did better on essays related to dietetics or primary education.

Age prejudice

People hold negative stereotypes of the young, the old, the middle-aged – in fact, about all age groups. Such stereotypes may be held by people of all ages, including peers.

Progress check

1 What is 'ingroup favouritism'?
2 Which explanation of prejudice can account for the hostility sometimes associated with prejudice?

2 Realistic conflict theory or authoritarian personality.

1 The perception of your own social group as being more desirable/capable/successful.

OCR core study: Ethnocentrism

Tajfel (1970) Experiments in intergroup discrimination

Aims Is it possible to create discrimination (ingroup favouritism and outgroup negative bias) even where no prejudice exists? This would demonstrate social identity theory.

Experiment 1

Procedures A laboratory experiment with eight groups of boys, aged 14 to 15, from a school in Bristol.

1 **Establishing the ingroup:** The boys were told that the purpose of the experiment was to investigate visual judgements. They were shown slides of dots and for each slide asked to estimate the number of dots. They were then told whether they were over- or under-estimators (arbitrarily).

2 **The matrix game:** Each boy went to another room on their own, and was given a booklet containing 18 pages. On each page there was a matrix such as the one in the table below. Each boy had to tick one column in the matrix. For example, in the matrix below, the arrow indicates a choice of the column holding the numbers 4 and –9 (so member 74 would gain 4 points and member 36 would lose 9 points). This column choice would then determine the number of points awarded to members named on the left of the matrix (in our example, members 74 and 36). At the end each boy would receive their total number of points in real money.

Member no. 74 overestimator	12	10	8	6	4	2	0	–1	–5	–9	–13	–17	–21	–25
Member no. 36 underestimator	–25	–21	–17	–13	–9	–5	–1	0	2	4	6	8	10	12

Matrix used in Tajfel study (1970)

OCR core study *(continued)*

Findings When the matrix involved making an *inter*group choice, the boys tended to give more money to members of their own group.

When the boys had an entirely ingroup (or outgroup) choice to make, they tended towards the point of maximum fairness (this would be 0 and –1 in the example above).

Conclusions Boys awarded points on the basis of ingroup favouritism alone.

Experiment 2

Participants 48 boys in three groups of 16.

Procedures This time the groups were ostensibly divided on the basis of aesthetic preference (liking for art) of paintings by Paul Klee and Wassily Kandinsky. Different matrices were used in this second experiment because this time Tajfel did not want to look at the effect of relative weight in pulling decisions one way or the other. Instead, he wanted to assess three things:

- **Maximum joint profit (MJP):** the largest possible award for 2 people
- **Maximum ingroup profit (MIP):** largest possible award to ingroup member
- **Maximum difference (MD):** largest possible difference in gain between a member of ingroup and a member of outgroup, in favour of the former.

An example of one of these matrices is shown in the table below.

Member no. 74 of Klee group	19	18	17	16	15	14	13	12	11	10	9	8	7
Member no. 36 of Kandinsky group	1	3	5	7	9	11	13	15	17	19	21	23	25

In this case, if the participant was a member of the Klee group:
- *MJP would be a choice of 7 and 25*
- *MIP would be 19 and 1*
- *MD would be 19 and 1 (favouring the Klee group).*

Findings MJP exerted hardly any effect at all. In other words, boys did not make their choices on the basis of trying to give both parties their best joint deal.

MIP and MD exerted a strong effect. Participants always tried to give their ingroup members the best deal at the cost of the outgroup member.

In a situation where the choice was between two outgroup members, participants' choices were not as near the MJP as when choosing between two ingroup members. Participants were simply less fair with outgroup members.

Conclusions The experiments demonstrated the ease with which outgroup discrimination could be triggered, based on only minimal social identity.

Criticisms However, the participants were all adolescent boys (a biased group), they knew each other well, and there was not a great deal at stake.

OCR Revision question
a) From the study by Tajfel on discrimination, what are the key features of ethnocentrism? [2]

b) According to Tajfel, what are the minimum conditions for creating ethnocentrism? [2] (1999 Paper 1, question 10)

6.3 Social influence: Conformity and minority influence

Research into conformity

True independence is following one's conscience rather than being non-conformist. For example, Galileo's resistance to ideas of his time was healthy non-conformity (independence) whereas going round a roundabout in an anticlockwise direction is foolish.

Apparent non-conformity occurs when an individual is apparently not conforming to group norms but is, in fact, conforming to a different set of group norms. For example, wearing 'punk' clothes is conforming to another set of norms.

Definitions

Key Term   Social influence is the effect that other people have on each other. Psychologists study how these influences affect our behaviour and thoughts.

Key Term   Conformity (majority influence) is a change in behaviour as a result of real or imagined group pressure or norms. Kelman (1958) suggested that there are three kinds of conformity:

- **Compliance** – conforming with the majority, in spite of not really agreeing with them; public but not private change of opinions.
- **Identification** – conforming to the demands of a given role because of identification with that role, as in the behaviour of a traffic warden and in Zimbardo's prison study (see Haney *et al.* OCR core study on p.143). This kind of conformity generally extends over several aspects of behaviour. There still may be no change to personal opinion.
- **Internalisation** – personal opinion does change because the new norms are internalised.

Norms are the rules established by a group to regulate the behaviour of its members.

Empirical studies

Informational social influence

In many situations, especially social ones, there is no 'right' answer and therefore we look to others for **information**. This may change private opinion because the individual now regards the majority opinion as the correct answer.

Allport (1924) and Jenness (1932) found that people behaved differently in groups than when they were working alone. Participants shifted their individual judgements (about the pleasantness of odours or number of beans in a bottle respectively) towards group means after having group discussions.

Sherif (1936) used the autokinetic effect (a point of light moves erratically when viewed in total darkness) to demonstrate group influence. He showed the light to individuals and asked them to estimate how far and in which direction it moved. After about 100 trials the individuals had reached a consistent level of judgements. Sherif then asked groups of participants to work together. They were not asked to arrive at a group estimate but nevertheless, after a few exposures, the judgements of the group tended to converge and persisted when the individuals were tested later. The group performance had created a socially determined standard or norm. This convergence towards a norm is useful in ambiguous situations. It helps us know how to behave (i.e. **informational social influence**).

One psychologist asked a group of his students to try the following: go up to a stranger on an underground train and ask for their seat, offering no excuse. They all said they couldn't do it, which reveals the enormous inhibitory anxiety that ordinarily prevents us from breaching social norms (Tavris, 1974).

Normative social influence

People also conform because they want to be liked by the other members of the group, and also want to avoid being rejected. This may have played a part in Sherif's study. Normative influence is not likely to change private opinion. It may occur in various situations:

* In an **unambiguous** situation: see Asch's study, in the key study below.
* When conforming to **social roles**: see Haney *et al.*'s core study on p.143.
* Under **anonymous conditions** (public opinion not expressed). Crutchfield (1955) used a more efficient method than Asch, testing 600 participants using the **Crutchfield apparatus** (a cubicle with switches and lights). Participants are given a question, they can see the selection made by other (non-existent) participants, and are asked to register their own choice. When the question was clear-cut, 30% conformed. If the question was an insoluble mathematical one (therefore ambiguous), conformity was 80%. If the question asked for agreement or disagreement with a statement of opinion, 58% conformed. This demonstrates both informational and normative conformity.

Progress check

1 Define conformity.
2 What kind of conformity results in a change of personal opinion?.

2 Identification.

1 Change in behaviour as a result of real or imagined group pressure or norms.

AQA (A) Key study: Conformity (majority influence)

Asch (1952) Opinions and social pressure

Aims Asch suggested that Sherif's results were due to the fact that the stimulus was ambiguous. What would happen if there was no ambiguity? Would people still conform to majority opinion even if the answer required of them was clearly wrong? What would be the effect of social pressure?

Procedures This was a laboratory experiment that involved deception. The participants were 123 male college students, each paid $3. They were asked to take part in a study of visual perception. They were tested in groups of 7–9 participants. Each group was shown 2 pieces of card. One had a 'standard' line on it, the other had 3 lines of varying length. Each member of the group was asked to say out loud which line they thought was the same length as the standard.

In fact, all the members of the group except one were confederates. The true participant was the last but one to answer. On each trial the answer was clear. On the third trial, and several later ones, the confederates unanimously gave the wrong answer. There were 12 trials in all, half of which were 'critical' (the confederates gave wrong answers).

 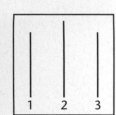

Participants were shown the line on the left and asked to state which of the three lines on the right was the same length.

Findings Approximately 75% of the participants conformed at least once, 5% conformed all of the time, 24% never conformed. The average rate was 37%.

Participants were interviewed afterwards and gave one of three reasons for why they did conform: (1) **distortion of perception** – they really did think their wrong answers were right, (2) **distortion of judgment** – they felt doubt about the accuracy of their judgment and therefore yielded to the majority view, (3) **distortion of action** – they didn't want to be ridiculed and therefore went along with the majority.

Conclusions This was astonishing evidence that some people are extremely willing to conform with group norms even when the answer is clearly wrong. However, it should be remembered that on two-thirds of the trials the participants remained independent, which is also clear evidence that people resist the pressure to conform at least in situations of certainty.

Criticisms This was a highly artificial situation. The consequences of complying were not harmful and the pressure to comply was great. In some real-life situations this would not be true. Venkatesan (1966) found that in some situations reactance is displayed – a reaction against a group norm (see page 146). In this study, groups of students were asked to select one of three identical suits. The true participant (last to register an opinion) conformed to majority opinion except when most of the confederates made statements strongly favouring one suit. When individuals feel forced to conform they may react by asserting their independence.

The participants' behaviour was due to normative social influence which is strong in a group of strangers, where the need to establish social contact is greater than the need to be correct. The same might not be true for established groups, though there may be other pressures to conform. However, Williams and Sogon (1984) found that conformity was even higher when they tested participants who all belonged to the same sports club.

Later variations

Asch conducted a number of subsequent variations and found the following.

- A group of three was sufficient to create the effect; larger numbers did not increase conformity.

- The presence of one dissenter cut conformity rates by 25%, even when the dissenter disagreed with the participant as well as the group. This is an example of minority influence (see below).

- Conformity increased if the group members were regarded as of high status.

- Conformity decreased if the participants were not face-to-face (see also Crutchfield, above).

OCR core study: Prison simulation

Haney, Banks and Zimbardo (1973) Stanford study of prisoners and guards

Aims Zimbardo questioned whether prison guards' behaviour was caused by the situation, or by the personality of the guards (a situational or dispositional explanation respectively).

Procedures This study involved role play and observation. A college newspaper advertisement sought male volunteers for a psychological study of 'prison life', to be paid $15 a day. There were 75 respondents who were given a series of psychological tests and interviews. The 24 most stable men were selected and randomly assigned to being a prisoner or a guard. There were 2 reserves and 1

OCR core study (continued)

This study first appeared in a scientific journal called the *Naval Research Reviews* (by Haney, Zimbardo *et al.*) because it was funded by the Office for Naval Research. Why do you think they might want to know about the behaviour of guards and prisoners?

dropped out, finally leaving 10 prisoners and 11 guards. They were all students, and largely middle-class.

The 'prisoners' were unexpectedly 'arrested' at home. On entry to 'prison' they were put through a delousing procedure, searched, given a prison uniform with ID number, nylon stocking caps, and an ankle chain. They were told to refer to each other only by number. They were in prison 24 hours a day.

The guards only referred to the prisoners by number. The prisoners were allowed certain 'rights': three meals a day, 3 supervised toilet trips, 2 hours for reading or letter-writing, and 2 visiting periods and movies per week. They had to line up 3 times a day to be counted and tested on the prison rules.

The guards had uniforms, clubs, whistles, handcuffs and reflective sunglasses (to prevent eye contact).

Findings Both guards and prisoners took, alarmingly, to their roles. For example:

Zimbardo's study is sometimes used when discussing obedience. The guards and prisoners were **conforming** to roles but the prisoners were also **obeying** the guards.

- The guards grew increasingly tyrannical. They woke prisoners in the night, locked them in a closet and got them to clean the toilet with their bare hands.
  Even when participants were unaware of being watched they played their roles – for example, prisoners talked among themselves as if they were prisoners.
- Five prisoners had to be released early because of extreme depression (crying, rage and acute anxiety). In fact the whole experiment was ended after 6 days, despite the intention to continue for 2 weeks.

Haney *et al.* tested the participants' personality and found no differences between the prisoners and guards. They did find that the participants who left early tended to have less conforming personalities.

Conclusions This was a remarkable demonstration of the strength of social norms and people's reluctance to 'disobey' them. Participants' behaviour was the result of normative social influence and identification rather than internalisation. It is most accurate to say that the participants complied rather than showed 'true' conformity (internalisation) since they probably did not change their personal beliefs.

The concept of **deindividuation** refers to losing one's sense of personal identity in certain situations, such as being in a crowd or when wearing a uniform or mask.

Haney *et al.* suggested that three processes can explain the prisoners final 'submission':

- *deindividuation:* the prisoners lost their sense of individuality. They even referred to themselves by number.
- *learned helplessness:* the unpredictable decisions of the guards led the prisoners to *give up responding.*
- *dependency:* the fact that the prisoners depended on the guards for everything emasculated the men and increased their sense of helplessness.

Learned helplessness is a condition where an individual learns to stop responding because, in the past their responses were ineffective. Therefore they learn that there is no point trying.

Criticisms *Ethics:* Participation in this study must have caused all participants emotional distress. One defence of this is that the extremes of behaviour could not have been anticipated at the outset.

Artificiality: It is possible that participants took on very specific role behaviours because that is what they were asked to do (**demand characteristic**). In real life a person might adapt a role to suit their personal beliefs and the requirements of the situation.

OCR Revision question In the prison simulation study by Haney, Banks and Zimbardo, features of the procedure led to the prisoners becoming dependent on the guards.

a) Identify **two** behaviours for which the prisoners were dependent on the guards. [2]

b) Describe **one** psychological effect this dependency had on the prisoners. [2]
(January 2001, Core Studies 2, question 3)

Evaluation of research into conformity

Experimental artefacts

This refers to features of the experiment which are artificial, for example:

- **Demand characteristics.** Participants behave in certain ways because features of the experiment 'demand' a typical response.
- **Desire to please the experimenter.** In Crutchfield's (1955) conformity experiment many participants said afterwards that they hadn't wanted to spoil the results so they had gone along with the others.
- **Experiments are social situations.** In Asch's (1955) study the participants expressed how much of an outsider they felt by dissenting. Belonging to the group is more important than correctness.

Ecological validity

To what extent do the results generalise to other situations and real life?

- **In real life** people sometimes have the option to simply do nothing, which may not be possible in an experiment.
- All of the experiments involved **strangers**. We may behave differently with individuals or groups who know us and we know them.

Child of the times

Social norms are always changing.

- Perrin and Spencer (1980) replicated Asch's study using British students but did not obtain evidence of conformity – concluding that today people may have learned to be more self-reliant.
- Doms and Avermaet (1981) did reproduce the same results as Asch and suggest that Perrin and Spencer's use of science and engineering students could have biased their results. It is also possible that Asch's findings became generally known (i.e. people have become aware of the tendency to be over-conformist in certain situations) and this new general knowledge has influenced the behaviour of participants in the more recent studies.

Ethical issues

These are discussed in the next topic section on p.154.

Why do people yield to majority influence?

The term 'majority' refers to the greater number. Norms can be determined by a majority or a minority. Minority influence is considered later.

Informational social influence

People like to be right and assume that if most people share a particular view, it must be right. The majority are assumed to supply correct information. Informational social influence operates especially in situations of ambiguity and may lead to internalisation.

Normative social influence

People want to be accepted by social groups and therefore seek to conform to the norms for that group. Normative social influence operates most when with groups of strangers and is likely to lead to compliance rather than internalization.

Individual differences

Some people are more likely to be conformist. There is evidence that women tend to be more conformist – for example, Eagly and Carli (1981) claim that women are more easily influenced than men but Eagly (1978) suggests that women may be more oriented towards interpersonal goals and thus *appear* more conformist.

Progress check

1 What is 'majority' influence?
2 Name two factors which might increase your willingness to conform to a majority opinion.

2 E.g. to be liked by others, because you are uncertain of the right answer.
1 When more than half of the people in a group share an opinion and this influences other individuals.

Minority influence

AQA A   U3
AQA B   U2

Key Term Minority influence occurs when a minority of people within a group hold an opinion different to the majority. Through the use of consistent yet flexible arguments a minority may change the views of the majority.

Moscovici (1980) claims that the two processes of majority and minority influence are different.

- **Majority influence** is likely to result in a public change of behaviour but no private realignment.
- **Minority influence** produces conversion, i.e. a change of private opinion. This is because deviant ideas produce cognitive conflict and a structuring of thought. Innovation of ideas must occur through minority influence and therefore this may be the more important kind of social influence.

Empirical studies

Moscovici *et al.* (1969) demonstrated minority influence in a classic study described on p. 147. This showed that consistency was important and that private rather than public opinion was more likely to change.

Flexibility is also important. Nemeth and Brilmayer (1987) arranged for a group to role play a jury considering the amount of damages to be awarded for a ski accident. When a lone minority refused to change his position, he had no effect on the opinion of others whereas a person who was prepared to shift in the direction of the majority exerted more influence.

Situational factors have also been found to be important. Moscovici and Nemeth (1974) found that a person who expresses a minority opinion is more likely to be influential if seated at the head of the table.

Minority influence is probably of more importance than majority influence in terms of social change.

Why do people yield to minority influence?

1 Personal characteristics of the minority

The minority must be *consistent* in their opposition to majority opinion, but influence is most effective if they show some *flexibility*. The minority must not appear to be rigid and dogmatic. A consistent and committed minority will lead people to rethink their position. Majority influence involves the reverse: compliance but not conversion/internalisation.

2 Relevance

The minority will be more successful if their views are in line with social trends (called the *zeitgeist*) and if the majority can identify with members of the minority (*social categorisation theory* – people are more influenced by those with whom they identify).

3 Snowball effect (Van Avermaet, 1996)

Minority influence starts by affecting one member of a group, and this begins to create doubt in the minds of other group members until gradually the minority becomes the majority. Sometimes there is a significant time gap in this process so that by the time the views become those of the majority people have forgotten the initial source of the influence. Perez *et al.* (1995) called this *social cryptoamnesia*.

AQA A Key study: Minority influence

Moscovici *et al.* (1969) Calling a blue slide green

Aims Research has tended to focus on the importance of majority influence yet such influence doesn't actually explain how change in opinion (innovation) comes about. Majority influence maintains the status quo, yet opinions and social trends do change. To what extent do people respond to minority influence?

Procedures This was a laboratory experiment involving deception. There were 32 groups of 6 people with good eyesight. Females were preferred because of their 'greater involvement in evaluating the colour of an object'. Two members of each group were confederates. Each group was shown 36 blue-coloured slides. They were told that the experiment was about colour perception and that they would be asked to report the colour aloud.

- Experiment 1: Two confederates in the group (the minority) consistently said that the slides were green. The confederates either answered first and second, or first and fourth.
- Experiment 2: A further 10 groups followed the same procedure as in experiment 1 and then afterwards were asked to do a similar task individually, writing down their answers. Moscovici *et al.* proposed that some individuals might conform to the majority publicly but privately might show a change of opinion.
- Experiment 3: The confederates answered 'green' 24 times and 'blue' 12 times, i.e. they were not consistent.
- Control group: In each experiment there were also control groups with no confederates.

> Why is it necessary to have a control group?

Findings The participants agreed with the minority view on 8.42% of the trials (i.e. they said the slides were coloured green). 32% agreed at least once (which, of course, means that 68% never agreed). There was no significant difference in relation to the position of the confederates. In groups where very few members gave the response 'green' in public, there was a greater number of 'green' judgements privately. When the confederates were inconsistent, agreement was reduced to 1.25%.

> Compare the rate of conformity in this experiment with Asch's study. In which study did participants show greater conformity?

Conclusions This shows that minorities can influence majority opinion. Consistent minority opinion had a greater effect than inconsistent opinion. The minority influence was stronger on private opinion than publicly expressed opinion, which is the reverse of majority influence.

Criticisms Moscovici claimed that consistency was sufficient for minority influence but that may not be so. Nemeth *et al.* (1974) replicated the above study but varied consistency by changing the confederates' responses on different trials. In other words, they didn't always say 'green' – on some trials they said 'green' and on others they said 'green-blue'. The minority had no influence at all under these conditions whereas when the confederates said 'green' to every slide there was 21% conformity.

This again was an artificial task and thus lacks ecological validity. The findings may not apply to real-life settings where there may be many other factors at work.

Progress check

1 What is a 'demand characteristic'?
2 Name one factor which can explain minority influence.

2. E.g. consistency, or flexibility.
1 A feature of the experimental situation which invites participants to behave in a particular way.

6.4 Social influence: Obedience to authority

After studying this topic you should be able to:

- describe and evaluate research studies of obedience to authority, including Milgram's work
- discuss issues of ethics and validity in the context of obedience research
- explain the psychological processes involved in obedience
- explain why people may resist obedience (independent behaviour)

LEARNING SUMMARY

Research into obedience to authority

AQA A	U3
AQA B	U2
EDEXCEL	U1
OCR	U1, U2

Conformity and obedience both involve changing behaviour in response to social influence. Conformity is a response to group pressure (whether majority or minority). Obedience is to a single individual or law.

Obedience

Key Term Obedience to authority is behaving as instructed but not necessarily changing your opinions. Usually it is in response to individual rather than group pressure, though you might obey group norms. Obedience happens when you are told to do something, whereas conformity is affected by example.

Research studies

Milgram's laboratory research

Milgram's first study (1963, see OCR core study on p.150) showed surprisingly high levels of obedience: 65% obeyed every order even when it threatened the life of the 'victim'. Milgram (and others) conducted a number of subsequent variations, each of which inform us about the conditions under which obedience is likely to take place.

- **Proximity of 'learner':** If the 'teacher' was placed in the same room as the 'learner' and had to press the learner's hand on the shock plate, obedience fell to 30%.
- **Proximity of experimenter:** When instructions were given over the phone the 'teacher' often said they were giving the shocks when they weren't. Overall, 21% of 'teachers' continued to obey.
- **Perceived authority:** When the experiment was conducted in a run-down building rather than a prestigious university setting, obedience fell to 47.5%.
- **Individual differences:** The experiment was repeated with over 1,000 participants from all walks of life. It was found that educated participants were less obedient, and military participants were more obedient.
- **Social support:** If the 'teacher' was paired with two other 'teachers' who dissented, then only 10% of the real participants continued to 450 volts.
- **Deindividuation:** Zimbardo (1969) arranged for the learner to be introduced to the participant and to wear a name tag, or to wear a lab coat and hood. The latter condition led to more electric shocks.
- **Cultural differences:** Milgram (1961) repeated his research with French and Norwegian participants and found differences. Smith and Bond (1993) report a number of cross-cultural replications with different rates of obedience, for example 85% in Germany and 40% for male Australians. It is likely that such studies did not exactly replicate Milgram's study.
- **Gender differences:** Milgram found that female participants were equally obedient but Kilham and Mann (1974) found much lower conformity rates in Australian women (12% compared to males at 40%).

Field studies

- **Nurses:** Hofling *et al.* (1966) conducted a more real-life experiment where

People often express surprise at the unexpected results of these studies because people appear to be much more obedient than we expect. This is the result that is often overlooked: the surprise is that we are surprised by human behaviour! This is the value of psychological research compared with reasoned argument – we may produce counter-intuitive findings.

nurses were told to administer a drug to a patient. The instruction they received was contrary to their rules: nurses were not permitted to accept instructions over the telephone, nor from an unknown doctor, nor for a dose in excess of the safe amount. Nevertheless, 21 out of 22 nurses obeyed the order (95%). Nurses defended themselves by saying it often happens, a doctor would be annoyed if they refused. However, their behaviour might be interpreted as conforming to expected role behaviour rather than being obedient.

- **Obedience to a uniform:** Bickman (1974) arranged for experimenters to be dressed casually, or in a milkman's uniform, or a guard's uniform which made them look like a police officer and to issue orders to order New York pedestrians (e.g. 'Pick up this bag for me', 'This fellow is overparked at the meter but doesn't have any change. Give him a dime'). Participants were most likely to obey the experimenter dressed as a guard, which supports the finding that obedience can be related to the amount of perceived authority.

Role play

Meeus and Raajmakers (1995) told participants that they were investigating how interviewers handle stress. The participants were the interviewers and were given statements that aimed to humiliate the interviewees (confederates) such as 'This job is too difficult for you'. The confederates were instructed to appear progressively more distressed, finally pleading for the interview to stop and refusing to answer any more questions. Nevertheless, twenty-two out of the total of twenty-four participants delivered all 15 'stress remarks'.

Evaluation of obedience research

Milgram's study has been criticised because it lacked internal and external validity, and ignored ethical considerations.

Experimental validity

Key Term **Experimental validity** is the extent to which the experimental set-up is believable. Experimental validity includes both internal and external validity. 'Internal' refers to what goes on inside the experiment and 'external' refers to what goes on outside the experiment. If experimental validity is low then the findings of a study are meaningless.

Internal validity

- Orne and Holland (1968) claimed Milgram's participants must have been aware that **something didn't add up**. Why wasn't the experimenter giving the shocks himself? However, in a replication of Milgram's experiment by Rosenhan (1969), nearly 70% of participants reported that they believed the whole arrangement – i.e. that this was a genuine learning experiment.
- Orne and Holland also suggested that obedience was a **demand characteristic** of Milgram's experiment. Participants obeyed because they entered into a social contract, and also because obedience is a natural feature of the experimenter–participant role.
- **Mundane or experimental realism.** The artificiality of an experiment means that it lacks mundane realism (it doesn't seem real). However, this can be overcome if it has experimental realism, i.e. the experiment is so engaging that participants are fooled into thinking the arrangement is real rather than artificial. Milgram argued that his study had both. Obedience to authority is the same whether the setting is artificial or occurring more naturally outside the laboratory, therefore the experimental design does have mundane realism. The experiment must have been highly engaging in order for the participants to behave in the way that they did, therefore there is also experimental realism.

A demand characteristic is a feature of an experiment that invites participants to behave in certain, predictable ways. Participants are susceptible to such cues because they want to know how they are expected to behave.

External validity

Any aspect of a study which means we cannot generalise from the study to other settings, or other people, or to other periods of history threatens the usefulness or validity of the findings.

Key Term **Ecological validity** is the extent to which the experimental findings can be generalised to real life and other settings. Milgram's study has been said to lack ecological validity because it was conducted in a laboratory environment which lacks realism. However, the findings have been replicated in many other settings, which is not true of the study by Hofling *et al*. This latter study may apply only to the particular doctor–nurse relationship and thus lacks ecological validity whereas Milgram's study may apply to obedience relationships much more generally, and thus is higher in ecological validity.

Population validity is the extent to which experimental findings can be generalised to other people. Milgram's study lacked population validity because it concerned US men.

Ethical considerations

These are discussed in full in the next topic section on p.154. Using role play is an alternative to conducting an experiment. However, even though participants are playing a role, as in Meeus and Raajmaker's study (see above) and Zimbardo's study (see p.143–144), this did not overcome problems of deception or distress because participants experienced both. It is also difficult to know whether individuals don't actually *exaggerate* their behaviour in such situations and therefore the study would be low in ecological validity.

> Some people feel that field studies such as Hofling *et al*. have greater ecological validity than Milgram. However, this study only shows that *nurses* are obedient to *doctors* not that people in general are obedient to authority. In addition, attempts to replicate Hofling *et al*.'s study have not been successful (e.g. Rank and Jacobsen, 1977) and this suggests that the results cannot be generalised.

Progress check

1 Name one researcher who has investigated obedience, besides Milgram.
2 What is internal validity?

2 The extent to which an experimental arrangement/design is believable.

1 E.g. Hofling *et al.*, Zimbardo, Langer *et al.*

OCR core study and AQA (A) Key study: Obedience to authority

Milgram (1963) Behavioural study of obedience

Aims Obedience is generally reasonable except when it is to unjust authority. Will people inflict great harm simply because they are ordered to do so? History provides much evidence to suggest that they will, most infamously the behaviour of some Germans in response to their Nazi leaders. Would ordinary Americans behave in the same way, or are Germans different?

Procedures This was a controlled observation. Forty males, aged between 20 and 50, whose jobs ranged from unskilled to professional. They were all volunteers, recruited through newspaper advertisements or flyers through the post. When they arrived for the supposed memory experiment they were paid $4.50 at the onset and introduced to another participant, who was in fact a confederate of the experimenter. They drew lots for their roles, though the confederate always ended up as the 'learner' while the true participant was the 'teacher'. There was also an 'experimenter' dressed in a lab coat, played by an actor.

The 'learner' was strapped in a chair in another room and wired with electrodes. After he has learned his list of word pairs given him to learn, the 'teacher' tests

> This experiment is one of the most well known in psychology, probably for two reasons: first of all because of the 'shocking' findings and, second, because of the subsequent ethical objections to it.

him by naming a word and asking the 'learner' to recall its partner from a choice of four possible answers. The 'teacher' was told to administer an electric shock every time the 'learner' made a mistake, increasing the level of shock each time. There were 30 switches on the shock generator marked from 15 volts (slight shock) to 450 volts (danger – severe shock).

The learner gave mainly wrong answers and for each of these the teacher gave him an electric shock which was received in silence until they got to shock level 300. At this point the learner pounded on the wall and then gave no response to the next question. When the 'teacher' turned to the experimenter for guidance, he was given the standard instruction, 'an absence of response should be treated as a wrong answer'. After the 315-volt shock the learner pounded on the wall again but after that there was no further response from the learner – no answers and no pounding on the wall. If the teacher felt unsure about continuing, the experimenter used a sequence of 4 standard 'prods', which were repeated if necessary:

> It is questionable as to whether this study is an experiment. Can you identify an independent and dependent variable? An independent variable is one manipulated by the experimenter in order to observe its effect on some dependent variable.

- Prod 1: Please continue.
- Prod 2: The experiment requires that you continue.
- Prod 3: It is absolutely essential that you continue.
- Prod 4: You have no other choice, you must go on.

If the teacher asked whether the learner might suffer permanent physical injury, the experimenter said: "Although the shocks may be painful, there is no permanent tissue damage, so please go on."

If the teacher said that the learner clearly wanted to stop, the experimenter said: "Whether the learner likes it or not, you must go on until he has learned all the word pairs correctly. So please go on."

Findings

No one stopped below the level of intense shock. 22.5% stopped at 315 volts (extremely intense shock). 65% of the 'teachers' continued to the highest level of 450 volts.

> Would you have obeyed? The survey prior to the experiment suggests that people think participants wouldn't obey, yet, in reality, people do.

Prior to the experiment Milgram asked 14 psychology students to predict the naïve participants' behaviour. The students estimated that no more than 3% of the participants would continue to 450 volts.

The participants showed signs of extreme tension: most of them were seen to 'sweat, tremble, stutter, bite their lips, groan and dig their finger-nails into their hands'. Three even had 'full-blown uncontrollable seizures'.

All participants were debriefed, and assured that their behaviour was entirely normal. They were also sent a follow-up questionnaire. 84% reported that they felt glad to have participated, and 74% felt they had learned something of personal importance.

Conclusions

Participants showed obedience to unjust authority beyond what anyone expected. The sheer strength of obedience and the tension created by the social pressure to obey were surprising.

Criticisms

Milgram suggested various reasons why obedience was so high, such as the prestigious environment (Yale University), and that the participant believed the experimenter is earnest in pursuit of knowledge and therefore obedience is important. In short, features of the experimental set up enhanced the tendency to obey (demand characteristics).

Later variations

Further experimental variations (Milgram conducted 21 in all) and a full evaluation of the study are reported in the text. (See p. 148)

OCR Revision question

In this study of obedience, Milgram encouraged the participants to continue with the electric shocks.

a) Outline **one** way in which Milgram encouraged his participants to continue. [2]

b) Describe **one** way in which the findings of the Milgram study can be applied to social control in everyday life. [2] (January 2002 Core Studies 2, question 2)

Why do people obey?

AQA A — U3
AQA B — U2
EDEXCEL — U1
OCR — U1, U2

Obedience to authority does depend on what you are being asked to do. It is obedience to *unjust* authority which especially needs to be explained. In many situations obedience and conformity are healthy and appropriate responses.

Situational explanations

A socially obedient environment

In some environments it is the norm to obey authority, whereas in others it is not. Individuals have past experience of being rewarded for obedience, so we obey because that is what we have learned to do. There are roles that require obedience, such as being a nurse or being an experimental participant.

Graduated commitment

A person may be unaware of obedience before it's too late. In Milgram's study the shocks increased by only 15 volts each time, what does one more step matter? Having obeyed initially, to a small request, **binding factors** ensure continued obedience.

The agentic state

Milgram (1974) proposed that the participant becomes an 'agent' of the person in authority. When an individual is in an agentic state they cease to act according to their own conscience and lack a sense of responsibility for their actions. The opposite is true of an **autonomous state**.

Uncertainty

In some situations, such as the psychology experiment or many occasions in real life, we are not sure how to behave and therefore we respond to social cues (**demand characteristics**).

Dispositional explanations

The authoritarian personality

Adorno *et al.* (1950) proposed that some individuals are more likely to be obedient (and conformist) because of the way they were brought up – see p.138.

Need for social approval

Crowne and Marlowe (1964) used the Marlowe-Crowne Social Desirability Scale and found that those low in need for social approval were less likely to conform in an Asch-type experiment.

Resistance to obedience

AQA A — U3

There are some situations and individuals who do not obey. In Milgram's study 35% disobeyed. What factors explain independent behaviour?

Empirical studies

Gamson *et al.* (1982) showed that individuals will rebel against authority when there is the possibility of collective action. In this study, volunteers were placed in groups of 9 and each group asked to listen to evidence against Mr C. The participants were ostensibly employed by a (fictitious) public relations firm, MHRC, which was collecting evidence of community opinions to use against Mr C. The groups soon realised that they were being manipulated to produce a tape of false evidence. All of the groups rebelled (stopped producing evidence) but some still signed an affidavit giving MHRC permission to use the video tape in a trial. This shows that, when sufficient numbers take a rebellious stance, the whole group conforms to this. However, in some groups the majority of people did not have anti-authoritarian values. Therefore, despite the fact that some members had expressed rebellion, the whole group signed the affidavit.

Venkatesan (1966) found that in some situations reactance is displayed – a reaction against a group norm. In this study, groups of students were asked to select one of three identical suits. The true participant (last to register an opinion) conformed to majority opinion except when most of the confederates made statements strongly favouring one suit. When individuals feel forced to conform they may react by asserting their independence.

Why do people resist obedience?

The same reasons that can be used to explain obedience can be used to explain resistance – for example, the presence of an authority figure leads to obedience and the lack of sufficient authority leads to resistance. Other explanations include the following.

Rebellion

As in Gamson *et al.*'s study, (p.152) groups may feel more able to resist unjust authority because group members know there is a possibility of collective action.

Increasing one's sense of autonomy (reversing the agentic shift)

Individuals can be reminded that they (not the authority figure) are responsible for their actions. Hamilton (1978) found that under these conditions, agentic shift was reversed and sharp decreases in obedience could be obtained.

Past experience

One of Milgram's participants, Gretchen Brandt, rebelled because she said she had witnessed the ill-effects of obedience growing up in Nazi Germany. Milgram (1974) suggested that the painful memories had taken her out of her agentic state.

Individual differences

Krech *et al.* (1962) suggested that independent people tend also to exhibit the following traits: to be more intelligent, less anxious, have more realistic self-perception, be more self-contained and more original. Crowne and Marlowe (1964) found they had less need for social approval. Burger and Cooper (1979) found that non-conformers had a higher desire for personal control. Stang (1972) found that high self-esteem was related to independence.

Progress check

1 What is the 'agentic' state?
2 Suggest one personality characteristic associated with independent behaviour.

2 E.g. high self-esteem, high desire for personal control.

1 When an individual ceases to act according to their own conscience.

6.5 Critical issue: Ethical issues in psychological research

Ethical issues

AQA A	U3
AQA B	U1
EDEXCEL	U3
OCR	U1, U2, U3

Key Term Ethical issues are dilemmas that arise in psychological research where there are a conflicting set of values concerning the goals, procedures or outcomes of a research study. Examples include deception, lack of informed consent and protection from psychological harm.

Deception

Key Term Deception is dishonesty. Participants should never be deliberately misled without extremely strong scientific or medical justification. It is reasonable to expect to be fully informed when you agree to take part in psychological research. However:

Deception is sometimes relatively harmless

This is the case in some memory experiments, e.g. Mandler (see p.37) did not inform participants that their memory would be tested. Christiansen (1988) reported that participants don't object to deception as long as it isn't extreme.

Deception is sometimes necessary

In the conformity and obedience experiments, knowledge about the purpose of the research would have made the studies pointless.

On occasion deception can be justified

For example, when there are no alternative, deception-free ways of studying an issue.

How would you feel if you had been a participant in Asch's or Milgram's research? Would you feel aggrieved about the deception?

Debriefing is vital

After the study participants should be informed about the deception, and have the opportunity to withdraw their data. In field experiments (such as Bickman's p.149) this is not always possible. Both Milgram and Asch thoroughly debriefed their participants. Milgram's participants reported that they did not regret taking part but Freudian theory might explain this as an ego defence (dealing with anxiety through denial).

Informed consent

Key Term Informed consent should be given wherever possible. Participants should consent to take part and this should be based on having all the information necessary in order to decide whether or not to take part, i.e. being informed about the nature and purpose of the research and their role in it.

Participants can only give informed consent when they know:

- All aspects of the research that might reasonably be expected to influence their willingness to participate.

- Their rights, e.g. to confidentiality, to leave the study, and to withhold their data.

Such consent is not possible when:

- Deception is involved.
- Participants are unable to fully understand, such as is the case with children or participants who have impairments that limit understanding. An alternative is to seek informed consent of, for example, a parent.
- In field experiments or observational studies, when participants are not even aware that they are taking part in a psychological research.

Possible alternatives are:

- Presumptive consent – seeking approval from the general public prior to an experiment, as Milgram did. If others approve, then it is presumed the actual participants would also have agreed.
- Prior general consent – seeking general approval from participants. Gamson *et al.* (see p.152) asked all prospective participants if they would be willing to take part in research on any of the following:
  - brand recognition of commercial products
  - product safety
  - research where you will be misled about the purpose until afterwards
  - research involving group standards.

  When participants agreed to all four they were then informed that only the latter kind of study was in progress. They had agreed to be deceived.
- Role play or questionnaires – participants are asked to behave as if they were in a certain situation (role play) or to state how they would behave in certain situations (questionnaires). However, this is likely to be unreliable. Consider the findings from Milgram's prior survey (people *said* they wouldn't obey).

Compensatory procedures

- The right to withdraw – Milgram did tell participants that they could leave at any time and not forfeit their money. However, in reality, they were ordered to continue by the standardised 'prods'.
- The right to withhold data – during debriefing, participants can decide to withhold their data – in essence asserting their right to informed consent to have participated.

Aronson (1988) argued that there might have been no ethical objections to Milgram's research if the findings had been less distasteful. In other words, it was the findings rather than the methods which were distasteful.

Psychological harm

Key Term Protection of participants from psychological harm includes protecting participants from loss of self-esteem, ridicule, stress and anxiety. The risks should be no greater than in ordinary life.

- Baumrind (1964) criticised Milgram for the stress and emotional conflict experienced by participants. Milgram defended himself by saying that he expected very low levels of obedience; before the experiment he had asked psychiatrists, students and ordinary people how participants would behave. They thought that at most only 3% of the participants might go as far as 450 volts.
- Asch's participants also experienced distress. Evidence for this was obtained by Bogdonoff *et al.* (1961), who found that the participants in an Asch-type study had greatly increased levels of autonomic arousal.

Risks no greater than in ordinary life

This means that participants should not be exposed to risks greater than or additional to those encountered in their normal life styles. A classic study by Watson and Raynor (1920) involved making a loud and unpleasant noise near an infant's head and thus creating a fear response. They argued that the baby (Little Albert) was not exposed to anything more than an ordinary experience. However, Genie's mother (see p.72) objected to the extensive testing her daughter was subjected to, saying that it caused her undue distress.

Progress check

1 When is deception acceptable?
2 What is presumptive consent?

The use of ethical guidelines

AQA A	U3
AQA B	U1
EDEXCEL	U3
OCR	U1, U2, U3

Key Term Ethical guidelines are a set of rules produced by a group of professionals to 'police' themselves and deal with ethical issues. The British Psychological Society (BPS) has a set of ethical guidelines for human and non-human animal research, as well as for clinical practice. The same is true in other countries (e.g. the American Psychological Association). There are also Home Office regulations for the use of non-human animals in research.

The BPS guidelines for research with human participants

This is a summary of the main points.

Introduction

Ethical guidelines are necessary in order to clarify the conditions under which psychological research is acceptable. In all their work psychologists shall conduct themselves in a manner that does not bring psychology into disrepute.

General

The investigation should be considered from the standpoint of all participants. The best judge of whether an investigation will cause offence may be members of the population from which the participants in the research are to be drawn.

Consent

Participants should be informed of the objectives of the investigation and all other aspects of the research which might reasonably be expected to influence their willingness to participate. Special care needs to be taken with children or with participants who have impairments.

Deception

Intentional deception of the participants over the purpose and general nature of the investigation should be avoided wherever possible.

Debriefing

The investigator should provide the participants with any necessary information to complete their understanding of the nature of the research and should discuss their experience in order to monitor any unforeseen negative effects or misconceptions.

Withdrawal from the investigation

Participants should be aware from the outset of their right to withdraw from the research at any time. Participants also have the right to withdraw any consent retrospectively, and to require that their own data be destroyed.

Confidentiality

Subject to the requirements of legislation, information obtained about a participant during an investigation is confidential unless otherwise agreed in advance.

Protection of participants

Investigators have a primary responsibility to protect participants from physical and mental harm, no greater than in ordinary life.

Observational research

Studies based upon observation must respect the privacy and psychological well-being of the individuals studied. Unless those being observed give their consent to being observed, observational research is only acceptable in situations where those observed would expect to be observed by strangers.

Giving advice

During research, an investigator may obtain evidence of psychological or physical problems. An appropriate source of professional help advised.

Colleagues

A psychologist who believes that another psychologist may be infringing ethical guidelines should encourage the investigator to re-evaluate the research.

An evaluation of the use of ethical guidelines

How effective and useful are such guidelines?

Infringements

The severest penalty is disbarment from one's professional organisation.

Universal ethical truths

Ethical guidelines suggest some universal 'truths' yet the guidelines vary in different countries and with respect to changing social attitudes. For example, the French code concentrates on fundamental rights rather than on conducting research.

The cost–benefit analysis

Inevitably, ethical decisions involve weighing costs (e.g. harm to participants, infringement of rights, financial considerations) against benefits (e.g. what the research can tell us about behaviour). Diener and Crandall (1978) have identified the following problems with this.

- **It is difficult to predict costs and benefits prior to conducting a study:** In Milgram's study there was no expectation that participants would continue, and therefore the potential stress (costs) was not anticipated. Also, the ultimate findings (benefits) were not anticipated.
- **It is hard to quantify costs and benefits**, even after a study, because such judgements inevitably require subjective judgements (what one person regards as harm differs from another's view).
- Cost–benefit analyses tend to **ignore the rights of individuals** in favour of practical considerations because one is focusing on issues of, for example, benefits to human kind.
- Baumrind (1975) pointed out that **cost–benefit analyses inevitably lead to moral dilemmas**, yet the function of ethical guidelines is precisely to avoid such dilemmas.

Sample question and student answer

AQA A style question

(a) Outline **two** reasons why people yield to majority influence. [3 + 3]

(b) Describe the procedures and findings of **one** study that has investigated minority influence. [18]

(c) Outline ethical issues in obedience research and consider whether they have been dealt with effectively. [18]

A brief but accurate answer; the candidate has provided sufficient detail by using the technical language to gain 2+2 marks. For full marks examples might have been provided to give some extra detail to both explanations.

Many candidates make the mistake of simply writing everything they know about a study rather than focusing on the requirements of the question. In this case the candidate has provided accurate information about the procedures, though it could be more detailed. There is a minimal amount of information about findings (though there is no requirement for procedures and findings to be in balance). The final sentence is irrelevant. This answer would get 4 marks.

The candidate has structured this response nicely by identifying ethical issues and, at least sometimes, showing where these occurred in obedience research (the paragraph on informed consent is rather minimal). However, the first paragraph is largely a waste of time because they are no links to ethical issues except the last sentence which is little more than a list. This is followed by a number of good points made about deception and whether it was dealt with effectively in the context of three studies. Some further commentary is offered on harm. The final 'issue' is actually a guideline rather than an issue. However, this still leaves three creditworthy issues. Altogether the commentary is reasonable though slightly limited (AO2 = 10 marks). The ethical issues have been identified but not much descriptive detail is offered (AO1 = 4 marks). This may seem rather low marks for a long essay but it is not well focused on the question set. It could have been more exactly organised according to the question's demands.

(a) People yield to majority influence because they want to be right. This is called informational social influence. The second reason is that they conform because they want to be liked and fit in. This is called normative social influence.

(b) Moscovici asked people to describe what colour they thought a picture was. Six people took part and two of them were confederates. The two confederates always described the slides as green whereas they were actually blue. This minority of two affected the responses of the others. 32% conformed at least once. This is less than in Asch's experiment but it is a lot considering they were clearly wrong.

(c) Milgram found that 65% of his original participants were willing to administer the highest level of shocks to the 'learner'. For all the participants knew, they could have killed the person they were giving shocks to. In Milgram's film, one of them clearly said he thought he'd killed them. The ethical objections to this research include the issues of deception, informed consent, harm, and the right to withdraw.

The participants were deceived because they were not told the true purpose of the research. However, there would be no point conducting the study if they did know the true purpose. The ethical guidelines say that deception is acceptable if there is no alternative. Other studies of obedience have also had to use deception such as Hofling *et al.* and Bickman. Therefore it would seem inevitable that deception is used in this study.

One way to compensate for deception is to debrief participants afterwards so they do know the true aims of the experiment and they have an opportunity to withhold their data if they want to. Debriefing also provides an opportunity for the researcher to find out if the participant was harmed and to offer any extra support. Milgram did all of this after his experiment. However, in a field study such as Bickman's this was not possible.

One difficulty with this debriefing is that participants may feel even worse when they discover they have been cheated, and upset that they fell for the deception.

The second ethical issue is informed consent. If an experiment involves deception obviously participants can't give their informed consent because they do not know what is actually involved.

In terms of psychological harm, all obedience research involves high levels of anxiety and stress for participants. Just having to decide whether to obey, even though someone else is suffering, imposes great stress on a participant. Just debriefing someone afterwards doesn't remove the stress that they felt. They might say that they feel OK but they may be denying their true feelings. They may feel quite depressed about the way that they behaved. It is true that most of Milgram's participants said that they were glad to have participated and had learned something valuable.

The final ethical issue is the right to withdraw. Milgram told participants that they were free to go, yet the standardised prods made it very difficult for them to leave. In the field experiments such as Hofling's or Bickman's, participants were not aware of this right and couldn't exercise it anyway. [417 words]

TOTAL: 22 out of 30 marks

Practice examination questions

1

(a) Outline **two** psychological processes that might be involved in obedience. [3 + 3]

(b) Describe how psychologists have dealt with **two** ethical issues that have been evident in social influence research. [3 + 3]

(c) Consider whether findings from studies of conformity can be applied beyond the research setting. [18]

AQA A style question

2

(a) Explain what is meant by the term *compliance* when it is used to describe a type of conformity. [2]

(b) Give **three** examples of social norms which occur among groups of school pupils. [3]

(c) Describe **one** study in which obedience was investigated. Indicate why the study was conducted, the method used, results obtained and conclusion drawn. [5]

(d) Melvin is a member of a team of experts who are judging an art competition. Melvin favours a landscape painting for first prize. The majority of the group prefer an abstract painting, and try to persuade Melvin to agree.

Discuss **at least two** psychological factors which might influence whether or not Melvin will yield to group pressure. Refer to empirical evidence in your answer. [10]

AQA B May 2002

3

(a) Outline **one** reason why Milgram's study has been so controversial. [2]

(b) Outline **one** justification why Milgram carried out his study. [2]

OCR Core studies 1 January 2002

A 'theory' counts as any set of interrelated facts which in some way account for the behaviour. When you describe a theory you can draw on material about its implications.

4

(a) Define what is meant by the term obedience. [2]

(b) (i) Name **one** theory of obedience. [1]

(ii) Describe this theory of obedience. [4]

In this question the theory in parts (b) and (c) need not be the same one. Be sure to describe both a strength and a weakness.

(c) Evaluate **one** theory of obedience in terms of one of its strengths and one of its weaknesses. [4]

Edexcel specimen paper

Chapter 7

Research

The following topics are covered in this chapter:

- *Quantitative and qualitative research methods*
- *Research design and implementation*
- *Data analysis*

7.1 Quantitative and qualitative research methods

After studying this topic you should be able to:

- *distinguish between quantitative and qualitative methods of research*
- *give examples of and evaluate quantitative methods of research*
- *give examples of and evaluate qualitative methods of research*
- *outline the ethical issues involved in these research methods*

Quantitative research methods

AQA A	U3
AQA B	U1
EDEXCEL	U3
OCR	U3

The term 'research' means the process of gaining knowledge either through the use of theories (to explain a behaviour) or empirical data collection. In this chapter we will look at the methods of **empirical data collection**. ('Empirical' means something which is based on observed facts, i.e. data that is collected through direct observation.)

In **quantitative** research, the information obtained from the participants is expressed in numerical form. It is concerned with how much there is of something – i.e. the quantity.

In **qualitative** research the emphasis is on the stated experiences of the participants and on the stated meanings they attach to the data. It is concerned with how things are expressed, what a behaviour feels like and what it means – i.e. the quality.

Experiments

In an experiment the relationship between two things is investigated by deliberately producing a change in the **independent variable (IV)** and recording what effect this has on the **dependent variable (DV)**. The main features of experiments are:

- **Causal relationships** between the independent and dependent variables can be demonstrated.
- **Greater control** – features of the experimental environment can be controlled by the researcher.
- **Replication** – the study can be repeated because all variables have been identified and operationalised.

The terms quantitative and qualitative actually refer to the data collected, not the research method. Quantitative data is concerned with 'how much' whereas qualitative data provides non-numerical information ('what something is like').

The laboratory experiment

Advantages

- This is the **ideal form** of the experiment because there is the possibility of good control of all variables, especially extraneous ones.
- **Replication** is good. The IV is the variable that is manipulated by the experiment and the DV is the one that is measured.

Disadvantages

- In reality, **total control is never possible**. The results may be affected by, for example: extraneous variables, experimenter bias, demand characteristics, volunteer bias, sample bias.
- The laboratory experiment is an **artificial situation**, therefore the results may not generalise to real life (it lacks **ecological/external validity**).

Ethical considerations

- **Informed consent** isn't always possible.
- Participants may not truly be able to exercise their **right to withdraw**.
- Participants should not be subjected to **stressful** or negative manipulations.

The field experiment

This is an experiment conducted in more natural surroundings, where the participants are unaware that they are participating in a psychology experiment. The independent variable (IV) is still manipulated.

Advantages

- Greater **ecological validity** (in general).
- The technique **avoids experimenter bias** and evaluation apprehension because the participants are unaware that they are part of an experiment.

Disadvantages

- Inevitably, extraneous variables are **harder to control**.
- Some **design problems** remain, such as sample bias.
- It is **more time-consuming** and expensive than laboratory experiments.

Ethical considerations

- It is not possible to gain **informed consent** or usually to give **debriefing**.
- Participants may be **distressed** by the experience (especially because they are not aware that it is 'make believe').

The natural experiment

When comparing laboratory and field experiments you can see that each has advantages. Field experiments tend to have higher external validity whereas laboratory experiments have higher internal validity because of the greater control.

Natural experiments are sometimes called 'quasi-experiments' because they are not genuine experiments – which is what 'quasi' means (not quite the real thing).

If conditions vary naturally, the effects of an independent variable (IV) can be observed without any intervention by the experimenter. The research is still an experiment in the sense that a cause and effect are being identified, but it is not a 'true' experiment because:

- **the IV is not directly manipulated**; this means that one cannot be certain that the IV is the *cause* of any observed effect
- **participants are not randomly allocated to conditions**; therefore participants in different conditions may not be comparable.

Advantages

- It is the **only way to study cause and effect in certain situations** – for example, where there are practical and/or ethical objections to manipulating the variables (such as looking at the effects of deprivation).
- There is greater **ecological validity** (in general).
- If the participants are unaware of being studied, the technique **avoids experimenter bias**.

Disadvantages

- It cannot confidently establish **cause and effect** because so many other factors may influence the dependent variable (DV).
- A **lack of control** reduces internal validity. There may also be a lack of a suitable control group.
- It is not easy to **replicate** such studies, and may not even be possible.
- It can **only be used when conditions vary naturally**. Such conditions are not always possible to find.
- **Participants may be aware of being studied** and show improvements just because of this (the **Hawthorne effect** – see p.171).

Ethical considerations

- A natural experiment may involve **withholding treatment** from one group, as when a new educational programme is being tested and the research requires that one group of students do not have the new teaching method.

- If participants are unaware they are taking part, there is the issue of **informed consent**.
- **Researchers need to be sensitive** to the problems of participants in unfavourable circumstances that may surround the behaviour being studied, as in the case of deprived children.

Progress check

1 Name one difference between a laboratory and field experiment.

2 Name one difference between a laboratory and a natural experiment.

2 E.g. in a laboratory study the IV is directly manipulated by the experimenter.

1 E.g. field experiments involve more naturalistic surroundings, participants are not aware of being studied.

What is the difference between an experiment and a correlational study? We study co-variables rather than an IV and DV, and cause and effect cannot be determined.

Investigations using correlational analysis

In this method a numerical value (coefficient) is calculated to represent the degree to which two sets of data are correlated. The terms IV and DV are not used because one does not depend on the other. The variables are called **co-variables**. Perfect positive correlation is +1.00, perfect negative correlation is –1.00.

Advantages

- Can be used where **experimental manipulation would be unethical** or impossible.
- Indicates **possible relationships** between co-variables, and might suggest future research ideas which would look at possible causal relationships.
- Can **rule out causal relationships** – if two variables are not correlated than one cannot cause the other.

Disadvantages

- Does not establish **cause and effect**.
- The relationship may be due to other **extraneous variables**. For example, in an experiment trying to establish a relationship between diet and IQ, the extraneous variable might be parent's IQ because intelligent parents might supply a better diet.

Ethical considerations

- Causal inferences shouldn't be made but often this **misinterpretation** of the data does happen.
- This is especially important with relation to **socially sensitive issues**, such as IQ, which tend to rely on correlational data.

Interviews can produce qualitative data: in fact, **unstructured interviews** are *more* likely to produce qualitative data. So, it is difficult to categorise interviews and questionnaire surveys as being exclusively either quantitative or qualitative methods.

Interviews and questionnaire surveys

Interviews can be highly structured or little more than an informal 'chat'; they may be conducted face-to-face (interviews) or require written answers (questionnaires).

The structured interview

In these, all or most of the questions are decided beforehand. The questions may have a limited range of answers (e.g. 'Yes', 'No', 'Don't know').

Advantages

- Can collect information about people's **feelings and attitudes**, which cannot be obtained through observation or experiments.
- Requires **less skill** than unstructured interviews.
- Can be conducted on the **telephone**.

Disadvantages

- The interviewer's **expectations may influence** the interviewee's performance

The **halo effect** is the tendency to think that someone with one desirable characteristic also has other desirable characteristics, e.g. thinking that an attractive person is probably also nicer and more intelligent than someone who is less attractive.

Confirmatory bias refers to people's preference for things that confirm their existing stereotypes.

(halo effects, confirmatory bias, racial/sexual/ageist prejudices).

- People often don't actually know what they think and therefore their answers are **influenced by suggestion and response biases.**
- The method relies on self-report, which is open to problems such as **social desirability bias** (providing answers that make the interviewee 'look good').
- In comparison with unstructured interviews, the data collected will be **restricted** by a pre-determined set of questions.

Ethical considerations

- **Deception** may be necessary.
- Questions may concern **sensitive and personal issues.**
- **Confidentiality and privacy** must be respected.

The unstructured interview

The interviewer has a few questions, and lets the interviewee's answers guide subsequent questions. Clinical psychologists use this method with patients.

Advantages

- **Rich data** can be obtained.

Disadvantages

- It requires **well-trained interviewers,** which makes it more expensive to produce reliable interviews.
- Interviews may not be comparable because different interviewers ask different questions (**low inter-interviewer reliability**). Reliability may also be affected by the same interviewer behaving differently on different occasions.
- It is more affected by **interviewer bias.**

The questionnaire survey

Respondents record their own answers.

Advantages

- **Large amounts of data** can be collected at relatively little cost – both financial and in terms of time.

Disadvantages

- Answers may not be truthful (**social desirability bias**).
- Only **suitable for certain kinds of participants** – those who are literate and willing to spend time filling in a questionnaire, creating a biased sample.
- Designing questionnaires requires **considerable skill** (see p.169).

Progress check

1 What are the variables called in a study that uses correlational analysis?
2 What kind of interview is likely to produce the more qualitative kind of data?

2 Unstructured interview.

1 Co-variables.

Qualitative research methods

AQA A	U3
AQA B	U2
EDEXCEL	U3
OCR	U3

Observational studies

Naturalistic observation

Behaviour is observed in the natural environment. All variables are free to alter and interference is kept to a minimum. No IV is manipulated.

Advantages

- Study behaviour for the first time – observation is needed to **establish possible relationships.**
- It offers a way to study behaviour where there are **ethical objections** to manipulating variables.
- Gives a more **realistic picture** of spontaneous behaviour. It has high ecological validity.
- If the observer(s) remain undetected, the method **avoids most experimental effects,** such as experimenter bias, and evaluation apprehension.

Disadvantages

- It is not possible to infer **cause and effect.**
- It is **difficult to replicate** and therefore you cannot be certain that the result was not a 'one off'.
- It is not possible to **control** extraneous variables.
- **Observer bias:** the observer sees what he 'wants' to see.
- Where participants know they are being watched (disclosed observations) they may **behave unnaturally.** Even non-participant observers, by their mere presence, can alter a situation.

Ethical considerations

- Undisclosed observations preclude the right to **informed consent.**
- Disclosed observations may affect the individuals observed, creating **distress.**

Other kinds of observation

- **Experimental (controlled) observation:** Some observational studies are conducted in a controlled, laboratory environment. For example, Ainsworth's Strange Situation (p.62) and Milgram's 'experiment' (see p.150).
- **Participant and non-participant observation:** The observer may be a participant as well or may watch (non-participant).
- **Disclosed or undisclosed observation:** Participants may be observed through a one-way mirror (undisclosed) as in Bandura *et al.*'s study (see p.24).
- **Content analysis:** A detailed analysis of written or verbal material. Indirect observation of behaviour using, for example, books, diaries or TV programmes and counting the frequency of particular behaviours.

> Remember that observations may produce highly **quantitative** data. This is especially true for a content analysis.

Case studies

These are detailed accounts of a single individual, small group, institution or event. They might contain data about personal history, background, test results, and the text of interviews.

Advantages

- Only option when a behaviour is **rare.**
- Provide insights from an **unusual perspective** and rich data.
- Relate to real life (**high ecological validity**).

Disadvantages

- Usually involve recall of earlier history and therefore are **unreliable.**
- Close relationship between experimenter and participant introduces **bias.**
- **Cause and effect** are difficult to establish.
- Not a rigorous methodology: often unstructured and **unreplicable.**
- Limited samples, lack generalisability (**low in ecological validity**).
- **Time consuming** and expensive.

Ethical considerations

Confidentiality and **privacy** must be protected. Individuals should not be named.

7.2 Research design and implementation

After studying this topic you should be able to:

- *describe and use different kinds of hypothesis formulated when planning research and describe different sampling procedures*
- *outline issues around the identification and control of variables in research*
- *discuss methods of experimental design*
- *identify the features of good research design*

Planning research

AQA A	U3
AQA B	U3
EDEXCEL	U3
OCR	U3

When planning a research study there are various considerations to think about and these are described below.

Aims and hypotheses

Research aims are the stated intentions of question(s) that are planned to be answered.

A **hypothesis** is a formal, unambiguous statement of what you believe to be true.

- The **null hypothesis** (H_0) is a statement of 'no difference' or 'no relationship' between the populations being studied.
- The **alternative hypothesis** (H_1) makes a prediction about the effect of the IV on the DV. In the case of a study using a correlational design, the alternative hypothesis makes a statement about the relationship between the co-variables.
- A **directional** (or **one-tailed**) **hypothesis** predicts the direction of the effect.
- A **non-directional** (or **two-tailed**) **hypothesis** anticipates a difference or correlation but not the direction.

> An example of a null hypothesis would be 'Any difference/relationship that is found is due to chance factors alone'.

> An example of an **alternative hypothesis** in an experiment could be 'Participants recall more words from list A than list B'. This is directional. (The DV would be recall, the IV would be differences between list A and list B.)

Progress check

1. Is the following an example of a null or an alternative hypothesis: 'There is no relationship between variable A and variable B'?
2. Rewrite the following hypothesis so that it is non-directional: 'Younger participants do better on the test than older participants'.

2 'There is a difference in the performance of young and older participants in terms of their test performance.'

1 A null hypothesis.

Populations and sampling

The following list explains the terms used in relation to selecting samples for use in research.

- **Sample:** part of a population selected such that it is considered to be representative of the population as a whole.
- The **population** is the group of people from whom the sample is drawn. The population may be unrepresentative – e.g. selecting a sample from one school.
- **Sampling bias:** this occurs when some people have a greater or lesser chance of being selected than they should have, given their frequency in the population.

Sampling techniques (methods of drawing a sample)

- **Random sample:** Every member of the population has an equal chance of being selected, therefore it is an **unbiased sample**. This can be achieved using random number tables or numbers drawn from a hat. However, be aware that the population the sample is drawn from may be biased, e.g. if you take names from the phone book this only includes those people with telephones.

- **Systematic or quasi-random sample:** For example, using every 10th case or the name at the top of each page in the phone book. There is no bias in selection, however, every person does not stand an equal chance of being selected (therefore quasi-random).
- **Opportunity sample:** Selecting participants because they are available – for example, asking people in the street. This is sometimes mistakenly regarded as random whereas it is invariably biased.
- **Volunteer or self-selected sample:** Participants who become part of an experiment because they volunteer when asked. The results are likely to suffer from a volunteer bias because such participants are usually more highly motivated and perform better than randomly selected participants.
- **Stratified sample:** The population is divided in sections or strata in relation to factors considered relevant, for example, social class or age. The researcher then randomly selects a preset number of individuals from each strata.
- **Quota sample:** This also uses stratified methods but the sample is not randomly determined, because the researcher seeks any 5 individuals satisfying each criteria.

> Most research involves opportunity sampling. It is the easiest method in terms of both time and money.

Progress check

1 What method of sampling is unbiased?
2 What method of sampling is most commonly used?

2 Opportunity sampling.
1 Random sampling.

Research design

AQA A	U3
AQA B	U1
EDEXCEL	U3
OCR	U3

> In a study of the effects of stress on performance, some participants are given an impossible puzzle to solve, whereas others do an easy puzzle. Then all participants have to do further test (task B). In this case, the IV is the difficulty of the puzzle (task A) and the DV is the performance on the task.

Variables

Experimental variables

These are the ones that we are studying.

- The **independent variable** (IV) is the one which is specifically manipulated so that we can observe its effect on the **dependent variable** (DV). The DV is usually the one we are measuring or assessing.
- **Operational definition** is necessary in order to make a variable measurable and unambiguous. The definition is based on a set of operations or objective components. For example, hunger might be defined in terms of the number of hours since a participant last ate or a rating scale of how hungry they feel.
- **Levels of measurement** – variables can be measured at different levels of detail. Each level expresses more information about the thing we are measuring:
  - **Nominal** – data is in discrete categories, such as grouping people according to which kind of foods they prefer (Italian, American, Indian, etc.).
  - **Ordinal** – data is ordered in some way, for example asking people to put various food products in order of liking: spaghetti could be 1st, followed by burgers, sausages and liver. The 'difference' between each item is not the same, i.e. the individual may like the 1st item a lot more than the 2nd one but there might only be a small difference between the items ranked as 2nd and 3rd.
  - **Interval** – data is measured using units of equal intervals. For example, when using a centigrade temperature scale or any 'public' unit of measurement. Many psychological studies use **plastic interval scales**

> The key issue in interval data is that the intervals are equal and not arbitrary. The intervals reflect a real difference.

(Wright, 1976) where the intervals are arbitrarily determined and therefore we can't actually know for certain that there are equal intervals between the numbers.

- **Ratio:** There is a true zero point, as in most measures of physical quantities.

Participant variables

This refers to features of the participants, such as their gender, age, social class, and education. These characteristics are important when assessing the extent to which a sample is representative, and are also used when matching participants in a matched participant design (see p.168).

Participant variables can be controlled using **random allocation** to conditions. Any bias in placing participants in experimental or control groups can be overcome by randomly determining the group they are placed in.

Situational variables

Features of the situation which may interfere with the effect of the IV on the DV and 'spoil' the research result.

- **Extraneous variable:** anything that may unintentionally affect the dependent variable. These need to be controlled (as described below).
- **Confounding variable:** an extraneous variable that has not been controlled. There are two kinds:
  - **Constant errors:** e.g. testing the effects of noise on memory, all of those tested in the noise condition are tested in the morning whereas those tested in no noise condition are tested in the afternoon. Time of day is a constant error. Better performance may be due to time of day rather than lack of noise.
  - **Random errors:** features of the experiment that occur with no pattern. They occur equally in both conditions and are assumed to cancel each other out. For example, if participants are randomly allocated to groups one would presume that any individual differences are randomly distributed and we would not find all the brightest or oldest individuals in one group.
- **Controlling extraneous variables**
  - **Standardised procedures** are used to ensure that conditions are equivalent for all participants, this includes the use of **standardised instructions**.
  - **Counterbalancing** to control **order effects**. Give half the participants condition A first, while the other half get condition B first. This prevents improvement due to e.g. practice, or poorer performance due to e.g. boredom.

Progress check

1 What is the difference between an extraneous and a confounding variable?
2 When is counterbalancing used?

2 When order effects may affect performance.
1 A confounding variable is one that confounds the findings because it acts as another IV, whereas an extraneous variable is one that was potentially confounding but has been controlled.

Experimental designs

Repeated measures design

In this design the same participant is tested before and after the experimental treatment. Therefore all participants are tested twice, for example doing a memory test with and without noise. Performance on the DV is compared to see if there was a difference before and after.

Advantages
- Good control for **participant variables**.
- Needs **fewer participants**.

Disadvantages
- **Order effects** (e.g. practice or boredom) can affect final performance.
- Participants may **guess the purpose** of the experiment after the first test.

Independent groups design

In this design comparison is made between two unrelated groups of participants. The participants are in groups. One group receives the experimental treatment, the other doesn't (control group) or receives a different experimental treatment. Performance on the DV is compared.

Advantages
- Used **where repeated measures are not possible** (because otherwise participants would realise the purpose of the experiment).
- **No order effects** and other problems of repeated measures.

Disadvantages
- **Lacks control** of participant variables.
- Needs **more participants**.

Matched participant design

In this design participant variables are controlled by matching pairs of participants on key attributes. One partner is exposed to the IV, and both are compared in terms of their performance on the DV.

Advantages
- **No order effects** or other problems of repeated measures design.
- **Participant variables** partly controlled.

Disadvantages
- Matching is **difficult**, time-consuming and may waste participants.
- Matching is **inevitably inexact**.

Design of naturalistic observations

Observational studies require methods of categorising behaviour to ensure consistency and to reduce time taken in situations where it is limited.

Methods of recording data
- **Rating system**: score each individual in terms of degree, such as amount of interest shown.
- **Coding system**: a system of symbols or abbreviations is developed as a shorthand. Tick occurrences of target behaviours. These categories may be derived from earlier research, for example **ethograms** (a record of the behavioural repertoire for a particular species).
- **Diaries**: participants and/or observers keep a diary of events, either at the time or at the end of the day.
- **Sketches or photographs**: showing who or what is where.
- **Tape or video recording**: keep record of all data for later analysis.

Sampling techniques
- **Event sampling**: a list of behaviours is drawn up and a record made every time they occur.
- **Time sampling**: observations are made at regular intervals, such as once a minute.
- **Point sampling**: observe one individual for a fixed period of time, such as five minutes, and then move on to the next individual.

Design of interviews and questionnaire surveys

Attitude scales

See p.131–132.

Structured interviews/questionnaires

- Develop research aims.
- Develop sub-topics to investigate. A 'top down' approach should be used in generating questions – start with broad questions and break each down into a number of different specific behaviours.
- Question style
  - Avoid complex, ambiguous, negative, emotive, and/or leading questions.
  - Open versus closed: Open questions can have an infinite variety of answers (e.g. 'How do you reduce stress?') and are best for obtaining maximum information. Closed questions (with a limited range of answers) are best for ease of scoring.
  - Forced choice questions (e.g. 'Do you smoke to reduce stress?' Yes/No) may bias the results because participants can't give their real answer. 'Don't know' categories may get overused.
  - Filler questions: it may help to include some irrelevant questions in order to mislead the respondent from the main purpose of the survey.
- Sequence for the questions: It is best to start with easy ones, saving difficult questions, or ones which raise emotional defences, until the respondent has relaxed. Also, respondents may resist answering 'yes' or 'no' too many times in a row (response set).
- Write standardised instructions, and debriefing notes.
- Pilot run: The questionnaire should now be tested on a small sample; use feedback to redraft the questionnaire.
- Decide on sampling technique (see p.165–166).

Progress check

1 Which method of experimental design avoids order effects?
2 Name one sampling technique used in observational studies.
3 What is meant by a 'closed question'?

3 One that only has a limited range of possible answers.
2 E.g. event, time, point sampling.
1 Independent measures.

Factors associated with good design

AQA A	U3
AQA B	U1
EDEXCEL	U3
OCR	U3

Pilot studies

These are smaller, preliminary studies which makes it possible to check out standardised procedures and general design before investing time and money in the major study. Any problems can be adjusted.

Reliability

Reliability is the extent to which something is consistent or stable.

Internal reliability

This is the extent to which a measure is consistent within itself. It can be checked using:

- **The split-half method:** test is randomly divided into two halves so that each half is equivalent. Internal reliability is demonstrated by participants' scores being similar on both halves.
- **Item analysis:** compare performance on each item with overall score. Good correlation suggests high internal reliability.

External reliability

This is the extent to which a measure varies from one use to another.

- **Test-retest:** the same person is tested twice over a period of time. Similar scores demonstrate high external reliability.
- **Inter-rater reliability:** the ratings from more than one person are correlated to check for agreement.
- **Replication:** any research study should produce similar findings if repeated.

Validity

Validity is the extent to which something is true.

Internal validity

This is the extent to which something measures what was intended to be measured.

- **Psychological tests:** Is the test 'true'? Does it measure what it says it measures? For example, in the case of a test of anxiety – does it actually measure anxiety? This can be assessed using, for example:
  - **Face validity:** the items look like they measure what the test says it measures, for example on a creativity test, do the items look like they are measuring creativity?
  - **Criterion validity:** do people who do well on the test do well on other things that you would expect to be associated. For example, does someone who does well on an intelligence test also do well at school?
- **Research studies:** Internal or **experimental validity** is the extent to which the experimental procedure is believable (see p.149). It is the extent to which all extraneous variables have been controlled and that we can be certain that any changes in the DV were due to manipulation of the IV. In order to maximise this validity, one should attend to experimenter bias, demand characteristics, order effects (in repeated measures designs), participant variables (in independent measures), and any other confounding variables.

> The more control an experiment has (high internal validity), the less ecological validity it may have.

External validity

This is the extent to which the experimental findings can be generalised to real life and other situations (see p.150).

Progress check

1 Why are pilot studies useful?
2 Name one method of assessing reliability.
3 What is the difference between internal and external validity?

3 Internal validity concerns what is happening inside the experiment (e.g. demand characteristics) and external validity concerns what is external.

2 E.g. split-half technique, item analysis, test-retest.

1 To test that your procedures work.

Relationship between researchers and participants

Examples of the influence of researchers on participants

Note that the **experimenter effect** is different from the **experimental effect**, which is the effect of the experimental treatment.

- **Experimenter (investigator) effect or bias:** an experimenter has expectations about the outcome of an experiment and may indirectly and unconsciously communicate these to the participant (human or animal). This affects the participants' behaviour. Rosenthal and Jacobsen (1968) provided empirical support for this self-fulfilling prophecy in their study of the effects of teacher expectations on IQ performance.
- **The Hawthorne effect:** a person's performance may improve, not because of the experimental treatment, but because they are receiving unaccustomed attention. Such attention increases self-esteem and leads to improved performance. The effect is named after the Hawthorne electrical factory where it was first observed.
- **The Greenspoon effect:** participants are subtly reinforced by the experimenter's comments. Greenspoon (1955) was able to alter participants' responses by using subtle reinforcement of 'right' or 'wrong' answers. He said 'mm-hmm' whenever the participant said a plural word or 'huh-uh' after other responses. This led to increased or decreased production of plural words in random word-generation.
- **Demand characteristics:** those features of an experimental setting that 'invite' the participant to behave in particular ways. They bias a participant's behaviour. One example is the participant's attempts (not necessarily conscious) to guess what the experiment is about, and to do (or not do) what is expected of them. Orne (1962) tested this by telling participants they were participants in an experiment investigating sensory deprivation. In fact, they were not deprived at all, yet they displayed the classic symptoms of being so. In other words, they did what they were expected to do.

Reasons why participants are likely to be influenced

- **The experiment is a social situation:** participants prefer to behave in a socially acceptable manner. This is true even when performing anonymously or when answering questions on paper.
- **Active participants:** Orne (1962) argued that the picture of the participant as automaton is a foolish ideal. Participants actively search for clues about how to behave.
- **Evaluation apprehension:** a participant is aware of being 'tested' and wants to appear normal and to create a good impression. In order to overcome anxiety and uncertainty, the participant tries to guess what the experimenter really wants.

Ways of overcoming researcher and participant reactivity

- **Single blind technique:** participants are not informed of the aim of the experiment until after it is finished. This attempts to control participant bias.
- **Double blind technique:** neither the participant *nor* the experimenter are aware of the 'crucial' aspects of the experiment. This aims to avoid both participant and experimenter bias. (The experimenter is the person actually carrying out the research, whereas the investigator designs and directs the research.)
- **Placebos** are a control for the effects of expectations because participants think they are receiving the experimental treatment when they are not. They receive a 'treatment' which appears the same as the real thing but does not have its critical effects.
- **Undisclosed observation:** in a field experiment, and in some natural experiments, the participant has no expectations because they are unaware of being part of an experiment.
- **Standardised instructions:** these help to prevent experimenter bias by controlling what the experimenter says to the participants.

7.3 Data analysis

After studying this topic you should be able to:

- outline methods of analysing qualitative data
- define and evaluate measures of central tendency and of dispersion
- describe a method of representing correlational data
- explain the appropriate use and interpretation of graphs and charts

Analysis of qualitative data

AQA A	U3
AQA B	U1
EDEXCEL	U3
OCR	U3

A common criticism of this form of analysis is that it tends to be subjective. However, when the same data are analysed qualitatively by various people it becomes more objective.

Interviews

These may have open-ended questions and/or questions which are unstructured. Foster and Parker (1995) suggest the following possibilities for analysing the data produced by these:

- **'Giving voice'**: represent and/or summarise what the interviewee has said using selective quotations and describing the key details of the entire interview.
- **Grounded theory**: use the text to develop theoretical accounts of the interview data. What you write is 'grounded' in the text; it is 'theoretical' in the sense that it is an attempt to produce a coherent account of the facts. You might identify certain themes which recur, or categorise types of behaviour.
- **Thematic analysis**: organising the interview material in relation to certain research questions or themes that had been identified before the research started. This differs from 'grounded theory' in that the themes arise *prior* to the research. (Grounded theory comes out of the interview text.)
- **Discourse analysis**: aims to reveal how the text is organised by a number of competing themes or discourses (see p.130).

Observation

- **Quantitative analysis**: analyse data from time, event and point sampling using descriptive and inferential statistics.
- Produce a **detailed record** of observed behaviour ('giving voice').
- Produce **interpretations** (as above for interviews, e.g. thematic analysis, grounded theory), which may lead to further quantitative analysis.

Measures of central tendency and dispersion

AQA A	U3
AQA B	U1
EDEXCEL	U3
OCR	U3

Descriptive statistics are ways of *describing* the data so that the meaning of the data becomes more apparent, e.g. by reporting the mean or drawing a bar chart: you can see at a glance the meaning of the data.

Measures of central tendency

'Central tendency' refers to ways of giving the most typical or central value.

- **Mean**: Add up all the values and divide by N. *Advantage*: it is a sensitive measure. *Disadvantage*: it can be misleading with extreme values.
- **Median**: The middle or central value in an ordered list (see box below). *Advantage*: it is not affected by extreme scores. *Disadvantage*: it is not as sensitive because not all scores are used in calculation.
- **Mode**: The modal group is the most commonly used group. Bi-modal means two modes. *Advantage*: it is the only measure appropriate for nominal data. *Disadvantage*: it is not useful in data with more than one mode.

Measures of dispersion

'Dispersion' refers to the spread of the data.

- **Range:** the distance between lowest and highest value. *Advantage*: it is quick to calculate. *Disadvantage*: it is affected by extreme values.
- **Standard deviation:** The difference between each value and the mean is calculated, and then the mean of these differences is worked out. *Advantage*: it is the most accurate measure because it takes the distance between all values into account. *Disadvantage*: it requires extensive calculation and it is also not immediately obvious (whereas the range is).

Progress check

1 Which measure of central tendency would be suitable for nominal data?
2 Which measure of central tendency uses most of the data?
3 Which measure of dispersion is easiest to calculate?

1 The mode. 2 The mean. 3 The range.

Correlational data

AQA A	U3
AQA B	U1
EDEXCEL	U3
OCR	U3

Scattergrams are used to plot correlational data. Each pair of values is plotted against each other to show if a consistent trend is present. The correlation may be positive (trend from bottom left to top right), negative (trend from top left to bottom right) or none (even spread).

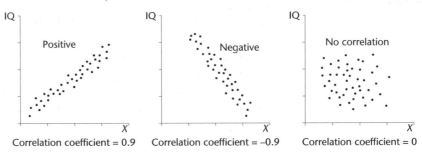

Correlation coefficient = 0.9   Correlation coefficient = –0.9   Correlation coefficient = 0

Graphs and charts

AQA A	U3
AQA B	U1
EDEXCEL	U3
OCR	U3

Methods which can be used with any level of measurement

- **Tables:** numerical data is arranged in columns and rows.
- **Bar charts:** a visual display of frequency, with the highest bar being the mode (see opposite). The data on the *x*-axis can be categories (nominal), i.e. not continuous. The *y*-axis represents frequency.

Spaghetti   Curry   Fish & chips
Fat food

Methods suitable for ordinal and interval data only

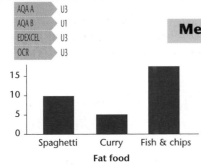

Score on memory test (out of 15)

- **Histogram:** this differs from a bar chart in that the area of the bars must be proportional to the frequencies represented, and the *x*-axis must contain continuous data (see opposite).

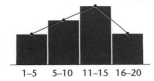

1–5   5–10   11–15   16–20

- **Frequency polygon:** the midpoint of each bar is joined to show continuous change; it is not suitable for data that is not continuous (see opposite).
- **Curved lines:** a sketch of an approximate line may be the best way to represent the data rather than using a jagged line graph.

Sample questions and student answers

A group of psychology students designed a memory experiment to investigate the effects of organisation on recall. Previous research has shown that organisation improves recall. The researchers gave one group of participants a list of words that was unorganised. A second group of participants were given the same words but the words were organised into categories.

After the list of words had been studied for 30 seconds, the word lists were collected back in and the participants were asked to write down as many words as they could remember. The findings from the study are displayed in Table 1.

Group 1: Unorganised list	Group 2: Organised list
10	15
11	16
11	16
13	17
14	18
14	19
16	19
18	20
18	21
27	23
	25
	25

Table 1: Number of words recalled after 30 seconds

(a) (i) Give an appropriate experimental/alternative hypothesis for this study. [2]
   (ii) State whether your hypothesis is directional or non-directional and justify why you choose this form of hypothesis. [3]

(b) (i) Name the experimental design used in this study. [1]
   (ii) Give **one** advantage and **one** disadvantage of this kind of design in the context of this study. [2 + 2]

(c) Suggest a suitable sampling method for this study and explain **one** strength of this method of sampling. [3]

(d) Identify **one** ethical issue that the students should have considered when designing their study and explain how they might have dealt with this. [1 + 2]

(e) Name **one** possible extraneous variable in this study and explain why this might affect the findings. [1 + 2]

(f) What measure of central tendency is most suitable to describe the data in Table 1? Explain your choice of measure of central tendency. [3]

(g) Explain what is meant by a pilot study and give **one** reason why it might be appropriate to use a pilot study as part of this investigation. [2 + 2]

(h) Give **two** conclusions that can be drawn from the data in Table 1. [2 + 2]

(a) (i) Participants will recall more words in the organised list condition than in the unorganised list condition. [2]

   (ii) This is a directional hypothesis. I used a directional hypothesis because past research suggests that organising word lists leads to better recall. [3]

(b) (i) Independent groups design. [1]

   (ii) One advantage is that there wouldn't be a practice effect, in a repeated measures design you would have to use different lists of words for both conditions and this could bring in an extraneous variable. One disadvantage is that you need to have a lot more participants. [2 + 1]

Only the first answer has been contextualised.

(c) An opportunity sample could be used. This is easy to conduct because you just take whoever is available. [3]

Debriefing does not count as an ethical issue – it is a means of dealing with the issue of deception.

(d) One ethical issue is debriefing. The students should have told the participants what was involved in the study and given them the opportunity to withdraw their data. [0 + 0]

(e) The participants in one condition might have been tested at a different time of day. People might have better memories earlier in the day and that would explain why they had better recall rather than the actual memory condition. [1 + 2]

(f) The median would be best because it is not affected by extreme values (there is one in Group 1) which would affect the mean. [3]

(g) A pilot study is a small-scale practice run of a study to check for any problems in methodology that might need adjusting. It would have been useful in this study to see whether, for example, the standardised instructions were clear and if 30 seconds is a long enough delay. [1 + 2]

Both answers are correct but require some further detail for full marks.

(h) One conclusion is that organisation does enhance memory. The second conclusion is that there are individual differences. [1 + 2]

Total marks for this question 25/30 marks

Practice examination questions

A psychology lecturer notices that he can clearly see one of the tables in a college coffee bar from an upstairs window. The lecturer decides to carry out an observation study to discover if males differ from females in the number of *friendly acts* displayed in their interaction with other people. *Friendly acts* are defined as smiling and touching. For interaction that was observed the lecturer recorded the number of smiles and incidents of touching displayed by each *participant*.

To qualify as a participant in the study, the person had to be at the table in the coffee bar and in full view of the lecturer. The participant had to be with only one other person (companion).

The lecturer conducted the observations over a two-week period for a total of 12 separate hours. The same number of male and female participants were observed. The following data were obtained.

		Gender of participant	
		Male	Female
Gender of companion	Male	102	140
	Female	184	225

Table 1 Number of friendly acts displayed by male and female participants when interacting with either a male or female companion.

(a) What type of observational study did the lecturer conduct? [2]

(b) Describe the data depicted in *Table 1*. What may be said about the patterns of friendly acts displayed by males and females when interacting? [3]

(c) There may be a danger that *observer bias* could be present in this study.
i) What is meant by the term *observer bias*? [3]
ii) Explain **one** way in which the lecturer might overcome this problem? [2]

(d) Name **two** variables (other than observer bias) the lecturer might have controlled for in his study. Why might it have been important to control for these? [4]

(e) Explain why the lecturer should be cautious about generalising his results to all males and females. [3]

(f) Discuss **one** ethical issue raised by this study. [3]

AQA B specimen paper Unit 1 Introducing psychology question 3

Index

Psychology

Cara Flanagan

Contents

Specification lists

AQA A Psychology

MODULE	SPECIFICATION TOPIC	CHAPTER REFERENCE	STUDIED IN CLASS	REVISED	PRACTICE QUESTIONS
Unit 4	**Section A: Social psychology**				
	Social cognition	1.1–1.3			
	Relationships	1.4–1.6			
	Pro- and anti-social behaviour	1.7–1.9			
	Section B: Physiological psychology				
	Brain and behaviour	2.1–2.3			
	Biological rhythms, sleep and dreaming	2.4–2.6			
	Motivation and emotion	2.7–2.9			
	Section C: Cognitive psychology				
	Attention and pattern recognition	3.1–3.3			
	Perceptual processes and development	3.4–3.6			
	Language and thought	3.7–3.9			
	Section D: Developmental psychology				
	Cognitive development	4.1–4.3			
	Social and personality development	4.4–4.6			
	Adulthood	4.7–4.9			
	Section E: Comparative psychology				
	Determinants of animal behaviour	5.1–5.3			
	Animal cognition	5.4–5.6			
	Evolutionary explanations of human behaviour	5.7–5.9			
Unit 5	**Section A: Individual differences**				
	Issues in classification and diagnosis	6.1–6.3			
	Psychopathology	6.4–6.6			
	Treating mental disorders	6.7–6.9			
	Section B: Perspectives				
	Issues: Gender bias, cultural bias, ethical issues, the use of non-human animals	7.1–7.4			
	Debates: free will and determinism, reductionism, psychology as a science, nature-nurture	7.5–7.8			
	Section C: Approaches	7.9			
Unit 6	Coursework				

(Chapter references include complete coverage of the specification)

Examination analysis

The specification comprises three units for AS (units 1–3) and three units for A2 (units 4–6).

Unit 4 **Five sections:** Social, Physiological, Cognitive, Developmental, Comparative; each divided into three subsections and one question set per subsection (15 questions). Candidates answer 3 questions. 1½ hours 15% of total A Level marks (30% of A2)

Unit 5 **Section A:** Individual differences (three subsections, one question set from each)
Section B: Issues and debates (two questions on issues, two on debates)
Section C: Approaches (two stimulus questions)
Candidates answer one question from each section (synoptic assessment)
2 hours 20% of total A Level marks (40% of A2)

Unit 6 Coursework: One 2000 word report plus project brief, centre-assessed. 15% of total A Level marks (30% of A2)

AQA B Psychology

MODULE	SPECIFICATION TOPIC	CHAPTER REFERENCE	STUDIED IN CLASS	REVISED	PRACTICE QUESTIONS
	Section A: Child development				
	Social development	AS 3.3, 3.4			
	Cognitive development	A2 4.1			
	Moral development	A2 4.3			
	Exceptional development	–			
	Section B: Psychology of atypical behaviour				
	Definition and classification of behaviours	AS 5.3, 5.4; A2 6.1			
	Anxiety and eating disorders	AS 5.5; A2 6.6			
	Mood disorders and schizophrenia	A2 6.4, 6.5			
	Treatments of atypical behaviours	A2 6.7, 6.8, 6.9			
Unit 4	**Section B: Health psychology**				
	Health and illness	AS 5.3, A2 6.7			
	Psychological aspects of illness	AS 4.5			
	Lifestyles and health	AS 6.2			
	Stress and stress management	AS 4.4, 4.5, 4.6			
	Section B: Contemporary topics in Psychology				
	Human relationships	A2 1.4, 1.5, 1.6			
	Psychology and paranormal phenomena	–			
	Substance abuse	–			
	Criminological psychology	A2 6.5			
	Section A: Perspectives in Psychology	A2 7.9			
	Section B: Debates				
	The scientific approach	A2 7.7			
Unit 5	Debates in Psychology	A2 7.5–7.8			
	Section C: Methods in Psychology				
	Inferential statistics; issues in research	AS 7.1, 7.2, 7.3			
Unit 6	Coursework				

(Chapter references cover some but not necessarily all of the specification)

Examination analysis

The specification comprises three units for AS (units 1–3) and three units for A2 (units 4–6).

Unit 4 **Section A:** Child development, one question set on each of four subsections
Section B: Options (Atypical behaviour, Health Psychology, Contemporary topics), one question set on each of 12 subsections
Candidates answer 3 questions, at least one question from each section.
1½ hours 17.5% of total A Level marks (35% of A2)

Unit 5 **Section A:** Perspectives (two questions set)
Section B: Debates (one question set from each subsection)
Section C: Methods (one compulsory question)
Candidates answer one question from each section (synoptic assessment)
2 hours 17.5% of total A Level marks (35% of A2)

Unit 6 **Coursework:** One 2000 word report, centre-assessed. 15% of total A Level marks (30% of A2)

Edexcel Psychology

MODULE	SPECIFICATION TOPIC	CHAPTER REFERENCE	STUDIED IN CLASS	REVISED	PRACTICE QUESTIONS
Unit 4	**4A: Clinical psychology**				
	Defining and classification	AS 5.3; A2 6.1, 6.3			
	Approaches and therapies	AS 5.4; A2 6.7–6.9			
	Specific mental disorders	AS 5.5; A2 6.4–6.6			
	4B: Criminological psychology				
	The legal aspects of crime	AS 2.4, 6.3, A2 1.1			
	Social and media influences	A2 1.1, 1.9			
	Treating crime	A2 1.7, 6.8			
	4C: The psychology of education				
	Theories of learning	A2 4.1, 5.2			
	Factors affecting student performance	A2 4.1			
	Assessment	A2 4.2			
	4D: Sports psychology				
	Individual differences and sport	A2 4.4, 4.5			
	Participation and motivation in sport	A2 1.1, 2.8			
	Influences on sport performance	AS 6.3; A2 2.7, 2.8			
Unit 5	**Part (a) 5A: Child psychology**				
	Attachment	AS 3.3			
	Deprivation and privation	AS 3.4, 3.5			
	Social development	A2 4.5			
	Part (a) 5B: Environmental psychology				
	Personal space and territoriality	AS 4.5			
	Stress, crowding and urban living	AS 4.5, A2 1.7			
	Changing behaviour to save the environment	AS 6.2			
	Part (a) 5C: Health Psychology				
	Health and substance abuse	AS 4.1			
	Stress	AS 4.4–4.6; A2 2.4			
	Health promotion	AS 6.2			
	Part (b) Research methods	AS 7.1–7.3			
Unit 6	Issues, perspectives and debates in Psychology	AS 7.1–7.3; A2 7.3, 7.4, 7.7–7.9			

(Chapter references cover some but not necessarily all of the specification)

Examination analysis

The specification comprises six compulsory modules (3 examination units).

Unit 4	**Applications of psychology.** Candidates select any two applications (4A–D), and answer all 3 questions set 1½ hours 16.7% of total A Level marks (33.3% of A2)
Unit 5	**Applications of psychology and research methods** Part (a) Candidates select any one application (5A–C), and answer all 3 questions set Part (b) Compulsory questions on research methods 1½ hours 16.7% of total A Level marks (33.3% of A2)
Unit 6	**Issues, perspectives and debates in psychology.** Candidates answer two from three questions (synoptic assessment) 1½ hours 16.7% of total A Level marks (33.3% of A2)

OCR Psychology

MODULE	SPECIFICATION TOPIC	CHAPTER REFERENCE	STUDIED IN CLASS	REVISED	PRACTICE QUESTIONS
Unit 4	Psychology research report				
Units 5 and 6	**Specialist choice: Psychology and education, e.g.**				
	Perspectives on learning	A2 4.1, 5.2, 6.8			
	Motivation and educational performance	A2 1.1, 2.8			
	Specialist choice: Psychology and health, e.g.				
	Adherence to medical requests	AS 6.2, 6.4			
	Stress	AS 4.4–4.6			
	Specialist choice: Psychology and organisations, e.g.				
	Motivation to work	A2 2.8			
	The quality of working life	AS 4.5			
	Specialist choice: Psychology and the environment, e.g.				
	Environmental stress, noise	AS 4.5; A2 1.7			
	Climate and weather	A2 2.4			
	Specialist choice: Psychology and sport, e.g.				
	Personality and sport	A2 4.4			
	Aggression in sport	A2 1.7			
	Motivation and self-confidence in sport	A2 2.8			
	Arousal and anxiety in sport	A2 2.7, 2.8			
	Attitudes to exercise in sport	AS 6.2; A2 1.1			

(Chapter references cover some but not necessarily all of the specification)

Examination analysis

The specification comprises three units for AS (units 1–3) and three units for A2 (units 4–6).

Unit 4   Psychology research report
 1 Practical project: one report, no more than 1400 words
 2 Assignment: applying psychological concepts to an everyday event (no more than 1000 words excluding references)
 Board-assessed (synoptic assessment)
 16.7% of total A Level marks (33.3% of A2)

Unit 5   Select one specialist choice
 Section A: Four short answer questions on a particular topic area, a choice of two topic areas
 Section B: One structured essay from a choice of two
 1½ hours 16.7% of total A Level marks (33.3% of A2)

Unit 6   Select a second specialist choice
 Section A: Four short answer questions on a particular topic area, a choice of two topic areas
 Section B: One structured essay from a choice of two
 1½ hours 16.7% of total A Level marks (33.3% of A2)

AS/A2 Level Psychology courses

How does A2 differ from AS?

The AS examination is designed to be half way between GCSE and the full A Level standard. The questions are set and marked with the notional 17-year-old candidate in mind. In general the AS assessment contains more AO1 (description) than AO2 (evaluation). These assessment objectives are described below.

The A2 specifications contain more options than AS, so you may have an opportunity to select the areas that you have found interesting and study them at greater depth. The A2 examination is set and examined with the notional 18-year-old in mind who has studied psychology for two years. The question style is different, usually fewer short-answer questions and more essays or structured essay questions. These A2 style questions shouldn't be 'harder' because you will have had a further year of study, and have developed greater knowledge and skills. You will be assessed on your knowledge of specific topics as well as your critical understanding of general issues in Psychology. This is called 'synopticity' and is discussed below.

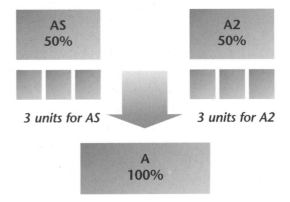

Unit tests

You may sit any unit in January or June and are allowed to resit any unit once, accepting your highest mark. The normal sequence of taking unit examinations will be AS units 1–3 in the first year of study (January and/or June), and A2 units 4–6 in the second year. However you may take them all at the end of the second year. The paper that includes synoptic assessment can be taken at any time of the candidate's course of study. It assesses his/her overall understanding of psychology.

Key skills

It is important that you develop your key skills throughout the AS and A2 courses that you take, as these are skills that you need whatever you do beyond AS and A Levels. To gain the key skills qualification, which is equivalent to an AS Level, you will need to demonstrate that you have attained Level 3 in Communication, Application of Number and Information Technology. Part of the assessment can be done as normal class activity and part is by formal test. It is a worthwhile qualification, as it demonstrates your ability to put your ideas across to other people, collect data and use up-to-date technology in your work.

Different types of questions in A2 examinations

All examination boards have produced specimen question papers and mark schemes for the new examination series. In addition, after each examination the boards publish the mark schemes for the examination. It pays to read these.

The example questions below have been selected from the specimen papers.

Essay questions (AQA A)

Example from AQA A specimen material

Discuss the role of genetic factors in the development of measured intelligence. (24 marks)

AQA A Unit 4, question 10

Structured essay questions (all boards)

Example from AQA A specimen material

(a) Describe **two** explanations of the formation of relationships. (12 marks)

(b) Assess the extent of cultural variations in relationships. (12 marks)

AQA A Unit 4, question 2

Example from OCR specimen material

(a) Examine what psychologists have learned about arousal and sport performance. (10 marks)

(b) Evaluate what psychologists have learned about arousal and sport performance. (16 marks)

(c) Using your psychological knowledge, suggest an anxiety management technique that could be used by an athlete to improve performance. (8 marks)

OCR question 3

Stimulus material (AQA A, AQA B, Edexcel)

Example from AQA B specimen material

Hazel was involved in a car crash that left her suffering from whip-lash injuries to her neck and shoulders. For some time after the accident, she was in terrible pain. Her doctor was concerned that, despite evidence that she had recovered from the physical damage caused by the crash, she continued to suffer pain in her neck and shoulders. Hazel was referred to a health psychologist so that she could be helped with her pain.

(a) Describe **one** physiological and **one** self-report measure that the psychologist could use to assess the extent of Hazel's pain. (6 marks)

(b) Compare and contrast **two** ways of managing pain that the psychologist might use with Hazel. Refer to psychological theory in your answer.

(14 marks)

AQA B Unit 4 question 11

> **IMPORTANT INFORMATION**
> (This book is based on the latest versions of specifications, however these do change and candidates should always consult the website of the appropriate examining board to check the latest versions.)

Exam technique

Examination injunctions

In order to write clear examination questions, it is necessary to define key terms (injunctions) that are used. This also enables you to know what you have to do to gain credit. Most boards publish a 'Glossary of terms' which defines all the injunctions used in that examination. The definitions given here are from AQA specification A.

AO1 terms

Describe Present evidence of what you know.

Outline Give a summary description in brief form.

Also: define, explain

AO2 terms

Evaluate Make an informed judgement of the value (positive or negative) of the topic area as far as possible, based on systematic analysis.

Also: analyse, assess, to what extent

AO1 and AO2 terms

Discuss Describe and evaluate with reference to different (contrasting) points of view. You may be asked to discuss with reference to particular criteria.

Critically consider 'Consider' (demonstrate knowledge and understanding) plus 'criticise' (evaluate strengths and weaknesses).

Also: compare and contrast

Other terms

Research Knowledge gained through empirical test (i.e. direct study) or theoretical examination.

Studies Empirical investigations.

Theory A complex set of interrelated ideas/assumptions/principles used to explain observed phenomena.

Model Less complex than a theory, usually comprising a single idea.

Evidence Empirical or theoretical material.

Findings The outcome of research.

Also: insights, concepts, methods

What the examiners are looking for

In Psychology examiners are looking for evidence of your knowledge. Often there are no 'right' answers, especially at A2. There are a range of correct answers and any of these will receive credit. It is a combination of having knowledge and using it effectively. Examiners are looking for *psychologically informed*, rather than 'commonsense' answers. The examiners mark your answers positively. They do not subtract marks when material is missing. Instead they aim to award marks for any material that is relevant and demonstrates a critical understanding of psychology.

How the exams are marked

In Psychology there are three assessment objectives.

Assessment objective 1 (AO1)

Knowledge and understanding of psychological theories, terminology, concepts, studies and methods in the core areas of cognitive, social, developmental, individual differences and physiological psychology, and communication of knowledge and understanding of psychology in a clear and effective manner.

At A2 candidates will be expected to extend their knowledge and understanding to psychological principles, perspectives and applications.

Assessment objective 2 (AO2)

Analyse and evaluate psychological theories, concepts, studies and methods in the core areas of cognitive, social, developmental, individual differences and physiological psychology, and communication of knowledge and understanding of psychology in a clear and effective manner.

At A2 candidates will be expected to extend their analysis and evaluation to psychological principles, perspectives and applications.

Assessment objective 3 (AO3)

Design, conduct and report psychological investigation(s) choosing from a range of methods, and taking into account the issues of reliability, validity and ethics, and collect and draw conclusions from data.

Quality of written communication (QoWC)

The quality of written communication is assessed in all AS and A2 assessment units where candidates are required to produce extended written material. Candidates will be assessed according to their ability to:

- select and use a form and style of writing appropriate for complex subject matter
- organise relevant information clearly and coherently, using specialist vocabulary when appropriate
- ensure text is legible, and spelling, grammar and punctuation are accurate, so that meaning is clear.

Synoptic assessment

Throughout your AS and A2 studies you have learned about discrete areas of psychology, such as memory, relationships, stress, sleep, mental illness, child development, and so on. Within these topic areas you have learned about how psychologists explain behaviour, and how they evaluate these explanations. How does all of this add up to 'psychology'? There are common threads that run across the specification and this is referred to as 'synopticity'.

A synopsis is a summary or outline, thus the synoptic element of psychology (or any subject) is your summative knowledge; your overview of psychology as a whole rather than the discrete elements that can be studied.

An understanding of synopticity can be demonstrated by using the knowledge, understanding and skills learned in all your psychology studies. In particular:

- knowledge and critical appreciation of different approaches and perspectives in psychology, such as learning theory (behaviourism) and the cognitive approach

- knowledge and critical appreciation of issues and debates in psychology, such as ethics and determinism
- appreciation of the different methodologies used in psychological investigations, such as experiments and observational studies
- the ability to forge links between topics across the specification
- Psychology-wide concerns such as reliability and validity, cultural variation and demand characteristics/participant reactivity (iatrogenesis).

In the examination you will be set questions which require you to bring together principles and concepts from different areas of psychology and apply them in a particular context.

In all A Levels synoptic assessment forms at least 20% of the final A Level mark, so it is very important to recognise and understand these common threads throughout the time you are studying A Level.

AQA A Marking criteria for Unit 4

AQA A uses a generic marking criteria to assess all essay questions. The key criteria, and marks are shown below.

For unit 4 Assessment objective 1 (AO1)

Band	Marks	Content	Relevance	Organisation and structure	Breadth and depth
3 (Top)	12–11	Substantial, accurate and well-detailed		Coherent	Substantial evidence of both and balance achieved
3 (Bottom)	10–9	Slightly limited, accurate and well-detailed		Coherent	Evidence of both but imbalanced
2 (Top)	8–7	Limited, generally accurate and reasonably detailed		Reasonably constructed	Increasing evidence of breadth and/or depth
2 (Bottom)	6–5	Basic, generally accurate but lacks detail		Reasonable	Some evidence of breadth and/or depth
1 (Top)	4–3	Rudimentary, sometimes flawed	Sometimes focused	Reasonable	
1 (Bottom)	2–0	Just discernible; weak/muddled	Wholly or mainly irrelevant		

For unit 4 Assessment objective 2 (AO2)

Band	Marks	Commentary	Use of material	Selection	Elaboration
3 (Top)	12–11	Thorough	Highly effective	Appropriate	Coherent
3 (Bottom)	10–9	Slightly limited	Effective	Appropriate	Appropriate
2 (Top)	8–7	Limited	Reasonably effective		Reasonable elaboration
2 (Bottom)	6–5	Basic	Restricted		Some evidence of elaboration
1 (Top)	4–3	Superficial and rudimentary	Not used effectively		No evidence
1 (Bottom)	2–0	Muddled and incomplete	Wholly or mainly irrelevant		

AQA B Marking criteria for unit 5

Assessment objective 1 (AO1) the maximum mark is 15 and, in addition to descriptors for content, relevance, organisation and structure, and breadth and depth, there is a synoptic criterion 'evidence of different theoretical perspectives and/or methodological approaches'.

Assessment objective 2 (AO2) the maximum mark is 15 and, in addition to descriptors for commentary, use of material, selection, and elaboration, there is a synoptic criterion 'critical commentary on the different theoretical perspectives and/or methodological approaches'.

Some dos and don'ts

Dos

Do know what you're talking about.

- There is no substitute for knowledge. Commonsense arguments do not attract credit. Your answers must be psychologically informed.

Do use your knowledge effectively.

- It is one thing to know something (AO1) but another skill (AO2) to be able to use that knowledge to present a coherent argument. Effective use of material is extremely important.

Do read all the questions first.

- If you have to choose between questions make sure you choose the right question for you, rather than panicking and doing the first one that seems OK.

Do answer the question set.

- This sounds obvious but, under examination conditions, most candidates feel very anxious and write about anything they can think of. They don't even read the whole question. They just look at the first few words and start writing.

Do use the mark allocation to guide you in how much you should write.

- Two marks is likely to mean two valid points. If you write lots and lots for a question with very few marks you won't get extra credit and you will leave less time for the other questions, or parts of the question.

Do write legibly and try to use technical terms and correct spelling.

- There are marks in the examination for your quality of written communication, and this includes the use of technical terms.

Don'ts

Don't present your 'Blue Peter answer' (the one you prepared earlier).

- Just because your essay got a good mark in class doesn't mean it will achieve the same mark for a slightly different question in the examination.

Don't leave out obvious material.

- It is very easy to think 'the examiner knows that' and therefore that you don't have to write down obvious things. However, the examiner cannot be sure that you know it unless you demonstrate it.

Don't write everything you know.

- Selectivity is also important. Don't simply include everything you know on a topic. Be selective in order to produce a well-structured response within the time limit.

Don't waste time.

- An examination has a finite length, don't spend time 'waffling' or describing three studies when the question asks for two. It is better to think for a few minutes about which two to choose.

Don't feel you have to include names and dates.

- You are not penalised for omitting these but they do help give the impression that you are psychologically informed, and may act as an aid to memory.

Four steps to successful revision

Step 1: Understand

- Study the topic to be learned slowly. Make sure you understand the logic or important concepts.
- Mark up the text if necessary – underline, highlight and make notes.
- Re-read each paragraph slowly.

GO TO STEP 2

Step 2: Summarise

- Now make your own revision note summary:
  What is the main idea, theme or concept to be learned?
  What are the main points? How does the logic develop?
  Ask questions: Why? How? What next?
- Use bullet points, mind maps, patterned notes.
- Link ideas with mnemonics, mind maps, crazy stories.
- Note the title and date of the revision notes
  (e.g. Psychology: Developmental psychology, 3rd March).
- Organise your notes carefully and keep them in a file.

This is now in **short-term memory**. You will forget 80% of it if you do not go to Step 3.
GO TO STEP 3, but first take a 10 minute break.

Step 3: Memorise

- Take 25 minute learning 'bites' with 5 minute breaks
- After each 5 minute break test yourself:
  Cover the original revision note summary
  Write down the main points
  Speak out loud (record on tape)
  Tell someone else
  Repeat many times.

The material is well on its way to **long-term memory**.
You will forget 40% if you do not do step 4. **GO TO STEP 4**

Step 4: Track/Review

- Create a Revision Diary (one A4 page per day).
- Make a revision plan for the topic, e.g. 1 day later, 1 week later, 1 month later.
- Record your revision in your Revision Diary, e.g.
  Psychology: Developmental psychology, 3rd March 25 minutes
  Psychology: Developmental psychology, 5th March 15 minutes
  Psychology: Developmental psychology, 3rd April 15 minutes
  ... and then at monthly intervals.

Chapter 1

Social psychology

Social psychology is concerned with how your behaviour can be explained in terms of the way that other conspecifics (members of your species) affect you.

- Other *individuals* may influence you. For example, you may imitate what others do (social learning theory) or you may obey someone else.
- *Groups* of people may influence you. For example, people conform to group norms.

- *Society* (culture) in general may influence your behaviour. For example, methods of child rearing tend to be cultural or sub-cultural.

At AS Level your study of social psychology may have focused on conformity and obedience, as examples of the way other people influence your behaviour.

At A2 you may select to study one or more of the following areas in social psychology.

Social cognition

    1.1   Attribution of causality
    1.2   Social perception
    1.3   Prejudice and discrimination

After studying this area you should be able to:

- *describe and evaluate theories of attribution, as well as the research evidence related to these theories*
- *discuss errors and biases in the attribution process*
- *understand social and cultural influences on interpersonal perception*

- *explain social perception in terms of impression formation, stereotypes, schema and social representations*
- *describe and evaluate theories of prejudice and discrimination*
- *critically consider ways to reduce prejudice, with reference to relevant research evidence*

LEARNING SUMMARY

Relationships

    1.4   Attraction and formation of relationships
    1.5   Maintenance and dissolution of relationships
    1.6   Cultural and sub-cultural differences in relationships

After studying this area you should be able to:

- *explain interpersonal attraction and describe relevant research studies*
- *discuss theories and research studies relating to the formation of relationships*
- *discuss theories and research studies relating to the maintenance of relationships*
- *discuss theories and research studies relating to*

- *the dissolution of relationships*
- *critically consider psychological explanations of love*
- *explain differences in relationships between Western and non-Western cultures, with reference to appropriate research studies*
- *discuss 'understudied' relationships, such as gay and lesbian and 'electronic' friendships*

LEARNING SUMMARY

Pro- and anti-social behaviour

    1.7   Nature and causes of aggression
    1.8   Altruism and bystander behaviour
    1.9   Media influences on pro- and anti-social behaviour

After studying this area you should be able to:

- *describe and critically assess social psychological theories of aggression, including appropriate research studies*
- *discuss research into the effects of environmental stressors on aggressive behaviour*
- *critically consider explanations of altruism and bystander behaviour, including relevant*

- *research studies*
- *discuss the effects of cultural differences on pro-social behaviour*
- *explain media influences on pro- and anti-social behaviour*
- *discuss research studies relating to media influences on pro- and anti-social behaviour*

LEARNING SUMMARY

Social cognition

1.1 Attribution of causality

AQA A   U4
EDEXCEL   U4
OCR   U5, U6

Attribution is the process of explaining causes of behaviour. We do not observe traits, we observe behaviours and infer personal attributes.

Does your mother ever say 'I think that jumper likes to be safely in your cupboard'? This is an example of anthropo-morphism – attributing human feelings to an inanimate object, a dispositional attribution.

An example of correspondent inference is when we assume that film stars have similar personalities to the roles they play.

'Personalism' is when behaviour is seen as directly intending to benefit or harm the perceiver. 'Hedonic relevance' refers to behaviour having specific effects for the perceiver.

Things that covary are things that tend to happen at the same time, such as grey clouds and rain, or drinking and hangovers. Their covariance leads us to expect that one causes the other.

All attribution theories assume that people make judgements in a *logical and rational* manner – which may not always be true.

Theories of attribution

Theory of naïve psychology: Heider (1958)

Commonsense or naïve 'theories' about behaviour are based on two sources:

- the *person* – internal or dispositional factors, such as a person's beliefs
- the *situation* – external or situational factors, such as social norms or luck.

Dispositional attributions are preferred (*fundamental attribution error*, FAE).

Research evidence

Heider and Simmel (1944) found that participants described objects (e.g. triangles) in a film in anthropomorphic terms, indicating our tendency to infer 'personalities' even when no causation could possibly be involved.

Ross *et al.* (1977) demonstrated the FAE. Observers rated questioners (quiz participants who made up the questions) as superior to answerers, a dispositional attribution even when situational factors were clearly involved.

Evaluation

- *Not a true theory* of attribution but inspired others to formulate theories.
- FAE is *not universal* (see below).

Correspondent inference theory: Jones and Davis (1965)

We infer that an individual has a corresponding disposition when a behaviour is: intentional, unusual, low in social desirability, has personalism and/or hedonic relevance.

Research evidence

Jones and Harris (1967) showed that participants judged an essay writer's opinion to be the same as expressed in their essay (pro- or anti-Castro) even if the raters knew the essay was written under no-choice conditions.

Evaluation

- Attribution may be *more complex* in real life. Jones and Nisbett (1971) gave additional information about essayists' opinions affecting judgements.
- Some behaviours are *not intentional* (e.g. clumsiness) but seen as dispositional.
- Some behaviours *confirm expectations* (e.g. stereotypes) but they lead to correspondent inferences.

Covariation model: Kelley (1967)

Kelley proposed that attributions are based on covariations:

- *consistency* – e.g. John always laughs at this comedian (high consistency)
- *distinctiveness* – e.g. John laughs at just this comedian (high distinctiveness)
- *consensus* – e.g. everyone laughs at this comedian (high consensus).

External attributions are made when there is sufficient evidence of all three. Internal attributions occur when distinctiveness and consensus are low and consistency is high.

Research evidence

McArthur (1972) used sentences with information (high or low) about all three axes. Participants attributed external/internal causes predicted.

Evaluation

- The evidence is based on *artificially created situations*. Real-life is different.
- Possible to *explain the results differently*, e.g. attending to salient features.
- We *often have rather incomplete information*.

Causal schemata: Kelley (1972)

Causal schemata (heuristics) provide rapid interpretation of ambiguous social data:

- *multiple necessary causes* – a group of behaviours are jointly necessary

A *heuristic* is a general guideline for solving a problem that doesn't guarantee a solution but tends to work well most of the time.

- *multiple sufficient causes* – attributions are made on the basis of only one instance of behaviour using, e.g. the *discounting principle* (select most obvious potential cause) or the *augmenting principle* (a behaviour 'against the odds' is given greater weight).

Evaluation

- Can explain how attributions are made when information is *incomplete*.
- However, the model lacks *empirical support*.

Three-dimensional model: Weiner (1980)

- *Locus:* external or internal (E or I).
- *Stability:* stable or unstable (S or U).
- *Controllability:* controllable or uncontrollable (C or U).

A person might explain their lateness to school: 'It always takes me a long time to walk to school' (locus: E, stability: S, controllability: C) or 'I'm just a born latecomer' (locus: I, stability: S, controllability: U).

Evaluation

- Includes *other dimensions* than just the internal/external.
- The model has *interesting applications* such as attribution retraining.

Errors and biases in the attribution process

A *bias* is a distortion, a systematic factor which overuses or underuses information providing errors in social perception.

Fundamental attribution error (FAE)

The overemphasis on dispositional rather than situational factors.

Research evidence

Ross *et al.* (1977), Jones and Harris (1967) above.

It is possible to explain the discrepancy between original expectations and actual behaviour in terms of the FAE.

Evaluation

- *Cultural bias.* Western cultures emphasise individualism. Miller (1984) found that Indian Hindus preferred situational to dispositional explanations.
- The *English language facilitates* dispositional explanations (e.g. we refer to an honest person but not an honest situation).

At AS Level you studied Milgram's obedience research. We automatically think of dispositional explanations (someone would only give strong shocks if they were inhuman) rather than situational ones (in a laboratory people may feel they have to obey).

Actor/observer bias

We prefer to explain our own (the actor's) behaviour in terms of situation and the behaviour of others (those we are observing) in terms of disposition.

Research evidence

Nisbett *et al.* (1973) asked students to explain, for themselves and a friend, the reasons for selecting a particular course. They made situational attributions about themselves.

Evaluation

- *Available information.* The actor knows about his/her own disposition but has to make inferences about another person, finding situational factors more salient.

Self-serving biases

We take credit for our successes and disassociate from our failures, blaming external factors. This protects self-esteem, and gives us a sense of control.

Research evidence

Jones *et al.* (1968) arranged for participants to teach two pupils. The 'teacher' attributed improved performance to themselves but blamed the pupil for failure.

Ingroup bias (the tendency to show a preference towards members of your own group) is an example of a self-serving bias because it enhances your personal self-esteem. Duncan (1976) showed White participants a video of a White or Black person violently pushing another during a heated conversation. Participants made internal attributions ('violent personality') when the pusher was Black and external ones for the White aggressor ('he was provoked').

Evaluation

- Explains why 'actors' sometimes explain their behaviour in situational terms (when it enhances self-esteem), the *reverse of the actor-observer bias*.
- *Depressed* individuals may behave in the opposite way. Abramson *et al.* (1978) suggested that depressives tend to attribute failure to themselves (internal) rather than to external factors, and as global rather than specific.
- *Cultural bias.* Kashima and Triandis (1986) found Americans explain successes in terms of high ability and failures in terms of external factors whereas the opposite was true of Japanese participants.

Practice essay 1.1

(a) Describe **one** theory of attribution. (12 marks)

(b) Evaluate the theory of attribution that you described in part (a) in terms of research evidence. (12 marks)

1.2 Social perception

AQA A ▸ U4

Impression formation

Impression formation consists of taking a limited amount of information and producing a global perception of another individual.

Research evidence

Asch (1946) gave participants descriptions of a person (e.g. energetic – assured – talkative – cold – ironical – inquisitive – persuasive). If key words were changed (e.g. 'warm' instead of 'cold') participants gave different descriptions of the target individual.

Kelley (1950) arranged real-life encounters where students were given a description of a substitute lecturer and, after the lecture, asked the students to assess the lecturer.

Biases in impression formation

- *Central traits*: Adjectives such as warm/cold or intelligent have greater weight than other words, such as polite and blunt.
- *Primacy/recency*: First impressions do count, though when there is a time interval the recency effect may come into play.
- *Halo effect*: A person who possesses one desirable characteristic, such as being physically attractive, will be assumed to possess other desirable traits.
- *Contrast effect*: When an object is contrasted with something even less appealing, in contrast it looks much better. Kenrick and Gutierres (1980) asked male students to rate a blind date. Those who did this after watching an episode of Charlie's Angels (with attractive girls) gave lower ratings than those who did the rating beforehand.

Stereotyping and schema theory

Both schema and stereotypes provide a means of organising information and generating future expectations which simplify our social perceptions. Stereotypes are more fixed and culturally determined.

Explaining stereotypes and schema

- *Cognitive misers*: Stereotypes/schema allow us to conserve cognitive energy because they summarise large amounts of information. Such simplified cognitive processing depends on *heuristics* and *categorisation* (identifying groups of individuals).
- *'Grain of truth' hypothesis*: At least some stereotypes are derived from experience and contain some truth. Once formed they are resistant to change possibly because they tend to be *self-fulfilling* leading to self-fulfilling prophecies. See also *confirmatory bias*, below.
- *Illusory correlations*: When two things co-occur people often perceive relationships where none exists, especially when the two things are unusual such as presence of a minority ethnic group and a crime being committed. This can explain negative stereotyping of minority groups.

Biases in stereotyping

- *False consensus effect*: Individuals overestimate the degree to which others think the same. Sherman *et al.* (1984) found that smokers estimated a higher percentage of smokers than did non-smokers (51% to 38%).
- *Confirmatory bias*: We seek out information which confirms rather than challenges our beliefs. Cohen (1981) found that people tended to remember data consistent with stereotypes when shown a video about a waitress or a librarian.

Evaluation

- Stereotypes *aid cognitive processing* but they are at least *partly inaccurate*.
- The *motivated tactician*. People don't always use heuristics, they can also act as a 'fully engaged thinker'. Kruglanski and Freund (1983) asked participants to assess the quality of dissertations attributed to individuals of different ethnic origins. When time was limited and there was no expectation of evaluation, participants were more affected by the ethnic origin of the writer. When given more time and told they would be assessed, participants thought more carefully and were less affected by stereotypes.

'Perception' describes the interpretation of available sensory data.

Social perception is concerned with how we interpret our social world from available data.

Interestingly, in these experiments no one said, 'How am I to know?' Participants do their best in experiments – but this may well result in *demand characteristics*.

A *schema* is a cognitive structure that contains knowledge about a thing, including its attributes and the relations among its attributes (Fiske and Taylor, 1991).

A nice illustration of the *self-fulfilling prophecy* was given by Guthrie (1938). A group of students played a trick on an unattractive female classmate, pretending that she was the most desirable girl in the college and taking turns asking her out. By the sixth date, the general opinion was that she had actually become more attractive. Presumably she came to believe she was attractive and this led her to behave differently.

It is clearly important to investigate when people act as 'motivated tacticians' because then we can avoid the influence of stereotypes.

- *Complex situations*. Most people are aware of the effects of stereotypes and try to control them but this may break down in complex situations. Darley and Gross (1983) showed videos of 'Hannah' playing in a high-class or run-down neighbourhood and asked participants to estimate her academic ability. If the information was minimal participants resisted the influence of stereotypes but when shown further videos (increasing the complexity of the task) their judgements were more affected by stereotypes.

Social representations

The concept of *social representations* emphasises the way that we represent *social* knowledge and how this knowledge is unconsciously shaped by *social* groups, i.e. such representations are social in two ways.

Cultural knowledge is constructed *and* transmitted via social representations. Moscovici (1981) first described social representations as shared beliefs that evolve within a social/cultural group and are used to explain social events. Social representations are more than schema because they include social dynamics.

How are social representations formed?

Moscovici (1984) suggested that social representations are the product of:

- *Anchoring* – unfamiliar objects and events are set in familiar contexts by using known classifications. For example, by labelling a behaviour as 'child's play' one is creating a host of expectations and understandings.
- *Objectification* – unfamiliar abstract concepts are made more accessible through *personification* (linking a concept to a person, e.g. Freudian principles), *figuration* (use of metaphorical images, e.g. Freud's concept of the id) and *ontologising* (making the abstract more material, e.g. discussing brain rather than mind processes).

Research evidence

Moscovici (1961) used the idea of social representations to explain how psychoanalysis moved from a scientific theory to a broader explanation of why society is like it is. The first, scientific phase, is when scientists use the theory. Second, the ideas become more widely known and finally, in the ideological phase, the concepts are applied to society in general.

Echabe and Rovira (1989) used the concept of social representations to explain distorted recall of AIDS-related information by individuals who had different beliefs about AIDS (conservative or liberal).

Evaluation

- The concepts of *schema* and *social representations* are complementary. Schema operate at a more individual level whereas social representations operate at more collective or macro level.
- Some critics feel that social representation theory *doesn't lend itself to scientific research*, which may be true in terms of the experimental tradition, but discourse analysis is more appropriate.
- Social representation theory may be *non-falsifiable* because any data can be interpreted in a way that is consistent with the theory.
- Social representations *may not be consensual*, a basic element of the concept. Litton and Potter (1985) analysed the St Paul's riots in Bristol and noted that the range of explanations offered by participants showed consensus but also individual variation – some people acknowledged but rejected the shared accounts.

Practice essay 1.2

Discuss the nature of social representations in social perception. (24 marks)

1.3 Prejudice and discrimination

AQA A ▶ U4

Theories of the origins and maintenance of prejudice and discrimination

Social identity theory (SIT)

Social identity is determined by categorisation (creates ingroups and outgroups, simplifies interpersonal perception), social comparison (ingroup favouritism and outgroup negative bias enhance social and personal esteem) and social beliefs (our beliefs/attitudes generate different social behaviours).

Research evidence

Tajfel (1970) conducted the minimal group experiments; Linville *et al.* (1982) demonstrated the illusion of outgroup homogeneity; Breakwell (1978) showed how group members react to threat.

Evaluation

- Good explanation of *ingroup favouritism*, generates a number of *testable propositions*, which in turn can support the theory, and can account for prejudice in situations of *minimal information*.
- Doesn't fully explain the *violence* associated with some prejudices.

Realistic conflict theory

Prejudice stems from direct competition between social groups over scarce and valued resources. Outgroup becomes the scapegoat.

Research evidence

Sherif *et al.* (1961) used the Robbers Cave Experiment to demonstrate conflict and super-ordinate goals; but Tyerman and Spencer (1983) didn't obtain the same results. Hovland and Sears (1940) found a negative correlation between number of lynchings and economic wealth.

Evaluation

- Prejudice is likely to exist prior to conflict, but *conflict is the trigger* to hostile behaviour. Can be applied to reducing prejudice (see the 'jigsaw method' page 21).

The authoritarian personality

Adorno *et al.* (1950) suggested that some individuals may be more prejudiced, conformist and obedient personalities as a consequence of parenting styles.

Research evidence

The F scale tested authoritarianism. It found that the authoritarian personality had a positive self-concept, rigid cognitive style, favoured law and order and tended to repress feelings. The parents of such individuals tended to give conditional love, strict discipline and expected unquestioning loyalty. Such experiences would create an insecure adult who respects authority, conforms readily, and who may increase self-esteem through ingroup favouritism. A person with repressed feelings will project these on to scapegoats (realistic conflict).

Evaluation

- Accounts for existence of *prejudices and the hostility element*.
- Sample was *biased*, and some data was *retrospective*. Questionnaires may have contained a response set. The study was *correlational*.

Reduction of prejudice and discrimination

Contact hypothesis

Contact may reduce stereotyping and prejudice.

Research evidence

Deutsch and Collins (1951) found that prejudice possibly increased when Black and White residents lived in separate buildings, whereas it decreased when they were randomly assigned apartments in the same buildings irrespective of race.

Sidebar notes:

Prejudice was discussed in the *Revise AS Guide*. This is a review of the information covered there.

Relative deprivation theory can also be used to explain prejudice. This theory is described on p.29.

The *F (Fascism) Scale* was designed to measure the attitudes of the authoritarian personality.

There may be cultural differences in authoritarianism. McFarland *et al.* (1992) found that authoritarian Russians tended to favour continuing communist control, a stance directly opposite to authoritarian Americans who tended to be politically conservative.

Evaluation

- Increased contact *may increase conflict*. Forced desegregation may have an effect opposite to that intended, increasing aggression through resentment.
- For the minority group, integration may lead to *lowered self-esteem* because it emphasises their inferior position, thus creating stronger hostilities.
- It is quite common for people to like individual members of an outgroup, *but still feel prejudiced towards the group as a whole*. For example, Stouffer *et al.* (1949) found that racial prejudice amongst soldiers diminished in battle but did not extend to relations back at base.

Pursuit of superordinate goals

Sherif *et al.*'s study (1961) found that cooperation and superordinate (shared) goals overcame prejudice.

Research evidence

Aronson *et al.* (1978) developed the *jigsaw method* to foster mutual interdependence. Schoolchildren worked in groups where each member had a piece of work to prepare and teach to other group members for an end-of-project test.

Evaluation

- In Aronson's study, there was some attitude change but it was limited, probably because time spent in the classroom is low compared with *home and cultural influences*.

> This is called the *jigsaw method* because each child contributes a piece of knowledge to the whole task.

Equal status

When the US Supreme Court declared segregation unconstitutional in 1954, they sought the advice of social psychologists who argued that equal status would be necessary to eliminate false stereotypes.

Research evidence

Minard (1952) found that Black and White miners were not prejudiced when they worked together below ground. However, above ground, when their positions were unequal, their attitudes changed.

Evaluation

- Equal status doesn't address the *hostility factor* from intergroup conflicts. Needs social and political change, which is at best slow.
- Equal status *may be impossible.* For example, Abeles (1976) suggests that even though conditions are improving for Blacks in America, the gap between the rich and the poor remains. A survey of Black people living in poor areas of America showed that they have rising expectations which leads to a sense of dissatisfaction and militancy.

Challenging stereotypes through the use of advertising and instruction

Phrases like 'Black is beautiful' try to create a positive bias. Direct campaigns about the danger of stereotyping have been mounted in America, using the caption 'We shouldn't infect children with poisonous stereotypes.'

Research evidence

Elliott (1977) gave a lesson in discrimination by telling her brown-eyed pupils that they were more intelligent and treating them more favourably. The blue-eyed children became the underdogs until she reversed her treatment. Years later the children said that this taught them to be more careful about discrimination.

Evaluation

- *Prejudice is inevitable.* Stereotype formation and social identity are processes basic to human nature and make the world more manageable.
- *Holding prejudices has benefits*: positive discrimination for the ingroup increases self-esteem and prejudices provide a means of displacing aggression.

Practice essay 1.3

Discuss **two** ways in which prejudice **and/or** discrimination might be reduced.

(24 marks)

Relationships

1.4 Attraction and formation of relationships

Explanations of interpersonal attraction

Physical attractiveness

Many studies show that people who are physically attractive tend to be treated better. For example, Landy and Sigall (1974) found that male participants rated essays thought to be written by a more attractive woman more highly.

The *matching hypothesis* predicts that people select partners of comparable physical attractiveness. This may be to maintain balance (see Equity Theory on page 28), or due to a fear of rejection, or because of the *halo effect*.

The *halo effect* describes how the possession of one desirable characteristic, such as being physically attractive, is extended so that we think the person possesses other desirable traits, such as intelligence and kindness.

Research evidence

Murstein (1972) asked dating couples to rate themselves in terms of physical attractiveness, and asked independent judges to rate them. He found that real pairs were more similar in terms of physical attraction than random pairs.

Silverman (1971) confirmed these findings in a field study, noting that the greater the degree of physical attractiveness, the more physical intimacy was displayed.

The computer dance experiment (Walster *et al.*, 1966) did not find support for the matching hypothesis. Nearly 400 male and female students were randomly paired at a dance, and later asked to rate their date. Physical attractiveness (which was independently assessed) proved to be the most important factor in liking, rather than similarity. It was also the best predictor of the likelihood that they would see each other again.

Evaluation

- *Individual differences*. Towhey (1979) found that individuals who scored high on the Macho Scale were much influenced by physical attractiveness.
- *Artificiality* in the computer dance. Walster and Walster (1969) found that when students met before the dance and had time to think more about their dates, they later expressed the most liking for those who were at the same level of physical attractiveness as themselves.
- Physical attractiveness is important in *initial attraction*, matching is more important later.
- The matching hypothesis has been extended to include matching in terms of *other highly attractive features*, such as intelligence or wealth.

Kerckhoff and Davis (1962) proposed a *'filter theory'* of relationship formation, where each of the traits listed here act as a filter in the initial selection of friends or partners.

Proximity

Physical closeness increases the probability of interaction and acquaintance.

Research evidence

Festinger *et al.* (1950) found that people who lived near the stairways (in the end apartments) in a U-shaped housing block had most passive contact with other residents, and had developed the greatest number of friendships with other residents.

Clarke (1952) found that 50% of the people living in Columbus, Ohio, married people who lived within walking distance of their house.

Saegart *et al.* (1973) gave participants the task of rating the tastes of various drinks, during which they came into contact with a stranger one, two, five or ten times; liking of the stranger was positively related to the frequency of meeting.

Studies on interpersonal attraction tend to be rather artificial and often use students as participants, who may form relationships for different reasons than other people.

Evaluation

- Proximity may *polarise relationships*. Ebbesen *et al.* (1976) found that most 'enemies' also lived close by.
- *Proximity can be psychological* as well as physical, explaining by Internet relationships.

Explanations also tend to overlook individual and cultural differences, and often focus on romantic relationships.

Similarity

Similarity reinforces our own attitudes, reducing uncertainty and anxiety.

Research evidence

Newcomb (1961) offered 17 male students rent-free housing; 58% of those paired with a room-mate with similar attitudes formed friendships as opposed to friendships between 25% of those with dissimilar room-mates.

Byrne and Nelson (1965) found a significant linear relationship between attraction and similar attitudes when participants rated people on the basis of seeing their responses to an attitude questionnaire.

Evaluation

• It is important to distinguish between similarity in attitudes, demographic characteristics and personality. Winch (1958) argued that people seek a partner whose personality is *complementary*.

Theories of relationship formation

> This is a learning theory account of relationship formation, as it is based on the concept of reinforcement.

Reinforcement-Affect Model (Clore and Byrne, 1974)

We learn to associate positive feelings (affect) with people or situations which reward us (reinforcement).

Research evidence

Veitch and Griffitt (1976) placed participants in a waiting room where they listened to either good or bad news with a stranger present. When they were asked to rate the stranger the degree of liking was related to the kind of news they had been listening to.

Evaluation

• Duck (1992) criticises such bogus stranger methods for being *artificial*.

Need satisfaction (Argyle, 1994)

There are seven basic motives or needs, each of which can be satisfied at least in part by interpersonal relationships: biological (e.g. eating together), dependency (e.g. being comforted), affiliation (seeking company), dominance (establishing social order), sex (reproduction), aggression (interpersonal hostility), and self-esteem (being valued by others).

Evaluation

• Presents a *one-sided picture*, omitting the behaviour of other people.

Sociobiological theory

Only those behaviours which increase an individual's reproductive success are naturally selected (see page 108). This theory would predict, for example, that women can increase their reproductive success by choosing high-status males who can control sufficient resources to provide for the offspring. Men use physical characteristics, such as youth and symmetry (= 'attractiveness') as a guide to reproductive ability.

Research evidence

Dunbar (1995) found that 'lonely hearts' ads supported this: women seek resources and offer attractiveness whereas the reverse is true for males.

Evaluation

• This approach is directed at *reproductive relationships* only, is *deterministic* and based on studies on non-human *animal behaviour*.

Practice essay 1.4

Discuss research studies related to interpersonal attraction.   (24 marks)

1.5 Maintenance and dissolution of relationships

Both social exchange and equity theories are sometimes called 'economic theories' because they explain relationships in terms of maximising rewards and minimising costs.

Relationships are also maintained through daily routines, which offer comfortable predictability.

Equity theory is a version of social exchange theory which attempts to quantify what makes a relationship fair. Both over- and under-benefits are not fair. Social exchange theory is only concerned with under-benefits.

In the initial stages of a relationship sensitive personal information is exchanged (reciprocal self-disclosure), later this changes to offering support for problems rather than by engaging in self-disclosure.

Social exchange theory would predict that dissolution is the result of an imbalance in rewards and costs; and/or a better alternative.

These stage models may be useful in marriage guidance, to identify the stage of dissolution reached and suggest appropriate strategies.

A strength of this model is the inclusion of repair strategies.

These models tend to apply mainly to romantic relationships.

Theories of relationship maintenance

Social exchange theory (Thibaut and Kelley, 1959)

Satisfaction (profit) is determined by exchange of rewards and costs. There are two comparisons: between actual and expected rewards (*comparison level*, CL), and the comparison level for alternatives (CLalt). Relationships develop through key stages:

- *sampling* – explore rewards and costs directly or indirectly (observing others)
- *bargaining* – prospective partners establish sources of profit and loss
- *commitment* – routines are established
- *institutionalisation* – norms and mutual expectations are established.

Research evidence

Rusbult (1983) found that 'costs' are only calculated after the honeymoon phase.

Simpson *et al.* (1990) found that participants who were dating rated members of the opposite sex as less attractive, demonstrating that they close themselves off from attractive alternatives.

Evaluation

- *Mechanistic* approach. In reality it is difficult to define rewards or costs precisely.
- The model doesn't *quantify* the point of dissatisfaction.
- *Relationship differences*. Clark and Mills (1979) argued that romantic relationships are communal rather than exchange relationships.

Equity theory (Walster *et al.*, 1978)

Balance is achieved more through perceived fairness, as in the *matching hypothesis*. Inequity results in striving to restore balance or in dissolution.

Research evidence

Hatfield *et al.* (1972) interviewed over 500 students about equity in their relationships. Three months later the inequitable relationships were more likely to have ended.

Evaluation

- Equity may be maintained by matching any *'attractive' characteristics*, such as physical looks, money or status.
- *Individual differences*. Individuals low in exchange orientation don't bother about equity (Buunk and VanYperen, 1991).
- *Cultural differences*. Equity is not a norm for all cultures.

Theories of relationship dissolution

Lee's (1984) stage model

Dissolution is a process taking place over a period of time:

- *dissatisfaction* – problems recognised
- *exposure* – problems identified and brought out into the open
- *negotiation* – discussion about the issues raised during the exposure stage
- *resolution attempts* – both partners try to find ways of solving the problems
- *termination* – if the resolution attempts are unsuccessful.

Research evidence

Lee (1984) studied over 100 premarital romantic break-ups, and drew up the five stages. Those relationships that had been the strongest took the longest time to work through the five stages of dissolution.

Duck's (1984) model of relational dissolution

- *Breakdown*: dissatisfaction leads to crisis. *Repair strategy*: correct own faults.
- *Intra-psychic phase*: thinking about the relationship; in private, then with confidants. *Repair strategy*: re-establish liking for partner.
- *Dyadic phase*: deciding whether to break up or repair. *Repair strategy*: express conflict, clear the air and reformulate rules for a future relationship.
- *Social phase*: including others in the debate, enlisting support for your 'side'.

Repair strategy: outsiders may help patch things up or encourage separation.

- *Grave dressing phase*: public and private post-mortem. *Repair strategy*: decide on a mutually acceptable version of events; salvage friendship.

Evaluation

- Lee's model is mainly concerned with *events leading up to* dissolution, whereas Duck's model concerns processes after breakdown.
- Neither model explains why breakdown occurs; they are *descriptive*.

Duck's (1982) risk factors

1 *Predisposing personal factors* (dispositional): distasteful personal habits, change in interests, poor role models (e.g. parents divorced), poor social skills.
2 *Precipitating factors* (situational): such as deception, boredom, relocation, conflict.

Evaluation

- These factors offer an *explanation* for dissolution.
- Many relationships are *stable* despite the presence of such factors.
- Some of the factors are *intervening variables*, for example lower educational levels may be associated with divorce but not the cause.

Felmlee's (1995) *'fatal attraction theory'* suggests that the same characteristic(s) which initially caused attraction ultimately lead to dissolution. Such characteristics might initially be exciting or different but later appear predictable or strange.

Psychological explanations of love

Romantic and companionate love (Bersheid and Walster, 1978)

Companionate love is an extension of liking. It develops through mutual rewards, familiarity, and tends to deepen over time.

Romantic/passionate love is based on intense emotions which often become diluted over time, and a mixture of emotions (e.g. excitement and deep despair).

Sternberg's (1986) triangular theory of love

- *Intimacy* (emotional component): mutual understanding and support.
- *Passion* (motivational): physical attraction, need for self-esteem.
- *Decision/commitment* (cognitive): short- and long-term decisions.

Rubin (1970) suggested that love could be measured in terms of three main factors: desire to help the other person, dependent needs of the other person and feelings of exclusiveness and absorption. Liking could be measured in terms of respect for the other person's abilities and similarity of the other person.

	Intimacy	Passion	Commitment
Liking/friendship	✓	✗	✗
Romantic love	✓	✗	✗
Companionate love	✓	✗	✓
Empty love	✗	✗	✓
Fatuous love	✗	✓	✓
Infatuated love	✗	✓	✗
Consummate love	✓	✓	✓

Evaluation

- Classifications can be used to identify *where changes can be made*.
- Some of the components are rather *vague*.

Three-factor theory of love (Hatfield and Walster, 1981)

(i) a state of physiological arousal (ii) an appropriate label for that arousal (cultural influence) and (iii) an appropriate love object.

See Schachter and Singer's (1962) cognitive labelling theory of emotion, page 56.

Research evidence

Dutton and Aron (1974) arranged for men to be interviewed by an attractive female either on a high suspension bridge (high arousal) or a low bridge. The high arousal condition led to greater attraction presumably because the men misattributed the arousal they felt as sexual attraction rather than fear.

Lee (1973) proposed six styles of love: Ludus (game-playing love), Mania (possessive love), Pragma (logical love), Agape (altruistic love), Storge (companionate love) and Eros (romantic love).

Evaluation

- Can explain *cultural differences* and 'love at first sight'.
- May only be *relevant to certain* love experiences.

Practice essay 1.5

(a) Describe **one** theory related to the maintenance of relationships. (12 marks)

(b) Evaluate the theory related to the maintenance of relationships that you described in part (a). (12 marks)

1.6 Cultural and sub-cultural differences in relationships

AQA A ▶ U4

AQA B ▶ U4

A *collectivist society* is one where individuals share tasks, belongings and value interdependence, unlike an *individualist society* which emphasises individuality, individual needs and independence.

Moghaddam *et al.* (1993) conclude that social relationships tend to be individualist, voluntary and temporary in Western cultures, whereas elsewhere they are collective, obligatory and permanent.

Hsu (1981) distinguished between Americans and Chinese individuals by saying that the former would ask 'How does my heart feel?', whereas the latter would ask 'What will other people say?'

Differences between Western and non-Western cultures

Individualist and collectivist

Many theories of relationships are more appropriate for individualist, Western, societies probably because they are based on research studies conducted there.

Research evidence

Argyle *et al.* (1986) compared the friendship rules selected by people from Japan and Hong Kong (collectivist cultures), and Italy and Britain (individualist cultures). They found evidence of universal features, for example all respondents distinguished between intimate and non-intimate relationships. They also found differences, such as the Japanese endorsing more rules for avoiding conflict, the Italians being more concerned with regulating intimacy, and there were more rules for obedience in the East.

LeVine *et al.* (1995) interviewed young people in 11 countries, asking them 'If a man/woman had all the other qualities you desired, would you marry this person if you were not in love with him/her?' In most collectivist societies the highest percentage was 'yes' (e.g. India 49%) whereas in England it was 7.3%.

Voluntary and involuntary

Moghaddam (1998) identifies the major difference between Western-style marriage and non-Western arranged marriages in terms of Sternberg's love triangle (see page 25). In Western, romantic marriages, passion is most important during the initial stages of a relationship but in arranged marriages commitment is, and that commitment involves the entire family.

Research evidence

Harris (1995) found that only 6 out of 42 societies world-wide gave individuals complete freedom of choice of marriage partner.

Ghuman (1994) studied Sikhs, Hindus and Muslims living in Britain and found that arranged marriages are common.

Yelsma and Athappilly (1988) compared happiness in arranged Indian marriages with both Indian and American love matches, and found satisfaction higher in the former.

Permanent and impermanent

Social norms affect the way individuals conduct their relationships.

Research evidence

Statistics indicate Chinese divorce rates are less than 4% and US rates are over 40% (US Bureau of Census, 1992). Divorce is likely to be higher in individualist societies because of the view that one should seek the ideal partner.

Brodbar-Nemzer (1986) found greater marital stability in traditional New York Jewish families (collectivist) than those who had assimilated more into the individualist US society. Over 4000 households were interviewed.

All Muslim men are permitted to have up to four permanent wives, Shi'i Muslims are additional allowed any number of temporary wives (lasting between 15 minutes and 15 years) (Haeri, 1989). This means that extramarital affairs are essentially condoned and more common than, e.g. in the US where 25% of men admit to such affairs (Gagnon *et al.*, 1994).

Sub-cultural differences in relationships

Research evidence

Risavy (1996) found that men tended to display Lee's love style called Agape (altruistic love) whereas women endorsed Pragma (logical love). Older men were generally more pragmatic than younger men. There were no social class differences.

Haskey (1984) reported that divorce rates were four times higher in unskilled manual families than in professional families.

Argyle (1994) noted a tendency for middle-class individuals to have friendships based on shared interests and attitudes, and with work colleagues.

Evaluation of cultural research

- Research conducted in different cultures is likely to suffer from *observer bias* and the use of *imposed etics* (such as the use of Western questionnaires to assess attitudes).
- Conclusions may be based on small and possibly *biased samples*.
- The *differences within cultures* may be as great as those between cultures.

'Understudied' relationships

Gay and lesbian relationships

Kitzinger and Coyle (1995) suggest that research on gays and lesbians has gone through three phases:

- *heterosexual bias* – heterosexuality is more natural than homosexuality
- *liberal humanism* – homosexual and heterosexual couples are basically similar
- *liberal humanism plus* – there are special characteristics of gay and lesbian relationships.

Research evidence

Similarities: Kurdek and Schmitt (1986) measured love and liking and found no significant differences in married, heterosexual cohabiting, gay and lesbian couples.

Differences: Blumstein and Schwartz (1983) interviewed couples who had been together for more than ten years; 22% of wives, 30% of husbands, 43% of lesbians and 94% of gay men reported having had sex with at least one person other than their partner. They also found that a lack of power equality was more a factor in the breakdown of lesbian and gay relationships than heterosexual marriages.

Kitzinger and Coyle (1995) point out that gay and lesbian couples have to survive in the face of considerable hostility from society. The longer duration of heterosexual relationships is likely to be due to the greater social support they receive.

Electronic relationships

Usenets

Discussion groups ('usenets') exist for sharing information (e.g. about sleep problems), seeking advice (e.g. counselling services), conversation (e.g. chat rooms) or playing games (e.g. MUDs – Multi-User Dungeons).

Cyberaffairs

Griffiths (1999) suggests that there are three types of cyberaffair:

- two people meet on the Internet and engage in an erotic dialogue
- relationships that are more emotional than sexual, leading to offline contact
- two people meet offline but maintain their relationship online, possibly because of geographical distance.

Young (1999) explains the appeal of such relationships with the ACE Model (anonymity, convenience and escape) and Cooper (1998) uses the Triple A Engine (access, affordability and anonymity).

Problems with electronic relationships

- Individuals may *masquerade* as something they are not.
- Internet relationships encourage *vulnerable individuals* to be seduced emotionally and sexually, and may *replace real-life relationships*; the latter are ultimately more complex and satisfying.

Any studies conducted in non-Western cultures are plagued with the difficulties inherent in cross-cultural misunderstanding.

Research into homosexual relations is an example of socially sensitive research, insofar as it is research that may have direct social consequences and concerns an area where there is little agreement and much bias.

Electronic communication (like snail mail) lacks important nonverbal signals which communicate emotion. There is a growing set of symbols to overcome this. Many people pepper their messages with 'emoticons' such as :-)) or :-(or ;-).

Fasgrolia (fast-growing language of abbreviations, initialisms and acronyms) are used as well, such as IMHO (In My Humble Opinion) and LOL (Laughing Out Loud)

You might consider how a relationship over the Internet differs from the more traditional relationship that exists with a penpal.

Practice essay 1.6

Discuss cultural and sub-cultural differences in relationships, with reference to 'understudied' relationships.

(24 marks)

Pro- and anti-social behaviour

1.7 Nature and causes of aggression

AQA A | U4
EDEXCEL | U4, U5
OCR | U5, U6

Aggression is a first act of hostility with the deliberate intention of harming another against their will.

Social psychological theories of aggression

Social learning theory (SLT)

We learn both aggressiveness and how to express aggression through direct reinforcement (conditioning theory) and indirect reinforcement (social learning). Bandura (1977) suggested that there are four steps in the modelling process.

- *Attention.* If a person (model) is prestigious or similar you will pay more attention.
- *Retention.* Actions must be remembered (i.e. cognitive processes involved).
- *Reproduction.* Vicarious reinforcement is not enough, imitation requires skills.
- *Motivation.* Imitation depends on direct and indirect reinforcements and punishments.

'Social' learning is learning that involves others.

Research evidence

Bandura *et al.* (1961, 1963) showed that, if children watched someone else behave aggressively towards Bobo-the-doll (punching it, shouting at it and hitting it with a hammer), they were more likely to be aggressive *and* to imitate specific actions when they were placed on their own with the doll (after being mildly frustrated). Other findings and later variations found that imitation was even more likely if:

- the model was *rewarded*
- the model had high *status*, for example, a favourite hero or heroine on TV
- the child *identified* with the model, for example same sex
- *live models* were more effective than a film or a cartoon
- the person had low *self-esteem*.

Aggressive video games provide an opportunity to observe the effects of models on behaviour. For example, Cooper and Mackay (1986) observed the free play of 9- and 10-year-old children after they had played aggressive video games, and found that aggressive behaviour increased in girls but not boys.

Evaluation

- Research findings may be due to *demand characteristics* in an unfamiliar social situation (the children had to look for cues of what to do with Bobo).
- Can explain *media influences* (see page 33).
- Can explain influence of *coercive home environments*. Parents solve disputes aggressively, children model their behaviour on this (Patterson *et al.*, 1989).
- Can account for *cultural* and *individual differences* between people.
- It explains the fact that people imitate *specific acts* of violence.
- *Oversimplified.* People are not consistently rewarded for aggression, often they are punished.
- *Environmental determinism.* Suggests that aggression is externally caused.

Deindividuation describes the loss of a sense of personal identity that can occur when, for example, in a crowd or wearing a mask. It is associated with a reduced sense of personal responsibility and increased anti-social behaviour.

Deindividuation

The presence of a crowd (or group) leads individual members to feel anonymous and act according to a different set of rules than they would normally.

Zimbardo (1969) suggested that:

- *individuated behaviour* is rational, consistent with personal norms
- *deindividuated behaviour* is unrestrained, acting on primitive impulses, leads to anti-social acts.

Zimbardo's classic *Stanford Prison Study* involved deindividuated behaviour from both prisoners and guards. It was described in the *Revise AS Guide*.

Research evidence

Zimbardo (1963) repeated Milgram's (1963) obedience experiments with participants either wearing a name tag (individuated) or in a hood (deindividuated). The latter gave more shocks.

Diener *et al.* (1976) observed the behaviour of over 1000 children on Halloween; the house owner asked some of the children to give their names. Those who remained anonymous were more likely to steal some money and/or extra chocolate when briefly left alone (i.e. behave anti-socially).

Evaluation

- In some instances deindividuation leads to increased *pro-social behaviour* .
- As with obedience, an individual can elect whether to behave *autonomously*.

Relative deprivation theory

The gap between what one has and what one feels one deserves leads to feelings of relative deprivation and aggression.

Runciman (1966) distinguished between two forms of relative deprivation:

- *egotistic deprivation* – derived from comparison with other similar individuals
- *fraternalistic deprivation* – derived from comparisons with other groups.

Research evidence

Abeles (1976) interviewed over 900 poor Blacks living in the US to find out why, when socioeconomic conditions were improving for Blacks, there were still so many urban riots. The respondents felt they were still worse off when compared with White counterparts whose incomes had also increased. They also had increased expectations.

Evaluation

- Can explain feelings of aggression expressed by a *whole group*.
- Can explain why some *well-off members* of minority groups continue to feel relative deprivation (fraternalistically rather than egotistically).

Effects of environmental stressors

Research evidence

Overcrowding: Calhoun (1962) described 'behavioural sink', a pathological response to overcrowding in rats. Co *et al.* (1984) studied prison populations and found as density increased so did disciplinary problems and death rates.

Temperature: Baron and Ransberger (1978) linked collective violence in the US and heat, up to a point. When it becomes very hot, people become lethargic.

Pain: Berkowitz *et al.* (1979) placed participants' hands in cold or warm water. They caused greater harm to a partner in the cold water condition.

Noise: Glass *et al.* (1969) found that unpredictable noise has a 'psychic' cost because it required attention, whereas constant noise can be 'tuned out'. Noise led to frustration.

Lack of control: Glass *et al.* (1969) found that when some participants were given a button, ostensibly to control the noise, they showed greater task persistence. Donnerstein and Wilson (1976) found angered participants gave greater shocks except when they had a control button.

Frustration-aggression hypothesis

Environmental stressors may increase frustration. Dollard *et al.* (1939) suggested that frustration always leads to some form of aggression and aggression is always the result of frustration.

Research evidence

Frustration triggers aggression. Geen and Berkowitz (1967) frustrated their participants using insoluble puzzles. If the participant then watched an aggressive film and the confederate used a name from the film ('Kirk' as in Kirk Douglas) then the number of shocks given to the confederate was greater.

Cues also trigger aggression. Berkowitz and LePage (1967) showed that when students received electric shocks from a confederate and then were given the opportunity to do the reverse, level of shocks were higher when a gun was close to the shock machine.

Evaluation

- General levels of arousal may be a better explanation (*arousal-aggression hypothesis*) since environmental stressors are physiologically arousing.
- Some events are physiologically arousing but lead to positive behaviour, such as loud music. Stressors may amplify mood (*density-intensity hypothesis*).
- This explanation *combines* biological and social factors (physiological arousal and learned responses to cues).

The feelings of aggression arising from relative deprivation exacerbate existing prejudices about outgroups, especially at times of economic hardship.

Trade union leaders are often well off themselves. They experience fraternalistic but not egotistic deprivation.

Sources of stress were discussed in the *Revise AS Guide*. This is a review of the information covered there.

Aggression can also be explained in terms of *disinhibition* – seeing someone else behave aggressively may reduce one's own inhibitions about behaving in this way.

The term '*weapons effect*' is sometimes used to describe cues to aggression, such as guns.

Practice essay 1.7

Critically consider **one** social psychological theory of aggression. (24 marks)

1.8 Altruism and bystander behaviour

Explanations of altruism

Biological and psychological altruism

> *Pro-social behaviour* is voluntary behaviour which benefits others.
>
> *Altruism* is putting the interests of others first, possibly with some risk or cost to the altruist.

- *Biological altruism*: The principle of natural selection predicts that individuals should behave selfishly to promote their own survival and reproduction. However, even though an altruistic act may decrease reproductive potential, it increases the survival of the genes; altruism is selfish at the levels of the genes. This is called *kin selection* (because one's kin are being favoured) and is referred to as 'apparent altruism' because it is actually selfish behaviour. (Other kinds of biological altruism are discussed on pages 109–110.)

- *Psychological altruism*: Altruism in humans is influenced by personal choice, empathy, morals and social norms. The behaviour of the bystander, Lenny Skutnik, who drowned while saving passengers from an aircrash in the Potomac River illustrates all of these.

> The empathy–altruism model suggests that people are not always motivated to behave selfishly.

The empathy-altruism hypothesis (Batson *et al.*, 1981)

People are more motivated to help when they feel empathy for a victim rather than just seeing the distress. Batson claims that empathy is an innate trait, like altruism.

Research evidence

Batson *et al.* (1981) asked female students to take the place of 'Elaine' who was receiving mild electric shocks. Those who were led to believe that a placebo drug they took led to empathetic concern offered to take the shocks whereas those who had been led to believe that they would feel distress were more likely to leave.

Evaluation

> It is also possible to explain altruism in terms of *social norms* (see cultural differences on p. 32).

- *Developmental evidence* suggests that children do become more altruistic as their empathy develops.
- Smith *et al.* (1989) proposed the *empathic joy hypothesis*, that we help another because empathy leads to shared feelings of joy. However, Batson *et al.* (1991) found those lowest in empathic concern were keenest to hear about their successful altruistic act, supporting the empathy-altruism hypothesis.

The negative-state relief model (Cialdini, 1987)

> The negative-state relief model proposes that altruism is ultimately a selfish act (called '*egotistic altruism*').

Altruists act because of a desire to reduce their own negative state of distress which has been created through empathising with the victim.

Research evidence

Cialdini *et al.* (1987) misinformed participants about the effects of a placebo drug – saying it would 'fix' their mood. They found, as predicted, that participants were less prepared to help a student who was receiving shocks if this wouldn't help them to reduce their own sad feelings.

Evaluation

- There is evidence that people *do not* always act out of *self-interest*. Lerner and Lichtman (1968) found participants would voluntarily receive electric shocks in place of their partner if told the other girl was scared or that she would leave the experiment unless she was the control.
- We may only feel distress when we are *attached* to the other person, therefore this model cannot explain all altruistic behaviour.

> The *bystander effect* describes the fact that the presence of others (bystanders) reduces the likelihood that help will be offered in an emergency situation.

Explanations of bystander behaviour

Bystander intervention is pro-social behaviour at minimal cost to the helper. The various studies by Latané and Darley were the result of questions asked after the tragic death of Kitty Genovese. She was fatally stabbed despite the fact that at least 38 people heard her screams. Why did no one act, even to phone the police?

Diffusion of responsibility

Darley and Latané (1968) arranged a conversation over an intercom between students.

One confederate said he suffered from seizures and later appeared to collapse. When participants thought they were the only listener, 85% helped; if there was one bystander 62% helped; with four bystanders 31% helped. It is worth noting that participants couldn't actually see if anyone else was helping.

Latané and Darley (1968) asked participants to fill out a bogus questionnaire in a room which filled with smoke. If the participant was alone 75% reported the emergency within six minutes; with two other participants this dropped to 12%.

Evaluation

* *Laboratory studies* may not represent real responses. In a field experiment on the New York subway Piliavin *et al.* (1969) demonstrated a reversal of the diffusion of responsibility effect. The more passengers in the immediate vicinity of the victim, the more likely help would be given. This may be because the costs of helping were low and not helping were high; it was also clearly an emergency and the victim could be seen (i.e. relatively unambiguous) and was less easy to ignore.

Pluralistic ignorance

Clark and Word (1972) arranged for a maintenance worker to walk through a room with a ladder while participants were filling out a questionnaire. Later a crash is heard. If this was followed by 'Oh my back, I can't move' everyone offered help, whether alone or in a group, whereas only 30% helped in the ambiguous situation when nothing was heard after the crash. In ambiguous or novel situations we look to others to tell us what to do. Each non-responding bystander is communicating: 'It's OK, no action needs to be taken.'

Evaluation apprehension

Latané and Darley (1976) tested all three explanations by observing participants' willingness to help a victim when they could (i) see the victim and be seen by other bystanders (diffusion of responsibility), (ii) see but not be seen (diffusion plus social responsibility), (iii) not see but be seen (diffusion plus audience inhibition), (iv) neither see nor be seen by onlookers (diffusion plus social responsibility plus audience inhibition). The likelihood of help was least in condition (v) and most in (vi).

Characteristics of the victim

Piliavin *et al.* (1969, above) found that when the victim carried a cane 95% of bystanders helped within 10 seconds, if he appeared drunk help came in 50% of the trials. Varying the race (Black or White) of the victim, or his attractiveness (presence of an ugly facial birthmark) also altered the likelihood of helping.

Bickman (1974) left a dime in a telephone box. If the experimenter was dressed in a suit he got the dime back 77% of the time, if he was wearing unkempt work clothes there was a 38% return rate.

Characteristics of the helper

Piliavin *et al.* (1969, above) found that men were more likely to help than women.

Bierhoff *et al.* (1991) found that helpers at the scene of a traffic accident were likely to have a high internal locus of control, held a belief in a 'just world', were more able to empathise, and were less egocentric than non-helpers.

Models of bystander behaviour

The decision model (Latané and Darley, 1968)

The factors which lead a person to decide whether or not to help in an emergency.

1 *Notice something is wrong.* Darley and Batson (1973) showed that students who were rushing to a lecture were less likely to help a man moaning and many said it was because they had not noticed.

2 *Interpret it as an emergency* (ambiguity). Shotland and Huston (1979) found that people were more likely to help in emergencies (e.g. a person needs an insulin injection) than non-emergencies (e.g. needing an allergy injection).

3 *Decide whether to take personal responsibility* (diffusion of responsibility), e.g. Darley and Latané (1968, above).

The more people there are, the less that help is forthcoming. Each individual feels less responsibility because it is shared and therefore spread out (diffused). This is opposite to the commonsense view that the more people present, the more that help should be forthcoming.

Pluralistic ignorance is a form of *informational social influence*, a concept introduced in the *Revise AS Guide* to explain conformity in ambiguous situations.

The bystander wants to avoid looking foolish. The larger the audience the more inhibited we feel (*audience inhibition*).

People are more likely to help some people than others. It may be related to 'deservingness'.

4 *Decide what type of help to give.* Bryan and Test (1967) showed that where a man stopped to help a stranded woman motorist, observers were more likely to do the same for another driver 5 minutes down the road. This is social learning.

5 *Implement the decision.* At any stage the decision may be 'no'.

Evaluation

- This model is a rather *mechanistic* approach to behaviour.
- People may not have the time for such apparently *logical decisions* and are more likely to act impulsively.
- Doesn't explain why people are helpful.

Arousal: cost-reward model (Piliavin *et al.*, 1969, above)

The decision to help is based on a cost-benefit analysis, driven by arousal.

1 *Physiological arousal.* The primary motive is the need to reduce the arousal created by seeing someone in distress.

2 *Labelling the arousal*, e.g. as personal distress or empathetic concern.

3 *Evaluating the consequences* of helping, consider costs of helping (e.g. effort, potential harm) and benefits of helping (e.g. social approval, self-esteem).

Evaluation

- *Arousal* has been shown to be an important component.
- This model does not explain *selfless behaviour*.

Cultural differences in pro-social behaviour

Identifying cultural differences

National differences

It is important to distinguish between a culture and a nation. Many studies of a culture are actually studies of a national group.

Whiting and Whiting (1975) measured altruism in six countries and found 100% of Kenyan children behaved altruistically compared with 8% of American children. The others (India, Japan, Philippines, Mexico) were in between the two extremes.

Gender differences

Eagly and Crowley (1986) concluded from past research that men are more likely to help when the situation involves some danger, or when there is an audience.

Individualist versus collectivist societies

An individualist society emphasises the rights and interests of the individual, in contrast with a collectivist one where individuals share tasks, belongings and income. The emphasis is on 'I' rather than 'we-ness'.

Nadler (1986) found that children raised on kibbutzim (collectivist society) were more likely to seek help on an anagram task than those raised in Israeli cities (individualist society).

Explaining cultural differences

Social norms and social learning

In different cultural settings, we learn different social norms for behaviour. People are more helpful in rural locations. Korte and Kerr (1975) found that 70% of the stamped postcards dropped in small towns around Boston were posted as compared with 61% of those dropped in Boston itself.

Research on cultural differences tends to be conducted outside laboratories and may demonstrate greater helpfulness than traditional bystander research because of the social context.

We model our own behaviour on others. See Bryan and Test (1967, above).

Childrearing practices

Children learn pro-social behaviour through parents and the media. For example, Rosenhan (1970) showed that helpfulness is learned from parents. Those who had warm relations with parents who were concerned about moral issues *and* the parents acted on this were more likely to behave altruistically.

Practice essay 1.8

(a) Describe **two** research studies related to bystander behaviour. (12 marks)

(b) Assess the value of these studies for understanding altruism **and/or** bystander behaviour. (12 marks)

1.9 Media influences on pro- and anti-social behaviour

The term 'media' refers to any medium of communication: television, films and video most obviously but also books, magazines, plays, songs and so on.

Explanations of media influence

Imitation

We learn to behave in a pro- or anti-social manner from observational learning and vicarious reinforcement (*social learning theory*). This is especially likely if the observer identifies with the characters. Bandura *et al.*'s research (see page 28) shows that children imitate specific acts and general levels of aggression increase.

Disinhibition effect

The media present social norms about what behaviours are common and acceptable. Normally we are inhibited about behaving in certain ways. These new social norms may alter our behaviour. In America, the lawyer for a 15-year-old who shot his neighbour in the course of a burglary claimed that the boy's sense of reality had been distorted through excessive exposure to television.

Desensitisation

Exposure to violence may desensitise us so that we tolerate it more easily in real life. Drabman and Thomas (1975) showed young children a film which was either violent or non-violent but exciting. The participants were then asked to monitor the behaviour of two younger children via a TV link. When the confederates started hitting each other, the children who were exposed to the violent film were slower to call for help.

Cognitive priming

Cues presented in the media may later trigger pro- or anti-social thoughts and feelings. Josephson (1987) showed a violent TV programme, involving a walkie-talkie, to one group of boys while another group watched a programme about a motocross team. Later, during a game of hockey, those boys who had instructions via a walkie-talkie *and* had watched the violent film were most violent.

Stereotypes

All media need to communicate a great deal of information in a relatively short time, so they use standard cultural stereotypes such as foreigners playing 'baddies', overweight people depicted as 'jolly', and wolves as big and bad. Such stereotypes may or may not reflect reality, and may be positive or negative.

Gunter (1986) found that people who watch a lot of television hold more stereotyped beliefs, suggesting that the use of stereotypes on television does have an influence. Alternatively, people (e.g. children) who have a more simplistic cognitive style and tend to use stereotypes may prefer to watch more television.

Many programmes use *counter-stereotypes* (such as a Black female doctor) to try to alter our stereotypical views. However, the deliberate manipulation of stereotypes, for good or bad, is ethically questionable because it presumes that certain stereotypes are preferable.

Displacement effect

A media bias would be less harmful if it was sufficiently counterbalanced by experience of the real world. However, people who spend a lot of time watching television or reading books have less time for real interactions. Gerbner and Gross (1976) found that people who watch a lot of television rate the outside world as being more dangerous and threatening than it actually is (*deviance amplification*).

Keith *et al.* (1986) found that children who watch far more television than average perform less well at school.

Stimulation hypothesis

Television is an ideal medium to present educational information, and is a resource much used by schools. *Sesame Street* provides preschool children with carefully considered material to promote emotional, social and intellectual development. The value of television and all media is related to what you actually watch, read or listen to.

Evaluation

- There are important *individual differences*. For example, people who are more aggressive may choose to watch anti-social programmes and/or are more influenced by them.

Media influences on pro-social behaviour

Friedrich and Stein (1973) studied American preschool children, who watched episodes of a pro-social television programme called *Mister Rogers' Neighbourhood*. These children remembered much of the pro-social information contained in the programmes, and they behaved in a more helpful and cooperative way than did children who watched other television programmes with neutral or aggressive content. They became even more helpful if they role-played pro-social events from the programmes.

Lovelace and Huston (1983) suggested three types of pro-social programming.

1 *Pro-social behaviour only*, e.g. Sprafkin *et al.* (1975) showed TV episodes to 6-year-olds, after which they had the chance to help some distressed puppies. Those children who watched a boy rescuing a puppy spent longer helping than those who watched a programme where no helping was involved. This shows that they imitated specific acts they had seen.

2 *Pro-social conflict resolution*. More typically pro-social programmes include conflict resolution. Paulson (1974) reported mixed effects of a *Sesame Street* programme that showed pro-social resolutions of anti-social behaviours.

3 *Conflict without resolution*. This may be better for older children, and requires someone to discuss the conflict with the child.

Evaluation

- Messages presented in an *artificial environment* may not generalise to real-life and are situation-specific.
- Children may model the *anti-social behaviours* that are resolved instead of the resolution.

> Greenfield (1984) found that *Sesame Street's* use of ethnic and disabled minorities helped children from minority groups have a greater sense of cultural pride.

Media influences on anti-social behaviour

Correlational studies

Robinson and Bachman (1972) found a positive correlation in adolescent self-reports of the number of TV hours watched and amounts of aggressive behaviour. Wiegman *et al.* (1992) followed 400 Dutch secondary school pupils over a period of three years, and found that positive correlations between watching television violence and aggressive behaviour disappeared if initial levels of aggression were taken into account.

Field experiments

Parke *et al.* (1977) looked at the effect of violent and non-violent films on Belgian and American male juvenile delinquents. Aggression increased on some measures in the 'violent-film' group but on other measures increased only in those who were naturally high in aggression.

> Anti-social behaviours include negative gender stereotypes. Manstead and McCulloch (1981) found that the majority of advertisements still use gender stereotypes, a potentially anti-social effect. Williams' (1985) study found that children's sex role attitudes became more traditional and sex-stereotyped after they had been exposed to Americanised television culture.

Natural experiments

In Williams' (1985) study of Canadians who had their first exposure to TV (the residents of 'Notel') it was found that levels of aggression increased physically and verbally. Charlton (1998) has documented the effects of Western TV on St Helena and as yet observed no increase in violence.

Longitudinal study

Huesmann *et al.* (1984) related the amount of television watched and levels of aggressiveness in some young children with the same information when the children were older. The amount of television violence watched at a young age was correlated with later aggressiveness (measured by the number of criminal convictions by the age of 30) and also with the amount of violent TV watched. This suggests that watching violent TV may be a cause of aggression and also an effect.

Practice essay 1.9

Discuss explanations of media influences on anti-social behaviour.

(24 marks)

Sample question and model answer

Discuss **one or more** explanations of the origins of prejudice **and/or** discrimination.   (24 marks)

Examiner's comments

Clearly your answer must focus on <u>causes</u> of prejudice and/or discrimination though you could consider methods of reduction as a means of evaluating explanations. The question does not require you to make any distinction between prejudice and discrimination. In terms of how many explanations to cover, you are offered the depth route (one explanation given in some detail) or the breadth route (more explanations but necessarily in less detail because of the time constraint). It may be preferable to give one explanation and use others as a means of evaluation. Of the total 24 marks, half are for your description of one or more explanations and half for the evaluation (discuss = describe + evaluate/comment).

Given that you have 30 minutes to write your answer you must be highly selective and present only material that is creditworthy rather than any background details.

Candidate's answer

Social identity theory is one way to explain the origins of prejudice. The basis of this explanation is that our self-image has two components: personal identity and social identity. Social identity is determined by three causal processes. First, is categorisation – we tend to group people into social categories, and this leads to the formation of ingroups and outgroups. This categorisation process makes social perception easier and puts less strain on our cognitive processes (we are cognitive misers). Second, we make social comparisons between groups in order to increase self-esteem. This leads to ingroup favouritism and outgroup negative bias both of which enhance social and therefore personal esteem. Third, we hold beliefs about social groups (the ingroups and outgroups) and these beliefs generate different social behaviours, such as prejudice.

The classic experiment used to support this theory was by Tajfel (1970), called the minimal group experiment. In this study he demonstrated that ingroup favouritism and outgroup negative bias can be created on the basis of almost nothing. Boys were divided into groups on the basis of a perception task (in fact the division was random). Despite this they still gave most points to those boys who they thought were in their group. In the real world this suggests that we are very ready to favour members of our own group because this increases our own social identity (because we identify with the group).

There have been criticisms of the study – for example that it involved schoolboys (a biased group) who knew each other well, and there was not a great deal at stake. The boys' behaviour may have been a demand characteristic (how else were they to behave?). On the positive side, a subsequent study by Billig and Tajfel (1973) still found ingroup favouritism when they <u>told</u> their participants that group membership was determined randomly. The results may be due to demand characteristics, but in real-life we sometimes have little other basis for determining our behaviour.

Social identity theory (SIT) offers a good explanation of why members of an ingroup favour themselves over an outgroup. Such favouritism, and the related social beliefs, might lead to prejudice but it can't explain the hostility that is associated with intergroup prejudices. For this reason SIT can't on its own explain the origins of prejudice.

A better alternative might be to use another theory in addition to SIT. For example, realistic conflict theory proposes that prejudice stems from direct competition between social groups over scarce and valued resources. This explanation assumes the pre-existence of social groups (SIT) but proposes that hostility arises because of competition and then the outgroup becomes the

Sample question and model answer (continued)

scapegoat for economic problems. This explanation is supported by various real–life studies such as Hovland and Sears (1940) who found that lynchings of Blacks increased in the southern US during periods when the price of cotton was low and therefore (presumably) farmers felt a greater sense of competition. In a more recent study Langford and Ponting (1992) interviewed non–Aboriginal Canadians and concluded that continuing prejudices towards Aboriginals (individuals who originated in that country) were positively related to perceived conflict over things like jobs. The study by Sherif *et al.* (1961) of the Robbers Cave camp also supported realistic conflict theory.

SIT might be good in situations where there is minimal information, and this is true for many prejudices because when people do get to know members of an outgroup their prejudices break down. One way to reduce prejudice is to increase contact between ingroups and outgroups. However, this doesn't always work. For example, Stouffer *et al.* (1949) found that racial prejudice amongst soldiers diminished in battle but did not extend to relations back at base.

[612 words]

Examiner's comments

This answer contains many features of a grade A essay. First, it is clearly constructed which demonstrates that the candidate has a clear grasp of what he/she is talking about. Essays often ramble as the writer recalls various bits of information with no clear sense of direction – this suggests a lack of understanding.

Second, the candidate communicates a detailed and clear knowledge of the chosen explanations, social identity theory and realistic conflict theory. Both are expressed succinctly.

Third, research studies are used well and accurately referenced. Note that the candidate has avoided the common pitfall of describing such studies in more detail than required but only selected relevant details. Some evaluation of the studies is included to help assess the value of the evidence.

The second explanation, realistic conflict theory, could be credited as evaluation but might attract more marks if taken as a second explanation – and the linking material is seen as commentary (AO2). The key point here is that both explanations are examined in terms of their value.

AO1
Accurate and well-detailed. The organisation is coherent and the content is substantial with sufficient depth and breadth given the time available (i.e. 15 minutes). Band 3 (top) = 12 marks.

AO2
The commentary is less developed. It is slightly limited but effective. Closer to 'reasonably effective' than 'highly effective' thus Band 3 (bottom) = 9 marks.

Total 21 out of 24 (see page 12 for band descriptors), equivalent to a Grade A.

Chapter 2

Physiological psychology

Physiological psychology seeks to explain behaviour in terms of body systems. The key assumption is that ultimately all behaviour can be reduced to and explained at the level of the functioning of physiological (body) systems. These systems include the central and autonomic nervous systems, the action of nerves and hormones, and the activity of individual cells.

At AS Level your study of physiological psychology may have focused on stress, as an example of a behaviour that can be explained using physiological processes.

At A2 you may select to study one or more of the following areas in physiological psychology:

Brain and behaviour

2.1 Methods of investigating the brain
2.2 Localisation of function in the cerebral cortex
2.3 Lateralisation of function in the cerebral cortex

After studying this area you should be able to:

- describe both invasive and non-invasive methods of investigating the brain
- assess the strengths and limitations of such methods
- describe functional organisation of the cerebral cortex
- describe the organisation of the primary motor, sensory and association areas of the cerebral cortex
- critically consider the extent to which cortical functions are distributed or localised
- explain lateralisation of function in the cerebral cortex, including language and other hemisphere asymmetries

Biological rhythms, sleep and dreaming

2.4 Biological rhythms
2.5 Sleep
2.6 Dreaming

After studying this area you should be able to:

- describe and evaluate research studies into circadian, infradian and ultradian biological rhythms
- explain the role of both endogenous pacemakers and exogenous zeitgebers in the control of biological rhythms
- discuss the consequences of disrupting biological rhythms, as in shiftwork and jet lag
- describe the stages of sleep
- discuss restoration and ecological theories relating to the function of sleep
- understand the implications of findings from research studies of total and partial sleep deprivation for such theories
- be aware of research findings relating to the nature of dreams (e.g. content, duration, relationships with stages of sleep)
- critically consider neurobiological and psychological theories of the function of dreaming

Motivation and emotion

2.7 Brain mechanisms of motivation
2.8 Theories of motivation
2.9 Emotion

After studying this area you should be able to:

- explain the process of homeostasis
- discuss the role of brain structures in hunger and thirst
- critically consider theories and appropriate research studies relating to hunger and thirst
- describe and assess physiological, psychological and combined approaches to explaining motivation
- discuss the role of brain structures in emotional behaviour and experience
- describe and assess physiological and combined physiological and psychological approaches to explaining behaviour and experience

Brain and behaviour

2.1 Methods of investigating the brain

Invasive methods of investigating the brain

Ablation and lesions

Ablation involves removal of parts of the brain. A lesion is a cut which may result in functional ablation (because areas are no longer connected). For example, in your AS studies the case of HM was due to ablation of his hippocampus; Lashley (1950) removed large sections of rats' cortex to discover what areas were important in learning; prefrontal lobotomies involve lesions severing the connections within the frontal lobes.

- You cannot be certain that a *primary cause* has been located.
- The damage caused in surgery *may not be limited* to specific parts of the brain.
- Conclusions drawn from animals may not always *generalise to humans*.
- *Ethical* considerations are important.

> Some techniques of investigating the brain are called 'invasive' because they involve going inside the brain and deliberately interfering with it.

> When brain lesions are produced surgically, the amount of tissue destroyed is typically less than with ablation.

Electrical recording

Implanting electrodes

Single-unit recording. A micro-electrode is inserted into the brain to obtain a record of electrical activity within a cell. For example, Hubel and Wiesel (see page 69) studied visual processing by placing single electrodes in individual cells of cats' visual cortex.

Multiple-unit recording. This uses larger electrodes and records activity from a few hundred cells instead of just one cell. It is less exact but possibly more reliable.

- *Very slow way* of understanding how the brain works.
- Mainly *limited to non-human* animals because of damage; such findings are not always applicable to humans.
- Difficult to keep single electrode *in position*.

Electrical stimulation of the brain (ESB)

A weak current is applied to a small region of the brain in a conscious patient to see what experience they report. Penfield (1955) produced recollections of specific memories and sounds by stimulating specific areas of the brain.

- *Very weak current* may not truly emulate a real nervous impulse.

Chemical methods

Temporary lesions

Sodium amytal, an anaesthetic, can be used to deactivate a hemisphere for short periods in a fully conscious patient (the *Wada test*).

- Invasive methods are *not always harmful*.

Neurotransmitter levels

Samples of neurospinal fluid (the fluid that bathes the brain) and of blood may be used to detect levels of neurotransmitters *in vivo* during, for example, certain sleep stages. Alternatively this may be done at post-mortem.

- We don't know whether raised levels of neurotransmitters are a *cause or an effect* of a condition.

> A *neurotransmitter* is a biochemical substance that transmits messages from one neuron to another.

Use of drugs

Drugs mimic the action of neurotransmitters, indicating what may be happening normally. For example, Grossman (1964) found that noradrenaline injected into a rat's brain elicited feeding, while acetylcholine elicited drinking.

- It is difficult to prove the precise effect of any chemical substance, particularly as the *effects vary* from one person to the next and most chemicals have more than one effect.

Non-invasive methods of investigating the brain

'Non-invasive' techniques involve observing the brain in action from the outside without disturbing its functioning.

Electrical techniques

EEG (electro-encephalogram)

Micro-electrodes are attached to the patient's scalp to detect electrical activity in specific parts of the brain; useful in understanding sleep stages.

- *Not very precise* because electrical activity over the whole brain is measured, and measurements are made through the skull.

Evoked potentials (event-related potentials or ERPs)

EEG records made more precise. A stimulus is presented several times, and the EEG recordings from each presentation are averaged.

When considering the precision of any method one can think of *spatial* precision (some techniques provide information about the functioning of particular neurons) or *temporal* precision (some techniques provide information about brain activity on a millisecond-by-millisecond basis).

Brain scans

Computerised axial tomography (CAT scans)

X-rays are passed through an individual's head and the level of radioactivity is detected. The denser the area the lower the radioactivity. A three-dimensional picture is constructed from repeated scans.

- *Useful* for detecting tumours and damaged parts of the brain.
- Can't *localise* areas and very *expensive*.

Magnetic resonance imaging (MRI scans)

Radio waves excite atoms producing magnetic changes which are detected by a large magnet surrounding the patient.

- Produces *very precise* 3D picture. Used to detect very small brain tumours.

Functional MRI (fMRI)

Provides both anatomical and functional information by taking repeated scans of brain in action.

- Very *fine resolution*. Provides information about brain function since brain is active.

Positron emission tomography (PET scan)

A radioactive form of glucose is injected into the body. This is taken up by active parts of the brain because they need glucose for energy. The scanner measures the positrons emitted from the radioactive glucose. Only tiny amounts of radioactivity are involved.

- PET scans show us the *brain in action*, but areas not identified with precision.
- PET scans taken over 60 seconds or more so they sum activity over a *prolonged time*.

Brain damage

Accidental damage

Phineas Gage's accident resulted in lobotomy, a form of psychosurgery still occasionally used to treat mental illness (see p. 143).

In 1848 Phineas Gage had a crowbar fired through his skull when working with explosives. He survived, but became obstinate and like a child, which led experts to suppose that prefrontal cortical damage was responsible for his changed behaviour.

Brain operations

Split-brain operations have been used to demonstrate the functional asymmetry of the brain (see page 43).

Brain illnesses and tumours

The brains of stroke or tumour patients can be examined with PET scans, and damage related to behavioural changes. Post-mortem brain examinations are made of people with known problems, as in the research by Broca and Wernicke (see page 41).

One common problem is that you cannot be certain that a primary cause has been located. For example, if you sever a person's vocal chords they cannot speak but that doesn't mean the chords are central to speech.

- Observations of human behaviour can *confirm the results of animal studies*.
- It is difficult to know whether a *primary cause* or effect has been identified.
- It is usually not possible to make *before and after comparisons* of patients.
- The process of brain injury is *traumatic*, which in itself changes behaviour.

Practice essay 2.1

(a) Describe **two** non-invasive methods of investigating the brain. (12 marks)

(b) Assess the strengths **and** limitations of these methods. (12 marks)

2.2 Localisation of function in the cerebral cortex

The functional organisation of the brain

The brain can be divided into the *forebrain*, *midbrain* (contains the *reticular activating system* (RAS) important in sleep), and *hindbrain* (contains the *cerebellum*, *pons* and *medulla*).

The *forebrain* contains, for example, the thalamus, hypothalamus, hippocampus and the cerebral cortex. The cerebral cortex is responsible for higher cognitive functions. It is divided into two halves (hemispheres) joined by fibres (including the *corpus callosum*). Each half has four lobes:

> The *cerebral cortex* is the surface few millimetres of the forebrain. It is like a tea cosy covering the brain but highly folded and accounts for 50% of the human nervous system.

- *frontal cortex* – fine voluntary movements; thinking and planning
- *parietal cortex* – somato-sensory; touch, pain, pressure and temperature
- *temporal cortex* – contains auditory cortex for hearing and balance; contributes to memory, language, emotion and perception
- *occipital cortex* – primarily responsible for vision (visual cortex).

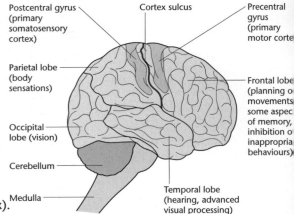

Motor functions

> The *central sulcus* is a deep fold separating the frontal and parietal lobes of the brain.

Motor neurons travel from all over the body to the spinal column and thence to the *primary motor area* in the frontal lobe, just in front of (anterior to) the *central sulcus*.

Topographical organisation

> The term '*topographical organisation*' describes how different regions of the motor area correspond to different parts of the body.

Penfield and Boldrey (1937) used ESB to stimulate different regions of the primary motor cortex and found that different parts of the body twitched. They were thus able to map the motor cortex. Some regions of the body are 'over-represented' such as the fingers and the mouth, for greater fine motor control.

Initiating movement

> Motor functions are also controlled *subcortically*, for example the cerebellum is very important in organising the sensory information that guides movement.

- An intention is formed in the *frontal lobe*, just in front of the primary motor cortex.
- The *secondary motor cortex* (between the pre-frontal area and the primary motor cortex) coordinates sensory inputs and motor outputs. This area consists of the supplementary motor area (SMA) and the premotor cortex.
- Messages are passed to the *primary motor cortex* to activate the actual muscles.

Sensory functions

> For most motor and sensory functions control is *contralateral*, the right hemisphere controls the left side of the body and *vice versa*.

Visual information is sent to the *visual cortex* (see page 68), auditory information is sent to the *auditory cortex*, and information from other body regions (such as that for touch, temperature, pressure and taste) is transmitted to the *somatosensory area*.

Primary auditory area

> Contralateral and ipsilateral input means that the sound heard in both right and left ears can be compared, which is important in identifying the direction of sound.

The primary auditory area lies in the temporal lobe. Most processing is *contralateral* (the left ear passes signals to the right auditory cortex) but some processing is *ipsilateral* (the left ear sends signals to the left auditory cortex).

Penfield also used ESB to stimulate the primary auditory cortex. He found that people would think they were hearing the ringing of a doorbell or a sound like a car starting.

The primary auditory cortex is organised in vertical functional columns. The neurons within a vertical column respond mainly to sounds of similar frequency.

Primary somatosensory area

This is located in the parietal area, just behind the primary motor cortex. Areas of the body are topographically represented. If a region of this strip is electrically stimulated it feels as if one is being touched on the corresponding region of the body.

Association areas

The remainder of the cerebral cortex, when you exclude the motor and sensory areas, is referred to as the *association cortex*. This is concerned with higher cognitive functions.

Motor association areas

There are motor association areas throughout the cortex. The frontal lobes are concerned with planning movement and coordinating sensory and motor input. People with brain damage to areas of the parietal lobe can describe what they see but have trouble using this information to guide their movements. People with damage to parts of the occipital lobe can't describe the shape and location of objects but can reach out and grasp such objects.

Sensory association areas

Visual agnosia refers to the inability to recognise objects and interpret their meaning.

The visual association cortex is concerned with, for example, movement, colour perception, object recognition and shape analysis. Damage to parts of the temporal cortex result in *visual agnosia*. Warrington and Taylor (1978) asked patients to match pictures. They matched a folded umbrella with a walking stick rather than an open umbrella because they could perceive form but not function.

Language

Language is usually controlled in the left hemisphere within localised regions.

Broca's area

Both of these regions are named after researchers who linked certain linguistic behaviours to brain damage in specific regions of the cortex using post-mortems.

Broca's area is in the anterior frontal lobe of the left cerebral cortex. It has sensory-motor connections and is involved in *speech production*. Broca's patient, Tan, could understand speech but only say 'tan'. These areas show damage when a patient is permanently unable to speak. Broca's aphasia results in, e.g. difficulty with language production (slow and poorly articulated, difficulties writing).

- When normal people speak, there is increased blood flow to Broca's area but also to the motor cortex, the left thalamus and basal ganglia. This shows that speech production is *not limited just to Broca's area*.
- Individuals with Broca's aphasia also have difficulties in *understanding*.

Wernicke's area

Damage to the connection between Broca's and Wernicke's areas is called *conduction aphasia*; patients can't repeat what others say, and can't name objects.

Wernicke's area is in the posterior temporal lobe of the left cerebral cortex. It is connected to the visual and auditory cortex and is related to *language comprehension*. Wernicke's aphasia is shown by poor language comprehension and difficulty finding the right word (*anomia*) but no difficulty with articulation.

Distributed versus localised functions

The term *localisation* refers to the idea that specific behavioural functions are governed by specific areas of the brain.

Lashley (1931) trained rats to learn a maze and then lesioned some parts of their cerebral cortex, finding that the effects were the same no matter where he made the lesions. He proposed the *principle of equipotentiality*: that all parts of the cerebral cortex had the potential to be equally involved in the storage of memories.

Lashley also proposed the principle of *mass action*: the more cortex you remove, the more severe will be the likely resulting memory deficit.

These principles suggest that memories are stored in a distributed fashion.

Why are some functions more localised than others? This is probably related to the complexity of the system. The more complex, the more the function is distributed.

While this may be true for memory in general, it is not true for other functions and it is not true for specific aspects of memory, e.g. declarative memory has been linked to the right hippocampus (Squire *et al.*, 1992).

The contradiction can be explained using the concept of *distributed control*. There are many interconnections between different localised functions and therefore damage to one specific region rarely results in a complete loss of function.

Practice essay 2.2

Discuss the extent to which functions are localised in the cerebral cortex. (24 marks)

2.3 Lateralisation of function in the cerebral cortex

Hemispheric asymmetries

Organisation of language

In most people language is organised in an asymmetrical fashion. It is controlled in the left hemisphere (see split-brain studies below).

Left hemisphere language dominance may cause some problems for left-handers because their dominant side is controlled by the right hemisphere. Therefore, for example, when writing the link between language centre and hand control is not as direct as in a right-handed person. The corpus callosum is 11% thicker in left-handers, presumably to facilitate cross-hemisphere communications (Kalat, 1998).

For example, for some left-handers writing is controlled by the right hemisphere (contralateral), this may explain strange inverted writing posture used by some left-handed people.

Not everyone has language centres on the left, when brain damage to either side of the brain results in impaired language this indicates bilateral language control which is the case for about 25% of left-handers (Satz, 1979). About 5% of right-handers have right-side language dominance. Kimura (1993) reports that speech is more bilaterally organised in women (see page 43).

Why is language lateralised?

Mixed dominance is associated with a variety of problems such as stuttering and dyslexia. Such language difficulties may be due to the presence of two competing language centres. The linguistic confusions (as between b and d) which are typical of some dyslexics may be due to having bilateral language centres.

Stutterers may have mixed dominance for speech. Jones (1966) used sodium amytal to establish where patients' speech centres were located so that he could operate on tumours (if they could still talk when the left side was paralysed, the centre must be on the right). He found that all patients with mixed dominance stuttered but after the left hemisphere centres were removed (with the tumour) their stuttering stopped.

Handedness

Handedness or hand preference is another characteristic which is asymmetrical. Hand preference has been observed in the womb in terms of thumb sucking (Stirling, 2000). About 10% of all people are either left-handed (dominant right hemisphere) or ambidextrous. Studies of prehistoric cave paintings show that this percentage has not changed, supporting the view that handedness may be innate. For some left-handers the whole brain may be reversed so that, for example, the language centres are in the right hemisphere. For other left-handers cerebral dominance is mixed.

Emotionality

The right hemisphere tends to control emotional expression and the understanding of other people's expressions. It contributes emotional content to speech. The left side of the face (controlled by the right hemisphere) generally smiles more broadly and expresses more emotion than the right side.

Gainotti (1972) studied brain-damaged patients. Those with left hemisphere damage experienced anxiety and aggression, whereas those with right hemisphere damage seemed relatively unemotional and indifferent.

Heller and Levy (1981) found that a face which is smiley on the left and neutral on the right is judged as happier than the reverse, presumably because the left side is processed by the right hemisphere.

However, Davidson *et al.* (1990) used EEG recordings and found that participants had greater left hemisphere electrical activity when experiencing pleasure (positive emotion) and more right hemisphere activity with feelings of disgust (negative emotion).

Spatial tasks

Visual and spatial tasks, such as imagery, artistic expression and pattern recognition are often performed better by the right hemisphere.

The cerebral cortex is divided into two sides or hemispheres.

The word 'lateral' means 'side'. Thus lateralisation refers to the fact that some functions are governed by one side rather than another. The result is asymmetry – the two hemispheres are not the same.

Language is also localised (see Broca's and Wernicke's areas on p. 41).

The term 'cerebral dominance' refers to the fact that one side of the brain has greater control over a particular function. In terms of motor functions, the left hemisphere is dominant for right-handed people.

When viewing a painting one might appreciate the artist's techniques (analytic) or one might appreciate the feelings conjured up by the whole painting (synthetic).

Analytic versus synthetic brain

It may be possible to explain many of the findings in terms of two general concepts: analytic (logical or bit by bit) versus synthetic (or holistic) processing. The left hemisphere is analytic and the right hemisphere is synthetic (Sperry, 1985).

Some psychologists have suggested that the left brain is scientific, rational, deductive and sequential whereas the right brain is creative, intuitive, immediate and artistic.

Gender and dominance

There is evidence that females are more likely to have bilaterality and that boys are more likely to have right-hemisphere dominance. For example, McGlone (1980) reported that damage to the right hemisphere was more likely to result in impaired visuo-spatial behaviour in men than women. Geschwind and Galaburda (1985) suggested that the male hormone testosterone may impair the development of the left hemisphere during early prenatal and postnatal development which could lead to, for example, dyslexia (linked with left hemisphere damage), which is more common in boys, and right hemisphere dominance.

Split-brain studies

If the fibres connecting the two cerebral hemispheres are cut, two functionally independent brains are created. This procedure is used in patients suffering from severe epileptic seizures.

The evidence from these split-brain studies demonstrates that language centres are in the left hemisphere.

Research evidence

Sperry and Gazzaniga (1967) tested patients' cognitive functions by placing them behind a screen with their hands free to handle objects unseen. If a word was flashed to the left side of the screen it was 'seen' by the right hemisphere only. If the participant was asked to pick up the object they could only do this with their left hand, and could not say what the object was. Patients learned ways of communicating between hemispheres, for example, if a letter was shown to the left visual field and the patient asked if it was 'A', the left hemisphere guessed the answer. The right hemisphere (which knew the answer) heard this and made a frown if the answer was wrong, the left hemisphere felt the frown and corrected the mistake (both sides control and feel the facial muscles).

How do 'split-brain individuals' cope? They learn strategies for ensuring information is received by both hemispheres but this doesn't always work. One patient had selected some clothes to wear and found her left hand independently choosing a second pair of trousers.

Jeeves (1984) reported that individuals who are born without a corpus callosum (fibres connecting cerebral hemisphere) can say words they see in either visual field (they probably have two language centres), they are slow on tasks requiring coordination of two hands and when asked to move the fingers of one hand they involuntarily move the fingers of the other hand.

Evaluation of split-brain studies

The split-brain procedure raises an interesting philosophical point (called *Fechner's question*), do split-brain patients have two minds or one?

- The problem with split-brain experiments is that they use a *small sample of abnormal individuals* (whose brains may have been damaged by the severe epilepsy). However, the findings have been confirmed in studies of normal individuals.

Split-field studies with normal individuals

Divided visual field. To test right and left visual fields in normal participants different information is very briefly presented to each field simultaneously. Right or left visual preference is shown by the fact that the participant reports one rather than the other image. Such experiments show right visual field (RVF) advantage (left hemisphere control) for words, letters and digits and LVF advantage for faces and patterns (Green, 1994).

Other support for split-brain findings comes from studies using the Wada test to anaesthetise one hemisphere, and also from studies of stroke patients who lose function of one hemisphere.

Dichotic listening tasks. Pairs of sounds are presented simultaneously to both ears. Such studies show right ear advantage (REA) for spoken words and digits, and LEA (right hemisphere) for recognition of environmental sounds and many aspects of music perception (Green, 1994).

Practice essay 2.3

Discuss research (theories **and/or** studies) relating to hemisphere asymmetries in the cerebral cortex. (24 marks)

Biological rhythms: sleep and dreaming

2.4 Biological rhythms

AQA A   U4
EDEXCEL   U5
OCR   U5, U6

A *biological rhythm* is a biologically driven behaviour that is periodically repeated.

The *suprachiasmatic nucleus* takes its name because it is located directly above the *optic chiasma* – the place where the optic nerves cross over.

The term '*zeitgeber*' is German for 'time-giver'.

The concept of 'adaptiveness' comes from evolutionary theory and refers to the idea that behaviours that persist are likely to be those that promote an individual's survival and reproduction.

Circadian comes from 'circa' (about) 'dies' (day). Circadian rhythms recur about once every 24 hours.

Body temperature also forms a circadian rhythm, reaching a low around 4 a.m. and a high around 8 p.m.

'Infra' means 'below'; infradian rhythms occur less often than once every 24 hours.

Control of biological rhythms

Endogenous (internal) pacemakers

In mammals the main endogenous pacemaker is located in the *suprachiasmatic nucleus* (SCN), a small group of cells in the hypothalamus. Rhythms are produced from protein synthesis and 'fine tuned' by light (input to the SCN comes directly from the eyes) and other stimuli. The SCN regulates production of *melatonin* in the *pineal gland*.

Biological rhythms are also endogenously regulated by *hormones*, e.g. menstruation.

Research evidence

Morgan (1995) removed the SCN from hamsters and found their circadian rhythm disappeared. The rhythm could be re-established using transplanted SCN cells.

There is evidence of separate internal clocks controlling the sleep–waking cycle and temperature. Folkard's (1996) study of Kate Aldcroft found that she developed a 30-hour sleep–wake cycle but a 24-hour temperature cycle.

Exogenous (external) zeitgebers

External stimuli may themselves be rhythmic. Day length is the dominant *zeitgeber*. Also important are the seasons, availability of food and social stimuli.

Research evidence

Miles *et al.* (1977) studied a blind man who had a 24.9 hour circadian rhythm despite being exposed to a variety of zeitgebers (such as the radio). He had to use stimulants and sedatives to coordinate his sleep–wake cycle with the rest of the world. This demonstrates that light really is the dominant time-giver.

Light cues can be overcome. Luce and Segal (1966) pointed out that people who live within the Arctic Circle still sleep for about 7 hours despite the fact that during the summer months the sun never sets. Social cues are dominant.

Evaluation

- It is *adaptive* for endogenous rhythms to be reset by external cues so that animals are in tune with seasonal variations, and day time/night time.
- It might be *life threatening* to be solely at the mercy of environmental cues, therefore endogenous cues are important too.

Circadian rhythms

Sleep–waking cycle

Siffre (1972) spent 6 months in an underground cave. His sleep/waking cycle settled down to 25–30 hours. It appears that light has a profound influence and that our 'free-running' cycle is not 24 hours, which means that we have to adjust our clocks each day.

Individual differences. Aschoff and Wever (1976) observed that some people, when isolated from daylight, maintain 24–25-hour cycles whereas others develop idiosyncrasies such as 29 hours awake and 21 hours asleep.

Evaluation

- Sleep–wake cycle *reverts* to an endogenous rhythm in the absence of external cues.
- It is normally *entrained* by external zeitgebers.

Infradian rhythms

Menstrual cycle

Endogenous hormone production may be regulated by the circadian rhythm of the SCN. Reinberg (1967) documented the menstrual cycle of a woman who spent three months in a cave. Her menstrual cycle became shorter.

Menstrual cycle can be synchronised by external factors. Russell *et al.* (1980) collected daily samples of women's underarm sweat, mixed it with alcohol and applied this to the upper lip of their female participants. The participants' menstrual cycles began to synchronise, probably due to pheromones.

Circa-annual rhythms

Migration

Gwinner (1986) kept wild birds exposing them to 12 hours of light and 12 hours of darkness. They still showed signs of migratory restlessness, suggesting endogenous control. Migration may also be triggered by the availability of food (exogenous cue).

Hibernation

Pengelly and Fisher (1957) artificially controlled squirrels' exposure to light (12 hours on/off) and temperature (0°C). Nevertheless the squirrel hibernated from October to April.

Seasonal affective disorder (SAD)

Darkness rather than temperature causes some people to become depressed at the onset of winter, probably because of increased production of melatonin (due to increases in darkness) which affects mood.

Ultradian rhythms

Sleep stages

Described on page 46.

Basic rest activity cycle (BRAC)

Klein and Armitage (1979) tested participants' performance through the day and found a 96-minute cycle, the same duration as the REM (rapid eye movement) cycle (see page 46).

Disrupting the biological clock

When external cues (such as light) change suddenly, we have to re-adjust our internal clock. In the interim our ability to cope may be harmed. Phase delay (delaying one's internal clock) is easier than phase advance (making one's internal clock skip ahead).

Shiftwork

On average it takes about three days to adjust to a 12-hour shift in time.

Hawkins and Armstrong-Esther (1978) studied 11 nurses during the first 7 nights of their duty. Performance was significantly impaired on the first night but improved through the week. Temperature was still not adjusted by the last night.

Improving shiftwork performance

Dawson and Campbell (1991) exposed participants to a 4-hour pulse of bright light on their first night and found that this helped their subsequent adjustment.

Czeisler *et al.* (1982) tested the effects of rotating shifts with the clock (phase delay). Workers in a chemical plant in Utah found phase delay led them to feel better. The management also reported increased productivity and fewer errors.

Jet lag

Klein *et al.* (1972) found that adjustment was faster for westbound flights (phase delay). Schwartz *et al.* (1995) found that East coast US baseball teams did better when travelling west than West coast teams travelling east.

On the other hand returning home may be easier than the outward journey because body temperature changes within a week but the rhythm of adrenocortical hormone production takes much longer so the body has never re-adjusted to the new time zone.

Practice essay 2.4

(a) Describe research studies that have investigated circadian rhythms. (12 marks)

(b) Assess the consequences of disrupting circadian rhythms. (12 marks)

2.5 Sleep

AQA A U4

> Sleep is not unconsciousness, it is an altered state of consciousness such that there is a decreased responsiveness to the external environment. It occurs daily (*circadian*) and has distinct stages (*ultradian*).

> Most sleepers complete about five ultradian cycles during a normal night's sleep (descending the 'sleep staircase') with progressively less SWS and more REM activity as morning approaches.

> Horne (1988) suggested that only some parts of sleep are essential (SWS and REM) and called this *core sleep*. *Micro-sleep* describes small periods of rest during the day which are too short to be noticeable but may allow certain restorative functions to take place.

> When an animal is deprived of REM sleep its subsequent sleep periods contain more REM sleep. This is called the *REM rebound effect*.

> The *flowerpot technique* involves placing an animal on an upturned flowerpot in water. Every time the animal enters REM sleep it starts to slip off the flowerpot and is awakened.

The nature of sleep

Sleep stages

- *Stage 1:* Relaxed state, brain waves change from awake beta waves to alpha waves (8–12 Hz) which are synchronised. The transition from stage 1 is often accompanied by a *hypnogogic state*, which may include hallucinatory images.
- *Stage 2:* Slower, larger, brain waves (theta, 4–8 Hz), short bursts of high-frequency *sleep spindles* and *K-complexes* (responses to external stimuli). Easily awoken.
- *Stage 3:* More slowing down of brain waves and bodily activity (e.g. heart rate). Long, slow, delta waves (1–5 Hz) with some sleep spindles.
- *Stage 4: Slow-wave sleep* (SWS). More delta waves than stage 3. Hard to be woken except by personally significant noise. Production of growth hormones.
- *Stage 5:* Stage 4 sleep is followed by stage 3, stage 2 and then stage 5: *rapid eye movement* (REM) *sleep,* and active (beta 13–20 Hz) brain waves. Jouvet called this *paradoxical sleep* because of the contradictions: eye movement, heart rate, etc., are increased but the body is in a state of near paralysis.

Sleep deprivation research

Total sleep deprivation

Non-human animal studies

Rechtschaffen *et al.* (1983) used EEG to detect when a rat was about to fall asleep at which point a disc started rotating and the rat would fall into the surrounding water, thus preventing sleep. These rats died within 33 days.

Human studies

Case studies. Dement (1972) reported the cases of a disc jockey, Peter Tripp, and a student, Randy Gardner, who spent over 200 hours without sleep. Towards the end Tripp experienced hallucinations and profound delusions but Gardner wasn't affected except finding it difficult to perform some tasks. Afterwards Gardner recovered one-quarter of his lost sleep time but this sleep consisted of mainly *core sleep* (stage 4 and REM). It's possible that he benefited from episodes of *micro-sleep.*

Lugaressi *et al.* (1986) studied a 52-year-old man who could hardly sleep at all, and died. Post-mortem examination revealed a tumour in part of the brain involved in sleep regulation. His death may have been due to sleeplessness or it might have been anxiety.

Controlled studies. Webb (1985) found that sleep loss over 48 hours had little effect on cognitive processing tasks, whereas attention measures suffered. Depressed performance may be due more to motivational than cognitive factors.

Effects over time. Hüber-Weidman (1976) reported that after one night total deprivation there is an increased urge to sleep, after four nights increased episodes of micro-sleep, after six nights a impaired sense of reality (*sleep deprivation psychosis*).

Partial sleep deprivation

Webb and Bonnet (1978) found that participants deprived of two hours per night were fine though they went to sleep more quickly. Through training they were able to reduce sleep to four hours a night after several months, without apparent ill effects.

REM sleep deprivation

Jouvet (1967) used the *flowerpot technique* to deprive cats of REM sleep. The cats become hypersexual and eventually died. Their death might be due to anxiety.

Dement (1960) woke eight volunteers during each REM episode. They needed progressively more REM sleep; they were woken 12 times on the first night and 26 times by the seventh night.

Remember:
1 All animals sleep, suggesting some vital function.
2 Different species sleep differently, suggesting evolutionary adaptations.

Functions of sleep

Restoration theory (Oswald, 1980, and Horne, 1988)

Sleep allows various physiological and psychological states to be recovered.

Physiological restoration

During slow wave sleep the body makes repairs, waste products are removed and there is increased production of growth hormone.

Stern and Morgane (1974) argue that the normal function of REM sleep is to restore levels of neurotransmitters after a day's activities. Antidepressants appear to reduce REM activity possibly because they increase neurotransmitter levels.

Psychological restoration

Berry and Webb (1983) found that when people slept well during a given night, their level of anxiety on the following day was lower than when they had slept poorly.

Evaluation

- *Deprivation research* partly supports the restoration view, though the effects of sleep deprivation seem as much about motivation.
- Should find *increased sleep in relation to increased activity*. Shapiro *et al.* (1981) found that marathon runners did require extra sleep, whereas Horne and Minard (1985) found that exhausted participants went to sleep faster but not for longer.
- On the other hand, Empson (1989) claims that it is simply *impossible to go without sleep* and remain OK, and Horne (1988) points out that sleep-deprived participants do show *a rebound effect*.
- Can explain deprivation research in terms of some recovery taking place during *micro-sleep or relaxed wakefulness*. It may be that only core sleep is essential.

Ecological (evolutionary) theory

Sleep is an adaptive response to environmental and internal demands.

Protection from predation (Meddis, 1975)

Animals have evolved an innate programme to protect them when they can't be gathering food (darkness) and at times of danger. The more dangerous your world, the less time you should spend sleeping. This is true for cats (predators who sleep lots), and gazelles (preyed upon, sleep little). It also makes sense if prey species are as inconspicuous as possible – many prey species sleep in burrows.

Hibernation theory (Webb, 1982)

Sleep is adaptive because it is a means of conserving energy in the same way that hibernation enhances survival by reducing physiological demands.

Evaluation

- It is *difficult to falsify* evolutionary theory.
- There are problems with applying this theory to *human sleep*. In the environment of evolutionary adaptation (EEA) sleep may have enhanced survival, but not now.
- Empson (1989) calls ecological theories '*waste of time*' theories because they propose that sleep happens in order to waste time. However, deprivation studies do suggest that lack of sleep has distinct consequences.

Conclusion

Neither theory accounts for why animals lose consciousness when sleeping. Sleeping may not be necessary for restoration, and from a safety (adaptive) point of view it makes little sense.

Horne (1988) made the important point that sleep probably serves different purposes in different species. Thus, no single theory is likely to be adequate.

Practice essay 2.5

(a) Describe **one** theory of the function of sleep. (12 marks)

(b) Assess the theory you described in part (a). (12 marks)

2.6 Dreaming

AQA A   U4

It is important to remember, when considering the function of dreaming, that REM sleep is not the same as dreaming. It is true that most dreaming takes place during REM sleep. Dreams do also occur in NREM sleep.

The nature of dreams

Dement and Kleitman (1957) established an objective method for studying dreams. They showed that REM activity was generally associated with dreaming by waking participants during REM episodes, 80–90% of the time they reported dreaming, i.e. most but not all of the time. Dreams were also recalled about 7% of the time when participants were woken from NREM sleep.

Content

> One criticism of the Dement and Kleitman study was that it took place in a laboratory and therefore sleep activity may not have been true-to-life.

Dement and Kleitman (1957) related eye movements to dream content as a means of demonstrating that REM activity is the same as dreaming. For example, when one participant displayed horizontal eye movements (which were quite rare) he reported that he dreamt he was watching two people throwing tomatoes at each other.

Duration

Dement and Kleitman found that REM periods lasted between 3 and 50 minutes. During that time the eyes were not constantly in motion but there were bursts of activity. There were individual differences in the intervals between REM activity. The average was once every 92 minutes.

Relationship with stages of sleep

> Research into dreaming is complicated by the fact that it largely depends on self-report.

Dreaming is an *ultradian* rhythm. REM activity occurs after the first four sleep stages. After stage 4, the sleeper ascends the sleep staircase (stage 3 then 2) and then enters stage 5, REM *(rapid eye movement) sleep* (see page 46). As the night progresses there is more REM activity and less deep sleep in each sleep cycle.

Neurobiological theories of dreaming

Activation-synthesis model (Hobson and McCarley, 1977)

An output blockade prevents brain signals causing actual movement, and also prevents processing of external stimuli. Internal, spontaneous and random activation (e.g. from sensory parts of the brain) is interpreted (synthesised) as if it was produced by external stimuli and this leads to the experience of dreaming.

Research evidence

> Periodic arousal of the brain may be necessary to maintain minimum levels of activity in the nervous system.

Hobson (1988) found evidence in cats of apparently random firing of cells during REM sleep, producing activation in the parts of the brain that are used in visual perception and the control of motor movements.

Evaluation

> When formulating a theory of dreaming one may be aiming to account for the physiological activity sometimes associated with dreaming (i.e. REM activity) and/or the psychological experience of dreaming.

- Based on detailed information of the *physiological activity* of the brain.
- Accounts for the *incoherent nature* of many dreams, but can't explain why dreams sometimes seem very clear.
- Also can't explain why dreams often *relate to current concerns* if they are based on random activity.
- *Can't explain NREM dreams*, though these may be the synthesis of different kinds of brain activity.

Reverse-learning theory (Crick and Mitchison, 1983)

> This theory uses a computer analogy to liken dreams to updating memory files and discarding redundant data. The actual content of dreams is an accidental by-product.

Dreams occurs when the brain is 'off-line' and can get rid of useless ('parasitic') information that is taking up valuable space. Unwanted elements are destroyed and the subjective experience of dreaming is a kind of 'read out' of the search and destroy activity.

Research evidence

Crick and Mitchison (1983) point to the fact that animals who do not have REM sleep have very large cortexes (such as dolphins and spiny anteaters). Possibly their large cortex means they can function effectively without unlearning. Alternatively, Winson (1997) suggests that the large cortex enables them to conduct unlearning while awake and thus removes the need for REM activity.

Evaluation

- Explains why we *rarely remember* our dreams.
- Doesn't explain why *some dreams are significant* – we would be less likely to be unlearning significant connections.
- Modern *connectionist ideas* about the brain suggest that we have a vast potential for information storage and there is no need to save space.

Psychological theories of dreaming

Psychoanalytic theory (Freud, 1900)

A key assumption of Freud's theory of personality was that anxiety-provoking thoughts are repressed into the unconscious. Dreams are the disguised fulfilment of unconscious desires. Such wish fulfilments are often unacceptable to the dreamer, and this leads the dreamer to produce:

- *Manifest content*: what the dreamer actually dreams.
- *Latent content*: the true meaning of the dream. 'Dream-work' transforms a forbidden wish into a non-threatening form, thus reducing anxiety and allowing the dreamer to continue sleeping.

Dream analysis can be used to uncover latent content partly through interpretation of universal symbols (e.g. a gun represents a penis) but is more likely to be based on personal symbols (if your star sign is Pisces you might represent yourself as a fish).

Research evidence

Hajek and Belcher (1991) showed that dreams are related to current concerns. People on a course to give up smoking had dreams that focused on smoking and anxiety about taking it up again. Such dreams seemed to help the ex-smokers; those who had the most dreams and most guilt about smoking were less likely to start smoking again.

Evaluation

- Freud lived at a time when many feelings were *repressed*, but it is not clear why this would be true today. Hayes (1994) points out that, if dreams have a wish-fulfilment function, then people today should dream more of food.
- Some dreams (*nightmares*) are frightening, and not wish-fulfilling at all.

Problem-solving (Webb and Cartwright, 1978)

Dreams are a way of working out personal and work problems. There are many well-known examples of this, such as the chemist Kekule who dreamt of a ring of snakes that revealed to him the ring-like atomic structure of benzine molecules.

Like Freud's wish-fulfilment theory, problem-solving theory also suggests that dreams are a way of coping with problems. However, in problem-solving theory, the manifest content of the dream is the true meaning of the dream, though the dream may rely on metaphor, such as the ring of snakes.

Research evidence

Hartmann (1973) found that people who were experiencing various kinds of problems had more REM sleep than the less troubled individuals.

Webb and Cartwright (1978) reported that participants who had limited REM sleep were less able to provide realistic solutions to problems.

Evaluation

- This approach cannot explain *why non-human animals dream*, if they do, and why some dreams are not related to solving problems.
- May explain *one kind of dreaming*.

Neurobiological theories only explain one kind of dreaming – REM activity – and they can't explain why dreams are meaningful except insofar as our cognitive processes have a tendency to impose meaning on any set of data.

Some psychologists think that dreams are psychological rather than physiological experiences, and therefore serve a psychological function. It may be just coincidental that many dreams are in REM sleep.

Freud called dreams 'the royal road to a knowledge of unconscious activities' enabling repressed desires or memories to become known.

Freud said, with reference to a dream involving a cigar, 'Sometimes a cigar is only a cigar', meaning that dreams require careful individual rather than universal interpretation.

Remember to use psychological theories as a means of evaluating neurobiological theories, and vice versa. They each account for different aspects of dreaming.

All *psychological* theories are uninformative about the physiological processes involved in dreaming.

Practice essay 2.6

Discuss **one** neurobiological theory of dreaming. (24 marks)

Motivation and emotion

2.7 Brain mechanisms of motivation

AQA A | U4
OCR | U5, U6

Hunger and thirst are *primary drives* and as such are good examples of motivated behaviour. Both are regulated by *homeostasis,* the process of maintaining a reasonably constant environment or steady state.

Brain structures and hunger

Hypothalamic theory

Ventromedial nucleus of the hypothalamus (VMH)

Hetherington and Ranson (1941) suggested that the VMH is a *satiety centre* (causes eating to stop). Lesions in this area cause overeating. Reeves and Plum (1969) performed a post-mortem examination of a patient who had doubled her body weight in two years, finding a tumour in the VMH.

Lateral nucleus of the hypothalamus (LH)

Anand and Brobeck (1951) suggested that the LH is a *feeding centre* (initiates food intake). Lesions in this area inhibit eating. Quaade (1971) found that electrical stimulation of the LH in obese patients led to reports of feeling hungry.

Evaluation

The hypothalamic theory is an *oversimplification.*

- Lesions to the LH affect drinking and therefore it is *not just a feeding centre.*
- Damage to VMH is *complex.* Teitelbaum (1957) found that rats with VMH damage continue eating but don't seem very hungry. Schachter (1971) found that rats and humans will eat more when food is easy to obtain but eat less when it is difficult.
- Animals with VMH damage *gain weight even if they don't eat.* Friedman and Stricker (1976) suggested that VMH damage causes overeating because food intake is converted to fat leaving glucose levels low and encouraging further eating. Han *et al.* (1972) found VMH-lesioned rats gained more body fat than controls given the same amount of food.

Glucostatic theory

There are *glucoreceptors* in the lining of the liver, the blood vessels and the hypothalamus. Tordoff *et al.* (1982) found that injections of glucose into the blood reduce food intake. Russek (1971) found that glucose injected into the liver affected food intake but not when injected into the main vein leading to the heart.

Evaluation

- Glucose is part of the story but *not the whole thing.* For example, levels of glucose don't change that dramatically even after long periods without food, and large doses of glucose don't always trigger eating behaviour.

Lipostatic theory

Body fat (lipid) is normally maintained at a steady level and therefore fat levels are monitored in the hypothalamus and affect sensations of hunger. Taylor (1990) suggests there are lipid-sensitive receptors in or close to the abdominal cavity.

It was thought that obese individuals have high *leptin* levels in the blood (as a result of having high fat stores) which reduces food intake. However, Stephens *et al.* (1995) found that in fact obese people are insensitive to leptin in the hypothalamus. The result is that neuropeptide Y (NPY) is released which increases feeding.

Evaluation

- This might explain why *short-term diets* do not effect long-term weight loss.
- There is probably *multiple control* over eating behaviour. Friedman *et al.* (1986) found that lipoprivation and glucoprivation individually produced small effects but jointly increased food intake.

Motivation is the internal state that *drives* or encourages an organism to act towards a goal.

Hypothalmus   Cerebrum

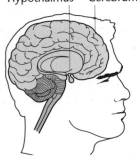

Note that these are all homeostatic theories of hunger, involving some hypothetical 'set-point'. Such set-points may be in part inherited and also may be dictated by early nutritional experience.

Glucose is produced when you eat carbohydrates. It is an important source of quick energy. Changes in blood glucose levels occur soon after eating and therefore would seem likely as a means of regulating hunger.

The problem is that in countries where food is plentiful, hunger is often related to learned cues and expectation rather than glucose or lipid levels.

Explanations for feelings of fullness

- *Cognitive.* 'I have eaten therefore I am full.'
- *Presence of food in the mouth.* Spiegel (1973) fed participants a liquid diet via a tube. Participants maintained regular body weight but found the meals unsatisfying. This shows that taste is not necessary for hunger regulation.
- *Presence of food in the stomach.* Cannon and Washburn (1912) demonstrated that there was a link between hunger pangs and stomach contractions using an inflated balloon in Washburn's stomach. Also stretch sensors in the stomach report fullness, which is why liquids make you feel full.
- *Physiological mechanisms.* The intestine produces *cholectystokinin* (CCK) in response to the presence of food. Injections of CCK curtail meal size (Antin *et al.*, 1978).

Brain structures and thirst

Intracellular and extracellular water

> Thirst occurs when water levels fall and the organism is motivated to take in more water.

The body's cells die without water (*intracellular water*). Water moves in and out of cells through *osmosis*. Water outside the cells (*extracellular*, i.e. in the blood) moves into the cells when osmotic pressure is lower inside the cell.

Thirst occurs either because of intracellular or extracellular deficits. Rolls *et al.* (1980) studied different species and found that intracellular deficits have more effect on drinking behaviour.

Water deprivation

> One way to evaluate these explanations is to consider other causes of thirst, such as the learned association between a tall glass of icy lager and feeling thirsty.

There are two different reasons why the body needs water: *osmotic thirst* and *hypovolemic thirst*.

Osmotic thirst

We lose extracellular water through, for example, sweating and breathing. This means that the intracellular water is drawn out of the cells because of osmotic pressure created by lower extracellular water. Osmotic pressure is also affected by greater salt extracellularly (salt stays in the blood and doesn't pass into cells because the semi-permeable cell only allows water to pass through).

> When you eat crisps it makes you thirsty because the increased salt creates intracellular water loss.

The cells of the brain are like all other cells. The decrease in osmotic pressure is detected by a group of *osmoreceptors* in the lateral preoptic area of the hypothalamus. Water balance is restored:

- *directly*, by creating a desire for water (i.e. osmotic thirst)
- *indirectly*, because antidiuretic hormone (ADH) is released causing the kidneys to excrete more concentrated urine, conserving water.

Volumetric thirst

> Take care to focus on how the *brain* is involved in hunger and thirst, rather than the body.

Animals also lose water through blood loss, such as a cut or a heavy menstrual flow. Reduced blood volume is detected by *blood-flow receptors* and blood-pressure receptors (*baroreceptors*) in the wall of the heart. This results in:`

- messages to the hypothalamus to stimulate drinking, and to release ADH
- release of renin from the kidneys which converts certain blood proteins into angiotensin which constricts the blood vessels, so increasing blood pressure (Epstein *et al.* (1970) found that injections of angiotensin into the preoptic area stimulated drinking.)

> Volumetric thirst is best relieved by drinking salty water.

- when salt levels fall, the adrenal gland releases aldosterone which leads the kidneys to reabsorb salt and water so reducing the loss of these substances in urine.

Practice essay 2.7

(a) Describe the role of brain structures in **one** motivational state. (12 marks)

(b) Assess the role of brain mechanisms in motivation. (12 marks)

2.8 Theories of motivation

AQA A — U4
EDEXCEL — U4
OCR — U5, U6

A theory is a systematic collection of interrelated facts put forward as an description and/or explanation of a set of observed phenomena.

Physiological approaches

Homeostatic drive theory

Cannon (1929) coined the term *homeostasis* to describe the organism's motivation to return to a state of balance when basic needs are not fulfilled. As we have seen in 2.7, there are homeostatic mechanisms involved in hunger and thirst.

Evaluation

- The principle of homeostasis is generally valid for *primary drives* but does not account for all biological needs, such as for vitamins.
- Animal motivation is also *governed by other factors*, such as learning.
- Human motivation is also *governed by higher order needs* (see below). Homeostatic drive theory makes no reference to *cognitive factors*.

'Arousal' refers to the state of being ready to respond.

Optimal level of arousal (OLA) theory

An animal has a drive to return to an optimum state of moderate arousal. OLA can explain behaviours that don't fit the homeostatic drive theory, such as curiosity. Hebb (1958) noted that monkeys do puzzles even if there is no external reward, i.e. they are motivated by the need to be moderately aroused. If arousal is too low then extra stimulation is sought; if arousal levels are too high, stimulation is avoided. This is a homeostatic mechanism.

- *Physiological level.* Moderate arousal is important for the nervous system.
- *Psychological level.* The *Yerkes-Dodson Law* (1908) states that when arousal is very low or very high, performance is poor. Performance is best at a medium level of arousal. Boredom (lack of curiosity drive) may have profound psychological consequences. Animals in zoos suffer from boredom because in the wild most of their time is occupied searching for food. Davis and Harvey (1992) found that major league baseball players performed less well in the closing stages of a game if the pressure was too great.

Zuckerman (1979) described 'sensation-seekers' as people who have a high OLA and engage in activities such as rollercoasters or bungee jumping. This is an individual difference.

Evaluation

- We can only establish OLA by observing behaviour, a *circular argument*.
- Explaining curiosity in terms of OLA *ignores the basic motive* for such behaviour which is cognitive development.

Physiological theories account for motivation in terms of bodily processes. It is likely that such theories will be more appropriate for non-human animal behaviour because human motivation is related to higher cognitive processes.

Combined physiological and psychological approaches

Drive-reduction (Hull, 1943)

- *Needs* (physiological), e.g. low glucose levels create a need for food.
- *Drives* result from needs and are psychological. The need for food increases activity which eventually leads to finding something which will satisfy the need (i.e. food).
- *Reinforcement.* Eating reduces the drive (hunger) thus reinforcing the behaviour which led to finding food (*operant conditioning*).

Drive-reduction (which is physiological) is reinforcing and leads to learning (which is psychological).

Hull believed that all human behaviour is a result of satisfying *primary* needs. Dollard and Miller (1950) extended this to *secondary* needs. When something becomes associated with satisfying a primary need that thing takes on the properties of the primary need and becomes reinforcing in itself (a *secondary reinforcer*).

This is called drive-reduction theory because behaviour is motivated by the attempt to reduce one or more drives, and this drive reduction is reinforcing.

Evaluation

- This theory offers a *useful distinction* between needs (physiological) and drives (psychological).
- It is limited to *biological, homeostatic mechanisms*, but the principle of reinforcement can be adapted to cope with secondary motives.
- It produces *testable equations* and does explain some behaviour. However, Blodgett (1929) demonstrated that learning can take place *without reinforcement* when rats had to learn a maze (see page 112).
- It does not explain behaviour which is *not drive-reducing*. Sheffield and Roby (1950) found that rats will continue eating saccharin for hours even though it has no nutritional value and even if it did, saturation must have been reached.

Psychoanalytic theory

Freud suggested that the infant and id are driven by innate, biological (sexual), forces, governed by the pleasure principle and homeostatic forces (tension is reduced by satisfying basic needs). As the child gets older, the ego and superego regulate the expression of the id's drives, and provide higher order motives learned from society.

Psychological approaches

Needs theory (Murray, 1938)

There are 20 different human motives (needs), such as for achievement (nAch), play, affiliation, aggression, sex, nurturance, and understanding.

The need for achievement (nAch) was measured by McClelland (1961). Koestner and McClelland (1990) suggest that societies with high nAch have higher levels of productivity than those with a low nAch, which was supported by a survey of children's books published in 40 countries between 1925 and 1950. These indicated a positive correlation between nAch and economic progress.

White (1959) described competence as the 'master reinforcer' because our capacity to deal effectively with and to control our environment is intrinsically rewarding.

Evaluation
- The humanistic approach can account for the influence of *social environment*, *individual differences* and *long-term goals*. It reflects the complexity of human behaviour, but is less relevant to animal behaviour.
- Measures of nAch have fairly *low reliability and validity*.

Hierarchy of needs (Maslow, 1954)

Physiological needs are *prepotent* (more powerful when unfulfilled) to intermediate and meta needs, resulting in a hierarchy of needs.

- *Levels 1 and 2 – physiological*
  Basic needs – physiological (food, water), safety (physical danger).
- *Levels 3 and 4 – intermediate*
  Psychological needs – love and belonging (affiliation), esteem (respect from achievement, competence).
- *Levels 5, 6 and 7 – meta*
  Self-actualisation needs – cognitive (knowledge, curiosity), aesthetic (order, beauty, art), self-actualisation (self-fulfilment, realising potential).

Maslow (1970) estimated that Americans satisfy about 85% of their physiological needs, 70% of their safety needs, 50% of their belongingness and love needs, 40% of their self-esteem needs and only 10% of their self-actualisation needs.

Aronoff (1967) compared fishermen (who had insecure but well-paid jobs) and cane cutters in the British West Indies, and found that only those whose security and esteem needs were met chose the more challenging and responsible job of fisherman, as predicted by the hierarchy of needs.

Evaluation
- A more *powerful and comprehensive* explanation than just a list of needs.
- There is some question about whether the *hierarchy is strictly followed*, for example many sports involve considerable danger.
- It is difficult to collect *empirical support*.
- The notion of self-actualisation is *vague*. It may be *culture-specific* and not achievable. Furthermore the link between creativity and self-actualisation is not established; many artists do not fit this category.

Psychological approaches address human motivation more appropriately than physiological approaches.

Humanistic psychologists suggest that humans have higher order needs as well as physiological ones.

Theories of motivation have real-world applications in the world of work. Goal-setting theory (Locke, 1968) attempts to relate the difficulty of goals to levels of performance.

The needs towards the bottom of the hierarchy are *deficiency* needs, because they are designed to reduce inadequacies or deficiencies. Needs towards the top of the hierarchy (intermediate and meta needs) represent *growth* needs.

Self-actualisation refers to the notion that each of us has an innate drive for growth and fulfilment of one's potential.

The more psychological approaches sometimes ignore basic, physiological, needs.

Practice essay 2.8

(a) Outline and evaluate **one** physiological theory of motivation. (12 marks)

(b) Outline and evaluate **one** psychological theory of motivation. (12 marks)

2.9 Emotion

AQA A ▶ U4

Emotion has many components: cognitive (perception), physiological (bodily changes), experience, expression and behaviour.

The role of brain structures

The Papez circuit (Papez, 1937)

The *Papez circuit* consists of the hypothalamus (emotional expression) and the *limbic system* (emotional feeling).

Theory based on non-human animal experiments where aggression produced by stimulating the hypothalamus and thalamus. Also based on observation that increased aggression associated with damage to the hippocampus in cases of rabies.

Evaluation

* The Papez circuit is *oversimplified*. Different regions of the hypothalamus respond differently, for example cats may show a quiet, biting attack when one area is stimulated, but vicious attack when another area is stimulated (Flynn, 1976).

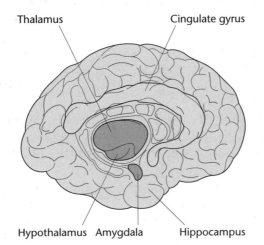

Thalamus   Cingulate gyrus

Hypothalamus   Amygdala   Hippocampus

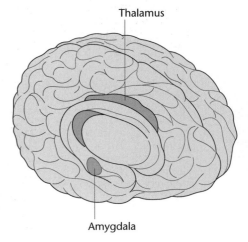

Thalamus

Amygdala

Papez–MacLean limbic model

MacLean (1949) suggested improvements to the Papez circuit, reducing the role of the cingulate gyrus, and increasing emphasis on the hippocampus and amygdala. Klüver and Bucy (1939) found that removal of the anterior temporal lobe (mainly the amygdala) in monkeys resulted in reduced fear and more sexual activity (the *Klüver–Bucy syndrome*). This model consists of:

* the *amygdala* and *hippocampus* – self-preservation, such as aggression
* the *cingulate gyrus*, *septum* and other structures – pleasure, sex
* the *hypothalamus* and *thalamus*: cooperative social behaviour, certain aspects of sexuality and motivation.

Aronson and Cooper (1979) studied male cats with lesions of the amygdala and found that they were not just hypersexual but became indiscriminate about partners. It appears that lesions do not simply cause or prevent a behaviour, but change how the animals interpret information.

Evaluation

* The theory accounts well for *non-human animal behaviour* but is less relevant to humans where experience is a key element of emotions.
* The model deals mainly with *high-intensity emotions*, such as rage and fear.

LeDoux's modified limbic theory (1995)

There are two separate brain circuits involved in emotion. Information is first received by the thalamus, and then passed simultaneously to the :

* *amygdala*: rapid emotional response, e.g. ANS changes which may then be interpreted by the cortex
* *cortex*: slower emotional response, affected by higher mental processes.

Emotion comes from the Latin meaning 'to move, excite, stir up or agitate'.

The physiological approach focuses on the bodily changes that accompany an emotional state and assumes that the experience is related to these.

The *limbic system* is a network of structures in the forebrain, including the hypothalamus, thalamus, hippocampus, and cingulate cortex.

The limbic system and hypothalamus stimulate production of *adrenaline*, which arouses the sympathetic branch of the autonomic nervous system (ANS). This creates a physiological response (e.g. increased heart rate) and a behavioural response (e.g. increased attention) in readiness to deal with the stimulus.

The ANS controls the body's involuntary activities and is largely automatic and self-regulating.

LeDoux (1989) suggests that the amygdala is the brain's 'emotional computer'. Monkeys with lesions in this area cannot assess the emotional importance of stimuli.

The famous case of Phineas Gage (p. 39), who lost a section of his frontal cortex in an accident with dynamite, suggested that emotional changes may be related to the cortex.

The subjective experience of emotion is a 'read-out' of the physiological state. Primary emotions (such as joy and sadness) are universal and innate; secondary emotions (such as contempt) are a blend of the former and are culturally determined.

In Laird's experiment participants were amused because they were smiling, not smiling because they were amused.

The cortex

Bard (1929) ablated the cerebral cortex in cats, which led to *sham rage*, a kind of 'cool' aggression. If the hypothalamus was also removed the rage stopped, suggesting that the cortex ordinarily inhibits and organises attacks, whereas the hypothalamus is necessary for expression of rage.

Jacobsen *et al.* (1935) removed the frontal lobes of an emotionally disturbed chimpanzee called Becky, reducing her temper tantrums. Moniz, impressed with these findings, developed the use prefrontal lobotomies (which include the temporal lobes and the limbic system) to treat human mental disorder (see page 143).

The physiological approach

James–Lange theory of emotion

James (1884) and Lange (1887) proposed that bodily changes come first and form the basis of an emotional experience.

Research evidence

Physiological activity causes subjective experience. Laird (1974) told participants that he was measuring activity of facial muscles using electrodes and instructed them to relax and contract muscles. Cartoons viewed when 'smiling' were rated as funnier.

For each emotion there should be a different physiological state. Schwartz *et al.* (1981) and Ekman *et al.* (1983) asked participants to imagine scenes involving primary emotions or to watch themselves in a mirror as they tried to look happy, sad, etc. Primary emotions had individual physiological 'signatures' (e.g. different combinations of heart rate and blood pressure).

There is no emotion without bodily changes. Hohmann (1966) interviewed patients with spinal-cord injuries who reported minimal experience of emotion. However, Bermond *et al.* (1991) found that most patients with spinal damage reported *increased* intensity of emotions.

The more intense the arousal the greater the emotion. White *et al.* (1981) found that male college students who ran for 120 seconds rated videos of attractive women more highly than those who ran for only 15 seconds, whereas the opposite was true if the woman was unattractive, suggesting that arousal enhances existing emotional states.

Evaluation

- A reasonable account of some of the evidence, but cannot explain emotion *before or without any arousal*, nor the *role of learning and cognition*.
- Emotional experiences occur rapidly yet the *ANS is slow to react*.
- It is difficult to *perceive different physiological states accurately*. People are not very aware of increases or decreases in their blood pressure (Valins, 1966).

Cannon–Bard theory of emotion

Cannon (1927) criticised the James–Lange view and put forward his own ideas, which were later modified by Bard. This model suggested that changes of emotional state and changes in the ANS occur simultaneously but independently, both caused by the arrival of the same sensory input at the thalamus.

James said you are frightened when you see a bear *because* you run, not the reverse, that you run because you are frightened. This is *not* the commonsense view.

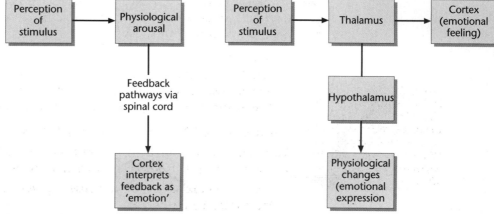

James–Lange theory   *Cannon–Bard theory*

Research evidence

Physiological changes can occur without any emotional experience. Marañon (1924) injected patients with adrenaline, 71% were aware of physical sensations but had no emotional experience, the rest used phrases like 'it's as if I was afraid'.

> This evidence can be taken as criticism of the James–Lange view.

Emotional states may occur without any physiological changes. Valins (1966) showed male participants slides of semi-nude women and gave them false feedback about their heart rate. Ratings of attractiveness were positively related to supposed increases in heart rate (the *Valins effect*).

Evaluation

- This fits in with *LeDoux's modified limbic theory* (see page 54).
- *Cognitive labelling theory* may better explain the role of arousal.

The combined approach

Cognitive labelling theory

Schachter and Singer (1962) proposed that all emotional experiences are preceded by a generalised state of arousal. The nature of the subjective experience is determined ('labelled') by the individual's cognitive assessment based on external, situational cues or internal ones such as imagination.

Research evidence

Schachter and Singer (1962) injected 185 male undergraduates with a 'new' vitamin, Suproxin (adrenaline) and placed them with a euphoric or angry confederate. Participants who were correctly informed (told they would feel aroused) were least affected by situational cues (the behaviour of the confederate) whereas the misinformed (told their feet would feel numb) and uninformed used the situational cues to 'explain' their arousal.

> One problem with this study was that the researchers excluded participants who did not report any physiological sensations. If their data had been included the results may not have been so significant. The research also equates drug-induced arousal states with real-life emotion.

Several studies have failed to replicate this finding (e.g. Marshall and Zimbardo, 1979).

Dutton and Aron (1974) arranged for attractive women to conduct a questionnaire on a high suspension bridge (high arousal) or a low bridge. Men in the high arousal condition were more likely to phone later and to interpret a picture in a more sexual way; presumably because they labelled their arousal as sexual attraction rather than fear (see three-factor theory of love, page 25).

Evaluation

- There are occasions when *cognition comes before or without arousal* (e.g. Valins effect, above).
- There are *different physiological states* (Schwartz *et al.* above).
- You can have an *emotional response with no cognitive awareness*. For example, McGinnies' (1949) research on 'perceptual defence' demonstrated an emotional response (galvanic skin response) to subliminal words.
- This view can explain *how emotions are learned* because an emotional 'label' is derived from previous experiences of emotion in a similar situation.

Cognitive appraisal theory

This is an extension of cognitive labelling theory. Lazarus (1991) suggested that the experience of emotion is related to how one appraises it.

Research evidence

Lazarus (1965) showed that participants who viewed a film of industrial accidents experienced less stress (emotion) if told that the characters were actors (denial condition) or were asked to consider the film in terms of its value for promoting safety at work (intellectualisation) than when given no instructions. This shows that the same event may be threatening or not, depending on how its contents are appraised.

Practice essay 2.9

Discuss the role of brain structures in emotional behaviour and experience. (24 marks)

Sample question and model answer

Describe and evaluate **one** theory of the functions of sleep.   (24 marks)

Examiner's comments

In this question 12 marks are available for a description of one theory and 12 marks for an evaluation of the theory. In some essay questions the AO2 (evaluate) is more difficult than the AO1 but in this essay it may be more difficult to have enough knowledge to write a description of a theory for about 15 minutes (the total essay time, including planning and thinking time, is 30 minutes). It is important that you write enough to maximise your AO1 marks rather than writing too much for AO2.

Candidate's answer

There are two main theories in psychology offered to explain the function of sleep. One is called the ecological or evolutionary theory. The basis of this theory is that the reason why all animals sleep (and it is a fact that all animals sleep) is because sleep serves some adaptive function. The notion of adaptiveness comes from the theory of evolution. The idea is that any behaviour that has continued in an animal's gene pool is because it must have been naturally selected because it, in some way, has helped promote the survival and reproduction of an animal possessing that characteristic.

So sleep is likely to serve some adaptive function. Meddis proposed that the function is a protective one. When animals do not have to be out and about finding food, then it would be adaptive for them to be quiet and hidden. At the same time animals that are likely to be preyed upon would be better off sleeping very little whereas predators can afford to sleep a lot because they are not in much danger. Observations of the animal world support this. Predator species, such as cats, sleep a lot more than prey species such as gazelles.

On the other hand, one might argue that predators need to spend a lot of time finding food so if they sleep a lot they may go hungry. In addition herbivores have to spend a lot of time finding food and will sleep little. The cow is not preyed upon and sleeps only a little. The point is that the evolutionary argument can be used to explain almost any sleep pattern!

Another evolutionary explanation was suggested by Webb. This is the hibernation theory. This theory suggests that sleep is adaptive because when an animal is asleep it is not using up energy. For most animals finding food is their biggest problem so that there is a vicious cycle, the more active the animal is, the more food has to be found; the more food finding, the more energy is used. When an animal hibernates or sleeps this reduces the amount of food that is needed and would increase survival.

Evolutionary theory can be used to explain why different animals sleep in different ways. For example one species of dolphin sleeps one hemisphere at a time possibly in order to maintain consciousness of debris in the environment in which they live.

Certainly some aspects of sleeping are adaptive; however, it may not be the main function of sleep. The alternative theory is the restoration theory, which proposes that all animals sleep because certain functions take place during sleep which help the animal restore itself physiologically and psychologically. Of course this in itself may be adaptive. Physiological and psychological restoration can take place when an animal is relaxing, so why then is it necessary to become unconscious during sleep? In terms of protection one would think it is more adaptive for animals not to lose consciousness. Perhaps the reason is that for good restoration to take place the brain has really got to go off-line.

An important consideration, when thinking about the function of sleep, is to distinguish between different <u>kinds</u> of sleep: core sleep and other sleep. The two most important kinds of core sleep are slow wave sleep and REM sleep. It is possible that each serves a different adaptive purpose.

Sample question and model answer *(continued)*

One of the key criticisms made, in relation to evolutionary accounts of sleep, is that many of them suggest that animals sleep in order to waste time (Empson called them 'waste of time' theories). Whereas the restoration view is that sleep is not wasting time but offers the opportunity for key functions to take place.

A second criticism is that evolutionary theories may not be suitable for explaining human sleep. Sleep may have been adaptive during the environment of evolutionary adaptation but this hasn't been true for a long time and one wonders why humans haven't evolved different patterns of sleep.

[655 words]

Examiner's comments

An excellent, thoughtful essay, perhaps slightly lacking in structure but lots of different descriptions of the evolutionary account. The different evolutionary accounts (counting as one theory) are each presented in some detail but perhaps greater breadth than depth.

The commentary is nicely interwoven into the narrative so that every point that is made is considered in terms of its value (the true meaning of 'evaluation').

Note that this candidate has used restoration theory explicitly as evaluation. Candidates are often tempted to use an essay such as this as a vehicle to describe all the theories they know. But marks are only available for the description of one theory. Therefore the restoration theory is only creditworthy insofar as it is a contrasting approach to understanding sleep. If you wrote 'An alternative theory is …' and then described your second theory this would be characterised as 'lacking effective use'. For AO2 you must know the points of evaluation, describe them and use them effectively.

AO1

Accurate and well-detailed. Given the time constraints the depth is sufficient for Band 3 (top) but 11 rather than 12 marks to reflect the fact that the balance is not always achieved = 11 marks.

AO2

The commentary is less developed. It is limited and reasonably effective. Closer to 'effective' than 'restricted' Band 2 (top) = 8 marks.

Total 19 out of 24 (see page 12 for band descriptors), equivalent to a Grade A.

Chapter 3

Cognitive psychology

Cognitive psychologists are primarily interested in thinking and related mental processes such as memory, perception, attention, forgetting, learning, thinking and language. The key assumption of the cognitive approach is that behaviour can largely be explained in terms of how the mind operates. Many cognitive explanations use the metaphor of information processing, assuming that the mind works in a manner that is similar to a computer: inputting, storing and retrieving data. Cognitive psychologists see psychology as a pure science.

At AS Level your study of cognitive psychology may have focused on memory and forgetting, and how such research might be applied to eyewitness testimony.

At A2 you may select to study one or more of the following areas in cognitive psychology:

Attention and pattern recognition

3.1   Focused attention
3.2   Divided attention
3.3   Pattern recognition

After studying this area you should be able to:

- describe and evaluate studies of focused (selective) attention
- critically consider explanations of focused attention, including early and late selection models
- discuss explanations of divided attention
- describe and evaluate research into controlled and automatic processing
- comment on research related to action slips that arise from automatic processing
- discuss explanations of pattern recognition, including the role of biological mechanisms and context
- describe and critically assess studies and theories of face recognition

LEARNING SUMMARY

Perceptual processes and development

3.4   The visual system
3.5   Perceptual organisation
3.6   Perceptual development

After studying this area you should be able to:

- describe the structure and function of the visual system
- critically consider research into visual information processing (such as contrast, colour and patterns)
- discuss direct and constructivist theories of visual perception
- understand and evaluate explanations of perceptual organisation, such as the perception of depth and movement, and visual constancies and illusions
- describe and evaluate research into the development of perceptual abilities, including infant and cross-cultural studies
- critically consider explanations of perceptual development, with reference to the nature–nurture debate

LEARNING SUMMARY

Language and thought

3.7   Language and culture
3.8   Language acquisition
3.9   Problem-solving and decision-making

After studying this area you should be able to:

- critically consider research into the relationship between language and thought, including the linguistic relativity hypothesis
- discuss social and cultural aspects of language use
- describe and evaluate research into the process of language acquisition
- discuss environmental (learning) and nativist theories of language development
- critically consider research into problem-solving, including Gestalt approaches, means-ends analysis and analogy
- critically consider research into decision-making, including risk-taking behaviour and errors in thinking about probability

LEARNING SUMMARY

Attention and pattern recognition

3.1 Focused attention

Early selection theories

Single channel filter model (Broadbent, 1958)

Data arrives at a *sensory buffer*. This model proposed (1) a bottleneck (filter) prior to perceptual analysis, (2) messages are filtered on the basis of physical characteristics.

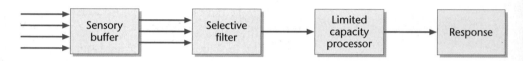

Research evidence

Cocktail party phenomenon. Cherry (1953) presented two auditory messages to participants. If they *shadowed* one message they were unaware of the content of the non-attended message (e.g. they didn't notice if it was in a foreign language) but they did notice physical characteristics, such as sex of speaker.

Broadbent (1958) used the *dichotic listening task*, presenting three different digits to each ear (e.g. 493 and 852). Participants usually recalled the digits ear by ear (493852) rather than in the sequence heard (489532). This shows single channel, *serial processing*. However, Gray and Wedderburn (1960) and found participants recalled by meaning rather than ear by ear (DEAR AUNT JANE and 534 rather than DEAR 5 JANE 3 AUNT 4).

Evaluation

Consider the following research studies:

Moray (1959) found that information played to the 'deaf' ear was not remembered even if it was repeated 35 times. However, if the non-attended message contained the person's name it was remembered one third of the time.

Von Wright *et al.* (1975) conditioned participants by pairing target words with an electric shock. In a later shadowing task the participants produced a GSR when these words, or their synonyms, were presented to the non-attended ear, indicating some semantic processing of the non-attended message.

- Far more processing takes place on the non-attended message than Broadbent's *rigid system* allows. The filter acts on meaning as well.
- However, Broadbent's filter model was *historically important*. All later filter models are essentially modified versions of this, the difference lies in where the filter is placed.

Attenuation model (Treisman, 1964)

Incoming signals become progressively attenuated (weakened) as they pass through successively more sophisticated filters. If a weak signal triggers a person's 'dictionary' of important words, the signal is enhanced. If there is insufficient capacity in the system (due to other demands) the 'higher' filters are omitted.

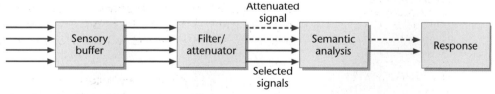

Research evidence

Treisman (1960) arranged for bilingual participants to listen to a speech given dichotically in French and in English with a time delay. As the offset was reduced, the participants realised they were the same. This suggests they were processing more than the physical characteristics of the non-attended message.

Treisman (1964) showed that ease of shadowing a message (passage from a novel read by a woman) was related to the degree of similarity between attended and non-attended messages (either read by female or not; either same passage or passage from

---

Sidebar notes:

Shadowing involves two auditory messages, one given to each ear. The participant is asked to attend to just one of the messages and repeat it back out loud while ignoring the other message.

In the *dichotic listening task* two different sets of information are presented simultaneously to each ear. Participants are asked to recall the data in whatever order they prefer.

The term *serial processing* describes dealing with one piece of information at one time, as distinguished from *parallel processing* where several pieces of information are dealt with at the same time.

GSR (galvanic skin response) is a measure of sweating and indicates activity in the autonomic nervous system, i.e. emotion.

Attention is the concentration of mental effort. *Focused (selective) attention* refers to the ability to pick out (or focus on) a particular set of stimuli in a mass of information. *Divided attention* describes the ability to allocate attention to two or more tasks at the same time.

a biochemical text, or in a foreign language, or nonsense syllables).

Evaluation

- This model is more flexible but is still essentially a *single channel theory*.
- The attenuation process is *not precisely specified*.

Late selection theories

Deutsch and Deutsch (1963)

> This is more a model of parallel than serial processing.

All stimuli are analysed fully; the most relevant stimulus determines the response. The bottleneck is closer to the response end of the processing system.

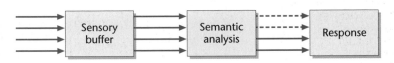

Research evidence

> Von Wright *et al.*'s study (above) also shows that the non-attended message only *appears* as if it isn't being processed whereas it is, but the processing isn't always accessible.

McKay (1973) played an ambiguous sentence to participants' shadowed side, e.g. containing the word 'bank'. Another word was played to the non-attended ear, e.g. either 'river' or 'money'. Participants had no recall of the non-attended words but their interpretation of the ambiguous sentence was affected.

Evaluation

- This model allows for the effects of *context*.
- *Unnecessarily complicated*; the attenuator model can account for the same evidence.

Attenuator vs late selection models

> All of this research concerned attention in a laboratory environment and may not reflect real-life attention. In addition experimental participants may have been influenced by experimenter bias.

Treisman and Geffen (1967) asked participants to shadow one message and tap whenever they detected a target word in either message. Attenuation theory would predict reduced ability to respond to signals from the non-attended message, which is what was found (detection rate for attended message was 87%, against 8%).

> This model is a compromise.

Deutsch and Deutsch (1967) claimed that in fact their theory assumes that only *important* inputs lead to responses, whereas the shadowed targets were more important than the non-shadowed ones. Treisman and Riley (1969) asked participants to stop shadowing and tap whenever they detected a target in either message. Many more target words were still detected in the shadowed message.

A flexible model (Johnston and Heinz, 1978)

> An example of the words in Johnston and Wilson's study would be socks paired with 'smelly' or paired with 'punches' (both appropriate targets), or paired with a neutral word such as 'Saturday' (an inappropriate target which impaired recognition).

Selection occurs as early in processing as possible, depending on the prevailing circumstances and task demands. Semantic processing makes a greater demand on resources than physical messages and therefore makes early filtering necessary.

Research evidence

Johnston and Wilson (1980) asked participants to shadow words belonging to certain categories, e.g. clothing. The words were ambiguous, and each was paired with a non-attended word that would bias interpretation. If the non-attended message *was* processed this would affect the interpretation of the target word. In the divided attention condition (participants did not know in which ear the targets would arrive), target recognition was improved by appropriate non-targets and impaired by inappropriate non-targets. In a focused attention condition, target detection was unaffected by the non-target word. Therefore processing is adjusted to suit the task.

> All of these theories are examples of the *information processing approach*, one which presumes that mental *processes* are similar to computer processes. Such theories are reductionist and tend to overlook social and emotional factors.

Evaluation

- *Explains all research data*, and offers a *link to divided attention*.
- Is a model of focused attention necessary at all?

Practice essay 3.1

(a) Describe **two** studies of focused (selective) attention. (12 marks)

(b) Evaluate the contribution of such studies to our understanding of focused attention. (12 marks)

3.2 Divided attention

The term *dual task performance* is used to describe what happens when a person tries to do two things at once. Dual-task performance is affected by: task similarity, task difficulty and practice.

Task similarity. McLeod (1977) asked participants to manually respond to a tracking task with one hand and, at the same time, to make a verbal or manual response (with their other hand) to a tone. They could do the verbal response better than the manual one. It is difficult to test task similarity because it is not always possible to decide how similar two tasks are (e.g. playing the piano and singing a song).

Task difficulty. Sullivan (1976) arranged for participants to shadow one message and report the presence of target words in the non-shadowed ear. If the shadowing task was made more difficult, the performance with the non-shadowed ear fell.

Practice. Allport *et al.* (1972) noted that expert pianists could play from seen music and shadow auditory messages, demonstrating the effects of practice.

Automatic processing, like attention generally, is a way to use resources efficiently.

Explanations of divided attention

Bottleneck theory (Welford, 1952)

Performance is severely limited when a person has to make two decisions almost simultaneously (a bottleneck).

Research evidence

Psychological refractory period effect. When one stimulus is presented shortly after another, response to the second stimulus is slower. Pashler (1993) showed that the effect remains even after practice and even when the stimuli and responses are very different, e.g. a tone requiring a vocal response and a visual letter requiring a button-push response.

Evaluation

- *Practice* facilitates dual-task performance, which doesn't support the model. Spelke *et al.* (1976) trained two participants to perform two quite complex tasks simultaneously (read for comprehension and take down dictation).
- A bottleneck *cannot be the only explanation*.

Central capacity model (Kahneman, 1973)

A central processor allocates one central pool of attention. The amount of capacity varies with circumstances: you have more attentional capacity when wide awake, different tasks take up different capacity and motivation increases capacity. When two tasks do not overload capacity, they do not interfere with each other.

Research evidence

Bourke *et al.* (1996) gave participants dual-task assignments. A random letter generation task (no real words allowed) interfered *most* with other tasks (because of greatest demand on central resources) whereas the tone identification task interfered least. When the two tasks were very different they did not interfere with performance.

Evaluation

- Can explain both *focused and divided attention*.
- The concept of 'central capacity' is rather *vague*.
- Can account for the effects of *task difficulty and practice*. However, it cannot handle some of the effects of task similarity. Segal and Fusella (1970) combined image construction (task A) with signal detection (task B), both in visual (C) and auditory (D) modes. They found that the auditory image task (B) interfered more than the visual one (A) with auditory signals whereas the opposite was true for the visual signal task, in both cases due to task similarity.

Modular theory (Allport, 1989)

There are various specific processing mechanisms (modules), each of which is independent and has limited capacity.

Research evidence

Neurophysiological evidence. For example, individuals with tumours in Broca's area lose specific linguistic abilities (see page 41).

Evaluation

- This model can account for task interference on *similar tasks* and lack of interference on different or automated tasks.
- This is a difficult theory to *disprove*. It also does not explain how modules are *coordinated*, unless there is a central processor.

Controlled and automatic processing

Automatic processes:

- are fast
- make no demands on attention
- are not available to consciousness
- are unavoidable (Eysenck and Keane, 2000).

Research evidence

The Stroop effect. Stroop (1935) found the task of naming the colour of a conflicting colour word (e.g. RED is written in green) is slower than naming the colour when the word and ink are the same. It is claimed that the Stroop effect is due to the automatic tendency to read words. However, Kahneman and Henik (1979) found that the Stroop effect was less likely to occur when distracting information (the colour name) was in an adjacent location, which suggests that the effect is not entirely unavoidable and therefore not fully automatic. Logan and Zbrodoff (1979) showed that practice could reduce the effect in a study where participants had to say the position of the word 'ABOVE' or 'BELOW' when it appeared above or below a line.

Skill acquisition. A skilled typist can make one keystroke every 60 milliseconds (Fitts and Posner, 1967). This is an automatic process because it is fast and requires little conscious control.

A theory of controlled and automatic processes

Shiffrin and Schneider (1977) proposed a distinction between:

- *controlled (attentional) processes* – limited capacity, serial processing, focused attention, and can be modified easily
- *automatic processes* – no capacity limitations, do not require attention, parallel processing, and are difficult to modify once learned.

Research evidence

Schneider and Shiffrin (1977) asked participants to memorise a set of consonants. Then they were shown a list of items (visual display) and had to decide rapidly if each item was in the memory set. If the display was numbers (*consistent mapping* task), then experience at distinguishing between letters and numbers meant they could do this automatically. If the memory set and visual display consisted of consonants and numbers (*varied mapping*), it was not possible to use automatic processes.

Schneider and Shiffrin found that the number of items in the memory set and visual display had very little effect on decision time with consistent mapping, but had a large effect with varied mapping, i.e. automaticity enhanced task performance.

Shiffrin and Schneider (1977) trained participants (2100 trials) to do the consistent mapping task with consonants. It then took a further 1000 trials for the learned automatic response to be extinguished, indicating how hard it is to unlearn automatic processes.

Evaluation

- It is a *descriptive* rather than explanatory account.
- Automatic processes do place *some strain* on attention. Shiffrin and Schneider (1977) found increased items in the consistent mapping condition did affect speed. Therefore, Norman and Shallice (1986) suggested that controlled and automatic processes should be located on a continuum: fully automatic processes at one end and fully controlled processes at the other end, with partially automatic processes resolved by *contention scheduling* in between.

Instance theory (Logan, 1988)

Explains *how* automatic processes develop through practice:
- a memory trace is stored after each experience
- practice further strengthens this memory
- this knowledge base allows rapid retrieval of relevant information when the appropriate stimulus is presented.

Action slips

Research evidence

Diary study. Reason (1979) asked 35 people to keep diaries for two weeks. Of the 400 errors reported 40% were storage failures (intentions/actions were forgotten or recalled incorrectly), 20% were test failures (diversions from a planned activity) and 18% were subroutine failures (small alterations of a well-used routine).

Laboratory study. Reason (1992) asked participants to respond quickly to questions, for example, 'What do you call the white of an egg?', 85% said 'yolk' because the misleading context activates an automatic response.

The fact that we possess both automatic and controlled processes allows us to respond rapidly and appropriately to most situations.

Contention scheduling is an automatic process which determines the amount of attention any task should receive. Without this, automatic processes would disrupt behaviour.

Logan (1988) described automatic processes as memory retrieval: 'performance is automatic when it is based on a single-step direct-access retrieval of past solutions from memory'.

Action slips (absent-mindedness) are the performance of an unintended action. They are the price we pay for automatic processes.

Action slips tend to occur during highly practised and over-learned activities, rather than, as one might expect, during learning.

Theory of action slips (Reason, 1992)

There are two modes of control over motor performance.

- *Closed-loop* (feedback) method of control used during skill acquisition to monitor motor performance and provide feedback; attention is required.
- *Open-loop* methods of control result from practice. Subroutines (predetermined sequences of action) are performed automatically (without attention) thus freeing central resources. Sometimes a person who is operating in open-loop mode may fail to return to closed-loop mode (direct attention) when necessary, resulting in an action slip because the wrong motor programme is activated or runs on.

The concept of schemas is used throughout psychology as a means of explaining cognitive activity. A schema is a cluster of facts about one thing or plan of action, stored in long-term memory.

Schema theory (Sellen and Norman, 1992)

Actions are determined by hierarchically arranged *schemas* or organised plans. The highest level is the overall intention, and the lower levels are like Reason's subroutines. At any time an intention or environmental cue will trigger a particular schema, which is performed with attentional control. According to schema model there are three reasons why action slips occur:

- errors in forming the intention to do something, e.g. discrimination errors
- faulty activation of a schema leading to the performance of the wrong schema, e.g. storage failures
- faulty triggering of active schema, e.g. programme assembly failures.

The study of action slips has important applications as action slips may explain the causes of many accidents, such as pilot and machine-operator errors.

Evaluation

- Schema theory suggests that action slips are a *normal by-product* of the attentional system rather than being specific to one mechanism of action.
- Action slips don't just occur with automatic processes, they are much more common with *actions of minor importance* and very unlikely when conducting a dangerous but routine activity.

Practice essay 3.2

Discuss research (theories **and/or** studies) into automatic processing, including slips associated with automatic processing. (24 marks)

3.3 Pattern recognition

AQA A ▶ U4

Explanations of pattern recognition

Template theory

A set of templates is matched against a stimulus item. This works if the stimulus is predictable, such as the detection of the numbers on cheques.

How do we recognise that A ⒜ a A A are all the same letter?

For human pattern recognition the number of templates would have to be vast. One possibility is that the stimulus undergoes a *normalisation* process. (*Normalisation* refers to producing an internal representation in a standard position, size and so on.) Alternatively we would have to have more than one template for each item, to accommodate different variations.

Pattern recognition concerns identifying an arrangement of parts as a known item.

Research evidence

Larsen and Bundesen (1992) studied machine recognition of handwritten digits. If 5 templates were stored for each digit, the machine recognised 69% of them; this rose to 89% when 60 templates were stored. Human participants averaged 97%.

Evaluation

- Template theory works with *simple stimuli* but not ill-defined or complex stimuli (such as types of bridge).
- Template theory doesn't account for *context effects* (*top-down* processes).
- Template matching may explain the end of the process.

Prototype theories

A prototype is an idealised abstraction of a pattern.

Patterns are matched against the stimulus but an endless store of the letter 'A' is not necessary, only one prototype.

A study by Palmer (1975) illustrates *context effects*. Briefly presented pictures (e.g. a cup) could be identified more accurately when they were preceded by a picture of an appropriate context (e.g. a kitchen) than by no context.

There are *feature detectors* in the brain as part of the visual system (see Hubel and Wiesel's research, on p. 69). This supports feature detection theory.

Selfridge (1959) described a *pandemonium model* of feature detection. Image, feature and cognitive demons 'shout' progressively louder the closer the input is to their own feature or pattern. A decision demon selects the one shouting loudest.

Essentially this is a more flexible template model.

Biederman claims there are 36 different geons. Lund (2001) reports that just 3 geons can be arranged to produce 1.4 billion objects.

Evaluation
- A more *economical* way of explaining the matching process.
- Can better explain the *speed* of the pattern recognition and how we can deal with *novel stimuli* for which there would be no previous template.
- Cannot explain the effects of *context*.
- Some prototypes (e.g. 'B' and 'D') might be *hard to distinguish* between yet we are generally very accurate.

Feature detection theory

A pattern consists of a set of specific features which are combined in unique ways.

Research evidence

Neisser (1964) found that visual search was slowed if participants were asked to search for a 'Z' embedded in a list of 'distractor' letters with similar *features* (e.g. M and V rather than O and G).

However, Harvey *et al.* (1983) showed that letters that shared features (e.g. 'K' and 'N') were not confused when participants were shown very brief presentations, but letters with similar spatial frequencies but few common features were confused.

Evaluation

- *Relationships* among features are important (\ / – is not perceived as 'A').
- Feature theories ignore the effects of *context* and of *expectations*. This can be seen in the *object-superiority effect*. The *object-superiority effect* was demonstrated by Weisstein and Harris (1974) where participants were better able to detect a feature if it was embedded in a three-dimensional form.

Template and feature detection (Larsen and Bundesen, 1996)

Research evidence

Larsen and Bundesen (1996) programmed a machine on this basis and found 95.3% accuracy with an average of 37 templates per type of digit.

Evaluation

- Template theory is more effective when information from *all templates* is assessed rather than the *one* producing the closest match to the input stimulus.

Recognition-by-components theory (Biederman, 1987)

Geons (geometric ions) are basic three-dimensional shapes such as cylinders and wedges. Any pattern or object can be broken down into component geons which are then recognised with templates. The collection of geons including their relationships, is matched to complete object descriptions.

Research evidence

Biederman *et al.* (1985) tested how participants dealt with *degraded* information (objects missing certain geons); they were still 90% accurate in their identifications, supporting the theory. Biederman (1987) also found that, when information about contours was missing, recognition was more difficult, demonstrating the importance of concavities. Edge information was more crucial than colour.

Evaluation

- More *economical* in terms of storage than other models.
- There is no *direct evidence* of the 36 geons.
- Object recognition should be *impaired* if objects divided up so that geons difficult to detect but this was not found by Cave and Kosslyn (1993).

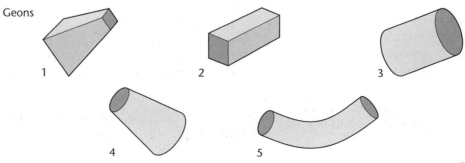

Geons

1   2   3

4   5

> The process of face recognition differs from object recognition in major ways.

> Feature-by-feature recognition is an example of *bottom-up processing*, processing based on the physical stimulus itself rather than expectations.

> *Top-down processing* (context) can explain why it is easier to recognise a shop-assistant in the shop than in the street.

> It has been suggested that the recognition of unfamiliar faces involves feature detection (as in Identikit photographs) whereas familiar face recognition involves configural recognition (Yin, 1969).

Face recognition

Farah (1994) showed that a patient with prosopagnosia (LH) could recognise ordinary objects but not faces. Some patients cannot even recognise their face.

Research evidence

Feature-by-feature recognition. Bradshaw and Wallace (1971) constructed Identikit faces. Participants could distinguish between two faces faster the more differences there were. They must have analysed each feature separately.

Configuration. Young *et al.* (1987) constructed faces by combining the top half of a famous person's face with the bottom half of another famous person. The more closely aligned the two halves, the harder recognition was of the two individuals. The close alignment produced a new configuration which interfered with recognition.

Motion. Bruce and Valentine (1988) filmed a face with lights attached. Participants could identify the facial expressions in the films and sometimes could identify the person on the basis of the movements only.

Familiar faces. Bahrick *et al.* (1975) showed that after 34 years ex-students were still able to name 90% of the photographs of their classmates.

Theory of face recognition (Bruce and Young, 1986)

- The *recognition of familiar faces* depends mainly on structural encoding, face recognition units, person identity nodes and name generation.
- The *recognition of unfamiliar faces* involves structural encoding, expression analysis, facial speech analysis and directed visual processing.

Research evidence

Malone *et al.* (1982) tested a patient who appeared able to recognise photographs of famous statesmen but coped poorly with matching unfamiliar faces.

Young *et al.* (1985) reported a diary study of face recognition. There was not one case where a participant reported being able to put a name to a face without also knowing something else about the person, but often they could remember a lot about the person but not their name.

Evaluation

- One *amnesic patient*, ME, matched 88% famous faces and names but didn't know any information about them (de Haan *et al.*, 1991).
- The role of the cognitive system is *not well specified*.
- Burton and Bruce (1993) presented a *more precise version* of the model that has been used in computer simulations. The new model has no separate store for names and familiar face recognition is at the person-identity node rather than at the face recognition unit.

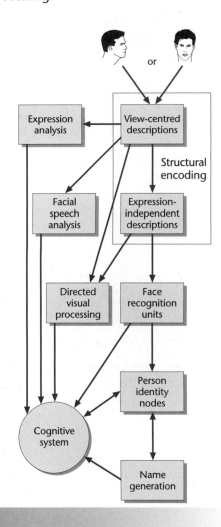

Practice essay 3.3

(a) Outline **two or more** explanations of pattern recognition. (12 marks)

(b) Assess the explanations you outlined in part (a). (12 marks)

Perceptual processes and development

3.4 The visual system

Structure and function of the visual system

The eye

> Vision is critical for survival and therefore it is not surprising that the eye is a very intricate organ.

The iris is the coloured part around the pupil, muscles control the amount of light admitted. The cornea and lens bend incoming light so that it is focused on the *fovea*. The lens is round for near focus (attached muscles contract) and flat for distant vision (muscles relax). This is called *accommodation*.

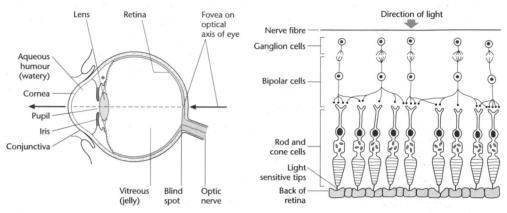

> Light has to pass through all three layers of the retina until it reaches the photoreceptors. The reason for the inverted structure of the retina is that the eye is an outgrowth of the brain.

The retina

The retina is a thin sheet of interconnected nerve cells.

Outermost layer: photoreceptors

Photoreceptors are photosensitive, they convert light (sensory transduction) into a nervous impulse.

> It is adaptive to detect movement 'out of the corner of your eye' in case it is a predator about to attack. Precision vision is only necessary in the centre of the retina (the *fovea*).

* *Rods*. Rod-like photosensitive cells (124 million of them) respond to shades of grey, to movement and edges. They function in conditions of low lighting and are concentrated in the outer parts of the retina.

* *Cones*. Cone-shaped cells, sensitive to colour, function in daylight conditions. They (12 million of them) are not present in the outer parts of the retina.

The *fovea* is specialised for detailed vision, it contains densely packed photoreceptors, mainly cones.

Second and third layer: bipolar and ganglion cells

Every photoreceptor is connected to more than one *bipolar cell*, and each bipolar cell receives impulses from more than one photoreceptor. In the second layer there are also *amacrine* and *horizontal cells*. One or more bipolar cells are connected to each *ganglion cell*, the third layer closest to the light source.

> If you draw two black dots about 6 inches apart, and focus on the left one while covering your left eye, the other circle should disappear as you move the paper towards you. This is because of your blind spot.

The optic nerve

Ganglion cells are bundled into the *optic nerve*. The area of the retina where the optic nerve passes through is called the *blind spot* or optic disc, it generally doesn't disrupt vision because the brain 'fills in gaps' in data.

The visual system

Pathways of the optic nerve

The *optic chiasma* is where the optic nerves from each eye crossover. The *lateral geniculate nucleus* (LGN) is a relay station, nerves from the retina synapse with nerves to the visual cortex. The *retina-geniculate-striate* system has two independent channels:

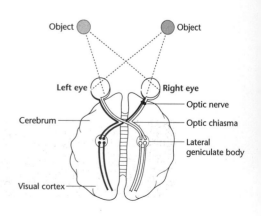

- the *parvocellular* (or P) *pathway*: sensitive to colour and to fine detail; most of its input comes from cones
- the *magnocellular* (or M) *pathway*: sensitive to information about movement; most of its input comes from rods.

The visual cortex

The visual *association cortex* (see page 40) is in the *occipital* cortical lobe (at the back). The *striate cortex* is the primary visual cortex surrounded by the *parastriate cortex*. The primary visual cortex passes data to at least 30 different areas of the brain for higher order processing (Stirling, 2000).

Visual information processing

Sensations are the raw data of the perceptual system, the unaltered record of the physical stimulus.

Sensory adaptation

When an eye is kept in a low light for some time, it grows more sensitive and a given light will then appear to be brighter. This is *dark–light adaptation*. Eyes also adapt to over-bright conditions.

This happens for two reasons:

- the pupil dilates in darkness, and this allows more light into the eye
- the photopigment *rhodopsin* breaks down when exposed to light but quickly recovers unless there is a lot of light and then recovery takes longer.

Contrast processing

> The retina collects 136 million points of light; there is little point processing all this data. Some information is summarised at the retina by the bipolar and ganglion cells.

> Usually light adaptation is faster than dark adaptation.

> *Lateral inhibition* is another means by which retinal information is reduced.

When any photosensitive cell is stimulated, it inhibits activity in surrounding cells (*lateral inhibition*). This emphasises the borders between light and dark, enabling edge detection and contrast processing.

The *ray figure* (right) is disturbing to look at probably because it 'upsets' the visual system by over-stimulating the edge detectors. The *white diamond* illusion (bottom right) is created because the white areas closest to the square will be least inhibited, whereas the area equidistant between all four corners is inhibited by surrounding cells. Therefore one appears to see dark diamonds at the crossroads.

The perception of colour

> This is also called the *trichromatic theory* because three types of colour-sensitive cell are proposed.

Young–Helmholtz theory (Young, 1802, von Helmholtz, 1896)

There are three types of cone: red-, green- and blue-sensitive each of which contain photopigments which respond maximally to particular wavelengths (short, medium and long respectively).

This account explains how the perception of colour is created by mixing signals from each receptor and is supported by evidence of only three types of cone pigment. However it cannot explain colour blindness (why is it rare to be green-blue colour blind?), nor why people who are red-green colour blind can recognise yellow (which is dependent on red and green receptors), nor explain *negative afterimages*.

> A *negative afterimage* occurs when you look at an red object and then look away and see a green afterimage – the opponent colour.

Opponent–process theory (Hering, 1870)

There are three pairs of receptor systems, red–green, blue–yellow and black–white, which work in opposition. Stimulation of one of the pair results in inhibition of the other. It is probable that when information leaves the cones (i.e. bipolar and ganglion cells) it is then coded in the opponent-process fashion.

Opponent-process theory can account for negative afterimages and colour blindness, which occurs when there is damage to the cells responsible for the perception of red + green, or yellow + blue. This is why one finds red/green or yellow/blue but not green/blue colour blindness.

The Young–Helmholtz and Hering theories describe different aspects of the same process. The three cone types of the Young–Helmholtz theory send signals to the opponent cells of the Hering theory, and this produces the perception of colour.

Synthesis

This combined theory is supported by the finding that people who are red–green colour blind have fewer medium- or long-wavelength cones (Zeki, 1993).

Retinex theory (Land et al., 1983)

This accounts for the fact that colour constancy depends on simultaneous contrasts; if you wear red-tinted glasses you still perceive colour differences but if you focus on a blue object it will start to look red because there is no contrast. The visual cortex compares the wavelengths of light coming from different parts of the retina at a given time and determines a colour perception for each object.

Feature processing

Hubel and Wiesel's discovery of cells that respond to lines of particular orientation is in line with feature detection theories of pattern recognition (see p. 65).

Hubel and Wiesel (1962) placed micro-electrodes in different parts of a cat's and monkey's visual cortex. They found that each cell (*simple cells*) only fired when the cat was shown a line of unique orientation in a particular part of the visual field. They also found cells sensitive to other features (e.g. a stationary or moving dot, or a moving line), *complex cells* which responded to several simple cells, and *hypercomplex cells* which responded to simple patterns or shapes (such as angles). These cells are organised into *functional columns* which may predispose the brain to be able to make certain comparisons, such as those used in depth perception.

Practice essay 3.4

(a) Outline the structure of the visual system. (12 marks)

(b) Assess the contribution made by the visual system to the process of perception. (12 marks)

3.5 Perceptual organisation

AQA A   U4

Theories of visual perception

Direct theory (Gibson, 1979)

Direct perception involves *bottom-up* or *data-driven* processing.

The amount of data contained in the retinal image (the *optic array*) is underestimated. It is sufficiently rich in information to explain perception.

Optic flow patterns are produced as we move around the environment; thus movement produces perceptual data.

Gibson felt movement (action) was a key part of perception.

Invariants. Some aspects of the optic array remain the same when you move, such as the pole (point towards which someone is moving), *horizon–ratio* relation, and *texture gradients* (provide information of depth from sensory data alone). We collect this invariant data in an automatic way – called *resonance*.

We collect visual data in the same way that a radio collects radio waves: perceptual data 'resonates' in the environment and this data is perceived by the viewer. We do not have to do anything in order to perceive it.

Affordance explains how the meaning of an object is perceived directly because its use is obvious. One look at a postbox and you can 'see' its meaning (a place to put letters).

Research evidence

Lee and Lishman (1975) built a swaying room so that they could manipulate optic flow patterns. Children typically fell over but adults were able to adjust, showing that sensory and motor processes are linked and that we learn to adjust them.

This theory is sometimes called the *ecological theory* because perception is explained solely in terms of the environment.

Evaluation

- Explains *animal perception* and some aspects of human perception, particularly where data is *unambiguous* (e.g. when lighting conditions good).
- Can explain 'seeing' but not '*seeing as*' (attaching meaning to what you see).
- Can't explain *perceptual set*, the lack of recovery of *cataract patients* (see page 73), and some constancies and illusions. However *illusions are artificial* and do not represent perceptual behaviour in the real world.
- Can't explain *concept-driven processing* or internal representations. Menzel (1978) showed monkeys 20 hidden food items, which they could later locate. They must have relied on cognitive maps and not solely on sensory data.

Perceptual set is the tendency to respond in a certain manner to a sensory stimulus, in line with expectations built on past experience.

This theory is *top-down* or *concept-driven* processing. Perception is primarily determined by 'best guesses' based on past experience.

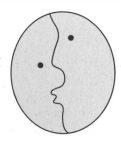

This theory can be applied to understanding certain accidents, such as when an airplane pilot makes an error because what he 'sees' is affected by preconceived ideas.

Bottom-up and top-down processing can be seen as complementary. The former may represent innate sensory mechanisms whereas the latter depend on learned experience. Their relative importance varies with particular circumstances.

These are monocular cues because you only need one eye to see them. They are all examples of direct perception.

Aerial reconnaissance uses *stereopsis* to detect images.

Convergence, accommodation and stereopsis are only effective cues for depth perception over relatively short distances.

Systematic movements in the visual field give cues of movement.

Constructivist theory (Gregory, 1966)

A perceived object is a hypothesis, which is suggested and then tested by sensory data. The stimulus provided to our senses is often incomplete or ambiguous; perception must rely on cognitive expectations.

Research evidence

Visual illusions illustrate perceptual inaccuracy and can be explained in terms of mistaken hypotheses (*misapplied size-constancy theory*, see page 71).

The *Ames room*. One person looks smaller because we don't expect the room to be a strange shape (see page 71).

Schafer and Murphy (1974) rewarded participants each time they saw one face and punished them for the other face over 100 trials. When shown the ambiguous image (left) they were more likely to 'see' the face that had been rewarded.

Evaluation

- Explains *perceptual constancy* and *set*, and how incomplete and ambiguous visual stimuli are perceived.
- Can't explain why vision is generally so *accurate* even in novel situations.
- Can't explain why the system is sometimes *slow to adjust* (as in inverted images) and sometimes faster (as in seeing ambiguous images).
- Can't explain how the system *reacts so fast* when having to search through a store of cognitive schemas.

Analysis-by-synthesis or cyclic model (Neisser, 1976)

Perception starts with a sampling of available information (bottom-up), for example, four legs might generate the hypothesis 'dog'. Attention is directed towards specific features which are generated from existing cognitive schema (top-down), e.g. a wet nose and a hairy body. If these are not found, the original hypothesis must be modified, and the process restarted.

Evaluation

- Gibson would argue that it is not necessary to *complicate matters*.
- Such a perceptual cycle would be *slow*.

Perceptual organisation

Depth perception

Monocular cues

Relative size (more distant objects are smaller), *linear perspective* (parallel lines converge), *texture gradients* (distant things appear denser because the constituent parts are closer together), *shading*, *brightness* (a brighter object appears closer), *relative clarity* (things in the distance are less in focus and bluer), *interposition* (one object overlaps another), *motion parallax* (things which are closer move faster with respect to those farther away).

Oculomotor cues

Depth is perceived using cues from the muscles around the eyes: *convergence* (the closer an object the more both eyes turn inwards to focus), and *accommodation* (thickening of the lens when focusing on a close object).

Binocular cues

Binocular disparity (*stereopsis*) is the slight difference between two retinal images produced when viewing an object. Julesz (1964) produced computer-generated random dot patterns with some of the dots in one picture shifted horizontally in relation to corresponding dots in the other picture so that, when viewed stereoscopically, an illusion of depth is created and an 'image' emerges. Binocular cells in the visual cortex compare corresponding points from both retinas and compute depth from the disparity.

Perception of movement (location constancy)

Environmental information, e.g. optic flow, motion parallax.

Effect of expectations: *phi phenomenon* (sequence of lights flashing appears to be moving) is due to 'best guess' that temporally related events are likely to be one object in motion.

The movements of the head and eyeball flicker give the appearance of movement, therefore the perceptual system needs muscle feedback to eliminate this data.

Perceptual constancy

Shape constancy. Book 'looks' rectangular from any angle.

Brightness constancy. White shirt 'looks' white in any light.

Colour constancy. Blue shirt 'looks' blue in red light ('Retinex theory', page 69).

Size constancy. Size is determined by apparent distance (as in *the Ponzo illusion*, on the left). In the *Ames Room*, one person appears larger because constancy cues are confused. One corner of the room is actually further away but the ceiling is adjusted to maintain the appearance of a rectangular room. If the person in the far corner is very familiar, the size effect disappears and the room is seen as distorted.

> We 'see' the same object despite changed retinal images.

Ponzo illusion and railway lines

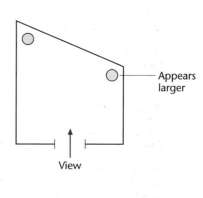

Appears larger

View

The Ames room

Perceptual illusions

Misapplied size constancy theory

Gregory (1970) suggests that size constancy rules for 3D objects are sometimes applied inappropriately to the perception of 2D objects. This can only explain some illusions (e.g. Ponzo illusion). It doesn't fully explain the *Müller–Lyer illusion*, e.g. when fins are replaced with circles the effect persists; DeLucia and Hochberg (1991) used 3D models (so real depth cues available) and the effect persisted.

Incorrect comparison theory

Matlin and Foley (1997) suggest that our perception is influenced by parts of the figure that are not being judged, thus explaining the Müller–Lyer inconsistencies above. Coren and Girgus (1972) found the Müller–Lyer illusion was greatly reduced when the fins were in a different colour to the vertical lines, because it was easier to ignore the fins.

'Good figure' theory

Gestalt psychologists explained perception as making best sense out of sensory data, e.g. we tend to see a row of dots as groups (e.g. .. ..). Illusions cause one feature to stand out. This can explain e.g. faces-goblets figure.

Physiological confusion theories

Carpenter and Blakemore (1973) suggest that converging or angled lines produce asymmetrical regions of lateral inhibition (see white diamonds effect on page 68) and this leads to distorted perception.

The effects of action

Gibson suggested a close link between perception and action. Wraga *et al.* (2000) found no Müller–Lyer effect when participants indicated the length of a 3D model of the lines by walking blindfolded.

> Gregory (1978) identified four major categories of visual illusions: ambiguous figures (e.g. the Necker cube), paradoxical figures (e.g. the Penrose triangle), fictitious figures (e.g. Kanisza triangle), and distortions (e.g. Ponzo illusion).

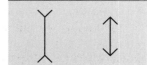

Müller-Lyer illusion

> There are also auditory illusions, for example Warren and Warren (1970) showed that, if a sentence is tampered with so that a bleep occurs instead of a particular phoneme, listeners still 'hear' the phoneme even when they know it's missing (*phonemic restoration*).

Practice essay 3.5

Discuss **one** theory of visual perception.   (24 marks)

3.6 Perceptual development

> Is perception an innate process (*nature*) or do we have to learn how to interpret sensory data (*nurture*)?

> At birth the human visual system is sensitive to colour, brightness, movement and visual patterns which have sufficient light/dark contrast.

> Changes that occur after birth may be due to maturation (nature) rather than learning (nurture).

> Perceptual development is the beginning of cognitive development, learning to make sense of the mass of sensory data – James (1890) called this 'one unanalysed bloom of confusion'. However, Fantz (1966) suggested that research findings run counter to James' view of visual confusion. In fact the neonate can distinguish many features of his or her environment.

> Studies of human neonates suggest that many perceptual abilities are innate. If this view is correct, and abilities such as depth perception are inborn, then we should find that all people develop these abilities regardless of their different personal experiences.

Research studies

Human infant studies

Size and shape constancy

Bower (1966) conditioned 6–8-week-old infants to turn their heads towards a certain sized or shaped cube by rewarding them with a game of 'peek-a-boo' every time a correct response was made. When he changed the distance or angle (retinal image changes), they continued to produce the conditioned response, thus demonstrating size and shape constancy. If infants had a patch over one eye, their performance remained the same, but not when the objects were shown as slides, indicating that the infants were using *motion parallax* to determine depth.

Depth perception

Bower *et al.* (1970) observed infants' (6–20 days old) response to an approaching object. If infants had no depth perception their response to a large disc stopping further should be the same as the response to a smaller, closer one because both objects create the same retinal image. In fact the infants were so upset by the smaller, closer one that the experiment was abandoned.

Gibson and Walk (1960) used the *visual cliff* with infants aged 6 to 14 months. Most of the infants (92%) refused to crawl over the 'cliff' even if they had a patch across one eye, which showed that they were using monocular cues only. This may be due to learned rather than innate factors, though when younger infants (2 months) were placed on the deep side their heart rate slowed showing interest and an ability to detect depth (Campos *et al.*, 1978).

Pattern recognition

Fantz (1961) showed that neonates (up to 6 months old) could discriminate certain visual forms. They preferred more complex patterns and a real face rather than a scrambled set of the same features. An interest in complexity may be important in stimulating the visual development of the brain; however, the preference for a face cannot be solely due to pattern complexity because the scrambled was less preferred. It may be due to a liking for things which are symmetrical or it may have adaptive importance (recognising and responding to one's own species).

Tracking

Aslin (1987) showed that neonates can follow a moving object with their eyes, but this ability improves considerably with practice.

Cross-modal perception

Cross-modal perception refers to using one sensory modality to recognise a stimulus familiar through another modality. Kaye and Bower (1994) gave day-old infants one of two dummies to suck and an image of the dummy was shown on a screen. If the infant stopped sucking the other dummy would be shown. Babies controlled their sucking to keep the first image on the screen showing an innate ability to match visual and tactile modalities.

Evaluation of human infant studies

- Testing a somewhat *immobile and unresponsive participant* is difficult and prone to subjective interpretation and experimenter bias.
- Research tends to be *laboratory based* and possibly atypical.
- *Separating maturation from learning* is difficult. An ability may still be innate even if an infant has not developed it yet.
- Sensorimotor *learning takes place even before birth,* in the womb, so we can't be sure whether abilities present at birth are innate or learned.

Cross-cultural studies

Depth perception

Turnbull (1961) described how a pygmy guide thought a herd of buffalo grazing in the distance were insects. Turnbull presumed that the guide, having lived in a forest all his life, had acquired no knowledge of depth cues nor of size constancy.

Hudson (1960) tested over 500 children and adults, Black and White, from southern Africa. He showed them pictures of a hunting scene or a flying bird and found that the 'school-going' participants interpreted the depth cues correctly whereas the 'non-school-going' participants did not, suggesting that the ability to decode depth cues is learned. Inability to interpret depth cues may be because the pictures are presented on paper. Deregowski *et al.* (1972) found that the Me'en in Ethiopia did not respond to drawings of animals on paper but they did if they were on cloth.

Interpretation of pictures

Drawing is not a direct representation of the real world. We learn cultural forms of representation. Aborigines (natives of Australia) represent people using a semi-circle (Cox, 1992). The *split-style drawing* technique is used by some Africans (Deregowski, 1972).

Visual illusions

Segall *et al.* (1963) found the Müller–Lyer illusion would only be perceived by those with experience of a *carpentered environment* (straight lines and rectangles); rural Zulus did not show the Müller–Lyer illusion. Allport and Pettigrew (1957) found that rural Zulus showed the horizontal–vertical illusion to a greater extent than Europeans, presumably because of greater familiarity with large open spaces.

However, Gregor and McPherson (1965) found no differences between Australian Aborigines living in carpentered or open-air environments in terms of Müller–Lyer or the horizontal–vertical illusion. Cross-cultural differences in visual illusions may relate more to training and education than environment.

Evaluation of cross-cultural studies

- Cross-cultural studies are fraught with *difficulties* such as biased interpretations by observers and limited samples.
- This research has focused on *limited aspects of perception* (e.g. visual illusions) and may tell us little about cultural differences in everyday perception.

Other research

Human deprivation studies

Banks *et al.* (1975) found that if children with squints are operated on before the age of three, they subsequently develop normal vision but if the operation is left any later the deprivation appears to result in some degree of abnormal binocular vision.

Deprived environments

Wiesel (1982) sewed one eye of a kitten shut. If this is done early enough the eye becomes blind, suggesting that experience is necessary to maintain the innate system.

Restricted environments

Held and Hein (1963) showed that the effects of visual deprivation are tied to sensorimotor experiences. When one kitten is allowed to walk in a kitten carousel its sensorimotor coordination develops normally whereas a yoked control, kept in a basket and not allowed to walk, has no such coordination.

Blakemore and Cooper (1970) placed kittens in a drum which had only vertical or only horizontal lines. The kittens later were virtually blind for the contours perpendicular to those they had experienced. Examination of their visual cortex showed that no cells responded electrically to the orientation not experienced by the cat, supporting the view that physical degeneration in the visual cortex took place.

Cataract studies

Gregory and Wallace (1963) studied SB who was blind from birth due to cataracts. In later life they were removed but he was never fully able to use his newly acquired sight though he was not blind. Von Senden (1932) found the same in other cataract patients.

Distortion studies

Stratton (1986) and Snyder and Pronko (1952) experimented with goggles which turned the world upside down. Within a few days the world appeared right way up. This suggests that experience leads to new interpretations of visual data by the brain, a feature not present in a fully innate system.

There is a tendency, in psychology, to confuse 'culture' with 'country'. A cultural group shares a set of beliefs, values and practices. Within any one country there may be many cultural groups.

Sensory deprivation has major emotional effects, which could explain the physical effects of sensory deprivation.

Cataract patients may have undergone physical and psychological trauma when their eyesight was restored, and may also have learned to rely on other senses.

The conclusion from studies of deprivation is that experience modifies innate abilities.

Explanations of perceptional development

Theories of perceptual development

Enrichment theory

Piaget suggested that perceptual (and cognitive) development depends on the individual enriching their sensory input using cognitive schemas.

Differentiation theory

Eleanor Gibson (1987) proposed that sensory information alone and without the influence of expectations can account for perceptual development. The infant learns to differentiate between the distinctive features of different classes of objects and to ignore irrelevant features. Bower (1982) suggested that infants can *register* most of the information that adults can, but are unable to handle it. Therefore perception is innate and direct.

Nature and nurture

The process of differentiation or bottom-up processing may explain innate systems of perception whereas enrichment or top-down processing is related to those perceptual abilities which are learned. In any one situation the relative contributions of each will vary according to particular circumstances.

The empirical evidence suggests that innate systems may be incomplete at birth and require experiential input to be maintained and to adapt to changed circumstances (nature and nurture).

> This mirrors the distinction between direct and constructivist theories of perception.

> Milner and Goodale (1998) propose that visual perception is processed in the brain in two different streams: the ventral ('what') stream processes recognition (related to constructivist theory) and the dorsal ('where') stream deals with action (direct perception theory).

Practice essay 3.6

'Is perception due to nature or nurture, or both?' Discuss the nature–nurture debate in the context of perceptual development. (24 marks)

Language and thought

3.7 Language and culture

 AQA A   U4

Language and thought

Language is thought

Watson (1912) suggested that thinking occurs in the voice box. Dr Smith (Smith *et al.*, 1947) demonstrated that he could think even when paralysed by a drug. Furth's studies of the deaf (1966) show that people can have no speech but still are able to think and use language.

Strong position: language determines thinking (linguistic determinism)

Whorf (1956) and Sapir (1958) proposed the Whorfian (Sapir–Whorf) hypothesis, that a person's thoughts are determined by the categories made available to them by their language.

Research evidence

Carroll and Casangrande (1958) found that Navaho children were better at form recognition than American counterparts, and suggested that this was because their language stressed the importance of form. However, these differences may be due to experience as much as language.

Evaluation

- This extreme position is *unlikely*, as the evidence below suggests.
- The terms 'language' and 'thought' are *relatively loosely defined* which makes the hypothesis difficult to test.

> Miller and McNeill (1969) suggested that there are three different hypotheses concerning the effects of language: the strong, weak and weakest hypotheses.

> Whorf (1956) said 'We dissect nature along lines laid down by our native language'.

> George Orwell wrote in his classic book *1984* of a language called 'Newspeak' which was a form of thought control.

Weak position: language affects thinking

Language may alter conceptualisation (*linguistic relativity hypothesis*), a position later taken by Whorf.

Research evidence

The *Great Eskimo Vocabulary Hoax*. Languages may have a large vocabulary for certain concepts (e.g. the Eskimos and words for snow) which enables native speakers to make cognitive distinctions not available to speakers of other languages. However, Pinker (1994) points out that the Eskimos actually only have around 12 words for snow rather than the 50 or so that has been claimed, and that there are about the same number of 'snow words' in English (e.g. sleet, blizzard, powder).

Whorf (1956) also claimed that *grammars* vary between language, based on his study of Apache language which led him to conclude that they must think differently (though he didn't interview any Apaches).

Evaluation

- It is the *cognitive need to make distinctions* which influences the vocabulary that a person develops rather than the other way round.

Weakest position: language affects some cognitive processes

Symbolic processes are affected by the codes used to represent meaning.

Concept formation

Vocabulary helps young children make discriminations; learning a new skill generally involves learning a new vocabulary. At the very least language aids concept formation.

Memory

Work on 'leading questions' shows how language can alter perception. For example, Loftus and Zanin (1975) showed how the use of 'a' or 'the' in a question changes the way people answer a question. 'Did you see the broken headlight?' assumes that there was a broken headlight whereas 'Did you see a broken headlight?' is more open-ended.

Perception

Carmichael *et al.* (1932) gave two groups of participants different descriptions for the same set of drawings, e.g. a picture which looked like a thin crescent moon was described as a 'crescent moon' or 'the letter C'. Subsequent recall was related to the labels.

Schooler and Engstler-Schooler (1990) found that memory for colours was affected if participants were asked to give names to colours.

Stereotypes are perpetuated by the 'labels' people use to describe certain groups of people. Hartland (1991) claims there are 200 words for sexually promiscuous women but only 20 for men.

Thought is independent of language

Some concepts may exist independently of the language we use, and are based on innate discriminations.

Research evidence

Perception of colour is independent of language. Rosch (1978) tested the Dani (from New Guinea). They have only two colour words, equivalent to black and white. Dani participants were quicker at learning a new colour category based on 'fire-engine' red (which is closest to the pigment in the retina) than a category based on an 'off-red'.

Berlin and Kay (1969) found that native speakers of different languages selected the same colours from a selection of 300 as the best example of each of their 'focal colours'.

Davies (1998) asked English (11 basic colours), Setswana (5), and Russian (12) speakers to sort 65 colours into similar groups. Their selections were remarkably similar.

Evaluation

- A modified Whorfian hypothesis (Hunt and Agnoli, 1991) would propose that some languages *lend* themselves to certain ways of thinking but this does not preclude a speaker of another language from having the same thought.

Margin notes:

Even if Eskimos did have more words, it wouldn't be surprising because the more contact one has with a particular kind of thing the more one has concepts to represent finer distinctions.

The term grammar refers to the rules used to combine words to produce meaning.

Vygotsky (1987) pointed out that the acquisition of a new word is the beginning of the development of a concept rather than the finish.

Mentalese (Pinker, 1994) is the sensation of knowing what 'you meant to say', which means you had the thought without language.

Piaget and Vygotsky's theories of cognitive development are discussed on pp. 84–86.

The developmental view

Piaget: thought produces language

Cognitive changes precede and underlie linguistic advances. Sinclair-de-Zwart (1969) found that children who could not conserve also showed differences in their linguistic development: they used absolute rather than comparative terms such as 'big' rather than 'larger' and used a single term for different dimensions such as 'small' to mean 'short', 'thin' or 'few'. She tried to teach the nonconservers the verbal skills they were lacking but 90% of these children were still unable to conserve, supporting Piaget's view that cognitive maturity is a prerequisite for linguistic development.

Vygotsky: language and thought are separate

Thinking originates in the need to restructure a situation (pre-linguistic thought) whereas language starts with the need to communicate (pre-intellectual language). Language shapes thought when it takes on a thinking function.

Social and cultural aspects of language use

Sociolinguists claim that language normally functions in a social context.

Social aspects of language use

Social markers

Language communicates social position. Giles and Powesland (1975) found that individuals using received pronunciation (RP) English were more favourably evaluated in terms of status and competence than non-RP speakers.

Speech accommodation theory (Giles, 1984)

People modify their speech to suit the context. Bourhis et al. (1975) suggested that convergence of speech markers (e.g. accent) between two people signals liking (bilateral convergence). If a low-status speaker wants to be upwardly mobile he/she may adjust speech (unilateral convergence) but a high-status speaker may resist (unilateral divergence). Hogg (1985) found that female students shifted their speech style upwards towards that of their male partners.

Ethnolinguistic identity theory is related to social identity theory, the view that group membership affects self-image.

Ethnolinguistic identity theory (Giles and Johnson, 1981)

Language is part of group (social) identity because it distinguishes between groups and enhances group esteem. This can explain the revitalisation of some languages that were on the verge of disappearance, such as Gaelic and Welsh, and resistance to 'invented' languages such as Esperanto.

Sub-cultural differences in language use

Bernstein's view was that a restricted linguistic code limits cognitive development. This is an example of socially sensitive research.

Verbal deprivation theory

Bernstein (1961) argued that only a certain kind of language (elaborated code) allows users to articulate abstract concepts, and that children who use a restricted code are unable to engage in this kind of intellectual activity.

If this verbal deprivation theory is correct then it follows that enriched language experience should increase cognitive development in lower-class children.

Research evidence

Schwartz et al. (1967) found significant differences in language between a group of socially disadvantaged primary school children who received enriched schooling for two years and those who didn't. However, the study by Sinclair-de-Zwart (1969, see above) suggests that linguistic enrichment may not affect cognitive development.

Hart and Risley (1995) observed words used in families with 3-year-old children. Those in professional families had up to 15 000 more words directed towards them in a week than did the children from families on welfare.

Evaluation

Labov also noted data are inevitably flawed when White interviewers assess Black speakers.

Labov (1970) pointed out that Bernstein's conclusions were due to a failure to recognise the subtleties of some forms of non-standard English and a confusion between social and linguistic deprivation. Labov (1972) studied Black English vernacular in New York and concluded that the differences between this and standard English were trivial.

Practice essay 3.7

Discuss research (theories **and/or** studies) related to the linguistic relativity hypothesis.

(24 marks)

3.8 Language acquisition

AQA A ▸ U4

Research into the process of language acquisition

Stages of language acquisition

Pre-linguistic (under 12 months)

Communication is through cooing, crying, babbling, echolalia, gestures. Paralinguistics is shown in turn-taking, for example Trevarthen (1974) observed that young babies 'take turns' in conversations.

Bates *et al.* (1979) found that 10-month-olds used gestures to say 'What's that?' or 'Look at that.' These are part of the pragmatics of language.

One-word utterances (12–18 months)

Nelson (1973) found that first words tended to be for objects which were prone to change (movement), such as 'ball'. She also found that, from the beginning, children used all types of words and ones which were quite specific such as 'pigeon' rather than 'bird'. Vocabulary was typically 10 words at five months, and 200 words by 2 years.

First sentences

Bee and Mitchel (1980) distinguished two stages.

- *Stage 1 grammar* – two-word utterances, telegraphic speech. Braine (1963) described a pivot grammar: pivot words (e.g. 'see') combined with 'open' words.
- *Stage 2 grammar*: Complex sentences with MLU of 4.

Brown *et al.* (1973) recorded the speech development of Adam and Eve, observing the following features of early *grammar*.

- *Imitation preserving word order.* The mother might say 'He's going out' whereas the child would repeat 'He go out'. Order (grammar) not content was preserved.
- *Reduction of sentence length* is not because of memory limitations, otherwise children would only repeat the first two or three words. The key words sustain meaning.
- *Imitation with expansion.* The mothers responded to telegraphese by expanding the sentence with the order preserved. This is a 'meaning check' for the mother and a lesson in how to create detailed meaning for the child.
- *Overgeneralisations.* E.g. 'goed', and 'sheeps'.
- *Overextension* (using one word to refer to more objects it they should, e.g. 'Spot' for all dogs) and *underextension* (the meaning given to a word covers too few objects, e.g. 'car' only for family car).

Later speech

Increased complexity (e.g. embedded sentences 'Here is the book I was reading yesterday) and use of metalanguage in poems and jokes (e.g. 'How can you make time fly?').

Explanations of language development

Environmental (learning) theory (Skinner, 1957)

Language is acquired in the same way as any other behaviour: child imitates words (*echoic response*) and makes demands (*mands*) which are selectively *reinforced* by the child getting what it wants, such as a biscuit or attention. A *tact* is involved when the child is rewarded for correct pronunciation and correct grammar.

Research evidence

Gelman and Shatz (1977) found that children are helped by an adult's use of *motherese*, a special form of language which uses a simplified grammar (e.g. 'pat the doggie').

Evaluation

- Explains *some aspects* of language acquisition such as learning speech sounds, simple meanings, vocabulary and accent.
- Slobin (1977) noted that adults reinforce *incorrect grammar*. Brown *et al.* (1969) found that mothers reinforce meaning rather than grammatical structure.
- Cannot account for *overgeneralisations* nor the *universal sequence* of acquisition.

Babble reflects the sound of adult speech, Bates *et al.* (1987) say that babies are 'learning the tune before the words'.

There is a difference between vocalisations (making a noise) and verbalisation (using language).

A *holophrase* is one word which is used to express a more complex meaning. For example, 'milk' might mean 'I want some milk.'

'Grammar' refers to the rules of how words are combined to provide meaning. An infinite number of meanings can be generated from a finite set of sounds (*phonemes*).

MLU=mean length of utterance measured in *morphemes*; 'to' is one morpheme, 'toes' and 'today' are two.

Shaping involves successive reinforcements for behaviours that are progressively closer and closer to the desired behaviour.

For political correctness, motherese is also called parentese or the Baby Talk Register (BTR).

Language acquisition is biologically driven. We acquire language in the same way that we 'learn' to walk – because we inherit this facility.

'The peasants are revolting' has two deep structures; 'the cat chased the dog' and 'the dog is chased by the cat' have the same deep structure.

Nativist theory (Chomsky, 1959)

Humans have an innate capacity to generate the rules of grammar (linguistic rules) from a native vocabulary (i.e. acquire language). The language centres of the brain contain a *language acquisition device* (LAD, later just called a 'universal grammar') which produces *transformational grammar* – the ability to move between *surface structure* (the actual words and phrases expressed) and *deep structure* (the meaning).

Research evidence

Berko (1958) showed children a picture of a 'wug', and then a picture of two; children easily completed the sentence: 'There are two...', demonstrating grammatical knowledge.

Studies of non-human animal language (see page 118) suggest that animals cannot acquire grammar which is probably due to innate neurophysiological differences.

Lenneberg (1967) suggested that, if language is biologically controlled, it must be acquired within a *sensitive period* (before puberty), or the ability disappears. Genie (Curtiss, 1977) emerged from an early life of privation at age 13 and was unable to acquire language. She used words but not combined in meaningful ways ('shoe tie' and 'tie shoe' meant the same thing). Privated children 'discovered' earlier could acquire language (e.g. Isabelle).

Singleton and Newport (1993) studied two deaf parents who only learned sign language after the age of 15 and never could use it grammatically. Their son, Simon, was able to generate a grammatical system from this defective linguistic input. Pinker (1994) described how a group of older deaf Nicaraguans invented their own sign system (LSN) when deaf schools opened for the first time. Younger deaf children were able to develop a grammatical version, called ISN from the ungrammatical input.

Newport (1994) found that Asian immigrants to the US were better able to learn complex rules of grammar and other aspects of English the younger they were.

McNeill (1966) argued that the evolution of a language relies on the reformulation made by children as they acquire language, each new generation of children reinvent and simplify the linguistic corpus.

Pinker (1994) noted that all human societies develop language and that, while 'there are Stone Age societies, ... there is no such thing as a Stone Age language'.

This theory does not contradict other theories, it is an addition.

Evaluation

- Chomsky's views were *revolutionary*, opening up the study of language.
- Fits with the fact that there are *linguistic universals* (forms of speech which can be found in all languages, e.g. nouns, verbs, clauses) and there is a universal sequence of language acquisition (as described on page 77).
- Combines *nature and nurture* (innate grammar and learned vocabulary).
- *Explains* overgeneralisations, linguistic universals, the ease of acquisition even when working on an incomplete sample, the lack of true language in animals, sensitive periods and language localisation in the brain (see page 41).
- Children reared in *social isolation* don't develop language on their own, therefore exposure and innate potential are both necessary but not sufficient.

Functional theories (Halliday, 1975)

Chomsky's approach refers almost exclusively to structure and ignores function. Halliday points out that early language has functional importance: smiling, crying and eye-contact. Bruner (1983) proposed an innate acquisition system LASS (language acquisition support system) which includes social interaction.

Research evidence

Sachs *et al.* (1981) studied a young boy, Jim, whose parents were both deaf and couldn't speak. Jim heard language on TV and briefly at nursery school, but by the age of 4 his speech was backward. He lacked the necessary social context.

The Nicaraguan deaf children (above) did not learn sign language from their teachers but invented it themselves in the playground.

Vygotsky (see p. 85) also underlined the social importance of language.

Evaluation

- This model would predict that *stone age cultures* should have stone age languages, because language is a reflection of culture.
- Can't explain why *blind children* develop normal language despite limited social interactions.

Practice essay 3.8

Describe and evaluate **one** explanation for language development. (24 marks)

3.9 Problem-solving and decision-making

AQA A U4

Research into problem-solving

Learning theory

Thorndike (1898) explained problem-solving as *trial-and-error learning*. Hungry cats were placed in a 'puzzle box' with some food outside. They needed to pull a string dangling from the ceiling to escape. By trying various solutions which were incorrect (negative reinforcement) they eventually found the correct one (positive reinforcement).

Gestalt approaches

Reproductive problem-solving

Reproduction (e.g. trial and error learning) involves the re-use of previous experience which may hinder successful problem-solving.

Luchins (1942) showed that, if participants become accustomed to a particular solution on the *water jar problem*, they continue to use it when no longer effective.

Duncker (1945) showed how people become 'fixed' (*functional fixedness*) on an interpretation. Participants were given candles, drawing pins and a box of matches and asked to mount the candle on the wall; their problem-solving was blocked because they thought in terms of the box as a container rather than as a platform. When they were given an empty box, they found the solution more easily.

Productive problem-solving

Insight into a problem is achieved by productive *restructurings* of the problem.

Köhler (1925) set chimpanzees various open-ended problems to solve, such as trying to reach bananas outside a cage. The animals might appear to give up, but later they would solve it in a flash of '*insight*' (e.g. using a stick).

Maier (1931) used the pendulum problem to demonstrate insight in humans. Two strings hang down from the ceiling, too far apart to hold both at once. You can manage to tie them together if you use a pair of pliers to make a pendulum (restructuring).

Information-processing approach

Problem-space theory (Newell and Simon, 1963)

Individuals select the shortest route between a current state and goal state using *heuristic* methods. It is like finding your way through a maze, beginning at the entrance (initial state) and seeking the goal by moving through the whole space of possible paths (problem space) and making choices.

Means-ends analysis: one heuristic method (Newell and Simon)

• Note the problem space (distance between current and goal state).
• Create a sub-goal to reduce this difference.
• Select an operator which will solve the sub-goal.
• Recalculate the problem space and set a new sub-goal.

Empirical evidence

The *General Problem Solver* (GPS) was the computer program they wrote based on means-ends analysis. *Protocol analysis* can be used to show that the model does demonstrate problem-solving behaviour. This involves recording a protocol (a record of what a person is thinking when engaged in a task) and comparing this with the computer trace (record of the computer's activity).

Structuring a problem into various sub-goals improves overall performance. Egan and Greeno (1974) gave participants five- and six-disc versions of the Tower of Hanoi; those who had previous experience with four-disc versions were better than a control group.

Having sub-goals facilitates problem-solving. Simon and Reed (1976) gave participants a five missionaries and five cannibals problem. When participants were given a hint about different strategies this resulted in improved performance.

Evaluation

• The GPS was an early and *influential* computer program but it was *abandoned* because it couldn't be applied to human problem-solving.

Problem-solving and decision-making are examples of 'thinking'. We are conscious of our thoughts but usually not conscious of the processes involved.

Gestalt psychologists suggested that problem-solving behaviour is both *reproductive* and *productive*.

Birch (1945) found little evidence of this kind of insightful problem-solving in apes that were raised in captivity.

This is evidence of cognitive activity, a form of explanation rejected by behaviourists.

Heuristics are rules of general principle which, unlike *algorithms*, are not definite solutions for a problem but possibilities that will save a lot of time and effort.

People show characteristic differences in their approach to problem-solving. Hudson (1963) found that science-oriented pupils tended to have a linear, focused, style of reasoning ('convergers') whereas arts students were more divergent, intuitive or impulsive ('divergers').

An *analogy* is a means of explaining a concept by drawing a comparison with another situation, for example 'Amin's treatment of Ugandans was as bad as Hitler's treatment of the Jews.'

- Problem-space theory has *not been bettered* though it has been extended.
- Means-end analysis works with *well-defined goals* but in everyday life people have to solve problems with unclear goals and many ambiguities.

Analogy

Analogical thinking involves mapping the conceptual structure of one set of ideas (a *base domain*) into another set of ideas (the *target domain*).

Research evidence

Gick and Holyoak (1980) showed how past experience can be applied to a new problem (i.e. using analogy). Duncker's (1945) radiation problem (how to destroy a tumour when X-rays kill all tissue) can be solved by using lower dose X-rays to converge on the tumour. Only 10% of participants think of this; however, if participants are first asked to memorise a story about an army converging on a fort from many different directions, the success rate can rise to 80%.

Practical issues relating to decision-making research

Decision-making involves making choices and taking risks (weighing costs against benefits).

Risk-taking behaviour

Utility theory (Neumann and Morgenstern, 1947)

The expected utility (usefulness) of any decision = (probability of a given outcome) x (utility of that outcome).

Tversky and Kahneman (1987) used the example of two programmes that can fight a disease threatening 600 people: programme A will save 200 lives, whereas programme B offers a one-third probability that all will be saved. Both programmes have the same expected utility but, when asked, 72% of participants choose programme A. This shows that we don't always behave in line with expected utility, possibly because of:

Much of the theory assumes that we think logically. Dewey's 'trouble' theory of thinking suggests that most of the time we function on automatic pilot; it is only discrepancy that calls for thought.

- *Framing effect.* Programme A is 'framed' more positively. Johnson (1987) found that people prefer meat labelled 80% lean than 20% fat.
- *Loss aversion.* People are more sensitive to losses rather than gains. Kahneman and Tversky (1984) asked participants whether they would accept a bet that involved them winning $20 if a coin came up heads, but paying $10 if it came up tails. The bet should be accepted according to utility theory, but most of the participants rejected it.

Elimination by aspects theory (Tversky, 1972)

The decision-maker eliminates options by considering one relevant attribute after another. This theory implies that the option that is selected depends on the order in which the attributes are considered.

Satisficing theory (Simon, 1978)

Satisficing theory might help explain decisions such as about who you might marry.

A more appropriate explanation for situations where various options become available at different points in time. Decision-makers set a minimum acceptable level. The first option to reach that level is selected. Payne (1976) found that people, when choosing a flat, used elimination by aspects and satisficing to reduce the number of possibilities. They then focused on the remaining options in a more thorough way.

Errors in thinking about probability

Errors in decision-making may occur because the wrong probability heuristic is used.

Representativeness heuristic

The precise strategies that people use are likely to vary from problem to problem. Most strategies are not ideal but work well enough (i.e. they are *heuristics*).

When estimating probability a decision must be made about how representative a particular event is of the general population.

Kahneman and Tversky (1972) asked participants to identify a random distribution; they choose 4,4,5,4,3 rather than 4,4,4,4,4 seeing the latter as too orderly.

However, Tversky and Kahneman (1980) found that people don't always rely on the representativeness heuristic. A blue or green taxi was said to be involved in an accident; when some base-rate information (85% of accidents involve green taxis), was made obvious, participants' judgements were closer to the true probability.

Availability heuristic

We make decisions based on the most 'available' information.

Tversky and Kahneman (1973) gave participants a list of 19 well-known men and 20 even better-known women (this was reversed for another group). Participants, when asked how many men and women were in the list, greatly overestimated the number of women, presumably because the famous names were more available.

Evaluation

- It is useful to think of decision-making in terms of heuristics but this approach suggests that people are *less accurate* than they in fact are.
- The theory is based on *artificial laboratory studies*.

Practice essay 3.9

(a) Describe **two** studies that have investigated decision-making. (12 marks)

(b) Assess the extent to which these **and/or** other studies inform us about decision-making behaviour. (12 marks)

Sample question and model answer

(a) Describe **two** studies that have investigated slips associated with automatic processing. (12 marks)

(b) Assess the contribution of these, **and/or** other studies, to our understanding of attentional processes. (12 marks)

Examiner's comments

In part (a) you are required to select and describe two studies that have investigated slips associated with automatic processing. You should spend about 6 minutes on each study, trying to cover aims, procedures, findings and conclusions. Do not offer any evaluation of the studies as such material would not be creditworthy in an AO1 question.

In part (b) AO2 skills are required. This means that you must analyse and evaluate the studies – but a particular means of doing this has been identified, in terms of how such studies inform us (or not) about attentional processes. Your focus here should be on commentary and analysis and you should avoid descriptive material, which would not attract credit.

Candidate's answer

(a) James Reason (1977) conducted a diary study, where 35 participants recorded their action slips over a two week period. The aim of this study was to see what kind of errors people make in everyday life. Four hundred errors or action slips occurred during this period. Reason divided them into 5 categories. The most common error was storage failures. An example of a storage failure would be putting two teaspoons of sugar in a cup of tea when you usually only have one. Test failures accounted for 20% of the errors. An example of a test failure would be making a cup of coffee instead of tea. Subroutine failures accounted for 18% of the errors. These involve the reversal or accidental change of the order of component routines involved in completing a task, such as putting the water in a cup before the coffee. Discrimination failures (15%) involved using incorrect instruments in a task, such as a fork instead of a spoon to stir the coffee, and finally programme-assembly failures involved misplacing components involved in a task.

Reason did another study in 1984 with Lucas. They developed a questionnaire on absent-mindedness while shopping, based on an analysis of over 100 letters written by 70 individuals who felt they had been wrongly accused of shoplifting. The questionnaire was given to a control group of people not involved in shoplifting to see how often they experienced lapses while shopping. The comparisons suggested that the 'shoplifters' did have more lapses of attention.

Sample question and model answer (continued)

(b) Reason's first study identified the mistakes or slips that people make while doing everyday tasks. Reason constructed a theory based on this research. He suggested that we have two modes of control over motor performance: closed-loop control which is used during skill acquisition to monitor motor performance (it requires direct attention) and open-loop methods of control which occur when automatic processing takes place, requiring little direct attention. Certain activities are performed automatically (without attention) thus freeing central resources. Action slips occur when someone is operating in an open loop and fails to return to closed-loop mode.

An alternative theory was formulated by Sellen and Norman (1992) based on the idea of schemas. In this theory, an environmental cue will trigger a particular schema and then the schema (or plan for action) is performed with attentional control. The reason why errors occur is that the wrong schema may be activated or the environmental cue may not properly trigger a schema.

One of the problems with these theories is that, in fact, errors tend to occur when we are engaged in everyday activities. When we are doing something important our attention is more focused. This aspect of behaviour isn't incorporated into these models.

[454 words]

Examiner's comments

(a) *The examiner is looking for accuracy, depth and breadth (detail). Reason's diary study is reported in considerable detail and demonstrates good understanding of the concepts. The bulk of the material concerns the findings from the study thus restricting the breadth of material covered but there is more than enough detail overall.*

The second study is limited by the fact that the detail provided essentially relates to procedures, and even this is not complete. There is no requirement for the two studies to be provided in the same amount of detail in order to get full marks.

Overall the two studies would rate a mark in band three (bottom) as being 'slightly limited'.

(b) *The second half of this essay ended up as a second descriptive essay, offering an account of two theories of attention processing and not addressing the question set which was to consider what such studies tell us about attentional processes. In the first paragraph there was some link between the research study and our understanding of attentional processes but this information has not been used very effectively.*

The final paragraph is an attempt at analysis and evaluation, a consideration of the kind of behaviours that are not accounted for by the theories. This would have been improved if reference had been made to the fact that the studies have focused on minor everyday activity that is likely to produce just such a biased theory.

AO1
A mixture of 'substantial' and 'limited' which places the mark in band 3 (bottom), both studies are short on breadth but reasonably detailed = 10 marks.

AO2
This material can be described as 'restricted' though moving towards being 'limited' and there is coherent elaboration. The bottom line is that the material has not been used in a 'reasonably effective manner', so band 2 (bottom) = 6 marks.

Total 16 out of 24 marks (see page 12 for band descriptors), possibly equivalent to a weak Grade A or strong Grade B.

Chapter 4

Developmental psychology

Development refers to the changes that take place over a person's lifetime. These changes may be the result of:
- inherited factors (*nature*), which include events that occur as a result of maturation, such as puberty
- lifetime experiences (*nurture*), which include interactions with other people.

At AS Level your study of developmental psychology may have focused on attachments in development, and how such research might be applied to day care.

At A2 you may select to study one or more of the following areas in developmental psychology:

Cognitive development

4.1 Development of thinking
4.2 Development of measured intelligence
4.3 Development of moral understanding

After studying this area you should be able to:

- describe and evaluate theories of cognitive development, including those by Piaget and Vygotsky
- critically consider the application of these theories to education
- discuss research into the role of genetics in the development of measured intelligence
- discuss research into the role of environmental factors in the development of measured intelligence

- assess the importance of cultural factors in the development of measured intelligence
- describe and evaluate theories of moral development (Piaget and Kohlberg) and pro-social reasoning (Eisenberg)
- assess the influence of gender on the development of moral understanding
- consider cultural variation in the development of moral understanding

LEARNING SUMMARY

Social and personality development

4.4 Personality development
4.5 Gender development
4.6 Adolescence

After studying this area you should be able to:

- discuss psychodynamic explanations of personality development
- discuss social learning explanations of personality development
- describe and evaluate explanations of the development of gender identity and gender roles

- critically consider research into social development in adolescence, including the formation of identity
- discuss research into relationships between parents and peers during adolescence
- discuss cultural differences in adolescent behaviour

LEARNING SUMMARY

Adulthood

4.7 Early and middle adulthood
4.8 Family and relationships in adulthood
4.9 Late adulthood

After studying this area you should be able to:

- describe and evaluate theories of development in early and middle adulthood
- critically consider the role of crises and transitions in development in early and middle adulthood
- discuss factors associated with key life events: marriage (partnering), divorce and parenthood
- describe and evaluate research related to these life events

- consider gender and cultural differences in these life events
- critically consider cognitive changes in old age
- describe and evaluate explanations of adjustment to old age
- discuss factors associated with life events in old age: retirement and bereavement, including cultural differences

LEARNING SUMMARY

Cognitive development

4.1 Development of thinking

AQA A	U4
AQA B	U4
EDEXCEL	U4, U5
OCR	U5, U6

The development of thinking was discussed in the *Revise AS Guide*. This is a review of the information covered there with the addition of some further material.

A 'schema' is a cluster of related concepts that represent particular aspects of the world.

An 'operation' is an internally consistent, logical, mental rule, such as rule of arithmetic.

Pre-operational children focus on the appearance of things and not the reality (thus lacking internal consistency).

Horizontal décalage describes the fact that not all aspects of the same stage appear at the same time, for example the ability to conserve number and volume. Uneven cognitive performance is probably due to different learning experiences.

Piaget's methods involved naturalistic observation and semi-structured interviews, as well as experimental work with Inhelder.

When considering the research evidence, remember the following: the stage *sequence* remains unchallenged by this evidence.

Theories of cognitive development

Piaget's (1896–1980) theory of cognitive development

Cognitive development is the study of how mental activities develop. The cognitive-developmental approach focuses on how thinking changes in age-related stages.

Essence of Piaget's theory
- There are *qualitative* differences between child and adult thinking.
- It is a *biological approach*: biological readiness is the prerequisite for change.
- *Language* is the outcome of a generalised cognitive ability, rather than the view that language leads cognitive development.

The structure of the intellect

Variant cognitive structures develop with age: *schemas* and *operations*.

Invariant cognitive structure are *assimilation* (information taken in) and *accommodation* (schema adjusted). The process is 'driven' by *disequilibrium*.

Stages in cognitive development
- *Sensorimotor stage* (0–2). Early reflex activities, circular (repetitive) reactions coordinate sensory and motor activity.
- *Pre-operational stage* (2–7). Symbols used (such as language) but not adult logic (operations). Subdivided into: pre-conceptual (concepts not fully formed) and intuitive (appearance not reality is important).
- *Concrete operational stage* (7–11). Adult (internally consistent) logic but only in concrete situations. Problem-solving is random rather than systematic.
- *Formal operational stage* (11+ years). Abstract and systematic (scientific) thought.

Research evidence

Object permanence (sensorimotor stage). The realisation that objects continue to exist even when they cannot be seen. Piaget claimed that this developed after the age of 8 months. Bower (1981) found that infants 5–6 months old showed surprise when an object that had been hidden behind a screen was no longer there. Baillargeon and DeVos (1991) used the rolling car task to show that 3–4-month-old infants were aware of object permanence.

Egocentrism. Pre-operational children find it hard to take the perspective of another. Piaget and Inhelder (1956) used the three mountains task but Hughes (1975) achieved better performance with toy policeman.

Conservation (pre-operational stage) is the ability to understand that quantity is not changed even when a display is transformed. Piaget used counters, beakers and balls of clay to demonstrate children under 7 cannot conserve. Samuel and Bryant (1984) found younger children coped better with one question but there were still age differences. McGarrigle and Donaldson's (1974) study with 'naughty teddy' produced more convincing results that younger children could conserve, though Moore and Frye (1986) suggested that naughty teddy may have unduly distracted the children.

Formal operational thinking. Bryant and Trabasso (1971) showed that difficulty on transitive inference tasks may be due to memory failure rather than lack of ability. Piaget and Inhelder's (1956) beaker problem showed that formal thinkers are systematic. Shayer and Wylam (1978) found that only 30% of 15–16-year-olds had achieved formal operations.

The influence of *language on thought*. Sinclair-de-Zwart (1969) found that non-conservers have limited vocabularies but teaching new words didn't improve ability to conserve (see page 76).

Evaluation of the theory
- Piaget's theory was the *first comprehensive account* of cognitive development. It changed the traditional view of the child as *passive* and stimulated research.

- The influence of language and *social and emotional* factors was overlooked.
- Piaget's evidence often lacked *scientific rigour*.
- Piaget suggested that *disequilibrium* would be the driving force in cognitive development. However, conflict does not tell a child how to solve the problem.

Vygotsky's (1896–1934) theory of cognitive development

The essence of Vygotsky's theory

- Active and *social construction* of knowledge rather than passive conditioning (Pavlov).
- *Experts* move child through ZPD (*zone of proximal development*).
- *Language and other cultural tools* (*semiotic mediation*) are the means by which experts transmit knowledge.
- *Social and individual levels*. Knowledge first appears on a social level; gradually dialogues between expert and learner become internalised (the individual level).

The structure of the intellect

Elementary mental functions are innate capacities such as attention and perception, possessed by all animals. Cultural influences transform elementary functions into *higher mental functions*.

Stages in cognitive development

- *Pre-intellectual*, social speech (0–3).
- *Egocentric speech* (3–7 years). Language controls one's own behaviour.
- *Inner speech* (7+). Language serves for thought and social communication. Since social processes shape language, they also shape thought.
- Vygotsky identified four stages in concept formation: *vague syncretic stage* (no systematic strategies), *complex stage* (non-random strategies not very successful), *potential concept stage* (focusing on one feature at a time), *mature concept stage*.

Research evidence

Social construction of knowledge Gredler (1992) noted that counting system used in Papua New Guinea (a cultural influence) limits cognitive development. It influence counting on fingers, toes and other body parts and only goes up to 29.

Influence of experts Freund (1990) found that children who worked with experts (mothers) showed a dramatic improvement in their ability to perform a furniture sorting task.

Social and individual plane Wertsch *et al.* (1980) showed that, when mothers and children worked on a task (building a truck), social factors in the form of the mother's looking behaviour had much more impact on younger than on older children. Older children were presumably more self-regulating. In addition, as the younger children became more proficient at the task they became more self-regulating.

Inner speech Vygotsky (1934) demonstrated the importance of inner speech by deliberately introducing obstacles to a child's activity which resulted in an increase in inner speech. Berk (1994) recorded children's speech when working on school tasks. She found that children talked to themselves more when they were faced with a difficult task, when working by themselves, or when a teacher was not available to help.

The *influence of language* on thought. Sinclair de Zwart's research (on facing page) suggests that language is not critical.

Evaluation

- Comparatively little *empirical support* (so far) but lots of interest.
- Exaggerated the importance of the *social environment*. Motivation important too and social interaction may have negative effects.
- If the help of others was all that was required, learning complex skills *should be faster* than it is.
- May describe *a different kind of learner* – the Vygotskian learner is extrovert and cooperative, the Piagetian child is more introverted and competitive.

Lev Semenovich Vygotsky was born in pre-First World War Russia but his work was first published in English in 1962.

The ZPD is the distance between a child's current and potential abilities. The aim of instruction is to stimulate those functions which lie waiting in the ZPD.

An 'expert' is anyone with greater knowledge.

Vygotsky emphasised how knowledge is acquired through social interaction whereas Piaget described it as a process of self-discovery.

Piaget and Vygotsky need not be seen as opposites. Glassman (1999) argues that in fact the two theories are remarkably similar especially at their central core.

The notion of education includes not just teachers but extends to anyone who is expanding the knowledge and understanding of children, e.g. parents, playleaders and toy manufacturers.

'Each time one prematurely teaches a child something he could have discovered for himself, that child is kept from inventing it and consequently from understanding it completely' (Piaget, 1970).

'What a child can do with assistance today he/she can do by him/herself tomorrow' (Vygotksy, 1978).

Practical applications to education

Piaget's theory

- *Readiness.* Offer moderately novel stimuli when the child is ready.
- *Self-discovery* and self-motivation lead to complete understanding.•
  Individualised. Children mature at different rates.
- *Discovery learning.* Learning should be child-centred and active. The teacher's role is not to impart knowledge but to ask questions, thus creating disequilibrium and forcing children to make accommodations.
- *Logic* is not an innate mental process, it is the outcome of cognitive development. Logic, maths and science subjects facilitate cognitive development.
- *Concrete materials* to teach young children (stage of concrete operations).

Vygotsky's theory

- *Expert intervention* (by peers or adults) is most effective when the expert is aware of the limits of the child's ZPD.

- *Scaffolding.* An adult advances children's thinking by providing a framework (scaffolding) on which children can climb. Wood *et al.* (1976) found that when a learner runs into difficulty, the expert provides specific instructions. When the learner is coping well only general encouragement is needed. In time, we all learn to scaffold ourselves (self-instruction).

- *Peer tutoring* and *cooperative group work*. Peers can be experts. Bennett and Dunne (1991) found that children engaged in cooperative group work were less competitive, less concerned with status and more likely to use logical thinking.

Practice essay 4.1

Describe and evaluate Piaget's theory of cognitive development.   (24 marks)

4.2 Development of measured intelligence

AQA A   U4
EDEXCEL   U4

Intelligence is a hypothetical quality measured by intelligence tests. Such tests represent intelligence numerically (IQ or intelligence quotient) which in children is calculated by mental age divided by chronological age x 100.

Monozygotic (MZ) twins share the same genes whereas dizygotic (DZ) twins share 50% of the same genes. If MZ twins have more similar IQs this suggests that IQ is inherited.

The role of genetics

Twin studies

MZ twins have more similar IQs. Bouchard and McGue (1981) reviewed a number of studies and found an MZ correlation of .85 and DZ correlation of .58.

If MZ twins are reared apart they should nevertheless have very similar IQs. Shields (1962) found that the concordance for MZ twins reared apart was 0.77 and reared together was 0.76. This suggests little environmental influence. Pedersen *et al.* (1992) reported on the Swedish Adoption/Twin Study of Ageing (SATSA): MZ twins reared apart or together had IQ correlations of about .79, DZ twins reared apart were .32 and together were .22. This suggests that about 80% of IQ is inherited.

Evaluation

- Kamin (1974) criticised twin studies, suggesting that the *samples are relatively small* and in reality the twins had *often spent a substantial amount of time together*.
- If intelligence was entirely inherited, the *MZ correlations should be 1.00*; the fact that scores are lower shows a significant environmental component.
- A correlation is not evidence that one factor *caused* another. A third factor may be important such as home environment. See also heredity – environment interaction on page 159.
- The assumption that *MZ twins are identical is wrong*. Allen *et al.* (1976) found constitutional differences based on different birth and intrauterine experiences, and found that these could be related to different parental perceptions and expectations of the twins.

Familial studies

Bouchard and McGue (1981) surveyed over 100 studies looking at familial correlations of IQ, and found that the closer the genetic link, the higher the correlation between

IQs. For example, siblings reared together had a correlation of 0.45 and adopted siblings had a correlation of 0.31.

Evaluation

- This would seem to support the genetic position, but it could be taken *equally as evidence for environment*.
- Comparisons from one study to another involve *grouping together* many different tests.

Adoption studies

This is strong evidence for the influence of genetic factors.

Skodak and Skeels (1949) followed 100 adopted children and their natural mothers. At the age of 4 the IQ correlation was 0.28 and at 13 it was 0.44. The effects of environment become less with age, which may be due to early enrichment and extra attention levelling out, and genetic factors showing through.

It is best to think of genetic factors as a 'reaction range'; they provide a potential which is very much dependent on environmental influences as to whether it is maximised or minimised.

Horn (1983) reported on the Texas Adoption Study which looked at about 300 families with adopted children separated from mothers within one week of birth. The children at age 8 had a correlation of 0.25 with their biological mother (genetic link) and 0.15 with their adopted mother (environmental link). Plomin (1988) reported on the same children at age 10. They had a correlation of 0.02 with their adoptive siblings.

Evaluation

- Adoptions are often made to *similar environments*. Any differences tend to be in a positive direction.

Gene mapping studies

Chorney *et al.* (1998) identified a gene (IGF2R) found in 33% of 'super-bright' children but only 17% of 'average' IQs. Since intelligence is determined by many genes (polygenic), we are looking for an array of genes that are involved.

Environmental factors

Adoption studies

Current estimates suggest that up to 50% of IQ can be due to environmental influences.

Scarr and Weinberg (1977) found that on average adopted children have IQs that are 10 to 20 points higher than those of their natural parents.

Evaluation

- Adoptive families are generally wealthier and better educated than natural families, which would cause *environmental factors to appear stronger*.
- Early adopted children do better, favouring the idea that environment is important *under suitable circumstances*.

Family influence

Parent–child interactions affect the development of IQ. Yarrow (1963) found a correlation of .65 between IQ at six months and the amount of time the mother spent in social interaction with her child.

Birth order is related to parental attention. Zajonc and Markus (1975) examined the IQ data of 40 000 Dutch males, finding that IQ declines with family size and birth order. In larger families, each child has a smaller share of parental attention and resources.

Diet

Average IQ gains in Japan are 7.7 points over the last 10 years whereas they are 1.7 in the US. This can only be explained in terms of improved environmental factors, probably diet (Lynn, 1986).

Harrell *et al.* (1955) gave low-income, expectant mothers supplementary diets. When their children were tested at 3 years they had higher IQs than those whose mothers had been given placebos.

Benton and Cook (1991) found that IQ scores increased by 7.6 points when children were given vitamin supplements rather than a placebo.

Enrichment

If IQ was genetically fixed then enrichment programmes would not be effective.

Operation Head Start (started in 1965) resulted in initial IQ gains but these were small and short-lived. Follow-up studies such as Lazar and Darlington (1982) found that participants were less likely to become pregnant, need welfare assistance, become delinquent, to be employed after high school and/or to continue in further education.

The Milwaukee Project. Heber *et al.* (1972) worked with newborn infants and their mothers (low social class, low IQ). Half the group were 'controls'. The mothers in the experimental group were given help with job-related skills, parenting and housekeeping and their children were in regular day-care from the age of 3 months. At age 5, the experimental group had a mean IQ of 124 whereas the control group's IQ was 94. By the age of 10 there was still a 10-point IQ difference.

Evaluation

- The control groups may not have actually been comparable because allocation to such groups was not strictly random. Ramey *et al.* (1999) reviewed ten studies that randomly allocated children and concluded that there was firm evidence that Head Start did boost IQ.

Cultural differences

Culture bias in tests

Almost all IQ tests have been designed by White middle-class Westerners, and have been standardised on similar populations. Inevitably people from other cultures do less well on 'our' IQ tests.

Race and IQ

Jensen (1969) sparked off a controversy when he suggested that Black people have innately lower IQs because, on average, they scored 15 points less than White people. This may be due to test culture bias – we might expect White people to do poorly on Dove's (1968) Dove Counterbalance General Intelligence Test. Poor test performance may be due to lower stimulation, social deprivation and so on.

Mackintosh (1986) compared White and West Indian children in England. When the groups were unmatched there was a 9-point difference but when matched there was a 2.6-point difference, showing that environmental factors are important.

Social class

Bernstein (1961) introduced the notion of restricted language (code) as opposed to elaborated code (see page 76). Children from low SES (socioeconomic status) groups learn a limited form of language which lacks, for example, abstract concepts and limits their cognitive development and verbal intelligence. Labov (1970) rejected this idea and claimed that Bernstein was confusing social and linguistic deprivation.

Sameroff *et al.* (1987, 1993) conducted the Rochester Longitudinal study, following over 200 children from birth. They found a clear negative (about –0.60) association between IQ and risk factors including parental mental health, education, occupation, family support, stressful life events and family size (all are related to social class). At age 4, high-risk children were 24 times as likely to have IQs below 85. When a child is not exposed to risk factors, genetic factors will be important in determining intelligence. When there are risk factors, these will be of more importance than the inherited ones.

Motivation. Lower-class children may have less desire to do well. Zigler *et al.* (1973) found that such children improved their test performance by 10 points if they had a play session with the tester beforehand to increase familiarity and decrease anxiety, whereas middle-class children only gained 3 IQ points.

Evaluation

- It is impossible to conduct definitive research on race because we cannot *define race* nor can we exclude the *effects of deprivation*.
- Such research raises important *ethical issues* and is socially sensitive.

> What is intelligence? People from different cultural backgrounds would define, and assess, it differently.

> The concept of 'race' is in itself problematic as it is not true that, for example, Whites and Blacks form separate biological groups. There is more genetic variation *within* any so-called racial group than *between* racial groups.

Practice essay 4.2

Discuss research (theories **and/or** studies) into factors associated with the development of intelligence test performance. (24 marks)

4.3 Development of moral understanding

AQA A ▸ U4
AQA B ▸ U4

Both Piaget and Kohlberg's theories are cognitive-developmental, characterised by identifying innately determined stages of development.

Piaget's (1932) theory of moral development

Age (approx.)	Stage	Rules	Means of evaluating actions	Punishment	Stage of cognitive development
0–5 years	Premoral	Rules not understood			Pre-operational
5–9	Moral realism	Rules exist as real things	Consequences	Atonement: make up for damage done	Intuitive, moving into concrete operations
9+	Moral relativity	Rules mutually agreed and changeable	Intentions	Reciprocity: punishment fits the crime	Concrete and then abstract operations

Children in the stage of moral relativity recognise that morals are not absolute, for example there are some situations where it is acceptable to lie.

Piaget believed that moral development was in part due to maturation but also due to exposure to the views of others that cause the child to question his/her own values.

Research evidence

Realism vs relativism. Piaget (1932) talked with children about the rules for playing marbles. Children under 3 used no rules at all, by the age of 5 rules were seen as inviolable and from some semi-mystical authority, by the age of 10 children understood that people had invented the rules and they could be changed if all players agreed. Linaza (1984) found the same sequence of development in Spanish children.

Intentions vs consequences. Piaget presented pairs of moral stories to children where one story had greater consequences but the intentions were good. He asked who was naughtiest and why. The heteronomous younger child could distinguish between intentional and unintentional actions but based their judgement on the severity of outcome. The autonomous older child used the motive/intention as the means for judgement. However, Nelson (1973) found that even 3-year-olds can make judgements about intentions if the information is made explicit.

Evaluation

- The game of marbles is a *rather insignificant* example of moral behaviour.
- Piaget's moral stories *confound intentions and consequences,* making it especially difficult for younger children. Armsby (1971) manipulated the stories so that there was a small amount of deliberate damage or a large amount of accidental damage. He found that younger children did take intention into account.
- Cannot explain *moral inconsistency,* and ignores emotional influences.
- Piaget's work *introduced the idea of stages* that are related to cognitive maturity.

Hartshorne and May (1928) found little consistency in moral behaviour. A child who cheated in one situation didn't in another. They also found that immoral behaviour was more governed by the probability of being caught than any principles of morality.

Kohlberg's (1966) theory of moral reasoning

Kohlberg was more interested in why people made certain choices (moral reasoning) rather than what their choices were (moral behaviour). He devised a set of moral dilemmas, such as Heinz and the druggist who wouldn't sell a drug to save Heinz's dying wife. Kohlberg (1963) tested a group of 10–16-year-old boys, and used their responses to construct the classification scheme (below).

Level		Age	Stage	
I	Pre-conventional	6–13	1	Deference to authority, heteronomous
			2	Doing good to serve one's own interests, egocentric
II	Conventional	13–16	3	Care for the other, interpersonal conformity, 'good boy/girl'
			4	The primacy of social order, conscience, unquestioning acceptance of authority
III	Post-conventional or principled	16–20	5	Concern with individual rights, questioning authority in order to ensure justice
			6	Universal, ethical principles (later dropped because rarely, if ever, exhibited)

Research evidence

Colby and Kohlberg (1987) did a more careful analysis of the original data and found only 15% reached stage 5 and there was no evidence of stage 6 judgements.

Colby *et al.* (1983) followed Kohlberg's initial participants over 20 years, re-testing every 3 years. By the age of 36 participants were mainly reasoning at stage 4 (65% of their responses), stage 3 still accounted for about 30%, and stage 5 was 5%.

Delinquents. Fodor (1972) found that delinquents operate at a much lower level on the Kohlberg scales than non-delinquents.

Cross-cultural support. Snarey (1985) listed 27 different cross-cultural studies which found a progression from stages 1 to 4 at about the same ages. Very few studies found any stage 5 reasoning and where it occurred it was likely to be in urban areas.

Evaluation

- The notion of 'dilemmas' recognises the fact that people behave differently in different situations (*moral inconsistency*).
- May be the *best available approach* and has generated much empirical interest.
- This is a theory of *moral principles* not behaviour.
- Stages 5 and 6 may be *moral ideals*, never achieved by some people.
- *Gender bias.* The theory is biased towards male morality (justice) as the participants were male. Kohlberg claimed that women tended to be 'less' morally developed (see Gilligan below).
- *Culture bias.* Kohlberg claimed that the moral stages are universal. In fact the stages reflect Western values of democracy.
- *Age bias.* Some dilemmas are irrelevant to children.

Eisenberg's (1982) theory of pro-social reasoning

> Pro-social behaviours are those that aim to benefit others. There is a section on pro-social behaviour on pp. 30–32.

Other theories overlook 'pro-social' moral reasoning. Eisenberg emphasised role-taking skills (the ability to assume the perspective and take the part of another person) in moral development. Eisenberg *et al.* (1983) used moral stories where a child has to decide whether to help someone when the pro-social act would be at some cost.

Level	Age range (approx.)	Brief description
1 Hedonistic (self-centred)	Preschool and early primary	Pro-social behaviour most likely when it will benefit self in some way
2 Needs oriented	A few preschoolers, mainly primary	Sometimes considers needs of others, but not much evidence of sympathy or guilt
3 Approval oriented	Primary and some secondary	Pro-social behaviour in return for approval and praise from others
4 Empathetic or transitional	Older primary and secondary school pupils	Some understanding of abstract principles, duties and values, evidence of sympathy and guilt
5 Strongly internalised	A small number of secondary and perhaps a few primary	Internalised principles which are important to self-respect

Research evidence

Eisenberg *et al.* (1991) found that empathy (which develops during Level 4) plays an important role in producing pro-social thinking.

Evaluation

- A different perspective *emphasising emotional factors* and focusing on pro-social reasoning rather than wrongdoing.
- Other evidence suggests that *empathy appears much earlier*. Zahn-Waxler *et al.* (1979) found that children aged 18–30 months showed concern when they saw other children in distress.

Individual and cultural variations

Influence of gender

Gilligan (1982) suggested that Kohlberg wrongly assumed there was only one moral perspective, one of justice and fairness, whereas women tend to operate an ethic of caring. This was based on interviews with women facing real-life dilemmas (about abortions).

Gilligan and Attanucci (1988) asked a group of men and women to produce accounts of their own moral dilemmas. Overall, men favoured a justice orientation and women favoured a care orientation.

Eisenberg *et al.* (1987) found that girls aged 10–12 gave more caring responses than boys, though this may be because girls mature earlier.

Gilligan's stage theory of moral development

Stage	Justice perspective	Care perspective
1	Uphold moral standards and withstand pressure to deviate	Concern with what others say and how choices might might affect relationships with others
2	Justice tempered with mercy; principles are most important but one should consider feelings	Sacrificing one's own concerns to the welfare of others; relationships are more important than conventional rules
3	Everyone is best served by universal laws, though there are some exceptions to the rule	Aiming for a balance between valuing the individual and trying not to hurt anyone

If a man's moral perspective was assessed using Gilligan's stage theory, he might appear to be morally inferior.

Evaluation

- The findings may be due to *demand characteristics*. Eisenberg and Lennon (1983) found that, if participants knew researchers were looking at empathetic behaviour, they portrayed themselves more empathetically.
- Kohlberg's theory *may not be as gender biased* as claimed. Funk (1986) found that women scored higher than men using Kohlberg's dilemmas.

Kohlberg suggested that moral thinking was related to innate tendencies. Therefore we would expect to find that people think in the same way all over the world.

Cultural variations

Ma (1988) constructed a Chinese version of Kohlberg's stages, including the 'Golden Mean' (behaving as most people in society behave) and 'Good Will' (acting in a way that complies with nature). This shows similarities and differences.

Miller *et al.* (1990) found that people in India tend to give priority to social duties whereas Americans give priority to individual rights. Berry *et al.* (1998) report that behaviours were more similar where serious moral issues were concerned.

Where we observe cultural variations, these must be related to learned social behaviours.

Whiting and Whiting (1975) found that 100% of Kenyan children behaved altruistically whereas only 8% of American children did. Eisenberg and Mussen (1989) found that children living on Israeli kibbutzim (communal farming communities) were more cooperative than North Americans. Korte and Kerr (1975) found that stamped-addressed letters left lying in the street were more likely to be placed in a post box if the street was in a rural rather than an urban location.

Practice essay 4.3

Critically consider **one or more** theories of the development of pro-social reasoning.

(24 marks)

Social and personality development

4.4 Personality development

AQA A — U4
EDEXCEL — U4
OCR — U5, U6

Psychodynamic explanations of personality development

Freud's (1856–1939) psychoanalytic theory

The structure of the personality

Personality consists of those relatively enduring aspects of individuals which distinguish them from others and which make them unique.

- The *id* (or 'it') is the primitive, instinctive, unconscious, part. It demands immediate satisfaction and is governed by the *pleasure principle*.
- The *ego* (or 'I') is the conscious and intellectual part. It regulates the id and is governed by the *reality principle*, the need to behave in acceptable ways.
- The *super ego* (or 'above I') is the ethical and moral component, learned from others, particularly parents. It gives rise to a conscience.

'Psychodynamic' refers to a theory that seeks to explain what drives or motivates (i.e. dynamics) personality development.

Psychosexual stages

- The *oral stage*. In the first year the id is dominant, the organ-focus is the mouth. Tension is reduced through satisfying basic needs. Pleasure is gained through sucking. Any disturbance of this may result in a permanent fixation on the oral channel for gratification, for example smoking, overeating, thumb-sucking.
- The *anal stage*. At the age of about 2, the anus becomes the favoured pleasure

Freud used the word 'sexual' to refer to physical pleasure. At each stage the *libido* (life energy) is focused on one physical region of the body.

zone. Pleasure is derived from expelling and withholding faeces. Fixations may be caused by either exceptionally strict toilet training or intense pleasure associated with taboos such as smearing faeces on the wall. The anal/obsessive character wants to make a terrible mess and therefore must build defences against this, for example orderliness, rigidity, hatred of waste.

- The *phallic stage*. Around the age of 3 children's libido focuses on their genitalia and their opposite-sex parent. In boys this is the *Oedipus conflict* (Freud termed it *penis envy* in girls and Jung called it the *Electra complex*). Resolution is through identification with the same-sex parent and is important for an appropriate gender concept and a conscience. The conflicts may result in homosexuality, authority problems and rejection of appropriate gender roles if not resolved.
- The *latency period*. Up to the start of puberty personality development is on hold.
- The *genital stage*. In adolescence the main source of pleasure is again the genitals. Focus is also on the development of independence. If some issues remain unresolved, the individual can't shift focus from their immediate needs to larger responsibilities involving others.

The dynamics of personality

Threats to the ego (such as feelings of anxiety) are dealt with through *ego defence mechanisms* (sublimation, repression, denial, displacement, projection) which remove threats from conscious awareness.

Unconscious thoughts are expressed in, for example, dreams (see page 49), neurotic symptoms (e.g. hysterical paralysis), Freudian slips (parapraxes).

Research evidence

One of Freud's greatest contributions was to identify the role of the unconscious as a motivating force in personality. He proposed three levels of the mind: the conscious, the preconscious, and the unconscious.

Freud recorded case studies of patients undergoing psychoanalysis and used these to support his theory. He also used self-analysis.

Repressed memories. Myers and Brewin (1994) found that 'repressors' (individuals classed as low on anxiety and high on defensiveness) took much longer to recall negative childhood memories and actually reported *more* painful memories. Williams (1994) tracked down women who had received hospital treatment for sexual abuse; 17 years later 38% said they had no conscious recollection.

Perceptual defence (repressing emotionally threatening perceptions). McGinnies (1949) showed that participants took longer to recognise emotionally threatening words such as 'raped'.

Evaluation

- A *revolutionary* theory in its time, and has lasted – something must be right.
- Can explain *inconsistency* ('part of me wants to, but the other part doesn't').
- It is a theory of normal personality development based on experiences of *disturbed individuals*, who were White Viennese, middle-class, Victorian women.
- Largely omitted *social influences* and promoted a *deterministic*, *biological* view.

Erikson's (1902–1994) psychosocial theory

Erikson was a 'neo-Freudian', someone who has adapted traditional psychoanalytic theory.

The individual experiences conflicts between maturation and the expectations of society. This conflict leads to various crises which need to be resolved for healthy development. A purely negative outcome only is unhealthy, a mixture of negative and positive is balanced.

Age	Life crisis	Positive outcome	Negative outcome
0–1	Trust vs mistrust	Trust	Suspicion, insecurity
2–3	Autonomy vs shame	Sense of autonomy, self-esteem	Shame and self-doubt
4–5	Initiative vs guilt	Initiates activities	Fear of punishment, guilt feelings
6–11	Industry vs inferiority	Competence and achievement	Inadequacy and inferiority
12–19	Identity vs role confusion	Strong personal identity	Confusion
20–40	Intimacy vs isolation	Ability to experience love	Isolation
40–64	Generativity vs stagnation	Wider outlook	Boredom, self-involvement
65+	Integrity vs despair	Satisfaction, self-acceptance	Regrets, fear of death

Research evidence

Erikson based his theory on clinical evidence gained as a practising psychoanalyst, and reflections on interviews with the Dakota Indians.

Vitaro *et al.* (2000) found that, if your best friend is a delinquent, your own chances of delinquency are increased, except if you have a good-quality relationship with your parents. This mediation was predicted by Erikson's theory.

Evaluation
- De-emphasised biological influences and focused on *social influences*.
- Influential particularly because it introduced the idea of development *throughout life*.
- It is *difficult to test* this theory and some concepts *vague*, e.g. how a crisis resolved.
- The stages are meant to be universal but there are gender and culture differences.

Social learning explanations of personality development

Social learning theory (Bandura, 1977, 1986)

Steps in the modelling process
1 *Attention.* You pay more attention if the 'model' is attractive, prestigious, competent, more like yourself, e.g. parents, peers and the media.
2 *Retention.* Is necessary to remember what to do; this involves cognitive processes (setting SLT apart from learning theory).
3 *Reproduction.* Imitation requires personal skills – one can't imitate everything.
4 *Motivation.* The likelihood that a behaviour will be repeated is related to direct/indirect *reinforcement* or *punishment*.

Reciprocal determination
Each individual selects what behaviours to imitate, based on their personality, beliefs and cognitive abilities. These selections then affect what behaviours are reinforced. We choose how we interact with the environment and this selectively reinforces behaviour.

Self-efficacy
An individual's sense of perceived effectiveness (*self-efficacy*) influences what is learned, and depends on: previous experiences of success and/or failure in that situation, relevant vicarious experiences, persuasion from someone else and emotional arousal.

Research evidence
Bandura *et al.* (1963) demonstrated how aggressiveness is socially learned (see page 28). Bandura and Cervone (1983) found participants high in self-efficacy exerted more effort, especially if they had been dissatisfied with initial performance.

Evaluation
- Not specifically a *developmental* theory.
- Rather sketchy on the details of *how* we influence our environment.

Situationalism (Mischel, 1968)

Personality is not consistent at all; behaviour is specific to certain situations (*behavioural specificity*) due to *selective reinforcement*. There are individual differences in the way we learn (*person variables*) so that it is not simply the situation that affects behaviour but the individual's prior learning experience.

Research evidence
Mischel and Peake (1982) asked individuals to rate the behaviour of 63 students in various situations. They found almost zero correlation between the different situations.
Abernethy (1940) showed that learning was enhanced if testing took place in the same room, i.e. context mattered.

Evaluation
- The view of *many selves* may be correct.
- This denies *free will*.
- There is evidence that *people are consistent* and do generalise learning across situations, e.g. Small *et al.* (1983).

The research you studied at AS on attachment can be used to argue that trust vs mistrust is indeed the concern of the infant.

Social learning theory (SLT) proposes that behaviour is learned through direct and indirect (vicarious) reinforcement. We observe others and model our own behaviour on this. This contrasts with the psychodynamic approach which combines social factors and innate, biological processes. SLT is concerned solely with external social experiences.

Bandura (1977) said self-efficacy judgements are concerned 'not with the skills one has but with judgements of what one can do with the skills one possesses'.

We may think that people are consistent but that is because we impose structure and predictability on the world around us to make it easier to cope.

Mischel's view was that people possess different 'selves', each reinforced in different situations. Our sense of a single, integrated self is an illusion.

Practice essay 4.4

Describe and evaluate **one** psychodynamic explanation of personality development.

(24 marks)

4.5 Gender development

The biological approach

Research evidence for

Biological differences. Young boys have a higher metabolic rate, girls develop motor skills earlier. These differences influence behaviour and psychological development.

Hormones. Hormones control many sexual behaviours, such as ovulation and parenting behaviours. The presence of male hormones during prenatal development leads to masculinisation of the brain. Dörner (1974) injected rats with male hormones during prenatal development and they showed male behaviours.

Androgenital syndrome. Money and Ehrhardt (1972) studied a group of girls whose mothers had received male hormones during pregnancy to prevent miscarriage. As a result the girls developed male genitalia and, through childhood, their behaviour was described as tomboyish, presumably due to the prenatal androgens, though it may be that the girls were responding to the expectations of others (parents and teachers) who knew about their condition.

Twin study. Diamond and Sigmundson (1997) reported that the twin studied by Money (whose penis was damaged while being circumsized and was raised as a girl) eventually elected to go back to being a man, despite prolonged attempts to socialise him into being a girl. This indicates the strength of biological factors.

Cultural relativism. Mead (1935) initially concluded from her studies of three tribes in New Guinea that gender was culturally determined. Later (1949) she changed her view to one of cultural relativism – some behaviours are innate and universal. In all three tribes, all the men were more aggressive in comparison with the women.

Research evidence against

Social influences. Goldwyn (1979) described the case of Daphne Went, an XY individual with Testicular Feminising Syndrome (TFS). Mrs Went was content with her female role. It may be that her brain was also insensitive to the male hormones.

Evaluation

- Some gender differences are *clearly biological*, therefore the biological approach must be part of any account.
- Case histories show that genetic sex and gender *need not correspond*. Therefore biological explanations are not sufficient on their own.

Social learning theory (SLT)

Gender role identity is learned through reinforcement and modelling; a child is directly rewarded for sex-appropriate behaviour and punished for sex-inappropriate behaviour. Behaviour is learned indirectly through modelling, for example, parents.

Research evidence for

Parental reinforcement. Smith and Lloyd (1978) gave mothers feminine-, masculine- and neutral-type toys. When a 6-month-old baby was dressed and named as a boy, the mothers encouraged more motor activity and gave masculine-type toys.

Peer reinforcement. Lamp and Roopnarine (1979) observed preschool children at play. Children generally reinforced same-sex peers for sex-appropriate play and were quick to criticise sex-inappropriate play.

Television reinforcement. Williams (1985) studied the effects of the arrival of TV on Notel. He found that the children's sex role attitudes became more traditional and sex-stereotyped after two years of exposure to TV.

Stereotypes. Maccoby and Jacklin (1974) reviewed more than 1500 studies of gender differences and concluded that gender differences observed are minimal and that most popular gender-role stereotypes are 'cultural myths' which are self-perpetuating.

Research evidence against

Real gender differences. Jacklin and Maccoby (1978) introduced unfamiliar 2½-year-olds to each other and dressed them in neutral clothing; they found that interactions were most lively and positive with same-sex pairs.

A person's sex is the biological fact of being male (XY) or female (XX).

Gender is the maleness and femaleness of a person's behaviour.

Gender identity is one's awareness of being male or female.

Gender role is the behaviour expected of an individual on the basis of their gender (masculinity or femininity).

TFS is an insensitivity to testosterone which results in female external genitalia.

Lamp and Roopnarine's study suggests that children already know what is sex-appropriate, their peers are just reinforcing that knowledge.

Male/female preferences may well reflect an early incompatibility between girls and boys, partly based on biological differences such as boisterousness and partly due to learned preferences for toys and activities.

Variable reinforcement. Fagot (1985) found evidence that teachers reinforce 'feminine' behaviours in both boys and girls such as being quiet, but only girls acquire them.

Evaluation

- Reinforcements are *not sufficiently consistent* to explain all observed differences, but gender appropriate behaviours are clearly reinforced.
- Explains *cultural differences* and accounts for the influence of *stereotypes*.
- It *overlooks biological* (innate) factors.

Cognitive-developmental theory

Kohlberg (1966) argued that gender identity is a combination of social learning mediated by maturational and cognitive factors. Gender identity is the result of a child's active structuring of his/her own experience, not the passive product of social learning.

Children attend to same-sex models because they have already developed a consistent gender identity, not vice versa (as suggested by SLT).

Kohlberg proposed 3 stages:

1 *Basic gender identity* (2–3½ years) gender known but child still believes it is possible to change sex.
2 *Gender stability* (3–4½ years) awareness that gender is fixed.
3 *Gender consistency* (4½–7 years) that superficial changes don't alter gender.

Research evidence for

Slaby and Frey's study shows how children actively seek information which will help them develop gender-appropriate behaviour.

Slaby and Frey (1975) showed preschool children a film with men on one side and women on the other. Those children who had previously been rated as having gender consistency watched more same-sex models.

Ruble *et al.* (1981) found that TV ads had more effect on children high in gender consistency. Supports Kohlberg's view.

Research evidence against

Maccoby (1980) found that 3-year-olds learn many gender role stereotypes long before they attend to same-sex models.

Evaluation

- *Combines a social learning approach* with some aspects of *biological* development.
- Basic gender identity *appears between 2 and 5*, in line with cognitive development.
- This view assumes that *development proceeds in stages*, and that gender identity is mediated by cognitive factors. This may not universally be true.

Gender-schema theory

In Kohlberg's theory, a child must recognise the permanence of gender before he/she can begin to imitate same-gender models. In gender-schema theory, gender schema begin to be formed as soon as the child recognises that there is a difference between men and women.

Martin and Halverson (1981) suggested that once a child has a basic gender identity they are motivated to learn more about the sexes and incorporate this information into a gender schema. This serves to organise relevant information and influence behaviour.

Research evidence

Martin and Little (1990) found that preschool children had only very rudimentary gender understanding, yet they had strong gender stereotypes.

Fagot's (1985) study, above, can be explained with gender schema theory insofar as children are only processing information which is consistent with their gender schema.

Masters *et al.* (1979) showed that children aged 4–5 were more influenced in their choice of toy by the gender label (e.g. 'It's a girl's toy') than by the gender of the model seen playing with the toy.

Evaluation

- A *middle ground* between social learning and cognitive-developmental theories.
- Explains how *gender stereotypes persist*, because people are more likely to remember information that is consistent with their schemas.
- Explains how gender behaviours occur *before gender identity*.

Practice essay 4.5

Discuss the development of gender identity. (24 marks)

4.6 Adolescence

Social development in adolescence

Erikson's (1968) identity crisis

Erikson proposed psycho*social* crises (rather than Freud's psycho*sexual* crises). The child has an identity but this is thrown by the major physical changes at puberty. The task for adolescents is to resolve the conflict between *identity* and *role confusion*. Successful resolution results in a new, enduring and unified sense of identity or self. Failure results in a lack of personal identity (i.e. role confusion), which may lead to:

Hall (1904) described adolescence as a time of 'storm and stress' when the adolescent has to experience the volatile history of the human race before reaching maturity (called *recapitulation theory*).

- *negative identity* – e.g. delinquent, permits some sense of control
- *lack of intimacy* – avoids close relationships but may worship a pop star
- *time perspective* – avoids making plans because idea of adulthood creates anxiety
- *industry* – compulsive overwork or difficulty concentrating.

Erikson defined identity as a subjective sense of sameness and continuity.

Research evidence

Whitbourne *et al.* (1992) found that intimacy and identity increased after adolescence.

Smith and Crawford (1986) found that more than 60% of students in secondary school reported at least one instance of suicidal thinking, and 10% had attempted suicide; supporting the notion of crisis in adolescence.

Evaluation

- *Useful focus* on identity formation and crisis.
- Mainly concerned with *adolescent males*.
- Not very suitable for *empirical research*.

Marcia's (1966) theory

Developed Erikson's ideas further, suggesting that there are different ways that adolescents can fail to achieve a stable sense of identity. Each adolescent has an identity status. To investigate this status Marcia interviewed adolescents about occupational choice, religion and political ideology, and asked whether alternatives were considered (i.e. crisis point reached) or they had made a firm commitment. Marcia concluded that there are four possible identity statuses:

Marcia argued that adolescent identity formation involves both crisis and commitment.

- *identity diffusion* – confusion, possible rebellion
- *identity foreclosure* – uncertainties avoided by committing self to safe, conventional, goals without exploring alternatives, potentials not realised
- *identity moratorium* – decisions about identity put on hold
- *identity achievement* – individual emerges with firm goals, ideology, commitments.

Research evidence

Meilman (1979) interviewed males from 12 to 24 and found that identity achievement did rise steadily from age 15, but only 50% of those at 24 had reached this point.

Waterman (1985) found a decrease in diffusion status and an increase in identity achievement with age. Moratorium was quite uncommon at all ages, and a total of 33% were in foreclosure.

Evaluation

- The statuses may be specific to a *particular historical period and culture*. Waterman and Waterman (1975) studied fathers and sons. The sons were mainly classed as identity moratorium or identity diffusion. The fathers were in identity foreclosure.
- *May be oversimplified*. Archer (1982) found that only 5% of those interviewed were classed in the same identity status for all concerns, 90% were in two or three different statuses (e.g. in identity confusion for sexual attitudes, but identity achievement for occupational choice).

Coleman's (1980) focal theory

Coleman (1980) disagreed that adolescence was a time of identity crisis. The 'normal' adolescent focuses on one issue at a time; crises only occur when issues accumulate.

Coleman and Hendry (1990) questioned 800 children aged 11–17 and found that different issues peaked at particular ages. For example, young boys focus on heterosexual relationships but later are concerned about conflicts with parents.

Research into relationships between parents and peers

Parental relationships

Blos (1967) suggested that adolescence is a time of reindividuation, the adolescent must separate from his/her parents. However, the evidence suggests that many adolescents have continuing good parental relationships.

Rutter *et al.* (1976) studied over 2000 14–15-year-olds on the Isle of Wight. The teenagers reported a higher frequency of conflict, but rarely reported serious disagreements or criticised their parents. Apter (1990) found that most of the 65 adolescent girls interviewed said that the person they felt closest to was their mother aside from minor quarrels. Carlo *et al.* (1998) found that parents who were highly supportive had adolescent children with fewer emotional and behavioural problems; less-supportive parents tended to have more angry, aggressive and anti-social adolescents. Ryan and Lynch (1989) point out that securely attached adolescents, like infants, find it easier to become independent.

Peer relationships

Peer culture has a strong influence in adolescence. Palmonari (1989) found that 90% of adolescents surveyed considered themselves to be part of a peer group.

Parental influence is exchanged for peer influence. Floyd and South (1972) found low peer orientation and high parent orientation at age 11, but the reverse by age 17 with a crossover at 15.

Conformity is typical of adolescent peer groups. Constanzo and Shaw (1966) used an Asch-type conformity test and showed that conformity peaked around 11–13 years.

Delinquency: Children who are not achieving at school turn to other sources to define success, thus forming delinquent sub-cultures. Reicher and Emler (1986) argue that the peer context is critical in constructing social and personal identity and, for some adolescents, delinquency is their main route to do this.

Cultural differences in adolescent behaviour

Historically

Shaffer (1993) claimed that adolescence is an 'invention' of the twentieth century; before that, older children went to work alongside adults so there was no in-between period. Adolescence is therefore historically a new conception.

Individualist and collectivist societies

Markus and Kitayama (1991) note that individualist societies have an independent construal of self whereas collectivist societies have an interdependent construal of self where many life choices will be made by others. In such societies, the whole nature of adolescence is different from that in individualist societies.

Research evidence

Mead (1928) in her book *Coming of Age in Samoa*, suggested that turmoil may be due to growing up in an industrialised society. She observed that, in Samoa, sexuality is dealt with in an open, casual manner and therefore children are spared the guilt, anxiety and confusion which we experience. Freeman (1983) argued that Mead only saw what she wanted to see and did not get totally honest responses from the natives.

Condon (1987) observed that the harsh life of the Inuit Indians might explain why childhood led immediately to adulthood. There was no time for identity consideration.

Bronfenbrenner (1974) found that Russian adolescents showed less of the anti-social behaviour common in American adolescents. This may be because Russian youths are able to integrate with adult society whereas American youths are more segregated.

Adolescence is also a stressful time for some parents, coping with a physically and psychologically different person and the conflicts of dependence and independence. Perhaps the observed stress in adolescents is due to their parents' stress at this time of change.

In some cultures puberty is marked by *rites of passage*. Gennep (1960) describes these as having three stages: isolation, hardship and finally reinstatement where the adolescent is brought back into the community as an adult.

An individualist society is one which values the rights and interests of the individual whereas a collectivist society shares tasks, belongings and income.

Eccles *et al.* (1993) suggested that the reason many adolescents experience stress is due to the mismatch between their developing needs and the opportunities afforded to them by their social environments. It may be the case that other cultures offer more to adolescents than we do.

Practice essay 4.6

(a) Describe **one** theory of social development in adolescence.　(12 marks)

(b) Assess the contribution of this theory to our understanding of social development in adolescence.　(12 marks)

Adulthood

4.7 Early and middle adulthood

AQA A ▷ U4

The crisis approach

Psychosocial theory (Erikson, 1950)

> Erikson proposed eight crises during the whole lifespan (see p. 92). The last three crises are described here

- *Early adulthood* (20–30 years): intimacy vs isolation. Commit to a love relationship or remain isolated. Social focus is on friendships.
- *Middle adulthood* (30–60 years): generativity vs stagnation. Productive valuable work (including having children), or become stagnant and self-centred.
- *Old age* (60 years onwards): integrity vs despair. Make sense of life and become wise, or experience despair. The social focus is on humankind.

Research evidence

> Erikson suggested some gender differences, such as men typically achieve a sense of identity before they achieve intimacy with a sexual partner during the stage of early adulthood.

Erikson based his theory on detailed biographical case studies, such as Gandhi and Martin Luther, as well as more ordinary people.

Hodgson and Fisher (1979) found female undergraduates rated as identity achievers, also had achieved intimacy, though half of those who weren't identity achievers had also achieved intimacy. It may be that women achieve intimacy before identity.

> The main problem with any stage account is that it suggests that all people develop in the same way and at similar times.

Livson (1981) compared individuals originally classed as traditionals or nontraditionals during adolescence. At age 40, the traditionals were resolving the issue of intimacy; age 50 they were in the generativity stage. The nontraditional women appeared to be having a mid-life identity crisis at age 40, a throwback to adolescence. This did not hamper development because they went on to be the best adjusted at age 50.

Evaluation

> See other criticisms of Erikson's theory, on p. 93.

- Somewhat *sketchy*; one stage lasts 30 years.

The transition approach

Seasons of man's life (Levinson 1978, 1986)

> This theory is an alternative to stage theory. 'Seasons' implies no progression just change.

The scheme was based on interviews with 40 men aged 35–45 (ten novelists, ten biologists, ten factory workers, ten business executives). They were interviewed again two years later, as well as most of their wives. The theory concluded that everyone proceeded through the same eras (life cycles) at about the same ages.

- A *life structure*: the underlying pattern at a given time.
- A *life cycle*: an underlying order spanning adult life, consisting of a sequence of eras. The move from one era to another is not smooth, there are cross-era *periods of transition*, which last for about five years.

> This approach promotes the view of a 'mid-life crisis' at age 40.

Levinson's seasons of man's life

Era of pre-adulthood (0–22 years): era of rapid development.	**Era of middle adulthood (40–65 years):** moving on from illusions of eternal youth; time to act on decisions made during mid-life crisis.
17–22 *Early adult transition.* Make life decisions, establish a home and select a career. The person's dream is formed.	45–50 *Entering middle adulthood.* A time to build on past decisions or start a new occupation.
Era of early adulthood (17–45 years): era of greatest energy and greatest contradiction.	51–55 *Age 50 transition.* Tension between attachment and separation.
23–28 *Entering the adult world*, constructing an adult lifestyle.	56–60 *Culmination of middle adulthood.* Less inward looking, may take greater interest in family.
29–33 *Age 30 transition.* Some people experience self-doubt, a sense of life becoming more serious.	61–65 *Late adult transition.*
34–40 *Settling down.* Becoming one's own man (BOOM), looking for recognition and self-sufficiency.	**Era of late adulthood (60+ years):** final acceptance of one's life; may be a crisis or may be calm acceptance.
41–45 *Mid-life transition.* May be a difficult period for those who have not realised their initial dreams.	65+ *Late adulthood.* An acceptance of the inevitability of physical decline, and of what life has been.

Research evidence

Valliant (1978) followed a group of about 100 men from the time they were undergraduates (in 1940) to when they were in their late 40s. Nearly all of those classed as 'best outcomes' at age 47 had married before the age of 30 and stayed married. Conversely, those who were 'worst outcomes' had either married after age 30 or separated.

Roberts and Newton (1987) found that women often established an occupation or marriage at a time beyond the early adult period.

Valliant (above) found few radical changes during the mid-life period; for some people it is the happiest time of their life, when they are reaching the peak of their career.

Livson (above) found an interaction between lifestyle and personality which determines whether a person has a mid-life crisis. 'Nontraditionals' often found it difficult.

Evaluation

- *Gender biased* but data on women has been presented which fits this scheme.
- The empirical data is *limited* to middle adulthood but is rich in detail.
- The data may suffer from a *cohort effect*.
- *Mid-life crisis may not be universal*. Rutter and Rutter (1992) reported that individuals who did not go through this crisis still remained psychologically healthy.

The evolution of adult consciousness (Gould, 1980)

Extended Freud's theory to adulthood. To grow up you have to give up the fictions (false assumptions) of childhood.

Research evidence

Gould based his stage theory on the responses of over 500 white, middle-class, people aged 16–50 years old to a questionnaire. The questionnaire was developed by observing outpatient therapy groups and collecting statements characteristic of the different age groups. These statements are called *false assumptions*, beliefs that need to be challenged during each phase of adult development for continuing healthy development.

Evaluation

- This is a *culture-biased account*, and age-limited.
- Data was collected by inexperienced students and may have been *unreliable*.

A cohort effect is when behaviours are assumed to apply to all individuals whereas they are in fact specific to a particular generation who had unique problems or experiences.

We hold these false assumptions because they give us the illusion of safety and protect us from anxiety, but they prevent evolution (development) of adult consciousness.

Gould's false assumptions

18–21 *False assumption*: 'I will always belong to my parents and believe in their world.' Marriage at this age is an attempt to gain independence but may fail because such marriages are too dependent.	**28–34** *False assumption*: 'Life is simple and controllable. There are no significant coexisting contradictory forces within me.' One must recognise the contradictory pressures from within and without.
22–28 *False assumption*: 'Doing things my parents' way, with willpower and perseverance, will bring results. But if I become too frustrated, confused or tired or am simply unable to cope, they will step in and show me the right way.' This dependence on parents (or a loved one) prevents independence and ultimately leads to feelings of hostility.	**35–45** *False assumption*: 'There is no evil in me or death in the world. The sinister has been destroyed.' One must come to terms with mortality. Men have to recognise that success and hard work cannot protect them from dying, women may strike out on their own as a means of challenging man as the protector and coping with their own mortality.

Practice essay 4.7

Discuss **one** theory that explains development in early **and/or** middle adulthood.

(24 marks)

4.8 Family and relationships in adulthood

> Studying common life events offers a different approach to understanding the experiences of adulthood.

> In your AS studies, you may have learned about *life events*, as measured by Holmes and Rahe's Social Readjust-ment Rating Scale (SRRS).

> Many studies of marriage were conducted some time ago. Things may be different today.

> There is further research on cultural differences in marriage on p. 26.

> Even where arranged marriages are not the norm, there is some guidance offered to couples in their choice of partner.

> Divorce scores 73 LCU (2nd) on the Holmes and Rahe Scale, separation 65 LCU (3rd) and reconciliation 45 LCU (9th).

> The benefits gained from marriage, such as social support, are lost when one divorces. This means that much of the same research can be made relevant.

Research into factors associated with marriage (partnering)

Satisfaction

Argyle and Furnham (1983) found three main factors which determine people's level of satisfaction with different kinds of relationships: material and instrumental help, social and emotional support, and common interests. Spouses were rated higher than partners in any other kind of non-sexual relationship on all three factors.

Bradburn (1969) found that married people were happier than never-marrieds (about 35% as compared with 18%). The separated, divorced or widowed were even less happy (7%). However, it may be that happy people tend to stay married.

U-shaped relationship between marital satisfaction and the length of the marriage. Glenn and McLanahan (1982) found that marital satisfaction declines sharply with the birth of the first child, and rises again when the last-born child leaves home.

Mental and physical health

Cochrane (1988) found that the rate of admission to mental hospital was only 0.26% for married people whereas it was 0.77% for singles, 0.98% for widowed and 1.4% for divorced. It may be that divorced people divorce because of mental disease.

Lynch (1977) found that married people were much less likely than single, divorced or widowed individuals of the same age to die from several kinds of physical conditions.

Social support

The benefits of marriage may be due to social support. Kiecolt-Glaser *et al.* (1984) found that students with more social support suffered less reduction of their immune responses.

Tache *et al.* (1979) found that cancer was less common in married adults than those divorced, widowed or separated; probably because of greater social support, though it is possible that stress increased vulnerability in the non-married adults' health.

Gender differences

Vaillant and Vaillant (1993) found that husbands' level of marital satisfaction stayed the same over a 40-year longitudinal study whereas their wives showed a steady decline. It may be different for women today.

Lynch (1977) found the beneficial effects of marriage on physical health were rather stronger in men than in women.

Cultural differences

Levine *et al.* (1995) found that members of individualist societies regarded love as being more important in marriage.

Harris (1995) surveyed 42 societies and found that in only 6 was there complete freedom of choice of marriage partner.

Yelsma and Athappily (1988) compared American marriages with Indian arranged marriages, finding few differences and similar levels of happiness.

Research into factors associated with divorce

Bohannon (1970) proposed the following six stages in divorce: *emotional* (marriage ends with accompanying emotions), *legal* (marriage is dissolved), *economic* (financial arrangements are made), *co-parental* (arrangements are made for the children), *community* (relationships with friends and family are adjusted), *psychic* (adjustment to being single and return of autonomy).

Mental and physical health

Kiecolt-Glaser and Glaser (1986) found poorer immune functions where persons were suffering marital disruption.

Carter and Glick (1970) found increased rates of various illnesses, and suicide in women, among the divorced.

Psychological loss

Clulow (1990) argued that divorce is similar to death, both for the couple and their children. It involves grief, sorrow and anger.

Plomin (1997) reported that identical twins whose co-twin has divorced are more likely to become divorced than identical twins whose co-twin has not divorced. This suggests that some aspects of divorce are inherited.

In China 4% of couples divorce whereas about 40% divorce in the US (US Bureau of Census, 1992).

People in individualist societies are more likely to divorce because of the belief that one should seek the best for oneself.

Pregnancy scores 40 LCU (12th) on the Holmes and Rahe Scale, a new family member scores 39 LCU (14th) and a child leaving home scores 29 LCU (23rd).

Stress may be due to an identity crisis (divorce involves reorganisation of routines and social circles) and/or legal issues (equitable distribution of possessions, including children; the process will be expensive and often creates considerable antagonism).

Effects on the children

Amato *et al.* (1995) conducted a longitudinal study of over 2000 married people, and interviewed nearly 500 adult offspring. The children were coping better if their parents divorced but only if there had been high conflict. In low-conflict situations, staying together is best. This appears to suggest that conflict is worse than divorce.

Gender differences

Cochrane (1988) found that men were slightly more affected than women in terms of admissions to mental hospital after divorce.

Cultural differences

Brodbar-Nemzer (1986) compared traditional (collectivist) Jewish families in New York with those who had become more individualist, finding more stability in the former.

Kaffman (1993) found that divorce was associated with less stress among Kibbutz dwellers because most of the factors that exacerbate stress (legal, parenting, financial) are less problematic. Divorce remains equally emotional for non-Kibbutz families.

Research into factors associated with parenthood

Positive experience

Turner and Helms (1983) see parenthood as positive (1) children provide a sense of achievement (Erikson's generativity), (2) they allow parents to give and receive love, (3) having children is a cultural expectation, (4) children give parents a sense of importance.

Stressful experience

Hultsch and Deutsch (1981) found that 50–80% of adults described the birth of their first child as a moderate to severe crisis.

Parenthood causes marital problems, possibly because people sometimes have children as a way of patching up their difficulties and also through conflicts over childrearing.

The empty nest. Another effect of parenthood is when it ends; this is often seen as part of a mid-life crisis, but it may also be a time of increased wealth and freedom. Most parents look forward to extending their parenting into grandparenthood.

Intervening variables

Heinicke and Guthrie (1992) found that couples whose interactions were most positive during the months of pregnancy, and who showed respect to each other when conflicts arose, dealt most successfully with their roles as parents.

Gender differences

Brown and Harris (1978) found that women who don't work and have several children to look after at home are far more likely to become seriously depressed.

The impact of a baby on its parents depends on numerous factors, such as social and financial status.

The life events approach tends to emphasise crises as the main force in personality development and de-emphasise individual differences.

Cultural differences

Social class differences. Russell (1974) found that middle-class parents were more dissatisfied than working-class parents. This may because they start with higher ideals and the mother is more likely to have to give up a career.

In non-Western cultures, there is less decline in satisfaction. This may be related to the extended family and collectivist societies, and/or different cultural practices. For example, Mexicans practise a family ritual, *La cuarentena*, where the first 40 days after birth involve considerable support for mothers (Wadeley, 2000).

Practice essay 4.8

Describe and evaluate research (theories **and/or** studies) into factors associated with marriage (partnering).   (24 marks)

4.9 Cognitive changes in late adulthood

AQA A ▷ U4

Cognitive changes

Intelligence

Wechsler (1955), in compiling the normative data for WAIS (Wechsler Adult Intelligence Scale), found that intelligence reaches a peak around the age of 30. Schultz *et al.* (1980) found declines in fluid intelligence and spontaneous flexibility with age, but some older participants were the best of all. Whereas Burns (1966) reported a longitudinal study where a set of people were tested at age 22 and again when they were 56; on average their IQs were higher.

Studies of IQ may suffer from the *cohort effect* if they compare one generation with another; older generations inevitably have lower IQs due to poorer diet. People today are smarter. Schaie (1983) found, from a longitudinal study in Seattle, that cohort effects equal or exceed age differences.

Studies of IQ may fail to distinguish between kinds of intelligence. Baltes and Baltes (1990) claim that *fluid intelligence* actually declines with age but that *crystallised intelligence* may increase with age. Arlin (1977) suggested a fifth stage of cognitive development: divergent thinking or problem-finding (rather than solving).

Memory

Talland (1968) found that participants aged 77 to 89 remembered less than half the number of items that a 20–25-year-old age group can recall on a short-term memory task, and also forgot more in the initial 90 seconds after presentation of a three-letter word. Kimmel (1990) suggested that there may be dramatic declines shown in laboratory memory experiments and some everyday memory skills, but older people show highly competent memory skills in other areas, such as long-term recall or expert memory skills.

Problems in assessing ability

Health. Some elderly have decreased abilities due to the effects of strokes and other progressive illnesses. Birren *et al.* (1963) examined a group of men aged 65–91; some had no obvious symptoms of disease but, on close medical examination, they in fact had certain mild diseases which would subtly affect performance.

Social deprivation. Decline may be due to lack of stimulation rather than old age *per se*. Institutionalised elderly people may suffer similar ill-effects to children in orphanages. Rubin (1973) found that elderly people living in their own homes performed better on Piagetian tasks than those living in institutions.

Cohort effects. Observed differences between older and younger participants may be due to generational differences.

Explanations of adjustment to old age

Social disengagement theory (Cumming and Henry, 1961)

Psychological well-being is promoted by a gradual withdrawal from personal contacts and world affairs.

Research evidence

This was based on a five-year study of nearly 300 individuals aged between 50 and 90. They observed that older people gradually lose contact with others, have fewer roles and are freed to play the roles they wish.

Havighurst *et al.* (1968) found that some of those studied by Cumming and Henry were *disengagers*; for example individuals who have always been rather reclusive tend to disengage in their later years.

Evaluation

- This would lead to a *policy of segregation* for the elderly (Bromley, 1988).
- It may be that disengagement *is forced on* to an individual by ill-health or lack of money.
- Havighurst *et al.* (1968) also found that some of the original sample remained active and content, in fact the *most active were the happiest*.

Fluid intelligence is proposed to be a kind of general intellectual capacity, whereas *crystallised intelligence* is knowledge from experience.

Motivation is probably of importance, and some older participants may be less motivated to do well.

Graham and Baker (1989) found that the status level of an 80-year-old was equivalent to that of a 5-year-old. This drop in status may explain why older people find adjustment difficult.

Erikson (1963) characterised the ageing years as a time of integrity versus despair (see p. 98). This view describes old age as a continuing period of development.

Atchley (1977) argued that most people continue to do the same things in retirement that they were doing before. Their social relationships continue at similar levels to before.

Activity theory (Havighurst *et al.*, 1968)

Continued or new interests and involvements maintain psychological health and long life. Havighurst *et al.* felt it was important for the elderly to maintain a 'role count', the number of social roles they have to play.

Research evidence

Rubin's research (above) demonstrates how deprivation can lead to mental deterioration. Langer and Rodin (1976) found that the more active elderly living in nursing homes lived longer than those who were less active.

Evaluation

- *Individual differences*. Some individuals are 'disengagers' so activity is inappropriate.
- There are *factors other than activity level* which contribute towards the adjustment made to old age, e.g. physical health, financial security, close relationships and a strong social network.

Social exchange theory

Dowd (1975) suggested that an individual 'agrees' to give up certain things (being a financially active member of society) in exchange for their increased leisure time and pension. This informal 'contract' contains expectations about how an older person will behave (see also 'Social exchange theory' as an explanation of relationships, page 24).

Life events

Coping with retirement

Phases of adjustment (Atchley, 1982)

Typical experience of retirement:

- *pre-retirement phase* – think of potential changes, such as loss of earnings
- *honeymoon phase* – period of relative enjoyment and euphoria
- *disenchantment phase* – looked-forward-to activities fail to measure up to expectations, failing health may mean less is possible
- *reorientation phase* – a more realistic approach developed, seek new roles
- *stability phase* – life takes on an orderly routine again
- *termination phase* – poor health requires significant lifestyle changes.

Coping with bereavement

Health

Hinton (1967) found a higher incidence of death in recent widows than a sample of married women of the same age. Parkes (1987) found that 75% of widows sought medical advice within six months. However, Mor *et al.* (1986) suggested that this may be because illness may have been ignored in the period leading up to a spouse's death.

Symptoms

Clayton *et al.* (1971) interviewed widows, whose symptoms were crying, lack of concentration, sleeping and poor memory. Abnormal grief may occur as a response to extreme circumstances.

Lindemann (1944) described reactions after the Coconut Grove night-club fire: somatic distress, guilt, hostility, sense of unreality and preoccupation with the deceased.

The bereavement process

Bowlby (1980) distinguished five phases of grief and mourning:

- initial shock, denial, concentration on the deceased
- anger
- appeals for help
- despair, withdrawal, disorganisation
- resolution, reorganisation and new focus.

This has parallels with the dying process. Kübler-Ross (1969) interviewed over 200 dying patients and identified five processes which characteristically occurred. The aim is to provide a framework for helping people through the dying process:

- denial and isolation (others often avoid the dying or bereaved individual)

Prescriptive theories, such as activity or disengagement, suggest what old people should be doing to promote well-being, whereas in fact there are the same individual differences as at any stage of life.

The experience of retirement depends on whether it is voluntary and looked forward to, and how much the individual enjoyed work and the company of co-workers.

An understanding of these phases may be useful in helping individuals prepare more successfully for retirement.

Death of spouse scores 100 LCU (1st) on the Holmes and Rahe Scale, the death of a close family member 63 LCU (5th) and of a close friend 37 LCU (17th).

Bereavement varies with a person's own feelings about death and their emotional type, the type of death, the age of the deceased, relationship with the deceased (closeness, dependency, duration). Where interpersonal problems were unresolved the grieving is much harder.

Mourning usually lasts between one and two years, which is reflected in the historical practice of wearing black for a year.

> These stages may not follow in a sequence, but may come and go.

- anger (the beginning of acceptance)
- bargaining (trying to find a little extra time or some way out)
- depression (important to allow individuals to express their sorrow in order to reach a final acceptance)
- acceptance.

Cultural differences

Gender (a kind of cultural difference). Barrett (1978) found that widowers had a lower morale, expressed greater dissatisfaction and required more help than widows. Many men rely on their wives for domestic care and for friendship, and therefore experience greater loss. Some women experience greater sense of loss than others, depending on how much they defined themselves in terms of their husband (Lopata, 1979).

Rites of passage vary from culture to culture.

Collectivist cultures have extended families. Lonely elderly may find bereavement more difficult.

Practice essay 4.9

Outline and evaluate **two or more** explanations of adjustment to old age. (24 marks)

Sample question and model answer

Discuss **one** theory of cognitive development. (24 marks)

Examiner's comments

This may look like a simple, straightforward question and it is – it follows the predictable format of AQA A-style questions. However there are hidden dangers. The likely choice of theory will be Piaget's theory of cognitive development. You have 15 minutes to demonstrate your knowledge and understanding of this theory which is why the question uses the term 'outline' rather than 'describe'. You must carefully select what information to include in order to use your 15 minutes for this half of the question profitably. Rather than list all the ages and stages it would be preferable to cover several different aspects of the theory, such as the structure of the intellect and how knowledge is acquired. A 'list-like' answer will be unlikely to get more than 8 out of the 12 marks.

You can evaluate elements of the theory as you go along, for example when describing certain stages of development you can present evidence that supports or challenges the stage. Remember to use such evidence as effective commentary rather than simply describing the studies.

Alternatively you can present the commentary/evaluation all in one section of your answer, as the candidate has done here.

Candidate's answer

Piaget's theory is the best-known and most comprehensive theory of cognitive development. It has been called an 'ages and stages' theory because Piaget identified the stages that an infant and child pass through as they develop cognitively. The key point about these stages is that they represent differences in biological maturation. As the child gets older they are capable of progressively different <u>kinds</u> of thinking rather than just having an increase in their general knowledge (a quantitative change). A child moves from one stage to another when their minds are mature enough. The first stage is sensori-motor, when the infant is learning to coordinate what he sees/hears with what his body is doing. The infant repeats actions (circular reactions) in order to establish these sensori-motor links.

At the end of the first year the child starts to use language and this is the beginning of the second stage, the pre-operational stage. 'Operations' are mental rules of logic. In this second stage children cannot cope with internally consistent logic. They have their own form of logic but it wouldn't be any use in mathematics. They are 'fooled' by the appearance of things and mistake that for reality. This explains why they find the conservation task difficult.

The third stage is the stage of concrete operations (age about 7) where children can now cope with conservation and with logical operations – but only if they are presented in a concrete form rather than abstract form. The child's problem-solving abilities also tend to be rather random. The game called 'Mastermind' is one way to demonstrate this because younger children can't deduce the solution using logical steps. Nor can they cope systematically with the pendulum task.

At the age of 11 children move into the formal operational stage, when they are capable of abstract and systematic (scientific) thought. It may not be a universally achievable stage.

There is another, equally important, aspect to Piaget's theory which is his description of how a child (and adult) acquires knowledge. We are born with certain 'schema' – little programmes for how to do things, such as a sucking schema. Through our lives we adapt these to accommodate new experiences and thus build up our knowledge. Each new experience can either be assimilated into an existing schema (assimilation) or has to be changed (accommodation) to produce a new schema. Accommodation occurs because of a sense of disequilibrium. If a new experience doesn't match existing schema then there is a sense of imbalance and we have a drive to return to a state of balance.

Piaget assembled some of his own research evidence and his work has generated lots of other research – often in an attempt to show that Piaget had it wrong.

Piaget's own methods largely involved naturalistic observation of his own children. He may have been biased in making observations and exaggerated things that they could do. He also used semi-structured interviews. These are good for eliciting unexpected information because there are no preset directions to take. However, the way an interviewer asks a question may bias the response that a child gives.

In the area of object permanence, Piaget claimed that infants were only aware of this after the age of 8 months. However, a study by Bower showed that younger infants were surprised when a screen was lifted and an object was not there. This suggests that Piaget underestimated the age that infants could achieve this cognitive step, thus challenging Piaget's evidence.

Piaget's research on conservation has been especially challenged. One suggestion has been that the fact that he used two questions may have confused younger participants who thought that if there is a second question, there perhaps is a second answer. Therefore they changed their answer in the second condition. Older children were less confused which is why they appear to do better on the conservation task. Research by Samuel and Bryant supports this, showing that younger children are more capable than Piaget suggested – however there still are age differences.

McGarrigle and Donaldson (1974) had a different idea. They wondered whether the task itself was confusing. So they used 'naughty teddy' to mess up the row of counters. Again younger children did cope better but then other research by Moore and Frye suggested that naughty teddy may have unduly distracted the children and so they simply didn't notice that any transformation had taken place and that's why they did apparently better.

Piaget's theory claimed to be a biological and therefore universal theory of

Sample question and model answer (continued)

behaviour yet most of the research has been done on American and British children, and in laboratories. Some of this research may not generalise to the real world though its usefulness in education suggests that it does have a place there.

[788 words]

Examiner's comments

The answer is coherent and well structured, and also well detailed – though, as this question requires an 'outline', it is breadth which matters more than depth (detail). The candidate has attempted to present each stage in outline and avoided getting bogged down in lots of detail about particular behaviours but there is still too much on stages at a sacrifice of more information about other aspects of Piaget's theory.

The commentary begins by considering some of the methodology used by Piaget. Piaget's research has also been challenged by other psychologists because he may have confused his participants. However, these studies show nothing more than an underestimation of what children can do – an assessment of the studies that have criticised Piaget. Finally, there is a brief consideration of the culture-bound nature of the research though this lacks elaboration. On the negative side, it is not clear that this is an analysis of evidence that has <u>supported</u> Piaget's theory. In a way, some of the essay reads more like a look at evidence that has challenged Piaget. A slight shift of emphasis would have been preferable.

AO1
Accurate and well detailed, coherent but slightly limited. Band 3 (bottom) = 10 marks.

AO2
Commentary is thorough and used in an effective manner. There is evidence of appropriate selection and coherent elaboration. It is not thorough but closer to this than 'slightly limited'. Band 3 (bottom) = 10 marks.

Total 20 out of 24 marks (see page 12 for band descriptors), equivalent to a Grade A.

Chapter 5

Comparative psychology

Comparative psychologists seek to make comparisons between the behaviours of different animals, with the intention of gaining insights into human behaviour. Much of the research relies on observations of animals in their natural environment. Experimental research has the drawback of not necessarily being applicable to real-life behaviour, as is the case throughout psychology.

At A2 you may select to study one or more of the following areas in comparative psychology:

Determinants of animal behaviour

5.1 Evolutionary explanations of animal behaviour
5.2 Classical and operant conditioning
5.3 Social learning in non-human animals

After studying this area you should be able to:

- describe and critically assess evolutionary explanations of non-human animal behaviour
- discuss biological explanations of apparent altruism
- describe and evaluate both classical and operant conditioning
- discuss the role of conditioning in the behaviour of non-human animals

- critically consider explanations and research studies of the role of social learning in the behaviour of non-human animals, for example imitation and foraging
- critically consider the evidence for intelligence in non-human animals, including self-recognition and theory of mind

LEARNING SUMMARY

Animal cognition

5.4 Animal navigation
5.5 Animal communication and language
5.6 Memory

After studying this area you should be able to:

- critically consider research studies into animal navigation, including homing and migration
- discuss explanations of animal navigation
- describe and assess the use of different signalling systems in non-human animals, including those based on visual, auditory and olfactory channels
- critically consider research studies of both natural

animal language and attempts to teach language to non-human animals
- describe and evaluate research studies of memory in non-human animals, with reference to navigation and foraging
- discuss explanations of memory in non-human animals

LEARNING SUMMARY

Evolutionary explanations of human behaviour

5.7 Human reproductive behaviour
5.8 Evolutionary explanations of mental disorders
5.9 Evolution of intelligence

After studying this area you should be able to:

- discuss the relationship between sexual selection and human reproductive behaviour
- describe and assess evolutionary explanations of sex differences in parental investment
- critically consider evolutionary explanations of human mental disorders, including schizophrenia,

depression and anxiety disorders
- discuss evolutionary factors in the development of human intelligence
- critically consider the relationship between brain size and intelligence

LEARNING SUMMARY

Determinants of animal behaviour

5.1 Evolutionary explanations of animal behaviour

AQA A ▶ U4

Darwin's theory of evolution

The theory of natural selection

Variation. Individuals within a species vary. Some of this variation is inherited.

Competition. Between individuals for scarce resources (e.g. food, mates).

Fitness. The individuals who are best adapted to their ecological niche are fittest, and are most likely to survive and reproduce.

Selective pressure. Selective pressure is the force by which one individual is favoured over another, i.e. naturally selected. Any behaviour that promotes survival and reproduction is adaptive and will be naturally selected.

Ongoing. Environmental change means that new characteristics are continually being selected.

Understanding evolution in terms of genetics

In the nineteenth century Mendel conducted experiments with plants and demonstrated that particles (genes) explained heredity.

The total set of genes is an individual's *genotype*. Some genes are dominant and some are recessive. Dominant genes mask recessive genes that are not expressed but may be be passed to offspring.

An individual's *phenotype* is the external character of an organism. Recessive genes are not expressed unless they occur as a pair.

Research evidence

Comparative studies. For example, most living and fossil vertebrates share similar bone structure in their arms providing evidence for evolution.

Studying the effects of geographical isolation. Darwin observed the physical differences between members of the same species living on different islands of the Galapagos, and related these to their environmental niche. Finches with thick beaks lived where there were hard-shelled seeds; finches with elongated beaks foraged for insects under rocks. These physical differences are due to selective pressure.

Studying the effects of environmental change. Industrialisation in Britain led to a blackened environment, and darker moths had an adaptive advantage in terms of camouflage. The peppered moth was light-coloured until a mutant darker variety appeared in 1850; by 1900 it had virtually replaced the lighter form (industrial melanism). Kettlewell (1955) demonstrated this by recording the frequency that birds took different types of moths on darker and lighter trees. Similar selective pressures have occurred with insecticides and antibiotic-resistant strains of bacteria.

Artificial selection experiments. Manning (1961) bred fruit flies which were fast and slow maters; the progeny had combined characteristics showing inheritance. Selective breed-ing programmes are successfully used by farmers with both plants and animals.

Evaluation

- Much of the empirical support is from *natural experiments*, which cannot truly demonstrate causal relationships.
- How are *intermediate stages* of evolution selected? For example, when a species evolves a form of brightly coloured protective mimicry, there is a period during which the mimicry is not yet fully developed and the bright coloration must act as a positive disadvantage.

Other theories of evolution

Lamark's theory

Lamark (1809) proposed that characteristics which are acquired during an organism's lifetime are inherited by subsequent generations. For example, a blacksmith's son

---

Sidebar notes:

Evolution is a fact, living things evolve (change). A theory is an explanation of the facts.

The phrase 'survival of the fittest' refers to the fact that an animal with greater competitive edge is more likely to survive. Fitness is measured in terms of the number of offspring produced by an individual.

Only characteristics which are inherited can be naturally selected.

It is *genotype* which is naturally selected; however, selective pressure works on *phenotype*.

It is possible that the baseline data is erroneous. The evidence that there were only a few dark-peppered moths in the late nineteenth century comes from moth collections. It may be that collectors avoided collecting ugly black moths.

Ontogeny describes those changes which occur through experience whereas *phylogeny* are the changes which are genetically based.

would inherit large muscles developed during the father's lifetime. This cannot explain evolution because natural selection can only work on genetically determined characteristics.

Group selection (Wynne-Edwards, 1962)

A group with more favourable characteristics would be more likely to survive to reproduce. However, selection takes place at the level of individual genes.

Sociobiological explanations (e.g. Hamilton, 1964)

Sociobiologists explain social behaviour (e.g. altruism) in terms of *evolutionary* processes. Any behaviour must serve some adaptive function. Sociobiologists extended Darwin's concept of individual fitness to *inclusive* fitness. Selective pressure acts on the genes (*kin selection*) rather than the individual.

Evolutionarily stable strategies (ESS) are species-specific strategies which have evolved to a point where they cannot be bettered by any feasible alternative and therefore can not be invaded by a mutant gene. For example the hawk–dove strategy (Maynard-Smith, 1976), a balance between hawks (individuals who fight to kill) and doves (individuals who will threaten but avoid serious fighting).

Cultural inheritance

Cultural inheritance is a form of evolutionary change related to natural selection. Behaviours which are successful or adaptive are imitated and passed on to future generations (ontogeny). Cultural transmission is more powerful and flexible because it is faster (see page 113).

Apparent altruism

Darwin's theory of evolution would predict that altruistic behaviour would not be naturally selected because it decreases the fitness of the altruist. The fact that animals do behave altruistically is a paradox. Why does it occur?

Kin selection

Behaviour may be unselfish at the level of the individual, but at the level of the genes it is selfish because it promotes the perpetuation of the gene (*kin selection*). It increases the individual's inclusive fitness. This can explain why parents protect offspring, why there are lookouts in a squirrel colony, sterile workers in an ant colony and helpers at the nest (e.g. meerkats).

Kin recognition

Kin selection presupposes that individuals can recognise their relatives.

Recognition by place. 'Any individual in the nest is kin.' The hypothesis is likely to be correct but it allows for brood parasitism as in cuckoos.

Association mechanism. Individuals learn to recognise each other, usually during early experience (imprinting). Holmes and Sherman (1982) reared squirrels in four groups: siblings reared together or apart, and non-siblings reared together or apart. When the squirrels were later placed together they found that animals reared together rarely fought, regardless of genetic relatedness. They also found that, of the animals reared apart, the true siblings were less aggressive towards each other.

Phenotype matching. External appearance, such as odour (phenotype rather than genotype), is evidence of apparent relatedness. Kalmus and Ribbands (in Ridley, 1986) found that inter-hive fighting decreased when bees fed on the same flowers and smelled the same. When they divided a hive and fed each half different diets, intra-hive fighting increased.

Green beard effect. Dawkins (1976) proposed that kin possess certain features which promote recognition. It is an unlikely possibility.

Evaluation

- Kin selection presupposes that individuals *can recognise* their relatives.
- Assumes that genes *directly cause* behaviour.
- *Speculative accounts*, but they are supported by extensive observation.

Selective pressure *includes* close genetic relations (kin selection). *Inclusive fitness* is measured in terms of the number of surviving descendants and relatives as opposed to direct descendants.

Beware of explanations which sound as if the genes are actively developing strategies; evolutionary strategies are the passive result of natural selection.

Biological altruism is behaviour which increases the survival potential of another while decreasing the altruist's survival and future reproductive potential. Human or psychological altruism is somewhat different (see p. 30).

Dawkins (1976) argued in his book *The Selfish Gene* that altruism is actually a selfish behaviour, at the level of the genes. Thus we use the term '*apparent* altruism'.

Reciprocal altruism (Trivers, 1971)

One individual helps another organism, at some risk to themselves, in anticipation that the favour will be returned at some later date. For example, Packer (1977) documented how non-dominant male olive baboons take it in turns to act as lookout while one of them copulates with a female.

Axelrod and Hamilton (1981) proposed that reciprocal altruism was an ESS, as illustrated by the Prisoner's dilemma. Individual A and B can either choose to cooperate or defect. If they both cooperate, they both gain some reward. If one defects but the other cooperates the defector gets a large reward. If everyone defects there is no pay off. Under such conditions it pays occasional individuals to defect, but over a long period the ESS will be cooperation.

> An ESS (evolutionarily stable strategy) is one that persists because it can't be bettered.

Evaluation

- It is *adaptive* because of mutual benefit.
- It is *vulnerable to cheating* and therefore may only evolve in species where individuals can recognise each other.

Mutualism

Two animals behave in altruistic ways towards each other because there is a net gain in terms of survival and reproductive benefit. Non-relatives may collect food together because they offer increased protection from predation (as in geese grazing) or more effective capture techniques (as in lions hunting). This is not true altruism because both individuals benefit.

Manipulated or induced altruism

> This is altruism in Darwinian terms (selfish individual interest).

What looks like altruism on the part of the host is manipulation by the recipient. Manipulated altruism can be interspecies (as in the cuckoo or any parasite) or intraspecies (as in cliff swallows which place their eggs in the nests of other females and avoid any further parental investment).

Practice essay 5.1

Discuss **one or more** evolutionary explanations for the behaviour of non-human animals.

(24 marks)

5.2 Classical and operant conditioning

AQA A — U4
OCR — U5, U6

Classical (Pavlovian) conditioning

Learning to associate a stimulus with a response. Pavlov observed that dogs came to salivate (a reflex response) when they heard a door opening, presumably because this sound had become associated with the likelihood of food.

> In the case of classical conditioning learning is based on a existing response (a reflex) whereas in the case of operant conditioning a new response is being learned.

Before conditioning		
NS (neutral stimulus, bell)	→	no response
UCS (unconditioned stimulus, e.g. food)	→	UCR (unconditioned response, e.g. salivation)

During conditioning
NS and UCS are paired by occurring together

After conditioning		
CS (conditioned stimulus, bell)	→	CR (conditioned response, salivation)

Features of classical conditioning

Extinction. If the stimuli stop being paired, the CR is extinguished.

Spontaneous recovery. If there is a rest interval after extinction, the CR will reappear. Suggests that extinction is just a temporary suppression of the CR.

> Conditioning takes place with no conscious activity. A conditioned response is acquired through association (classical) or reinforcement (operant).

Generalisation. The CR may occur in response to stimuli which are similar to the CS. For example, if the UCS was a circle, then other shapes (e.g. ellipse) may also elicit the CR.

Generalisation gradient. The similarity between the new object (e.g. ellipse) and the original one. The more similar they are the stronger the response.

Guthrie (1935) suggested that in fact all learning takes place on a single trial – the reason it appears to take longer is because a large number of simple components are being acquired.

The concepts of generalisation, discrimination and extinction also apply to operant conditioning.

Most classical conditioning experiments involve passive learning whereas, in real life, learning involves active involvement with the environment. Nevertheless, classical conditioning does explain some natural behaviours.

Discrimination. If the circle continues to be paired with the food and the ellipse is shown without food, the organism learns to discriminate.

One trial learning. Usually the NS and UCR have to be paired more than once for learning to take place, but under some conditions one trial is sufficient, for example one fearful incident in childhood may lead to a lifelong fear of dogs.

First-order conditioning. Initially conditioning acts on reflex responses.

Higher-order conditioning. The CS from the original (first-order) conditioning series is used as the UCS in a new series. For example, a bell might be the first CS which can then be associated with a time of day.

Timing. The strongest CR is produced when the NS appears half a second before the UCS and remains during the UCS (delayed or *forward conditioning*). If the NS comes after the UCS (*backward conditioning*) very little learning takes place.

Research evidence

Pavlov (1927) investigated digestion and salivation by redirecting dogs' salivary ducts through their cheek. The dogs would salivate before they were given food. He demonstrated conditioning using a bell, a metronome, the odour of vanilla, apomorphine (a drug which causes vomiting) and a rotating object as the UCS.

Menzies (1937) asked participants to put their hands in ice-cold water whenever a buzzer sounded; the cold temperature caused vasoconstriction (constriction of the blood vessels). Eventually the vasoconstriction occurred just in response to the sound of the buzzer.

Marquis (1931) showed classical conditioning in ten newborns. By associating a buzzer with the presence of a bottle, they began sucking at the sound of the buzzer.

Watson and Rayner (1920) conditioned Little Albert to fear white furry objects by pairing the presence of a rat with a loud noise, creating a CER (*conditioned emotional response*). Albert's fear generalised to other white furry things including Santa Claus.

Operant (instrumental) conditioning

Learning due to the consequences of a behaviour (response). The probability of a behaviour being repeated depends on strengthening or weakening stimulus–response (S–R) links.

Thorndike (1913) first described this as the '*law of effect*', behaviours are stamped in or out depending on their consequences.

Skinner (1938) introduced the term *operant* because the learner operates on their environment, which brings certain consequences (in classical conditioning the learner responds, respondent behaviour).

A (antecedents) ➔ B (behaviour) ➔ C (consequences)

Features of operant conditioning

Reinforcement. Both positive and negative reinforcement strengthen the likelihood of a future response. Negative reinforcement is the absence of, or escape from, a negative stimulus.

An example of negative reinforcement would be learning to get out of the way of an electric shock. You are likely to repeat this behaviour because the consequences are pleasant.

Punishment may be counter-productive because the attention associated with it is actually rewarding.

Shaping can be used to explain how a trainer teaches a circus animal to perform a complex trick.

Avoidance learning can be used to explain phobias.

Punishment is the presence of a negative stimulus (or removal of something positive, e.g. not having a chocolate treat because you did something wrong).

Shaping. It takes a long time for an organism to perform the right behaviour to receive a reward. This would suggest that learning is a time-consuming process, which it isn't. Therefore Skinner proposed that operant behaviours are gradually built up through progressive reinforcement as each behaviour becomes closer to the final goal.

Avoidance learning. A type of operant conditioning where a response is learned as a means of avoiding an unpleasant (aversive) stimulus. However, the organism never has the chance to discover if the painful stimulus is still there, so it can't be extinguished.

Reinforcement schedules. Variable reinforcement schedules are more resistant to extinction. This may be because, under fixed rate reinforcement, the organism 'expects' it regularly and therefore 'notices' its absence more quickly.

Primary and secondary (conditioned) reinforcement. Things which act as primary reinforcers are innate, such as food or fear. Secondary reinforcers work because at some time they have been paired with a primary one. The classic example is money. An example of a negative secondary reinforcer is a hot cooker.

Research evidence

Skinner (1938) placed a pigeon in a Skinner box. If it pressed a lever (UCS), a door would open and food (reinforcer or reward) was delivered. The pigeon first pecks randomly around the box as part of its natural exploratory behaviour (*operating* on the environment). Accidentally it presses the lever a few times and receives food. Each experience strengthens the S–R link. Reinforcement is both positive (when the lever is pressed) and negative (when pecking elsewhere no food appears). The lever becomes the CS and pressing the lever is a CR. Behaviour has been brought under stimulus control. If the pigeon learns to press a button whenever it is lit to get food, it is learning to discriminate the state of the button (*a discriminative stimulus*).

Skinner claimed that the effects of punishment were short-lived. Estes (1944) trained rats to lever press for food, then gave one group a shock on every lever press, which extinguished the response for a while. The other group merely had no food given. In the long run the two groups produced the same number of responses, showing that punishment doesn't result in lasting learning or true extinction.

Skinner believed in *equipotentiality* – that any response could be conditioned in any stimulus situation. However, Breland and Breland (1961) tried to train pigs to insert a wooden token into a piggy bank for reward but the pigs handled the token like they would treat any object – tossing it up and rooting with it. What animals learn tends to resemble their instinctive behaviour (*instinctive drift*).

Wolfe (1936) developed the *token economy system*, used in behaviour modification (see page 144). Chimpanzees were given vending machines and learned that putting in tokens led to getting a grape. Even when the machine was not present the monkeys worked to get tokens (*secondary reinforcers*).

Seligman (1975) demonstrated *learned helplessness*. Dogs were exposed to unavoidable shocks. Later they were placed in a situation where they could escape from shocks but they didn't. They had learned to respond passively to unpleasant stimuli. Dogs not previously exposed to the unavoidable shocks learned quickly to jump away from the shocks on the sound of a warning tone.

> Learned helplessness has been used to explain depression (see p. 139).

Evaluation of conditioning (learning) theory

Learning theory cannot explain the following.

Innate learning. Seligman (1970) suggested that a species is biologically predisposed to acquire certain conditioned responses more easily than others (*preparedness*). Garcia and Koelling (1966) demonstrated that rats had a predisposition to learn quickly to avoid substances which made them feel sick.

> There would be an adaptive advantage to individuals who avoided unfamiliar foods or sampled them cautiously. This 'bait shyness' can explain why rat poison isn't very effective.

Latent learning. Learning without reinforcement and in behavioural 'silence'. Blodgett (1929) demonstrated that rats that received no reward when placed in a maze did not appear to learn anything but when, after six days, food was placed in the goal box, they learned to go to that arm of the maze more rapidly than rats who had been rewarded from the beginning of the experiment. During the period before reward they had wandered around the maze and must have stored a *cognitive map* of the maze.

Insight learning. Some learning may take place because of a flash of insight, rather than by trial-and-error (see page 79). In defence of conditioning, this behaviour could occur through generalisation.

> Are classical and operant conditioning different? In the classical conditioning experiment is food a UCS or a reward? The bell is a signal that the food is coming, salivating is an anticipatory response to food. If the bell comes immediately after the food it should still result in conditioning (backward conditioning) but such conditioning is rare, which suggests that the food is a reward and this paradigm is operant conditioning.

The transfer of learning. Positive transfer occurs when learning task A has a positive effect on learning task B, negative transfer occurs when learning task A interferes with learning task B. Both imply some cognitive activity is mediating performance.

Imitation or observational learning. See social learning theory, pages 28 and 93.

Practice essay 5.2

(a) Describe the nature of classical conditioning. (12 marks)

(b) Evaluate classical conditioning as an explanation for the behaviour of non-human animals. (12 marks)

5.3 Social learning in non-human animals

AQA A   U4

Group (social) living leads to social learning because: (1) the opportunity is there, and (2) group life creates problems that need solving, and this leads to learning.

Social learning is superior to trial-and-error learning because (1) it is much faster and less costly because mistakes aren't made, and (2) it enables cultural transmission.

The role of social learning in behaviour

Imitation

Kawai (1965) observed Japanese snow monkeys. Sweet potatoes were left on the beach for the monkeys, one of whom (Imo) 'invented' the idea of washing the sand off the potatoes in the sea. Soon other monkeys imitated her, and this was passed to subsequent generations. Imo also invented a way of washing wheat.

Imitation and stimulus enhancement

Nagell *et al.* (1993) suggested that the behaviour in Kawai's study could be explained in terms of *stimulus enhancement* rather than imitation. When the other monkeys observed Imo washing potatoes this drew their attention to both the potatoes and the water, and enhanced the monkeys' ability to solve the same problem.

Sherry and Galef (1984) compared the effectiveness of stimulus enhancement versus imitation using Canadian black-backed chickadees (related to tits). If birds are left in a cage with individual portion milk containers, some of them learn to open them (4 out of 16). Those birds which failed to do this were placed in one of three conditions: (1) had the opportunity to watch a 'tutor' (one of the birds who had learned), (2) given an open container (stimulus enhancement), or (3) left on own as before. In groups 1 and 2, three-quarters of the birds learned the trick whereas one did in group 3, suggesting that stimulus enhancement is as valuable as imitation.

Imitation and tutoring

Imitation is a passive process where the individual animal doesn't deliberately perform an action so it can be imitated; tutoring is an active process where the tutor is modifying its behaviour to accommodate the needs of the learner.

Boesch (1991) observed tutoring in chimpanzees. Mothers sometimes intervened when offspring were having difficulties cracking open nuts. The mother might leave a 'hammer' nearby (stimulus enhancement) or might place the nut in a better position (tutoring).

Foraging

Optimal foraging theory (OFT) (MacArthur and Pianka, 1966)

Animals develop strategies which maximise benefits (e.g. calories gained) and minimise costs (e.g. energy expenditure, risk of attack).

Zach (1978) observed that crows which eat whelks (dropping them on to rocks to get the food) prefer larger whelks (more food and easier to break shells but greater weight to carry). Zach suggested that this may be socially learned through imitation.

Searching for food

Search behaviour may be innate, or learned through trial-and-error. Smith (1974) experimented with thrushes by arranging pastry 'caterpillars' in different spacings. When food is clumped, the thrush will do well to stop and eat what's nearby, when food is evenly spaced out a straight path is a more efficient search strategy.

Recognising food

Innate recognition. Toads have a diet mainly restricted to small insects. If you move a small dark piece of paper in front of a toad, it will snap at it. The toad's predisposition to snap at anything small, dark and moving works well in the natural environment because anything answering this description is invariably an insect.

Learned recognition. Animals with more varied diets need a search image. They have to learn to distinguish between food and background. Dawkins (1971) dyed grains of rice: some were a different colour from the background and therefore easy to see, some were the same colour as the background and therefore hard to see. Chickens took a few minutes to peck at the camouflaged ones. They had to learn a search image.

Cultural transmission enables a group of animals to possess a large body of useful knowledge that promotes survival and reproduction. It is also faster.

Imitation involves learning a complex set of behaviours.

Just copying a simple behaviour would not be considered 'imitation', such as when a flock of sheep follow a leader running to another part of a field. This is social contagion.

Great tits and blue tits were first observed removing the foil tops of milk bottles and drinking the milk in 1921, within ten years the habit had spread throughout Britain. The new behaviour was not due to natural selection because the change was too rapid.

Tutoring incurs some costs, perhaps just in terms of time, and therefore in order to remain adaptive there must be some long-term benefit for the tutor.

A 'tutor' probably needs to have some idea of what the learner is thinking, which involves a *theory of mind* (see p. 114).

Aspects of foraging behaviour rely on social learning, though some foraging behaviours are innate.

One of the benefits of group rather than solitary living is being able to coordinate hunting activities. An organised group of lions can hunt more efficiently and tackle larger prey.

Hunting in groups

Caro (1980) documented how mother cats teach their kittens to capture prey. First the mother brings dead prey and eats it, then leaves the kitten to eat it, then brings injured but live prey for kitten to play with, and finally live prey for kitten to catch.

Evidence for intelligence in non-human animals

Intelligence can be defined as the ability to acquire information, to think and reason well, and to deal effectively and adaptively with the environment.

Self-recognition

If one can recognise oneself, this implies a self-concept which is a mentalistic state.

Mentalistic abilities are those that involve some form of mental activity or 'intelligence'. Stimulus enhancement and conditioning are non-mentalistic abilities. Self recognition and theory of mind involve mentalistic (intelligent) behaviour.

Gallup (1971) used the mirror test to demonstrate self-recognition. A red mark is placed on an animal's forehead (when anaesthetised). Comparison is then made between how often the animal touches this mark without and with a mirror. Gallup (1977) found that chimpanzees and orang-utans are capable of self-recognition but not other primates or non-primate animals.

However, Epstein *et al.* (1981) found that pigeons can learn to use a mirror to help them remove bits of paper stuck to their feathers, which suggests self-recognition. So does the mirror test really demonstrate *mentalistic abilities*?

Theory of mind (ToM)

A 'theory of mind' is not a formal psychological theory, but a collection of ideas that each individual formulates when trying to understand what is going on in other people's minds.

To possess a theory of mind is to have an understanding of others' thoughts and emotions, recognising that they are different from one's own. This ability enables one to make predictions of how others will behave.

Role-taking

Role-taking concerns the ability to watch the behaviour of another person and understand their intentions.

Premack and Woodruff (1978) showed videos of people solving problems to a female chimpanzee (Sarah) in order to see if she could understand their language (they were teaching her to use human language). The video was stopped just before the solution and Sarah shown two pictures of possible solutions, she consistently selected the only one that would work, suggesting that she understood the intentions of the actors.

Deception or Machiavellian intelligence

In order to deceive another individual intentionally one has to have an understanding of what they know, or don't know.

Premack and Woodruff (1979) arranged for a chimpanzee to see a trainer place food under one of two containers that were out of reach. A second trainer entered the room in a green coat (chimpanzee trained to know he was cooperative) or a white coat (known to be competitive). On most trials the chimpanzees manipulated both trainers to obtain food – they helped the cooperative trainer and deceived the competitive one. The chimpanzee knew that the competitive trainer would act on their false information, evidence of a ToM.

Perspective-taking

Perspective-taking involves being able to understand that another individual has a different perspective to oneself. The *Sally–Anne test* is used to test children.

The *Sally–Anne test* involves two dolls, Sally and Anne, and an observer. Sally puts a marble in her basket and then leaves the room. Anne removes the marble and places it in a box. Sally returns and the observer is asked, 'Where will Sally look for her marble?' If the observer answers 'in her basket', this is a false belief and demonstrates that the observer has got a ToM.

Hauser (1998) devised an 'ape-version'. A monkey observes an actor watching an object being hidden. A screen is then placed between the actor and the hiding place. The monkey sees a second actor move the object. The fact that the monkey stares longer at the first actor when he looks in the new location rather than the original hiding place is evidence of ToM because the monkey knows the actor is looking in the wrong place.

Evaluation

- All of the evidence can be explained in terms of *associative learning*, and the extent that *intention* is involved is debatable.
- The extent to which *ToM is intelligence* is debatable. Intelligence is also defined as the *ability to solve problems* and all animals have this capacity.

Practice essay 5.3

Discuss psychological evidence for intelligence in non-human animals.   (24 marks)

Animal cognition

5.4 Animal navigation

AQA A ▷ U4

Navigation

Navigation involves: location-finding (map) and direction-finding (compass).

Navigation by location

Use of local landmarks

Tinbergen and Kruyt (1938) placed a circle of pine cones around the entrance of a digger wasp's burrow. After a few days, they moved the circle a few metres away. When the wasp returned it looked for its burrow where the pine cones were.

However, pigeons don't appear to follow local landmarks. Walcott and Schmidt-Koenig (1971) placed translucent lenses on pigeons and found they still could find their way home. Keeton (1974) observed that *clock-shifted* pigeons have flown in completely the wrong direction even though their home loft is visible.

Clearly the conclusion must be that some animals do use local landmarks to guide them while others rely more exclusively on direction-finding.

Smell

Salmon return to the same river they were born using smell. Hasler (1960) plugged the noses of salmon and found that they homed less accurately than untreated controls. Grier and Burk (1992) exposed young salmon to one of two artificial odours before being released into Lake Michigan, and then scented two streams with the artificial odours. More than 90% of the recovered fish went to the stream that had the odour to which they had been exposed when young.

Papi *et al.* (1972) demonstrated that pigeons without smell can't home in on their loft (by cutting olfactory nerves and also using local anaesthetics). However, it may be the discomfort endured by the pigeons that affected their homing behaviour. Kalmus and Ribbands (in Ridley, 1986) showed that bees recognise their own hive by smell.

Note that many animals, such as dogs and otters, mark their territories using smell. This is not an example of homing.

Sound

Spallanzani (1793!) noted that bats use echolocation to recognise their locality. They emit high noises which bounce off objects creating recognisable patterns. When bats are homing over long distances they may well use magnetic information, but their actual home is recognised by familiar sound patterns.

Navigation by direction

The sun (celestial navigation)

Santschi (1911) shielded ants from direct sunlight and used a mirror to reflect sunlight from the opposite direction. This caused the ants to turn around and walk in the opposite direction until the shade was removed.

Bellrose (1958) found that mallards became disoriented on cloudy days. In contrast, Lednore and Walcott (1983) found that pigeons can navigate without the sun, though they use it when it is present. Keeton (1974) used artificial lighting to fool pigeons into 'thinking' it was six hours earlier (called '*clock shifting*'). When the pigeons were released on a sunny day, they set off about 90° away from the homeward direction but showed normal homing behaviour on overcast days.

The stars (stellar navigation)

Bellrose (1958) also tracked mallards at night by attaching small flashlights to their feet. They were disoriented on cloudy nights but OK when the sky was clear.

Emlen (1975) used the *stamp-pad technique* to show that indigo buntings in a planetarium respond to alterations in the night sky.

Magnetic information

Gould *et al.* (1978) turned a bees' honeycomb round thus disorienting them so they

---

To navigate means to find one's way.

Navigation is not just a matter of route-finding. It is important to compensate for any displacement.

Clock shifting entails using a light to move an animal's internal clock forward or backward so that they misinterpret the sun's position when released into the wild.

Salmon probably use a sun compass to navigate across the ocean but, once they are at their home coast, they distinguish between rivers using smell.

What ethical concerns are raised by studies where researchers interfered with the natural behaviour of animals?

Animals who navigate using stars must recognise patterns. Such memory abilities are considered on p. 119.

The *stamp-pad technique* involves placing a bird in a funnel. When the bird is restless it will jump up the sides of the funnel and, because its feet have been inked by the stamp pad, marks are made showing the intended direction of travel.

Lednore and Walcott found that inexperienced pigeons are much less able to navigate accurately on the basis of magnetic information alone. This indicates a role for learning.

We may know what information animals use for direction-finding but we don't know how they use it.

In the case of migration, animals may travel over great distances and will use both navigation and local landmarks to orient themselves.

An animal uses homing behaviour to locate its home (nest, burrow, hive, etc.), origin or food store. This may require travel over land, air or sea.

could not use their sun compass. However, it did not take long for them to reorient using their magnetic compass and then reset their sun compass.

Lednore and Walcott (1983) attached an electromagnetic coil to pigeons' heads, thus disrupting their ability to use magnetic information. The pigeons could return home on sunny days but not cloudy days.

Walcott and Green (1974) also used electromagnetic coil caps. When they reversed the polarity on cloudy days, the pigeons flew in the opposite direction.

How are magnetic fields detected? It is possible that *magnetite*, which is found in some species, acts as a magnetic sense. Beason (1989) found evidence of magnetite in a region of the brain just behind the nose in bobolinks (a bird). However, Wiltschko and Wiltschko (1988) argue that magnetite can't be used to detect the earth's magnetic force. Detection may involve the visual system.

Migration

Migration may be innate. It would otherwise be hard to explain the mass annual migration of Monarch butterflies from Canada to Mexico. Such insects have minimal learning capacity. Perez *et al.* (1977) clock-shifted Monarch butterflies which resulted in changed flight orientation. Cocker (1998) claims there is evidence of magnetite in their bodies. This suggests that they have an innate ability to use the sun and magnetic information for homing.

Storks also have an innate sense of direction findings. Schuz (1971) moved stork eggs from their nests in eastern Europe to western Europe. The young storks flew in a southeasterly direction, rather than the southwesterly direction of storks whose parents were from western Europe.

Other research has shown how learning is involved as well. Perdeck (1967) followed starlings flying from the Baltic Sea to Spain. They were caught over Holland, ringed and released in Switzerland (a southerly displacement). The juveniles continued to fly south-west to France and Spain, using only compass navigation. The adults flew north-west to their usual winter grounds in northern France; they used true navigation (compass) and then landmarks (map) as the destination approached, showing innate and learned influences.

Why do animals migrate? It uses up energy and is dangerous, but maximises food resources, may offer relief from predation and reduces competition. Migrants return home because they are better adapted to their home environment. Migration is triggered by changes in day length, temperature and availability of food. There may also be internal mechanisms (see Gwinner, on page 45).

Homing

The most widely studied example is homing pigeons. In familiar terrain pigeons use physical cues. There is some debate about whether they ever truly experience unfamiliar terrains because they have a maximum range and within this range there may always be familiar landmarks. If they do use true navigation it might be based on the following:

1 The *position of the sun in the sky*; making allowance for daily changes using an internal clock. Experiments have shown that pigeons make predictable errors when trained on a artificial light/dark schedule and are then exposed to the sun.

2 A *'map' strategy*; pigeons work out latitude and longitude to home in on their target using magnetic information.

3 A *magnetic compass*; pigeons with bar magnets on their head navigate incorrectly on cloudy days. This suggests that they do use magnetic fields and that they use this in conjunction with the sun.

4 *Smell*; the pigeon may remember and orient to home odours. It has been found that pigeons do not home accurately if their noses are blocked.

Practice essay 5.4

(a) Describe **two** research studies into animal navigation. (12 marks)

(b) Assess what these studies can tell us about homing and/or migration. (12 marks)

5.5 Animal communication and language

> All animals use signalling systems but there is a distinction between these and true language.

> A signal is any behaviour or feature which has the effect of changing the behaviour of another animal, through sensory perception rather than force. The message may not be intended.

> Some animal vocalisations involve a vocabulary. For example Seyfarth and Cheyney (1980) noted three different types of alarm call in vervet monkeys, each related to a different predator (eagles, leopards and pythons).

> Olfactory signals often rely on *pheromones*, biochemical substances that are produced by one individual and have an effect on target individuals.

Use of different signalling systems in non-human animals

Sensory modalities

Visual signals

- *Location of food*, e.g. dance of honey bee (see next page).
- *Threat and dominance displays*, e.g. facial expression (bared teeth, staring eyes).
- *Mood*, e.g. the octopus changes colour to indicate pleasure or anger.
- *Deceit and mimicry*, e.g. spots on caterpillars communicate danger to predators.
- *Danger*, e.g. rabbits raise their tail exposing a white patch as an alarm signal.
- *Sexual displays communicate readiness*, e.g. female primate's genitalia.

Strengths and limitations. Visual signals are instantaneous and can communicate a lot of information. However, they are only effective under reasonable lighting conditions and of no use over long distances. Visual displays are 'expensive' in terms of energy.

Auditory signals

- *Mating and territorial defence*. Krebs and Dawkins (1984) replaced pairs of great tits with loudspeakers or nothing. Where loudspeakers played a full repertoire of the bird song it took longer for new pairs to occupy the territory.
- *Alarm call*. Tyack (1983) played tape recordings of excited whales to a group of other whales, who all dispersed.
- *Sociality*, e.g. a group of humpback whales all sing the same song.
- *Parent–young call*, e.g. parents call in order to locate their young.

Strengths and limitations. Auditory signals are effective over distances and in water, and in the dark or poor lighting. They are generally fast and efficient but use a lot of energy, can be detected by predators and may be distorted over long distances.

Olfactory signals

- *Mating*, e.g. female silk moths produce bombykol.
- *Location of food*, e.g. ants leave a trail of pheromones from food to nest.
- *Identification*, e.g. sweat bees have colony odours to distinguish friends and foes.
- *Marking territory*, e.g. urination in dogs and defecation in hippopotamuses.

Strengths and limitations. Odours can communicate effectively over both time and space. They are hard for predators to detect and interpret, and can be used in the dark.

Kinaesthetic (touch) signals

- *Sociality*, e.g. grooming is an important social signal for bonding and dominance.
- *Parent–young*, e.g. mouth-to-mouth contact elicits feeding.
- *Electrical signals* are largely related to locating prey, as in the duckbilled platypus.

Strengths and limitations. Touch does not depend on complex structures but can only be used in situations in which direct contact is possible.

The origins of communication and rituals

Necessary acts inevitably take on a communicative function: intention movements (e.g. first moves in aggression become a signal for hostility), displacement activities (e.g. self-grooming when experiencing conflict), autonomic displays, i.e. emotion (e.g. bristling hair communicates arousal), sexual displays (communicate fitness).

Honest or dishonest?

A signal may be naturally selected because it is:

Honest. Signals evolve into ritualised and less ambiguous forms, to benefit both signaller and recipient.

> Examples of dishonest signals include mimicry of poisonous prey, the behaviour of the cuckoo, and displays of aggression.

Dishonest (*manipulation hypothesis*, Dawkins and Krebs, 1978). Some animals use signals to manipulate the behaviour of other animals into doing things for the benefit of the signaller. The signaller's fitness is increased at the expense of the receiver. When instances of dishonest signals outnumber honest versions, the signal becomes devalued and will no longer be effective. Therefore it progressively evolves into more and more extravagant forms.

Research studies of animal language

Hockett (1958) suggested certain 'design features' of language including: *semanticity* (units have meaning and meaning communicated by order, i.e. *grammar*), *arbitrariness* (units may be arbitrary), *displacement* (in time and space), *prevarication* (using language to tell lies), *productivity* (novel utterances, infinite number of expressions). Each of the design features is apparent in signalling systems, for instance urination in dogs is an example of communication across space and time. The issue is whether all are present.

Studies of natural animal language

Dance of the honey bees (von Frisch, 1914)

A returning forager performs the 'waggle dance' to tell other bees how far away the food is from the hive. The 'round' dance indicates the direction. If the dance is performed on a vertical surface, the line represents the angle between the hive, the position of the sun and the food.

Bird-song

Bird species vary in the extent that their song development is innate. Some birds have almost no facility for learning and the full adult song is present even in birds raised in isolation, for example the alder flycatcher. Most birds need to hear the adult song to develop their innate version. Slater (1981) showed that chaffinches produce only a very basic song repertoire if hand reared and tend to copy the song of any bird they hear.

Marine mammals (cetaceans: whales and dolphins)

Dolphins use their clicks and whistles for social coordination, to warn of danger and for quite complex information. Bastion (1967) kept two dolphins in separate tanks, able to hear but not see each other. One dolphin was taught to press a paddle to receive a reward. When the other dolphin was given the same equipment, it knew the solution.

Chimpanzee

Menzel (1974) showed that chimpanzees could convey specific information. One chimpanzee watched him hide something and then communicated the location to the others. If a snake was hidden, they approached more cautiously. If two kinds of food were hidden, they usually went to the better one. This suggests that the 'leader' chimpanzee was communicating some very specific information.

Attempts to teach human language to non-human animals

Psychologists have sought to teach animals to use human language in order to determine the extent to which it is a species-specific ability. If it is, this supports the nativist view of language acquisition (see page 78). A second purpose of this research is as a means of differentiating humans from animals. This is especially important in terms of the ethical rights we accord to animals (see page 155).

Research studies

Gardner and Gardner (1969) raised a female chimp, Washoe, and used operant conditioning (rewards such as tickling) to teach her American Sign Language (ASL), much of which is iconic, but some is arbitrary. Washoe was treated like a child. By the age of five she had 133 signs and she spontaneously combined signs into strings of two to five words and talked about things which were not there. Her language appeared to be grammatical, for example she overgeneralised. 'Overgeneralisation' refers to the application of grammatical rules to irregular situations, such as when a child says 'He goed home.' This shows that the child has an understanding of grammar because such expressions have not been imitated.

Fouts (1973) continued work with Washoe to see if she would teach ASL to an adopted son, Loulis (cultural transmission). The researchers never signed directly to Loulis but, by the time he was five years old, he had learned 51 signs.

Patterson and Linden (1981) taught Koko, a gorilla, ASL. After seven years he knew almost all 700 signs. He produced some novel sentences (his own form of swearing, 'you big dirty toilet') and invented his own combinations of signs, such as 'runny nose'. Others claim that his grammar wasn't consistent.

Terrace (1979) worked with a chimp called Nim Chimpsky who never reached Washoe's level possibly because he wasn't home-reared and lacked social interactions.

Any mode of communication can be a language. It does not have to be vocal.

'Grammar' refers to rules of how words are combined to provide meaning. A grammar allows an infinite number of meanings to be generated from a finite set of sounds. This is discussed on p. 78.

The units of communication used by bees are arbitrary and information is communicated across time and space.

Bird-song demonstrates cultural transmission.

Whale songs demonstrate novel utterances.

Premack and Woodruff (1979) demonstrated prevarication (deception), see p. 114.

Terrace *et al.* (1979) claimed that Washoe was only imitating her trainer's signs and also may have been cued, like the horse 'Clever Hans' who appeared to be able to add up.

Nim Chimpsky was named after Noam Chomsky, who proposed the innate theory of language acquisition, see p. 78.

Terrace (199) says Kanzi is simply 'going through a bag of tricks in order to get things'. Others claim Kanzi doesn't really understand what he is saying but has just been conditioned.

Other animals have been taught as well. For example, Pepperberg (1983) taught her parrot Alex to name 40 objects. Herman *et al.* (1990) worked with dolphins and Schusterman and Gisiner (1988) taught sea lions.

Many of the attempts to teach non-human animals to use human language may have failed because it was not done in a social setting. Humans also fail to acquire language under such conditions (see p. 78).

Premack (1971) taught Sarah (a chimp) a language based on plastic, arbitrary symbols (lexigrams) to reduce memory requirements. She was able to interpret messages left for her on a magnetic board and to respond by placing the appropriate shapes on the board. (See also page 114 for more research with Sarah.)

Savage-Rumbaugh (1991) used lexigrams with Kanzi and Panbanisha (Bonobo apes), using language in the course of everyday life. The results were a rich use of language: 90% accuracy in being able to identify pictures, novel combinations of words and prevarication. Kanzi's skills were compared, on film, to the progress of a 2½-year-old child; they both showed correct comprehension about 75% of the time.

Evaluation

- Non-human animals acquire *certain features* of human language, e.g. the ability to name objects, some novel utterances and spontaneous production. Terrace (1979) suggested that primates reach a plateau due to intellectual rather than linguistic competence.

- Non-human animals never acquire language without extensive training, unlike the *speed and ease* with which humans acquire language. This suggests that they do not have the same innate capacity.

- *Grammatical.* Washoe's grammar was never consistent; she would interchangeably say 'sweet go' and 'go sweet'. But Aitchison (1983) suggested that this may have happened because she was not rewarded for grammatical expressions.

- *Subjective interpretation.* The question of whether an expression is grammatical or novel depends on the interpretation of the researcher.

- *Experimenter bias.* The animals may be responding to inadvertent cues from their trainers. However, the Gardners (1978) tested Washoe with questions to which they didn't know the answer, she was correct 72% of the time. Kanzi was tested with Savage-Rumbaugh behind him and performed well.

- *Ethics.* Do the ends justify the means? Teaching language involves enculturation.

Practice essay 5.5

Describe and assess the use of **two** different signalling systems in non-human animals.

(24 marks)

5.6 Memory

AQA A U4

Memory is the process of retaining information when the original thing is no longer present. There are close links between learning and memory, except 'memory' requires reference to internal mental processes – a non-behaviourist approach.

Memory in navigation

Navigation by location requires a recall of landmarks, smells or sound (see page 115).

Feature-by-feature recall

Baerends (1941) found that digger wasps used distant landmarks to guide their homeward journey, such as a stone wall. As soon as the wasps identified the start of a sequence of visual cues, they homed in on their target but didn't appear to have any concept of the interrelationships between the cues as in a map.

Spatial representation (cognitive maps)

Blodgett (1929 see page 112) demonstrated that rats that received no reward when placed in a maze did not appear to learn anything but later when food was placed in the goal box, they learned more rapidly than rats which had been rewarded from the beginning. During the period before reward they and must have stored a *cognitive map* of the maze.

Spatial adaptation model (Sherry et al., 1992)

Spatial memory evolves because it is adaptive for some animals, such as one who travels over longer distances. Gaulin and FitzGerald (1989) studied meadow moles. Males have larger territories than females and demonstrated better maze-learning abilities, suggesting better spatial memory as would be predicted by the model. In prairie voles the male and females share the same size territory, and they also are fairly equal in their ability to learn a path through a maze. It appears that spatial abilities are related to environmental demands.

Gould (1987) argued that there is an adaptive trade – off. It would be more useful to remember a map but this requires a lot of memory. A list of visual cues is sufficiently useful.

As part of your AS studies, you learned about human memory. There are aspects of non-human animal memory which are similar. For example, non-human animals are also likely to have *procedural* and *declarative* memories. It is also likely that the same regions of the brain are involved, such as the hippocampus.

Foraging behaviour was discussed on p. 113.

Non-human animals are able to remember many things: dogs recognise their owners, sheep recognise the smell of their lambs and bees find their way back to their hive.

Pliancy model (Day et al., 1999)

Alternatively, male meadow moles have better maze abilities because they have evolved more flexible (or pliant) memories. This can be seen in lizards (Day *et al.*, 1999). One species studied had prey that were clumped together (requires good spatial memory to locate them), second species had more mobile prey (spatial memory offers no adaptive advantage). Both species were equally good on maze-learning task but first species were better on a non-spatial visual discrimination task. Suggests that environmental demands were associated with an ability to perform more complex processing rather than just more complex spatial memory.

Neurological basis of spatial memory

Jarrard (1995) found that rats with damage to their hippocampus could locate a platform slightly submerged in murky water but, unlike normal rats, were unable to remember the location from one trial to another. This indicates a role for the hippocampus in spatial memory. In humans, Maguire *et al.* (1997) found that taxi drivers' right hippocampus was active when they were recalling routes around London but not when recalling information about landmarks.

Bingman and Mench (1990) found that pigeons with a damaged hippocampus were not disoriented when direction-finding but when they got close to home they had more difficulties (spatial memory).

Memory in foraging

When foraging, an animal may need to remember where food was found (to save time in future) and to remember where it was hidden (food cache).

Locating food

Menzel's (1971) study of chimpanzees suggests that they use spatial representation rather than visual cues. They followed a researcher as food items were hidden along a trail. Later they went straight to the hiding places rather than following the series of visual cues on the trail.

Srinivasan *et al.* (1977) gave honey bees food in a tunnel lined with black stripes on the wall. If the food source was removed, the bees flew back and forth in diminishing circles until they landed where the food should have been. If the number of stripes was changed this didn't affect their homing but it did if the stripes were horizontal rather than vertical. This suggests that their spatial memory was related to how much of the world they had passed.

Food caches

Balda and Kamil (1992) found that birds were able to locate food caches up to 40 weeks after they had hidden the food in a special laboratory environment.

Manning and Dawkins (1998) found that birds which don't store food tend to do less well on tasks involving spatial memory.

MacDonald (1977) found that red squirrels, which are less reliant on food caches, were less accurate in relocating food caches than grey squirrels. This suggests that grey squirrels have evolved superior spatial memories to cope with their need to store food.

Squirrels may use smell rather than location. Jacobs and Liman (1991) replaced some buried nuts with new nuts (devoid of the correct smell). The squirrels were more likely to recover their nuts than new nuts placed in the old locations.

Smulders *et al.* (1995) found that black-capped chickadees had larger hippocampal regions during late autumn, a time when the birds are caching food for winter and therefore would be making large demands on their spatial skills. In general, food-storing birds have been found to have larger hippocampal regions than non-food storing animals (Krebs *et al.* 1989).

Practice essay 5.6

Discuss the importance of memory in non-human animal navigation.   (24 marks)

Evolutionary explanations of human behaviour

5.7 Human reproductive behaviour

AQA A   U4

Sexual selection and human reproductive behaviour

Anisogamy

> Darwin proposed sexual selection as a variation of natural selection.

In general, each sex behaves differently because of different selective pressures. These pressures start from the differences between eggs and sperm. *Anisogamy* means different gametes. The egg and sperm are gametes. At the most basic level females (eggs) select and males (sperm) compete.

Sperm

> Sexual selection is the selection for traits which are solely concerned with increasing mating success. For example, if a peacock's tail increases his chances of being selected as a mate then the trait becomes perpetuated – it has been sexually selected.

Males produce millions of sperm and can potentially fertilise hundreds of females at a minimal cost to future reproductive potential. Natural selection will favour strategies which maximise the number of fertilisations, leading to *intrasexual* (within the same) competition and polygamy.

Eggs

Female investment is greater because the egg contains nutrients. Eggs are produced in limited numbers and females need to be more careful to ensure that each reproduction is successful (e.g. seek good mate, high parental investment and monogamy). Natural selection will favour discrimination in females which leads to *intersexual* (between the sexes) selection strategies.

Male (intrasexual) strategies

> Darwin claimed sexual selection was the basis of sexual dimorphism (two forms, male and female) because only competition makes dimorphism necessary.

Dimorphism

When females are a scarce resource, males compete for their attention and/or for nesting sites. Therefore males evolve elaborate weaponry (e.g. antlers) and are bigger for fighting. Males also develop adornments to advertise their fitness, such as the peacock's tail.

The testicular effect

Short (1991) argued that where male competition is high, males need to produce more sperm (and have larger testicles) in order to enhance the likelihood of reproductive success. Chimpanzees have relatively huge testicles in comparison with gorillas, and live in mainly *polygynandrous* society (high competition) whereas gorillas live in harems. Human male testicles are intermediate between chimpanzees and gorillas suggesting *serial polygyny*.

Sneak copulation

> It is important, when discussing human reproductive behaviour, to use studies of non-human animal behaviour with caution.

A non-dominant male discreetly copulates when the first male is not looking. Some male elephant seals pretend to be females and are then able to join a harem and sneak copulation when the bull is occupied elsewhere.

Ridley (1993) found that over 20% of UK children are offspring of males other than their presumed father. However, Sasse *et al.* (1994) found, in a study in Switzerland, less than 1.4% of the children's presumed father was not their biological one. Unpartnered males gain from sneak copulation. Women may gain from varied partners by increasing the quality of their offspring.

Rape

> Williams (1966) suggested that courtship is a contest between male sales-manship and female sales resistance.

Thornhill and Thornhill (1983) controversially argued that men who are unable to mate are driven to select an alternative strategy. Thornhill (1980) cites the behaviour of the male Panorpa scorpion fly which inseminates unwilling females by securing the female's wings in an abdominal clamp.

Female (intersexual) strategies

A female wants 'good genes' so that her offspring are fitter. Male fitness is assessed through adornments and/or courtship routines. For the male there is a benefit (increased reproduction because they are chosen) and a cost (energy and predation). Why do these characteristics evolve into extravagant forms?

Runaway process (Fisher, 1930)

Females select males with attractive characteristics because they will produce sons who inherit those characteristics, increasing the sons' reproductive success (and continuance of mother's genes). Initially the characteristics would have had some survival value (e.g. long tail) but, because females actively select mates with this feature, it becomes exaggerated. Andersson (1982) extended or shortened the tail length of long-tailed widow birds and found that breeding success was positively related to longer tail length. As long as the advantages outweigh the disadvantages the 'bizarre' characteristic will be perpetuated.

Handicapping theory (Zahavi, 1975)

Females prefer mates with handicaps (such as an over-long tail) because this is evidence of their superior genetic quality. Critics point out that the same might apply to males who have been injured, but this 'handicap' would not be heritable and in fact individuals which get injured tend to be weaker to begin with.

Revisions of handicapping theory (Hamilton and Zuk, 1982)

Sexual displays are indicators of genetic resistance to disease. Only males who are disease free can fully develop secondary sexual characteristics. Møller (1990) studied barn swallows, a species troubled by the blood-sucking mite. He found that parents with longer tails had offspring with smaller mite loads even when they were reared in a foster nest (where the mites could not be passed on through contact).

Møller (1992) suggested that symmetry is a handicap because it requires a great deal of precision. Only good genes can produce a symmetrical body and this could explain why symmetricality is attractive.

Non-genetic benefits

Females may also select males on the basis of their non-genetic characteristics. For example, a male with a good nesting site or a male which can supply food during courtship bodes well for rearing offspring later.

Human females look for resources whereas males seek signs of fertility. Buss (1989) found that, in 37 cultures, males preferred younger females (good reproductive potential) and females preferred older males (more likely to have good resources). Davis (1990) found that when women place adverts for males they emphasise their physical beauty and seek a high-status, wealthy man. Men emphasise their wealth or other resources.

Mating strategies (monogamy versus polygamy)

Both sexual selection and parental investment are related to particular mating strategies. The choices are: one (mono) mate or many (poly) mates; 'gamy' refers to joining, 'gyny' refers to females and 'andry' is male.

Mating systems

Monogamy. A single male pairs with a single female, both take part in care of offspring and tend to be similar in size (because there is less competition). *Serial monogamy* describes bonding for prolonged periods but not for life.

Polygyny. A single male mates with several females, as in a harem. In *serial polygyny* one male stays with one female for a period but, over a breeding season, has other mates. Found in many songbirds, such as the pied flycatcher. In many cultures men are permitted to have more than one wife simultaneously. This has advantages for the male (increased reproduction) and may benefit the female where mates and/or resources are limited. Females can also share care of offspring.

Polyandry. One female mates with several males, and often develops bizarre characteristics. The male usually cares for the young, e.g. Tasmanian native hen.

Polygynandry or promiscuity (forms of polygamy). Both males and females mate with different members of the opposite sex. There is increased reproduction (for males) and sperm competition (for females). Human females may choose promiscuity because they can marry someone for resources but mate with someone with 'good genes'.

Mating strategies

It is more adaptive to have alternative strategies which are selected as a response to prevailing conditions. Davies and Lunberg (1984) found that dunnocks exhibited all four mating systems, each having different costs and benefits.

Side notes:

This explanation is also called the 'sexy sons' or 'good taste' hypothesis.

This explanation is also called the 'good genes' or 'good sense' hypothesis.

The fact that diseases continue to evolve means that this mechanism would be particularly advantageous.

A mating system describes a set of behaviours which maximise reproductive success.

When the male:female ratio is high, males are unlikely to succeed at polygyny because of intersexual rivalry.

Polyandry occurs rarely in human societies, though in Tibet a woman may marry two or more brothers. This is probably necessitated by the harsh living conditions where it takes at least two men to manage a farm. With two brothers, all parents share a genetic interest in all the children (Dickemann, 1985).

The fact that humans exhibit dimorphism is evidence of competition and polygyny but the differences are not as great as in some animals (such as peacocks) which suggests only a low degree of polygyny. Altogether this suggests that humans are serial monogamists/polygamists. Like all species, humans have a set of alternative strategies which are selected in relation to prevailing conditions. Grier and Burk (1992) report that studies across different cultures show humans tend towards polygyny.

> The high divorce rate may reflect humans' natural tendency to be serial polygamists.

> Trivers (1972) used the term 'parental investment' to describe the balance between effort (time and resources) and reproductive success. Mating reduces a parent's future reproductive potential, therefore it is important to offset this by increased success.

Sex differences in parental investment

Eggs and sperm

Parental investment begins with the gametes; female investment is greater. Either sex may use one of two strategies: r or K.

r strategy. Many eggs/sperm and devote little extra care, survival is ensured through numbers alone, or by having several mates and leaving the partner to care.

K strategy. Relatively few eggs (female) and mate with one partner. Devote more energy to ensuring survival.

Which sex cares?

Mode of fertilisation may be a way of explaining which sex becomes the carer.

Paternity certainty hypothesis (Ridley, 1978)

Males are more likely to care for young when fertilisation is external because the care increases the certainty that the offspring are his own. In the case of internal fertilisation the male can desert, knowing (or thinking) that the offspring are his.

> In mammals, offspring have a prolonged period of gestation inside the female and, after birth, the young depend on the female's milk. The male may stay and feed and protect the female.

> External fertilisation does not always result in male care, nor does internal fertilisation always lead to maternal care. For example, the female jacana lays a clutch of eggs for each male in her harem and then leaves them for the male to incubate and rear entirely on his own.

Order of gamete release hypothesis (Dawkins and Carlisle, 1976)

Both sexes prefer not to be left 'holding baby' because this decreases future reproductive potential. Internal fertilisation allows the male to get away first, with external fertilisation the female can leave first.

Association hypothesis (Williams, 1975)

The adult who is left in close proximity to the embryo tends to care for the young. Where external fertilisation takes place this is the male, with internal fertilisation this is the female.

Practice essay 5.7

Discuss the relationship between sexual selection and human reproductive behaviour.

(24 marks)

5.8 Evolutionary explanations of mental disorders

AQA A U4

General explanations for the evolution of mental disorders

Selective advantage

Apparently maladaptive genes may offer some benefit to the possessor and/or their offspring. Sickle cell anaemia is an example. If an individual possesses two recessive genes this leads to sickle-shaped cells in the blood which may cause brain damage and even death. If only one defective gene is present this promotes resistance to malaria and is adaptive, which explains why sickle cell anaemia is most common among African-Americans.

> If mental disorders are maladaptive and they have a genetic basis, then how do we explain why the genes for such disorders remain? One would expect that such genes would reduce reproductive potential and therefore disappear.

> Human stress responses, which were covered in the Revise AS Guide are an example of possible genome lag.

Genome lag

Most of our inherited behaviours stem from the time of the *environment of evolutionary adaptation* (EEA), between 35 000 and 3 million years ago. Some of these behaviours are not especially adaptive but have insufficient effect on reproductive potential to be eliminated through selective pressure.

It could be argued that the environment today is not sufficiently different from the EEA for this explanation to make sense.

Recessive genes

Selective pressure may not act on a recessive gene which is rarely expressed and therefore would not affect reproductive potential.

Specific theories of the evolution of mental disorders

Schizophrenia

Group splitting hypothesis (Stevens and Price, 1996)

Certain schizophrenic traits (e.g. bizarre beliefs, delusions) serve an adaptive function under certain conditions. When social groups become too big they are more at risk from predation and have more difficulty with food. A 'crazy' individual may act as a leader and enable one sub-group to split off from a main group.

Origin of language theory (Crow, 2000)

Schizophrenia is due to a disruption of language mechanisms (see page 136). This is supported by the fact that schizophrenics often believe they are hearing voices and/or may use strange language (e.g. word salads). Language is normally highly adaptive but it might be that sometimes the brain malfunctions, giving rise to abnormal linguistic functions. Schizophrenia is the price that humans pay for language.

Depression

Rank theory (Nesse and Williams, 1995)

Depression is an adaptive response to losing rank because it prevents further injury from re-engaging in combat. Conflicts are common in any social group and depression helps the individual to accept losing and accept an inferior role.

In time, depression became associated with other kinds of loss, such as loss of a loved one. 'Clinical depression' is seen as a pathological outcome of an adaptive emotional mechanism.

Genome lag (Nesse and Williams, 1995)

Depression may occur increasingly more because we are not adapted to live in urban situations. In addition, there are high commercial and achievement pressures in modern life which are stressful, leading to depression because of inability to cope with such aspects of modern life, things that we are not adapted for.

Manic depression

The manic phase of bipolar disorder has been related to creativity and charismatic leadership, and thus would be an adaptive trait. Many artists and famous leaders have been manic-depressives (e.g. Winston Churchill, Abraham Lincoln, Vincent Van Gogh).

Anxiety disorders

Phobias: preparedness (Seligman, 1970)

Individuals may be biologically predisposed to acquire certain conditioned responses more easily than others, e.g. a fear of snakes or heights. These fears would increase the individual's survival but may become a basis for phobias through conditioning (see page 141).

Bennett-Levy and Marteau (1984) found that fear was highly correlated with certain aspects of an animal's appearance – the more the animal's appearance was different to human form the more the animal was feared. This suggests some innate preparedness. Garcia and Koelling (1966) demonstrated that rats had a predisposition to learn quickly to avoid substances that made them feel sick, an adaptive fear.

Obsessive-compulsive disorder (OCD)

OCD patients develop compulsive rituals which relieve them from obsessive thoughts. Ritualistic behaviours often concern hygiene (e.g. repeated handwashing) and may be adaptive insofar as extra vigilance with cleanliness might promote survival.

Side notes:

Contrasting explanations of all three disorders are discussed on pp.136–141, including the symptoms and some possible causes of each disorder.

There is strong evidence that a predisposition for schizophrenia is inherited, and then life experiences trigger the condition (the *diathesis-stress* model).

There are two forms of depression: unipolar or major depression, and bipolar or manic-depression. There is stronger evidence of genetic factors in the latter.

Anxiety is an adaptive response in certain situations. It becomes maladaptive when disproportionate to any problem experienced.

Genome lag could explain why innate fears tend not to relate to modern dangers.

One should remember that evolutionary explanations for mental disorders are based on the assumption that such disorders are inherited, or at least a predisposition for the disorder is inherited.

Practice essay 5.8

Discuss **two or more** evolutionary explanations of human mental disorders.

(24 marks)

5.9 Evolution of intelligence

Evolutionary factors in the development of human intelligence

Intelligence is the ability to deal effectively and adaptively with the environment. An animal which can respond more effectively to environmental challenges will be more likely to survive and reproduce. What factors can explain why intelligence is adaptive and has evolved?

Foraging demands (Ecological theory)

> This has been called the 'ecological theory' because environmental (ecological) demands are related to the development of intelligence.

Intelligence may enhance survival and reproduction because it underlies the ability to be a good forager. Foraging (see page 113) and hunting require memory, planning and coordination. They also require tool use, which involves considerable intelligence. A good hunter is likely to have been popular as a mate, thus enhancing reproduction of such genes.

However, Humphrey (1976) noted that gorillas are fairly intelligent yet have few foraging demands. They eat leaves that grow in abundance.

Demands of group living (Social theory)

> *Theory of mind* is likely to be favoured by natural selection insofar as it promotes social relationships.

Animals live in groups because there are advantages (e.g. for foraging, reproduction, predation) but group living also presents problems (e.g. conflicts, interrelationships presumably between group members, cooperation). An individual who can solve social problems is more likely to survive and reproduce. One particular facet of sociality is the ability to understand the intentions of others (*theory of mind*) and the ability to cheat (*Machiavellian intelligence*) and detect cheats. Both are evidence of intelligence (see page 114).

Research evidence

Cosmides (1989) showed that participants, when doing the *Wason four card selection task*, find it easier to cope with a concrete example that involves social relations because our intelligence is adapted to cope with such problems. The abstract task consists of four cards, e.g. D, F, 3, 7. What cards do you need to turn over to prove the rule 'if a card has a D on one side then it has a 3 on the other'? The task is easier if the rule is 'If a person is drinking beer then he must be over 20 years old'. This shows that people are adept at solving social puzzles and looking for cheats. Deception is related to intelligence.

Dunbar (1993) found no relationship between the size of the *neocortex* (involved in higher order thinking) and environmental complexity in a range of different primates, but did find a strong correlation between size of neocortex and group size (an indicator of the complexity of social relationships). This supports social theory.

Sexual selection theory

> A more intelligent male is more likely to be chosen by a female and therefore has increased reproduction.

Intelligence may be sexually selected. Females prefer intelligent men as mates because they are, e.g., better hunters. Such sexually selected traits become more and more exaggerated (see e.g. the runaway process, page 122). There would therefore be selective pressure on males to be more intelligent. There would also be selective pressure on females in order to appreciate the writing, jokes, etc., produced by men.

Research evidence

> Such research is rational rather than empirical.

Miller (1992) argues that this would explain why people rate intelligence so highly as a trait for a prospective partner, despite the fact that it is not indicative of reproductive success. The explanation is further supported by the fact that men have larger brains, proportionately. It also explains the rapid change in brain size in both males and females (trebling in the last 3 million years) can be best explained in terms of sexual selection because brain size directly affects reproductive success. The question of whether brain size is related to intelligence is considered on the next page.

Miller (1998) points out that this theory can explain why men have historically been more creative in the arts because this allows them to demonstrate their intelligence.

Brain size and intelligence

Is brain size related to intelligence?

Larger animals have bigger brains because of the problems of coordinating their bodies. Therefore brain:body ratio is important.

Bigger brains have disadvantages. They require more energy and make birth more difficult. Therefore it is likely that there is some adaptive advantage to a proportionately bigger brain.

Research studies

Comparative studies. Rumbaugh *et al.* (1996) found that primates with proportionately larger brains were better able to cope on a task requiring intelligence (they were trained on two tasks, if one set of learning facilitated the second task then this was taken as evidence of intelligence). However, poorer performance may be because an animal is asked to perform a task which comes less naturally to it (consider instinctive drift, page 112) rather than because it is less intelligent.

Relative brain size may not be related to intelligence. The spiny anteater has a larger neocortex comparatively than a human, yet not a greater intelligence.

Human studies. Early studies found no correlation between brain size and intelligence but that may be because they couldn't measure brain size accurately (they used skull size). Willerman *et al.* (1991) used brain scans and correlated IQ scores of college students with brain size, finding a positive correlation of 0.51 between IQ and brain:body ratio. A further study by Andreasen *et al.* (1993) used a more representative sample (advertising through a newspaper) and found a lower but significant correlation.

> Any study that looks at IQ has the potential for being socially sensitive research.

Is organisation more important than size?

Albert Einstein's brain, when examined at post-mortem, showed no size advantage but there were some differences in terms of organisation such as more tightly packed neurons in his prefrontal cortex. Holloway (1979) claims internal structural complexity is more important in the evolution of intelligence.

Sex differences. Men, on average, have larger brains than women but do not have higher IQs. This is not because men are larger, because smaller people do well on IQ tests. This suggests that size is not a key factor in intelligence.

Johnson *et al.* (1996) found that women's brains are better organised, e.g. they have a larger corpus callosum (see page 40) which enables faster interhemispheric communication. So female brains may be smaller but more efficient.

Organisational changes

> Human brains are more highly organised than the brains of other animals. But it's impossible to know whether such brain organisation is a cause or an effect of intelligence.

There is also clear evidence that, in the course of the evolution of the human brain, its organisation has changed and this is likely to be related to increased intelligence. The organisation has changed in terms of the development of gross structures (such as language centres) and also in terms of fine structure, because the interconnections of neurons have changed dramatically.

Is brain size inherited?

Is intelligence inherited? If brain size and intelligence are related then both must be affected by similar factors. The size and organisation of the human brain is partly genetic because the human brain differs consistently from that of other animals. Brain size is also partly due to environment, e.g. Lucas *et al.* (1992) found that babies who are breastfed have higher IQs probably because breastmilk contains fatty substances that are important to brain growth.

Self-feeding co-evolution (Dawkins, 1998)

Mental abilities and brain growth have co-evolved. As the demand for greater intelligence (software) increases, the organisation and size of the brain (hardware) co-evolves to cope with the new demands.

Practice essay 5.9

Discuss evolutionary factors in the development of human intelligence.   (24 marks)

Sample question and model answer

Discuss research studies of non-human animal language. (24 marks)

Examiner's comments

Most examination questions are taken directly from the specification, as is this one, and are thus highly predictable. Take care, however, to avoid producing a prepared answer which may not be entirely appropriate. It is likely to be apparent to the examiner that this is what you have done and you may lose marks for not answering the exact question set.

'Discuss' is an AO1 and AO2 term (see page 10) and requires you to both describe research studies and to evaluate them, i.e. consider their value or usefulness in terms of any criteria you wish. Note that it is 'research studies' and not simply 'research' that is required. It would be legitimate to use studies of natural language and/or studies of attempts to teach human language to non-human language.

Candidate's answer

There has been considerable interest in the question of non-human animals and their ability to use language. First of all, what is language and can animals be taught language? How is their language different?

Hockett (1950s) identified 16 features of language including such things as traditional transmission, which is an ability to pass language from generation to generation, rapid fading (once we've spoken it doesn't last for long) and we string single units together to form meaningful sentences. But do these features relate to only human language or do animals also possess these abilities?

The largest area of research in this field is with apes, concentrating on whether they can use human language. As their vocal chords are not the same as ours they can't produce words as such and so research has centred on teaching them to use American sign language. Gardner and Gardner (1960s) taught a chimpanzee Washoe to use American sign language by moulding her hands into the shapes of words and rewarding the correct use of signs. By 5 years old Washoe could produce 133 signs and in independent tests was able to produce 72% accuracy. The Gardners also claimed that Washoe had the ability to string together signs to form meaningful sentences, for example when a doll was placed in a cup Washoe reportedly signed 'Baby in my cup.' However, a film clip showed Mr Gardner signing the same sentence to Washoe just seconds before.

Patterson (1970s) trained a gorilla Koko and got similar results, this time taking the use of language further because she could talk about an incident which occurred days earlier when Koko had bitten Patterson. When asked why, Koko signed 'Sorry, bite scratch, wrong.' These findings lead back to the work by the Gardners supporting the ability of these apes to produce language.

Terrace et al., however, did not have such success with their chimp Nim. It was discovered that a child of Nim's age possessed a much greater ability at signing. Terrace also reported that Nim could not string together more than two words at any time. These findings are quite contrary to the Gardners and Patterson.

Roger Fouts (1970s) claimed that Terrace's failing to find better results had nothing to do with Nim's ability but was rather the fault of inexperienced trainers and a lack of a stimulating environment for Nim. Even so, Terrace's findings led to an investigation of the Gardner's film footage which brought about the finding about the 'baby in my cup' sentence.

The American sign language research has also been criticised as it is argued that chimps don't show an understanding of the words, only the ability to cope with shapes and forms. This has led to the introduction of the lexigraph in recent studies. This piece of equipment requires the animals to show an understanding of the words before using them. Savage-Rumbaugh (1988) had a great deal of success with Kanzi (an ape). Using the lexigraph Kanzi was able to

Sample question and model answer (continued)

have conversations over the phone about past experiences, and show a depth of knowledge required to produce multiple word sentences. However, this has not been replicated in other studies and is still a relatively new method.

The biggest criticism for this research is the question, do we have the right to judge non-human animals, namely apes, on their ability to produce human language when they are clearly not designed to use it? For example, cognitive behaviour in chimps does not meet standards needed to produce spontaneous actions. Wouldn't it be better to concentrate on trying to understand the language/communication used by other species such as dolphins, so that human understanding can develop through a mutual bond with other species rather than teaching language to animals which are clearly not adapted to its depth and complications?

Honey bees for example have shown features of Hockett's 16 features in their own communication patterns. Worker and scout bees possess the ability to show the rest of the hive where they have found nectar and the waggle dance demonstrates direction and proximity. These dances show 5 of Hockett's design features and are a clear example of how, if we stopped concentrating on teaching our language to other species, we can learn from others.

In conclusion it would seem that animals do possess the ability to use human language and that it is not a species – specific characteristic.

[733 words]

Examiner's comments

This feels like a prepared answer because the candidate starts with Hockett's 'theory'. Such material may have been appropriate had the question been 'Discuss <u>research</u> into animal language' (and a theory is a form of research), but here the focus is on research studies. Hockett's criteria might have been used as a means of evaluating the research but this hasn't been done.

Nevertheless, most of the answer is relevant. The descriptions of studies are well detailed, and a fair number covered and reasonable detail provided for each.

The commentary is also good. Note how each paragraph ends with some reference to what the research showed, and some paragraphs begin with commentary. This is what examiners are looking for as evidence of AO2. There is also a paragraph near the end evaluating the general usefulness and ethics of such research studies. More consideration might have been made of the methodology.

AO1
Accurate and reasonably detailed, coherent but perhaps slightly limited – not substantial evidence of depth and breadth. Band 3 (bottom) = 10 marks.

AO2
Commentary is effective, and appropriately selected. It is coherently elaborated. Approaching the top of band 3, therefore 10 marks.

Total 20 out of 24 marks (see page 12 for band descriptors), equivalent to a Grade A.

Chapter 6

Individual differences

This approach focuses on the way that people differ. Traditionally, this has involved the study of personality and intelligence. However, there are many other ways that individuals differ: such as in terms of hair colour, skin colour, willingness to conform, gender and mental health. It is mental health and disorder that is the focus of this chapter.

At AS Level your study of individual differences may have focused on definitions and models of abnormality, and how such explanations might be applied to understanding eating disorders.

At A2 you may select to study one or more of the following areas in individual differences:

Issues in the classification and diagnosis of psychological abnormality

> 6.1 Classificatory systems
> 6.2 Multiple personality disorder (dissociative identity disorder)
> 6.3 Culture-bound syndromes

After studying this area you should be able to:

- describe and evaluate the current versions of ICD and DSM as examples of classificatory systems
- critically consider research into the reliability and validity of classification and diagnosis
- describe and assess case studies of multiple personality disorder (dissociative identity disorder)
- discuss the extent to which multiple personality

disorder is a spontaneous or iatrogenic phenomenon
- describe and assess case studies of syndromes apparently bound by culture
- critically assess arguments for and against the existence of culture-bound syndromes

Psychopathology

> 6.4 Schizophrenia
> 6.5 Depression
> 6.6 Anxiety disorders

After studying this area you should be able to:

- discuss three mental disorders: schizophrenia, depression and phobic disorders (as an example of an anxiety disorder)
- in each case be able to describe the clinical characteristics of the disorder

- in each case be able to assess biological and psychological explanations critically
- discuss the evidence on which the explanations are based

Treating mental disorders

> 6.7 Biological (somatic) therapies
> 6.8 Behavioural therapies
> 6.9 Alternatives to biological and behavioural therapies

After studying this area you should be able to:

- describe the use and mode of action of biological (somatic) therapies, including chemotherapy, ECT and psychosurgery
- critically consider issues surrounding the use of biological therapies
- describe the use and mode of action of behavioural therapies, including those based on both classical conditioning (behaviour therapies such as aversion therapy and systematic desensitisation) and operant conditioning (behaviour modification such as token

economy and modelling)
- critically consider issues surrounding the use of behavioural therapies
- describe the use and mode of action of an alternative therapy, such as psychoanalysis
- critically consider issues surrounding the use of psychoanalysis
- discuss issues about evaluating and comparing the effectiveness of therapies

Issues in the classification and diagnosis of psychological abnormality

6.1 Classificatory systems

AQA A   U5

AQA B   U4

EDEXCEL   U4

A classification system is a set of diagnostic criteria that allows a diagnosis to be made. There are classification schemes for both physical and mental disorders (as well as for other things).

Jointly all five axes provide a description of the patient and their condition.

Reliability is determined by looking at the extent to which different psychiatrists agree on a diagnosis using the classification scheme (*inter-judge reliability*).

Validity concerns the extent to which a diagnosis represents something real.

Other countries have produced their own classification schemes, for example there is a Chinese Classification of Mental Disorders (CCMD).

In this part of AQA specification A synopticity is assessed. Synopticity can be shown in the different ways that you draw comparisons and make links across the specification.

Diagnosis is the identification of a disease by its symptoms, using a scheme of classification.

Classificatory systems

Diagnosis involves: (1) identifying symptoms in a patient, (2) recognising that certain symptoms tend to co-occur and can be identified as *syndromes* (by a classification scheme), (3) prescribing an appropriate treatment.

Diagnostic and Statistical Manual (DSM)

DSM-IV (1994) is produced by the American Psychological Association and used in the US. DSM-IV is a *multi-axial system*; the patient is evaluated on five different axes:

Axis 1: clinical disorder diagnosed, e.g. eating disorders, schizophrenia, depression, phobias, dissociative disorders.

Axis 2: personality disorders and mental retardation. A patient may have long-term patterns of impaired functioning, e.g. anti-social personality disorder.

Axis 3: general medical conditions, e.g. diabetes or Alzheimer's, that might explain mentally disordered behaviour.

Axis 4: psychosocial and environmental problems: any significant stressful events in last 12 months is taken into consideration.

Axis 5: global assessment of functioning (GAF) on a 100-point scale.

Evaluation

- *Reliability* is reasonably high (e.g. +0.81 for schizophrenia, +0.63 for anxiety disorders).
- *Validity*. If a diagnosis results in a successful treatment then the diagnosis must have been valid, which can be claimed (see page 142) for example with somatic treatments.
- *Comorbidity*. Validity is also related to the ability to distinguish between discrete disorders. This is poor, e.g. many patients with an anxiety disorder are also diagnosed with one or more other anxiety disorders (Eysenck, 1997).

Internal Classification of Diseases and Health Related Problems (ICD)

ICD-10 (1993) is produced by the World Health Organisation and used in Europe. It is primarily designed for research and data collection, not for clinical diagnosis. ICD-10 lists 11 major categories of mental disorder: organic (e.g. Alzheimer's), schizophrenia, psychoactive substance use, mood (affective) disorders, neurotic disorders (e.g. phobias), behavioural and emotional disorders of childhood and adolescence (e.g. ADHD), disorders of psychological development (e.g. autism), mental retardation, disorders of adult personality (e.g. gender disorders, gambling), behavioural syndromes (e.g. eating and sleep disorders), unspecified mental disorder.

Comparisons between DSM and ICD

- DSM is a diagnostic tool whereas ICD is designed for statistical data collection.
- Recent revisions have aimed to be more similar.
- DSM-IV is probably more reliable than ICD-10 because of greater symptom specificity. DSM-IV has 16 categories whereas ICD-10 has 11.
- Both are related to the *medical model* of abnormality (covered as part of AS studies). There are classification systems for other models, e.g. Goldfried and Davison (1976) devised a system related to behaviour (for behavioural therapies).

Limitations of classification and diagnosis

Usefulness

The main intention of classification and diagnosis is to identify a suitable form of treatment. Classification schemes also enable research into disorders to be conducted, and are useful in assessing any later improvement or deterioration.

It is important to remember that even diagnosis of physical illness is not 100% reliable. However, physical illnesses have a, usually known, physical cause and therefore diagnoses of physical illnesses have the *potential* for greater reliability and validity.

You can demonstrate synopticity by noting the various different research methods used in this study.

The lack of agreement between psychiatrists demonstrates low reliability.

Reliability

Early forms of DSM/ICD were less reliable. For example, Beck *et al.* (1962) found that the agreement amongst diagnosticians was at about the level of chance. Current forms are more reliable (see above).

Validity

Heather (1976) claimed that the same diagnosis had a 50:50 chance of leading to the same or a different treatment, which suggests that diagnoses lack validity.

Zigler and Phillips (1961) found that the symptom of depression was just as likely to be found in someone diagnosed as manic-depressive as in someone labelled 'neurotic', and in 25% of those termed schizophrenic. This suggests that a diagnosis may convey little information about a patient.

Low validity was demonstrated by Rosenhan (1973). He arranged for eight 'normal' people to be examined by psychiatrists. The 'pseudopatients' behaved normally except for reporting that they heard a voice. All except one was admitted as schizophrenic, and later released (up to 52 days later) as schizophrenics in remission. It would seem that the context mattered more than the symptoms. Though it might be a case of a *type II error* – psychiatrists preferred to call a healthy person sick rather than a sick person healthy.

What would happen if the hospital knew some patients were pseudopatients? Rosenhan arranged for hospitals to expect one or more pseudopatients over a period of three months. In that time 193 patients were admitted and all staff were asked to rate the likelihood of whether they were 'real'. In fact all patients were genuine but more than 20% were judged as pseudopatients by one member of staff and 10% were judged so by two members of staff (a *type I error*).

Ethical considerations

Labelling

Labels related to mental illness are global (a person becomes a schizophrenic rather than an individual with schizophrenia) and 'sticky' (hard to remove). Rosenhan (1973) showed how people behave differently towards the mentally ill. Pseudopatients received curt or no response to their requests to medical staff.

Culture bias

Western classification systems are culturally biased. The symptoms of a disorder are often culture specific (see page 135) and therefore members of other cultural groups may be identified as ill when they exhibit behaviours normal within their own culture (e.g. hearing voices). Cochrane (1977) found that more people in the UK of African-Caribbean origins were diagnosed as schizophrenic than Whites (possibly seven times as many). Diagnosis rates for African-Caribbeans are not as high elsewhere in the world. It may be because members of minority ethnic groups in Britain have more stressful lives.

Culture bias applies to *social class*. It is possible that lower-class people receive less favourable diagnoses and treatment because of professional biases. Johnstone (1989) found that lower-class patients were more likely to spend longer in hospital, be prescribed physical rather than psychological treatments, and had a poorer prognosis.

Gender bias is a further problem. Histrionic personality is more often diagnosed in females whereas obsessive-compulsive disorder is more common in males. Ford and Widiger (1989) gave psychiatrists written case studies. Histrionic personality disorder was correctly diagnosed 80% of the time when the patient was said to be female, and 30% of the time when male.

Conclusion

The fact that diagnoses can be unreliable and inaccurate (invalid) suggests they should not be used. However, the same is at least partly true of medical diagnosis generally, yet we wouldn't suggest abandoning that. There are alternatives, e.g. using a more *idiographic* approach which doesn't require classification (which is *nomothetic*).

Practice essay 6.1

Discuss research (theories **and/or** studies) into the reliability and validity of classificatory systems.

(30 marks)

6.2 Multiple personality disorder (dissociative identity disorder)

Multiple personality disorder (MPD)

DSM-IV identifies the following clinical characteristics of MPD:

- two or more distinct identities, each relatively enduring
- each identity recurrently takes control of the person's behaviour
- inability to recall important personal information
- no other explanation, e.g. drug abuse or epilepsy.

Case studies of multiple personality disorder (MPD)

The three faces of Eve (Thigpen and Cleckley, 1954)

'Eve White' sought medical help for severe headaches and blackouts. Since there appeared to be no physical cause she was referred to a psychiatrist. A few months into treatment, a new mischievous identity, 'Eve Black', emerged. Eve Black was aware of all that Eve White did but the same was not true in reverse. Eve Black was scornful of Eve White's life, and her husband and child.

Psychological tests

There were minor differences in IQ. Eve White had an IQ score of 110 and a high memory function. Eve Black scored 104 with a lower memory function. Eve White was found to have a hysterical tendency and to be emotionally repressed. Eve White was the more dominant personality and the only one who could be hypnotised.

History

When Eve White's twin sisters were born she felt rejected by her parents; however, she loved them dearly whereas Eve Black hated them. Eve Black embodied all the angry feelings enabling Eve White to be a nice, loving, daughter.

Eve White's husband reported strange, inexplicable, episodes confirming Eve Black's presence earlier on.

During therapy things improved for Eve White for a while but then the blackouts returned. During one therapy session a third persona appeared, Jane, who was more mature and bold than Eve White. 'Evelyn' appeared at another crisis in Eve's life. Altogether there may have been 22 personalities.

Sybil

Sybil was a troubled young adult who sought help from the psychiatrist Dr Cornelia Wilbur in 1954. During treatment more than a dozen distinct personalities emerged, including two males ('Mike' and 'Sid'), and a baby ('Ruthie'). During childhood, Sybil had been abused by her mother.

Suspicions

Rieber (1999) analysed tapes of Wilbur's conversations with Sybil and concluded that Wilbur did not allow the separate identities to emerge spontaneously but encouraged their creation (probably unknowingly). Patients in a hypnotic state are highly suggestible and it may be that this is especially true of MPD sufferers.

Spiegel (1997) reported that, when he stood in for Wilbur, Sybil asked him if he wanted her to become one of her personalities. When he left it to her, she said she would prefer not.

Ken Bianchi

Ken Bianchi was arrested in 1978 for the rape and murder of 12 women. He claimed he was elsewhere when the murders were committed but when this alibi failed, he claimed that he invented it to explain a time gap in his memory. When hypnotised, an '*alter*' (Steve) appeared. Bianchi entered a plea of not guilty by reason of insanity, due to MPD.

Experts decide

Experts had to decide whether this claim was valid. Bianchi was identified as a fake because Steve's personality tended to change, i.e. was not stable, whereas alters usually have very clear personalities; a third personality (Billy) emerged after Bianchi was told

---

The terms MPD (multiple personality disorder) and DID are interchangeable. DSM-IV uses the term dissociative identity disorder, to signal commonalities with the other dissociative disorders such as amnesia.

Synopticity can be demonstrated through presentation of a variety of different case studies, a consideration of different methodologies within the case studies, and links to other parts of the specification (for example, consideration of split-brain studies, p. 43, and/or schizophrenia, p. 136).

It may have been that Eve was merely acting; however, Thigpen and Cleckley argued that the fact that the therapy took place over such a prolonged period makes this doubtful.

The real Eve, Mrs Chris Sizemore, wrote about her experiences and reported that eventually she learned to assimilate all her separate selves.

Think of the definitions of abnormality covered in the *Revise AS Guide*. In what way do you think that MPD is abnormal?

The term '*alter*' is used to refer to alternative identities.

Some people may act as if they are hypnotised ('*simulators*'). One way to detect this is to ask the person to imagine there is a chair in the middle of the room. A truly hypnotised person actually walks round the chair whereas a simulator bumps into it.

that MPD usually involves many identities; no friends or family could give examples of any lapses of memory evidence; and when hypnotised Bianchi's behaviour was like a '*simulator*'. It was decided that Bianchi wasn't an MPD sufferer, and it transpired that he had committed most of the crimes with his cousin, Angelo Buono.

Jonah (Ludwig *et al.*, 1972)

Jonah, aged 27, was admitted to hospital because of severe headaches and blackouts. It was observed that, at these times, he underwent personality changes. Four distinct identities were found, each with a special role and each having emerged in response to certain events.

Jonah was the central personality.

Sammy was the rational and responsible one. He first appeared when Jonah was 6 when his parents were fighting. Sammy was aware of all the identities.

King Young emerged soon afterwards as a response to Jonah's mother dressing him in girls' clothes. King Young was the ladies' man.

Usoffa Abdulla was the warrior and protector, who emerged at age 10 when Jonah was attacked by a gang of boys. He was only aware of Jonah.

Ludwig *et al.* (1972) found that each personality had distinct brain waves.

'Iatrogenic' means a disorder produced unwittingly by a therapist due to prior expectations.

Spontaneous or iatrogenic?

Research evidence supporting the 'spontaneous' view

There are cases where MPD hasn't been diagnosed when it should have been. Salley (1988) described a man who had experienced blackouts from age 6 and exhibited personality changes. He had been variously diagnosed as having an organic brain condition, schizoid personality, undifferentiated schizophrenia and seizure disorder. He was finally diagnosed with MPD at age 37.

There are valid explanations for the condition, e.g. a series of traumatic events in early childhood combined with the inability to escape lead to MPD, especially where an individual is capable of self-hypnosis leading to dissociative amnesia. In support, Putnam *et al.* (1986) reported that 97% of MPD patients have experienced child abuse.

The *neo-dissociation theory* of hypnosis (Hilgard, 1986) suggests that hypnosis is an altered state where consciousness is split into several streams somewhat independent of each other. This fits with evidence from MPD.

A second explanation relates to the *situational theory* of personality (see Michel, 1968, page 93) and context-dependent learning. MPD sufferers may learn that certain behaviours are appropriate in certain situations.

Coons (1989) reports that most MPD patients have never been hypnotised, suggesting that the effects of hypnosis can't be used to explain all MPD cases.

Research evidence supporting the 'iatrogenic' view

Clearly some cases of MPD are iatrogenic or even fake, but this doesn't mean that some cases are not spontaneous.

Modestin (1992) found very few cases of MPD in Switzerland but half were accounted for by three psychiatrists. This suggests that some psychiatrists may convey certain expectations to the patients through suggestion and social reinforcement, and this leads to higher rates of MPD.

Eve appears to have been a genuine and spontaneous case whereas Sybil's MPD may have been unwittingly manufactured by the therapist (*iatrogenic*) through selective attention and a form of experimenter bias.

Spanos *et al.* (1985) tested the effects of suggestion. Students were asked to pretend they were an accused murderer. Group A (full suggestion) were hypnotised and the suggestion made that another 'part' might want to communicate with the therapist. Group B (part suggestion) were hypnotised and told that hypnosis can access hidden thoughts. Group C (no suggestion) were simply hypnotised. More than 80% of the participants in group A and 30% in group B presented another personality. This indicates that personalities may emerge in response to suggestion, though this may only pertain to role-play.

MPD may be partly or completely a *social construction*. It may be that the underlying condition is real but the symptoms are culture-bound (see page 134), and created by the widespread media coverage.

Practice essay 6.2

Discuss whether multiple personality disorder is a spontaneous condition. (30 marks)

6.3 Culture-bound syndromes

AQA A ▷ U5
EDEXCEL ▷ U4

A *culture-bound syndrome* is a recurrent, locality-specific pattern of aberrant behaviour that may or may not be linked to a particular DSM-IV diagnostic category.

A syndrome is culture-bound if the symptoms are primary as opposed to being 'grafted on' to an underlying primary mental disorder, such as anxiety or depression.

There are a large number of potential CBSs. Humphreys (1999) has identified at least 36 including zar, brain fag, pibloktoq and witiko.

In 'quasi-amok' the individual only engages in minor attacks with non-serious consequences.

One suggestion is that sleep paralysis may underlie alien abduction experiences, where individuals very often report paralysis, out-of-body experiences and fear of alien abduction.

Case studies of culture-bound syndromes (CBSs)

Koro (genital retraction syndrome)

Found in south and east Asia. Symptoms include extreme anxiety linked to a fear that one's penis or labia will recede into the body, and possibly cause death.

Rare cases have been recorded outside Asia. Bernstein and Gaw (1990) described the case of a Cantonese man living in the US, and Tobin (1996) observed a case of koro in an Irish man. He had recently become impotent and believed that his genitalia were shrinking and that further shrinkage was going to kill him. The man had a family history psychotic and affective illness, and had recently experienced stress.

Culture-bound?

Devan and Hong (1987) suggest one can distinguish between *true koro* and a *koro-like state*, where symptoms of koro are associated with another mental disorder (as in the above cases). The former is relatively easy to treat with reassurance, which is not true of the latter. This suggests that true koro is a cultural-bound disorder. However, this can't explain a koro epidemic in India (Dutta, 1983) where media reports of a disease resulted in numerous cases of koro. Treatment was easy and the illness quickly subsided with no suggestion of underlying mental disorder.

Amok

A form of mental disorder found in south-east Asia where the individual behaves in a wild and aggressive manner for a limited period of time. It begins with a period of dismal brooding, and ends with an outburst of aggression against random victims, and possibly the attacker's death.

It is argued that Malay culture 'creates' such behaviour because outbursts are strongly sanctioned. Thus individuals occasionally engage in outbursts when they can no longer control their emotions, leading to amok.

Culture-bound?

Carr and Tan (1976) reported very little evidence of mental disorder either before or after an attack of amok, whereas Schmidt *et al.* (1977) claimed that all the cases they studied did show signs of an underlying primary mental disorder, such as schizophrenia.

Cases of amok have been recorded in other cultures, for example Michael Ryan's murderous attack on the town of Hungerford in 1987. He had no history of mental disorder and shot himself. The same can be said of recent murders in US schools, such as Columbine High. In a different case Charles Whitman gunned down 16 people from a tower on the Texas university campus in 1966, and was later found to have a brain tumour, suggesting that organic causes should not be excluded.

Dhat

A sex neurosis of Indian males, where physical and mental exhaustion is blamed on the presence of semen in the urine. The origins of this may lie in the Hindu belief that semen is produced in the blood, and that the loss of semen will result in mental and physical illness.

Culture-bound?

Chadda and Ahuja (1990) examined a number of patients with dhat and concluded that they were either suffering from neurotic depression or anxiety neurosis, i.e. an underlying primary mental disorder.

Qi-gong psychotic reaction

An acute, time-limited episode characterised by dissociative, paranoid or other psychotic or non-psychotic symptoms. The Chinese include this in their classification scheme. It may have its roots in qi-gong, a form of martial art and exercise regime. Westerners have described this as 'sleep paralysis' because of some of the symptoms.

Culture-bound?

Lim and Lin (1996) documented the case of a Chinese-American man who had engaged in qi-gong for problems with kidney stones. He began hearing voices telling him how to practise qi-gong, and believed that he had contacted beings from another dimension. A psychiatrist diagnosed schizophrenia.

Anorexia nervosa

Eating disorders primarily occur in Western cultures. It may well be that the predisposition towards a mental disorder exists in certain individuals and the form of this disorder is affected by culturally familiar behaviours.

Culture-bound?

Holland *et al.* (1988) found that in some cases where one twin suffered from anorexia, the other twin had either anorexia, bulimia or another form of mental illness, suggesting that eating disorders are symptoms of an underlying primary illness.

Lee *et al.* (1992) found that the incidence of bulimia was increasing in Hong Kong, possibly because exposure to Western media is growing, teaching indigenous people new ways of expressing underlying illnesses.

Do culture-bound syndromes exist?

Absolute

> Synopticity can be shown in the different ways that you draw comparisons and make links across the specification.

This is the view that mental disorders are the same in all cultures. However, this is unlikely, even those which are specific to organic states vary in expression and can be linked to cultural expectations. For example, in the 1920s schizophrenics complained of mind invasions by radio waves, in the 1950s this was TV signals and, in cultures where witchcraft persists, the invasion is by spirits.

Universal

There are identifiable categories of mental illness that are found world-wide, though symptoms are *expressed* differently in different cultures. Yap (1969) claims that latah (from Malaya) and susto (from Peru) are both brought on by a sudden or frightening stimulus, and are simply different cultural expressions of a 'primary fear reaction', a condition recognised by Western classification schemes.

> This challenges the universal nature of Western classification schemes.

Culturally relative symptoms

Mental symptoms are unique to certain cultures. The symptoms presented in DSM/ICD are relative to our own culture, and are as biased as those for dhat and amok.

Culture-bound conditions

Mental disorders are unique to certain cultures and can only be understood within the values of that culture, possibly 'true' koro is an example of this.

> This can explain why some ethnic groups are overdiagnosed with certain conditions, because their symptoms have been misinterpreted. For example, Cochrane (1977) found that more people of African-Caribbean origins were diagnosed as schizophrenic than Whites.

Practical importance

Culture-specific interpretations of behaviour

It is important to interpret behaviours in their cultural context in order to understand them. Symptoms, such as hearing voices, may or may not be representative of mental disorder. This means that no classification scheme can be applied universally because the symptoms given are culturally relative.

Culture-specific interventions

Different cultures use different methods of treatment (e.g. folk medicines) which may be equally valid or even superior to Western treatments. However, such treatments are excluded if one relies on Western classification systems.

> *Ethnocentricsm* is the tendency to view one's own culture as superior or central.

Ethnocentricsm

Fernando (1991) argues that the idea of CBSs suggests that Western syndromes (as identified within DSM/ICD) are the standard, and syndromes from other cultures are anomalies.

Practice essay 6.3

Discuss arguments **for** the existence of culture-bound syndromes.　　　　(30 marks)

Psychopathology

6.4 Schizophrenia

Psychopathology is the study of the nature and development of mental disorders.

Synopticity is assessed in this section of the specification. Ensure that you can present material that represents the links across the specification, as well as different approaches, perspectives and methodologies.

Schizophrenia means literally 'split-mind' but is wrongly confused with multiple personality disorder. Schizophrenia refers to a group of psychoses which are not enduring disorders of the whole personality.

Description of schizophrenia

Clinical characteristics

Thought disturbance (*positive* symptoms) such as thought insertion (e.g. thoughts controlled by aliens), hallucinations (e.g. hearing voices) and delusions (e.g. of grandeur).

Disturbances of affect/volition (*negative* symptoms) such as withdrawal, flattened and inappropriate affect, reduced motivation and difficulty planning and carrying out actions.

Psychomotor disturbances such as catatonia (immobility, bizarre statues), stereotypy (e.g. rocking) and frenetic activity (e.g. strange grimaces).

Language impairments are also characteristic. Patients may repeat sounds (echolalia) or use invented words (neologisms).

Diagnosis

Two or more of the above symptoms present for more than six months, along with reduced social functioning.

Categories

A distinction has been made between type I (positive/acute/functional cause) and type II (negative/chronic/organic cause) schizophrenia. DSM-IV identifies three main subtypes:

Paranoid type – positive symptoms. Awareness and language are relatively unimpaired.

Disorganised type – the most severe form, disorganised speech and behaviour, vivid hallucinations, flat emotion and inappropriate affect, onset in early adulthood.

Catatonic type – apathy and psychomotor disturbances.

Prognosis

Approximately one-third of cases have only a few acute episodes followed by full recovery. Another third have periodic acute episodes throughout life but lead a relatively normal life during remission. The final third (disorganised type) shows persistent deterioration which may be partly alleviated by drug therapy.

Biological explanations of schizophrenia

A predisposition for schizophrenia may be inherited.

The abbreviation MZ stands for monozygotic (identical) and DZ for dizygotic (non-identical or fraternal).

Evolutionary explanations of schizophrenia are discussed on p. 124; such explanations are biological.

Synopticity can be demonstrated through the use of different kinds of research evidence, and also a range of different ways of evaluating the research.

Genetic

Research evidence

Twin studies. Gottesman (1991) summarised about 40 studies, concluding that the concordance rate is about 48% for MZ twins but only 17% for DZ twins, indicating some environmental influence but a larger genetic component.

Finnish adoption study. Tienari (1991) followed 155 adopted children whose natural mothers were schizophrenic. In adulthood 10.3% had developed schizophrenia compared with only 1.1% of those without schizophrenic mothers.

Family studies. Kendler *et al.* (1985) found that first-degree relatives of schizophrenics are 18 times more likely to be similarly diagnosed.

Copenhagen high-risk study. Parnas *et al.* (1993) followed 207 children (aged 10–18 at the start) with schizophrenic mothers. At a 27-year follow-up 16% had been diagnosed as schizophrenic compared with 2% in a low-risk group.

Gene mapping. Sherrington *et al.* (1988) found evidence for a cluster of genes on chromosome 5, which might make an individual susceptible. Subsequent studies have not confirmed this.

Evaluation

- High concordance rates in MZ twins may be because they are *treated more similarly* (Loehlin and Nichols, 1976).
- Family similarities can also be explained by *shared environmental influences*.

• Genetic factors are involved but are *not solely responsible.* Less than 50% of children where one parent was schizophrenic develop the disorder (Fish *et al.,* 1992). The *diathesis-stress model* can be used to explain this.

Neurological

Research evidence

Neuroanatomical evidence. Post-mortems show schizophrenic's brains are 6% lighter and have fewer neurons in the cortex. PET and CAT scans show that schizophrenics have larger ventricles in their brains and a smaller than normal frontal cortex.

Neurochemical evidence (*dopamine hypothesis*). Drugs used to alleviate schizophrenic symptoms (neuroleptics) block dopamine synapses. Post-mortem examinations of schizophrenics show abnormally high levels of dopamine.

Evaluation

• Neurological differences may be *cause or effect.*
• Neurological differences may be genetic or could arise from birth complications, i.e. *nurture rather than nature.* Harrison (1995) found that at least some schizophrenics may have experienced brain damage from anoxia at birth.
• Neuroleptic drugs block dopamine fairly rapidly, yet they are *slow to reduce* the symptoms of schizophrenia.
• A new drug, clozapine, is more effective in reducing schizophrenic symptoms but *blocks dopamine activity less.*

Psychological explanations of schizophrenia

Social and family relationships

Schizophrenogenic families. Fromm-Reichman (1948) proposed that some families have high emotional tension; the mothers are cold, the fathers are ineffectual.

Double-bind theory. Bateson *et al.* (1956) proposed that schizophrenia is a learned response to mutually exclusive demands being made on a child. Laing (1959) also regarded schizophrenia as a sane response to a disordered environment.

Social causation hypothesis. Members of lower social classes have more stressful lives, and this makes them more vulnerable to schizophrenia. However, it may be that developing schizophrenia leads to reduced social status (*social drift hypothesis*).

Evaluation

• Family relations *may be an effect.* Studies of schizophrenogenic families usually occur after the onset of the disease and therefore the dynamics have probably been altered by the stresses of having an ill son/daughter.
• Family abnormalities may be a *reasonable response* to an unusual child.
• If the family is at fault, *all children should develop the disorder.*
• Environmental factors may be more important in understanding the *course rather than the cause* of schizophrenia. The *EE model* proposes that expressed emotion (EE) is linked to poor recovery. Some families are overcritical and overconcerned. Vaughn and Leff (1976) found 51% relapse in schizophrenics returning to high EE homes compared with 13% relapse for those returning to low EE homes.

Behaviourist: labelling theory (Scheff, 1966)

Schizophrenia is the result of learning that escape to an inner world is rewarding. Individuals who have been labelled as schizophrenic then continue to act in ways that conform to the label. Bizarre behaviours are rewarded with attention and sympathy for behaving bizarrely; this is known as *secondary gain.*

Evaluation

• The success of *token economies* (see page 144) offers modest support.

If schizophrenia is genetic then there should be neurological differences.

Cognitive explanations Many symptoms of schizophrenia relate to cognitive malfunction (e.g. hallucinations, disordered thinking). This may be caused by physiological abnormalities. Park *et al.* (1995) found that both schizophrenics and their first-degree non-schizophrenic relatives had working memory disorders.

The *diathesis-stress model* proposes that mental disorders occur when there is a *genetic vulnerability* (diathesis) which is triggered by environmental conditions (stressors). This combines biological and psychological models. However, Rabkin (1980) found that schizophrenics do not report significantly more stressful episodes during the months preceding the initial onset of the disorder.

The psychodynamic view is schizophrenics have regressed to a state of primary narcissism (or great self-interest) which occurs early in the oral stage. Schizophrenics experience a loss of contact with reality because their ego is no longer functioning properly.

General evaluations of the behaviourist approach can be used here.

Practice essay 6.4

(a) Outline the characteristics of schizophrenia. (5 marks)

(b) Outline and evaluate biological explanations of schizophrenia. (25 marks)

6.5 Depression

AQA A   U5

AQA B   U4

EDEXCEL   U4

There are two forms of depression: unipolar (or major) depression and bipolar (or manic-depressive disorder). The AQA A specification requires only that you study the former.

Depression is a disorder of mood or affect. It may exist on its own or is often just one symptom of a more involved disorder.

There are times when we all feel depressed. The symptoms of clinical depression are similar to 'normal' depression, but more intense and long-lasting.

Synopticity can be demonstrated through the range of differing explanations considered under the umbrella of the term 'biological'.

Noradrenaline, serotonin and dopamine are all neurotransmitters of the monoamine group, which explains the phrase 'permissive amine'. Under normal conditions these neurotransmitters are involved in arousal and mood.

Evolutionary explanations of unipolar and bipolar depression are discussed on p. 124; such explanations are biological.

PPD may be due to 'normal' hormonal cycles, or may be a reactive rather than endogenous disorder – caused by lack of emotional support, low self-esteem and unrealistic ideas about motherhood.

The hormone cortisol is produced when an individual is stressed or anxious.

Description of depression (unipolar disorder)

Clinical characteristics

- *Emotional* – sadness, melancholy, self-involvement, guilt, thoughts of suicide.
- *Motivational* – passivity, loss of interest and energy.
- *Cognitive* – hopelessness, pessimism, lack of self-esteem.
- *Somatic* – loss or increase of appetite and weight, sleep disturbance (insomnia or oversleeping).

Diagnosis

DSM-IV requires that the diagnosis of a major depressive episode requires that five symptoms occur nearly every day for a minimum of two weeks.

Categories

It may be useful to distinguish between *endogenous* depression (e.g. related to hormone changes) and *reactive depression* (triggered by external events).

Prognosis

Chronically depressed patients usually recover spontaneously after about three months. About 10% of patients remain depressed. Drug therapies have proved useful (see page 142).

Biological explanations of depression

Genetic

Research evidence

Twin studies. Twin studies indicate some genetic component, but generally more environmental. For example, Kendler and Prescott (1999) studied nearly 4000 US twin pairs and found 39% heritability for depression. This study found no gender differences whereas Bierut *et al.* (1999) found a stronger genetic component in female twins' depression.

Adoption studies. Wender *et al.* (1986) found that biological relatives of adopted depressives were about eight times more likely than adoptive relatives to have had major depression themselves.

Neurochemical

The *permissive amine theory* of mood disorder (Kety, 1975) suggests that depression is caused by a deficiency of noradrenaline. Noradrenaline is controlled by serotonin and dopamine. When levels of the latter are low, noradrenaline may fluctuate wildly.

Research evidence

Teuting *et al.* (1981) analysed the urine of depressed and normal people and found lower levels of products associated with noradrenaline in the former.

Anti-depressant drugs (e.g. MAOIs) increase levels of noradrenaline and serotonin.

Evaluation

- It is hard to know whether neurotransmitter changes are a *cause or effect*.
- The effects of anti-depressants *aren't the same* for everyone.

Hormonal

Some forms of depression are linked to hormonal changes. There are endogenous disorders such as *post-partum depression* (PPD) and *pre-menstrual syndrome* (PMS), and reactive disorders, e.g. *seasonal affective disorder* (SAD) (triggered by changing day length, causing changes in melatonin levels, see page 45).

Research evidence

Abramowitz *et al.* (1982) found that 41% of women who were admitted to psychiatric hospital entered on or within a day of the start of their menstrual period.

About 20% of women report moderate depression in the first weeks after giving birth.

Cortisol tends to be elevated in depressed patients. Carroll *et al.* (1980) showed that dexamethasone does not suppress cortisol in 50% of depressed individuals, whereas it does in normal individuals. This may be because levels of cortisol are so high in depressives that they can't be suppressed.

Evaluation
- Hormonal changes could be an *effect rather than a cause.*
- Hormonal changes may act as a *predisposing factor,* depression occurs when there are other stressors as in PPD (the *diathesis-stress model,* see page 137).

Psychological explanations of depression

Psychodynamic

Freud suggested that loss in early life leads to depression later. Repressed anger towards the lost person is directed inwards towards the self, reducing self-esteem. If loss is experienced later in adult life, this leads to re-experiencing early loss.

Bowlby (1973) suggested that separation from a primary caregiver in early childhood may increase susceptibility to depression later.

Research evidence

Bifulco *et al.* (1992) studied 249 women who, under the age of 17, had experienced maternal loss, either through separation (for more than a year) or death. These women were twice as likely to suffer from depressive or anxiety disorders as adults, and this was particularly true where death occurred before the age of 6.

Evaluation
- The evidence is *inconsistent*, e.g. Paykel (1981) reviewed studies and found that half weren't supportive of early loss as an explanation.

Behaviourist

Learned helplessness (Seligman, 1974)

If an animal finds that its responses are ineffective, then it learns that there is no point in responding and behaves passively (see learned helplessness page 112). This was further developed by Abramson *et al.* (see below).

Maier and Seligman (1976) found evidence for learned helplessness in humans, but these findings haven't always been replicated.

Reinforcement (Lewinsohn, 1974)

Depressed persons become trapped in a cycle of social withdrawal which leads to a lack of positive reinforcement, perpetuating depression. Socially unskilled individuals may be more prone to depression.

Cognitive-behavioural

Attributional style (Abramson et al., 1978)

A further development of learned helplessness, suggesting that depressed individuals have an attributional style where they tend to attribute failure to themselves (internal) rather than to external factors, and such individuals see these attributions as unchanging (stable) and as global rather than specific.

Seligman (1974) found that students who made stable, global, attributions stayed depressed for longer after exams. However, Ford and Neale (1985) found that depressed students didn't underestimate their sense of control, contrary to the predictions of the theory.

The cognitive triad (Beck, 1967)

Depressed individuals hold negative thoughts about:
- *themselves* – they regard themselves as helpless, worthless and inadequate
- the *world* is seen to contain obstacles that cannot be handled
- the *future* – one's worthlessness prevents any improvements.

Evaluation
- The success of *cognitive-behavioural therapies* (see page 145) offers support.

Sidebar notes

> Hormonal causes of depression may explain why more women than men suffer from depression.

> Bowlby's views on separation were discussed in the *Revise AS Guide.* Spitz (1945) used the term *anaclitic depression* to describe the severe and progressive depression found in institutionalised infants, resulting from a loss of attachments.

> General evaluations of the behaviourist approach can be used here.

> Attribution theory is discussed on pp.16–17. Such material offers the opportunity to be synoptic by making links across the specification.

> Such negative cognitions lead to depression and are self-defeating. The problem is in the way that individuals *think* about their life.

Practice essay 6.5

Discuss **one** psychological explanation of depression including the evidence on which it is based.

(30 marks)

6.6 Anxiety disorders

AQA A U5
AQA B U4
EDEXCEL U4

> DSM-IV includes a number of anxiety disorders, such as post-traumatic stress disorder, phobic disorders and obsessive-compulsive disorder. The AQA A specification requires that you only study one anxiety disorder.

> Anxiety, like depression, can be an adaptive response to stress.

> Evolutionary explanations of phobias are discussed on p. 124; such explanations are biological.

> Kendler *et al.* (1992) concluded that specific phobias have a small genetic component whereas agoraphobia appears to be more related to genetic vulnerability. Both involve additional exposure to negative environmental influences (the *diathesis-stress model*).

> About 75% of those who suffer from agoraphobia are female.

Description of phobic disorders

Clinical characteristics

A phobic disorder involves extreme, persistent and irrational fear with lack of control, which is strongly out of proportion with the danger.

- Exposure to the feared stimulus nearly always produces a high level of anxiety.
- The individual recognises that the fear experienced is excessive.
- The feared situations are either avoided or responded to with great anxiety.
- The phobic reactions interfere significantly with the individual's working or social life, or there is marked distress about the phobia.
- Possibly recurrent unexpected panic attacks.

Diagnosis

In the case of panic attacks, substance abuse should be ruled out as a cause.

Categories

Three categories are distinguished by DSM-IV:

- *agoraphobia* – fear of open spaces or public places. In most cases, the panic disorder starts first; fear of having another attack makes the individual feel insecure about being in public

- *social phobias* such as talking or eating in public, extreme concern about one's own behaviour and the reactions of others

- *specific phobias* – such as zoophobias (animals), fear of water, heights, etc. Specific phobias generally have little impact on overall quality of life.

Biological explanations of phobic disorders

Genetic

Twin studies. Torgersen (1983) found 31% concordance for panic disorder with agoraphobia in MZ twins versus zero concordance in DZ twins, though none of the MZ twins shared the same phobias.

Family studies. Solyom *et al.* (1974) found that 45% of phobic patients studied had a family history of the disorder compared with 17% of 'normal' controls. Ost (1989) in a study on blood phobics found that 64% had at least one close relative who also suffered from blood phobia.

Evaluation

- Individuals who are related may acquire phobias through *imitation*.
- The genetic explanations for phobias suggest that some individuals are *predisposed* to form phobias but that life experiences are important too.

Biological preparedness (Seligman, 1971)

People have an innate predisposition to develop certain fears (see page 124), e.g. it might be natural to feel fearful about social situations because of potential dangers from strangers; spiders may be poisonous.

Research evidence

DeSilva (1988) found that 88 phobic patients studied in Sri Lanka tended to exhibit fears that were biologically based, demonstrating the universal (and thus innate) nature of such fears.

Evaluation

- This can't explain fears of *harmless situations* or things, such as slugs.

Psychological explanations of phobic disorders

Synopticity can be demonstrated by considering a range of different psychological explanations, as well as different forms of evaluation for such explanations.

This case study method is described in detail in the *Revise AS Guide.*

Psychodynamic

Freud (1909) suggested that phobias arise when anxieties are displaced on to the phobic object which symbolises the initial conflict. If the conflict is resolved the phobia will disappear.

Research evidence

Case study of 'Little Hans' who feared horses. Freud (1909) suggested that the fear represented the boy's unconscious fear of his father.

Evaluation

- Hans might have developed his fear through *classical conditioning.*
- Freudian explanations lack *falsifiability*. Falsifiability refers to the ability to prove a theory wrong. It is possible to present a Freudian explanation to fit any facts.

Behaviourist

Classical and operant conditioning are explained on pp.110–111.

Classical conditioning

Watson and Rayner (1920) conditioned 'Little Albert' to fear white furry objects by pairing a loud noise with a furry object. It is likely that most phobias are learned through the association of trauma with some neutral stimulus. In addition, the fact that phobics avoid their feared situation means the response is never extinguished.

Stimulus generalisation (see p. 110) could be used to explain how a negative experience with one object has transferred to a fear of something else.

However, some fears may be innate (see above) and not everyone who is exposed to such conditioning develops phobias (e.g. DiNardo *et al.*, 1988, found that as many people without dog phobias as with reported negative experiences with dogs).

Operant conditioning

Mowrer (1947) proposed that the first stage involves classical conditioning followed by operant conditioning (*two-process theory*), because avoidance of the phobic stimulus reduces fear and is thus reinforcing.

Neo-behaviourist (social learning theory)

Fears may be learned through imitation. Mineka *et al.* (1984) found that monkeys could develop snake phobia simply by watching another monkey experience fear in the presence of a snake.

Cognitive-behavioural

Cognitive explanations centre on irrational thinking and faulty cognition.

Phobias may be the result of irrational thoughts. For example, the sensation of crowding in a lift may develop into a cognition that lifts are associated with suffocation.

The success of behavioural and cognitive-behavioural therapies in treating phobias supports their value as explanations.

Eysenck (1997) reports research on biological challenges (e.g. breathing a mixture of carbon dioxide and oxygen). This often provokes a panic attack in patients suffering from panic disorder with agoraphobia, but rarely in normal controls. Panic attack patients may differ in the way they *interpret* their bodily symptoms.

Social factors

Kleiner and Marshall (1987) report that 84% of agoraphobics had experienced family problems in the months before they had their first panic attack. This further supports the diathesis-stress model.

Gerslman *et al.* (1990) suggested, on the basis of a literature review, that phobics (especially social phobics and agoraphobics) have lower than normal parental affection and more parental control or over-protection. This might increase their levels of anxiety.

Evaluation

- Data collection in such studies relies on *retrospective recall* which may be unreliable.
- Such data is *correlational* and doesn't demonstrate a causal link.

Practice essay 6.6

Describe and evaluate **one or more** psychological explanation for any **one** anxiety disorder.

(30 marks)

Treating mental disorders

6.7 Biological (somatic) therapies

AQA A ▸ U5
AQA B ▸ U4
EDEXCEL ▸ U4

Somatic treatment (soma = body) is justified if one believes that mental illnesses have a physical basis like physical illnesses (the biomedical approach).

The biological (medical) approach as a model of mental illness was covered in the *Revise AS Guide*.

A drug is any substance that has an effect on the body.

The '*revolving-door phenomenon*' refers to patients being continually discharged and readmitted.

Ethical issues in general are considered on p. 154, and in the companion *Revise AS Guide*. Many, such as informed consent, apply to the treatment of mental disorders.

ECT was a popular treatment prior to the advent of drug therapies and gained a bad reputation for its indiscriminate use and lack of refinement in application.

Synopticity is assessed in this part of the specification. One way to demonstrate such synopticity is to consider a range of different issues surrounding the use of a therapy.

Chemotherapy (drug therapy)

Mode of action

The main classes of drugs are:

Antianxiety drugs (minor tranquillisers), e.g. barbiturates, benzodiazepines (e.g. Valium, Librium), reduce activity in the nervous system. Side-effects include drowsiness and addiction. Buspirone has fewer side-effects.

Antipsychotic drugs (major tranquillisers or neuroleptics), e.g. chlorpromazine, used to treat schizophrenia. They block dopamine receptor sites (see page 137). Possible side-effects include blurred vision and a decrease in white blood cells (can be fatal).

Antidepressant drugs, e.g. monoamine oxidase inhibitors (MAOIs), tricyclics, selective serotonin reuptake inhibitors (SSRIs, e.g. Prozac). They promote activity of noradrenaline and/or serotonin, leading to increased arousal (see page 138) but can be affected by rebound (depression after initial euphoria). Side-effects include dizziness.

Antimanic drugs, e.g. lithium carbonate, used to control mania in bipolar depression. Side-effects include damage to the cardiovascular system.

Issues surrounding the use of chemotherapy

Appropriateness

The use of drug therapies has offered significant relief to many sufferers, leading to de-institutionalisation. In 1955 there were 560 000 patients in American psychiatric institutions. By 1977 this had declined to 160 000.

However, there are problems of addiction and dangerous side-effects (as indicated above). Drugs are not cures, they are short-term remedies which may become long-term. Chemotherapy leads to the *revolving-door phenomenon*.

Effectiveness

Effectiveness varies between individuals, detracting from its power as a therapy. For example, Spiegel (1989) found 65% of depressed patients improved using tricyclics.

Gerbino *et al.* (1978) report that manic-depression is controlled by lithium in about 80% of patients and has considerably reduced the suicide rate.

Drugs can be effective when used in conjunction with psychotherapy; they relieve disabling symptoms, allowing the contributing psychological factors to be dealt with.

Ethical considerations

Drug therapies are chemical-straitjackets, infringing individual rights. The use of chemotherapy may prevent the use of other methods. Alternatively it may enable patients to be receptive to other methods (see above).

Drugs may be necessary as a means of protecting society at large from individuals who are dangerous. However, patients living outside institutions may fail to take their medication and pose a serious danger.

Electroconvulsive therapy (ECT)

The origins of ECT lie in the observation that epilepsy and schizophrenia do not co-occur. Cerletti and Bini (1938) introduced the use of electric shock.

Mode of action

A patient is given an anaesthetic and muscle relaxant. A sub-lethal (70–130 volt) electric shock is applied to the non-dominant cerebral hemisphere (unilateral) to produce a seizure. The individual awakens and remembers nothing of the treatment, but may suffer long-term memory loss. A course of treatment usually involves six sessions.

Current understanding suggests three possible explanations for its effectiveness:

1 *Punishment*. ECT extinguishes undesirable behaviours because it is seen as a punishment which weakens the S-R link. However, sub-convulsive shocks do not appear to change behaviour but are equally unpleasant.

2 *Memory loss* allows restructuring of disordered thinking. However, unilateral ECT leads to minimal memory disruption yet is still effective.

3 *Biochemical changes*. The shock activates noradrenaline transmission, reduces serotonin re-uptake and increases sensitivity of dopamine receptors, all of which may help alleviate depression (see page 138).

Issues surrounding the use of ECT

Appropriateness

There is some discomfort about using a method which cannot be explained; it may not be the seizure which is important at all.

The method has some risk. Drug therapies are safer but ECT offers faster relief than drugs, which is important for suicidal patients.

Effectiveness

ECT is now rarely used for schizophrenia; however, it appears to be successful for cases of severe depression. Janicak *et al.* (1985) found that 80% of all severely depressed patients respond well to ECT, compared with 64% given drug therapy.

However, Sackheim *et al.* (1993) found that there was a high relapse rate within a year suggesting that relief was temporary and not a cure.

Ethical considerations

In the past ECT involved broken bones and severe memory loss; the treatment today is more humane but is still regarded by some as abusive.

Psychosurgery

Jacobsen *et al.* (1935) removed the frontal lobes of an emotionally disturbed chimpanzee called Becky, reducing her temper tantrums. Moniz (1937) was inspired to reduce anti-social behaviour in humans in a similar manner.

Mode of action

Prefrontal lobotomy, introduced by Moniz. Large portions of frontal cortex are removed or the fibres running from the frontal lobes are cut, making a patient more controllable. Side-effects included apathy, diminished intellectual powers and even death.

Prefrontal leucotomy involves drilling two holes in either side of the skull and inserting needles to sever specific nerve fibres.

Stereotactic neurosurgery: small opening made in skull, and a system of precise coordinates are used to lesion very specific parts of the brain using an electrical current, e.g. the amygdala (*amygdalotomies*) or cingulate gyrus (*cingulotomies*), both of which are areas involved in anger and emotion.

Issues surrounding the use of psychosurgery

Appropriateness

In the 1950s and 1960s some amygdalotomies resulted in patients who were confused, lacking in motivation and unable to work (Eysenck and Eysenck, 1989).

Effectiveness

Prefrontal leucotomies are occasionally used in cases of severe depression, obsessive-compulsive disorder or pain where all other treatment has failed (Griest, 1992). Minimal intellectual damage is caused because of refined techniques.

Cosgrove *et al.* (1996) report successful treatment of patients with depressive or anxiety disorders using *cingulotomies*. These patients had not benefited from all other available therapies.

Ethical considerations

It is irreversible, and the effects are not consistent. Informed consent is an issue.

It is difficult to make comparisons between therapies because different therapies have different goals. Each therapy may be effective in terms of its particular goals.

Psychosurgery involves either the removal of sections of the brain or lesions (cuts) are made so that areas of the brain become 'functionally' removed.

From 1935 to 1955 about 70 000 lobotomies were carried out. Moniz received a Nobel prize for his work but it is ironic that he was shot in the spine by one of his own lobotomised patients.

The accidental brain damage caused to Phineas Gage's frontal lobes (a iron rod was blasted into his head by an explosion, see p. 39) also showed that personality changes followed damage to this area. In this case the once responsible and mild-mannered man became violent and impulsive.

It is possible that psychosurgery can be effective if it is performed precisely and on the right patients.

Practice essay 6.7

Discuss the use of **two or more** biological (somatic) therapies.   (30 marks)

6.8 Behavioural therapies

AQA A	U5
AQA B	U4
EDEXCEL	U4
OCR	U5, U6

Behaviourism as a model of mental illness was considered in the *Revise AS Guide*. The perspective in general is discussed on p. 160.

Classical and operant conditioning are discussed in detail on pp. 110–111.

The behavioural therapies based on *classical conditioning* are referred to jointly as *behaviour therapies*. These techniques work best with behaviours that are difficult to control voluntarily.

Success may be due to *reciprocal inhibition:* not being able to maintain incompatible emotional responses simultaneously (anxiety and relaxation).

Cognitive restructuring is a cognitive-behavioural therapy, described on p. 145.

The problem of *symptom substitution* is an issue for all behavioural therapies. Of course, behaviourists argue that the symptoms are all that matter.

The behavioural therapies based on operant conditioning are referred to jointly as *behaviour modification techniques.* These techniques work best with behaviours that are under voluntary control.

Behavioural therapies based on classical conditioning

Aversion therapy

Patients are trained to associate their undesirable behaviour (e.g. sexual desires) with an aversive stimulus (e.g. electric shock). Unconditioned stimulus (shock) paired with neutral stimulus (undesirable behaviour) will now produce the conditioned response (pain).

Used to treat alcoholics. They are given a drug that makes them vomit when drinking; eventually the nausea becomes a conditioned response to the presentation of alcohol (conditioned stimulus). Though this doesn't explain why more people don't give up drinking when it has made them sick.

Issues surrounding the use of aversion therapy

Effectiveness: Meter and Chesser (1970) found that at least half their patients abstained for a year after therapy. However, the drop-out rate tends to be high and there are doubts about its long-term effectiveness. It may work in the therapist's office but not generalise to other situations.

The use of an unpleasant stimulus is ethically questionable. A variation, called *covert sensitisation*, involves the patient simply imagining unpleasant consequences.

Systematic desensitisation (SD)

Used for phobias. The patient learns to pair the feared thing with relaxation rather than anxiety; called *counterconditioning*. Wolpe (1958) described the following steps:

1 patient learns deep muscle relaxation
2 patient constructs a hierarchy of increasingly threatening situations
3 patient asked to imagine each scene while deeply relaxed
4 at any time, if the patient feels anxious, the image is stopped and relaxation regained.

Issues surrounding the use of systematic desensitisation

Marks (1973) suggests that SD works because of exposure to the feared stimulus, not the relaxation. The technique can be explained in terms of *cognitive restructuring* rather than classic learning theory.

Implosion therapy or flooding

Both techniques aim to present the patient with maximum exposure to the feared stimulus; exposure continues until their fear subsides, thus extinguishing the conditioned response. This can be done in one's imagination (*implosion therapy*) where the person imagines a very fearful situation such as being in a room full of spiders. There is evidence that real life exposure (*flooding*) is more effective but it does involve placing the patient in an intensely anxiety-provoking situation.

Virtual reality may be a useful alternative with fewer anxieties. A classic example of flooding is locking a claustrophic in a lift.

Issues surrounding the use of implosion therapy/flooding

Ost (1989) found 90% improvement after one session of flooding with patients with specific phobias, and this was maintained for an average of four years. Van Oppen *et al.* (1995) reported much less success with obsessive-compulsive disorder.

Simple elimination of symptoms doesn't mean that the condition is cured. If there is an underlying problem this may lead to *symptom substitution*.

Behavioural therapies based on operant conditioning

Token economy (TE)

Institutionalised patients are given tokens as *secondary reinforcers* (see page 111) when they engage in correct/socially desirable behaviours. The tokens can then be exchanged for *primary reinforcers* – food or privileges. This mirrors the system of rewards used by parents.

Issues surrounding the use of token economy

Allyon and Azrin (1968) used TE to control the behaviour of 45 chronic schizophrenics who had been institutionalised for an average 16 years. They were given tokens for making their beds or combing their hair. The number of chores the patients performed each day increased from about 5 to over 40.

The drawback to this therapy is that it often fails to transfer to life outside the institution because of *context-dependent learning*. However, Woods *et al.* (1984) found that short-term changes did lead on to more fundamental long-term ones possibly because newly acquired behaviours are 'trapped' by social reinforcers.

The effectiveness of tokens may be due to other factors, such as being positively reinforcing for the nursing staff, who feel they are making positive gains and therefore are stimulated to persist. They also help to structure the situation and ensure consistent rewards.

> Biofeedback, which was covered in the *Revise AS Guide*, is based on operant conditioning – positive feedback is rewarding.

Modelling

For example, a patient first watches the therapist experiencing the phobic situation calmly, then the patient does the same. This is based on *social learning theory* (see page 28).

> Modelling works best when the model is similar to the patient.

Issues surrounding the use of modelling

Bandura *et al.* (1969) found that this therapy was most effective when working with a live example of the feared object (such as a real snake) rather than a symbolic representation.

Social skills training

This is an extension of modelling, used where individuals lack social skills, e.g. bullies.

Issues surrounding the use of social skills training

Lovaas *et al.* (1967) trained autistic children in language skills using shaping and positive reinforcement.

> Synopticity is examined in this part of the specification which means that you must always ensure that your answers consider overarching issues and links across the specification, such as context-dependent learning.

Cooke and Apolloni (1976) used live models to demonstrate social skills (e.g. smiling, giving compliments) to excessively shy or solitary children. The children's social behaviours increased, including behaviours that had not been shown by the model.

Cognitive-behavioural therapies

Cognitive-behavioural therapies are a combination of a cognitive explanation and a behavioural treatment that aims to restructure the way clients think about their problem. A number of cognitive-behavioural therapies were described in the companion book *Revise AS*. This is a brief summary.

> A cognitive-behavioural therapy is *not* the same as a behavioural therapy but it can be used as a means of evaluation insofar as cognitive-behavioural therapies are a development of behavioural therapies.

Cognitive restructuring therapy (Beck, 1976)

The therapist identifies the patient's self-defeating assumptions and substitutes more adaptive ones. This is especially for depressed patients but may also be effective with eating disorders and even schizophrenia.

Rational-emotional therapy (RET) (Ellis, 1962)

Clients hold a set of irrational beliefs which lead them to react to situations with undesirable emotions (ABC – Activating event – Beliefs about the activating event – Consequences). The therapist is directive and aggressive and challenges beliefs.

Stress inoculation therapy (Meichenbaum, 1975)

The therapist first identifies the patient's maladaptive coping mechanisms for a stress situation (cognitive preparation), second, the patient learns more adaptive responses and self-statements (skill acquisition), and third, the patient applies these.

> The success of behavioural therapies may be quite unrelated to learning theory, for example it may be a matter of giving increased attention.

Evaluation of cognitive-behavioural therapies

In general these therapies are quick, and are becoming increasingly popular.

Practice essay 6.8

(a) Describe **two or more** behavioural therapies based on classical conditioning. (15 marks)

(b) Assess the behavioural therapies that you described in part (a) in terms of the issues surrounding their use.

(15 marks)

6.9 Alternatives to biological and behavioural therapies

AQA A   U5
AQA B   U4
EDEXCEL   U4

There are various alternatives to biological and behavioural therapies, most notably psychoanalysis, cognitive-behavioural therapies and humanistic approaches such as counselling (client-centred therapy).

> The AQA A specification requires that you study only one alternative therapy.

Psychoanalysis

Psychoanalysis was first developed by Freud and later adapted in various ways by Freud's followers. Freud believed that abnormal behaviour is largely the result of repressed conflicts that threaten the ego. Repression results in regression typically back to a stage at which the person had previously fixated. Therapy involves making unconscious thoughts conscious and thus freeing repressions and fixations.

> Repression serves the function of reducing the level of anxiety experienced by the client. Repressed memory was considered in the *Revise AS Guide*.

Mode of action

Hypnosis. In Freud's early work (with Breuer) he used hypnosis, but stopped because he found it was not always possible to hypnotise a patient, and that the information produced under hypnosis was too unreliable to be useful.

> The ultimate goal of psychoanalysis is to provide the client with insight, but this is met with considerable resistance because such insight creates anxiety.

Free association. The therapist introduces a topic and the client talks freely about anything that comes into his/her mind on the assumption that fragments of repressed memories will emerge. Such recall is blocked by *resistance* – though a skilled therapist interprets pauses as resistance and thus gathers clues about important information.

Analysis of dreams. Dreams express the innermost workings of the mind. In Freudian therapy dreams are repressed 'wishes'; in Jungian analysis dreams reflect attempts to solve particular problems. Freud distinguished between the actual dream (*manifest content*) and the underlying repressed ideas (*latent content*).

> If a client accepts the therapist's interpretation of his/her behaviour, this confirms the interpretation. If the client rejects the therapist's interpretation, this may be seen as resistance – and thus evidence that repressed feelings have been identified. This makes Freudian explanations non-falsifiable.

Rich interpretation. The therapist explains the client's thoughts and feelings using Freud's dynamics of personality development.

Transference. The client transfers his/her feelings about others on to the therapist. These displaced feelings may then be an object of analysis in themselves and permit the client to gain useful insights.

Related approaches

Ego analysis. Several neo-Freudians (e.g. Horney, Anna Freud and Erikson) introduced this modified form of psychoanalysis. Therapy focuses on strengthening the ego or rational mind, rather than on the conflicts created by the id. Ego analysis focuses more on the client's current social and interpersonal problems than on their childhood experiences.

> The terms 'client' and 'patient' are interchangeable but the former emphasises the individual's active role in therapy.

Psychodrama. Participants act out each other's emotional conflicts. Moreno (1946) developed this as a means of enabling individuals to express deep and irrational feelings.

Transactional analysis (TA). Berne (1964) suggested that there are three ego states: the child which is impulsive, the adult state which is rational and the parent state which stands for social prohibitions. In normal social intercourse transactions are at an adult–adult level but sometimes the interactions are crossed. Berne suggests crossed transactions are 'games'; one person is manipulating the other. TA looks at the games people play and uses role play to uncross the transactions.

Play therapy. Children are given the same opportunities as adults to work through their anxieties and repressed feelings using play as a medium for communication.

> The distinction between *neuroses* and *psychoses* is no longer part of the classification systems in use but the terms generally refer to conditions where insight is retained (neuroses, such as phobias) and those where it is not (psychoses, such as schizophrenia).

Issues surrounding the use of psychoanalysis

Appropriateness

Psychoanalysis is only suitable for mental illnesses where some insight is retained, i.e. *neuroses* rather than *psychoses*.

> Some therapists practise a 'short form' of psychoanalysis, such as Malan's (1976) brief focal therapy which requires weekly sessions over 30 weeks.

Psychoanalysis requires regular weekly or even daily sessions, over months or years. This requires time and money. It is also necessary to be articulate. Garfield (1980) claimed that psychoanalysis works best with clients who are young, attractive, verbally skilled, intelligent and successful (YAVIS).

Freud's psychoanalytic theory of personality development is discussed on pp. 91–92, and the psychodynamic model of abnormality was discussed in the companion *Revise AS Guide*.

These are some general issues, some already mentioned, that apply to evaluations of all therapies.

Effectiveness

Eysenck (1952) analysed two outcome studies and found that 66% of control patients improved spontaneously, whereas only 44% of the patients receiving psychoanalysis improved. However, when Bergin (1971) reanalysed his results using different outcome criteria the psychoanalysis success rose to 83% and the control group fell to 30%.

Ethical considerations

Some clients may find the process painful.

Evaluating and comparing effectiveness of therapies

Is any one therapy better than another one? Therapy *outcome studies* are used to try to establish this but they are fraught with difficulties, such as described below.

What constitutes a cure or improvement?

Improvements in therapy may not carry over into real life or be long-lasting. The concept of 'cure' varies from one approach to another. For example, a psychoanalyst would not regard removing the symptoms as evidence that underlying problems had been cured, whereas a behaviourist would.

What measures are valid for assessing effectiveness?

The client's self-report may suffer from the *hello–goodbye effect*. People tend to exaggerate their unhappiness at the beginning of therapy to convince the therapist that they are in genuine need. At the end of therapy the reverse is true; in order to express thanks to therapist, the client exaggerates his/her well-being. The therapist is not likely to be an objective judge. Psychometric tests may be unreliable, and self-report methods rely on client honesty.

Changes in a target behaviour can be used, such as counting the time an agoraphobic spends away from home or hours of sleep in a depressed client. However, in the long-term, it is difficult to obtain such information reliably.

How do we know what caused the change?

Spontaneous remission. In the case of depression particularly, time alone may affect an improvement. Eysenck (see above) found evidence for *spontaneous remission*. However Smith *et al.* (1980) reviewed 475 studies which compared patients who underwent therapy with an untreated control group and concluded that the average patient showed greater improvement on such measures as self-esteem, anxiety and achievement than 80% of the untreated patients.

A *placebo* is a drug that has no physiological effects.

Placebo effect. If a patient believes a therapy will cure them, the expectations themselves may be the cause of success. Increased attention (*Hawthorne effect*) may account for any change; all methods involve this.

The *Hawthorne effect* describes a change in participants' behaviour as a result of knowing that they are being observed. It is named after the Hawthorne electrical factory in America where it was first observed.

Ethical and practical considerations

Obtaining a control group is difficult. If a waiting list exists, it may be possible to withhold therapy from some patients for a while but this still does not permit random allocation to therapies because this would be unethical. The alternative is to ask participants to volunteer, which introduces a volunteer bias. The information required may be considered confidential.

Are they comparable?

Each therapy works best with a particular set of problems, therefore it is inappropriate to try to compare them. Rosenhan and Seligman (1995) concluded that: anxiety disorders are best treated with systematic desensitisation, cognitive-behavioural therapy and drugs; depression is best treated by cognitive-behavioural therapy, ECT and drugs; and schizophrenia is most effectively treated with drugs and family interventions.

Practice essay 6.9

Compare and contrast **two** alternative therapies for treating mental disorders
(e.g. biological, behavioural, psychodynamic or cognitive-behavioural).   (30 marks)

Sample question and model answer

'Research into schizophrenia shows there is a major genetic component but the fact that concordance rates between identical twins is never 100% means that there must be environmental contributions.'

Discuss biological explanations of schizophrenia. (30 marks)

Examiner's comments

'Discuss' is a term that includes both AO1 and AO2. There is no specific requirement to address the quotation.

This question focuses specifically on biological explanations, which should be described and evaluated. Further AO2 credit can be achieved through a consideration of alternative, psychological (and environmental), explanations. However, you must take care not simply to present further descriptive passages about the alternative explanations but to use them as an evaluation of genetic accounts. One linking sentence would be helpful (and creditworthy) but the more you can integrate your commentary on alternative explanations, the more credit you will gain.

Many candidates have a vast knowledge of research related to the causes of schizophrenia and are likely to write an essay which reads rather like a list. This may prevent them achieving higher marks because of insufficient detail in their descriptions. A further, common difficulty is that the evaluations tend to be rather repetitive (e.g. instead of 'this can't explain all cases of schizophrenia' you could consider methodological problems, ethics, potential biases and so on).

In this question, you will be assessed on synopticity for both AO1 and AO2. To gain credit you should ensure that your explanations cover a range of possibilities (while ensuring detail) and seek to make links across the specification. Your assessment should also seek for breadth by using a range of different evaluative techniques, as already suggested.

Note that for Unit 5 there are three questions and you have 2 hours, i.e. 40 minutes per question.

Candidate's answer

Schizophrenia is a psychiatric disorder involving loss of contact with reality and a range of symptoms. There is considerable evidence that genetic factors are involved. This view considers that certain individuals possess certain genes which predispose an individual to schizophrenia. This means that it is inherited and we would expect to find that relatives have similar chances of developing the disorder. Indeed research has found that first degree relatives of people with schizophrenia are 18 times more likely to be affected than the general population.

Identical (monozygotic, MZ) twins would be expected to have a similar chance of having schizophrenia since they carry the same genes. Research by Gottesman and Shields has found higher concordance rates (where both twins have the disorder) in MZ twins than DZ (dizygotic) twins who only share 50% of their genes. However, if schizophrenia was solely caused by genes then we would expect 100% concordance in MZ twins. Since this is not found then other factors must be involved.

MZ twin studies have the advantage of controlling for genetics but the disadvantage of not controlling for environment. One way to get round this is to study MZ twins reared apart. Twin studies show similar concordance rates even when they have been reared apart but the samples used in these studies tend to be rather small and family problems may have been the reason for the separation.

A genetic predetermination could lead to abnormalities in the brain. There is strong support for the idea that high dopamine levels are involved in schizophrenia. Dopamine is a neurotransmitter in the brain and post-mortems have found higher levels than normal in the brains of schizophrenics. Research on

Sample question and model answer *(continued)*

amphetamines supports this because they increase dopamine and have been found to worsen schizophrenic symptoms. One study found that rats which were given amphetamines displayed schizophrenic-type behaviour, though there is no reason to suppose that humans react the same way as rats. It has also been found that those drugs which are known to reduce dopamine (antipsychotic drugs) also reduce schizophrenic symptoms. However, this evidence tends to be correlational and we can't know whether the dopamine levels cause schizophrenia or schizophrenia causes high dopamine levels.

MRI scans have found that schizophrenics have enlarged ventricles in their brain and post-mortems have found that the brains of schizophrenics are lighter. This could reflect loss of cells in the brain and could explain the cognitive symptoms such as poor attention, distractability and poor memory. This again could be a cause or effect of schizophrenia.

Abnormal brain structure could be caused by genes or it might be the result of brain damage during pregnancy or birth. There is evidence that where only one MZ twin is schizophrenic this twin had suffered birth complications and this would explain their schizophrenia.

Viruses might also be involved as they could invade and disrupt brain development in the foetus. Research by Mednick has found a higher rate of schizophrenia in people exposed to flu in the second trimester of pregnancy, a time when there is greatest cortical development. Crow suggested that a retrovirus was incorporated into DNA and this was transmitted between generations. This would explain the fact that there is gradual brain damage and why schizophrenia spontaneously appears in families.

Adoption studies support the genetic explanation for schizophrenia. Tienari found that children who had been adopted away from a schizophrenic biological mother were still more likely to get it than children adopted from non-schizophrenic parents, despite being raised in a different environment. Marcus also found that 22/50 children from one or two affected parents got it, and only 4/50 from healthy parents did. This supports the view that genetics has a strong role. However, not all high-risk participants got it, indicating that other factors are involved.

The importance of factors other than genetics is indicated in a range of studies on the effects of certain family behaviours. For example, Laing proposed that the disorder involves a 'divided self' as the person's internal and external worlds are split, so the person cannot identify reality. This could result from conflicting demands and breakdown in communication within the family. Bateson proposed the concept of 'double bind' to explain how a child can become confused and doubtful from parents giving conflicting demands – e.g. criticising for not giving hugs and then rejecting the child's hug. Although family factors could not explain why all children in a family do not get the disorder.

Lidz also suggested that family environment has a role – Lidz thought that skewed marriage can influence the child when one parent dominates and does not consider the needs or emotions of other members of the family. Schismatic marriage is also thought to lead to a schizophrenic child when both parents try to dominate and use the child as a pawn in a power game.

This view of an environmental contribution is further supported by research evidence that schizophrenia often occurs in disrupted families. Marcus found that all those in his study had parents who were rated high on hostility, overconcern and inconsistency. Tienari found that all those in his study who got schizophrenia were from families rated as 'disturbed'. He had used tests and interviews to rate the families but personal opinions are subjective and this may have caused a bias in the ratings.

Sample question and model answer (continued)

The diathesis–stress model is one way of combining genetic and environmental explanations. The model suggests that individuals are born with a predisposition towards certain behaviours, such as a mental disorder. They inherit the susceptibility. However, the disorder may not appear except under certain circumstances which act as a trigger or stressor. Family environment may act as such a stressor. The problem here is disentangling genetic family influences from environmental family influences. If one of your parents is schizophrenic you may inherit the disorder or you may be affected by living with someone with such a disorder. Adoption studies suggest that both factors may be important as not all children whose parents were schizophrenic acquire the disorder.

Finally we should remember that some environmental triggers or stressors are actually biological, such as birth injuries or viruses. In answer to the original question 'Discuss biological explanations of schizophrenia' we must conclude that biological factors are clearly very important but there remain other contributory factors as well. This is important for individuals who have relatives with the disorder because it means that they will not necessarily develop the disorder.

[1060 words]

Examiner's comments

This candidate clearly has an extensive knowledge of explanations of schizophrenia, and can make informed judgements about the value of the explanations and the research on which they are based. Every paragraph offers a description of relevant research followed by one or more evaluative comments. This gives the essay a nice sense of discussion – evaluation embedded in the description.

The candidate has sensibly restricted the psychological explanations and tried to use them as evaluation. It is creditworthy to evaluate such explanations for further AO2 marks. The evaluative material was well elaborated; most points stretch to more than one sentence; however, there might have been more consideration of strengths rather than just weaknesses.

In terms of synopticity, the range of different biological explanations explored provides evidence for AO1 and the variety of different kinds of commentary is credited within AO2.

The candidate wisely returned to the original question at the end of the essay, to remind her/himself of the point of the essay. Perhaps a bit more time might have been devoted to this in order to ensure that the essay was focused on the question set rather than just saying everything the candidate knew about research into the causes of schizophrenia.

AO1
Accurate and well-detailed, the organisation and structure is coherent. There is evidence of depth and breadth but in some cases the detail is not substantial and therefore the mark is not at the very top of band 5. Band 5 = 14 marks.

AO2
The evaluation of explanations is effective. It is perhaps slightly limited in comparison with the more substantial AO1 component and could have been more synoptic. Band 4 = 12 marks.

Total 26 out of 30 marks (the bands for Unit 5 are slightly different to those on page 12. There are 5 bands in total, using similar descriptors as those on page 12), equivalent to a Grade A.

Chapter 7

Synoptic: perspectives and approaches

This final chapter is concerned with the issues, debates and approaches which have been embedded in your whole A Level course: both AS Level and A2 studies. Some general considerations are presented here but the bulk of your knowledge must come from your studies of other areas of the specification.

'Perspectives and approaches' assesses your understanding of psychology as a whole as well as your ability to make links across the different areas of psychology.

Questions set on material from this chapter, and from chapter 6, are assessed on *synopticity*. This is described on page 11. You must ensure that you can demonstrate synopticity in your answers to the examination questions.

In the AQA A examination, you must answer one question on Issues and Debates (two are given on issues and two on debates) and one question on Approaches (you are given a choice of two).

Issues

7.1 Gender bias	**7.3** Ethical issues
7.2 Cultural bias	**7.4** The use of non-human animals

After studying this area you should be able to:

- describe and evaluate instances of gender bias in psychological theory and research
- understand the value of feminist research
- describe and evaluate instances of cultural bias in psychological theory and research
- understand the issues of ethnocentrism and imposed ethics
- critically consider ethical issues involved in psychological investigations using human participants

- discuss the means by which such ethical issues may be resolved
- understand the particular problems surrounding socially sensitive research
- describe the use of non-human animals in psychological investigations
- present arguments for and against the use of non-human animals in psychological investigations from a scientific and ethical point of view

LEARNING SUMMARY

Debates

7.5 Free will and determinism	**7.7** Psychology as a science
7.6 Reductionism	**7.8** Nature–nurture

After studying this area you should be able to:

- explain the concepts of free will and determinism
- discuss the arguments for and against the existence of free will and determinism, with reference to examples in psychological theory and research
- explain the concept of reductionism
- discuss the arguments for and against reductionist explanations, with reference to examples in psychological theory and research

- define the concept of science, and consider varieties of science
- discuss arguments for and against the claim that Psychology is a science
- explain the concepts of nature and nurture, and describe the historical roots of the debate
- discuss different views regarding the relationship between nature and nurture

LEARNING SUMMARY

Approaches

7.9 Biological, behavioural, psychodynamic and cognitive approaches

After studying this area you should be able to:

- discuss the assumptions of the four main approaches in psychology: biological, behavioural, psychodynamic and cognitive
- use the concepts related to each of these approaches to explain behaviour
- identify and evaluate the research methods used by these approaches

- critically consider the value of each approach in explaining behaviour

Note: you are allowed to use **any** approach when answering the examination question – evolutionary, humanistic, sociological, philosophical and so on; the approaches identified here are the most likely to be used

LEARNING SUMMARY

Issues

7.1 Gender bias

AQA A   U5

Gender differences

Maccoby and Jacklin (1974) reviewed over 1500 studies and found: girls are marginally superior on tests of verbal ability; boys are marginally better on tests of visual/spatial ability and on tests of arithmetic reasoning; boys are physically and verbally more aggressive than girls; there is little difference in overall intelligence. They concluded that most gender stereotypes are 'cultural myths' that are perpetuated by expectations.

Observed psychological differences may be due to the following:
* *socialisation* – girls have lower self-expectations and learn feminine behaviours.
* *Androcentric research* – many theories are derived from studies using male participants and then presented as an account of human behaviour (e.g. Kohlberg's theory of moral development, page 89). This often results in female behaviour being seen as abnormal (see 'Feminist psychology').

Alpha bias

The tendency to identify or exaggerate gender differences. Examples:
* evolutionary theory tends to emphasise gender differences
* theories of moral understanding – Gilligan suggested that females operate an ethic of care whereas men base morality on justice (page 90)
* psychoanalytic theory – Freud's theory suggests that males are superior (page 91).
* theories of mental disorder, e.g. depression is more common in women.

Beta bias

Beta bias is a tendency to ignore or minimise gender differences. Some theories are based on studies which used only male or female participants, yet they assume that the findings apply to all humankind thus ignoring any potential differences.

All male participants

Milgram and Zimbardo's studies (AS Level studies); Rahe *et al.* and Friedman and Rosenman's studies of stress (AS Level studies); Schachter and Sugar (page 56).

Mainly or all female participants

Freud's patients (page 91); Moscovici and Hofling *et al.*'s studies of social influence (AS Level studies); Darley and Latané's studies of bystander behaviour (pages 30–33).

Beta-biased theories

Kohlberg's theory of moral development used male participants but was applied to all behaviour (page 89). Erikson conducted research on males and presented a stage theory of human development (page 92). Levinson used all males (page 98).

Beta-biased research

Experimenters ignore differential treatment in experiments (e.g. different expectations). Rosenthal (1966) reported that male experimenters were more pleasant, friendly, honest and encouraging with female participants.

Feminist psychology

The traditional approach in psychology is to emphasise internal, individual, causes. This perpetuates myths about gender differences. In order for social change to occur research needs to focus on how social constructions shape our perceptions.

Bem (1993) proposed the '*encultured lens*' theory; the view of gender we receive from our culture misshapes how we see men and women. Explanations of behaviour often rely on male interpretations, resulting in a view of female behaviour as abnormal (e.g. pre-menstrual disorders).

Sidebar notes:

Gender is one means of defining a sub-cultural group (see the definition of 'culture' on p. 153), therefore some of the material on cultural bias applies to gender biases.

A 'bias' is a tendency to focus on certain aspects of experience rather than on others.

Alpha bias is more common than beta bias.

Much psychological research has used White, male, middle-class college students. In fact the whole of psychology may essentially be a psychology of that particular population!

Gender differences in an alpha- or beta-biased theory may be real or culturally-determined.

The fact that women may be more conformist, and females were used in Moscovici's research on minority influence, suggests that the theory may be beta-biased.

Feminist psychologists propose a new psychology which focuses on the individual and on social context.

Practice essay 7.1

Discuss gender bias in psychological theory and research.   (30 marks)

7.2 Cultural bias

AQA A   U5

Culture refers to the beliefs, values and practices shared by one group of people. Segall *et al.* (1990) defined it as the '[hu]man-made part of the environment'.

There is a tendency, in psychology, to confuse 'culture' with 'country'.

Cultural bias in research

Our understanding of our own and other cultures is gained through research, yet such research is inevitably biased.

- Researchers from another culture ('outsiders') may not understand the language or may misinterpret an action.
- Outsiders' own cultural biases produce expectations which alter what they 'see'.
- Outsiders use methods derived from an alien culture (see *imposed etic*, below).
- The sample of participants may be biased. It is also wrong to imagine a culture as being a homogeneous group of people; differences within a culture (sub-cultures) may be as large as those between cultures.

Cultural bias in theory

Many theories have been criticised for their inherent cultural biases, largely as a result of the fact that they are derived from research evidence collected in one culture. Examples include theories of social influence and attachment (see the companion book, *Revise AS*), relationships (page 26), moral development (page 90) and psychopathology (page 135). However, psychologists have attempted to redress this balance and use cross-cultural data as a means of validation.

Sources of bias

Ethnocentric refers to the belief that one's own group is superior to other cultures. *Eurocentric* is a specific form of this.

The Western world-view emphasises individuality, independence, survival of the fittest and control over nature (*individualism*); whereas Africans value cooperation, similarity, survival of the tribe and one with nature (*collectivism*).

Racial bias is a particular form of culture bias. This is discussed on p. 88.

Ethnocentric and eurocentric perspectives

Our view of behaviour is inevitably blinkered by our historical and cultural vantage point, and by the restricted sample of participants used in psychological research (middle-class, White, European, male undergraduates).

Nobles (1976) equates the domination of Western psychology with nineteenth-century colonialism, because it is a tool of oppression and domination. This can be seen in the Western view of Black intelligence (see page 88) and the self-concept.

Individualist–collectivist distinction

Discussed, for example, in relation to: attribution theory (page 17), relationships (page 26), pro-social behaviour (page 32), development in adolescence and old age (pages 97 and 104).

Ecological fallacy (Hofstede, 1980). One must take care when distinguishing between individualist and collectivist cultures not to assume that any two individuals selected at random from these cultures will differ in this way.

Emic–etic distinction

Emics are cultural specifics, as in 'phonemics', the study of universal sounds as they contribute to meaning in a particular language. *Etics* are universals of behaviour, as in 'phonetics', the study of universal sounds independent of meaning.

The main issue is that Western psychologists have been insensitive about their cultural bias. They have used Western culture as the standard by which everything else is measured.

Imposed etic

A technique or theory which is rooted in the researcher's own culture and used to study other cultures. Examples include: the Strange Situation (see the companion book, *Revise AS*), intelligence tests (page 86), moral dilemmas (page 89), the diagnosis and treatment of abnormal behaviour (pages 142–147).

Berry (1969) suggests that a derived etic, as used in ethnographic anthropology, can resolve the problem. It is a series of emic studies in several different cultures using local people and focusing on culture-specific phenomena.

Practice essay 7.2

(a) Describe **two or more** examples of cultural bias in psychological theories. (15 marks)

(b) Assess the extent to which such bias has affected our understanding of human behaviour.

(15 marks)

7.3 Ethical issues

AQA A ▷ U5
EDEXCEL ▷ U6

Ethical issues in psychological research, and the use of ethical guidelines, were discussed in the *Revise AS Guide*. This is a review of the information covered there.

To what extent are ethical guidelines universal? Schuler (1982) identified three common principles: physical harm, psychological harm and confidentiality. Every country has its own psychological association with its own ethical guidelines.

Participants should not be exposed to risks greater than to those encountered in their normal lifestyles. Watson and Rayner (1920) argued that the harm experienced by Little Albert was no more than in real life.

Socially sensitive research is that which has direct social consequences and often concerns issues where there is little agreement, much bias and serious implications.

Much psychological research has the potential for social manipulation, such as the treatment of mental illness.

Ethical issues in psychological research

Morals refer to our everyday standards of right and wrong, such as honesty. *Ethics* are a set of moral principles used by professionals, such as doctors. Ethical issues include damage to individuals, questions regarding privacy and also damage to the profession.

Ways to resolve ethical issues: ethical guidelines

The British Psychological Society (BPS) has a set of ethical guidelines for human and non-human animal research, as well as for clinical practice. Ethics are determined by a balance between ends and means, or a *cost-benefit analysis*.

The main points concern: deception, informed consent, protection from physical and psychological harm (including loss of self-esteem), privacy and confidentiality. Psychologists have wider responsibilities towards other psychologists and towards society.

Remember: deception is sometimes relatively harmless (e.g. memory research), deception is sometimes necessary (e.g. obedience research), informed consent is not always possible (e.g. participants not able to understand what truly is involved).

Lack of informed consent/deception can be overcome through, for example: debriefing, presumptive consent and prior general consent, and participants' right to withdraw or withhold data.

Limitations of ethical guidelines

- The greatest penalty is *disbarment* from one's professional organisation.
- Guidelines remove the need for individuals to *think for themselves*.
- Ethical principles become *enshrined*, and long-term effects may be overlooked.
- The cost-benefit analysis suggests that it is *possible to predict costs and benefits* prior to conducting a study, and that costs and benefits can be quantified (from whose perspective?).

Socially sensitive research

'Alternative' sexuality

Hamer *et al.* (1993) found evidence of a 'gay gene' by looking at the genes of homosexual brothers. If this is true, it could lead some people to test and abort unborn children.

Race-related research

This kind of research inevitably involves the use of an 'imposed etic' (see page 153). Jensen's research concluded that Black Americans were intellectually and innately inferior; this would have important implications for education (page 88). Other race-related psychological research may be more positive, such as attempts to understand prejudice and how to reduce it (page 20).

Intelligence tests

IQ tests were an early psychological contribution to society but the results have the potential for misuse. Gould (1982) reported on how highly flawed IQ data was used to argue against immigration in the US. Burt's (1955) data was used to support the 11 plus test, and later the date was suspected to be fraudulent.

Eyewitness testimony

Some socially sensitive research is of real benefit to society. Research into eyewitness testimony (see the companion book, *Revise AS*) demonstrates the unreliability of such evidence and has had an important effect on police and legal practices.

Practice essay 7.3

Discuss the ethics of socially sensitive research in psychology.   (30 marks)

7.4 The use of non-human animals

AQA A ▷ U5
EDEXCEL ▷ U6

Remember that investigations with animals include both laboratory experiments and naturalistic observations.

Studies of brain activity that use invasive techniques rely on non-human animals, e.g. Hubel and Wiesel's study of the visual cortex (p. 69).

Consideration of medical research that uses non-human animals is not relevant here.

Speciesism is a form of discrimination based upon differences between species. Ryder (1991) argues that discrimination on the grounds of having four legs is no different from discrimination on the grounds of skin colour.

Attempts to teach human language to non-human animals suggest that there are qualitative differences (pp. 118–119).

Koestler (1970) coined the term *ratomorphism* to describe generalisations which are made from non-human animals.

Anthropomorphism is attributing human feelings and characteristics to animals.

Are non-human animals preferable as research participants?

Yes
- Non-human animals are cheaper, less susceptible to experimenter bias and demand characteristics, and their behaviour is less complex.
- One can study instinctive behaviour in animals because the effects of learning are often minimal whereas in humans innate behaviours are masked by experience.
- Their use poses *fewer* ethical problems.

No
- It depends on the kind of behaviour being studied. In some situations animal research would have no relevance (e.g. reading) or minimal relevance (e.g. stress).

Is non-human animal research relevant to human behaviour?

Yes
- Some aspects of behaviour are unquestionably the same, for example, nerves.
- Even if the results are not directly applicable, comparisons can be made which are at least useful, as in the case of evolutionary theories and comparative studies.
- The results of non-human animal studies may point the way to possibly fruitful research with humans (e.g. Harlow's research see *Revise AS* Guide).
- Behaviourists argue that different species differ only quantitatively because they have all evolved from common ancestors and share the same 'building blocks'.

No
- Humans are qualitatively different from animals, because of (possibly) unique features, such as consciousness and language.
- Simply because structures are the same doesn't mean they perform the same function (see research on the brain and emotion, page 54).
- Humans rely more on cultural transmission so the same rules do not apply.

What is ethical in terms of the use of non-human animals?

Benefits must be weighed against costs. Harlow's work with monkeys had important consequences in child institutions. Gray (1985) argues that we owe a special duty to members of our own species, and it is acceptable to inflict a fairly high level of suffering on non-human animals to avoid a smaller level of suffering by humans, up to a point.

Psychological investigations of non-human animal behaviour may contribute directly to improving the life of animals, as in protecting the environments of endangered species.

Suffering needs to be assessed without being anthropomorphic. Do rats have the same feelings as primates? What about plant life?

Even research which involves a very low level of suffering, such as genetic engineering and selective breeding, raises ethical questions about humans interfering with nature.

The facts about non-human animal research

Coile and Miller (1984) found that only 7% of US studies had been primarily concerned with non-human animals. The Animals Act (1986) has laid down strict guidelines for animal research. The British Psychological Society (1985) strongly advises psychologists to: avoid, or at least minimise, discomfort to living animals; discuss any research with a Home Office inspector; be familiar with the requirements of the species they are studying; minimise the number of participants used; consider the relative costs and benefits.

Practice essay 7.4

Critically consider the use of non-human animals in **two or more** psychological investigations.

(30 marks)

Debates

7.5 Free will and determinism

AQA A US
AQA B US

Determinism

Kinds of determinism

Environmental determinism. The behaviourist view is that we are controlled by external forces. Skinner said that freedom was an illusion.

Physiological determinism. Behaviour may be determined by internal (biological) factors, e.g. physiological accounts of motivation (pages 50–52), emotion (page 54) and gender development (page 94).

Psychic determinism. Freud thought that freedom was an illusion, because the actual causes of our behaviour are unconscious and therefore hidden from us.

Genetic determinism. Ethologists argue that we are born with innate characteristics which inevitably lead to certain behaviours, such as altruism (page 30 and 109), mental disorder (page 124).

Issues related to determinism

Moral responsibility. When a person commits an anti-social act, the cause of their behaviour may be due to biological (inherited) or social (e.g. the media) causes. We cannot hold individuals legally responsible for their actions if the causes were outside their control.

Lack of determinism. Heisenberg's *uncertainty principle* (1927) and Hilborn's *chaos theory* (1994) suggest that even in a hard science such as physics there are no purely deterministic relationships.

Free will

Individuals are active in determining their behaviour, i.e. they are free to choose.

Issues related to free will

Assumptions of science

Science is based on the assumption that one thing causes (determines) another. Scientific research can be used to predict behaviour and manipulate it, e.g. reducing prejudice (page 20). Free will denies such relationships.

Personal responsibility

Rogers believed that it is only by taking responsibility for all aspects of one's own behaviour that one can be well adjusted and capable of self-actualisation.

Sartre, an existentialist philosopher, said we are 'condemned to be free'; freedom is a burden because we each are totally responsible for our behaviour. The law embodies this view.

Reconciling determinism and free will

Soft determinism

James (1890) suggested that there is a distinction between behaviour that is highly constrained by the situation (and appears involuntary i.e. determined) and behaviour that is only modestly constrained by the situation (and appears voluntary).

Freedom within constraints

Absolute free will means that behaviour is not determined in any lawful way. Heather (1976) suggested that much behaviour is predictable though not inevitable, individuals are free to choose their behaviour but this is usually from within a fairly limited repertoire.

Remember that all the units in this chapter are assessed in relation to synoptic knowledge. This means that you should be 'eclectic' in your essays – for example, by using material from diverse areas of the specification.

Where do you think a cognitive psychologist would stand on the free will–determinism debate?

The *uncertainty principle* states that the act of making an observation changes the observation, thus no objective research is ever possible. *Chaos theory* proposes that very small changes in initial conditions can result in major and unpredictable changes later.

Behaviour can be *determined* by internal or external forces.

At any time, would your behaviour have been different if you had willed it? Believers in free will say 'Yes'.

Humanistic psychologists (such as Maslow and Rogers) believe we exercise choice in our behaviour.

Practice essay 7.5

Describe and evaluate the free will and determinism debate as it is presented in **two or more** psychological theories.

(30 marks)

7.6 Reductionism

AQA A ▷ U5
AQA B ▷ U5

Reductionism is any attempt to reduce a complex set of phenomena to some more basic components. Many psychological accounts which are determinist are also reductionist.

A debate is an argument between two alternative positions. None of the debates studied in this section is simply 'one *or* the other', it is a question of weighing up the relative strengths and limitations of each side of the debate.

Holism is an argument or theory which proposes that it only makes sense to study a system as a whole rather than its constituent parts.

Some examination questions require you to 'analyse'. This means to break the problem down into its constituent parts, much like a chemist might do when analysing a compound.

This part of the specification assesses your ability to display synopticity – your awareness of links across the specification.

Legge (1975) gave the example of a person signing their name to illustrate how reductionist explanations fail to provide a complete account of behaviour.

Rose suggested that if reductionist explanations are used to 'explain away' psychological phenomena, then the result is unsatisfactory.

Kinds of reductionism

Environmental reductionism. Reducing behaviour to the effects of environmental stimuli, as in behaviourist explanations of relationships (page 23), and mental illness (page 139). Overlooks innate influences and has potential for abuse through social manipulation.

Physiological reductionism. Explaining behaviour in terms of physiological mechanisms, e.g. emotion (page 54), dreams (page 48), mental illness (page 137). However, this diverts attention from other explanations and can result in over-use of biochemical methods of control.

Evolutionary reductionism. Explaining behaviour in terms of evolutionary principles, e.g. reproductive behaviour (page 121), altruism (page 109), intelligence (pages 86–87). However, evolutionary explanations lack falsifiability and genetic components of behaviour are rarely more than 50%.

Machine reductionism. Explaining behaviour in information-processing terms. However, interconnectionist networks have been described by Penrose (1990) as holist.

Experimental reductionism. The use of controlled laboratory studies to gain understanding of similar behaviours in the natural environment. Lacks ecological validity.

Alternatives to reductionism

Holism. Gestalt psychologists argued that the whole does not equal the sum of the parts. Humanistic psychologists (e.g. Rogers, 1951) believe that the individual reacts as an organised whole, rather than a set of stimulus–response (S–R) links.

An eclectic approach. Relevant data is gathered together from various disciplines, e.g. understanding the causes of schizophrenia involves both reductionist and holist explanations (pages 136–137), or using data from brain scans to understand cognitive processes (see *Revise AS Guide*).

Arguments for and against reductionist explanations

For
- Reductionism may be a necessary part of understanding how things work.
- Reductionist arguments are easier to test empirically, and easier to discuss.
- Reductionist explanations may be correct or appropriate; the reason they are incomplete is because psychological research has yet to identify all the facts.
- Reductionist accounts should be part of all explanations, e.g. psychological theories of pattern recognition (page 64) should match physiological accounts.

Against
- Reductionist explanations may oversimplify complex problems, taking attention away from other levels of explanation so that we fail to usefully understand behaviour.
- Reductionist explanations may not answer the question. Valentine (1992) suggests that physiological explanations focus on structures whereas more holist explanations are concerned with process (see 'levels of explanation').
- Reductionist explanations are necessary but not always sufficient.

Levels of explanation

Rose (1976) suggested that reductionist explanations are one form of discourse and that physical explanations are at the bottom, moving through chemical, anatomical-biochemical, physiological, psychological (mentalistic), social psychological and, finally, sociological explanations.

Practice essay 7.6

Discuss **two or more** examples of reductionism in psychological theory. (30 marks)

7.7 Psychology as a science

AQA A	U5
AQA B	U5
EDEXCEL	U6

Data can be collected *empirically* (direct experience or observation) or *rationally* (by constructing reasoned arguments).

Popper (1969) argued that it was the possibility of falsification that separates science from religions and pseudo-sciences.

The word 'science' refers both to the body of knowledge and the methods used to obtain that knowledge.

This part of the specification assesses synopticity, which can be demonstrated in this area by discussing contrasting research studies and methods.

Kuhn's conception was that science develops through pre-science, to science and then to revolution.

Psychology is defined as the *scientific* study of behaviour and experience. It differs from commonsense insofar as it seeks to collect objective and verifiable facts.

Discourse analysis examines people's social conversations in order to understand how they perceive the world.

Triangulation is achieved by comparing the findings from a number of different studies or using different methods within one study. Close agreement confirms the validity of the findings.

What is a science?

The objective collection of facts and the organisation of these facts into theories.

1 *Making observations*, producing 'facts' (data about the world).
2 *Constructing a theory* to account for a set of related facts.
3 *Generating expectations* (hypotheses) from the theory. ←
4 *Collecting data* to test expectations.
5 *Adjusting the theory* in response to the data collected.

The scientific method consists of a cycle:

- *inductive phase*: observation, generalisation, theory
- *deductive phase*: hypothesis-formation, data collection, theory adjusted.

The key concepts of a science are: objectivity, control and manipulation of variables, replication (to confirm validity) and *falsification* (being able to reject a hypothesis).

The laboratory experiment is the best but not the only means of hypothesis testing, e.g. naturalistic observations use the scientific method.

Evaluation

Science may be an impossible ideal, no investigator is truly objective as indicated by Heisenberg's *uncertainty principle* (page 156).

Social representation theory (page 19) suggests that scientific knowledge is not a timeless concept but a feature of a particular group of people at a particular time in history. Scientific beliefs are subject to the same group pressures of other groups.

Is psychology a science?

Yes. Psychologists apply the scientific method and conduct well-controlled, repeatable, scientific experiments. They use the results of such experiments to develop theories which then generate new hypotheses.

No. The problems of bias in science are especially problematic in psychology. Experimental artefacts, such as *experimenter* bias and *demand characteristics* mean that it may be impossible to conduct objective and repeatable research.

Pre-science? Kuhn (1970) suggested that psychology has not yet evolved into a science because there is no single paradigm which encompasses all of human behaviour research.

On the other hand, Palermo (1971) argued that, far from being a pre-science, psychology has already undergone several paradigm shifts, such as behaviourism and information processing. It is now in the revolution phase.

Are the goals of science appropriate to the study of human behaviour?

Even if one accepted that psychology is scientific, we must ask what relevance this approach has to the understanding of human behaviour. The more controlled a study is (good science) the less it is *ecologically valid*. All scientific research is based on restricted samples; in psychology these are culturally and socially biased, producing theories which are not *universally valid*.

Humanistic psychologists feel that objective data can tell us little about subjective experience. It has statistical but not human meaning. New research methods are needed properly to investigate human behaviour, e.g. *discourse analysis*.

Social constructionists challenge the notion of a physical reality and suggest that the reality that we construct socially is more relevant. More subjective methods of research can be validated through, for example, *triangulation*.

Practice essay 7.7

Discuss the question of whether psychology is a science. (30 marks)

7.8 Nature–nurture

AQA A ▷ U5
AQA B ▷ U5
EDEXCEL ▷ U6

Nature refers to behaviour that is determined by inherited factors whereas *nurture* is the influence of environmental factors including learning.

This debate is sometimes called the 'heredity versus environment debate'.

'*Empirical*' means to discover something directly through one's own senses. Empiricists argue that all behaviour is acquired directly through experience.

Both Piaget and Freud suggested that development is 'driven' by biological changes. Adult characteristics are the consequence of the interaction between these and experience (nature and nurture).

Other examples of nature and nurture are perceptual development (p. 72) and attachment (see *Revise AS Guide*).

The history of the nature–nurture debate

Nativism

The Greek philosopher Plato believed that human characteristics are largely native to an individual. The French philosopher Rousseau believed that children should be allowed to follow their natural inclinations. This European view led to, e.g., Piaget's theory.

Empiricism

Locke, a 17th-century philosopher, suggested that newborns' minds are a blank slate (*tabula rosa*). Their development is passively moulded by empirical experiences. This view developed, e.g., into behaviourism.

Nature or nurture?

Nature

Explanations of behaviour where inherited factors are seen to be uppermost, e.g. nativist theory of language acquisition (page 78), gender identity (page 94), IQ (page 86).

Practical implications

If behaviour is entirely due to heredity then intervention would have little effect on development. Herrnstein and Murray (1994 *The Bell Curve*) argue that we can't significantly change IQ and therefore intervention programmes are a waste of money.

Nurture

Explanations which account for behaviour in terms of environmental factors, e.g. social learning theories of personality (page 93) and aggression (page 28).

Practical implications

There is evidence that intervention programmes, such as Head Start, can be used to boost IQ (see page 87).

An interaction

Hebb (1949) pointed out that the question 'nature or nurture' is like asking whether a field's area is determined more by its length or by its width.

Views on the relationship between nature and nurture

The *diathesis-stress model* (p.137) uses this concept of potential or susceptibility which is different to actual behaviour.

Questions on this part of the specification credit synopticity, therefore you must ensure that you make links across the specification in your answer and refer to different approaches and ideas.

MZ twins share 100% of the same genes, therefore in terms of nature they are the same.

Genotype and phenotype

Gottesman (1963) described a *reaction range*, e.g. our potential height (*genotype*) is inherited but actual height is determined by e.g. diet (*phenotype*).

Phenylketonuria (PKU) is an inherited metabolic disorder where phenylketones cause brain damage unless the child is given a diet (nurture) low in phenylalanine.

Heredity–environment interaction (Plomin *et al.*, 1977)

1 *Passive*. Parents' genetic character determines the environment the child grows up in.

2 *Reactive*. Adults behave differently towards different innate characteristics.

3 *Active*. As each child interacts with his/her environment it is altered and this in turn affects the behaviour of the individual (see *reciprocal determination*, page 93).

Methodological problems

One cannot study nature (genotype) directly. Twin studies are a form of natural experiment, comparing MZ and DZ twins; but this is flawed: MZ twins are treated more similarly and create similar *micro-environments*.

Practice essay 7.8

Discuss the different views of the nature–nurture debate that have been presented in psychological theory and research.

(30 marks)

Approaches

7.9 Biological, behavioural, psychodynamic and cognitive approaches

AQA A   U5
AQA B   U5
EDEXCEL   U6

This 'approaches' section of specification AQA A differs from all others because it is examined with a different style of question (see p. 165). You are given a short piece of text describing someone's behaviour, and then asked to offer a possible explanation for the behaviour using any named approach. You must pretend to be a biological psychologist, or a behaviourist, or a psychoanalyst, and so on.

The methods used in the physiological approach are discussed on pp. 38–39, such as lesions and brain scans.

The biological approach

Biology refers to the study of living organisms. *Physiology* is concerned with the functioning of body parts. *Genetic* explanations are biological but not physiological.

The physiological approach

Key assumptions of the physiological approach

All behaviour can be explained in terms of the nervous system and other parts of the body (physiological systems).
It makes sense to reduce behaviour and experience to this level (e.g. consciousness must have a physiological basis).

Key concepts of the physiological approach

Central nervous system: the brain (localisation and lateralisation).
Autonomic nervous system: hormones, endocrine glands, and sympathetic and parasympathetic action.
Activity of neurons: electrical and chemical transmission, neurotransmitters, synapses.

Evaluation of the physiological approach

- Objective, deterministic, reductionist, mechanistic, oversimplified explanations; more appropriate for some kinds of behaviour (e.g. vision) than other kinds where higher order thinking is more involved (e.g. emotion).
- Objective, reductionist nature of physiological explanations facilitates experimental research; can be used successfully to treat behavioural problems (e.g. drug therapies).

The genetic approach

Methods used in the genetic approach

Naturalistic observation.
Twin studies. Comparing MZ and DZ twins and/or twins reared together or apart.
Adoptive studies. Comparing adopted children with natural families.

An assumption is something which is taken as being true without any proof. It is the basis of an approach or belief.

Reproduction is the key. An individual who does not reproduce will not perpetuate its genes. Therefore traits that promote reproduction are highly adaptive.

The evolutionary approach is discussed on pp. 108–110.

Key assumptions of the genetic approach

A *gene* is a unit of inheritance which forms part of a chromosome.
Behavioural characteristics are inherited in the same way that physical characteristics are – through the *genetic code.*
Behaviours that promote survival and reproduction are '*naturally selected*'.

Key concepts of the genetic approach

Evolutionary theory. Environmental change means that new traits are needed to ensure survival. New genetic combinations produce adaptation and the individual who best 'fits' the environmental niche will survive and reproduce (survival of the fittest). Your *genotype* is your genetic constitution, whereas *phenotype* refers to observable characteristics due to gene–environment interaction.

Evaluation of the genetic approach

Explains many behaviours, e.g. attachment, sleep, reproductive behaviour.
Deterministic: assumes 1:1 correspondence between genes and behaviour whereas there is a difference between genotype and phenotype.

The behavioural approach

The behavioural approach is based on learning theory: classical and operant conditioning.

Pavlov, Watson, Thorndike, and Skinner are well-known behaviourists.

Key assumptions of behaviourism

Animals only differ *quantitatively*.
It is sufficient to be concerned with *external and observable behaviour* only.
All behaviour can be explained in terms of *conditioning theory* (S–R links).
All behaviour is determined by *environmental influences*, i.e. learning. We are born as a blank slate.

Behaviourism is so-called because it focuses exclusively on observable behaviours.

Key concepts of behaviourism

Classical conditioning: learning by association (UCS + NS → CR).
Operant conditioning: learning through consequences (positive and negative reinforcement/punishment stamp a behaviour in or out).
Generalisation: animals respond in the same way to similar stimuli.
Extinction: new response disappears.
Shaping: gradual learning through progressive reinforcement.
Reinforcement schedules: partial reinforcement schedules most effective.

Methods used in the behaviourist approach

Laboratory experiments, observing stimulus–response behaviour, lack ecological validity.
Non-human animal learning experiments, e.g. Skinner's box. May not be applicable to humans.

Methodological behaviourism is the view that all approaches in psychology use behaviourist concepts to some extent.

Evaluation of behaviourism

* Pervasive influence (*methodological behaviourism*); practical applications; good for scientific research.
* Mechanistic; excludes cognitive, emotional and innate factors; deterministic; reductionist; largely based on work with non-human animals; ethical concerns over behaviour manipulation.

Social learning theory extended behaviourism to incorporate vicarious reinforcement, a more powerful form of learning (page 28). It is sometimes called *neo-behaviourism*.

The psychodynamic approach

'Psychodynamic' refers to any approach which emphasises the processes of change and development, i.e. dynamics.

Freud's psychoanalytic theory is the best-known psychodynamic theory (page 91). Erikson (page 92) is another example of a psychoanalytic theorist.

Key assumptions of psychoanalysis

Psychoanalysis is both a theory of personality and the therapy derived from it.

Development is a *dynamic* process – it is motivated by certain forces.
Behaviour can be explained in terms of *unconscious* influences.
Infants are born with *innate biological drives* and these interact with early experience to produce adult personality.

Freud (1920) gave the following example of the *Freudian slip*: a British MP was speaking of his colleague from Hull but said 'the honourable member from Hell', thus revealing his private thoughts about the other MP.

Anxiety leads to *ego defence mechanisms*, e.g. repression where anxiety-provoking thoughts are made unconscious.
Anxiety may also lead to *regression*, typically back to a stage at which the person had previously fixated.

Key concepts of psychoanalysis

Structure of the personality. The id (motivated by the pleasure principle), ego (motivated by the reality principle), superego (an outcome of the Oedipus conflict).
Psychosexual stages of development. Oral, anal, phallic, latency and genital.
Ego defence mechanisms, e.g. repression, displacement, projection, intellectualisation.
Therapy (psychoanalysis) involves making unconscious thoughts conscious and thus freeing repressions and fixations, e.g. through dream interpretation and free association.

The three strands of Freud's theory of development are: the driving force (e.g. pleasure principle), personality structure (e.g. the id) and the organ-focus (e.g. oral).

Methods used in psychoanalysis

Case studies (e.g. Little Hans): rich data but may be unreliable.
Clinical interviews: maximises information collected but interviewer bias.
Analysis of symbols in dreams: latent and manifest content.

Evaluation of psychoanalysis

An idiographic approach is one that emphases individuality and unique insights.

* Recognised early, unconscious influences; highly influential; idiographic.
* Lacks objective evidence; reductionist and determinist; overemphasis on innate biological forces.
* Neo-Freudians (e.g. Erikson and Jung) emphasised social and cultural factors.

Cognition is the activity of internal mental processing. Cognitive psychologists are primarily interested in thinking and related mental processes such as memory, perception, attention, forgetting, learning, thinking and language.

Cognitive psychologists use the *information-processing metaphor*.

Many ideas from cognitive psychology have been used elsewhere in psychology, such as the cognitive-developmental approach, or in the treatment of mental disorders.

The cognitive approach

Key assumptions of the cognitive approach

Behaviour can largely be explained in terms of how the *mind* operates, i.e. the way we think about things.

The mind is like a *computer*: inputting, storing and retrieving data.

Cognitive psychologists see psychology as a *pure science*.

Key concepts of the cognitive approach

A *schema* is an organised packet of information, which stores knowledge and expectations.

Information-processing concepts: input, parallel and serial processing, output, modularity, distributed networks.

Methods used in the cognitive approach

Laboratory experiment. Lacks ecological validity, e.g. focus on explicit memory. Some field and natural experiments used. These have greater ecological validity but can't truly claim that cause and effect demonstrated.

Case studies of brain-damaged patients. Lack generalisability.

Imaging techniques: CAT, MRI and PET scans. Can conduct research on functioning of active, normal, brains.

Evaluation of the cognitive approach

- Mechanistic because cognitive explanations based on the behaviour of machines; therefore inevitably lacking in social and emotional factors.
- Useful applications, e.g. eyewitness testimony, air traffic control (attention).

Practice essay 7.9

You should write about 200 words on each approach

'Some people hate playing games like football or basketball whereas others greatly enjoy taking part in team sports. It isn't just the sporting aspect but the chance to belong to a group and share the ups and downs with your friends.'

(a) Describe how **two** approaches might try to explain why some people enjoy playing team games. (6 marks + 6 marks)

(b) Assess **one** of these explanations of why some people enjoy playing team games in terms of its strengths and limitations. (6 marks)

(c) How would **one** of these approaches investigate why some people enjoy playing team games? (6 marks)

(d) Evaluate the use of this method of investigating why some enjoy playing team games. (6 marks)

Sample questions and model answers

1

This question illustrates the issues and debates section of Unit 5.

(a) Outline ethical issues involved in psychological investigations using human participants. (15 marks)

(b) Assess psychologists' attempts to deal with such issues. (15 marks)

Examiner's comments

Part (a) requires a summary description of ethical issues (restricted to human participants only). The use of the term 'outline' means that breadth is rewarded rather than depth, though an answer that is simply a list of ethical guidelines will not receive high credit as the question specifies 'issues' rather than 'guidelines'. Clearly there is an overlap – for example, informed consent is both an issue and a guideline.

In part (b) the evaluative component of the question requires that you assess the extent to which psychologists have been able to deal with ethical issues. You are no longer required to identify the issues but to assess the way that psychologists have dealt with them. This might involve consideration of specific issues, such as informed consent, or a wider evaluation of the cost-benefit approach or cultural differences. As this question is on the synoptic paper, credit will be given for your ability to make reference to a variety of different areas of investigation within psychology, and a variety of different ways of coping with ethical issues.

Candidate's answer

(a) Ethics are the way that professional groups resolve their moral problems. The ethical problems that face psychologists concern the risks that are posed to participants, to other psychologists and to society at large as a consequence of psychological research.

What are the risks for participants? The most important risk is probably physical harm though this is rare in psychological experiments. Nevertheless it is clearly something that psychologists must be aware of. Related to this is psychological harm, which is very much a problem in psychological investigations as many of studies do leave participants feeling a loss of self-esteem, or more frustrated, or simply changed. The best-known example of this is Milgram's study where participants had to shock Mr Wallace. The participants were observed to dig their fingernails into their hands and sweat and look uncomfortable. Although many of them said, when interviewed later, that they had found the experience worthwhile, it still may have changed the way they felt about themselves. Aronson (1988) said that participants should leave the research situation in 'a frame of mind that is at least as sound as it was when they entered'.

In relation to psychological harm we might consider the issue of how people behave towards each other after taking part in psychological research. Take the example of the study of obedience by Hofling *et al*. After the experiment was completed, and the psychologists had gone away, the nurses and doctors still had to work with each other. This is an ethical issue. The psychologists might have thought about the potential harm they were doing to work relationships.

Another important issue in psychological investigations is confidentiality and privacy. It is vital that participants feel protected. If an IQ test is done they would assume that the results would not be made known to anyone. The question of privacy is usually resolved by saying that it is OK to observe anyone, for the purposes of psychological research, in a public situation where they would normally expect to be observed by others. But a real problem here is that people in field experiments or observational studies, like the one by Piliavin *et al*. on the New York subway, have no opportunity to give their informed consent.

Sample questions and model answers (continued)

At a wider level, psychologists have an ethical responsibility towards the profession of psychology as a whole. If they bring the name of psychology into disrepute it will harm all psychologists. Burt's invention of data is an example of this. It turned out that he had invented some if not all of his data. This would lead people to be suspicious of all psychologists and to lose respect for the profession.

Psychological research also has the potential to harm society. Burt's research was used as the basis of the 11-plus examination. If his data was invented then the whole premise of the British grammar school system is potentially flawed and generations of school children have been subjected to a system that masquerades as scientific. This is an example of socially sensitive research – research that has the potential to affect social practices and concerns areas of human behaviour over which there is much debate. Psychologists have to be extra careful when providing apparent 'facts' on such issues as they may lead to major social changes.

(b) In the second half of this essay I intend to assess psychologists' attempts to deal with these issues. The main way that they are dealt with is through the use of ethical guidelines. But how effective are these guidelines and what are their strengths and limitations?

Guidelines are there to protect participants and also balance the needs of the individual and society. We should remember that there are many benefits to psychological research, such as studies that have investigated how to reduce prejudice.

The cost–benefit approach has certain associated drawbacks. First, it is difficult if not impossible to predict both costs and benefits prior to conducting a study. This means that when you think you are weighing up costs and benefits, you aren't really. Second, it is hard to quantify them even after the study, partly because it varies depending on who is making the judgements (the participant, the researcher or a member of society). It also depends when you make the judgement – benefits may be judged differently in years to come.

In terms of individual ethical issues, one of the most important is that of informed consent. Like cost–benefit analysis this may be less possible in reality than in principle. First of all you may tell a participant (or their guardian) what is involved in a research study but even a very knowledgeable person may not fully understand the implications until the study is underway. Of course participants do have the right to withdraw at any time but this may be easier said than done. They may only realise the harm done when they reflect on the research study later. They can withdraw their data but this doesn't prevent the harm that has been done to them.

The second problem with informed consent is that many investigations rely on lack of knowledge from the participant so you can't tell them beforehand what is involved. Psychologists have developed various alternative techniques, such as presumptive consent, where the researcher asks other people what they think about the study and whether they would participate, and then presumes that the participants would have said the same. However, it is different saying you would do something and actually doing it. Another way round the informed consent problem is to use prior general consent. Gamson did this in a study on conformity, where participants were asked to agree to a whole list of studies including 'Research in which you will be misled about the purpose until afterwards.' So they essentially agreed to be deceived.

This leads us on to the issue of deception. A key moral principle is that of honesty, yet many psychological experiments rely on deception. Does this practice bring the psychological profession into disrepute? Deception is widespread in psychological research. Menges (1973) considered about 1000 experimental studies that had been carried out in the United States. Full information about what was

Sample questions and model answers (continued)

going to happen was provided in only 3% of cases. However, we should remember that many cases of deception are relatively harmless, as in memory experiments – though participants may come away with bad feelings about being duped.

There are certain important limitations to these ethical guidelines. In terms of effectiveness, we must remember that guidelines are not laws. The worst that can happen is that a psychologist is disbarred from the profession. This may mean the loss of someone's livelihood but perhaps it is less of a deterrent than a prison sentence.

Guidelines also remove the need for individuals to think for themselves and they make it appear as if certain behaviours are indisputable principles, whereas in fact ethical principles vary from one country to another. The Canadians have a more practical code which may make it easier for psychologists to resolve their ethical dilemmas. [1100 words]

Examiner's comments

This is an extensive and well-informed essay. In part (a) the candidate has taken a less usual approach to ethical issues by considering the risks posed to participants, psychologists and society at large. Examples are given of different research studies, displaying synopticity in terms of links across the specification. It is a competent outline of issues but perhaps there is too much detail and not sufficient breadth.

In part (b) the candidate has aimed to consider the effectiveness of guidelines rather than falling into a second descriptive section. The candidate has very briefly considered the benefits of guidelines but the remainder of the essay focuses on limitations and negative criticisms.

AO1
Well-structured but slightly limited. Band 4 = 12 marks.

AO2
Commentary is thorough, informed and effective, but lacks balance in terms of strengths and limitations. Band 4 = 12 marks.

Total 24 out of 30 marks.

2

This question is an example of the kind set for section C on Unit 5 of the AQA A examination, the 'approaches question'.

'People all over the world smile and laugh, fall in love and have babies, eat and drink too much or too little. But there are differences in the *way* they do all these universal activities. In other words, there are cultural similarities and differences.'

(a) Describe how **two** approaches might try to explain cultural similarities
and differences. (6 marks + 6 marks)

(b) Assess **one** of these explanations of cultural similarities and differences. (6 marks)

(c) How would **one** of these approaches investigate cultural similarities and differences? (6 marks)

(d) Evaluate the use of this method of investigating cultural similarities and differences. (6 marks)

Examiner's comments

The 'approaches question' is different to the usual essay question. The question begins with some stimulus material, followed by a fixed set of questions. Part (a) of this question aims to test your understanding of approaches in psychology as distinct from your knowledge of other people's explanations, such as those of Freud or Skinner. Both men applied their principles to explaining specific behaviours, such as gender development – and that is what you must do for whatever behaviour is described in the stimulus material. No credit will be given to published theoretical accounts or actual studies.

Sample questions and model answers (continued)

In parts (b), (c) and (d) your knowledge of topics across the specification (synopticity) is also assessed. In part (b) you are asked to demonstrate some critical appreciation of one of your approaches. You might refer to the other approach as a contrast but you should only evaluate one of them. In part (c) you are asked to consider how the problem might be investigated. You might describe all the elements of your proposed investigation. The method of investigation must be suitable for the approach. Part (d) is again an evaluative task.

In all parts of this question it is essential that you engage with the stimulus material; that you apply your knowledge and understanding to this situation. If you do not do this marks will be lost.

Candidate's answer

(a) The behavioural approach in psychology suggests that we are born as a blank slate. This would mean that everyone the world over is born identical. Both similarities and differences would be explained in terms of learning, by a behaviourist. Conditioning theory includes both classical and operant conditioning. Some behaviours result form learned associations (classical) whereas others are learned because they are rewarded in some way. For example you might learn to be kind to others because your parents praised you (a reward) when you behaved like that. In another, more aggressive culture parents might give rewards for aggressive acts and thus children would grow up this way. It is fairly easy to see how cultural differences arise through learning but similarities would be because people the world over respond the same way to certain behaviours. For example, if someone smiles at you, you smile back and this is rewarding so they do it more. The behavioural approach also suggests we learn through punishment, though less effectively. If you are punished you are discouraged from doing the same thing again.

The biological perspective takes a different view. According to this approach the reason we find that people behave the same way the world over is because people are born with those characteristics, they inherit them. For example, it could be argued humans have an innate characteristic to fall in love. This is because those individuals who fell in love were more likely to reproduce and thus their genes were perpetuated. The genes of people who didn't fall in love were less likely to be perpetuated. The biological approach explains that inherited characteristics determine the physiological functioning of our bodies and thus we can explain something like love as a physiological experience. It is arousal that is mislabelled as love. All sorts of other behaviour can be explained in the same way, such as eating and drinking which both have known physiological mechanisms. Clearly at one level such physiological explanations are appropriate.

[332 words]

Examiner's comments

The candidate has used two approaches and given a reasonable account for both, avoiding the pitfall of describing actual theories and instead engaging reasonably well with the stimulus material to explain cultural similarities and differences as a behaviourist or a biological psychologist. Both descriptions are reasonably thorough and presented coherently. They tend to be rather general and not always fully engaged with the stimulus material. Some evaluative remarks are made which would not attract credit. The behavioural one is slightly better, giving a mark of 5 + 4 = 9 marks.

Candidate's answer

(b) The problem with the behavioural account as we have seen is it has difficulties accounting for why people all over the world are similar. Why would all people smile when someone smiles unless there was something innately appealing in a smile? This means that we are not born as a completely blank slate but we are actually born with a number of inherited characteristics. This doesn't negate the behavioural account entirely, it just means that it cannot be the whole account of behaviour.

Sample questions and model answers (continued)

A further problem with the behaviourist account is that it ignores the workings of the mind. It assumes that all behaviour is learned through conditioning theory whereas it is clear that many behaviours are learned through indirect reinforcement. A child will pick up many cultural practices by watching others and imitating their behaviour especially when they have been rewarded for that behaviour. Similarly they may learn from seeing someone else punished. Thus cultural differences are explained in terms of social learning theory, an adaptation of the behaviourist approach.

The behavioural approach also is highly determinist, assuming that each individual has no control over what happens but is passively controlled by the environment. The social learning approach suggests that social influences are as important as environmental ones. It also suggests that each individual plays an active part in what they learn because it is the particular characteristics that they possess which affects the interactions that they have, and thus what they learn.

[227 words]

Examiner's comments

There is a slight tendency in this answer to give a rather general evaluation of the behaviourist approach rather than, as the question requires, assessing the behavioural explanation as an account of cultural similarities and differences. More emphasis might also have been given to the strengths of the behaviourist approach. The commentary is coherent and reasonably thorough but slightly limited by the inconsistent lack of engagement with the stimulus = 5 marks.

Candidate's answer

(c) A behaviourist is likely to design a well-controlled laboratory experiment in order to test his (or her) beliefs. Initial investigations might be done using non-human animals to demonstrate that rewards are an effective way to shape behaviour. In order to look at how cultural influences occur, the experimenter might reward one group of rats for aggressive behaviour and another group of rats for grooming behaviour. We could then see if the rats differed in their practices. A behaviourist would generalise these results to human behaviour, arguing that human and non-human behaviour differs only quantitatively. It would be possible to conduct similar experiments with humans as long as the rewards were for rather 'trivial' bits of behaviour, to avoid ethical objections. So an experiment might be designed where two groups of children were rewarded for sharing their sweets with a friend (they might be given an extra sweet) and the other group was rewarded for smiling. An unbiased observer might record smiling and sharing behaviours in both groups and we could see if they differed as predicted.

[117 words]

Examiner's comments

The candidate has described some appropriate investigations and provided a reasonable commentary. The analysis might have been more thorough, considering other aspects of an investigation such as sampling and design considerations. There is evidence of coherent elaboration and enough for the full 6 marks.

Candidate's answer

(d) Not all psychologists agree with behaviourists that we can generalise from studies of non-human animals whose behaviour is far less complex than humans. Just because animals can be conditioned to show 'cultural' differences does not mean that we can then leap to the conclusion that the same is true for humans whose behaviour is actively controlled by the mind.

Conducting behavioural research with humans is subject to ethical objections because by rewarding a behaviour one is manipulating that individual and they

Sample question and model answer (continued)

may never go back to what they were before. In the example above both behaviours that were encouraged were desirable but it is still social manipulation. It also means that we cannot generalise to learning undesirable behaviours.

A focus on cause and effect research devalues other possible means of collecting valid data, particularly when studying cultural similarities and differences. It might be more appropriate to conduct cultural observations of different child-rearing practices. Or even use discourse analysis.

On the positive side the behaviourist approach produces well-controlled experiments and the principles of conditioning have been confirmed in their widespread applications in society.

[184 words]

Examiner's comments

A number of valid points are made and valiant attempts to tie the answer to the question of investigating cultural similarities and differences. The commentary is effective and coherent, a good Band 2 (top) = 5 marks.

Total 25 out of 30 marks, equivalent to a weak Grade A.

Practice essays: guidance for answers

Chapter 1 Social psychology

Social cognition

1.1 Attribution of causality
It would make best sense to select Kelley's theory because it provides a wealth of descriptive material – especially if you present the first and second version as one theory. Try to be selective with the material you choose to use in part (b) so that you have the opportunity to engage with the 'evaluation' rather than just describing research evidence.

1.2 Social perception
For AO1 you should describe social representations, using examples. For AO2 you could evaluate by contrasting this with other explanations of social perception, or using research evidence. A good essay should be clearly organised rather than a list of possibly relevant points.

1.3 Prejudice and discrimination
There are two key features of this essay: first you should only describe two ways, and second, these must be related to reduction of prejudice not causes. If you describe more than two ways only the best two will receive credit. If you use other 'ways' explicitly as evaluation they may receive further credit. Description is likely to involve examples from research studies, and evaluation might then assess the validity of such research, as well as the viability of the proposed ways to reduce prejudice/discrimination.

Relationships

1.4 Attraction and formation of relationships
You should describe relevant studies (i.e. not those related to maintenance or dissolution). Evaluation may be in terms of theoretical formulations and/or methodological factors. A good essay will balance strengths and weaknesses.

1.5 Maintenance and dissolution of relationships
In part (a) you need to ensure both depth and breadth in your description. It might be useful to argue that social exchange and equity theories are essentially one theory, thus accessing a broader theory. In part (b) if you use studies and/or theories as your evaluation be careful to *use* these as part of an argument to establish the value of your first theory.

1.6 Cultural and sub-cultural differences in relationships
Your answer must include 'understudied' relationships. The specification gives gay and lesbian relationships as an example and these could form the basis for a discussion of sub-cultural differences. You may choose to argue that other cultural differences are also 'understudied'. Description of the differences is straightforward. Evaluation (AO2) might consider the extent to which such differences are important and what the practical implications are.

Pro- and anti-social behaviour

1.7 Nature and causes of aggression
One theory only must be described though other theories may be introduced as long as this is done explicitly as evaluation; description of further theories will attract no credit. 'Critical consideration' means description and evaluation. Evaluation can be done with reference to studies, practical applications and logical and/or methodological flaws.

1.8 Altruism and bystander behaviour
Studies can be described as at AS level: aims, procedures, findings and possibly conclusions (though these may be used in part (b)). Any criticisms of the studies would only receive credit in part (b). Part (b) is mainly concerned with the issue of the extent to which your selected studies increase (or not) our understanding of pro-social behaviour. It is important, in order to attract marks, that your assessment takes the form of an argument rather than a further descriptive passage.

1.9 Media influences on pro- and anti-social behaviour
You are required to focus on explanations rather than research studies, though clearly the latter will form part of your answer either as a means to elaborate the descriptions or as a means of evaluating the explanations. Your focus should be on anti-social behaviour though contrasts/ comparisons with pro-social effects could be made relevant.

Chapter 2 Physiological psychology

Brain and behaviour

2.1 Methods of investigating the brain
Ensure that the methods you select are non-invasive, and if you're not sure, offer a justification for your choice (though just saying 'they are non-invasive' wouldn't count!). If you describe more than two methods, only the best two would receive credit and you would have done better to write a sentence more for each of your chosen methods. In part (b) you must present both strengths and limitations.

2.2 Localisation of function in the cerebral cortex
In order to discuss this question you need to describe localised functions and then consider the extent to which

such functions are actually localised or might, more accurately, be considered to be distributed. You must ensure that you cover both description and evaluation equally in this essay to access the full marks available.

2.3 Lateralisation of function in the cerebral cortex
'Research' may be used to refer to theories and/or studies. The most likely area will concern split-brain research but you might also include other asymmetries, such as emotion and spatial abilities, to increase the breadth of your answer. Evaluation could include mention of both strengths and weaknesses of the research and might refer to methodological flaws or practical applications. The

advantages/disadvantages of asymmetry might also be considered.

Biological rhythms: sleep and dreaming

2.4 Biological rhythms
In part (a) you must describe two or more research studies (because studies is plural). There is a depth–breadth trade-off. If you write about a number of studies (breadth) then the level of detail is necessarily limited, and vice versa. For top marks a good balance between depth and breadth is required. In part (b) you are not required to describe the consequences of disrupting circadian rhythms but to assess the effects of such disruption. It is important to use your material effectively to present an appropriate response which is not descriptive.

2.5 Sleep
In part (a) you will not receive extra credit for writing about more than one theory of sleep but it would be possible to include several theories under the umbrella of evolutionary theory. You need to work at the explanation in order to provide sufficient detail for the full 12 marks. In part (b) you could offer contrasts with other theories of sleep. In both cases description is to be avoided; marks are awarded for effective use of material.

2.6 Dreaming
Credit will be given only for a description of one neurobiological theory; this can include description of associated research. For AO2 you could look at the strengths and limitations of this theory, which may include contrasts with other theories (neurobiological or otherwise). It is not sufficient to simply say 'I will evaluate my theory with another theory' and then offer a second description. Marks are

awarded in relation to the genuine effort that is made to use alternative explanations as a point of contrast and evaluation.

Motivation and emotion

2.7 Brain mechanisms of motivation
The one motivational state is likely to be hunger or thirst. Your description should refer only to the role of brain structures; other physiological mechanisms may be used in part (b), though here you must resist too much description and engage with the instruction to assess the role of brain structures. It will also be relevant to consider external influences and the influence of higher cognitive influences such as expectations.

2.8 Theories of motivation
The injunction 'outline' is used to signal the fact that less detail is required. As each theory is only a quarter of the total marks (i.e. 6 marks each and about 6 minutes of writing time) you obviously have no time for more than an outline; breadth but not detail. For each theory you also must offer some evaluation, such as reference to research studies. You need to maintain coherent elaboration and informed commentary to attract marks so endeavour to be selective in the material you use in evaluation.

2.9 Emotion
As in the earlier question on motivation, your description should refer only to the role of brain structures as distinct from other physiological mechanisms such as the action of the ANS. Evaluation may be in terms of research evidence and methodological criticisms of these. You may also contrast brain state explanations with alternative explanations, especially the influence of situational cues.

Chapter 3 Cognitive psychology

Attention and pattern recognition

3.1 Focused attention
When describing research studies you can follow the AS guidelines of including aims, procedures, findings and conclusions. Criticisms will not attract credit in part (a). Ensure your accounts are well detailed. In part (b) you can use any studies to consider the question of how they contribute to understanding focused attention. You are not required to describe the studies but to use them effectively.

3.2 Divided attention
'Research' refers to theories or studies, thus there is a large body of knowledge to draw upon in this essay. If you try to include everything you know it is likely to read like a list and lack sufficient detail (AO1) and elaboration (AO2). Thus it will be important to be selective. You must ensure, however, that you include reference to slips associated with automatic processing.

3.3 Pattern recognition
'Outline' requires a summary description only, breadth but not depth. Two explanations will be sufficient for full marks but you can present more than this. Leave enough time to do justice to part (b) where you should assess your explanations. You must assess at least two of these.

Perceptual processes and development

3.4 The visual system
An 'outline' requires less detail and more breadth than description. Diagrams are likely to be part of your outline but must be accompanied by text to demonstrate understanding. In part (b) you must use your knowledge about the visual system to argue how this contributes to perception (as distinct from sensation). Ensure you are not just describing the visual system further.

3.5 Perceptual organisation
It is likely that you will describe either constructivist or direct theory and then use the other as a means of evaluation, but ensure you do use the second theory as evaluation and not present both theories in a descriptive sense. Research studies may form part of your description and then might be evaluated in terms of their validity. Further commentary may be achieved through a consideration of practical applications and/or theoretical implications.

3.6 Perceptual development
You are not required to address the quotation but you may gain some ideas from it. Your discussion of the nature–nurture debate is likely to involve a description of evidence for both points of view and an analysis of the value of this evidence. AO2 may also be achieved through commentary on the debate and how it might be resolved.

Language and thought

3.7 Language and culture
'Research' refers to theory or studies. You may describe the variations of the hypothesis and use research evidence to evaluate it, or include the research evidence in your description and assess the extent to which this supports the various versions of the hypothesis. Methodological criticisms would be relevant as well.

3.8 Language acquisition
It is likely that you will select the nativist explanation of language acquisition for description as this will provide sufficient breadth and depth for AO1. Evaluation could be in terms of strengths and limitations and might include reference to research studies plus comparisons with alternative explanations, some of which can be seen as refinements to nativist theory.

3.9 Problem-solving and decision-making
When describing studies you can follow the AS guidelines of including aims, procedures, findings and conclusions. Criticisms would not attract credit. Ensure your accounts are well detailed. In part (b) you need to construct an argument relating studies to the theory. How much do such studies tell us about decision-making in the real world? The danger will be that you will engage in further description rather than commentary.

Chapter 4 Developmental psychology

Cognitive development

4.1 Development of thinking
Piaget is named in the specification so it is permissible to ask a question specifically about his theory of cognitive development (but not his theory of moral development). In your description ensure that you avoid a list of 'ages and stages' and present a well-detailed but varied account of the theory. Evaluation may be in terms of studies that support the theory, or otherwise, and also might include contrasts with other theories as well as practical applications. There is a vast amount of relevant material, so selectivity will be important for a balanced answer.

4.2 Development of measured intelligence
'Research' refers to theories or studies but in this case is most likely to be studies that are described. The evaluation might consist of methodological considerations and commentary on what such studies tell us about the development of intelligence. A well-balanced answer will look at genetic and cultural influences.

4.3 Development of moral understanding
Theories of pro-social reasoning differ subtly from those of moral development. It might be possible to argue that Kohlberg's theory does relate to pro-social reasoning but a more appropriate theory would be Eisenberg's. It is creditworthy to describe more than one theory if you feel you don't know enough to write about 300 words on one theory.

Social and personality development

4.4 Personality development
It is important to ensure that your answer includes both breadth and depth, in balance, for good marks. This means giving more than an outline of the main features of your chosen theory, and therefore it may be necessary to select key features and make these well-detailed. Strengths of the theory may be in terms of research support, or applications in psychoanalysis. Weaknesses may be related to the quality of the research evidence and/or contrasts with other theories that are less biological.

4.5 Gender development
This is a fairly open-ended question and the danger then is that you have too much to write and end up with a rather unstructured account that lacks detail. Both are signs of a weak essay. Be selective and focus on only a few explanations. It is helpful to be clear at the outset about what gender identity is.

4.6 Adolescence
It is possible to argue that both Erikson's and Marcia's theories (and Blos') are psychodynamic, and therefore they could all be included as one theory. Don't however end up with too much to write and an imbalanced essay in terms of depth and breadth. The AO2 component is likely to rely on research evidence to determine whether the theory can account for real-life experiences. You might go beyond the parameters of the theory to question, for example, whether it can explain peer influences and cultural differences.

Adulthood

4.7 Early and middle adulthood
Levinson's or Gould's theories are the likely choices and one may be used to evaluate the other. It is important when using a theory evaluatively not to engage in further description but to use it for comparisons and contrasts.

4.8 Family and relationships in adulthood
'Research' includes theory and studies. In this case it is likely that you will discuss research studies of marriage (and/or partnering). This might generally relate to the findings from such research or the aims, procedures and conclusions as well. It is important to achieve a balance between depth and breadth. Research can be evaluated with reference to methodological difficulties, ethical problems, practical applications, theoretical implications and so on.

4.9 Cognitive changes in late adulthood
The injunction 'outline' means that a summary description only is required and therefore you may consider a number of different explanations as breadth is more important than detail. If you only present one explanation there would be a partial performance penalty of 8 marks maximum for AO1 and the same for AO2.

Chapter 5 Comparative psychology

Determinants of animal behaviour

5.1 Evolutionary explanations of animal behaviour
One explanation of evolutionary behaviour will be enough for full marks but you would need to provide sufficient detail. Alternatively, you can go for multiple explanations. This is the 'depth–breadth trade-off'. For high marks you must achieve a good balance between depth and breadth. Evaluation is required for the AO2 element of the essay. This may refer, for example, to research evidence and/or issues of plausibility.

5.2 Classical and operant conditioning
Your description should communicate understanding of the various aspects of classical conditioning. Evaluation can be achieved through research studies, and contrast with operant conditioning or other explanations of learning. The intention is to consider how much of non-human animal behaviour can be explained in terms of classical conditioning, so a balanced answer will show that it is part of the story. Note that human behaviour is excluded unless it can be made relevant in some way.

5.3 Social learning in non-human animals
'Discuss' is an AO1 and AO2 term requiring a description of selected evidence for intelligence in non-human animals, plus an evaluation of such explanations which is likely to be achieved in terms of the quality of such evidence. A good answer will be well structured, with a coherent argument presenting the case for and against intelligence in non-human animals.

Animal cognition

5.4 Animal navigation
In order to achieve sufficient detail for your two research studies it may be useful to use the AS guidelines of aims, procedures, findings and conclusions. Criticisms of the study will not be creditworthy in part (a) but might be used in part (b). In part (b) you are required to outline the implications of such studies for homing/migration which can include a consideration of their validity. It would be legitimate, when making your assessment, to introduce other research studies as a means of support or otherwise for your initial two studies.

5.5 Animal communication and language
You can select two different modalities, such as vision and hearing, as different signalling systems, or you could examine the various signalling systems used by two different animals. In either case your evaluation could consider strengths and weaknesses of the systems, and may make comparisons with alternative systems.

5.6 Memory
The injunction 'discuss' requires you to describe the role of memory in navigation, and additionally to evaluate this role, i.e. determine the extent to which memory is important. For example, in the case of some animals (such as the monarch butterfly) no memory is involved in navigation.

Evolutionary explanations of human behaviour

5.7 Human reproductive behaviour
The starting point is likely to be a description of the relationship between sexual selection and human reproductive behaviour, i.e. a consideration of how traits that are solely concerned with increasing an individual's mating success are related to human reproductive behaviour. The AO2 element might involve a consideration of the implications of this relationship and/or the related research evidence (though this would be AO1 if it is purely descriptive).

5.8 Evolutionary explanations of mental disorders
You have the option of describing and evaluating general explanations, such as genome lag, or specific explanations such as the rank theory of depression. The minimum required is two explanations. As you increase the breadth of explanations you necessarily decrease the depth, and reduce the quality of your answer. There is a balance to be struck. Such explanations can be evaluated with reference to research studies and alternative biological or psychological explanations, or even alternative evolutionary explanations. The implications and practical applications would also count as evaluation.

5.9 Evolution of intelligence
You are required to describe evolutionary factors and consider the value of such explanations. The description is relatively straightforward. Evaluation may be in terms of alternative explanations, research evidence and the validity of such evidence, and/or a general consideration of evolutionary explanations.

Chapter 6 Individual differences

Issues in the classification and diagnosis of psychological abnormality

6.1 Classificatory systems
In this essay research is likely to refer to studies, though it can include theories. Such studies should be described (AO1) and evaluated (AO2) in terms of, for example, what conclusions we can draw, any methodological constraints or practical implications. As this part of the specification is assessed additionally with synoptic criteria you must aim to include different perspectives in your answer and make links, where possible, across the specification.

6.2 Multiple personality disorder
In order to consider the question of spontaneity, you first need to describe the evidence for this position. This is likely to involve descriptions of appropriate case studies (as these are referred to in the specification). Marks will be awarded for an answer that uses the case studies to describe the debate rather than simply describing case studies with little sense of direction. Further evidence might be drawn from explanations of possible causes of MPD and general support for, for example, the psychodynamic or behavioural view. Reference to such approaches will increase the synoptic element of the essay. Evidence for iatrogenesis may count as AO2 as long as it is given as counterpoint to AO1 points and not simply described.

6.3 Culture-bound syndromes

A balanced essay will examine the arguments and evidence in favour of culture-bound syndromes as well as those against. But argument 'against' must be juxtaposed against arguments 'for' in order to attract AO2 credit. If such arguments are merely described rather than used as effective commentary, they will gain no marks. AO1 is likely to involve a description of the syndromes and arguments 'for'. AO2 might further involve reference to case studies or other research to support the contrasting views.

Psychopathology

6.4 Schizophrenia

The AO1 marks are here divided between parts (a) and (b). In part (a) the mark allocation suggests no more than 7 minutes should be spent on a summary description (breadth not detail) of the characteristics. In part (b) this leaves 10 AO1 marks for an outline of biological explanations. This could include neuroanatomical, neurochemical and genetic accounts. Research evidence may form part of your description or may be used more evaluatively. Alternative psychological explanations may be presented as long as the focus is on evaluation and not further description. Such contrasting views may be useful in terms of synopticity.

6.5 Depression

The descriptive content of this essay is limited to one explanation. The evidence can also form part of the description as well as being used for critical commentary. Evaluation is likely to be in terms of alternative explanations (e.g. neurochemical or evolutionary) but these must be used effectively as points of contrast.

6.6 Anxiety disorders

The specification only requires that you study one anxiety disorder so the descriptive element of this essay is restricted to one disorder but any number of explanations, as long as they are psychological. You can use the biological explanations as a form of evaluation, which will also enhance the synoptic element of your answer. Explanations of other anxiety disorders might be used as further commentary.

Treating mental disorders

6.7 Biological (somatic) therapies

It is likely that you will describe all three named therapies, but bear in mind the 'depth-breadth trade off' – the more therapies you cover, the less detail can be provided and both are required in balance for top marks. At the same time breadth is useful for synopticity. The evaluation is likely to be in terms of the appropriateness and effectiveness of such therapies, which might involve comparisons with other therapies (thus increasing links across the specification). You also might consider more general issues such as how therapies can be evaluated.

6.8 Behavioural therapies

In part (a) you are only permitted to describe those behavioural therapies based on classical conditioning. If only one is described, you will lose marks because of partial performance. It is important to ensure sufficient detail in your response. Part (b) restricts evaluation to the issues surrounding the use of therapies described in part (a).

6.9 Alternatives to biological and behavioural therapies

It is permissible to ask a question that covers the whole of a sub-section ('treating mental disorders') rather than just one of the topics, as is the case here. The injunction 'compare and contrast' can be dealt with in two ways. The first is to describe both therapies for the AO1 marks and then consider their similarities and differences for the AO2 marks. The second possibility (a more difficult approach) is to describe the similarities and differences for the AO1 marks and then comment on these similarities and differences for the AO2 marks. Whichever approach you choose there are no marks for any general evaluation of the therapies.

Chapter 7 Synoptic: perspectives and approaches

Issues

7.1 Gender bias

The essay title is very general and therefore part of your task will be to decide on a structure for your answer and you will need to be selective in the material you present. The descriptions should be of instances of gender bias in psychological theory and research. The evaluation might consist of the effect this has had on such theories or on society in general. You might also consider ways to remedy this problem. A balanced answer will consider both positive and negative views.

7.2 Cultural bias

In part (a) you should describe a minimum of two examples of culture bias (it can be argued that gender bias is an example of this). The more examples that you include the greater the breadth and also synopticity, as you will increase the links you make across the specification. However there is a limit to the usefulness of this because your aim is to achieve a balance between breadth and depth. Part (b) requires consideration of how much such biases have affected our understanding of human behaviour. It is desirable to consider both possible answers – yes it has, and no it hasn't affected our understanding. Though the question only refers to psychological theories, you can argue that these are based on research studies, which may be biased, and thus include such studies in your discussion.

7.3 Ethical issues

The AO1 element must focus on social sensitive research with ethical issues in general. Note that 'ethics' is different to 'ethical guidelines', which are a means of resolving ethical issues. Thus the guidelines, and other means of coping with ethical problems, might form part of the evaluation in this discussion. Other evaluative material might include suggestions about what to do with the results of such research and whether to allow it in the first place. You should consider both the benefits and drawbacks of such research.

7.4 The use of non-human animals

'Critically consider' is an AO1 + AO2 term requiring you to describe and evaluate the use of non-human animals. Your discussion should be presented in the context of at least two psychological investigations but it is important to avoid overlong descriptions of the investigations themselves and instead you should focus on the use of non-human animals in such investigations. You might consider ethical arguments or you might consider the usefulness of non-human animals. Evaluation should not be of the study but should consist of commentary on the arguments you present – for example, you might describe a reason for the use of non-human animals in a particular study and comment on this by presenting a counterargument.

Debates

7.5 Free will and determinism

The AO1 element of this essay concerns examples of free will/determinism in specific psychological theories and provides you with the opportunity to develop links across the specification (synopticity). It will be important to limit the time you spend on description (no more than 20 minutes) in order to access the marks for AO2 as well. The evaluation might concern the problems created for each theory by being deterministic or not, as well as ways of resolving these problems. For example, Bandura's concept of reciprocal determination offers a way to reconcile behaviourist determinism with some degree of 'will'. Do not simply evaluate the theories.

7.6 Reductionism

The two most common mistakes made when answering questions like this is either that candidates write an essay about reductionism in general rather than focusing more specifically on examples of reductionism in psychological theory, or that they describe and evaluate psychological theories which are reductionist and provide little information about the reductionist aspects of the theories. It is not enough to say 'This theory is reductionist' and then discuss the theory. Commentary might look at the advantages or disadvantages of reductionism in the theory and possible alternative, and less reductionist, approaches.

7.7 Psychology as a science

There are various ways to consider this topic. First is the issue of what a science is, and then the question of whether psychology (and even other, more 'physical', sciences) can fit this bill. Third, is the question of whether all psychologists feel that the goals of science are appropriate to the study of psychology, and a consideration of alternatives. Techniques, such as discourse analysis, aim to be subjective yet there are attempts to make them more objective (i.e. scientific). A balanced response will recognise that there are no simple answers.

7.8 Nature–nurture

The question is framed in such a way as to encourage you to make links across the specification (synopticity) and use examples of the nature–nurture debate to form the basis for your discussion. The AO1 element will be satisfied by a description of different examples and the stance taken as regards nature and nurture within these examples. The AO2 element is concerned with an evaluation of whether nature or nurture has the greater role in your different examples. Wider issues might also be explored, such as the nature of nature–nurture interactions.

Approaches

7.9 Biological, behavioural, psychodynamic and cognitive:

The actual form of this question will be different in the examination (see page 165) but you might try, for practice, to suggest how a biological, behavioural, psychodynamic and cognitive psychologist might explain the behaviour described. For example, a behavioural psychologist would use concepts such as reward and punishment to suggest that some individuals learn to like team games when they are younger because they are rewarded by being successful and gaining the admiration of peers. Another individual might be rewarded through negative reinforcement – playing team games means that he or she has to do less schoolwork. A third individual might find the experience of standing around on a windy football pitch so unpleasant that the mere mention of football results in avoidance behaviour. The concepts of the behavioural approach will be important and also the assumptions, for example that all behaviour is learned and research with non-human animals is justified because they are only quantitatively different. The key issue to remember is that you must engage with the stimulus material, and not just present a general essay on your selected approach. You must use your knowledge effectively.

The same applies to the other parts of this question: (b), (c) and (d). The evaluation must not be a global one for, say, the behavioural approach. It must be an evaluation of the extent to which the behavioural approach works in this context. Such an evaluation should consider both strengths and weaknesses. You might even offer contrasts with other approaches.

In part (c) you need to identify a typical methodology and analyse the steps involved in any investigation. Finally, in part (d) you should consider the strengths and weaknesses of such an investigation.

Index